Embassy, Emigrants, and Englishmen

The Three-Hundred-Year History of a Russian Orthodox Church in London

Christopher Birchall

Holy Trinity Publications
The Printshop of St Job of Pochaev
Holy Trinity Monastery
Jordanville, New York
2014

Printed with the blessing of His Eminence,
Metropolitan Hilarion, First Hierarch
of the Russian Orthodox Church Outside of Russia

Embassy, Emigrants, and Englishmen: The Three-Hundred-Year
History of a Russian Orthodox Church in London

HOLY TRINITY PUBLICATIONS
The Printshop of St Job of Pochaev
Holy Trinity Monastery
Jordanville, New York 13361-0036
www.holytrinitypublications.com

ISBN: 978-0-88465-381-3 (Hardback)
ISBN: 978-0-88465-336-3 (Paperback)
ISBN: 978-0-88465-382-0 (ePub)
ISBN: 978-0-88465-383-7 (Kindle)

Library of Congress Control Number 2014942139

Cover Art and Design: James Bozeman
Engraving: The Russian Embassy Chapel
in Welbeck Street: *Illustrated London News*, April 1865.
(Source: Holy Trinity Monastery Archive)

Printed in the United States of America

CONTENTS

FOREWORD

This history of the Russian Orthodox Church in London is a long anticipated treatise which fills a large gap in historical and ecclesiastical studies concerning the Orthodox presence and activity in the West. It is with great pleasure that I welcome this work of Protodeacon Christopher Birchall on this very moving chapter in the history of Russian–English relations. Being himself a native of England and a spiritual son of the Russian Orthodox Church in London, Father Christopher accepted the call for such an extensive work when we celebrated the Millennium of the Russian Church in our parish in London in 1988. In order to complete this endeavour he had to overcome immense difficulties in locating materials pertaining to the development and life of this parish, as well as a personal relocation to Canada. Occasional visits to his homeland made it possible for him to dive further into the seemingly endless and bottomless factual material which survived in the most unexpected places.

This fascinating history reflects the ups and downs of 300 years of Church life in what would often involve the most adverse circumstances. The difficulties of the Orthodox clergy in the early times as they attempted to establish an Orthodox church in a non-Orthodox country, patient explanation of the Orthodox faith to English people who were drawn towards it, the burden of exiles and refugees after two World Wars, not to mention the difficulties of survival during the Cold War, and finally, of course, the peaceful time after the collapse of the anti-Christian Soviet empire, are all reflected in this history of one parish, its clergy, and its faithful.

Both ecclesiastical and secular historians will be grateful for this extensive presentation. We, as clergymen and parishioners of the Russian Orthodox Church Abroad, and, in particular, of its English diocese and London parish, are deeply indebted to the author for a moving account of Church history which would otherwise easily have fallen into oblivion. May our Lord reward him a thousandfold.

Munich, January 2012
+MARK, Archbishop of Berlin, Germany, and Great Britain

SCOTLAND
ENGLAND
Isle of Man
Preston
Leeds
Bradford
Manchester
Liverpool
Nottingham
Walsingham
Wolverhampton
Birmingham
WALES
Cambridge
Colchester
Oxford
London
Bristol
Portsmouth
Plymouth
Isle of Wight

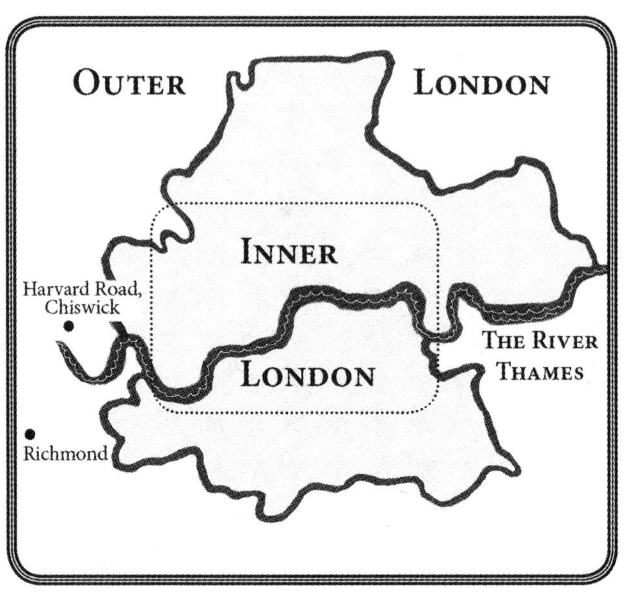

DETAIL OF INNER LONDON

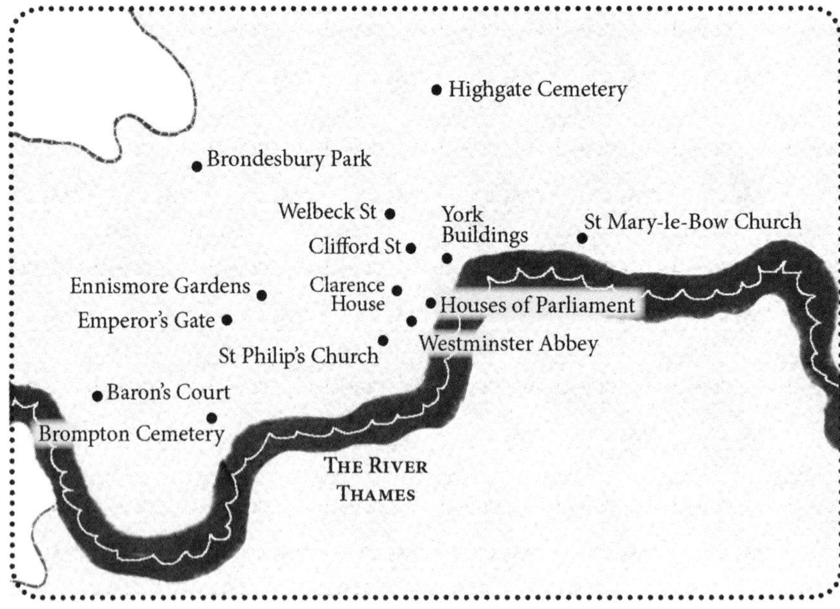

Approximately 10 miles

INTRODUCTION

Millennial Celebrations

Ideally history should be written backwards rather than forwards, because the past becomes interesting, at least initially, as it explains how we have arrived at the present. We find the recent past more compelling because we can more easily see how it explains our present situation, whereas events that occurred several centuries ago often seem remote and disconnected from our lives today. For example, the story behind the building of the Russian Church of the Nativity of the Mother of God at Harvard Road in Chiswick in West London has many fascinating and inspiring elements, not least of which is its connection with the living tradition of the ancient Pskov style of church architecture. This in turn raises questions about why the church was built in Chiswick, where the parish was located previously, and why it had to move. From there we can go further back to explore whether the church was established by refugees after the Russian Revolution of 1917, and we find that by then it had already existed for some two hundred years, founded by Greeks at the initiative of the Russian Emperor, Peter the Great. Nevertheless, due to constraints of grammar and literary convention, it will be more practical to follow the normal approach and begin at the beginning, that is, 1713.

This text began its life on April 26, 1987. The following year, 1988, would mark the Millennium of Russian Christianity, being the thousandth anniversary of the baptism of St Vladimir and the people of Kiev. As it was uncertain what celebrations, if any, would be allowed in the Soviet Union, the Russian Orthodox Church Abroad felt a particular responsibility to mark this event in a fitting fashion. In April 1987, then Bishop Mark, recently appointed to lead the parishes of the Russian Orthodox Church Abroad in Great Britain, held a meeting with some parishioners to discuss how best to honour this millennium. At that meeting I agreed to do some research on the history of the Russian Orthodox Church in London, with a view to preparing a brief account that the bishop could print at his monastery in Germany, and that would be ready in time for the celebrations the following year.

I circulated an appeal for information. In reply I received many suggestions of who to ask, but had trouble gaining concrete information; each person referred me to someone else or suggested I should have asked someone who had recently died. Then I was told that all the old parish records were lodged in the Public Record Office (now the National Archives), at that time located in Chancery Lane in London. This seemed to me rather improbable, but, as I was working near Chancery Lane at the time, I thought I might as well see if there was any substance in this idea. To my astonishment, I found an entire section of the archives categorized as "Non parochial Registers," which contained numerous files described as "Archives of the Russian Orthodox Church in London," covering the period from 1713 to 1926. Some of the earlier materials were in Greek and others were in English, but the vast majority were in Russian. In many cases, the files kept in London contained rough, handwritten drafts in spidery writing, using pre-Revolutionary Russian spelling, of reports that had evidently been transcribed into a fair copy before being sent on to St Petersburg. Archival materials speak to the reader on various levels. First, there is the specific information contained in the document, which may be difficult to interpret without knowing its exact purpose and the context in which it was written. But second, there is also the unwritten content—the tone of the document and the presumptions that lie behind it. Amid the bureaucratic reports there is some very valuable material, such as a letter from Metropolitan Philaret of Moscow about Anglican beliefs, and the reports of Father Eugene Popoff about his visits to Russian soldiers held in prisoner of war camps in England during the Crimean War. The most vivid and fascinating material was the minutes of the meetings held in 1919 as the Embassy church was reorganized as a parish in accordance with the directives of the Russian Church Council held in 1917–1918 (see Chapter 7).

Locating this archive was the breakthrough that convinced me that research into the history of the parish could produce something interesting and substantive. This material, however, did not extend beyond 1926. Gradually, additional information came to light about more recent times. At first it formed an incomplete patchwork, but with time a more complete picture began to emerge as links between different periods were filled in. It soon became apparent that completing this project in time for the millennium celebrations would not be a realistic objective. A four-page brochure was printed and distributed at the special church service held in July 1988 and given to guests at the banquet that followed. This provided a brief overview of the history of the parish with promises of a more complete study becoming available in the near future.

The 1988 pamphlet did not, of course, hint at how long it would take for the book to be completed. The lack of information at the early stages was replaced by an overwhelming volume of material of all kinds—documents from the past, lovingly preserved cuttings from old newspapers in various languages, accounts written in the past, and newer accounts written in response to my appeal for information—all of which would help to preserve the memory of people who would otherwise be forgotten. However, to sort all this and incorporate it into the already partially drafted text became a daunting task. For this and various other reasons, work ground to a halt in the early 1990s. After the fall of Soviet Communism, from time to time I received enquiries from Russia about specific individuals who had spent time in London. Then in 2009, two factors combined to help push this work to a conclusion. First, there were celebrations of the twentieth anniversary of the fall of the Berlin Wall—a vivid reminder of the passage of time since work on this history had begun. Second, I renewed my acquaintance with an old friend, Nicolas Mabin, who had recently retired from a professional career in the City of London. He agreed to help me shape the manuscript into passable condition, proofreading and preparing it in a form suitable for submission to a publisher. At this point, some of the text was in the form of a typed manuscript, some had been typed on a computer using an old Word Perfect programme, and some took the form of incomplete handwritten drafts. With the passage of time, I had also added two final chapters dealing mainly with the building of the new church in Chiswick. The delay has allowed me to bring the account to a more satisfactory conclusion. In 1988 the parish faced an uncertain future, as it was on the verge of having to leave its church premises because the lease had expired. By 2009, however, the new church was substantially complete pending finishing touches and consecration.

A Microcosm of Russian Church History in the Emigration

I persevered with this history in part because I began to realize that the material that had come into my hands was more than just a family history. As I wrote in the 1988 millennium brochure,

> The research into past history became increasingly fascinating, as the materials studied gave access to a series of "lost worlds"—in particular the church of the Imperial Russian Embassy in the 19th century and the

> Russian émigré community between the wars. Yet these are not really "lost worlds," because the Orthodox Church sees herself as the unity of all present and past generations of Orthodox Christians, who are bound together by bonds of love and prayer, while the unchanging nature of Orthodoxy gives a permanent value to the examples and teachings of past generations.

The Russian Orthodox community in England, especially after the Revolution, was part of a larger worldwide emigration and experienced many of the same joys and sorrows, as well as the same achievements in establishing their communities and church life in a new land. Many Russian churches in different parts of the world had their beginning in pre-Revolutionary times and were connected with embassies, consulates, or other Russian institutions abroad. However, focusing on one specific community, while at the same time placing local events in their wider historical context, enables us to witness these developments in a more intimate and real fashion than would be provided by a broader overview. The strength and weakness of history is that by the time it is written we know what happened and how it ended. But those who lived through these same events often were shaken and swept off their feet by happenings they did not understand, with no idea of where they would be tomorrow or when, if ever, they would be able to return home.

Looking closely into the life of one parish also allows us to share more intimately in experiences that were common to most émigré parishes all over the world. At the same time, the history of the London parish has a number of interesting and unique features of its own. Among its leading clergymen were Archbishop Nikodem, a former White Army general who later became a monk and then a bishop; Father Michael Polsky, who slipped away from custody in the 1920s and wandered the length and breadth of Soviet Russia before escaping and becoming a warm hearted and much-loved émigré pastor; Father Eugene Popoff, who was not only a caring pastor of Embassy officials but also worked extensively with Anglicans and converts to Orthodoxy; Father James Smirnove, who did double service as a diplomat; and Father Eugene Smirnoff, who presided over the transition period after the Revolution, including the transformation of the chapel in Welbeck Street into a parish of the Russian Orthodox Church Abroad.

Thus the book covers three distinct periods: (1) The period from 1713 to 1917, when the London church was connected with the diplomatic mission of Imperial Russia; (2) the period from 1917 to 1991, when it was a church of refugees from communist Russia and their descendants; and (3) the period since then, when it has become a church primarily of people who have come to England voluntarily, principally from the former Soviet Union and Eastern Europe. While the circumstances of the church in London were very different after the Russian Revolution, we note a distinct continuity among people who had served the Embassy church for decades under the Imperial regime and continued to do so after the Revolution. This is partly because the Embassy church was never located in an embassy building (which the Soviet regime would have taken over and closed down, as happened in Germany) but had a distinct independent origin and always served the needs of people other than just the embassy staff.

After the Second World War, parishes started opening in provincial centres as well as London, which became the centre of a deanery and then a diocese of the Russian Orthodox Church Abroad. At various times there were parishes in Manchester, Bradford, Leeds, Nottingham, Dublin, and Walsingham. More recently parishes have opened in Felixtowe, Colchester, Mettingham (Suffolk), Wallasey (near Liverpool), and Stradbally (in Ireland). These parishes are mentioned as they affect the life of the London parish and its clergy, but we cannot cover the life of each of them in detail.

The chapters are of uneven length and differing content. This reflects both the kind of material that was available and also the differing functions of the church over these periods. During the periods when the church served refugees, prayers were continually offered for the "suffering land of Russia" and individually for peoples' relatives who died during periods of bloodshed or disappeared without a trace. To some extent, refugees cannot help but live in the past, and I have devoted considerable space to what could be called the "backstory"—the experiences of refugees before they arrived in England. Chapter 7 includes material about the Russian Revolution and Civil War, including the various routes by which exiles reached London. Chapter 11 includes extensive extracts from Father Michael Polsky's own accounts of his experiences in Russia before he escaped over the frontier into Persia. Chapter 12 includes descriptions of displaced persons in Germany after the Second World War and their attempts to escape repatriation to the Soviet Union with the help of clergymen of the Russian Orthodox Church Abroad who later served in England. Chapter 15 draws on the published and unpublished memoirs of Galina von Meck, daughter of a pre-Revolutionary railway magnate who settled in London after the Second World War.

The copy of Father Michael Polsky's book *Положение Церкви в Советской России* [The situation of the Church in Soviet Russia], from which I took the extracts presented in Chapter 11, was given to me in 1970 by Maximilian Albrecht, a parishioner who had received the autographed copy from the author himself. Because it was an old and worn-looking book, and my Russian was not very good at the time, I did not pay much attention to it and soon forgot about it. However, when working on the initial draft of this chapter in 1988, I went up into the loft of the house in Teddington where I was then living, to look through some boxes of old papers to see if I had anything relevant. I found the old book inscribed to Maximilian Albrecht and took it downstairs. I found it was written with such a vivid style that I could not put it down and stayed up half the night reading it. This was the first book Father Michael wrote after leaving Russia in 1931. All his opinions were supported by direct personal experiences and meetings with leading ecclesiastical figures, some of them during his time confined in the Solovetsky prison camp, so I had no hesitation including extensive extracts from this first-class historical material. After returning to Canada in 1991, I mentioned this to Metropolitan Vitaly, then First Hierarch of the Russian Orthodox Church Abroad, who was also the Archbishop of Canada and had known Father Michael during his time in London and had an immense respect for him. I gave my copy of the book to the metropolitan, and he had it reprinted at his printing press in Montreal. Later, it was further reprinted in Russia. The original of the book disappeared during the reprinting process, but it was good to know that its contents could again be made known after spending so many years hidden in a box in Teddington.

Inevitably, the results of historical research depend on the person who carries it out. Another person might not have climbed up into a dusty loft but might have discovered other information that I did not. In particular, some might think that this book overemphasizes the clergy by comparison with the laypeople who made up the parish. Another person with better contacts might have found out more than I have about the faithful families who made up the body of the church from one generation to the next, and indeed about other aspects of the life of the church in London which I have overlooked. While I hope readers will find this account interesting and edifying, I make no claim to completeness.

Metropolitan Anthony Bloom

For many people who have heard anything about the Russian Orthodox Church in London, the one name that they associate with it is that of Metropolitan Anthony (Bloom). Therefore, it may come as a surprise and disappointment that he is mentioned here only in passing. As more fully explained in Chapters 8, 12, and 14, the Russian Orthodox Church in London was affected by the divisions among Russian Orthodox believers after the Revolution that ultimately led to a schism in 1926. From that point forward, this history is concerned primarily with the Russian Orthodox Church Abroad, otherwise known as the Russian Orthodox Church Outside Russia or the Russian Orthodox Church in Exile. The other parish formed in 1926 belonged to the Patriarchate of Constantinople, and then, at the end of the Second World War, transferred allegiance to the Patriarchate of Moscow. Metropolitan Anthony, who had grown up as an émigré in France, was sent to London in 1950 to lead the parish under the jurisdiction of the Moscow Patriarchate, first as a priest and later as a bishop. He remained in this position until his death in 2003. In 2007, following the reconciliation between the Russian Orthodox Church Abroad and the Patriarchate of Moscow, the two London parishes entered into eucharistic communion, although each has retained its separate organizational structure.

For periods after the Revolution and the 1926 schism, the focus of the present study is on the presence of the Russian Orthodox Church Abroad in London. After the reconciliation in 2007, I considered the possibility of adding some information about the history of the Patriarchal parish. However, in the end I decided this would be unduly time-consuming and even somewhat presumptuous. The Patriarchal parish at Ennismore Gardens has from time to time published articles dealing with its own history, but it would take extensive further research to write additional chapters to add to this book. Metropolitan Anthony himself was a well-known figure and much has been written about him already, both by Orthodox and non-Orthodox writers. To do justice to his many-facetted personality appears to have been somewhat of a challenge even to those who knew him well. In Chapter 17, I describe the process of unification between the Russian Orthodox Church Abroad and the Moscow Patriarchate, including meetings between clergy of the Russian Orthodox Church Abroad and Metropolitan Anthony toward the end of his life. His memory will be preserved by others in numerous articles and books already written. The focus of this book is on other edifying and fascinating personalities whose memory is already beginning, undeservedly, to fade.

Research and Sources

This book is based primarily on unpublished materials—papers held in the National Archives, personal interviews, and parish records—as well as church and émigré periodic publications. Other published sources have been consulted primarily for background information. In books on historical topics I observed a wide variety of different practices in citing sources. At one extreme, the author provides a footnote supporting virtually every statement made, while at the other, there are no footnotes at all but simply a "Select Bibliography" as a guide for further reading. I think that a text where every page is knee-deep in footnotes can be difficult to read, while a lack of information about sources can be perplexing and confusing. The present text consists of seventeen chapters, each representing a period—generally the incumbency of a particular clergyman as rector of the parish. Each chapter is further subdivided into sections, each dealing with a particular aspect or development of church life during that period. After the last chapter I have provided a list of sources for the entire book. For each section of each chapter I have indicated the main sources of the information presented in that section. For materials in the National Archives I have identified the exact file references, while for published sources I have given the normal citations of author, title, date, and place of publication.

Appendixes of Supplementary Material

Four appendixes contain material that I think is important but might otherwise interrupt the flow of the narrative. Rather than use the Library of Congress system for transliterating Russian names that indicates how the name was spelled in the original Russian alphabet, I chose to translate names in a way that better indicates how they are pronounced. Where possible, I used the English spelling people actually used for their own names. I have also provided a chart explaining ecclesiastical ranks both for married and monastic clergy.

Christopher Birchall
Deacon of the Russian Orthodox Church

Chapter 1

[1713–1725] The Delegation from Alexandria

The Archives

In 1917 and the years immediately following the Revolution, Russian exiles were scattered all over the world as refugees from the militant atheism that seized control of their country. Wherever they went, these refugees organized and built churches, often with limited resources at their disposal. In some European towns and cities, however, Russian Orthodox churches had been established through the efforts of the Imperial Russian government. Most were embassy chapels or churches built in the resorts and spa towns favoured by the Russian aristocracy in the nineteenth century. The church that refugees came upon in London—which became the first parish church of the Russian Church in Exile in 1919—had a unique history as the second oldest Russian church in western Europe.[1] The London church was founded during the reign of the Russian Emperor Peter the Great, thanks to a combination of events in the ecclesiastical world that occurred at that time.

The church archives tell little about the church's origin. Throughout the nineteenth century, in order to satisfy the demands of the St Petersburg bureaucracy, the church's rector was obliged to file a detailed report every year about the church and its clergy. These reports did not simply describe the events of the past year; they repeated everything covered in the earlier years' reports and also brought the history up to date for the current year. The first question to be answered was always, when and by whom was the church first established? The answer given was always the same: it is not known with any certainty when and by whom the Church of the Dormition of the Mother of God attached to the Imperial Russian Embassy in London was established. The reports explain that the oldest register in the church archives does not go back beyond 1749, although they indicate that the church existed long before that date. They contain several pages written in Greek and headed in Russian, with the following explanatory note: "Copy of the register written during the time of Archimandrite Gennadius and Priest-monk Bartholomew Cassanno, clergy of the Graeco-Russian Church in London. This is now copied from the original manuscript, which has completely decayed." The earliest entry in this Greek register is of a baptism performed on April 21, 1721. The annual reports conclude, "But whether the church was founded in 1721, or whether it had existed earlier—concerning this there is absolutely no information either in the archives or in the library of the present church in London." By comparing the annual report for 1885 with that written in 1910, one sees that this vague account of the church's origins is repeated verbatim for twenty-five years. In 1910 the clerk used a typewriter, while in 1885 it was copied by hand.

Although these reports were signed by Archpriest Eugene Smirnoff, rector of the Embassy church, there are indications that he knew more about the church's origin.[2] Thus, in 1897, when Archbishop Anthony of Finland visited England in connection with Queen Victoria's jubilee, Father Eugene greeted him at the entrance to the Embassy church with a speech. In that speech, he said that the church had been founded in 1716 through the initiative of the "Great Reformer" (Peter the Great) and in the interest of acquainting Western Christians with the Orthodox Church. This information would have come not from the records of the church in London, but from the synodal archives in St Petersburg. These archives contained (in addition to the original copies of the annual reports so meticulously sent in by Father Eugene and his predecessors) a number of rare and interesting documents relating to the early days of the church in London.[3] The earliest of these documents seems, at first sight, to be an unlikely source of information about the Russian Church in London. It is a letter from a Greek deacon, Simon Nomikos, who worked for twenty-five years as an assistant to Metropolitan Arsenius, Bishop of Thebes, a town in upper Egypt within the Patriarchate of Alexandria. In this letter he describes how, in 1712, he accompanied the metropolitan when he was sent by Patriarch Samuel of Alexandria to England on a fund-raising mission. For a more complete account of this delegation to England, additional sources pieced together include letters in the synodal archives written by Deacon Simon Nomikos and the Protosyncellus James, another member of the delegation, and a series of letters written by Metropolitan Arsenius to the Patriarch of Jerusalem. Also included are various Anglican sources that record the metropolitan's dealings with representatives of the Church of England. Stephen Runciman summarizes these Anglican sources in his book *The Great Church in Captivity*. Taken together, these texts provide a picture of the metropolitan's fund-raising journey, which acquired a missionary character reflecting his attempts to bring Orthodoxy to the English people. These attempts inspired him to build an Orthodox Church in London and resulted in establishment of the "Graeco-Russian" Church—the first permanent Eastern Orthodox church in the British Isles.

Metropolitan Arsenius and the Non-Jurors

In 1712, the Patriarchate of Alexandria was in exceptional financial difficulties and hoped to appeal to pro-Greek and pro-Orthodox sympathies that Patriarch Samuel knew existed in England. Metropolitan Arsenius of Thebes was sent armed with letters addressed to Queen Anne and accompanied by an impressive delegation of clergymen. These included Archimandrite Gennadius, the senior abbot of the patriarchate who was a Cypriot by birth; Deacon Simon Nomikos and another deacon; the Protosyncellus James, a translator; and Bartholomew Cassanno, assistant to Archimandrite Gennadius. According to Nomikos, they left Alexandria in 1712 and arrived in England in 1713; other sources give the year of their arrival as 1714. Nomikos said that they arrived in London in 1713, during the reign of Queen Anne, and went to see the Anglican bishop of London, who granted permission to celebrate Orthodox Divine Services. He then went on to say that the Jesuits began to slander them, spreading rumours that they had actually been sent by the Pope, and so "for one and a half years we could not hold services, and lived under house arrest." The metropolitan asked his consul for protection, and they were then allowed to hold services in private.

Strangely enough, neither Metropolitan Arsenius, in his letters, nor the Anglican sources quoted by Runciman make mention of these initial difficulties encountered by the delegation. Possibly, the period of house arrest accounts for the discrepancy of one year between the dates of arrival recorded in the different sources. The metropolitan wrote, "During the three years[4] in which I lived in England, both I and my retinue always walked about in our robes, and they held us in great favour, both the civil authorities and the ecclesiastics." Runciman recorded simply that

> . . . they were well received. They made friends with the Antiquary, Humphrey Wanley, . . . and he and his circle entertained them hospitably. . . . In 1715 Arsenius published a touching tract entitled *Lacrymae et Suspiria Ecclesiae Graecae: or the Distressed State of the Greek Church, humbly represented in a Letter to Her late Majesty, Queen Anne*. In response the Bishop of London, John Robinson, sent them a few months later £200 provided from Queen Anne's Bounty and £100 given by King George I, but with the

> expressed hope that they would then leave the country. He had procured another £100 for them, but held it back until they should announce their departure. They were, however, enjoying themselves too well to take this clear hint that they had outstayed their welcome. Wanley still entertained them. . . .[5]

The Anglicans' interest in their Greek visitors stemmed from the long-standing hope, which had existed in some Anglican circles since the Reformation, of re-establishing communion with the Orthodox churches of the East. Throughout the seventeenth century, there were contacts between the Anglicans and the Greeks, and as recently as 1701, a Greek bishop had visited Cambridge. Defining dogmatic questions in Western terms, the Anglicans were anxious to satisfy themselves that the Orthodox did not subscribe to any papal errors and were continually frustrated when they felt that they were not receiving a "straight answer" from their visitors. For example, in the doctrine of the Eucharist, the Orthodox believe that the elements undergo a real change into the Body and Blood of Christ; however, they are reluctant to define this change any more closely. Dr John Covel, the master of Christ's College, Cambridge, who had had dealings with the last Greek delegation to come to England in 1701, wrote to Wanley from Cambridge to warn him that Metropolitan Arsenius and his associates "would be no more reliable theologically than previous Greek visitors and would be certain to say that they did not believe in transubstantiation."[6] Runciman confirmed that "Arsenius avoided that trap. Wanley wrote back to Covel to say that the Greek hierarchs modestly declared that: 'they believed as Saints Basil and Chrysostom believed, and they would not meddle in what did not concern them.'"[7]

"Meanwhile," wrote Deacon Simon Nomikos, "some of the most prominent Englishmen began to come over to our faith." This surprising statement is explained, in part, by the interest shown in the Greek visitors by a dissident movement within the Church of England known as the Non-Jurors. In contrast to the lukewarm attitude toward Orthodoxy shown by the official representatives of Anglicanism, the Non-Jurors were far more determined in this regard. In fact, it was the metropolitan's dealings with this group that has focused the attention of church historians on his visit to England.

The name of the Non-Juror movement is derived from the fact that its followers refused to swear allegiance to King William III, who came to the throne in 1689 following the overthrow of King James II at the end of 1688. However, their main differences with mainstream Anglicanism were religious rather than political. The Non-Jurors rejected the Protestantism that was becoming entrenched as the official doctrine of the Church of England in favour of a more traditional theology, and they referred to themselves as the "Catholic remnant of the British Church." Their attitude is summed up in the last will and testament of Thomas Ken, former Bishop of Bath and Wells and one of the original Non-Juring bishops, who died in 1711. He wrote, "I die in the holy and apostolic faith professed by the whole Church before the division of East and West." His followers saw it as almost a sacred duty to attempt a union with the Orthodox. They were never very numerous, but their leaders were vigorous and enterprising. They therefore seized the opportunity presented by the visit of an Orthodox hierarch to England. Runciman recorded,

> [I]t was in July 1716 that the Scottish Non-Juror, Archibald Campbell, happened to meet Arsenius and spoke to him of the possibilities of a closer connection. . . . Arsenius was sympathetic. So Campbell and Jeremy Collier, *primus* of the English Non-Jurors, together with Thomas Brett, Nathaniel Spinkes, James Gadderer and a few others, met to prepare proposals for transmission to the Eastern Patriarchs.
>
> It was probably early in 1717 that a copy of the proposals was given to Arsenius, who despatched it to Constantinople. It was a lengthy document, translated into elegant Greek by Spinkes, with the help of Mr Thomas Rattray of Craighall. The proposals numbered twelve, but they were supplemented by a list of twelve points on which the Non-Jurors believed themselves to be in complete agreement with the Orthodox and five points on which they disagreed and on which discussion would be necessary.[8]

This letter was entrusted to the Protosyncellus James for transmission to Constantinople. It was more than three years before a reply was received.

It was the interest in Orthodoxy shown by English people, including the Non-Jurors, that inspired Metropolitan Arsenius to build an Orthodox church in London. His aspirations were not limited to effecting ecclesiastical union with the Non-Jurors as a group; rather they took on a clearly missionary character. Later, when negotiations with the Non-Jurors were foundering, Metropolitan Arsenius wrote to the Patriarch of Jerusalem:

> I myself was not concerned about those bishops. My desire was only to complete and found a church, because, during the time I was in England,

> many people came to talk with me, that I might receive them as communicants of the Orthodox Church. But I had to refuse them since I had no church. However, in spite of all that, I did receive a few people into Orthodoxy, and all of them secretly. But I celebrated openly and fearlessly before many English people, for every Sunday and feast-day many of the English, and women also, and some of their clergymen came to church. . . . In England there is freedom for our religion. Whoever desired to do so could frequent our preaching. Only the Latins are forbidden. Indeed during the three years I lived in England, I and my assistants walked about in our proper dress, and both the authorities and the clergy held us in great respect. That is why I longed that there should be an Orthodox church in that country.

Although his primary motivation for building a church in London is clear, another factor must have influenced the metropolitan to some extent. This is the presence of a Greek colony in London. During the seventeenth century, Greek merchant communities were being established in many major European cities, as Greek people sought greater opportunities than could be found under the oppressive conditions of Turkish rule. In fact, a Greek Orthodox church was built in 1677 in Soho, just off Charing Cross Road (then known as Hog Lane), through the initiative of Joseph Georgirenes, Archbishop of Samos, who was then living in England. The church also had a resident priest, Daniel Vulgaris. The church's brief but stormy existence came to an end in 1682 when the archbishop attempted to sell the church building in order to move the church to London,[9] which, as the commercial centre, was becoming the main focus of the Greek community. It proved that the Greeks had no sound title to the land on which the building stood; they held it under a complicated series of leases and, in reality, the land belonged to the Church of England. Under the prevailing political and religious climate,[10] the Anglicans were disinclined to help, and early in 1682 the building was seized from the Greeks by the parish of St Martin-in-the-Fields. In Constantinople, the British ambassador explained to the patriarch that it was "illegal for any public Church in England to express Romish beliefs and that it was just as bad to have them professed in Greek as in Latin." The Archbishop of Samos left England soon afterward. It may be assumed that when Metropolitan Arsenius went to England thirty years later, some of the Orthodox Greeks who had formed the congregation of this church in Soho would have begun attending the Divine Services celebrated by him and his clergy. According to Deacon Simon Nomikos, the Englishmen who had "started coming over to our faith" advised Metropolitan Arsenius to ask permission to have a public church "for the merchants and sailors who were arriving"—evidently he was referring to the growing Greek expatriate community.

Russian Support for the Church in London

In 1716 services were attended by one particularly distinguished visitor—Prince Boris Kurakin, who had been sent to London by Russian Emperor Peter the Great as his first ambassador to England. Deacon Simon Nomikos related, "In 1716 the Ambassador, Prince Kurakin, came to London. He came to the Church services, and there he was presented with the Englishmen's desire to erect a church in which services should be held in three languages (English, Russian, and Greek), and to be under the protection of the Russian Emperor." Kurakin advised the metropolitan to speak to the Russian emperor about this in person. He also said that an opportunity would soon present itself because Peter would be visiting Holland on his way back to Russia after a state visit to Paris. Metropolitan Arsenius duly set off for Holland, accompanied by Archimandrite Gennadius.[11] Nomikos continued, "Peter promised to help. He ordered the Metropolitan to go to Russia, since the project could not be accomplished at once. He also ordered Gennadius to return to England, and gave him an official document which entitled him to receive a salary of 500 roubles from Russia." Thus, Metropolitan Arsenius's stay in England came to an end. He left for Russia, accompanied by Deacon Nomikos. (It is not known whether he ever received the £100 promised by the Bishop of London upon his departure.) From Moscow and St Petersburg he wrote to Patriarch Chrysanthus of Jerusalem that he had come to Russia to raise funds for the building of a new church in London: "I came to these parts hoping to be able to build the church there. . . . Two or three Lords of the Council [in England] who were friends of mine asked me if I would like them to build me a Romaic[12] church. But I considered that by coming to this country I could render the church more secure, and I came for that purpose."

In fact (and contrary to what some later writers have assumed), no church was ever built. Nevertheless, Archimandrite Gennadius returned to London and, with the protection and financial support of the Russian government, established a church, known as the Graeco-Russian Church, on rented premises.

Peter the Great was, in his own way, a devoted son of the Orthodox Church, although his policies did much to weaken the Church and the canonical basis of its administration in Russia. Consequently, it is impossible to gauge how sincerely he supported the idea of building an Orthodox

Prince Boris Kurakin, ambassador to Great Britain, helped to establish the first Graeco-Russian Church in London.

church in London. Orthodox historians severely criticized Peter's policy of Westernizing Russia and his increasing contacts with the West. Nevertheless, it must be acknowledged that were it not for this policy, the Russian government would probably not even have known about the small church in London, let alone taken an interest in it and been able to offer financial support through an ambassador.[13]

The role of Metropolitan Arsenius during this visit has been subjected to varied interpretation. Runciman commented that "the Greeks were beginning to repay the generosity of their hosts by intriguing with the Non-Jurors."[14] Michael Constantinides commented that the metropolitan "was not noted for his intelligence, and showed no ability in the handling of the question" of the Non-Jurors. Admittedly, it was a very long time before the Non-Jurors received a reply to their letter to the Eastern patriarchs, but this was largely due to circumstances outside the metropolitan's control. The Protosyncellus James, who had been sent to Constantinople with their missive, wrote that he arrived there in August 1717 and then began the return journey with the patriarchs' reply in October 1718. He stayed in Smyrna until December due to adverse weather conditions and then had what he called a "fivefold battle with the Hagarenes," evidently some type of unpleasant encounter with the Turkish authorities. He reached Holland in April 1719 and was met by Prince Kurakin and told that Metropolitan Arsenius was now in Russia. Accordingly, he set out for St Petersburg in July 1719, where he was delayed until August 1721. It was at that time that he finally received instructions from the Russian Synod to return to England with the reply from the patriarchs and further communications from the Russian Church.

Not surprisingly, the Non-Jurors were disappointed with the long-awaited response. They had treated certain points of dogma as open to negotiation, while the Patriarchs simply restated the Orthodox belief and invited the Non-Jurors to concur. The Non-Jurors identified the following five principal areas of dogmatic disagreement: the authority of the seven œcumenical councils, the real presence of Christ in the Eucharist, the veneration of the

Mother of God and the saints, and the veneration of icons. They also proposed that the Patriarchate of Jerusalem be given precedence over the other patriarchates and that the British Church restore the old English Liturgy. To this, the patriarchs replied that they could see no reason to change the order of ecclesiastical administration laid down by the œcumenical councils and that they could not give their approval of the "old English Liturgy" because they had never seen it. On May 29, 1722, the Non-Jurors sent a reply to the patriarchs in which they conceded many, but not all, of the points they had previously disputed. The reply was again entrusted to the Protosyncellus James, who was to deliver it to Metropolitan Arsenius, now in Moscow, with a cover note asking him to transmit copies to the patriarchs, the tsar, and the Russian Synod. In February 1723, Archbishop Theodosius of Novgorod, the first vice president of the Holy Synod, invited the Non-Jurors to send two of their members to Russia for further discussions. However, it was at this point that the negotiations foundered. There was a delay in identifying two representatives of the movement who were able and willing to go to Russia. This was problematic because everything was being kept secret from the British government. Then, in January 1725, Peter the Great died, and his successor, Catherine I, had no further interest in the matter. Meanwhile, the Non-Jurors received a reply from the Eastern patriarchs that included a copy of a confession of faith written fifty years earlier by Dositheos, Patriarch of Jerusalem. This left no room for compromise over the questions of the veneration of the saints and of icons or of the real presence of Christ in the Eucharist. Later, in 1725, Patriarch Chrysanthus of Jerusalem received a letter from the Archbishop of Canterbury, who had finally found out about the correspondence with the Non-Jurors, warning him that he had "been intriguing with a small and schismatic body in Britain which in no way represented the Anglican Church." This effectively put an end to the whole affair.

Metropolitan Arsenius had backed the wrong horse, so to speak. The Non-Jurors, despite their desire to be the "Catholic remnant of the British Church," were not prepared to adjust their outlook and beliefs in light of the living tradition of Orthodoxy from which their church had been separated for seven hundred years. Nevertheless, there is little evidence to suggest that the metropolitan acted other than according to his archpastoral conscience as an Orthodox hierarch. It appears he did everything in his power to assist this small but determined group of Englishmen who had evinced such a strong sympathy for the Orthodox Church. He might have been well served by a closer knowledge of Anglicanism, but the same could be said of many well-intentioned hierarchs of the Russian Church over the following two centuries, particularly those who came into contact with the Anglo-Catholic Movement in the nineteenth century. After the death of Peter the Great, Metropolitan Arsenius returned to Egypt, having been away for more than ten years. Patriarch Samuel had died, and the original fund-raising mission on which he had been sent by the patriarch had been forgotten. Consequently, the little money that he did bring back with him was greeted with surprise and gratitude.

While still in Russia, he wrote despondently to the Patriarch of Jerusalem, "I considered that by coming to this country I could render the Church more secure. However the Evil One was jealous of the good work, and with the disorder of the times I have succeeded in doing nothing up to now." Certainly his grander scheme of reunion with the Non-Jurors had come to nothing, yet his visit to England was far from fruitless. While in England, as he himself recounted, he received a few people into the Orthodox Church. Also, after his departure, Archimandrite Gennadius established the Graeco-Russian Church on a more permanent basis, with the support of the Russian government.

So the year 1713, when Metropolitan Arsenius and Archimandrite Gennadius arrived in England, effectively marks the beginning of the Orthodox Church in London, serving both Greeks and Russians, which later became attached to the Imperial Russian Embassy.

Chapter 2

[1725–1780] The Beginning of Orthodox Church Life in London

The Graeco-Russian Church at York Buildings

Early documents give the location of the church as York Buildings, transliterated into Russian as "Yark Buildings." Although much of London has been rebuilt since the beginning of the eighteenth century, there remains a small side street near Charing Cross Station with this name. Thus, it is reasonable to assume that this is where the church was located.

All indications are that everything about the church was on a very modest scale. No descriptions are extant from the time of Archimandrite Gennadius, but information can be gleaned from later reports. In 1737 the Russian ambassador, Prince Antioch Kantemir, reported that there was no "public" church; he said it was located in a rented house. In 1749, the priest Stephen Ivanovsky made an inventory of the property that he took over from his predecessor, which provides the first detailed description. He said there were "eight fixed icons, without any frames, painted on wood." The word "fixed" (*naméstny* or *mestny*) is used to describe the icons on an iconostasis, so this indicates that the church was properly set up with an iconostasis separating the altar area from the rest of the church. He also said there were "four icons in the altar without frames," which confirms the existence of a separate altar area. Sixty-five items including books, vestments, sacred vessels, and other "appurtenances" were listed. The size of the house can be gathered from a list of certain objects that appeared to have gone missing during the tenure of his predecessor: "From the front room . . . from the back room . . . from the upstairs . . . from the kitchen." The list of furniture and household objects indicates that the house was well equipped for the time.

The early church registers, beginning in 1721, show that the pastoral work undertaken by Archimandrite Gennadius was mostly among the Greek community. However, his influence extended further afield. He is mentioned favourably in a letter written on January 28, 1723, by a group of

Non-Jurors to Metropolitan Arsenius, who had by then left for Russia. In addition to the usual records of baptisms, weddings, and funerals, the register contains a section with the heading "Those received and chrismated[1] into our Holy Church." Here some very English names make their appearance: "1731, December 25, chrismated Mr. Robert Bright with his spouse Elizabeth and their children Robert and Sarah, and united them to our Holy Church." Entries under the same heading for 1732 include Miss Sarah Jackson on January 9, Mr William Scott on April 2, and Mr William Thomas with his spouse and two children on October 29. On September 30, 1733, Miss Susanna Spicer is listed; on January 20, 1734, Mr Edward Pepper and his niece Martha Pepper; and on June 16, 1734, by Hanna Bright, mother of Mr Robert Bright. Beyond the names of these eighteenth-century converts, little information about them has survived. However, there is slightly more information about Philip Ludwell, who was received into the Church by chrismation on December 31, 1738. After his reception, he sailed back to his native Virginia, then one of the British colonies in America; he did not return again to London until 1760.

A number of English language service books are mentioned in Father Stephen Ivanovsky's church inventory: "No.56. Priest's service book in English translated from Greek, in manuscript; No.57. Two English Liturgies translated from Greek, in manuscript; No.58. Prayer at the Blessing of the Waters, translated into English from Greek, in manuscript; No.60. Symbol of the Faith (Creed) written in Greek and English." A cryptic note in the margin by this last entry reads, "Between the Greeks and the Non-Jurors who wanted to be united with the Greek Church." Item 62 is described simply as "one box containing English and Greek manuscript items." Some items, such as the translated priest's service book, could indicate that services were conducted in English, but this is not certain; the items could have been aids to help converts follow the services.

It is not known whether Archimandrite Gennadius had a command of the English language. However, the classical education that was common in England at the time meant that the Greek language was at least somewhat accessible to many educated English gentlemen, even though the classical Greek that they would have studied differed to a certain extent from the Byzantine Greek used in the services and, even more markedly, from the spoken Greek of the early eighteenth century.

Archimandrite Gennadius continued his service in England for twenty-one years and received his annual salary of 500 roubles from the Russian government until his death on February 3, 1737. He was buried in St Pancras

Cemetery, which was the burial ground reserved for foreigners at that time. His nephew, Father Bartholomew Cassanno, continued his work as parish priest.

Reporting to St Petersburg on the archimandrite's death, the Russian ambassador to Great Britain, Prince Kantemir, wrote that the church in London, dedicated to the Dormition of the Mother of God, was necessary for the Greeks coming from the archipelago and for the "greater glory" of Her Imperial Highness, the Empress of Russia, and therefore a young and well-educated priest should be sent to assist Father Bartholomew. In Russia there were still clergymen who had been in England and they were more than willing to return. These included the Protosyncellus James and Deacon Simon Nomikos, both of whom had been part of the original delegation from Alexandria in 1712. Deacon Nomikos gave a report to the Holy Synod of Russia in which he described the origins of the church in London and the local interest in Orthodoxy. This so inspired members of the Holy Synod that they resolved, "for the greater glory of Russia and for the expansion of the Orthodox Church and the Church Ceremonial," to appoint an impressive delegation of clergymen, including an archimandrite, two priest-monks, a deacon, two chanters, and an altar server at a combined annual salary of 1,750 roubles. When he heard of this scheme, Prince Kantemir pointed out that it was wildly excessive; after all, the church in London was located in a small rented house and there were only a few English Orthodox and perhaps ten Greeks. He said the church had very little income and there were no Russian merchants in London at the time. This altered the Holy Synod's decision. Finally, a single priest-monk, Father John Yastrembsky, was appointed, and he was accompanied by two psalm-readers, Alexei Kaminsky-Parchikaloff and Stephen Ivanovsky. Father Yastrembsky remained in London for only a few months. He was unable to work peacefully with Father Bartholomew and so was transferred to Holland.

Thus, Father Bartholomew continued to look after the little parish single-handed. He had been in England continuously since 1713, as assistant to Archimandrite Gennadius. He was ordained to the priesthood in 1726. The church registers record that on August 15, 1724, "Elizabeth, wife of Mr. Bartholomew Cassanno" was received into the Orthodox Church. Elsewhere in the records, he is referred to as "Priest-monk Bartholomew." Presumably he received the monastic tonsure later in life, following the death of his wife. Before his ordination, Cassanno assisted Metropolitan Arsenius in his negotiations with the Non-Jurors. The intent was that he accompany the proposed delegation of Non-Juror representatives to Moscow in 1723 to act as interpreter. From this it can be concluded that he knew Russian and English, as well as Greek, which must have made him well suited to carrying out his varied duties. He persevered at his post until his death in 1746 at the age of forty-nine. He was also buried in St Pancras Cemetery.

First Russian Clergy: Father Stephen Ivanovsky and the Move to Clifford Street

With the passing of Father Bartholomew, the church in London ceased being served by Greek clergymen. To ensure its continued existence, it was necessary to send clergy from Russia. From 1746 to the Russian Revolution in 1917, some remarkable individuals occupied the post of rector of the Embassy church in London, particularly after 1780 when Father James Smirnove (1780–1840) was appointed, followed by Father Eugene Popoff (1840–1875) and Father Eugene Smirnoff (1877–1922). However, before this period, there were some who did little to promote the "greater glory of Russia," let alone the "expansion of the Orthodox Church and Church Ceremonial." During the eighteenth century, the Church in Russia was going through a very difficult time, suffering from the successive anti-ecclesiastical policies of Peter the Great and Catherine the Great, which left the Church with meagre resources to attract and train an idealistic younger generation of clergy. London did not seem to have been regarded as a high priority, although this attitude changed in the next century. London was a distant posting for which few willing candidates could be found. Consider Father John Yastrembsky, sent to help Father Bartholomew, who remained in London for only a few months.

The first Russian clergyman sent as permanent rector of the church in London, Archpriest Antipa Martemianoff, seems to have been a rather disastrous choice, although his stay in London lasted only two years. His crossing from Russia was stormy, and all his baggage went to the bottom of the sea. From London he submitted a petition, signed by ninety-eight people, to the Imperial government asking that a new Orthodox church be built outside the city, one big enough to hold three thousand people. However, Ambassador Count Chernysheff reported that there were nothing close to three thousand Orthodox in England, and added that

> You would be lucky to find even the 98—they are all sailors, paupers and all kinds of riff-raff who never come to church. In England it is not easy to obtain permission to build a church; there is not a single Catholic church, while those belonging to the Lutherans [*sic*] and the other confessions were all built long ago. As for what the building would cost—without a plan

> this cannot be calculated exactly, but it would clearly be very expensive. There is absolutely no need for it. The church which now exists is very small, in a dirty, shabby side street, and even this one stands empty. It is regrettable, though, that Archpriest Martemianoff keeps it in a very dirty condition. In order to situate the church in a suitable location it would be necessary to assign 600 roubles a year instead of just 200. However, it would be better simply to improve the old church.

He concluded that the idea of building a new church was simply a way of obtaining funds for rogues and villains.

In 1749 Father Antipa became ill and recommended that, in the event of his death, one of the psalm-readers, Stephen Ivanovsky, be ordained in his place. In fact, Father Antipa recovered, but shortly thereafter he was summoned back to Russia, where he was put on trial for embezzlement and debt. In his book, *Russian Churches and Other Institutions Abroad*, Father Alexei Maltseff recorded, "The existing church was some distance away from the Ambassador and he started one of his own, but there were disagreements with the priest, so in 1749 the archpriest was sent back to Russia." This reference to a second church becomes clearer in light of Maltseff's entry for the Russian Church in Berlin, where he said that in 1747 Count Chernysheff took his private chapel away with him to England when he was transferred there as ambassador. There is no further information about a second private chapel existing in London. Rather, the Church of the Holy Dormition became known as the Embassy church, although it always served the needs of more than just the embassy personnel. The ordination of Stephen Ivanovsky proceeded as Father Antipa had recommended; he returned from Russia to England accompanied by Ivan Vasilievsky, who was to occupy his former position as psalm-reader.

Thus, Stephen Ivanovsky was in England for ten years as psalm-reader, and he remained for another seventeen years as priest. Although he was not the first priest of Russian extraction to be appointed to London, he was the first Russian priest to stay in London for more than a brief spell and to make a significant contribution to the work of the Church there. On his death in 1765 he was described by the ambassador as having been "quiet, pious, and learned." Little information about his pastoral service has survived. As is so often the case, the life of the Church proceeding in a quiet and orderly fashion does not constitute "history" as such. Fortunately, Father Stephen put the church records in order. He initiated the large folio volume that is the earliest source of information about the Church in London. He began by making a legible copy of the worn-out records written in Greek by his predecessors. He also compiled the first inventory of church property, which has been referred to already. English converts were received in London into the Church from time to time, including Catherine Copeland in 1751 and Maria Bradley in 1753. Father Stephen was also an iconographer; he painted an icon of the feast of the Dormition that was the patronal icon of the church for many years. It held a relic—a thread from the robe of the Mother of God—set under a silver plate.[2]

The church in York Buildings became increasingly dilapidated. In 1755 the Russian government decided to make an annual allocation of 600 roubles toward its repair. Then in 1756 the decision was made to move the church to a more suitable location. In the church record book, Father Stephen noted that on December 26, 1756, the Graeco-Russian Church in London was moved "from its old courtyard" to a new house in Clifford Street, Burlington Gardens. Clifford Street still exists just behind Regent Street in the West End of London.

Some details about the new church are recorded in the registers. The iconostasis was made of carved wood and painted white. In addition to the usual icons of Our Saviour and the Mother of God, it had an icon of Aaron on the north door and an icon of Moses on the south door. The upper tier of the iconostasis held four icons: Abraham about to sacrifice his son Isaac, the nativity of Christ, the baptism of the Lord, and Moses receiving the tablets of the law on Mt Sinai. On the royal doors, in addition to the usual icon of the annunciation, was a depiction of the "Greeting" or "Salutation" by Elizabeth of the Virgin Mary (Luke 1:39–41) as well as the four evangelists. All of these icons were painted on canvas and set in gilded frames. Above the royal doors was a gilded wooden ornament, to which the blue silk altar curtain was attached. At the highest point of the iconostasis was a large wooden cross, also gilded. Beside it were "three carved, gilded Seraphs' heads." On the wall behind the holy table, above the high place, was a large icon of the Mother of God in a gilded frame. On the holy table was a folding icon bearing depictions of the Saviour, the Mother of God, and St Anne. The sacred items in the new church included "the entire floor, on which the altar is built, which belongs to the church." Although this is not clear, it seems probable that in dismantling the old church, the floor beneath the altar, which is the most sacred part of the church, was removed and set up in the new location. There is no indication of the size of this house. Annual rental payments were approximately £70 until 1767, when a new lease was signed and the annual rent increased to £80.

The Church of the Holy Dormition remained the only Orthodox church in London until 1837, when a separate Greek church was established near Finsbury Circus. Until that time, the church served the needs of Greeks as well as Russians, even though the clergy were Russian. It is not clear whether Greek was ever used in the services. Certainly Father Stephen Ivanovsky knew some Greek to be able to make new copies of the old church registers written in Greek. Today a Greek visitor to a Russian church is struck by the difference in the type of singing: the harmonized Russian choral singing differs markedly from the ancient Byzantine chant executed by a small group of chanters, or even a single chanter, to which one is accustomed. In the eighteenth century, however, when harmonized choral singing was not nearly as widespread in the Russian Church as it is today, the differences would not have seemed so great.

In Russia then, as in Greece today, it was normal for services to be conducted in parish churches by a priest and a single chanter, known as the *psalomshchik*, or, more colloquially, as the *diák* or *diachók'*. Thus, in assigning clergy to London, the Russian church authorities insured from the outset that, in addition to the priest, there would be at least one chanter, or psalm-reader. This position was filled by individuals with a limited amount of theological education, primarily knowledge of the order of church services. They received a modest salary, but it was not enough to live on. Although presumably they had time to spare between services, as foreigners they had limited opportunities to find additional employment to supplement their income. For example, three years after his arrival in 1743, Father Stephen, who originally went to England in the capacity of psalm-reader, asked permission to return to Russia because while in London he had been forced to incur debts that he could not repay. In his case the crisis passed and he remained at his post.

This situation changed in the nineteenth century with the expansion of the Imperial Russian Embassy and the development of trade missions and other Russian government institutions in London. One psalm-reader in the late nineteenth century, Nicolas Vasilievich Orloff, translated liturgical texts into English that are still used today. Meanwhile, in the eighteenth century, the church records and synodal archives record a number of different problems that involved psalm-readers who were appointed to the London church. Alexei Parchikaloff, who had come to England at the same time as Ivanovsky and served with him as psalm-reader, appeared to have been overcome by jealousy at Father Stephen's ordination, after which he was unable to work peaceably with him. In 1752 he left London for Mt Athos. In the church inventory, Father Stephen noted, "on the day after the departure of the Diachok Parchikaloff from London, this item was not present in the church." Obviously, the implication is that Reader Alexei made off with some of the valuables. To make matters worse, the other psalm-reader, Vasilievsky, who had accompanied Father Stephen on his return from Russia after his ordination, proved to be incapable of fulfilling his duties and returned to Russia in 1751. During the next twelve years a succession of unsatisfactory individuals was sent to occupy this post, culminating with the Novgorod seminarian Silas Kirilovich Barkhatoff, whose unruly behaviour resulted in a prison sentence. The church register records, "On 28 January 1763 the Diachok Silas Barkhatoff died in the Gate House Jail in the City of Westminster, where he had been serving a one-year sentence since 29 June 1762. He was buried in a churchyard near the jail on Thursday, 30 January 1763." Prokhor Zhdanoff, who studied at the Moscow Theological Academy, succeeded him and served faithfully for a number of years.

Father Stephen died in 1765 after seventeen years as priest of London's only Orthodox church. The church register states, "The priest Stephen Ivanovsky, who initiated this church record book, passed away in London, in the church house in Clifford Street on Sunday, 13 February 1765, and was buried by the church of St James in the street known as Piccadilly." Two priest-monks, Gennadius and Jeremias, came from Mt Athos to continue the services in London on a temporary basis, aided by the chanter Prokhor Zhdanoff. The Church authorities decided that a priest with knowledge of the Greek language was needed for London, which is evidence of the continuing importance of the church for the Greek community. The candidate selected for the post was Priest-monk Ephrem Diakovsky, a former instructor and preacher from the Kiev Theological Academy. He was accompanied by psalm-reader Andrew Afanasievich Samborsky, who had studied at the same academy. Father Ephrem did not stay long, however. In 1767 he became ill and wrote to the Holy Synod complaining that the "uncouth and insolent" English populace mocked him because of his priestly clothing. He recommended that only widowed members of the white (or married) clergy be appointed to London in the future. Without waiting for a replacement, he left secretly for Hungary, where his uncle was a priest; from there he returned to Russia.

The Ludwell and Paradise Families

Little information has survived concerning any of these eighteenth-century clergymen, and even less is known about the laypeople who attended the Embassy church, beyond the names recorded in the church registers. An exception to this tantalizing dearth of details is the case of John Paradise and, to a lesser extent, Philip Ludwell, two individuals who caught the attention of secular historians. The church register shows that Philip Ludwell was received into the Orthodox Church on December 31, 1738, by Father Bartholomew Cassanno. In a letter written in April 1791, Russian Ambassador Count Simeon (Semyon) Woronzow referred to Ludwell as follows: "An Englishman . . . who had some property in Virginia, took it into his head to read in the original all the Fathers of the Church, and became convinced that our religion was the only true one; he forsook his own to study it and brought up in it his only daughter."[3] In 1760 Ludwell returned to England from Virginia (then still a British colony), and his three Virginia-born daughters—Hannah, Frances, and Lucy—were received into the Orthodox Church on April 3/14, 1762. An annotation in Father Stephen Ivanovsky's church inventory indicates that on August 20/31, 1762, a copy of the New Testament (apparently in Church Slavonic) "was given to Mr. Ludwell, an Englishman belonging to our faith, for the spiritual edification of himself and his three daughters."

In 1762 Ludwell published his translation of the *Orthodox Confession* by Peter Moghila, a seventeenth-century Orthodox Metropolitan of Kiev, with the title *The Orthodox Confession of the Catholic and Apostolic Eastern Church; Faithfully Translated from the Originals*. (It was reprinted in 1898 with an introduction by J. J. Overbeck, a later convert to Orthodoxy.) Today this work is generally not considered one of the best expositions of the Orthodox faith because it suffers from Western influences that are seen as alien to the Orthodox tradition. Nevertheless, these influences should not be exaggerated. Patriarch Nectarius of Jerusalem pronounced himself satisfied that it was a pure and correct confession of the faith, without any taint of Latin or Protestant heresies. It diverged from the Orthodox patristic tradition by attempting to provide a systematic and, in consequence, rather lifeless exposition of Orthodoxy in the form of a catechism. If Ludwell was as well versed in the Fathers of the Orthodox Church as Woronzow indicates, he could not fail to have been struck by the contrast between the inspired words of the ancient Fathers and the dead scholastic tone of the eighteenth-century writer. Nevertheless, he likely considered it a good introduction to Orthodox teaching because it was in a form familiar to Western readers and contained, in a single volume, answers to many questions that must have been posed by his acquaintances. Certainly, because the eighteenth century represented perhaps the nadir of Orthodox enlightenment in Russia, it is clear that in offering this work to the English public, Philip Ludwell was making the best effort he could and, in accordance with the understanding of the times, sharing his Orthodoxy with his fellow countrymen.

At some point in the 1760s, Ludwell's health began to fail. An entry in the church register for September 17/28, 1766, records that "The sick Mr. Philip Ludwell received Holy Communion at his home in the afternoon." Priest-monk Ephrem Diakovsky performed these ministrations to the dying Ludwell during his short stay in London. On February 22/March 5, 1767, Ludwell again received confession and Holy Communion at his home; Father Ephrem then performed the rite of Holy Unction, assisted by the reader Andrew Samborsky. The entry for March 14/25, 1767, records that "Mr. Philip Ludwell, English gentleman, died at 5 o'clock in the afternoon." The next day prayers for his departed soul were said at the Embassy church, and on March 22/April 2 he was buried in his family vault at St Mary's Church, Stratford-le-Bow.

Before his death, Ludwell appointed his good friend Peter Paradise as guardian to his daughters. The youngest, Lucy, was only fourteen at the time. The church records note that on March 31/April 11, 1767, Peter Paradise confessed and received Holy Communion, together with Hannah Ludwell, Frances Ludwell, and Lucy Ludwell, as if strengthening themselves for the new difficulties and responsibilities that lay ahead. The two families evidently remained close; in 1769 Lucy Ludwell married Peter Paradise's son, John. There is no reference to this wedding in the church register. It is not known if it was performed by the new priest, Father Andrew Samborsky, who succeeded Father Ephrem Diakovsky, or by a visiting clergyman, or whether, like Father Andrew before his ordination, they travelled to another European city to find a functioning Orthodox church in which to be married. The wedding is recorded in the extensive biography by Dr Archibald Bolling Shepperson, *John Paradise and Lucy Ludwell of London and Williamsburg*.

Peter Paradise was the British consul in Salonika, Greece, where he also carried on successful business enterprises. His wife was the daughter of a Greek woman and of Philip Lodvill, an Anglican clergyman.[4] Their son, John, was born in 1743. Count Woronzow describes him as follows: "He is English, born in Salonika, Greece, where his father was British Consul and, having married a Greek lady, adopted his wife's religion and brought up in it his only son, of whom I am now speaking." Thus, although Peter Paradise converted to Orthodoxy, his son was brought up in the faith from childhood. John received his early education at the University of Padua in Italy, where one of his tutors was the respected Greek theologian Nicephorus Theotokis.[5]

After Padua, John Paradise went to study law at Oxford. He developed wide interests in various academic and literary pursuits.

After finishing his studies at Oxford, John Paradise set up house in the West End of London, first in Cavendish Square and then in Margaret Street. His house became a favourite meeting place for social, literary, and political Londoners. In 1773 he met Dr Samuel Johnson, the great lexicographer, and this acquaintanceship developed into a firm friendship. When Dr Johnson had a stroke ten years later, he wrote to a friend that nobody had shown him more kindness during his disability than Paradise. John Paradise was also on close terms with James Boswell, an author best known for his biography of Dr Johnson. Paradise was elected a member of the Royal Society, where he met the famous scientists of the day, although he himself never performed any experiments. A contemporary visitor described his house as "the crowded rendezvous of foreigners of distinction, and on Sunday evenings open to almost every stranger." In the words of his biographer, John Paradise was "a man who numbered among his closest friends many of the greatest statesmen of England and America and who probably had a wider acquaintance among the intellectuals of continental Europe than any Englishman of his day, but who offered in return no more than gracious hospitality, personal charm, and a genius for friendship."

Lucy Paradise, in contrast, is described as "lively, superficial, ambitious, and shrewish." Mrs Thrale, a friend of Dr Johnson, referred to her as "that tiresome, silly woman, who talked of her family and affairs till she was sick to death of hearing her," to which Dr Johnson retorted, "Madam, why do you blame the woman for the only sensible thing she could do—talking of her family and affairs? For how should a woman, who is as empty as a drum, talk upon any other subject?" In Shepperson's view, Lucy effectively ruined John Paradise's life.

If Lucy did not inherit her father's wisdom and intellect, she was nevertheless heir to some of the Ludwell family estates in Virginia. These brought in some income for a time, but disaster struck in 1775, when the American Revolution broke out. Their properties were occupied in turn by loyalist and by revolutionary armies, and all revenues from the properties ceased. Paradise wanted to sort out their affairs in Virginia, and was at pains to demonstrate his loyalty to the new independent regime. It seems this was not mere opportunism; he had a genuine sympathy for the libertarian ideals that sparked the American Revolution. In 1780, Paradise went to Paris where he established close relations with Benjamin Franklin (who was a friend of John's father-in-law, Philip Ludwell) and acquired American citizenship. On the eve of the ceremony, John sent Franklin a note in which he wrote, "What higher pleasure, indeed, can be felt by a man, who may without vanity profess himself a lover of liberty and virtue, than to be admitted as an affectionate and zealous citizen by one of those illustrious states, who by the noblest exertions of unexampled virtue, have established their liberty on the surest basis." In London, Lucy Paradise became known in society as "a strenuous American republican." Nevertheless, they were unable to set sail for Virginia, and their financial situation worsened. In 1786 they met Thomas Jefferson during his visit to London. Jefferson became increasingly involved in the Paradise family and their financial troubles, and did his best to help them. Lucy Paradise kept up a lengthy correspondence with Jefferson for many years. She tried to have her husband appointed American minister in London or somewhere on the Continent, but these efforts came to nothing. Finally, in 1787, they made their long-awaited visit to Virginia. This did not help them financially, however, because they were unable to secure the return of their property. On returning to London, John and Lucy learned that their younger daughter had died during their absence.

It was at this troubled time that John and Lucy Paradise made the acquaintance of Count Woronzow, the new Russian ambassador, who was appointed to London in 1785. They met at the Embassy church, which Paradise continued to attend regularly. Woronzow wrote,

> John Paradise was in close relations with Dr. Franklin and Sir John Pringle who disapproved, just as my friend did, of the American War, during which he stayed here and wrote against it. In the meantime he received no revenue from his lands in Virginia which were overrun by friendly and hostile armies, and this obliged him to live on what he possessed here, and that he ate up completely. He has nothing left but his wife's property in Virginia. On my arrival here, having often seen him at our Church, and heard of the kindness which he had always shown to our compatriots, especially to our late Cousin, I made his acquaintance which I found of infinite use to me, for it enabled me to meet many highly esteemed scholars; and he also gave me information which I cannot obtain elsewhere.

In return for his services, Woronzow obtained modest remuneration for Paradise from the Russian government. In time, John Paradise became part of the closely knit group of people connected with the embassy and the Embassy church, which assisted Woronzow in his diplomatic and political activities.

Archpriest Andrew Samborsky

Archpriest Andrew Samborsky, rector of the Embassy church from 1769 to 1780, was a renowned expert in modern agricultural methods. (Source: Author's archive)

After the departure of Father Ephrem Diakovsky in 1767, the Embassy church was left temporarily without a priest. Andrew Samborsky, the psalm-reader who had accompanied Father Ephrem to England, married an Englishwoman, Elizabeth Fielding (the wedding took place in Amsterdam), and was happy to stay in London. In 1769 Samborsky visited Russia and was ordained to the priesthood.

Father Andrew was initially sent to England as part of a project to improve Russian agriculture, initiated by Russian Empress Catherine the Great. Having reasoned that in a Russian country village, the most authoritative person was generally the parish priest, she decided that some of the more promising graduates from the theological academies should be sent to England to learn about English agricultural methods, which they would then teach to their parishioners after ordination. During his early years in England as a psalm-reader, Samborsky was entrusted with supervising the Russian youths who were studying agriculture and other sciences. After his ordination, he devoted himself to their pastoral care as a priest.

During the next ten years, Samborsky acquired a reputation as a zealous pastor, while at the same time becoming an expert in agricultural matters. He later wrote, "When I was not performing my religious duties in church, I employed all my remaining time not for my own profit but for the general good, using every opportunity and means for the advancement of Russian artists, shipbuilders, sailors, and agriculturalists." As a result of this secular interest, some information about him has been preserved in both English and Russian works on agriculture. He made the acquaintance of John Arbuthnot and Arthur Young, who were leading English agriculturalists of the day, both of whom helped with the placement of Russian students on their own farms—Arbuthnot at Mitcham and Young in Essex and at Bradfield in Suffolk. Father Andrew is even mentioned in Arthur Young's autobiography, where he is referred to as "Sambosky." He recalls how Samborsky

> . . . wrote to me at Bradfield earnestly requesting that I would go to London and examine all the young men, that he might take them or send them to St Petersburg. This I accordingly did, and examined them very closely, except one, who refused to answer any questions from a conviction of his absolute ignorance. I gave a certificate of the others' examination, and I asked Sambosky what would become of the obstinate fool who would not answer. He replied that without doubt he would be sent to Siberia for life, but I never heard whether this happened.

Little detailed information about the Embassy church during this period has survived. It is known that in 1770 the vestry, sacred vessels, and service books were overhauled and replaced where necessary, but no further inventories of church property were made until the arrival of Father Eugene Popoff in 1842. In about 1770 the chanter Prokhor Zhdanoff was summoned back to Russia by order of a government minister, but without the knowledge of the Holy Synod. Theodore Grigorievsky, a singer from one of the Imperial chapels, replaced him.

In 1780 Empress Catherine the Great recalled Father Andrew Samborsky to Russia in recognition of his zealous pastoral service. He settled in the Imperial village of Tsarskoye Selo, near St Petersburg, where he was appointed spiritual adviser to the Imperial family and teacher of English to the Grand Dukes Alexander (the future Alexander I) and Constantine. He also wrote a book titled *A Description of Practical English Agriculture* (*Opisanie prakticheskogo anglinskogo zemledeliya*[6]), which was published in 1781. He implemented some of the modern agricultural techniques he had learned in England at a school of practical agriculture set up by Emperor Paul I in 1797 and also on his estate. Father Andrew died in 1815 at the age of eighty-three.

Father Andrew is an interesting example of the paradoxes that affected the Orthodox Church in Russia in the eighteenth century. Although he was a graduate of the Kiev Theological Academy, it appears that he was at least as interested in agriculture as he was in theology. It seems that he viewed agriculture as a way to improve the lot of ordinary people by helping to alleviate food shortages. By the time he returned to Russia, the empress had lost interest in her agricultural projects. However, in Tsarskoye Selo, using English methods, Samborsky established a model farm that included fishponds and an orchard where he gave demonstrations of efficient plowing techniques. He was also instrumental in redesigning the estate, including the construction of a new church. However, when the metropolitan of St Petersburg arrived to consecrate the church, he initially refused to let Father

Andrew take part in the service because he had shaved off his beard while in England and did not look like an Orthodox priest. It is interesting to note that although Father Andrew was the first Russian clergyman in London of whom there is a portrait, he looks more like an English country squire than a Russian Orthodox priest.

Before leaving England, Father Samborsky wrote, "I prepared at my own expense a worthy successor." In 1776, during a visit to Russia, he recruited four students from a seminary in his home region of Kharkov, Ukraine, to come to England, serve in the Embassy church, and study English agricultural methods. Concluding his description of his encounter with the Russian students (described earlier), Arthur Young wrote, "One of them, much the ablest, remained in England, and became in time Chaplain to the Russian Embassy, in which situation he is at the present time, and held in general esteem." This individual was James Smirnove, who assumed the position of rector of the Embassy church in 1780 and remained at his post until his death in 1840.

Chapter 3

[1780–1840]
Archpriest James Smirnove

A Priest and a Diplomat

"Out of all the officials attached to our mission in London there was only one remarkable man: he was the priest of our church, Yakov Ivanovich Smirnove, who was also used in the diplomatic sector," wrote Count Evgraf Komarovsky, a diplomatic courier who visited London in 1787, just seven years after Father Smirnove's ordination. Father James (Yakov) Smirnove[1] is the first of the London clergymen about whom enough information has survived to provide an impression of the actual person, not just a shadowy collection of names and dates.

In 1795 the journalist and author Peter Ivanovich Makaroff, who commented that he always made a point of visiting Russian priests on his travels "since they are intelligent people and generally well informed about the country in which they have long been resident," described his meeting with Father Smirnove:

> I was led into a room which was very well furnished and some minutes later there appeared a man who was fairly young, fairly handsome, tall, well-built, erect, impressive in bearing and dressed with the greatest care but without the least hint of unbecoming foppishness: in a word, a young, well educated Lord—and this Lord was Mr. S-v, the Russian priest at the Embassy.

On making his acquaintance, Makaroff found that Father Smirnove was

> . . . very intelligent; he knows Latin very well, speaks French, German and English and (if I am not mistaken) Italian. He has read a great deal and himself translates and writes. He has an extreme love of Englishmen, for

which the English in turn love him. I do not think he would wish to live in any place other than London.

Father James's command of spoken English was far from perfect, according to a letter written in May 1803 by a young Englishwoman on her way from Ireland to stay with Princess Dashkova in Russia. From London she wrote to her father, "The Russian Chaplain Mr. Smirnove has Call'd upon us here; and seems to take an interest for me I cou'd not have expected. The Elderly lady who is going to see her daughter at Petersburgh he told us is a Mrs. Delmain under whose care 'I cou'd go in the most agreeable manner, dat he was very sure Madlle wou'd much like his countree, and she wou'd be relish'd there.'"

In addition to the impressions left by Russian travellers, this period is generally better documented because the documents are more recent and therefore better preserved, and also because of the increasing requirements for reports to be submitted to the Church authorities in St Petersburg. In 1804 Ambassador Count Simeon Woronzow received a letter from the Ministry of Foreign Affairs of the Russian Empire asking him to "inform the priest attached to your mission, that every year he should send to the Holy Synod a signed list of births, marriages and deaths of members of the Graeco-Russian [i.e., Orthodox] Confession living locally, while at the same time leaving in the church a copy of this list also attested by his signature." As a result, starting in 1804, there are reasonably complete lists of births, marriages, and deaths preserved in the London archives of the Russian Orthodox Church. In June 1835 a decree was received from Russia announcing the requirement that annual reports include a service record (*formulyarnaya vedomost*) for each member of the clergy attached to the church. The record was to contain a brief curriculum vitae and information about the clergy's conduct. This was required because of cases of embassy clergy being called back to Russia to face investigations of alleged misconduct and the authorities having no information about them on file. Although repetitive, these annual reports provide much of the basic information about the church and its clergy, beginning with those who were in office in 1835.

The first report indicated that James Smirnove first went to England in 1776. He was the son of a priest and had studied at the Kharkov Collegium. On October 20, 1780, at the age of twenty-six, he was ordained to the priesthood by Archbishop Innocent of Pskov, to replace Father Andrew Samborsky, who was returning to Russia from London. The ordination certificate was dated October 1780 and signed by the Most Reverend Gabriel, Archbishop of Novgorod and St Petersburg. Father James Smirnove had five children, all born in England: Constantine, born in 1782; Elizabeth, born in 1788; Sophia, born in 1791; Ivan, born in 1794; and Catherine, born in 1798.

Continuing his report, Father James gave some detail of his income and expenditures. Three times a year he received his remuneration by courier from St Petersburg. The amount received in September 1835 was £427 1s. 3d.,[2] which included, in addition to his basic salary as a priest, various annual grants awarded by the Imperial Treasury in recognition of his valuable service. He used these funds to support himself and his family; maintain the church and the church house; pay for various church supplies such as charcoal, firewood, incense, prosphora, and wine; and pay for services that included such innovations as street lighting, the community police force, and "delivery of water to the house in pipes."

Faced with these expenses, Father James reported that he was able to spend his time in England without incurring any debts only by observing the strictest economies and by carefully watching all expenditures. In fact, Father James was not the only Russian in England who found it hard to reconcile the enormous expense of living in London with the modest stipends received from Russia, often after considerable delays. Many had no alternative but to go into debt, which led to an inevitable crisis when they were recalled to Russia. Even Count Woronzow, the ambassador, considered moving out of London because of the high cost of living there. Father Smirnove observed that the latter experienced particular difficulties because of his large family, "for the education and care of whom he is obliged to maintain in his home more people than the high cost of living, which is increasing from year to year, allows him." Father James wrote in his 1835 report,

> Almost from the very day of my arrival in London to take up my duties at the church here I have been entrusted with various tasks, principally in connection with the care of Russian subjects who have been sent to England to study various technical subjects. Besides this, I have had the honour to be used from time to time by the Russian Plenipotentiary Minister here [i.e., the Ambassador] for various other matters of government service.

One would think that with the intentionally vague phrase "other matters of government service," Father James was alluding to his extensive involvement in diplomatic affairs, which in his case grew naturally out of his long service as embassy chaplain. In fact, such was his prominence outside the purely ecclesiastical sphere that references to him can be found in many contemporary sources, including the memoirs of Russians travelling in Europe.

In addition to Count Komarovsky and P. I. Makaroff, other travellers who mentioned Father Smirnove include Pavel Ivanovich Sumarokov and Alexander Ivanovich Turgenev, brother of the famous novelist. Turgenev recorded that he was escorted on his visit to Parliament in 1826 by "the respected Smirnove, whose appearance was in accord with his calling and good reputation." Theodore Ivanovich Iordan, who later became rector of the Academy of Arts in Russia, provided a description of Smirnove in 1830, when he would have been seventy-six years old, which recalled Makaroff's impressions of thirty-five years earlier:

> Tall, with the accent of a Ukrainian from the Kharkov region, dressed in a black coat of an old-fashioned, Quaker-like cut. . . . Ya. I. pleased me greatly, dressed like a lord of an earlier age: in a long frock coat with tails which reached down almost to his heels, with buckles on his shoes, in gaiters, with a low, wide-brimmed hat and carrying a large sturdy stick with a silver knob. His whole appearance inspired sincere respect. He walked along quietly, describing circles with his stick, and with his respectable appearance, and his hair in a plait, heavily powdered and brushed back at the temples, he seemed to me a living portrait of the seventeenth-century Dutch school.

From these descriptions it is clear that Father James did not normally wear the clerical attire of an Orthodox priest nor, it would seem, was he expected to do so; he made no attempt to present an ecclesiastical appearance when he met his fellow countrymen. Evidently, at that time, it was felt that one should simply conform to the customs of the country in which one lived. It was not noted in any of these traveller's impressions, nor by A. G. Cross, from whose article the extracts are taken, that in his choice of attire Father James was not trying to appear quaint or old fashioned, and was trying still less to look like a Quaker. He was evidently trying to approximate, as closely as possible, the appearance of an Orthodox priest while keeping within the conventions of Western dress, hence the choice of black clothing and the long coat reaching "almost to his heels." The "wide-brimmed" hat was often worn by Russian nonmonastic clergy in place of the traditional *skoufiya*. Even the stick with the silver knob recalls the staff traditionally carried by Orthodox bishops and some senior clergy. Doubtless, the result was an acceptable appearance for attending debates in the House of Commons. However, the overall impression was of a curious, hybrid effect that was somehow symbolic of the many facets of Father Smirnove's long career. His diplomatic and other involvements, which are discussed later in this chapter, were extensive; still he was able to combine these with his primary responsibility, that of a priest ministering to the small Orthodox community in London.

The Russian Church Community in London

According to the 1835 report mentioned earlier, three psalm-readers, or chanters—referred to as *tserkovnik* rather than *psalomshchik*—assisted Father James. This alternative designation implies that their duties included general care of the church as well as assisting at services. The oldest, Leonty Ivanovich Litkevich, lived in England almost as long as Father James. He studied at the Kharkov Collegium and later was in the cathedral choir of Bishop Aggei of Belgorod and Oboyan. In 1780 Archpriest Andrew Samborsky summoned him to England and appointed him *tserkovnik* for the London church. He was at least eighty years old by 1835 and received his salary directly from the Imperial government in Russia.

His younger colleague Ivan Fyodorovich Kvitnitsky, who had been appointed to his post in London on February 16, 1814, was married and had a large family. He had studied theology in Kharkov and then was a singer in the bishop's choir in the Kharkov diocese. On September 27, 1832, he received a grant from the Imperial Treasury in recognition of his long and honourable service. However, it is doubtful that he found it easy to support a family on his earnings as psalm-reader. The path to ecclesiastical advancement opened for him in 1838 when his wife, Elizabeth, and seven daughters converted from Protestantism to Orthodoxy.[3] Father James Smirnove translated the service of reception into English for their benefit. They were received into the Orthodox Church by chrismation. A document was then drawn up in Russian and English declaring that "We, the undersigned, solemnly promise to observe the dogmas [of the Orthodox Church] steadfastly unto the end of our lives." It was signed by Kvitnitsky's wife, Elizabeth, and his seven daughters, Ariadna, Sophia, Catherine, Marianna, Daria, Alexandra, and Helen. Shortly thereafter, Father James sent a letter of recommendation to the diocesan authorities commending Kvitnitsky's long service and stating that he wished for him to be ordained to the priesthood, adding that his wife and family concurred with his wish. However, this ordination never took place.

In 1834 the clergy of the Embassy church were assigned a third psalm-reader, or *tserkovnik*, Alexander Belyaeff. He was the son of a minor clergyman and had studied in St Petersburg. As of 1835, he was unmarried.

Judging from the registers of births, marriages, and deaths, which are extant from 1804, and from the confession lists[4] that survived from 1831 onward, the Russian community to which Father James ministered was a small one, consisting of the ambassador and a few embassy staff as well as the clergy. For example, 1804 saw no births and no deaths and a single wedding. Major General Nicholas Alexandrovich Sabloukhoff (apparently a permanent member of the embassy staff) was married to the "noble and well-educated English spinster Juliana Angerstein." Fifteen people were recorded as having been to confession in 1831. Because of the firmly entrenched practice in the eighteenth and nineteenth centuries of receiving confession and Holy Communion once a year, the confession lists provide a register of Orthodox who were in "good standing" and attending a particular church. However, this would not have been the extent of the congregation as some churchgoers received the sacraments even less frequently than once a year. In addition to the clergy and their families, and the above-noted Major General Sabloukhoff, the list includes Ivan Smirnove, a *Pridvorni Sovetnik* (roughly, court counselor). This was Father James's son who, by 1831, was thirty-seven years old and, at that time, working in the London Embassy. He was also a Fellow of the Royal Society and contributed articles on Russian literature to British journals. In 1836 he was appointed Russian Consul-General in Genoa.

Count Simeon (Semyon) Romanovich Woronzow was the most prominent figure in the Russian community in London during Father James's tenure. Coming from an aristocratic family that had a distinguished record in the foreign and diplomatic service of the Russian Empire, he was appointed ambassador in 1785. His brother, Alexander, was Russian envoy to the Court of St James in 1762. Simeon Woronzow began his career as a soldier during the Russo-Turkish War. He was involved in the treaty negotiations with Turkey in 1774, where he launched his diplomatic career.

After a short period as envoy in Venice, Count Woronzow was offered an ambassadorial post either in Paris or London. He chose London largely through the influence of his elder brother, from whom he had learned to respect England and her institutions and acquired a firm belief in the need for Anglo-Russian friendship. Except for one short visit to Russia in 1802, Count Woronzow stayed in England continuously from his arrival in June 1785 until his death in 1832. In 1808 his daughter, Catherine, married George, the Earl of Pembroke. His son Mikhail also lived in England with his family. Count Woronzow's enemies accused him of being "more English than Russian," although this is likely not justified because, despite his growing affection for his country of domicile, he never properly mastered the English language, written or spoken. He was fluent in French, which was the international diplomatic language at the time and spoken by many upper-class Russians. In fact, much of his private correspondence is in French.

Although he remained a loyal servant of the Russian state, Count Woronzow's attachment to England grew with the passage of time. He was firmly committed to the alliance between England and Russia, and in matters of politics, he was an idealist rather than an opportunist. As the tide of international relations ebbed and flowed, he found himself alternately in and out of favour, which in the long run proved detrimental to his career. Woronzow formed a close and lasting friendship with Father James Smirnove, with whom he shared the dual affection for his native Russia and his country of residence. Woronzow remained in England even after his retirement as ambassador.

Apart from the permanent Russian community in London, the church registers indicate that it also ministered to travellers and other transient Orthodox who found themselves in England as a result of the Napoleonic wars and other upheavals of the time. In perusing these entries one is struck by the pervasive awareness of social class. For example, it is recorded that on April 26, 1806, Prince Ivan Ivanovich Bariatinsky was married to "the most well born and well brought up English lady, Frances Dutton, spinster, daughter of Lord Sherbourne." On August 21, 1807, Princess Natalia Theodorovna Galitzine, née Princess Shakhovskoy, died in London and was buried on September 8, 1807, in the church of St Marylebone in vault number 7. Then, in 1809, her remains were returned to Russia at the request of her family. It was noted that on November 2, 1833, Dmitri Sergievich Lanskoy, privy councilor and knight, died in London at the age of sixty-seven. The correspondence related to this has deep black borders, in keeping with nineteenth-century customs of mourning. By contrast, entries relating to the lower social orders leave no doubt as to their status. On June 1/13, 1809, the peasant Gregory Evdokimoff, son of Simon, died and was buried. On November 11/23, 1812, two serfs, servants of Baron Pavel Andreyevich Nikolai-Kondrati Dmitriev, son of Lopoukhoff and Evdokia Kirillova, daughter of Volkoff—were married. On January 6, 1817, a sailor, Simeon Sharoukhin, a native of the town of Mezen and a free man, died and was buried. On January 26, 1818, there is recorded the death of Naum Gnazdareff, servant of His Excellency, General of Infantry, bearer of many Russian orders and Knight, Count Simeon Romanovich Woronzow. Note that more space is devoted to the titles and distinctions of his master than to the deceased himself!

Although these entries may be amusing today, in eighteenth- and nineteenth-century Russia, every member of the population was assigned a specific rank, which was thus a matter of law as well as social status. Precise record keeping was expected by the Russian authorities, as can be seen in a letter Father James received in 1831 from St Petersburg complaining that copies of the registers had not been sent as required. Kondrati Dmitriev, the serf of Baron Nikolai who had married in London in 1812, applied for a divorce, and confirmation of the marriage details was required.

As the only Orthodox church in London, the Russian Embassy church continued to serve the needs of the Greek Orthodox community, which began to grow after 1815 as several Greek commercial houses were established in the city. The first of these was known as Argenti, Thomas and Company, followed by Ralli Brothers, founded by Pandia and Eustratius Ralli. These names are all found in the registers of the Embassy church. For example, on May 22, 1825, the Greek Eustratius Ralli married a Greek woman, Maria Mavrogordatos, offspring of another illustrious Greek merchant family. The following year, their first child was baptised; in 1828 was the baptism of their son Stephen, followed in 1830 by the baptism of another son, John. The year 1831 saw the baptism of Anthia, daughter of John Argenti, and in 1827 was the baptism of Alexander, son of the Greek John Mavrogordatos. The mother's sister, "Mrs Ralli," was one of the godparents. Other Greeks who sought the ministrations of the Russian Church included sailors and an employee of the Turkish consular service. Eventually, in 1837, the Greeks established a church of their own. This was the Church of the Saviour, which was located at London Wall, near Finsbury Circus. Ralli, Argenti, Mavrogordatos, and other Greek merchants in the city were prominent as organizers and benefactors of this new church.

The Earl of Guilford: An Extraordinary Convert

There is little evidence of English people converting to Orthodoxy during Father Smirnove's tenure. Exceptions arise chiefly in the case of converts through marriage, such as the Kvitnitsky family mentioned earlier. Lord Frederick North, Earl of Guilford,[5] is possibly the only member of the English aristocracy ever to have converted to the Orthodox faith. Concerning the Earl of Guilford, the church registers contain the following entry, which was made by Father James: "1827, October. Before his death, Lord Guilford informed me that in 1792 he had accepted the Greek faith of the Eastern (Orthodox) Church. At baptism he had been named Dimitri—his former name was Frederick." The case of Lord North has been carefully researched; following is a closer examination.

Frederick North, subsequently the fifth Earl of Guilford, was born in 1766. He was the third son of Frederick North, the second Earl of Guilford, who, as head of the British government from 1770 to 1782, failed to prevent the loss of the American colonies. Frederick North the younger was always weak in health and spent much of his childhood abroad at health resorts. In 1782 he went to Christ Church, Oxford, and later set out on a European tour that took him to Venice and the Greek island of Corfu, which at that time was under Venetian rule. As a young man he shared the enthusiasm for things Greek that was common among many of his contemporaries. This interest was generally inspired by sympathy for the Greek people suffering under the Turkish yoke and support for the growing Greek independence movement. The English Philhellenes, as they were known, were enthusiastic about the Hellenic culture of ancient Greece but knew little of the Orthodox Christian heritage of Byzantium. In this regard, the young Lord North differed from his contemporaries. There is evidence that even before his visit to Corfu, North had studied Greek theological works by St Symeon, the New Theologian; Patriarch Dositheos of Jerusalem; and Meletios Syrigos.

When he arrived on Corfu, the local inhabitants were immediately struck by his behaviour, which was quite different from that of the usual young Englishman making his "grand tour." He treated the local inhabitants with genuine respect. One observer, Nicholas Arliotis, noted in his diary,

> He speaks a little modern Greek, but with a difficult pronunciation different from our own. He loves our church services and is closely familiar with the Orthodox ritual. He has attended the Liturgy in the churches of the Most Holy Mother of God Spiliotissa and of St Spiridon, and he delights to hear the Constantinopolitan chanting. In church he repeatedly makes the sign of the cross as if he were a monk, which is scarcely consistent with the outlook and character of the English.

George Prosalendis, an elderly member of the local Corfu nobility who was well versed in the Orthodox faith, befriended Lord North. The two would meet in a coffee shop and discuss religious topics such as the validity of Anglican baptism. Before long, North asked to see Prosalendis privately and expressed his desire to receive Orthodox baptism. He was introduced to the senior priest on the island, the protopriest Dimitrios Petrettinos. In requesting baptism, North asked that it be performed in strict secrecy. He explained,

> For many years I have been convinced, through my study of the Old and New Testaments, the Holy Œcumenical Councils and the Holy Fathers, that I find myself in error. But the social and economic circumstances of

> myself and my family have led me to shrink back. Eventually I decided to travel round the world, in the hope that the Lord would show me some way of giving my soul to Him, while still preserving the civil status of my family. . . . I desire my Baptism to be secret, because of the social and economic commitments of my family.

Prosalendis, who had consented to be godfather at the baptism, was far from happy at this request for concealment, and the protopriest shared his sentiments. It was accepted only as a short-term arrangement, as Prosalendis wrote,

> This is to be regarded as a temporary concession, until he himself shall indicate that the proper moment has come for making the matter public. Firmly committing his conscience, he promises that he will indeed announce it himself by an oath before God, that, since for the time being for reasons of expediency he does not wish to confess the truth until the right moment shall come, he will feign ignorance when others question him out of curiosity; but under no circumstances will he actually deny the truth.

The baptism was held in the priest's house in the late evening of January 23/February 3, 1792. North drew up a profession of faith in Italian. The priest Spyridon Montesanto, in whose company North had sailed from Venice to Corfu, celebrated the service. Prosalendis described the service as follows:

> The doors of both the outer and the inner rooms were closed, and the nobleman withdrew to the inner bedroom, where the curtains were drawn. Here he removed his outer garments and emerged clothed only in his shirt, as the rubrics prescribe. At once Father Montesanto began the service, with the protopope standing on the nobleman's right and myself on his left. First the exorcisms were read, and then the questions about renouncing the devil and accepting Christ; the nobleman gave the answers himself and recited the Creed three times. The protopope named him by his own name "Frederick," and I by the other name that he wished to receive (as Father Montesanto had told me), "Dimitrios." Then, with the two of us as sponsors holding him by the arms and with the priest going in front, he was led unshod to the holy font, and the sacrament of Baptism was administered to him. After this he received the seal of the gift of the Holy Spirit through anointing with the Holy Chrism, and all the ceremonies were performed exactly as prescribed by the service book and by the tradition of the Holy Orthodox Eastern Church. Throughout the service from start to finish he

was irradiated with marvelous devotion. . . . Afterwards we had a short talk, at which it was said that this holy action must be kept secret from everyone apart from the five of us.

Early the next morning, North received Holy Communion at a liturgy specially celebrated in a local church. Later in the day he was given a written baptismal certificate by the protopope. George Prosalendis expressed the hope that the right moment for public disclosure of the baptism would soon arrive. He also dreamt of an Orthodox movement within the English aristocracy, with North at its head: "Through the collaboration of this nobleman with other peers of the realm who have become secret Orthodox, there will be an increase of Orthodoxy in that kingdom."

Lord Frederick North, now the newly baptised servant of God Dimitrios, left Corfu eleven days after his baptism. He spent Lent of that year in a monastery on the island of Levkas, observing the fast with great strictness, and returned to England during the summer. However, the hopes that he would soon make his Orthodoxy known were not realized. From 1792 to 1794 he sat as a member of Parliament for Banbury, which would not have been possible if it were known that he was Orthodox. (He is probably the only sitting member of Parliament to have belonged to the Orthodox Church.) From 1798 to 1805 he was governor of Ceylon. After he succeeded as Earl of Guilford in 1817, he spent a large part of each year on Corfu. In the last years of his life his interest focused on the Ionian Academy, which was established to provide Greeks the opportunity to pursue higher education. For a time the academy was a cultural rallying point for the Greeks in their struggle for independence. However, even there, Lord North's status as an Orthodox believer was not generally known. In England he was regarded simply as an amiable eccentric with a passion for classical Greek antiquity.

There is no indication that he regularly attended services at the Russian Embassy church in London, although it is known that he was acquainted with Father James Smirnove. Lord North composed an ode in Greek in the ancient Pindaric style in honour of the Russian Empress, Catherine the Great; a copy, which is preserved in the British Library, bears the inscription, "Reverend J. Smirnove, with the Author's most affectionate Respects." However, it appears that Smirnove did not know of his Orthodoxy until just before his death.

In late summer of 1827, when Lord North returned from his annual visit to Corfu, his health was failing, and then a fall from his carriage brought on a fatal illness. His sister Ann, Countess Dowager of Sheffield, sent the following urgent note to Father James, which is preserved among the church archives:

Saturday

> Revd Smurnove
> 32 Welbeck Street
>
> My dear Sir,
>
> It is with great concern I write to say that my dear Brother is most dangerously ill and he wishes to see you as soon as you can possibly be so good as to come to him and he begs you will bring whatever is necessary for him to take the sacrament with you. I am my dear Sir very sincerely yours
>
> Sheffield

The date October 1/13, 1827, is marked on this letter, presumably by the priest. His visit to take Holy Communion to Lord North is described by Andreas Papadopoulos-Vretos, the librarian of the Ionian Academy, as follows:

> Perceiving that the last moment of his life was near at hand, he repeatedly asked for the chaplain of the Russian embassy chapel, his old friend Father Smirnove, and from his hands he received Communion, to the great displeasure of his relatives, and especially of his nephew the Earl of Sheffield, in whose house he died. The Earl of Sheffield tried in every way to prevent him receiving the ministrations of a priest of a foreign dogma, contrary to that of his forefathers.

He received Holy Communion in the presence of two Greeks, his personal physician and his valet, and then departed to the Lord on October 1/13, 1827. After his death his relatives tried to suppress the account of his baptism written by George Prosalendis, but it was eventually published (in Greek) in 1879. They also secured the return of most of the books that Lord North had contributed to the Ionian Academy. However, the fact remains that, imperfect though his confession had been, Lord North remained faithful to his Orthodox allegiance to his death.

Woronzow, Paradise, Father Smirnove, and the Crisis of 1791

In an article titled "Two Orthodox Englishmen of the 18th Century," Professor Gleb Struve compared Lord North with his contemporary, John Paradise.[6]

The Ludwell and Paradise families could hardly have been more different. Although North remained aloof from the life of the Embassy church, Paradise and his wife, Lucy, remained in close contact with Father James and Count Woronzow, the ambassador. Woronzow befriended Paradise shortly after his arrival in England, at a time when the latter was living through a series of personal and financial difficulties, following his abortive trip to Virginia to secure the return of his wife's property and the sudden death of his younger daughter. In the last few years of his life, Paradise offered Woronzow valuable assistance in his diplomatic work, for which he received some compensation from the Russian government.

Through his close connections with the embassy, Father Smirnove also became involved in these diplomatic and political activities, for which he showed a surprising aptitude. A year after his arrival in London, Woronzow provided the following account of Father James's varied activities in a letter to Count Bezborodko, Catherine the Great's secretary of state:

> By his knowledge, the respect which he has earned here in society, and his devotion to his country he is very necessary for all our compatriots who are sent here to study by the Admiralty College and other places; to secure teachers for them and all conceivable things for the success of their studies, he is obliged to travel ceaselessly about the city as well as to other places where they are studying. In addition he attends to all commissions for the various instruments which are requested by various institutions. He is so well known and loved here by scholars and craftsmen that out of friendship for him they accept our students to learn crafts to which foreigners have for some time been barred and he succeeded in placing only recently two men from Tula who had been sent by Prince Grigory Aleksandrovich [Potemkin] to study weapon and steel production. In brief, he has more work and worries than I and Baxter [Alexander Baxter, the Russian consul] put together. In addition, when Mr. Lizakevich [Vasily Grigorievich, a long-serving member of the embassy] is ill and I have something for coding, I am forced to use him for it, since there is no one else who is capable of doing it.

In his despatches, Woronzow commended the services of Father Smirnove and Lizakevich as well as John Paradise. Father James was involved in four political incidents in the late eighteenth and early nineteenth centuries, of which the most significant was probably the crisis of 1791, that is, Russia's war against Turkey, when England was on the verge of declaring war in support of Turkey. Russian armies advanced into Turkish-held territory, and the Orthodox peoples of the Balkans, who looked to Russia for help in achieving independence from the Ottoman Empire, or to at least attain to a measure of autonomy, greeted the Russian advances with enthusiasm. The politicians of western Europe had little sympathy for the Turks, yet they were always fearful that Russia would gain too great an ascendancy over Turkey and, in turn, upset their beloved "balance of power." As a result, in March 1791 the British government under William Pitt agreed to act jointly with the Prussians in sending an ultimatum to Catherine the Great, requiring the withdrawal of Russian troops from the Balkans. The text of the ultimatum was drawn up, but it was never delivered. William Pitt, an elected prime minister, had succumbed to mounting opposition both in Parliament and among the British public generally. Russian embassy staff, under the leadership of Count Woronzow, played a significant role in fostering this opposition.

Woronzow met with the foreign secretary, the Duke of Leeds, to whom he declared that because the British cabinet was blind enough to persist in its warlike measures, he was going to do all in his power to inform the British public of their government's intentions. "I have too good an opinion of the common sense of the British public not to hope that a general outcry in the country will make you abandon this unjust undertaking," he told the foreign secretary. Coming from a country with no democratically elected institutions, it took Woronzow many years to comprehend the intricacies of the British parliamentary system. However, he closely studied the system in anticipation of the day when he would be able to put his knowledge to good use. He approached Charles Fox, the leader of the Opposition, who needed no persuading because he was opposed to the war. Fox made his famous speech in opposition to Pitt in the House of Commons on March 29, 1791. This led to a dwindling of Pitt's majority and so forced him to withdraw his ultimatum, which was already on its way to Russia.

Nevertheless, the threat of war was not over. The fleet remained under sail off Portsmouth, and Pitt was still disposed toward military intervention. So for the next three months, Woronzow mobilized public opinion against the war by orchestrating a vigorous pro-Russian campaign. He had articles and pamphlets drawn up, translated, circulated, and published in newspapers throughout the country. "No War with Russia" slogans were chalked on walls in London and Westminster. Because the industrial and commercial interests of England were at stake in the event of a Russian war, public meetings were held in several big manufacturing towns. Using strictly democratic methods, public opinion was roused to such an extent that war became a virtual impossibility. In June 1791 Catherine the Great told her chancellor, "Write to Woronzow and ask him to get me a white marble likeness of Charles Fox. I should like to have it placed on my colonnade between those of Demosthenes and Cicero. By his eloquence he saved Russia and his own country from an unjust and groundless war."

The empress expressed her gratitude to the ambassador for his efforts and in reply Woronzow wrote,

> In all this I had helpers whose efforts were great, and I can truthfully say that I myself felt no burden. It was easier for me to give work than for them to carry it out. They were continually used by me on various errands, to various places and to various people; for many nights they went without sleep, composing various items for the newspapers and journals, writing pamphlets, translating a great deal from English into French and from French into English, in short for the last five months they have been ceaselessly involved.

Woronzow went on to mention the names of Lizakevich, Father James Smirnove, Joly (a Swiss who was his son's tutor), and John Paradise. Concerning Father Smirnove, he observed, "He has in his charge the City and the Stock Exchange where he has many friends; he acts as messenger between myself and Dimsdale and Jackson; he also goes to hear the debates in Parliament."

Woronzow described Paradise's part in the propaganda campaign (after mentioning two other Englishmen who had helped him):

> There is also a third whom you do not know, but who is well known here among scholars, in France, in Italy and in America where he has some property through his wife. It is a certain Mr. Paradise. All our compatriots who have been here for fifteen years know him well. He has rendered, and is rendering, me services which defy description. . . . This man, since Mr. Pitt's outburst against us, has acted with an amazing zeal, trying to convince many members of both Houses; he succeeded with regard to several, including Lord Hawke. Every day he writes specially several paragraphs for the newspapers with the object of making the nation see the danger into which Prussia's intrigues and acts of violence are dragging it. At present he is engaged in translating a pamphlet which Joly has written on the basis of the material I supplied to him. Since this pamphlet is

> supposed to be written by an Englishman, and since Mr. Paradise has a vigorous style, I hope that it will be effective. . . . To eliminate all suspicion that the pamphlet on which Joly and Paradise are working emanates from the Russian Legation, the facts which it reports, though true, are not given in the authentic form: the statements of our Court have been abridged and are not quite in the same form and wording as the original; nevertheless their meaning is correct, and they appear to have been extracted from the British papers. Since it is assumed all the time that it was an Englishman who wrote the pamphlet, the author does not approve of Armed Neutrality, but somehow seems to justify it all the same. Russia's commercial relations with England are set out quite clearly. . . .

A nineteenth-century historian commented that in this pamphlet the arguments against Pitt's Russian policy "found perhaps their most forcible and least exaggerated expression . . . the old test of commercial utility was applied against the Government's scheme with triumphant coldness and calculation." The Russian sources were never suspected. Woronzow continued,

> One thing which seems to me to be of unquestionable utility to the service of Her Imperial Majesty, is that she should grant a pension of 150 or 200 Pounds sterling to Mr. Paradise. So long as he lives he will be of very great use to me and my successors for the good of our service. We could never have either a better pen or a more zealous man, and if you will point this out to the Empress I feel sure she will grant this pension. . . .

Later that year Woronzow received 2,000 roubles from Russia to defray his expenses, out of which he set aside £150 to pay Paradise.

With the threat of war with England averted, the Russians advanced into Turkish-held territory; the Turks sued for peace after they lost the fortress of Ochakov on the Dniester River. However, the Russians dashed the hopes of those who thought that they would advance further into the Balkans and drive the Turks out of Greece.[7]

Next, Count Woronzow and the embassy entourage were involved in the events of 1793–1795, when Polish nationalists in Russian-occupied Polish territory, following the second partition of Poland, threatened an uprising. On this occasion, not surprisingly, British public opinion favoured the Poles, and the Russian Embassy made no attempt to influence it. In fact, Woronzow did not approve of his government's Polish policy, and he was particularly concerned about apparent links between Polish insurgents and the "revolutionary monster" of France. So Woronzow and his associates directed their efforts toward uncovering links between the French Jacobins and the Poles, in particular, regarding shipments of arms to the insurrectionists. In a despatch to the empress, Woronzow reported, "I asked all who were with me here in your Majesty's service to keep watch in theatres, various public places and coffee houses through their friends." The activities of Smirnove, Lizakevich, and Paradise were given special attention, but here it was the intelligence gathered by Father Smirnove, who made use of his contact with Robert Greenall, an Englishman who had lived in Russia, that was of crucial importance. Greenall told him of his meeting with two individuals who were attempting to ship arms to Lübeck for transport to Polish revolutionary groups. Smirmove encouraged him to remain in contact with the conspirators and to report back everything he discovered about their further plans and contacts in Poland. Greenall provided him with copies of some letters from Poland that he had obtained; Smirnove passed these letters on to Woronzow for transmission to the empress, together with his own reports on the background and reliability of Greenall. Finally, Smirnove identified a Russian merchant named Tarakanov who had agreed to deliver arms from Libau (a port on the Baltic, now known as Liepaja) to places within Russia. In the letter in which he reported on this, he commented that the plan was unlikely to succeed in the face of the recent Russian advances and victories. His assessment of the situation proved to be correct.

This was the last time that Paradise would help Woronzow with embassy work; he died on December 1/12, 1795. Paradise entered the Russian service at a time of financial and personal crisis. He did not see his activities as being in any way disloyal to England, although he did regard himself as an American citizen rather than British. His loyalty to Woronzow was based primarily on friendship and on their common Orthodox faith. Woronzow, for his part, seems to have regarded him as a friend rather than as an agent. On January 4/15, 1796, he wrote to his brother, "I had the misfortune of losing a friend: it is Mr. Paradise, who was strongly attached to me and who, liking my son, taught him geometry and read with him books from which Mishinka benefited a great deal." ("Mishinka" was the future general—Field Marshall Prince Mikhail Woronzow—who fought at Waterloo by Wellington's side and later became viceroy of the Caucasus, whom Leo Tolstoy portrayed in his novel *Hadji Murat.*) Among the nine legatees who received £16 from Paradise's will were Thomas Jefferson, Count Woronzow, and Lord Frederick North, who had accepted the Orthodox faith just a few years before Paradise's death. He also left £100 to Father James Smirnove. His life was aptly characterized by Thomas Jefferson, who wrote in 1788, "Sensibility [or sensitivity] of mind is indeed the parent of every virtue, but it is the parent of much misery too. Nobody is more its victim than Mr. Paradise."

Interestingly, Paradise's biographer, Dr Shepperson, made no mention of his work on behalf of the Russian Embassy. It seems that he found no trace of these activities in the vast manuscripts that he studied. In all likelihood, Lucy Paradise, possibly acting on the advice of Count Woronzow and Father James Smirnove, her spiritual father, carefully destroyed all such references. The information presented here was derived from *The Woronzow Papers*, which were published in 1887 but remained largely unknown to British and American scholars prior to Professor Struve's study,[8] published in 1949, from which additional information has been drawn.

Count Woronzow continued to treat Lucy Paradise with kindness and attention during her widowhood. However, on the personal level, there was little in common between the quiet, cultured diplomat and the somewhat unbalanced American widow. Mrs Paradise also relied increasingly on Father James Smirnove for moral support; she referred to him as "my priest" and in general turned increasingly to her Orthodox faith. Dr Shepperson commented, somewhat scathingly, "Mrs. Paradise, a convert to Orthodox Catholicism, had become increasingly ardent as life had heaped more and more ills upon her ever-troubled spirit, and like so many other women she discovered in religion a consolation and a cure for the mental disturbances which seized her at this crucial stage of her existence." In 1805 Lucy Paradise returned to her native Virginia. Dr Shepperson quotes from a letter she wrote to then-President Thomas Jefferson, dated August 27, 1805, the day her ship docked in Norfolk, Virginia. She wrote "with the Blessing of God I am now in good health, and with my Priest's Blessing and command who is the Revd. Mr. Smirnove." In her final years she became increasingly unbalanced and was eventually confined to a mental asylum in Williamsburg, Virginia, where she died in 1814.

The "Priest of Many Parts"

Father Smirnove's work on the diplomatic front continued unabated as the eighteenth century drew to a close and the nineteenth century began. In fact, the third political incident in which Father Smirnove was involved left him for a while as the only remaining member of the Russian diplomatic mission and de facto chargé d'affaires in London. This occurred as a result of the upheaval in international relations brought about by the Napoleonic wars. Initially Russia fought on the British side against the French. After suffering several defeats, Emperor Paul I, the successor to Catherine the Great, began to blame his allies and broke off diplomatic relations with Britain. Woronzow, a committed Anglophile, did not conceal his disapproval of this policy, and so was dismissed from his post in disgrace and deprived of his estates in Russia. Mr Lizakevich, who was appointed chargé d'affaires in his place, was soon transferred to Copenhagen, whereupon Father Smirnove received the following decree dated September 29/October 11, 1800:

> In the absence of all accredited personages at the London court you are instructed to inform the Emperor of all you can find out about the projects, armaments, movements, transfers of funds and trading transactions of the English during this autumn and winter. In this important commission you will perceive the Emperor's trust and its justification will depend on your efforts.

Father Smirnove was never formally accredited as a diplomatic representative. The British Consul General at St Petersburg, Stephen Shairp, was refused permission to reenter the country, and in retaliation, the British expelled the Russian Consul in London, Baxter. Shairp was detailed to monitor Smirnove's activities in London, and in December 1800 he reported, "I have the strongest reason to believe that Mr. Smirnoy the Russian Chaplain in London continues to carry on correspondence with his country." This was true; Smirnove sent back reports on political developments and proceedings in Parliament. Early in 1801, as a result of a British embargo on Russian ships and goods, the Russian government closed the embassy. However, after Paul I's murder in 1801, there was a change of policy. Smirnove wrote to Count Woronzow, "Calm your spirit, your Excellency, after its temporary unrest, Paul I has departed to his eternal rest." Woronzow was restored to his post as ambassador, and Britain and Russia once again became allies in the war against Napoleon.

Perhaps it was the value placed on his priestly functions by the Russian authorities that enabled Father Smirnove to avoid being recalled to Russia as most of his colleagues at the embassy had been. In early 1800, at the height of the crisis, Count Woronzow emphasized the need to maintain, at all times, an Orthodox church "so as not to give up the longstanding and useful object of furthering contact with people of the same faith." In addition to the Orthodox Greeks who attended the Embassy church, Woronzow also refers to "Croats" and Dalmatians.

Anglo-Russian relations again deteriorated as Napoleon advanced into Russia and the help that had been expected from the British never came. In

1807 the Russians and French signed the Treaty of Tilsit, and once again it seemed as if all diplomatic personnel in England, including the priest, would be recalled to Russia. In December of that year, Father Smirnove wrote to a former member of the embassy staff, "Our mission is leaving here; some are going to Paris, others returning via Sweden, and the rest as yet do not know where they are to go. I am to remain until further instructions." The following October he wrote that he had been instructed "to sell the Embassy house for the best price possible, and, taking the archive with me, to leave England." Woronzow wrote to Father Smirnove with words of encouragement, saying "the Russian God is great and certainly will not desert altogether our poor country which is perishing from stupidity, corruption and treachery." Once again, Father Smirnove remained in England, despite the political crisis, and services at the Embassy church continued.

In 1812, as the tide turned in the Napoleonic wars, Britain and Russia again became allies. Count Christopher Lieven, appointed as the new ambassador, worked closely with Father Smirnove for the next twenty-two years. And Count Woronzow, now living in retirement in England, wrote of "the enthusiasm which people here have for the Russians; generals, officers, soldiers, nobility, middle classes and ordinary people, all are respected, admired and praised." Father Smirnove was present at the grandiose celebrations arranged by the Corporation of London when Tsar Alexander I visited London in June 1814.

If Father Smirnove's diplomatic activities were concentrated primarily during the Napoleonic war period, his involvement in other secular areas continued throughout his time in England. The study of agriculture was one reason why he initially went to England. As embassy chaplain, he continued to supervise Russian students of agriculture. In time he acquired the reputation of an expert among English agriculturalists such as the Earl of Findlater, Sir John Sinclair (who appointed Father Smirnove to the Board of Agriculture), and Arthur Young, to whom he had been introduced by his predecessor, Father Andrew Samborsky, shortly after arriving in England. He remained in close contact with Arthur Young and turned this friendship to his advantage by carrying out various commissions at the request of Russian landowners who were anxious to implement English agricultural techniques on their own estates. In June 1802, for example, he wrote to Young, recommending a Mr Davidson, manager of a farm established by Alexander I near St Petersburg, "in Imitation of that of His Majesty the King of England," who had been sent, as Smirnove wrote, to "stock it with the various Objects proper to that Purpose, such as Implements, Cattle, seeds, workmen, Dairy-maid, *et hoc genus omne*." In September of that year Davidson successfully accomplished his mission; Smirnove wrote to Young again, urging him to "let the Bull go," which had been selected for the farm. Smirnove expressed his friendship and admiration for Arthur Young in a letter of 1802, in which he called him "my very worthy Friend and Master, the true original Source of all the rational agricultural Knowledge"; he continued, "Here my dear Sir Divine Providence is visibly raising, in the Person of His Imperial Majesty, a very powerful Instrument to spread about your benevolent Views, to 'speed the Plough.'" This letter also provided an indication of the ideals that inspired Father Smirnove in his interest in agriculture. He refers to Young as "the Man, who more than any other Individual without Exception, had ventured to point out to Mankind the true Foundation of their Comfort and real Happiness."

Food shortages were a constant problem facing the poor people of eighteenth-century Europe, and Russia was no exception. As the son of a village priest, Father Smirnove would have had firsthand experience with these difficulties, which were exacerbated by primitive agricultural methods. Modern farming techniques, such as those being pioneered in England, could bring real improvement to the lot of the average Russian peasant, and it was to this end that Father Smirnove seemed to be referring when he spoke of "comfort and real happiness." Although the subject is perhaps far removed from the spiritual concerns that one would expect to be of prime importance to an Orthodox priest, the idealistic appeal of this interest is clear, and it is evidently an interest and inspiration that he inherited from his predecessor, Father Andrew Samborsky.

He pursued other secular concerns with less enthusiasm. On one occasion he wrote to Count Woronzow that many Russians who had been to England "remember me after they have gone only when they want me to carry out some commission for them." He is mentioned in a letter written in 1783 by the renowned economist Jeremy Bentham: "Smyrnov was as busy as a bee packing up fine things in abundance for Count Soltakoff, the man that whilom [formerly] commanded a Russian army." Between 1818 and 1823 he was involved in attempts to obtain plaster casts of the Elgin Marbles on behalf of the St Petersburg Academy of Arts. On other occasions he obtained precision instruments, manuals for agricultural implements, and literary works that were not available in Russia, as well as more frivolous items for members of the Russian aristocracy.

Finally, Father Smirnove was known as a writer and translator. His functions at the embassy involved both skills, which came to particular prominence in the newspaper and pamphlet "war" of 1791. Otherwise, he is known principally for his translation of Pleshcheyev's *Survey of the Russian Empire,*

According to its Newly Regulated State, a work that provided the British public with detailed information about the geography and resources of Russia, particularly from an agricultural point of view. In many cases, he provided advice, assistance, and encouragement to others who were writing about Russia.

In recognition of his efforts, Father James Smirnove was advanced to the rank of archpriest in 1817 and, over the years, received numerous ecclesiastical and civil distinctions. When writing in English, by 1825 he was signing his official correspondence this way: "James Smirnove, Protopresbyter, Knight of Several Orders, Chaplain to the Imperial Russian Embassy in London." The "several orders" were, according to his report for 1835, the Cross of St Anne (2nd class) and the Order of St John of Jerusalem. He was also awarded a bronze cross, a gold cross, and a diamond-encrusted cross by the Holy Synod.[9] However, Father Smirnove received little financial recognition for his "extra-curricular" services on behalf of the Russian Empire. In 1791 he received £200 for the anti-Pitt campaign. In 1795 he received £150 as well as an annual salary increase of £50 for his part in uncovering the plans of the Polish insurgents. However, he received no compensation for acting as unofficial chargé d'affaires during 1801, despite Count Woronzow's petition on his behalf. Alexander I replied that he seemed to be already in receipt of substantial remuneration from different government departments. Perhaps by Russian standards it seemed substantial. However, the high cost of living in London meant that he had to watch his expenditures very closely in order to avoid going into debt.

The New Church at Welbeck Street

It is not known how long the Embassy church remained in Clifford Street, Burlington Gardens. The political events of 1801 and, in particular, of 1807, following the Treaty of Tilsit, significantly reduced the Russian diplomatic presence in England. By 1808 Father Smirnove was living not on Clifford Street but at 36 Harley Street, which was the embassy house. He was instructed to sell this house during the crisis of 1807–1808 when he received orders to leave England. It seems likely that the church house at Clifford Street had been given up, either during the 1801 crisis or during the crisis of 1807. In early 1813 Father Smirnove was still living at 36 Harley Street, and so that is probably where he conducted services on a temporary basis.

Once the tide turned in the Napoleonic wars, however, it again became feasible, indeed desirable, to look for a separate house where the Embassy church could be properly established. In 1813, the year before Alexander I's state visit to London, on March 8 Count Woronzow wrote in a letter to the

Duke of Portland, who held the freehold of large parts of central London: "We now have to lease a house for the Chaplain of the Imperial Russian Embassy with premises suitable for establishing a chapel of the Greek Rite. Mr Smirnove, who has been acting as our chaplain for thirty-six years, has set eyes on a house situated on a property at 32 Welbeck Street." He went on to say that the house had outbuildings, presently used as stables, that could be adapted to the required use, that is, converted into a church. James Lowe, Augustus Brown, and John Hillersden held the property on a lease from the Duke of Portland. The Marylebone rate book indicates that the property had been vacant at Midsummer[10] 1812 since the departure of the previous occupant, Lady Dolling. To make the planned improvements, a "license to build" had to be obtained from the freeholder. The duke was sympathetic toward the scheme but was also concerned about maintaining the value of his property and the effect the alterations might have on his surrounding tenants.

On March 5, 1813, Father Smirnove received a letter from the Duke of Portland in which he said that taking down the existing buildings and building a chapel would lessen the property value. He would therefore require a covenant that the buildings be restored to their former state when the Russians left, secured either by a deposit of £500 or by the guarantee of a responsible English person. A week later he wrote in more encouraging terms to Count Woronzow:

> Dear Count, In answer to your letter which you have done me the honour to write, I can only say at this moment that if the interests of those who occupy the adjoining houses (whose interests I consider myself obliged to protect) do not suffer, I shall be much pleased to permit the object you have in view. . . . Allow me, dear Count, to use this occasion to compliment you on the successes and glories of the Russian nation and to receive assurances of the high consideration in which these are held by your humble and most obedient servant, Scott Portland.

In short, now that Napoleon was in retreat, and the Anglo-Russian alliance was flourishing, the duke was happy to let the Russians build a church on his property. It is known from a solicitor's bill rendered "for attending Mr. Smirnove" that the residents of the area certified they had no objection to the proposed conversion.

Eventually the negotiations were concluded. On May 29, 1813,[11] a deed was drawn up and signed by Scott Portland in which he permitted

> . . . James Smirnove to alter and convert the stable offices belonging to and situate behind and adjoining the said mews [Marylebone Mews] into a private chapel for the celebration of Divine Worship according to the rites and ceremonies of the Grecian Church so long as occupied by the said James Smirnove or the chaplain for the time being of the Imperial Russian Embassy, and without the said James Smirnove being compellable at any time hereafter to restore the buildings to stable offices, on condition that there should be no other access or entrance than through the messuage or tenement numbered 32 Great Welbeck Street.

There was to be no further alteration to the external walls of the stable buildings than was strictly necessary to effect the conversion.

The conversion of the stable buildings into a church seems to have been effected very simply because there are no records of large expenditures being incurred at that time. Although the church was later rebuilt in 1866 at considerable expense, there was to be no separate entrance to the church; one could only enter through the "messuage or tenement"—in other words, through the front door of 32 Welbeck Street.

Initially the house was held on a sublease from Messrs Lowe, Brown, and Hillersden, which was on a lease due to expire in 1835. The annual rent was £130, and Father Smirnove received an allocation of funds directly from Russia to cover this cost. In 1825 the house was valued for insurance purposes at £2,000 and the annual premium was £29 11s. 6d. As the sublease drew to an end, Father Smirnove began negotiating a new lease directly with the Duke of Portland. In 1834 a firm of surveyors was called in; the team reported that the property was sadly in need of repair: "The house will require painting, papering and whitewashing throughout for an incoming tenant, and I should consider a Water Closet on the half space landing absolutely necessary before it could again be let." The duke wrote back that he was anxious to keep a good tenant and proposed a new lease divided into three periods of 7, 13, and 21 years, in accordance with the custom of the times. Perhaps due to Father Smirnove's negotiations over the need for water closets and other improvements or perhaps because the lease was enacted directly with the freeholder, the lease was at a lower rent than had been paid up to 1835. And so the Welbeck Street property remained the home of the Russian Church in London until after the Revolution. However, it was always held on a series of long-term leases and never owned outright by the Russians.

The first report made by Father Smirnove's successor, Father Eugene Popoff, included a description of the new church. In 1842 he reported that the church was

> . . . of a portable type. Although it has a raised altar area as is usual in Russian churches, the iconostasis is attached to it in separate sections with screws in such a way that, in case of need, it could be moved to another place. There is one single altar, dedicated to the Dormition of the Mother of God.

In another report Father Popoff said that the icons and general appearance of the church were exactly the same as in Father Stephen Ivanovsky's description of 1746, when the church was moved to Clifford Street. Evidently there were the same icons in gilded frames painted on canvas, many of them of Old Testament saints, before which Orthodox Londoners had already been praying for at least fifty years.

Blindness and Death of Father James Smirnove

In his report for 1836, forwarded to St Petersburg early in 1837, Father Smirnove noted that there had been no baptisms, weddings, or confessions during the year because he had been suffering from a cataract in one eye and could not read or write. During the previous summer, he had undergone surgery at the hands of Henry Alexander, whom he referred to as "the most skilled eye surgeon in the whole of Europe." Father Smirnove concluded that he hoped to regain his sight within a few months. He submitted to St Petersburg a copy and a translation into Russian of a letter from Mr Alexander dated June 17, 1836, shortly after the operation. In it, he stated, "Mr. Smirnove's eye continues progressively to improve, but is not yet in a state to enable him to resume his professional duties, and I do not think that he will be enabled to do so for several months to come, when finally a favourable restoration of his sight may be expected." The letter was signed "H. Alexander. Surgeon and oculist in ordinary to His Majesty and the Royal Family and surgeon to the Royal Infirmary for Diseases of the Eye."

There were further complications. In January 1837 Mr Alexander wrote that Father Smirnove's recovery was impeded by closure of a pupil, which would require an additional operation in the ensuing spring. In October of that year, he wrote that Father Smirnove was making a slow recovery but no further operation was possible until the next spring.

As a man of wide-ranging intellectual interests, Father Smirnove must have been keenly affected by the loss of his sight, which would have prevented him from conducting church services. So, at the age of eighty-three, he was finally forced to retire from active duties. In August 1837 Priest-monk Niphont was sent from Paris to relieve Father James. Father Niphont was about fifty years old and had spent the past eighteen years serving as priest at the Russian embassies in Madrid and Paris. He was the son of a clergyman, had studied in a seminary, and became a monk after graduating. He was tonsured and ordained in 1816 in the Holy Trinity-Zelenitsky Monastery and then transferred to the St Alexander Nevsky Lavra, a large and well-known monastery in St Petersburg. In 1819 he was appointed chaplain to the Russian Embassy in Madrid. In 1822, due to unrest in the Spanish capital, he was assigned temporarily as assistant priest at the Russian Embassy in Paris. In the following year, Father Niphont returned to Madrid, where he remained until 1836, when he was summoned back to Paris. In 1837 he went to England on what was essentially a temporary assignment.

Father Niphont set to work attending to the priestly ministrations that Father James had been unable to perform over the past year. The 1838 confession list, which Father Niphont prepared, records twenty people, while that for 1839 records thirty: fifteen clergy, eight embassy staff, four merchants, and three servants.

After the arrival of Father Niphont, the wife and seven daughters of the psalm-reader Ivan Kvitnitsky were received into the Orthodox Church. Father Smirnove translated the service of reception into English. Perhaps his eyesight had improved by then or perhaps the text was read to him and the translation dictated. Because Father Niphont's assignment there was temporary, it is possible that in recommending Kvitnitsky for the priesthood, Father Smirnove was attempting to provide for a successor as rector of the Embassy church.

Nicholas Ivanovich Gretch, a Russian visitor to England, provided a portrait of Father James Smirnove in the last years of his life. In 1839 he found him to be "still lively in spirit and body" and continued, "It seemed to me that I had visited a pious hermit living on a lonely island amidst the stormy waves of a foreign ocean. Russian icons, the portrait of Russian tsars, Russian books and a Russian heart—that is all he had saved from the shipwreck. Sufficient for this world—and the next." Certainly, this impression of a "pious hermit" is a far cry from the cosmopolitan, businesslike personality of earlier descriptions. Perhaps his loss of sight together with the natural infirmities of old age led the venerable clergyman–diplomat to turn inward and to spend his last days in prayer and reflection, preparing for the transition to the future life.

Archpriest James Smirnove died on April 16/28, 1840, at the age of eighty-six. He was buried at Kensal Green Cemetery.[12] Summing up his long career, A. G. Cross wrote,

> He had no aspirations to being a theologian, but there is no reason to doubt the depth and purity of his faith and his willing service to his Church. He was in many ways a parish priest, if an extraordinary one, extending his pastoral care and concern over all the wide-ranging activities of Russians in England. Like Samborsky, he had a veritable passion for agriculture, which he saw as the key to man's "Comfort and real Happiness" on earth. Only his "political" activity might be seen as conflicting with his calling as a priest, although that would be to introduce too fine a distinction in the general patriotic sentiments which moved him. He was to the end a loyal and devoted servant of Russia and a good friend of England, although his patience was tried and his intelligence pained by the antics of first one, then the other.

In Father James Smirnove's six decades as rector, the survival and development of the Orthodox Church in England was closely bound up—at least in earthly terms—with political developments. His most tangible legacy was the establishment of the church at 32 Welbeck Street. In terms of more strictly ecclesiastical or religious history, however, a better reward is found in study of the next thirty-five years, during which Father Smirnove's successor, Archpriest Eugene Popoff, was rector of the Embassy church.

Chapter 4

[1842–1875] Father Eugene Popoff, Pastor of the Embassy Church

The Priest and People of the Embassy Church

From its beginnings until the Revolution and possibly beyond, the life of the Russian Church in London reflected, as a microcosm, the changing influences affecting the Orthodox Church in Russia. In the wake of Peter the Great's onslaught against the Church, the eighteenth century had not been a time of great spiritual enlightenment in Russia, and in the London church, even the most zealous clergy did not always distinguish clearly between the two ideals set out in the Holy Synod's resolution of 1737, which included such phrases as "the greater glory of Russia" and "the expansion of the Orthodox Church and the Church Ceremonial." By the middle of the nineteenth century, however, the religious climate in Russia was changing. The ancient spiritual tradition of monasticism began to flourish again in centers such as the Sarov and Optina hermitages, where holy elders provided guidance to large numbers of laypeople as well as to those living in the monasteries. In the governing circles of the church, the collegiate "synodal"[1] system imposed by Peter the Great began to operate in a more truly ecclesiastical spirit. Power-hungry bureaucrats were replaced in the all-important post of procurator of the Holy Synod by men devoted to the Church and her mission, such as Count Alexander Tolstoy (1856–1862) and Count Dimitry Tolstoy (1865–1880). This was possible only because the monarchs of nineteenth-century Russia were, without exception, devoted sons of the Orthodox Church. Lay theologians of the Slavophile school such as Khomiakov, Mouravieff, and Kireeff supported a return to patristic sources in theology and a deeper understanding of the Church's Orthodox doctrine. However, the single greatest factor in "softening" the Synodal system in the mid-nineteenth century was the immense influence of Metropolitan Philaret (Drozdov) of Moscow, who occupied the see of Moscow from 1826 until his death in 1867. He had, practically speaking, the same authority as that of a duly elected primate of the Russian

Church. This was due to his spiritual stature, his wide erudition, and his fine intellect, which enabled him to understand and often resolve practical problems of the day in light of the teachings of the church fathers. Even Count Protasoff, the procurator of the Holy Synod (1836–1855) who was keen to promote the authority of his office, held the metropolitan in great respect and often asked his help in resolving complex practical matters. Among the many varied questions that gained the attention of this great hierarch was the issue of a possible rapprochement of the Anglican Church with Orthodoxy (a subject that is examined more closely in Chapter 5). This came to the fore in 1840–1841 when an English theologian, William Palmer, visited Russia and spoke to many Russian hierarchs and clergymen, including the metropolitan. It became apparent that there might be considerable interest in Orthodoxy in England. As a consequence, it was noted that the position of rector of the London Embassy church should be filled by an individual able to respond to these strivings toward the Orthodox faith.

In 1841, when Palmer departed from Russia, the post of rector of the London Church was essentially vacant. Following the death of Father James Smirnove, Priest-monk Niphont continued the services on a temporary basis. Having performed most of his priestly service in France and Spain, it is doubtful that he had any command of the English language. There are few documentary traces of his period in office. He maintained the church registers, and some decrees addressed to him were received from church authorities in Russia. For example, in 1841 he received a circular directing

> . . . that those coming to church should not stand in such places where they might interfere with the conduct of the service . . . should not permit themselves to stand by the iconostasis or in general on the raised area or in the space between the two readers' stands (*cliros*), excepting only those cases when they are coming up to the Holy Communion and the Holy Icons.

On February 12, 1841, a bill was received from Heatherington & Co., Cut Glass and Lamp Manufacturers, suggesting that Father Niphont was attending to the renewal and replacement of the icon lamps in the church.

Before leaving Russia, Palmer went to see Count Protasoff, the procurator of the Holy Synod. He recalled,

> On Friday, July 2 . . . I took leave of Count Protasoff. He said that the chaplaincy of the Russian Embassy was now vacant, and they wished to send a chaplain who might be able to learn our language, and to study our

> divinity; and intended to require him to make them reports from time to time on the state of ecclesiastical matters and opinions in the English Church; that they would be much obliged to me if I would call upon him when he came, and make his acquaintance, and put him in the way of becoming acquainted with religious matters and with some of our clergy. He said it would be necessary to send a young man, since after a certain age it is not easy to learn a strange language. He then expressed abundance of good wishes and interest about myself personally, and on bidding me good-bye, embraced me after the foreign way, and said he hoped that what was the wish of all of us would in due time be accomplished.

The candidate chosen to meet these expectations and appointed in March of the following year to the London Church was Father Eugene (Evgeny) Popoff.

Father Eugene was perhaps the most positive personality of all the clergy who served in London prior to the Russian Revolution. During his time in office, the London church became an "embassy" church in more ways than one: while continuing to serve the needs of the embassy staff, it also became an embassy for the Orthodox Church in England. From the reports and correspondence that have survived, as well as from recollections, albeit fragmentary, of contemporaries, there emerges the impression of a warm-hearted, outgoing individual who was quietly and firmly committed to his own Orthodox faith, but never to a point of narrow-mindedness. He was always ready to welcome and help others. He was not a missionary, as was Priest-monk Nicholas Kasatkin, priest at the Russian consulate in Hakodate who later became the first bishop of the indigenous Japanese Orthodox Church.[2] In this, Father Eugene possibly disappointed some of his ecclesiastical superiors.[3] In addition, he did not fulfill the wishes of some Anglicans who prematurely hoped for intercommunion with the Orthodox. One Anglican source describes Father Eugene as being "imbued with a spirit of placid resignation as to the inevitable divisions of Christendom, yet ready to welcome with fraternal cordiality any steps taken to extend the knowledge of their Creed and ritual." "Placid resignation" was perhaps sober realism, devoid of delusions over unrealizable schemes of Christian unity. His good command of English ensured that Father Eugene was able to help those enquiring about Orthodoxy, especially the few English people who expressed a desire to embrace the Orthodox faith. Father Eugene also possessed another essential attribute for one in his position—a keen sense of humor. He was particularly fond of the then current English expression "in joke and in earnest."

In March 1842, Father Eugene, at age thirty was appointed to the London church. He had been serving at the church of the Imperial Russian Embassy in Copenhagen since February 1838. Unlike his predecessor, Father James Smirnove, who came from "Little Russia," that is, Ukraine, Father Eugene was from "Great Russia," that is, central Russia. Born into a clerical family, he graduated from St Petersburg Theological Academy with a master's degree. From October 1835 until his ordination in 1838, he held various positions at the Tver Theological Seminary, including instructor of world history and of the French language. Father Eugene arrived in England with his wife, Anna Iakovlevna, and his three-year-old son Basil, who was born in Copenhagen. While in England the couple had three more children: Nadezhda, born in 1843; Eugene, born in 1849 (who died before reaching his tenth birthday); and James (Yakov), born in 1854. Over the years, Father Eugene received numerous ecclesiastical awards: in May 1842, shortly after his arrival, he was awarded the velvet purple *skouffia* (a form of headgear); in 1847, he was raised to the rank of archpriest; in 1860, he was awarded a gold cross; in 1866, he was awarded the right to wear a mitre; and in 1874, the year before his death, he was awarded a diamond and sapphire cross. He also received a number of civil awards, beginning with the Order of St Anne, 3rd degree, in 1851, and culminating with the Order of St Anne, 1st degree, in 1873.

Despite the special circumstances surrounding his appointment, Father Eugene remained officially the chaplain of the Imperial Russian Embassy and was therefore considered, for all practical purposes, an employee of the Ministry of Foreign Affairs of the Russian Empire. Of course, many aspects of his work, considered in this chapter and in Chapter 5, went beyond this official function. This work brought him into regular contact with diplomats and visiting royalty, as well as Russians of differing social classes who found themselves in London for a period of time. For thirty-three years, he ministered to the Russian community in England and came to be regarded as "the soul of the Russian colony."

Although Father Eugene did not become embroiled in political activities, as his predecessor had done, his life as embassy chaplain was influenced by the political developments of the day, particularly the ebb and flow of Anglo-Russian relations. During most of his time in England, the Russian ambassador to London was Baron Brunnow. Although Brunnow was a Protestant (of German extraction) and therefore not, strictly speaking, part of Father Eugene's flock, the two men had a close relationship of mutual respect that was similar to the one Father Smirnove enjoyed with Count

Woronzow a generation earlier. The 1830s and 1840s were periods of rising tension between Russia and Great Britain. The main cause was the competing Turkish and Russian interests in the Balkans. Russian thought in politics, as in other areas, was polarized into two camps: the "Slavophiles" emphasized Russia's solidarity with other Orthodox Slav nations. This, in turn, led to a greater Russian hostility toward the Turkish Empire, under whom the Slav peoples of the Balkans were living in oppressive conditions. By contrast, the "Westernizers" saw Russia's future to be closer to western Europe. In the realm of foreign policy this implied living at peace with the Western powers. Count Nesselrode, the Russian Minister of Foreign Affairs from 1826 to 1856, was a convinced Westernizer. Like Baron Brunnow, Nesselrode was also of German extraction. He supported the ideal of the "Concert of Europe," whereby Russia would act in harmony with the Western powers, rather than antagonize them by adopting an anti-Turkish stance in the Balkans.[4] Throughout the reign of Nicholas I, Nesselrode's efforts were devoted to patching up relations with England and France, which were constantly on the brink of deterioration in the face of various international incidents (such as the *Vixen* affair of 1836, when a Russian warship captured a British merchant vessel near the Circassian coast). Nesselrode finally admitted failure when the Crimean War broke out in 1853. By that time he was seventy-five years old and felt it not premature to retire. Prince Alexander Gorchakov, who followed a "national" or Slavophile policy, succeeded him as foreign minister under the new emperor, Alexander II.

Brunnow was a protégé of Count Nesselrode and was expected to succeed him as foreign minister. However, the change of mood in Russia that resulted from the Crimean War meant that the Westernizing school was now out of favour; Brunnow's path to further advancement was closed and he remained at his post as ambassador to London until 1874. Nesselrode had sent him to London in 1839 to take part in the negotiations that led up to the Straits Convention of 1840 (concerning the neutrality of the Bosphorus and the Dardanelles). Brunnow attended in the capacity of a senior official of the Ministry of Foreign Affairs of the Russian Empire, known for his pro-Western and Anglophile views. On his arrival in London, he took over the functions of ambassador from Count Pozzo di Borgo, the chargé d'affaires. Initially this was intended as a temporary measure, designed to facilitate the negotiations: Pozzo di Borgo was hot tempered and had, on a number of occasions, provoked Lord Palmerston (then British Foreign Secretary) into anti-Russian tirades. In fact, Brunnow remained in England after this conference, and his appointment as ambassador was confirmed as permanent.

Baron Brunnow's respect for Father Eugene is apparent in a letter he wrote on December 28, 1865, in connection with a polemic on religious matters that arose in the Russian and British newspapers occasioned by the visit of Prince Orloff from Russia. Brunnow wrote,

> He [Prince Orloff] came to see me, then, to speak of the object which brought him to England. I enjoined him to speak of it with absolute confidence to our worthy chaplain, Father Eugene. He knows this country well, as he has been studying it for twenty-five years. Here he enjoys a widespread reputation for wisdom and piety. His advice on these ecclesiastical matters would seem to me to be the best that Prince Orloff could follow. The meeting was held in complete confidence. . . .
>
> Prince Orloff's letter printed in the *Moscow Gazette* had acquired a certain notoriety. . . . This morning it was reprinted and commented on by *The Times*. I regret this kind of publicity. It is inspired by a spirit which does not wish us well. When our politics are attacked, I am little concerned. I am used to it. But this is the first time that the English papers are speaking of a subject which touches the Orthodox Church of Russia, and I am very upset by it, as I know the brutality of style of this country's newspapers. If a polemic really gets under way, the language which the English will use could deeply hurt religious feelings in our country. This is why I must point out to you the bad path on which we risk to tread if the newspapers of the two countries start quarrelling about the things which are of God, and which do not belong to the human spirit.
>
> I will limit myself to this observation, without entering any further into a religious question which imposes a respectful silence upon me. Father Eugene has already given an account to the Procurator of the Holy Synod of what passed at the meeting at which Prince Orloff was present.
>
> I will urge our chaplain to remain completely aloof from the manifestations of the press. He is answerable only to his ecclesiastical authority and to His Excellency Prince Gorchakov.

This reference to Prince Gorchakov, the foreign minister, is a reminder of the embassy chaplain's status as an employee of the Ministry of Foreign Affairs of the Russian Empire. The close respect that Father Eugene and Baron Brunnow shared also led to cooperation in practical matters. For example, on September 9, 1865, Brunnow wrote to Father Eugene from Brighton, "In today's edition of *The Times*, I read that a Russian Naval officer named Mikhail Sysoeff was buried at Portsmouth. . . . In what circumstances did this officer die and were you called to perform any ministrations at this death and burial?" On August 24, 1869, he wrote, "Do you know anything about Second Lieutenant [*Podporuchnik*] Mansuroff? Does he come to church?" The replies to these enquiries are not available; however, it is known that the exchange of information went both ways. On December 17, 1866, Father Eugene received a note from the embassy confirming that they knew nothing detrimental about Genrikh Cherkesky, a nobleman living at 14 Johannes Square, London NW, who had expressed a wish to become Orthodox.

The chaplain's position as a foreign office employee is clear in a letter received in 1848 in which the church house was exempted from rates by direct order of Lord Palmerston. He wrote to Baron Brunnow,

> The Undersigned, Her Majesty's principal Secretary of State for Foreign Affairs, has the honour to acknowledge the receipt of the Note which the Baron de Brunnow, Envoy Extraordinary and Minister Plenipotentiary of the Emperor of Russia, addressed to him on the 23rd of December last, in reply to his note of the 11th of that month, and in which the Baron de Brunnow has had the goodness to furnish the undersigned with further explanations respecting the exemption from taxes claimed by him on behalf of the Chaplain to the Russian Embassy at this Court.
>
> As it appears from the Baron de Brunnow's note that the Chaplain is named and appointed by direct order of the Emperor, and therefore strictly forms a part of the Diplomatic Establishment of the Embassy, and that the House No. 32 Welbeck Street, in a part of which the chaplain resides, is not his own house, but a house belonging to, and used as the Chapel of the Russian Embassy, paid for by the Emperor, in the possession of the Representative of his Imperial Majesty, and as fully under his control as the house in which the Russian minister himself resides, the undersigned has the honour to state to the Baron de Brunnow that directions will be given by the Lords Commissioners of the Treasury to the Commissioners of Stamps and Taxes to abstain from making any further claim upon the Chaplain of the Russian Embassy for rates and taxes in respect of his occupation of a portion of that house.
>
> The undersigned avails himself of this opportunity to renew to the Baron de Brunnow the assurances of his high consideration.
>
> Signed: Palmerston, Foreign Office, February 17 1848.

Even the church services contained frequent reminders of the church's links with the rulers of the Russian Empire. During the litanies of the

Orthodox Church services, it was the priest's duty to pray for the emperor and Royal Family: the list of royalty to be commemorated expanded over the years. By the mid-nineteenth century it took up an entire page of print, beginning "For our Most Pious, Most Autocratic, Great Sovereign, the Emperor Nicholas Pavlovich of All Russia. . ." and concluding "for all their court (*palata*) and armed forces, let us pray to the Lord." When there were births, marriages, and deaths in royal circles, a revised version of the commemoration was sent to the priest. So the names of the emperor and Imperial family were very familiar to all members of the Russian clergy; however, it was not often that they were honoured by visits from the royalty themselves. Nevertheless, the Church of the Holy Dormition on Welbeck Street, which served as chapel to the Russian Embassy, was honoured over the years by more visits from royal personages than most churches within Russia.

The most memorable of these visits occurred during Father Eugene's tenure when Emperor Nicholas I came in May 1844. Count Nesselrode arranged the visit as part of his policy of improving Anglo-Russian relations over the so-called Turkish question. According to Father Eugene's records, his Imperial Majesty attended services in London on May 21 and 28. Before leaving for Holland, he presented Father Eugene with a diamond ring and £20 each for the minor clergymen. A more detailed description of the visit is preserved in the diary of Dr Robert Lee, FRS, private physician to Prince Mikhail Woronzow (son of Count Simeon Woronzow, the former ambassador).

> Sunday, 2nd June 1844. The Emperor Nicholas arrived in England last night. I went at 11 this morning to the Chapel in Welbeck Street and saw him coming out of the Chapel. He had a kind of great military cloak around him—bald head, the profile extremely like that of Alexander. Baron Brunnow went into the carriage before him. In the evening I saw three or four of the Royal Carriages at the Ambassador's House to take him to Buckingham Palace to dine with the Queen.
>
> This morning Mr. Arnott has related to me a circumstance which occurred at Woolwich on the landing of the Emperor, showing how uncertain he felt at the reception he was to encounter here. Baron Brunnow went off in a boat to the steamer and returned with all the pomp of the Emperor and was taken for the Emperor and treated as such. At last when he saw all was quiet he said to Captain Collier "I trust you will excuse the deception which I have practised." When it was obvious that there was no danger, Nicholas came ashore.

Another contemporary account of the visit runs as follows:

> On Sunday, after an Orthodox service, Nicholas was received by Queen Victoria in the Great Hall at Buckingham Palace. The whirl of appearances and formalities began on Monday with a tour of London, and for the rest of the week, wherever he moved he was followed by a host of the fair and fashionable. The showy equipages of the nobility were in perpetual motion. . . . The streets were a *levy en masse*. . . . And Buckingham Palace, with its guards, cavalcades, musterings of the multitude, and thundering of brass bands, seemed to be the focus of a national revolution. There was a train ride to Windsor, two appearances at Ascot, a military parade, and finally on Saturday *a déjuner* in a salon decorated as a Turkish tent, an appearance at the opera with the Queen, and the royal leave-taking. On Sunday Nicholas departed aboard the steamer *Black Eagle*, to the roar of cannon from the batteries along the Thames.

Queen Victoria, in the seventh year of her long reign, did not share her subjects' enthusiasm for the emperor's looks, courtesy, and gallantry. "The expression of the eyes is formidable," she wrote to the king of the Belgians. "He gives the impression of a man who is not happy, and on whom the weight of his power . . . weighs heavily and painfully. . . . He seldom smiles."

In fact, in diplomatic terms, the visit achieved little. Later that year Count Nesselrode went to England, as he put it, "to clarify the Emperor's views." In fact the purpose of his trip was to soften the hostility that Nicholas had displayed toward Turkey. Nesselrode spent some time in England, visiting Brighton and Kew. Father Eugene recorded that in September 1844, accompanied by Baron Brunnow, he attended a memorial service (*panikhida*) held in the Embassy church for the repose of the Grand Duke Alexander Nikolaevich.

Despite the worsening relations between Russia and England, Father Eugene recorded a number of visits from Russian royalty throughout the 1840s and 1850s, up to the outbreak of the Crimean War. These included Grand Duke Mikhail Pavlovich (the emperor's brother) who visited the church on September 28, 1843. Father Eugene recorded that the grand duke became godfather to his recently born daughter Nadezhda. Upon his departure, the grand duke left a brooch as a gift for Father Eugene's wife. On May 10, 1847, Grand Duke Constantine Nikolaevich arrived with his entourage. Father Eugene recorded that the next day was the feast of Pentecost (Holy Trinity) and that the church had been decorated with flowers for the feast by a florist named Little, "who laboured from 4 o'clock until 12." The grand duke stayed in London for three weeks and then toured other parts of England and Scotland. He again attended church on July 20, St Elijah's Day, before joining part of the Russian fleet at Portsmouth. Upon his departure, he left another brooch, this one diamond, for Mrs Popoff.

In June 1852 the Grand Duchess Ekaterina Mikhailovna attended the church in London before continuing to the Isle of Wight. Before going back to Russia, she made a point of returning to the Embassy church to order a service of intercession (*moleben*) for a safe journey. The grand duchess was back in England the following summer, this time accompanied by the Grand Duchess Maria Nikolaevna and other members of the Royal Family. During that summer they frequently attended services at Welbeck Street, and Father Eugene noted that he went "no less than eight times to Torquay, South Devon, and twice to the Isle of Wight, near Ryde" to conduct services at their summer residences.

The register of those going to confession and Holy Communion gives some indication of the regular congregation to which Father Eugene ministered after the royal visitors had gone home. Numbers ranged from twenty-eight in 1852 to fifty in 1863, made up of embassy staff, military officers, and the clergy of the church and their families. From time to time the numbers were higher: in 1866 a group of twenty-nine people, apparently the crew of a ship, came for confession during the fifth week of Lent, and in 1863 there is an entry captioned "sailors of all ranks—109." As before, each person's rank in society was clearly given: "Prince Romanovsky, Captain Rehbinder, the merchant Mirokoff, the five factory workers Afanasieff, Savitkin, Povarenkin, Antipoff and Tyumendin, the freed serf F. A. Likacheff, the serfs Demianenko and Gargouzoff," and so on. The lists for 1856 and 1861 include "Maria Solomonovna Bering, née Martinoff, wife of Henry Bering, Member of the English Parliament." The other registers show approximately two baptisms and two funerals a year, most of the same mixture of aristocratic personages, military officers, and their servants.

Converts to Orthodoxy included not only a few English people but also Russian subjects of other faiths who embraced Orthodoxy while serving abroad. One example of this was the previously mentioned Genrikh Cherkesky of 14 Johannes Square. However, there was also at least one conversion in the opposite direction. This was the case of Countess Aponi, which so distressed Father Eugene that he reported the matter to the procurator of the Holy Synod, Count Alexander Tolstoy. His comments are of interest because they foreshadowed some of the difficulties the Russian Church

Abroad would face after the Revolution, that is, preserving faithfulness to Orthodoxy in the face of "denationalization" and mixed marriages.

> For the first time in all my twenty years of service to the Holy Orthodox Church I have the grievous duty of informing your Excellency that in our little Orthodox world here a most unhappy event has occurred. Countess Anna Aponi (née, if I am not mistaken, Countess Benkendorff), the wife of Count Aponi, the Austrian Ambassador here, has been attending our Orthodox church for about two years and, so it seemed, was joining together with us with love in Orthodox prayer.[5] Then, a few days ago, she informed me that she had, to use her own expression, *"Embrassé la réligion Catholique"* ("Embraced the Catholic religion").
>
> But for the dead there are no physicians, and so I limited myself to a brief reply: *"Comme c'est un fait dejà accompli, il ne reste qu'à le laisser dans les mains de Celui qui est notre Juge et Sauveur et qui seul voit la pureté de nos motifs."* ("As it is an already accomplished fact, it remains only to leave it in the hands of Him Who is our Judge and Saviour, and Who alone knows the purity of our intentions.")

She expressed the "joy at being united in prayer again with her family." Popoff observed that as she was forgetting the language of her own country and could no longer speak Russian, perhaps this event was hardly surprising.

There were also cases of people who had drifted away from Orthodoxy during prolonged residence overseas before returning to their ancestral faith. On March 29, 1866, the procurator of the Holy Synod, Count Dimitri Tolstoy, wrote to Father Eugene about one such case:

> Further to your reverence's letter of 15th March, I have enquired of the Metropolitan of St. Petersburg as to whether G. Dzhunkovsky, who was reunited with our Church last January, can now be married in our Church. During his time spent abroad, while turning aside from the Orthodox faith, he was married in 1861 to a Miss Montgomery according to the rites of the Anglican confession.
>
> I have now received a reply from the Most Reverend Isidore to the effect that there is no hindrance to Dzhunkovsky being married in the Orthodox Church. . . .

Anna Pavlovna, Queen of the Netherlands and a Russian princess married to the Dutch king, showed greater steadfastness; her name appeared toward the end of a page-long petition prescribed for commemoration of the Imperial family. She had her own private chapel in The Hague to which Father Eugene was sent from time to time to conduct services. He received a decree (*ukaze*) in 1842 that read, "If there is no priest at the royal chapel at our mission in The Hague, then, if required by the Queen of the Netherlands to conduct services in Her Highness's church, the London priest is to go over to Holland, but not for more than one month at a time."

Father Eugene made other journeys outside the United Kingdom that included a visit to Lisbon in 1856 to baptize the daughter of an embassy official. While there, he also conducted a funeral service. However, it does not appear that he maintained regular contact with the Russian community in Lisbon.

Of the thirty or so people listed as having been to confession each year, approximately nine, that is to say, about 30 percent of the total, were represented by the psalm-reader, or chanter, Ivan Kvitnitsky and his numerous family members. Kvitnitsky was one of the two readers[6] serving in the church when Father Eugene arrived. In his report for 1842 he noted, "The clergy of the church is established as one priest and two psalm-readers. For the support of the priest 4,000 roubles in silver are provided; for the readers, one thousand, five hundred silver roubles each." He went on to observe, "The psalm-reader's salary is mediocre even for an unmarried man, but for a man with a family, due to the unparalleled high cost of living here, it is quite inadequate." (Despite these comments, the salary levels listed in the 1874 report were exactly the same thirty-two years later.) He made this remark doubtless in an attempt to help Ivan Kvitnitsky, who had a wife and seven children to support. In 1838 Father James Smirnove recommended Kvitnitsky for the priesthood, after receiving his family into the Orthodox Church. Why this never came to pass is not clear. Possibly Kvitnitsky did not meet the requirements of the St Petersburg authorities, who were looking for someone who was qualified to explain Orthodoxy to the English to be a successor to Father Smirnove. On the other hand, Kvitnitsky's English wife may have been unwilling to leave England for a post in Russia or elsewhere in Europe. With only fragmentary evidence available, one can only speculate.

In 1857 Count Christovich (who replaced Brunnow as ambassador for a short time immediately after the Crimean War), in an attempt to alleviate Kvitnitsky's financial burden, had him exempted from paying English taxes. The following letter on this matter was received by Count Christovich bearing the personal signature of the Earl of Clarendon, then foreign secretary, and is reminiscent of Palmerston's letter exempting the church house from rates nine years earlier:

> Monsieur le Comte, I have the honour to receive the note which you addressed to me on the 28th ultimo, explaining, in reply to my note of the 23rd ultimo, the grounds upon which you are of the opinion that the two choristers of the chapel of the Russian Embassy referred to in your note of the 11th ultimo, are entitled to be considered as forming bona fide a part of the Russian Embassy, notwithstanding that one of them, Mr. Kvitnicki, [*sic*] resides elsewhere than in the chapel house.
>
> Having taken into consideration the arguments which you have advanced, I have the honour to state to you, Monsieur le Comte, that I think the two gentlemen in question ought to be considered as forming a part of your establishment, and I have accordingly recommended to the Treasury that the demand which you state has this year been made upon Mr. Kvitnicki be discharged, so far as it relates to the assessed taxes, which are payable to the Crown and under the control of Her Majesty's Government.
>
> With regard to parochial and other local rates levied under the authority of Acts of Parliament, Her Majesty's Government have not the same means of direct control. The demands for such rates may however probably be not persisted in, when those for assessed taxes shall have been withdrawn, but if this should not be the case, I shall be happy, on being apprized by you of the demand, to do all that is in my power to obtain exemption for Mr. Kvitnicki.
>
> I avail myself of this opportunity to renew to you the assurance of the highest consideration with which I have the honour to be, Monsieur le Comte, Your most obedient and humble servant. Signed: Clarendon.

Sadly, this financial relief came too late to be of lasting benefit to Ivan Kvitnitsky. Later that same year, on September 29, he died, having served as chanter in the London church for forty-three years. This, of course, brought even greater financial hardship on his family. On June 30, 1858, Father Eugene wrote to the St Petersburg Spiritual Consistory, enclosing a petition from

> ... the daughters of the deceased cleric of the Embassy Church in London, Ivan Kvitnitsky—the spinsters Marianna, Helen and others. Passports from the London Embassy are enclosed. They request the Consistory to

issue to each one of them separate permits (*bileti*) to live in St. Petersburg and certain other towns in the Russian Empire.

How would they manage in Russia if they had trouble supporting themselves in England? Twenty years earlier, when they were received into the Orthodox Church, the service had been specially translated for them, and their solemn undertaking to remain steadfast in the Orthodox faith was also written in English. So presumably the family had no knowledge of Russian. Possibly they would take positions as governesses in wealthy Russian families that wanted their children to be taught English. Nevertheless, the confession lists confirm the fact that they did go to Russia. The number of Kvitnitskys listed declines from seven in 1857 to three in 1858 ("Family of the deceased cleric Kvitnitsky"). Kvitnitsky's wife, Elizabeth, died on August 14 ,1859; thereafter, the number listed decreases to two ("Daughters of Kvitnitsky").

Katherine and Daria remained and were mentioned in a letter written on May 22/June 3, 1865, in which Baron Brunnow inquired about their plight. First, he asked Father Eugene to confirm that Katherine Kvitnitsky really was too ill to support herself and, second, to indicate how much money he really thought they needed. Father Eugene replied that Katherine was too ill to move and that her sister had to stay to look after her. Just over a month later, on July 15/27, 1865, a pension of 150 roubles was approved for Kvitnitsky's daughters.

These are the fragments of information about this family tragedy—one of the few cases where it is possible to piece together elements of a human story behind the impersonal lists of baptisms, marriages, deaths, and confessions. During most of his years in London, Father Eugene ministered primarily to the embassy community, dealing with a relatively small number of people, many of them members of the aristocracy. This peaceful existence changed suddenly in 1853 when the Crimean War broke out. Before long, boatloads of Russian prisoners were brought to England and interned in prisoner of war camps. For the short time that the war lasted, Father Eugene ministered to the spiritual needs of hundreds of prisoners, most of them ordinary soldiers, in place of the few dozen diplomats with whom he was used to dealing.

Far from being oppressed by this extra burden of responsibility, Father Eugene found encouragement and inspiration in this renewed contact with the faith and piety of the simple people and in his efforts to help them and uphold their spirits. Reports on his visits to the Russian prisoners describe their living conditions, but are also of interest in that they throw light on

Father Eugene's personality. Father Eugene did not retain copies of most of his outgoing correspondence, so these reports on the Crimean War prisoners are some of the few documents written by him that survived in the London archives.

The Crimean War Prisoners

In his Chronicle for 1854, Father Eugene noted,

> In January, when England and France declared war,[7] the Embassy left us, and in May the Consul-General was recalled as well. So now we are living quite alone, and find consolation only in correspondence with our dear fellow countrymen, which, fortunately, is still possible.
>
> In October of last year I had the good fortune to spend some time in St. Petersburg, and I travelled as far as Berlin with Her Imperial Highness the Grand Duchess Maria Nikolaevna. Accordingly, once I was there I also had the opportunity to see her on several occasions, and this eventually enabled me to meet the Royal Family. And so, six days before my departure, I finally had the good fortune to meet the Sovereign Emperor. Among other things, I heard him say the following: "What is the point of going there? It's as if they were all heathen, they are all for the Turks. I have done everything I could for peace; but there you are! Well, we will still do everything we can, with God's help!" His words proved to be right: England and France have gone mad, and *quis furor?*—we will have to wait, be patient and pray. 22nd June old style.

The Crimean War was the culmination of tensions that had been building between Russia and western Europe over the past several decades. The immediate cause was Russia's declared policy of protecting the interests of Orthodox Christians who were subjects of the Turkish Empire. The renowned issue of custody of the Holy Places in Jerusalem, to which the French, in particular, attached great importance, was just one aspect of this. Any altruistic motives of protecting fellow Orthodox were disregarded by the West, which saw only aggression and expansionism in the Russian policies. In late 1853 the Russian army entered the Turkish-held Balkan provinces of Moldavia and Wallachia (now Romania), over which it had certain rights of protection under the terms of an earlier treaty. The Western allies regarded this as a hostile act and, on March 28, 1854, Britain and France declared war on Russia. Hostilities initially concentrated on driving the Russians out of the Danubian provinces. When this was achieved, however, Britain and France invaded the Crimea for good measure. The famous battles of the Alma and Inkerman took place in September and November of 1854. However, hostilities were not confined to the Crimea. In August 1854 a British fleet under Admiral Sir Charles Napier sailed into the Baltic and captured the fortress town of Bomarsund on the Aland Islands.[8] Many, if not all, Russian prisoners interned in England had, in fact, been captured not in the Crimea but in Bomarsund when the whole garrison surrendered.[9] In September 1854 prisoners of war began arriving in England. Adopting a more formal tone, as if for the "official" record, Father Eugene made the following observations:

> 1854. 8th September. Our prisoners of war were brought from Bomarsund on two English ships to Sheerness and installed in two hulks moored in the Thames Estuary.
>
> 11th September. Archpriest Eugene Popoff and the cleric A. Peroff made their first visit to the prisoners of war in Sheerness to carry out church ministrations. However, due to the stormy weather, it was impossible to go aboard the ships, but a prayer service was held in the quarters of one of the officer prisoners.
>
> 14th September. The Hours and a service of intercession were held on the two ships where the prisoners of war belonging to the lower ranks were, with their families.
>
> October. In October the prisoners were moved from Sheerness and lodged in three different towns: the Russians in Plymouth, the Finns in Lewes, while those under arrest remained on the ship *Devonshire* at Sheerness. From this point on, until the prisoners were sent back to Russia on 1st April 1856, Archpriest Eugene Popoff travelled almost every week to these three towns to carry out church ministrations and to bring financial assistance.

The church archives contain voluminous records made by Father Eugene about his visits to the prisoners. He took great care to record the name and rank of every prisoner, together with the regiment to which he belonged; he maintained separate lists of those confessing and receiving Holy Communion. Father Eugene was, by his own account, the only member of the Russian diplomatic mission who remained in England. It is possible that he passed the information on to the Russian government or at least hoped it would help clarify the status of servicemen missing in action. For example, his list of prisoners of war of the lower ranks in Plymouth runs thirty-six pages with about twenty-five names per page—900 names in all. The list of those confessing and receiving Holy Communion in Plymouth during the Great Lent of 1855 runs eighteen pages with forty names per page—a total of 720 souls. It must have taken considerable stamina to attend to so many confessions under the strained wartime circumstances, which involved travelling considerable distances and arranging for church services to be held in the prison barracks.

Father Eugene described some of his visits in detail in reports addressed to Baron Brunnow, who had left England when the war broke out. Written primarily in Russian, but with frequent quotations given in English and some in French, the following report written at the end of 1854 is of particular interest:

> Your Excellency,
> Dear Baron Philip Ivanovich,
>
> Although there have not been any particular changes in the condition of our prisoners of war here since I last had the honour to report to Your Excellency, nevertheless, I will make so bold as to bring to your attention some additional details about their life here. I will also relate certain incidents which are not without their significance under the present circumstances.
>
> I a). The last time I had the honour to report to you, the local authorities, particularly in Plymouth, were being guided by more moderate rules over the confinement of our prisoners of war, and were making, so to speak, various attempts to ascertain how best and most easily to satisfy their needs and requirements. For example, they decided to give them black bread and to make *kvass* for them to drink; but it turned out that there is no black bread in England, and to bring it in from Germany would cost no less than the usual soldiers' biscuits. Consequently, five weeks ago it was resolved to give them the following rations: Daily: 1/4 lb. biscuits or 1/2 lb. soft bread, 2/3 lb. fresh beef and assorted greens or 2/3 lb. fresh pork with 1/3 pint of peas; 2/3 ounce chocolate or 1/6 ounce tea for breakfast; 1/6 ounce tea and 1/6 ounce sugar for supper; weekly: 1/6 pint oatmeal, 1/6 ounce pepper and 1/6 pint vinegar; monthly: 1/2 lb. soap and 1/4 lb. smoking tobacco.
>
> b) The changes affecting their accommodation are that for the winter gas heaters have been installed in all the barracks and gas lights have been hung up, and also the areas between the barracks have recently been paved.
>
> c) Finally, the orderly and, one might say, laudable conduct of the prisoners has earned them the privilege of being allowed (albeit under military guard) to take walks in the town or by the sea.
>
> d) The matter of clothing has still not been resolved. Shirts were issued while they were still in Sheerness. The questions of shoes (soldiers here are

not issued with knee-boots) and overcoats have yet to be clarified. The local authorities know how much money has been assigned for this purpose. However, it would appear that they would prefer not to touch this sum, but meet these requirements from their own resources. I am constantly taking it upon myself to remind the appropriate people that, using the funds available to them, the prisoners of war could easily make their own clothes and boots in the Russian style, since among them there are many bootmakers and tailors. (Many of them are continuing to work on their own initiative, and the more industrious of them make a few kopecks on the side, although they earn more money from making games known as "puzzles.") I have yet to receive a definite answer about this. The matter should be decided within a few days.

e) The prisoners' health does not appear to be suffering either from the change of climate or from the change of diet. In Plymouth only two of them have died, while there are no more than ten sick, of whom one is suffering from nothing more than the infirmities of old age.

f) I am pleased to be able to say that the change of place and circumstance has not had, at least so far, the same effects as, unfortunately, have broken out on the Île d'Aix. Perhaps your Excellency is familiar with the report from a certain M. Jannez to the effect that "disorders have broken out among the prisoners on the Île d'Aix, and that several of them have abandoned their colours." To my amazement, news of this has reached the prisoners here, but all my observations indicate that they have not yet been affected by such wicked and criminal thoughts. Since I seemed to be on good terms with the Commandant, I asked him, "in joke and in earnest" as they say here, about any so-called "foreign legion" but he assures me that, in his words, "there is nothing of the kind that he knows of."

There is, however, one fact which, perhaps without justification, nevertheless leads one to have certain suspicions. Until very recently the Roman Catholics have been praying together with our Orthodox people, but now the government has begun bringing a Roman Catholic pastor down from London to look after their needs. Apparently this pastor (who only comes occasionally) left Poland about two years ago. I do not know what impression he can be making on them; probably only in that he leaves them Polish prayer books printed in Paris, and talks of Paris.

g) Nevertheless, they have not lost the habit of praying together with us, and I hope they will continue to do so. Since the Orthodox are predominant numerically, they inevitably have a certain influence over the others. At the same time, our place of prayer has taken on the appearance of a real chapel, so it inevitably attracts the attention of those who wish to pray. A magnificent opening frame [*kiot*] has been made for the icons which I have brought with me. Before the icons, as in Holy Russia, burn whole rows of candles and a vigil lamp is almost always alight in front of them. Covers have been made for the table which is used as an altar table, which give it a properly ecclesiastical appearance; a curtain has also been made, hanging across the entire width of the room, which closes off the area where the holy icons are during the ordinary hours of the day; incense is also burnt in accordance with the custom. Finally, even the order of events follows that of Russia and the Russian Church: on one side stands the lamplighter while on the other side is a churchwarden with the candles, which are now being made there in moulds by one of the prisoners who came from a clerical family. Here (in London) we have just a [psalm-]reader, while there they have a whole choir to sing. Nor must I omit to mention the congregation in this little chapel. Sometimes the service with molebens and panikhidas lasts from 8 until 2, and throughout this time they all stand and pray, as if they did not feel tired at all. This fact is worth more than any sermon. Still, they listen to the sermon each time with absolute attention and silence.

Partly out of duty, and partly to uphold morale, I am continuing to visit them at least every two or three weeks. On my last visit, in order more fully and truly to share with them the joy of our National Church and our own festival of St. Nicholas Day, I stayed there with our young assistant clergyman [*prichetnik*] for three whole days, returning only yesterday.

II) Concerning this last visit I should like, if your Excellency permits, to report to you in more detail, especially in that there were some aspects of this visit which, while quite unexpected, proved to be most agreeable.

For a long time I had been wondering how to celebrate our own, so dearly loved, festival in a properly festive way—and not just in the purely religious sense—but somehow all my plans came to nothing. It was impossible, for example, to arrange for something special for them to eat, since it would necessitate a change in the arrangements with the contractors supplying the prisoners' food; alcoholic drinks are completely forbidden, even beer; distributing money is not an easy matter, particularly as the question of clothing has yet to be resolved. While I was pondering these weighty thoughts, suddenly, and beyond all expectations, I received the following letter from M. Jannez in Paris:

> "*Mon Révérend Père*" [the letter continues in French] Prince Demidoff would like to provide the Russian prisoners who are in England with the means of celebrating the day of St. Nicholas, which is,

> at the same time, his father's nameday, the Emperor's nameday and the feast of the Patron Saint of Russia. To this end he would like to add, for 6/18 December, something extra to the usual rations of the soldiers and noncommissioned officers, such as a ration of brandy [*eau de vie*] or a certain quantity of smoking tobacco, and to offer the officers a banquet which you would provide. etc. etc."

In order to implement such a good desire, I immediately began to make enquiries both in Lewes and in the next town, and what do you think happened? Suddenly all my old doubts came flooding back. The local commandant, a good old gentleman, too good natured too, but surely too much old fashioned and too much narrow minded, answered all my attempts in joke and in earnest, only by shaking his head. That was not all. In his "zeal not according to knowledge" he went back on his decision to let me see and talk to the Finnish prisoners, for the sole reason that on this occasion the translator was away. "Of course you will talk to them in Russian," he said, "which I do not understand." There was no point in becoming angry, and so, knowing the person I was dealing with, I ended the matter in a joke. One reason for this was clear: the government was sending a Swedish pastor to Lewes, so I could not go there at the same time.

Fortunately, Plymouth was more favourably disposed towards me. Everything was arranged according to our heart's desire. Arriving on Saturday, 4th December (o.s.), I served the Vigil service there. After the service on Sunday, I spoke as best I could to the Commandant, made a tour of all the barracks, found out as best I could about the morale of our prisoners of different ethnic origins; spoke about this and that to the innkeeper of the hotel where I usually stay, and in this way organized everything necessary to achieve our purposes. Sunday evening arrived. The Vigil service started earlier than usual on this occasion—at five o'clock to be precise. The icon of St. Nicholas which I had brought with me from our church visibly heightened the festive mood at the beginning of our celebration.

In the morning I arrived for the service before 8 o'clock, and this enormous, long barrack, with our chapel at the end, was already full of people, and rows of candles were lit before the holy icons. Truly, it then seemed to me as if we were all once more in our native land and under our own skies. The service began and, at the same time, the usual prayers or, we could say, more than the usual prayers. Despite the great numbers of people, one could hear no movements other than those of prayer. Probably the fear of losing their great treasure, the Holy Orthodox Church, had disposed them to particular reverence for the prayers of the Church. This is how the service began, and this is how it ended. Before the moleben, in fulfillment of my duty, I explained the meaning of the celebration for the Church and the Fatherland, and when I came to the end, and said that "The Holy Church does not celebrate its festival for the sake of idleness,[10] etc., nor does the Fatherland celebrate its festival for the sake of idleness, etc., and this shows and proves that even in a land of another faith we can preserve our love for the faith of our fathers, it shows and proves that even in a foreign land, we can preserve our love for our rulers and our beloved Emperor etc." Then, it seemed to me, although God alone knows the heart and mind of man, that these people were confirming, not only with the expression on their faces, but also in their innermost conscience, the vows which once they gave to the Church and the Tsar. It was especially good to hear how, as always, in their place of captivity as in our own land, the response to the prayer for many years which I proclaimed was the customary triumphant and triumphantly joyful *Mnogaya Lyeta!*—Many Years!

After that, as previously arranged, the Governor made a sign to the translator to begin a general roll-call. Each man answered and then came up to a certain place and received from my hands a shilling, given to them on the feast day and because of the festival. The fact that it was shared out evenly made a particularly favourable impression on them.

Obviously neither the hospital nor the families were forgotten. The Governor and his translator were good enough to accompany us round all the barracks and "did all what was in his power to make the most of the donation." At five in the evening a meal was put on for the officers in the Albion Hotel. This is the best hotel in the area, the landlord being quite famous locally—this is the same man who organized the famous banquet for the coming of age of Lord Mount Edgecombe's son last summer. As the officers did not have their full dress uniform, they came in civilian clothing, but I, as far as possible, and in order to continue the festivities and to preserve their significance, came just as I was, in clerical attire, *avec mes petites distinctions*. On this occasion the meal followed the English order—that is to say, the toasts which I had the honour to propose were drunk when the plate was removed. The toasts were as follows: 1. To our religion and the faith of our ancestors; 2. To His Majesty and family who are sharing the perils of war; 3. To families and absent friends; 4. To all those who are serving their country, body and soul.

The first toast, for the faith of our fathers, was received in silence, but this silence showed more than words that it was accepted wholeheartedly by all. The second toast—for the long life and wellbeing of His Majesty

> the Emperor, the Empress and all the Imperial Family,—called forth a unanimous "hurrah." In response to the third toast, many, many names were called out. The fourth caused many to give audible expression to the desire of their hearts—to live and die "For the Faith, the Tsar and the Fatherland." By the time tea was served, the good-natured commandant arrived—*en privé*—in a private capacity. At 10 p.m. we all left in good spirits and with no untoward incident.
>
> Time and circumstances will show when it will be best to organize such a celebration for the officers in Lewes.
>
> They have nevertheless been favoured with a visit from the good Duke, and in turn they had the honour to be presented to him at Brighton, where he has his permanent residence. (On this occasion I had made so bold as to remind them of this duty to make a return visit.) They tell me that among other things the Duke showed them with particular satisfaction various things he had been given by His Majesty the Emperor and the Grand Duchess Maria Nikolaevna. He is expected to come here for Christmas. Then I will not hesitate to convey my respects to him.

The visit to Lewes was not to occur, however. Shortly after completing this enthusiastic report, Father Eugene learned that doubts were being cast over his activities. As noted earlier, he was first refused permission to arrange any celebration at Lewes. Then, on the eve of his departure for Plymouth, he heard that he would be allowed to go to Lewes after all. So he wrote the following, in English (presumably correspondence in foreign languages was forbidden), to Colonel Grahn, the senior Russian prisoner at Lewes:

> This minute I was informed by the person known to you relatively the last time as I visited you and the other Gentlemen officers. The plan is not given up; the means are provided; but I don't see any possibility to come to you in person, neither to forward to you what may be requisite for the decent celebration of the day. Tomorrow morning I must go to Plymouth. What am I to do! Necessity, as they say, changes even the law. Have our feelings to remain unchanged, the difference of a few days cannot diminish the joys of our fête. Our meeting, if God grants, will be in the course of next week. Meanwhile be so good as to give my best respects . . . etc.

The letter was sprinkled with Russian equivalents, in parentheses, of words the colonel might have found difficult. This letter brought on the trouble. The intentional absence of proper names, perhaps compounded by the occasional grammatical error and insertion of Russian words, created the impression that something was being hidden, as if the Russian chaplain were using his privilege of visiting the prisoners by entering into secret communications with them. Father Eugene wrote a report[11] setting out his version of events, revealing at the same time his sense of frustration and bewilderment, and concluded as follows:

> So could one doubt the true meaning of my perfectly innocent letter? I regret infinitely that it was couched in such vague terms. It was however only to avoid the unnecessary publicity of using proper names for the general public; but as for the Governor, he could have obtained all the explanations he could have required from the gentlemen officers or, ultimately, from me myself, because he knew perfectly well that having received permission to make the little distribution of money to the prisoners, I would have had to present myself to him for that occasion. There was absolutely nothing hidden there at all! That is why I consigned my unfortunate letter to the post without a second thought.
>
> Your Excellency! I cannot express how unhappy this misunderstanding has made me. Please be so good as to look over the enclosed documents to convince yourself that there is not the slightest shadow of what has been suggested by the other version of my letter. No such idea had ever entered my head. Please, I beg of you, make your most generous efforts to justify me in the eyes of Her Britannic Majesty's Government. Meanwhile, I will renounce the most innocent pleasures of correspondence and limit myself to my most immediate duties. I will therefore await the advice of your Excellency before permitting myself to renew my communications with the prisoners at Lewes, even though there are some belonging to our church among them.
>
> I have the honour to be Your Excellency's most obedient servant, Eugene Popoff.
>
> 23rd December 1854
32 Welbeck Street,
London.

The difficulties must have blown over because later the following year Father Eugene was again visiting the prisoners at all three places of confinement. A report written in 1856, which was primarily about finances, gives some further insight into Father Eugene's work among the prisoners of war:

Your Excellency,
It was only unforeseen circumstances which prevented me from reporting earlier, since the orders of the Minister of War (concerning the distribution of money among our prisoners) that your Excellency has been so good to communicate to me arrived in good time; these same circumstances have also prevented me from submitting the enclosed account earlier, although it was ready in January. In short, among other things, I found myself obliged, for different reasons, to renew my regular visits to all the three depots where the prisoners of war are wintering. Almost immediately after that, I was obliged, following the orders of the aide-de-camp general Count Orloff, to go to Paris for the 18th of February,[12] primarily because the mourning vestments belonging to our chapel in Paris were inadequate for the occasion. On returning from Paris, I had to leave for Plymouth once again, in order to spend the first week of Lent with the prisoners. 420 of them have already made their customary devotions. Can I therefore hope that these circumstances, taken all together, can gain your Excellency's indulgence for me?

Henceforth the question of the distribution of money would seem to have been resolved to the complete satisfaction of all concerned. For my part I will attempt to carry out the orders given to me as fairly and accurately as possible.

As for the enclosed account, may I be permitted to make a few observations concerning it?

1. If the majority of the sums destined for the prisoners have been distributed in cash instead of, perhaps, being used in another way, such as for purchasing various articles of clothing, there were specific reasons for this, namely. . . .

Here Father Eugene summarized reasons that have been cited earlier: the prisoners themselves preferred cash; it would be hard to find out what else each one really needed; the British had undertaken to supply them with basic necessities; and many of things they might have wanted, such as brandy or beer, were forbidden.

2. If I permitted myself to keep the rest of the sum designated for 1854 and 1855, the only reason for this was that, if a new party of prisoners of war should arrive (as has always been expected, and as they are even now expecting the arrival of prisoners taken in Japanese waters) we could find ourselves in a very disagreeable position.

3. The financial assistance given to the prisoners from time to time by Councillor A. A. Demidoff is not mentioned in the enclosed account, because I have given him a separate accounting for these sums on each occasion, immediately after the distribution of cash was made.

4. As far as my travelling expenses are concerned, I consider it my duty to assure your Excellency that I have made every effort to keep them as low as possible. This is why I have been trying, whenever possible, to make my visits alone, without being accompanied by a psalm-reader. To this end I have also been trying to train readers and singers among the prisoners themselves. If, taking all this into account, and even then with the exception of what they call here the "bill of fare" the expenses really do seem to be high, this must be attributed to other causes. Firstly, in England railway fares are very expensive for passengers; secondly, the distance between London and Plymouth, where I have had to go the most often, is quite considerable, being 250 English miles, so that the journey takes me a whole day.

Although one can travel very well second class on the Continent, in England it is as good as reserved for the most needy people and, during wartime, particularly on the routes between Sheerness and London and Plymouth and London, the second class compartments are almost exclusively occupied by sailors and soldiers.

Justice requires me to add here that the banker M. who has advanced small sums to me from time to time on my own account has not been charging me interest, probably in consideration of the fact that he has been holding all the sums destined for the prisoners of war.

5. If any mistakes or errors should have slipped into the enclosed accounts, I hope that your Excellency, in your extreme goodness, will not attribute them to anything other than my inexperience in affairs of this nature, and will deign to permit me to rectify them.

Having submitted these observations for your Excellency's kind consideration, I consider it my duty, as usual, to add at the same time some comments about the prisoners themselves, even though there have been no new developments.

There is always about the same number of prisoners—that is to say, just over a thousand. As in the past, the majority are in Plymouth.

Their health is generally satisfactory. Here the baths which have been set up in the Plymouth barracks have helped greatly. However, an east wind has been blowing here for several weeks, which is extremely dry, penetrating and cold, and it has caused widespread rheumatism among the prisoners. Last week I found no less than 28 sick men in the hospital. They all received Holy Communion without exception.

They continue to be well treated; the concern of Governor Veitch and the doctor deserve to be praised forever, and this is recognized by the prisoners themselves, although the articles of clothing are far from exemplary—this is something for which no one seems to be responsible.

Poor Shishmanoff has almost recovered, although he is still weak. The unfortunate Finn at Lewes, so I am told, is still suffering, although less than he was. The six sailors from Sebastopol who were at Sheerness have entered into the service of commercial vessels.

A peace agreement was signed in March 1856, and eventually arrangements were made for the prisoners to be transported back to Russia. Following is Father Eugene's chronicle of these events, written as if for the "official record":

1856. 16th February. Archpriest E. Popoff was summoned to Paris to concelebrate at a panikhida for the late Emperor Nicholas I, who had reposed in the Lord.

18th March. From Paris, the place of the peace conference, official notification was received that peace had been signed.

7th April. All of our prisoners of war who had been in Plymouth, Lewes and Sheerness, set sail from Portsmouth for Libau [now Liepaja] on board the transport ship *Imperatritsa*.

On this occasion I spent several days in Plymouth, and then I spent the night on board the transport, which stood for some time in Portsmouth harbour, awaiting the prisoners not only from Lewes and Sheerness, but also from the China Sea, where many were captured. Among the prisoners captured on distant seas, I remember, were Captain Musin-Pushkin, and Prince Urusoff. After peace was made, at first the Ambassador was Count Christovich; but he did not stay more than a year. His place was taken by Baron Brunnow, who has now returned.

Father Eugene's efforts during the war earned him the gratitude of both Nicholas I and Alexander II. His service record enumerates some of the awards he received in this connection:

. . . 26th October 1854 had the honour to receive the gratitude of the Ministry of Foreign Affairs "for carrying out his tasks of giving spiritual consolation and distributing financial assistance to the Russian prisoners

> of war who were in England" and, on 25 November of the same year, for "carrying out in a completely satisfactory manner the tasks assigned to him concerning the Russian prisoners of war in England" had the honour to receive thanks in the name of the late Sovereign Emperor Nicholas I. On 20 August 1855, having regard to his outstandingly zealous service and as a reward for his zealous and truly compassionate activities in carrying out the tasks assigned to him in connection with providing assistance to the Russian prisoners in Great Britain, was granted the Order of St. Anne, 2nd degree.

Before long both Russia and England were to deeply regret the war. Alexander II saw that it was essential to make peace his first priority when he acceded to the throne in 1855. Russia had been strained to the utmost, and it soon became apparent how ill prepared she was to wage war. On the English side, disillusionment set in about the value of fighting a war to shore up the Turkish Empire. Later in the century, a diplomatic writer commented, "The treaty of 1856 was a huge diplomatic blunder. It freed Turkey from the fear of Russia and left her to misgovern her Christian subjects as she pleased, which she forthwith proceeded to do. . . . Within eighteen months of the treaty it was impossible to do anything with them [the Turks]." So, Anglo-Russian relations returned to their old pattern of alternating friendship and mistrust. Diplomatic relations were restored, and after the prisoners returned home, life at the Embassy church returned to its previous, quiet routine.

Rebuilding the Church at Welbeck Street

"We ought, by all means, to have a good church in London." Such was the parting comment made by a priest, Father Fortunatoff, to William Palmer as he left Russia and returned to England in 1841.

From the time of his arrival in London, Father Eugene Popoff felt it necessary to ensure that the church was properly maintained and adorned as befit the house of God. It was, of course, the centre of his priestly ministrations as well as the first point of contact for English people inquiring about Orthodoxy. In 1843, the year after his arrival, he ordered new vestments and other items from Russia with the assistance of Baron Brunnow. In 1845 extensive repairs were undertaken to the church and the adjoining house. In his Chronicle, Father Eugene wrote,

> During the summer months repairs were done to both the church and the church house. The work done on the church consisted of gilding the

> iconostasis and whitewashing the walls. In the house sundry repairs were carried out and painting was done. Of the 500 pounds sterling assigned for this work, barely thirty were left, although the architect adhered to his contract and did not, as I had expected, demand additional, so-called extra amounts, as is customary here.

In 1848 Popoff recorded that various items were donated for the church, including icon lamps and a Gospel book as well as small rugs to place before the altar table. These were given by the daughters of the late Archpriest James Smirnove. In 1850 Father Eugene visited St Petersburg and, with the support and approval of the ambassador, ordered a number of items for the church. These were received the following year and included festal vestments (of gold brocade trimmed with silver), Sunday vestments (made of green material with silver trim), a silver-gilded container for the Holy Gifts, a Gospel book, a priest's service book, and an Epistle book. In 1860 other items were donated to the church by Russian merchants who had been at the Great Exhibition of the Works of Industry of All Nations, which was held in the Crystal Palace in Hyde Park in 1851. Specimens of Russian ecclesiastical art and metalwork that had been exhibited and later donated to the Embassy church included a Gospel book inscribed by Metropolitan Philaret of Moscow, a cross, a chalice, a discos, a spear, two plates, and a censer. All were made by an individual named Savikoff and are described by Popoff as "the very finest work." From these few examples, it is evident that Father Eugene was constantly concerned with ensuring that the church was adorned with the appurtenances of Orthodox worship as an outward expression of its inner grandeur.

The church remained essentially as it was when Father Eugene inherited it from his predecessor. There was a small extension at the rear of the church house, which had formerly been a stable block. The iconostasis was portable, "attached to the floor in separate sections with screws in such a way that, in case of need, it could be moved to another place," which Father Eugene described in his first annual report in 1842. In September 1862 the Ministry of Foreign Affairs of the Russian Empire gave its approval for improvements to be made to the church. Presumably this was in response to the increased attention being focused on Orthodoxy by English people and the growing importance of the London Embassy. The original intent was simply to extend and improve the existing church. However, when work began in September 1863, it was discovered that three of the church's four walls had no foundations, making additional work based on the existing structure out of the question. The only option was to demolish the church and build a new one in its place.

This would, of course, be a major undertaking and far more costly than the original proposal. Because the property at 32 Welbeck Street was held on a long-term lease, there was always the risk that money spent on improvements would be lost if and when the property reverted to the freeholder. There was also the restriction imposed by the original lease that the church could not have its own separate entrance and that access could only be through the "messuage and tenement," that is, through the house itself. In fact, James Thomson, the architect hired to design the new church, initially recommended that an alternative site be found where a separate church could be built in the traditional way. The following letter from Thomson to Father Eugene provides a clear picture of the difficulties that, even in the nineteenth century, stood in the way of finding a suitable site.

57 Devonshire St., Portland Place
June 1st 1863

Dear Sir,

I promised you to enquire as to the possibility of obtaining Ground on which to build a new Chapel, and having done so I beg to report as follows.

The site which I alluded to at Knightsbridge as highly eligible would I find (by direct correspondence with the several parties interested) cost about £10,000 to secure, but until a portion of it has been put up at Auction it cannot be certainly known.

Then the Ground in Albany Street, Regent's Park (where is now a riding school) is unfortunately sold to persons who are unwilling to part with it again even at a liberal premium, which it is well worth.

Since my negotiations about there, I have applied at the Office of the Duke of Portland's Surveyor, and there ascertained that little chance exists of any Ground at Portland Street likely to come into their hands, but I have advised to place myself into communication with a builder who has just taken Ground in Westmoreland Avenue, a great part of which is being rebuilt and likely to become a better thoroughfare than hitherto.

In this situation there is a corner plot to be had, about 40 feet frontage in one street and 90 feet in the other, which would afford the opportunity of Building a Chapel more than double the size of your present Chapel (when enlarged) together with suitable Architectural features to the exterior of the Edifice.

The price I find would also be very reasonable viz. - £600-0-0, subject to a Ground Rent of 50 guineas to the Duke of Portland for 59 years, and there is moral certainty that the Duke would renew the Lease (for such a purpose) from time to time in perpetuity.

Such being the case, I venture to advise the consideration of so important a subject before any operations are commenced in Welbeck Street.

The proximity of the Site to your present Residence would probably render it advantageous also in that respect—I shall be happy to afford you any other information and remain, dear Sir,

Yours Faithfully,
James Thomson.

Evidently the Westmoreland Avenue site came to nothing because rebuilding eventually took place at Welbeck Street. However, if it seems surprising that such extensive work was undertaken at the rear of a leasehold property, it is interesting to note that the possibility of finding a more satisfactory site had been explored thoroughly before work commenced.

The final plan included a rectangular extension to the church house, approximately 50 feet in length. Entrance would only be possible through the front door of No. 32, but subject to this restriction, the building was to be as impressive as possible, with a round Byzantine dome topped with a cross that would be visible above the roofline of the surrounding buildings. Thomson's vision in constructing the rounded dome was "to reproduce in the form of the building the idea of the heavenly vault, in contrast to the type of church buildings normally found in England, which have either sharp Gothic spires or the flat Latin type of roof."

Father Eugene entrusted the design and construction to Thomson, while he remained in overall charge of the work. He also concerned himself with fund-raising because, although the Russian government subsidized the project, other sources of funding had to be found. The grant from the Imperial Ministry of Foreign Affairs was £1,550.0s.0d. An additional £110.11s.3d. was collected in church and £1,608.12s.4d. was collected from individual donors both in England and Russia. The subscription lists for these private donations included some familiar names: Baron Brunnow, who gave £100; Prince Woronzow (son of the late ambassador), who gave £50; and Elizabeth and Catherine Smirnove, daughters of the former rector, who gave £5 each. Many members of the nobility and senior staff at the embassy contributed larger sums; there were also numerous smaller donations of a few shillings each from humbler folk. Donations were also received from a number of business firms in Russia, including Maliutin's, which gave 500 silver roubles, and Sorokosumovsky's, which gave 600 silver roubles.

Her Imperial Majesty, the Empress Maria Alexandrovna, consort of Alexander II, showed particular interest in the London building project. In October 1864, through her secretary, she wrote to ask what she could most usefully contribute toward the new church: "Her Imperial Highness has been pleased to command me to ask your Reverence how, precisely, she can express her kind assistance—whether through a grant of money or a donation of church plate." A year later, on October 6, 1865, she sent a donation of £300 "to cover the deficit which has arisen on rebuilding the Orthodox church attached to the Imperial Embassy in London."

The total collected between September 1862, when the project was initiated, and May 1866, when it was completed, was £3,570.5s.7d. However, this was still not enough to cover all costs. The costs included various items such as carpets and candle stands, which were not covered in the original budget and came to £3,944.13s.11d. Despite the empress's intent to defray the deficit, there remained a shortfall of £374, which Father Eugene borrowed on a temporary basis from various people. As he later reported, "The deficit of £374.8s.4d. had been borrowed by me from certain private individuals in the hope that, since these loans are required to be repaid at different times, the said deficit will be made good sooner or later either by subscribers who have not yet paid in their pledged donations, or through church collections."

Work began in 1863 and was evidently well under way by the spring of 1864 when Father Eugene was unable to use the church for the Easter services. On April 24, 1864, the procurator of the Holy Synod wrote to Father Eugene, "In your letter of the 27 March, permission was asked by your Reverence to perform the Liturgy on the day of Holy Pascha for those of our faith in London in one of the rooms in the church house, due to the disruption of our church there." Father Eugene's letter was sent by courier and only arrived in St Petersburg on Good Friday and was not received by the procurator until Easter. Consequently, permission could not be asked or passed on in time. The procurator apologized for not replying sooner. It is unclear what arrangements were made for the Easter services that year.

It was not until 1866 that Father Eugene reported to the ambassador, "Finally, with God's help, not only is all the work on rebuilding the church of the Imperial Embassy here absolutely finished, but also all the bills relating thereto have been paid." Further, he commented,

> I will permit myself to say that the following people truly deserve reward and encouragement in the highest degree: Thomson, the architect, for his

> hard work and attention to duty in completing the building; the church readers Basil Troyansky and Basil Popoff, for their close involvement in areas where direction and supervision were required from a Russian servant of the church; and Nicholas Mironoff, a merchant, for his active zeal in the matter of collecting money for the church.

Consecration of the church took place on February 14, 1865,[13] performed by the rector, Archpriest Eugene Popoff.[14] He reported, "The church was consecrated and opened for worship on 14th February 1865, in the presence of the Ambassador and members of the embassy staff, and a large congregation made up of our compatriots, of Greeks who share our faith, and also non-Orthodox sympathetic to our church."

The New Chapel of the Russian Embassy

The new church also attracted the attention of the British press. The following description, which was written for the most part by James Thomson, the architect,[15] was printed in the *Illustrated London News* on April 29, 1865. Lengthy extracts from it were later translated into Russian and included in the annual reports for each successive year until the Revolution.

> For several years past the religious services of the Russian Embassy had been conducted in a small room at No. 32, Welbeck-street; but a new and beautiful chapel has now been built on the same site.
>
> Its form is a parallelogram, 50 ft. in length, in the centre of which is a quadrangle of four bold piers, having moulded bases and ornamental caps. From these piers spring semi-circular arches, each 20 ft. in diameter, with scrollwork and other enrichments of a Byzantine character. From the corbels in the spandrils of these arches rise four smaller arches at a higher level, to cross the angles and bring the square figure into an octagon. The whole of this is subdivided into compartments by small pilasters, whose bases rest upon steps of progressive rise, and are terminated by moulded caps or archivolts, somewhat resembling the external ornamentation of the celebrated Baptistery of Ani. An enriched cornice surmounts this octagonal drum; and above it is a hemispherical cupola, 21 ft. in diameter, formed of wrought iron ribs, and resting on a stone base. This is divided into compartments, having twelve arched lanettes, 5 ft. high and 3 ft. wide, between which are discs to contain heads of the Apostles, on gold grounds. A gilt band encircles the upper part of the cupola, on which is inscribed, in Slavonic characters: *Turn Thee again, Thou God of hosts, look down from*

heaven; behold and visit this vine and the place of the vineyard which Thy right hand hath planted.

At the east end is a semicircular apse, having a vaulted ceiling, painted azure and studded with gold stars, which are embossed on the surface, graduating and concentrating from the base towards the apex, where the monogram representing the name of Jehovah is placed. The fittings of the apse consist of the altar table, within the holy doors; the screen, or iconostasis, corresponding to the veil of the Temple and, behind the altar, a triangular pedestal of oak, fitted with a bronze socket, to hold the seven-branch candlestick. To terminate the apse, a freestone arch, supported on black marble pillars, with carved capitals, contains a stained glass window, representing the Saviour, at whose feet, upon a verde-antique marble slab, is inscribed, in Greek characters: *Come unto me, all ye that labour and are heavy laden, and I will give you rest.* A large niche on each side contains tables and small enshrined pictures formerly belonging to churches at Bomarsund, presented by the British Government.[16]

A credence or cupboard of oak, fashioned as a miniature ark, with sloping roof, contains the chalice, patens and other holy vessels used in the celebration of the Eucharist. The iconostasis is formed of solid freestone, having a range of arches supported by coloured marble pillars, with carved capitals of Byzantine character, each capital being of a different design. The whole is surmounted by a coved cornice, also carved with various devices of cruciform character. In the centre is a *dessus de porte*, of carved freestone, which contains a picture of the Last Supper, while the compartments below have pictures set in marble frames, the subjects consisting of the Saviour and the Virgin, with St. George terminating one end of the screen and St. Basil the other. The north and south doors are decorated with pictures of the Archangels St. Gabriel and St. Michael. The whole of these are painted by Mr. Varuchin, a member of the Imperial Academy of Arts at St. Petersburg, on frosted gold grounds, each having the nimbus of more transparent colour and surface. The holy doors, which are massive and elaborate both in design and execution, are of wood, carved and splendidly gilt, inlaid with metals of different hue, so as to relieve what might otherwise look monotonous. They contain small heads of the Evangelists and a picture of the Annunciation.

The folding of these doors is peculiar, and managed so that, when closed, they appear as an impassable barrier, which at the proper time the high priest is able to unfold with ease, so as to give access to the altar.

The base of the iconostasis has mosaic panels of marble and coloured tiles, and the sanctum is encompassed by a handsome dwarf railing, bronzed and

Interior of the former Embassy Chapel at Welbeck Street as it appears today. (Source: Nicolas Mabin, June 2010)

gilt, with folding gates, the whole being capped with a gunmetal handrail, placed on a stone plinth, with circular steps leading to the altar.

Two other pictures should be noticed, which are placed on the side wall, one representing St. Alexander Nevsky and the other St. Mary Magdalene; the latter figure bearing the alabaster box of precious ointment. In advance of all are placed two elegant banners of graceful pattern and rich material, mounted on brass standards 16 ft. high, with crosslets carved and gilt; upon them are painted, as medallions, representations of the Baptism and Resurrection. The polychromy has been carefully studied in this matter, so as to produce variety of tone, yet in harmony with the pictures, bronze and other decorative features.

Several persons of high rank and distinction joined the Imperial Ministry of Foreign Affairs in contributing to adorn this place of worship. It was the Grand Duchess Marie, President of the Academy of Arts at St. Petersburg, at whose suggestion the Slavonic inscriptions and other parts were introduced. We may mention, also, the Duke of Leuchtenberg, the Russian Ambassador and Baroness Brunnow, Count A. Stroganow, Field-Marshall Prince Bariatinsky; Prince Gregoire Gagarin, Vice President of the Academy of Arts, who contributed a general idea for the screen; Prince Woronzow, Prince B. Galitzin, Count and Countess Orlow-Davidow, his Excellency D. Longuinow and Mdme. Longuinow, Mdme. Chertcow,

Exterior of the dome of the Russian Embassy Chapel on 32 Welbeck Street. (Source: Nicolas Mabin, June 2010)

> Princess E. Kotchsubey, the Councillor of Embassy Salomow, Prince Michel Gortchacow, Baron Friedricksz, Colonel N. Novitsky, Mr. A. Takovleff, and Mr. A. Prehn: besides some of the commercial notabilities of St. Petersburg and Moscow—such as, Messrs. Belaieff, Polejaieff, Maliutin, Sorokosumovsky, the Russian Steam Navigation Company, and others.
>
> The whole work has been carried out under the superintendence of Mr. James Thomson, architect, except such pictures and decorations as have been presented from St. Petersburg by Mr. Gromoff.

This article was accompanied by an impressive engraving of the new church, which is the oldest picture of the Russian church in London to survive. The only other Orthodox church in London at the time was the Greek Church of the Saviour, which moved from 9 Finsbury Circus to a larger premises nearby on Winchester Street near London Wall in 1849. With its new building, the Russian Embassy church was better able to fulfill both its official function as chapel for the embassy staff and its unofficial function as an embassy for the Orthodox faith in England, where there was at the time a growing interest in Orthodoxy in certain circles.

The freehold of 32 Welbeck Street currently belongs to the Howard de Walden Estate, and the current tenant is Circle Health Limited. The building's structure has remained basically unchanged since the nineteenth century. Circle Health now uses the former dwelling house at the front of the property as office space. Even the plasterwork appears to be unchanged since Victorian days. The passageway leading to the church at the back of the property remains in place as described in the nineteenth-century documents. The church building is now used as a meeting room. While no longer a place of worship, the layout of the room is still intact, making it easy to imagine how it would have looked as a church. The end where the sanctuary used to be is still raised above ground level. In recent years the ceiling and arches were repainted so as to highlight the details and restore the iconographic depictions of the Apostles that were around the base of the dome. At the back of the sanctuary, where the bishop's throne would have been, is an emergency exit leading out into the mews, reminding the visitor that this is where the stables would have been before the church was built.

Chapter 5

[1842–1875] Father Eugene Popoff, Pastor to English-Speaking Converts

The Anglican Movement Toward Orthodoxy

It is time to consider the work of Father Eugene Popoff with the Church of England. As the embassy chaplain, Popoff was a key contact point between the Russian Orthodox Church and the Anglican Church and, importantly, he was also the pastor of those Anglicans who embraced Orthodoxy. First to be examined in some detail is Father Popoff's role in nurturing the growing desire among certain sections of the Church of England for rapprochement with the Orthodox Church.

"Will the idea of union of the churches, which has lit up the west like a glow on the horizon, remain just the glow of sunset in the west, or will it turn into an Eastern radiance of sunrise, in the hope of a brighter morning? Thou knowest, O Lord." Thus the great Metropolitan of Moscow, Philaret, expressed his hopes and, at the same time, his reservations concerning the growing interest in Orthodoxy in the West during the mid-nineteenth century.

In England this interest was inspired by the desire that arose in some Anglican circles to find a surer basis for their church's existence than the fact that it was established by law. Legal reforms between 1828 and 1832 removed many restrictions in civil life that applied to non-Anglicans, including Roman Catholics who were beginning to establish a stronger presence in England. While some turned away from the Church of England to nonconformist Protestant groups and others turned to the Roman Catholic Church, many sought a religious revival within the Church of England itself. The Evangelicals, or "Low Church" party, hoped to reform it in a more Protestant direction, while the Anglo-Catholics, or "High Church," sought to move away from Protestantism in a more "Catholic" direction. Many came to believe in the so-called branch theory of the Church, which held that the Catholic Church of Christ is divided into three branches: the Anglican, the

Roman Catholic, and the Orthodox. The origin of the Anglo-Catholic Movement, also known as the Oxford Movement, can be traced to a sermon by John Keble, given in Oxford in 1833 and titled *The Apostasy of the Nation*. A group of Oxford theologians headed by John Keble, Edward Pusey, and John Henry Newman sought to prove that the Church of England had always been a part of the Catholic Church. Turning to the *Book of Common Prayer* and other sources, they found that many forms of ritual, which had gone into disuse in England, were in fact not forbidden and that others, such as the use of liturgical vestments, were actually required. They sought to prove that the official doctrine of the Church of England had always been Catholic and patristic in nature and that the Protestantism that had crept in was simply a misinterpretation of these official teachings. The Oxford Movement was also known as the Tractarian Movement, after the ninety *Tracts for the Times* published between 1833 and 1841 that expressed their views. Unable to accept the inconsistency of this position within the Church of England, in 1845 Newman became a Roman Catholic (eventually being made a cardinal), and others followed his example. Pusey, Keble, and their followers remained Anglicans. A few turned their attention to the Orthodox churches of the East.

William Palmer, a deacon of the Church of England and a lecturer at Magdalen College, Oxford, showed a particular interest in the Russian Church. In 1840 he visited Russia. Partly as a result of this visit, Father Eugene Popoff was appointed to the London church. Palmer, who later corresponded with the respected theologian Alexis Khomiakov, appeared to be considering entry into the Orthodox Church. However, in 1855, to the great consternation of his Orthodox friends, he became a Roman Catholic.

Initially, he hoped to affirm the Catholic nature of his church by reestablishing communion with the Orthodox Church—the Eastern branch of the Catholic Church, according to Anglo-Catholic theory. In 1839 Grand Duke Alexander of Russia (the future Alexander II) visited Oxford. Palmer, encouraged by the president of his college, presented the following petition to the grand duke:

> Though it may be presumptuous, I venture to present a petition to your Imperial Highness. It is this: to obtain that there be sent hither some Russian ecclesiastic, capable of examining the theology of our churches. He could live in Magdalen College (I am authorized to say this), and I would myself teach him English, that so through him the contents of some of our best books may be made known to His Imperial Majesty and to the Bishops

> of the Eastern Communion. And, if, after a time, I should go to Russia, to study there the theology and the ritual of the Russian Church, I hope that I may obtain your Imperial Highness's protection. Assuredly, if the whole Catholic Church ought to aspire after unity, nothing can be more worthy of the piety of a great prince, than to seek to facilitate the reunion of two Communions, separated only by misunderstandings and want of intercourse.

The following year, Palmer made an extended visit to Russia and did not return to England until a year later. He took with him a letter of recommendation from the Reverend Dr Routh, the president of his college, in which he requested the Russian Church to admit Palmer to Holy Communion:

> Further, I ask, and even adjure in the name of Christ, all the most holy Archbishops and Bishops, and especially the Synod itself, that they will examine him as to the orthodoxy of his faith with a charitable mind, and, if they find in him all that is necessary to the integrity of the true and saving faith, then that they will also admit him to communion in the Sacraments. I would have him submit and conform himself in all things to the injunctions and admonitions of the Russian Bishops, only neither affirming anything, nor doing anything, contrary to the faith and doctrine of the British Churches.

The hope was to confirm the Anglo-Catholic concept of the church by establishing that, when in Russia, an Anglican should naturally receive Holy Communion from the Russian Church. Dr Routh thought Palmer had little chance of success; a friend of Palmer described him as "an ecclesiastical Don Quixote." It is interesting to note that the Archbishop of Canterbury declined to countersign the letter and that other members of Magdalen College protested "at the very idea of intercommunion with the idolatrous Greek Church."

Palmer traveled extensively in Russia and made many friends. His description of his visit, however, is not pervaded with the same warmth that characterized the writings of William Birkbeck, an Anglican visitor to Russia of a generation later. Palmer's description is mostly taken up with accounts of his discussions and arguments with numerous clergy and laypeople he met, all with a view to establishing that he was a true Catholic and so had the right and duty to receive Holy Communion from the Russian Church. Of particular interest are his visits to Count Protasoff, the procurator of the Holy Synod, and to Metropolitan Philaret of Moscow.

He was received with great respect and, one might say, enthusiasm. The metropolitan and the procurator both pointed out, among other things, the inconsistencies of belief within the Anglican Church. In particular, they asked why there were Anglican chaplains both in Kronstadt and St Petersburg, while, according to Palmer, Anglicans were supposed to attend the Russian Church when in Russia. Palmer said to Count Protasoff, "If you believe your own exclusive definition of the Church, and have only a spark of charity, you ought to send a mission to England to convert us." To which the count replied, "We would only send missions to places where there is a chance of success; my best hope is for you, that we must convert you, and make you a bishop, as we made that Missionary bishop for the Aleoutines when you were present the other day, and send you back so."

The metropolitan's own account of the meeting was summed up in a memorandum, later sent to Father Popoff in London, which put the Orthodox position with clarity and sobriety:

> The Metropolitan replied briefly to him that discussing the dogmas of the faith is not a matter for an individual bishop and an individual deacon of churches which are foreign to one another, but it is a matter for a whole Council (*Sobor*) made up of bishops from both sides. And so, if he wishes unconditionally to accept all the dogmas confessed by the Orthodox Church and to be united to her by the established rite, then he will be accounted worthy to receive the Holy Mysteries in the Orthodox Church. If this is not the case, however, it remains only to wish him the most speedy conversion to the path of truth.

Palmer returned to England, still a convinced Anglican, without having received Holy Communion from the Russian Church. A few years later, however, he entered into correspondence with the theologian Alexis Khomiakov, which continued for approximately fifteen years. The letters cover many points of difference between Anglicanism and Orthodoxy. Khomiakov accepted the fact that it would be more difficult for an Anglican to become Orthodox than to become a Roman Catholic because, he said, all Western confessions stem from the same root. In 1844 he wrote to Palmer about the difficulties, as he perceived them, that stood between a Westerner and the Orthodox faith:

> It is now more than a thousand years since Spanish bishops invented the Inquisition (in the time of the Goths), and an addition to the Symbol

> [Creed]. It is almost as much since the Pope confirmed that addition by his word of might. Since that time the Western communities have nurtured a deep enmity and an incurable disdain for the unchanging East. These feelings have become traditional and, as it were innate, to the Roman-German world, and England has all the time partaken of that spiritual life. Can it tear itself away from the past? There stands, in my opinion, the great and invincible obstacle to Unity. . . . It is an easy thing to say "We have ever been Catholics; but the Church being sullied by abuses, we have protested against them, and have gone too far in our protest. Now we retrace our steps." This is easy, but to say "We have been schismated for ages and ages, even since the dawn of our intellectual life" is next to impossible. It would require in a man an almost superhuman courage to say it, and in a nation an almost incredible humility to adopt that declaration.

In 1847 Khomiakov visited Oxford, where he met Palmer in person for the first time, and so they continued their discussions face to face for a short time. Khomiakov also visited London, where he attended a service at the Embassy church on Welbeck Street.[1]

From his letters to Khomiakov, it is evident that, with the passage of time, Palmer had become increasingly disillusioned with Anglo-Catholicism; he failed to obtain support for his ideas among the Anglican hierarchy and began talking about seeking admission to the Orthodox Church. However, two stumbling blocks stood in his path: the divergence of practice between the Greek and Russian Churches over the baptism of converts and the interference of the state in ecclesiastical affairs in Russia, including censorship laws, which meant, for example, that many of his works could not be published there. Khomiakov's explanation that these were secondary issues went unheard. In 1853 Palmer went to live in Rome, and in 1855 he entered the Roman Catholic Church.

Palmer wrote that after studying the question for more than twenty years, he had finally become convinced that the Orthodox teaching on the Procession of the Holy Spirit (the dogmatic question that lay at the heart of the separation between East and West) was the true one. Why, then, did he become a Roman Catholic? From a careful reading of his letters, it seems that his concern over the question of baptism went beyond a mere confusion over the difference between Russian and Greek practices. Was he not more concerned to obtain a clear agreement from the Orthodox Church that he was already properly baptised, and so should be received as a baptised Christian? There is some indication of this in his letters. For example, he wrote that if he were to receive baptism from a Greek bishop, he would be acting not only against the synodical decrees of the Russian Church but also, perhaps, against his own conscience. Palmer's conversion to Catholicism came against the background of the Crimean War, when anti-Russian feeling ran high in England. Paradoxically, he had just written a treatise defending the Russians' right to act as guardian of the Holy Places in Jerusalem. The apparent inconsistencies surrounding his conversion to Catholicism led to hopes that this was a temporary phase and that eventually he would join the Orthodox Church. That was not to be the case.

One of Palmer's greatest achievements, gained through his travels and correspondence, was that he made Russian churchmen and theologians aware of England and the peculiar circumstances of the Anglican Church. He also inspired in them a desire to draw the English closer to Orthodoxy. Although there are indications that Palmer had some contact with Father Eugene Popoff, no detailed accounts of their meetings have survived. This is despite Count Protasoff's comment to Palmer in 1841 that he would be obliged if he would call upon the new chaplain when he came, "and make his acquaintance, and put him in the way of becoming acquainted with religious matters and some of our clergy." Palmer's chief sources of information about Orthodoxy were in Russia. This was not, however, the case with another contemporary Anglican theologian who evinced a strong sympathy for Orthodoxy, John Mason Neale. Neale relied extensively on Father Eugene for information about the Orthodox Church; while working on his *History of the Holy Eastern Church*, he even wrote to a friend, "Popoff works like a horse for me."

Neale's interest in Orthodoxy stemmed from his involvement with the Oxford Movement. He first became acquainted with the Oxford tracts while studying at Cambridge in the 1830s. Together with Benjamin Webb and others who shared his Anglo-Catholic views, he founded the Cambridge Camden Society. In 1841 Neale was ordained in the Church of England and in 1846 appointed warden of Sackville College, East Grinstead, a seventeenth-century almshouse founded by the Earl of Dorset. He remained at this post until his early death in 1866 at the age of 48. He played a part in the revival of monasticism in the Church of England by founding the Society of St Margaret, which was a convent in East Grinstead. Neale introduced some elements of ritual into his services, for which he suffered the censure of his own bishop, the Bishop of Chichester, who suspended Neale from priestly functions for a number of years. The feelings against these "papal innovations" were so intense that they led to riots in the streets. However, by the end of his life,

Neale's bishop and the local populace accepted his liturgical practices, and they have since been widely adopted in Anglo-Catholic circles. Neale, who suffered from poor health all his life, was very erudite—even described as "buried beneath a mass of obsolete learning"—a prolific writer, and, at the same time, simple and kindhearted toward the old people in his care at Sackville College.

Neale began writing his *History of the Holy Eastern Church* shortly after his ordination; it remained unfinished at the time of his death. He became particularly absorbed in this work while in East Grinstead while troubles were arising from his liturgical practices. In part, he wrote to advance the cause of Anglo-Catholicism in England (by providing a concrete example of what a "Catholic," but not Roman, church should be like) and, in part, it seems, to find a refuge from the difficulties of his life as an Anglican clergyman by immersing himself in what he felt to be a holier realm. The work was conceived in four parts, one for each of the four Eastern patriarchates, to be prefaced by a *General Introduction*.[2] (He hoped, in vain, that his friend Benjamin Webb would write some of the parts for him.) The first part completed was on the Patriarchate of Alexandria; Neale obtained some of this information by visiting libraries in Alexandria and Constantinople. He then began work on the *General Introduction*. He complained constantly of how difficult it was to obtain information and noted that ancient manuscripts, once tracked down in distant libraries, were difficult to understand and interpret. He sought help in correspondence with William Palmer, R. W. Blackmore (former chaplain of the English Russia Company at Kronstadt), and Father Eugene Popoff. Neale's biographer, Eleanor Towle, wrote:

> With the Rev. Eugene Popoff his relations were of the most friendly description. He afforded incalculable service in explaining and defending the ceremonies and principles of the Greek ritual; and mutual respect in course of time engendered a sincere and affectionate esteem. In his visits to London Neale attended his services, and consulted him upon points which must have presented difficulties to any outside the Greek Communion. His *History of Alexandria* found warm admirers amongst its members, and any praise or criticism from Russia is at once recorded in his letters.

The *General Introduction* concentrated more on the faith and practice of Orthodoxy than on history, and it was here that Neale found the assistance of an Orthodox priest particularly valuable. With Popoff's help, he began to study Slavonic so that he could study the service books of the Russian Church. Neale wrote the following to Benjamin Webb:

> It is true that when I began the *History of the Eastern Church*, I had no idea how necessary it [Slavonic] was. . . . Directly I began the *Introduction* I wanted it, and in a clumsy way I had it. I had only to send any Slavonic to Popoff, or Blackmore, or Palmer of Magdalen, and I had the translation. But as early as p. 120 of the *Introduction* I began to use my own knowledge of it. I don't say learn Slavonic that you may understand my book, but if you don't learn Slavonic, don't set up to know much about the Eastern Church.

On March 29, 1849, Neale wrote, "The distinction of Saints in the [Russian] calendar is even more perfect than the Greek. I have now, thanks to Popoff, mastered the seven degrees of festivals in the Eastern Church." In 1850, as the *General Introduction* was nearing completion, Father Eugene wrote to Neale, "Shall I really congratulate you for the *finis qui coronat opus*? If so, I do it quite heartily. May I ask you to make me one favour? It would be to look on the whole work before it is quite out. Again, can you not make some kind of provision for some future accidental insertions, omissions or supplements?" A little later, Father Eugene wrote to Neale:

> Your *Introduction*, I suppose, is today at St. Petersburg. . . . I would be happy to see you on any day. The service on Sunday begins at eleven o'clock, though the Matins we read for ourselves much earlier. The Liturgie will be that of S. Basile, as it is on all Sundays in Lent. For the hearers, the difference between the Liturgie of S. Basile and that of S. Chrysostom is felt principally in the chanting. It is a very old one, and pure Church-chanting. As for the Liturgie of the Presanctified, it will be on Monday, Tuesday and Wednesday in our Passion week—your Easter week.

Of course, the church to which he was invited on this occasion was the old chapel at 32 Welbeck Street. One can only speculate as to whether Neale might have been among the "non-Orthodox sympathetic to our faith" who were present when the new church was consecrated in 1865.

The *General Introduction* described the "Holy Eastern Church" with great warmth and understanding. For example, he wrote,

> Uninterrupted successions of Metropolitans and Bishops stretch themselves to Apostolic times; venerable liturgies exhibit doctrine unchanged,

> and discipline uncorrupted; the same Sacrifice is offered, the same hymns are chanted, by the Eastern Christians of today, as those which resounded in the churches of St. Basil or St. Firmilian. . . . In the glow and splendour of Byzantine glory, in the tempests of the Oriental middle ages, in the desolation and tyranny of the Turkish Empire, the testimony of the same immutable church remains unchanged. Extending herself from the sea of Okhotsk to the palaces of Venice, from the ice-fields that grind against the Solovetsky monastery to the burning jungles of Malabar, embracing a thousand languages, and nations, and tongues, but binding them together in the golden link of the same Faith, offering the Tremendous Sacrifice in a hundred Liturgies, but offering it to the same God, and with the same rites, fixing her Patriarchal Thrones in the same cities as when the Disciples were called Christians first at Antioch, and James, the brother of the Lord, finished his course at Jerusalem, oppressed by the devotees of the False Prophet, as once by the worshippers of false gods, —she is now, as she was from the beginning, multiplex in her arrangements, simple in her faith, difficult of comprehension to strangers, easily intelligible to her sons, widely scattered in her branches, hardly beset by her enemies, yet still and evermore, what she delights to call herself, One, Holy, Catholic and Apostolic.

Such a moving description of the Orthodox Church would not have been found in any Russian or Greek writings of the time. It is not surprising then that Neale's work was received enthusiastically in Russian church circles. On June 10, 1851, Father Eugene wrote to Neale:

> My dear Sir, His Excellency our Ambassador, Baron de Brunnow, has kindly charged me to announce to you, that His Majesty, the Emperor of Russia, in acknowledgment of the value of your arduous and useful work on the *History of the Holy Eastern Church*, as well as an encouragement in its continuance, has been graciously pleased to grant you the sum of £100.

In 1859 Neale published a work titled *Greek Liturgies of SS. Mark, James, Clement, Chrysostom and Basil*. This was the first time that the complete text of these services were made available in English. In recognition of this work, the following year Neale received some icons and a Slavonic prayer book from Metropolitan Philaret that was inscribed, "God's blessing be on all those who study the ancient liturgies and rites of the Church in preparation for the future union of the churches. Ph. M. Moscow." He kept the icons in his study and later wrote to Benjamin Webb, "I wish you could see my glorious icons. The Archimandrite also sent a very pretty Madonna to our Mother [the superior of the convent]. I had no idea until now how big a man I was in Russia." This appreciation of his work by the Russian Church was of great importance to Neale, given that for years it met with little sympathy in his own country.

In 1863 Neale, George Williams,[3] and Henry Parry Liddon founded the Eastern Church Association, forerunner of the Anglican and Eastern Churches Association. Father Eugene Popoff and Archimandrite Constantine Stratoulias, rector of the Greek Church in London, were included in its standing committee. The aims of this body were as follows:

> To inform the English public as to the state and position of the Eastern Christians, in order gradually to better their condition through the influence of public opinion in England; to make known the doctrines and principles of the Anglican Church to our Christian brethren in the East; to take advantage of all opportunities which the Providence of God shall afford us, for Intercommunion with the Orthodox Church, and also for friendly intercourse with the other ancient Churches of the East; and to assist, as far as we are able, the Bishops of the Orthodox Church in their efforts to promote the Spiritual welfare and education of their flocks.

In 1865, after many years of opposition to his work, it finally became possible to lay the foundation stone for St Margaret's convent near East Grinstead. Neale was particularly gratified that Archpriest Eugene Popoff and Archimandrite Constantine Stratoulias were present to witness the ceremony. The archimandrite even pronounced a blessing while the congregation knelt. The following year, when news of Neale's death reached Russia, it is reported that the bell that tolled to mark the passing of high-ranking Orthodox ecclesiastics was tolled for Neale.

Neale's greatest achievement was likely his making information about the Orthodox Church far more readily accessible to the English-speaking reader than had previously been the case. In addition to his *History of the Holy Eastern Church* and numerous articles, which were widely read in Anglican circles, Neale is best remembered as a writer and translator of hymns. He translated many Orthodox liturgical texts, adapting them to the poetic form of Anglican hymns. The results were not suitable for use in Orthodox worship, but they did provide Anglicans with some contact with Orthodox liturgical prayer.

Over more profound theological issues, Neale also showed a surprising degree of understanding of the Orthodox position. Concerning the doctrine of the Procession of the Holy Spirit, he wrote to Webb in 1849, "Depend upon it, the Greeks are right." His *General Introduction* includes a most interesting passage condemning the *Filioque*[4] addition to the Western creed:

> English Churchmen will hardly deny that, let the dogma of the double Procession be never so true, its insertion in the inviolable Creed was an act utterly unjustifiable, and throws on the Roman Church the chief guilt of the horrible schism of 1054. It was done in the teeth of the veto passed in the sixth session of the Council of Ephesus, in the fifth of Chalcedon, in the sixth collation of the second of Constantinople, and in the seventeenth of the third of Constantinople. It was done against the express command of a most holy Pope, himself a believer in the double Procession, who is now with God. No true union—experience has shewn it—can take place between the Churches, till the Filioque be omitted from the Creed, even if a truly Œcumenical Synod should afterwards proclaim the truth of the doctrine. And I end therefore, as I commenced, with the words of our great Bishop Pearson: "Thus began the schism; never thenceforth to be reconciled, till the word Filioque be omitted from the Creed."

Nevertheless, in a letter to Webb shortly after the *General Introduction* was published, Neale wrote, "I suppose that Blackmore, Palmer and I are the only men in the English Church who are thoroughly convinced that the Latin doctrine is grievously erroneous, suspected of heresy, and even (if logically carried out) heretical."

Despite these clearly expressed views, and his awareness that they were not widely shared in the Church of England, it seems to have never occurred to Neale that there was any inconsistency in his remaining an Anglican. His goal in studying Orthodoxy remained firmly the Anglo-Catholic one of, on the one hand, confirming the Catholic status of the Church of England by establishing eventual intercommunion with the Orthodox Church and, on the other, enriching the life of the Church of England through contact with Orthodox theology and liturgics. While studying the ancient liturgies, Neale never came to terms with the full richness of the Orthodox liturgical cycle. In his *General Introduction*, for example, he complained of the "tedious repetitions, the endless canons, the immense prolixity of the services outside the Liturgy, which make them unedifying to the ordinary worshipper, and contrast most unfavourably with the well-chosen lessons, the beautiful antiphons, the short appropriate responses of the breviary."

Many of the ceremonial aspects that Neale introduced into the Anglican services, such as the Stations of the Cross and the office of Benediction, were based on Roman Catholic practice, from which he selected what he considered to represent the ancient Western tradition, rather than on Orthodox precedents. He was also an early adherent of the idea that the Church of Christ will be renewed by a second Pentecost. This idea was prominent in the ideology of the ecumenical movement but had no basis in Orthodox tradition. In his *General Introduction*, Neale wrote, "In the great regeneration of the Church, in the second and more blessed Pentecost, the Æcumenical Throne of the East will bear no small part."

Nevertheless, in the present century, when information about any subject is so readily available, it is easy to underestimate Neale's achievement in making Orthodoxy accessible to English-speaking readers. This is why his work was so highly regarded in Russia and why his death was marked not by Orthodox memorial services (which would have implied a unity of faith that did not exist), but by the simple tolling of a bell in Moscow.

Similarly, the reaction in Moscow and St Petersburg to Palmer's visit of 1840 was one of cautious optimism, leading to a resolve to study the Church of England further and ascertain whether there was a chance that it might wish to unite with Orthodoxy. One of Father Eugene Popoff's duties was to study these matters and report back to the Holy Synod. An idea of the scope of his work in this area can be gleaned from his correspondence.

Even before he was appointed to London, Father Eugene had been asked to provide information about religious life in his land of residence. A letter dated December 31, 1840, from the procurator asks him for general information on prevailing thoughts in Denmark, where Father Eugene was then living. In particular, the procurator was interested in opinions about the Orthodox Confession and the Eastern Church, how well it was understood, and to what extent those of other faiths were becoming acquainted with Orthodoxy.

In 1851 Father Eugene reported to Count Protasoff concerning a group of Anglicans who, in reaction to the infamous Gorham Judgment,[5] were considering seceding from the Church of England and seeking recognition from the Russian Church. This movement was short-lived and had no practical results.

Count Alexander Petrovitch Tolstoy, who was procurator of the Holy Synod from 1856 to 1862, was particularly interested in the possibility of Anglican unity with Orthodoxy. On June 30, 1854, he wrote to Father Eugene:

> The information received from you about those seeking a rapprochement with the Eastern Church is extremely interesting. One cannot fail to rejoice that the Most Reverend Makary's Dogmatic Theology is being translated into English. However, his *Introduction to Orthodox Theology* also deserves to be translated, perhaps even more so, since it permits the reader to become acquainted with the distinguishing features of our Church in a single volume. It would also be good to translate the talks of Amphiteatroff[6] which give an explanation of Orthodox prayers and rites.

On February 28, 1858, Count Tolstoy acknowledged receipt of a notebook from Father Popoff that contained "a translation of D. Wiese's letters on English education and extracts from various articles by the so-called Oxford movement. I have also received Metropolitan Platon's catechism translated into the English language."

On April 30, 1860, the count wrote to Father Eugene:

> I have received your letter of 2 March and the items enclosed: your articles on the Anglican Church and Neale's Liturgy, and the *1859 Report from the Ecclesiastical Commissioners for England.* Please accept my sincere thanks for all this. I intend to forward your articles to a new journal which has begun publication in Moscow under the name *Orthodox Review* (*Pravoslavnoye Obozreniye*), and I will be anxiously awaiting the continuation of these articles which you promised in your letter. For our poorly-informed readers any information about the Anglican Church will of course be most interesting, but, in writing about the contemporary Anglican theologians and of the different parties which currently exist within the Anglican church, you will, evidently, devote particular attention to the sympathy of the High Church party for the Eastern Church. This is, in itself, a most interesting phenomenon, and for many of our people it can also be instructive: should we not be ashamed not to accept truths of our own Church, when these are even recognized by the English?

The letter goes on to ask, at length, about the state of education in England; reforms were afoot in Russia at that time, and the procurator hoped to obtain information in this area from Father Eugene. His next letter, which was written a month later, is an indication that he was not disappointed. In that letter he thanked Popoff for information about the Anglican clergy's involvement in education and for a new article about the different parties in the Church of England. In March 1861 he again wrote asking about Sunday schools in England. In December 1863 the procurator wrote to request Father Eugene's consent to publish an article he had written about the restoration of monasticism in the Church of England.

Metropolitan Philaret of Moscow took a close personal interest in the Anglican question and studied Father Eugene's reports and articles. Following are extracts from Popoff's letters and translated articles and some "opinions"[7] expressed by the metropolitan that were sent to Father Eugene for his information:

a. **Archpriest Popoff had sent a translation of an article by Pastor Warburton, a member of the Anglo-Catholic Society. Warburton says that one Russian Orthodox Bishop states that he is quite satisfied with the Anglican forms of ordination, baptism, and consecration of Holy Gifts.**
   The Metropolitan says this should be treated with caution.
b. **Archpriest Popoff informs that the Greek Archimandrite Philip Schulati, who was in London to make a collection, had been present at an Anglican service, and afterwards said that he had taken part in the service. From this it had been concluded that communion between the churches already existed de facto.**
   The Metropolitan of Moscow observes that if this incident, as reported here, should become known in the East, the impression would not be agreeable. The lesson to be drawn from this incident is how carefully a member of the Orthodox hierarchy should define his contacts with the heterodox.
c. **Article by Father Popoff on [Arthur] Stanley's views[8] on the Orthodox Church.**
   The Metropolitan of Moscow says it shows Stanley in a very bad light. Stanley is happy to use the creed without the *Filioque* but he does not wish to be separated from the age-old lawlessness and wishes to use the *Filioque* as a private opinion. The Metropolitan of Moscow remarks that a strong warning against this will have to be made if it is proposed to print the article. The writer says that some of the Fathers recognize Procession from the Son, but the Metropolitan says that he knows of none, but only of certain misinterpretations. On these conditions the article can be made known, and can form the beginning of what is proposed in the dealings with the emissary sent by the American bishops.

d. **Another article sent by Father Popoff about the possibility of communion between the Eastern and Anglican Churches, and the significant admission made by an American bishop: "To enter truly into communion with the Eastern Church we have very much yet to learn." The writer was prepared to admit Unction but not the seven sacraments. He tries to find a common wording for transubstantiation (*metavoli*).**
The Metropolitan of Moscow thinks he is trying to enter into union with Orthodoxy while keeping the old distinguishing features of his church. The Metropolitan does not find it useful to print this, but it should be borne in mind by all those dealing with Anglicans.
e. **Extracts made by Father Popoff from a letter he had received from San Francisco, where there are as many as a thousand Orthodox Russians and other Slavs.**
The Metropolitan of Moscow says that of course a church should be built. The matter speaks for itself, that it should be done. Let the Russian Church say it should be done. Let Russia say it should be done. May this word not fall on barren soil.

In his earlier reports, Father Eugene showed that he hoped that union of the Anglican Church with Orthodoxy might become a reality; however, he became increasingly disillusioned in later years. Similar feelings were reflected in a report written for the Holy Synod in February 1865 by Archpriest Joseph Wassilieff, rector of the Russian Embassy Church in Paris. While in Paris, Father Wassilieff devoted much of his time and energy acquainting the West with Orthodoxy and, in particular, countering the claims of the Papacy.[9] In November 1864 Father Joseph was invited to England to attend a meeting of the Russo-Greek Church Committee of the Anglican Church, which had been established the previous year by the Canterbury Convocation.

On his arrival in England, Father Joseph first visited Oxford and Cambridge universities, where he had warm and friendly meetings with many ecclesiastics. However, he found that only the celebrated Dr Pusey was interested in discussing the theological obstacles to reunion. An initial meeting, during which many points of agreement were noted, was followed by a second session devoted to a long and unsatisfactory argument about the *Filioque* addition to the Creed. Dr Pusey began by condemning Patriarch Photius of Constantinople as "an evil man, who intentionally neglects the question of the procession of the Holy Ghost from the Son." Wassilieff noted that "the Doctor was not composed or comfortable" when presented with the evidence and testimony of the Church Fathers on this matter. In conclusion, Dr Pusey commented that even if the leaders of the Anglican Church were to agree to drop the word *Filioque* from the Creed, they did not have enough authority over their members to enforce this change. Father Wassilieff noted, "At this point I allowed myself to offer advice that it might be necessary to prepare the members of the Anglican Church through preliminary and frequent explanations of the matter," advice that, as Father Wassilieff himself was well aware, was easier to give than to carry out.

From Oxford, Wassilieff went to London to attend the meeting to which he had been invited, together with Father Eugene Popoff. Father Wassilieff's description of the meeting was perceptive and betrayed a sense of humour lurking beneath the dry style of an official report:

> The next day I had to hurry to a meeting in London with the so-called Russo-Greek Church Committee, to which I had been invited by its president, the canon and chancellor of Lincoln, Massingberd. Last year this committee was commissioned to communicate with a similar committee in America by the decree of the Upper House of Convocation, which is made up of Anglican bishops from the Canterbury metropolitan see. Their task was then to submit, beginning with the Lower House and going on to the Upper, a report about the direction being taken with regard to the question of the amalgamation of the Anglican American Church with the Eastern Orthodox-Catholic Church: naturally an explanation of things was anticipated at this meeting, which consisted of ten distinguished priests from different dioceses. The venerable archpriest of our ambassadorial church in London, Eugene Popoff, was also invited to this meeting. The Anglicans present showered me with great cordiality, emitting at my presence two approving cries ("hear, hear"); but they did not satisfy my expectation of hearing a clearer account of what had been happening. The meeting lasted two hours, and was confined by choice to a careful and brief exposition, an account of past circumstances, which concerned the sought-for relations between the two Churches, and a reiteration of the sincere desire "that Anglican and Orthodox Christians might share in the prayers and sacraments of both Churches without being unfaithful each to their own Church." On my observation that it is necessary to refer to preliminary agreement in the teaching of faith, without which the relations of the sacraments are inconceivable, they answered that this question was extremely delicate, and that the Committee had not obtained the authority to make a decision on this; all that is indicated at the moment

is the general movement and goal, but circumstances in the future will show what means should be used.

The fruit of this meeting of the Russo-Greek Church Committee was a report, and I had the honour of hearing it presented.

On the next day this report was presented with great ceremony by the Lower House to the Upper. A deputation of priests, consisting of the president and twelve other members, in many-coloured robes, and led by three administrators carrying silver maces, set out in an orderly procession through the courtyard of Westminster Abbey to the meeting of bishops. The archpriest Popoff and I followed after this procession, awaiting some decision, or at least some indication of the outcome. The event ended more modestly than anticipated: the president of the priests at the entrance of the Upper House, bent his step toward the primate chairman of the bishops (of whom there were ten) and in a low voice explained to him that he had brought the report on the matter of the desire for amalgamation of the Anglican Church with the Eastern Orthodox Church. The Archbishop of Canterbury took the paper with an affable smile and put it on the table. Meanwhile the Bishop of Oxford came over to me (I had met him a year ago in Brussels), also the Bishop of London, with whom I had conversed at some length in 1862 in our Paris church, also the Bishops of Edinburgh, Salisbury and Bristol, to whom I had been introduced in passing in Oxford; all of them shook my hand and spoke courteous salutations. The Archbishop of Canterbury beckoned for me to go up to him and he graciously spoke to me, pressing my hand in accordance with custom. On the matter of unity with the Orthodox Church not one of them said a single word. This meeting was confined only to various invitations handed out to me: dinner with the primate, three luncheons with the Bishop of Oxford, and an evening and dinner with the Bishop of London.

Father Wassilieff accepted several of these engagements in hopes that some of the bishops might be more open to frank discussion in an informal setting. However, the dinners and lunches proved to be little more than social occasions. At the Bishop of London's house he met William Gladstone, the future prime minister, who was an adherent of the Oxford Movement and expressed his approval of union with the Orthodox Church, although he felt that it was not proper for the government to take the initiative in church matters. An invitation to dinner with the Archbishop of Canterbury produced some interesting, if unanticipated, results:

> During the course of a splendid meal at the Archbishop of Canterbury's, at which there were fifteen personages around the table (mainly lay), there was no talk about the movement towards the union of the Churches. After dinner the honourable primate courteously showed me all the splendour of his palace (which had belonged to the royal family), and drew my attention to some valuable paintings which adorned the enormous walls of his halls. Then he inquired about various aspects of the Russian Church—the election and designation of bishops, as well as the judgement passed on guilty priests in the Church—rather knotty questions for the Anglican Church. Having satisfied the curiosity of His Grace, and having heard his approving opinion of our Church's methods of discipline, I brought the conversation around to the aspirations existing within the Anglican Church towards unity with the Orthodox Church. The archbishop answered that such thoughts do actually exist in significant sections of the Anglican Church, but that they have not yet been worked through and clarified. As far as he, the archbishop, is concerned, he has still to hold substantial discussions with his fellow bishops on this matter and has not attained for himself any sort of practical understanding about the means of achieving this desired goal. Then, having been listening to the sounds of the clavichord, the primate of England began to speak of his love of music and singing, and promised to entertain his guests by singing a romance. It seemed to me that I had not understood him; but I was quickly convinced that he was expressing himself correctly. Indeed the 65-year-old archbishop made his way to the clavichord and, together with his two daughters, sang in a quavering tenor an idyllic romance "about a prisoner and his trained bird." The guests were not surprised at the behaviour of their spiritual leader; probably this was an established English custom. Conversation about serious matters was not resumed, and at eleven o'clock in the evening I took my leave of the singing bishop, thanking him for his cordial hospitality.

The final section of his report provided a remarkably penetrating analysis of the Anglican strivings toward Orthodoxy. He summarized his findings as follows:

1. There does exist in quite a significant part of the Anglican Church a confused movement in the direction of the Orthodox Church.
2. Plans for union with the Orthodox Church are curiously conceived by those who promote this movement and they cannot be reconciled with Orthodox or any other theological approaches to their realization. Thus

the practical and mutual benefits of union are given preference over and against the necessity for a preliminary agreement in doctrine.

3. Only a few individuals recognize the necessity for unity of dogma and labour to reconcile the differences, but without decisive concessions on the part of the Anglican Church.
4. Thoughts of unity between the Anglican and Orthodox Churches seem to be entering a positive phase, judging by the fact that on the one hand the official Convocation of priests and bishops belonging to the Anglican Church have placed this subject within their sphere of activity, and on the other hand, the Eastern Church Association has been formed, with the elucidation of this longed-for concern as its aim.

Father Wassilieff was frustrated by the lack of any real desire to face the dogmatic issues and ascribed this, in part, to the fact that the Church of England had existed for centuries without any real unity of belief. Consequently, he assumed that union with the Orthodox could be achieved on the same basis. Part of the Anglican hierarchy would have liked to strengthen its position by being recognized by the Orthodox, but nothing could be done without the consent of Parliament and the laity, who would resist any change. "The past and its customs give support to any opposition," he wrote, "in England they are virtually idolised." Echoing the ideas of Khomiakov, he continued,

> One of the reasons for the Anglican's faithfulness to his tradition and establishment lies in an exaggerated sense of superiority before other people, and in personal and national pride. He also extends this feeling to his Church, which is a national creation and thus national property. It is extremely difficult for the Anglican to admit that his forefathers constructed the Anglican Church unsuccessfully, that this sphere of life is higher, truer and firmer in Russia and among other Eastern peoples, who in all other respects are less favoured than the English.

Another factor hindering unity, Wassilieff noted, was the Anglican Church's "enormous possessions and income."

> If only some of the Anglican bishops together with a number of priests and faithful would unite with the Orthodox Church in rejecting the 39 heretical Articles of the Anglican Church as ratified by Parliament, then the government might well consider this society a sect, and might deprive its pastors of their worldly benefits by which they profit in the Anglican

> Church and condemn them to a life which would be the more arduous since their present life is so full of abundance and luxury. For a bishop or a dean to renounce his salary, he would have to possess an immutable belief and an exceptional faith.

In conclusion, however, Father Wassilieff expressed hope for the future and gave his recommendations as to how to help the few individuals or small groups that might sincerely wish to be united to the Orthodox Church.

> It is impossible not to see that these impediments which I have indicated are extremely important for us, and that their conditional plans for uniting are not the direct route toward the realization of our aspirations. But is it therefore necessary to postpone on our part every hope and every care with regard to this important matter? We do not think so. All obstacles to unity lie in chance circumstances, whereas incentives toward unity come from vital needs. With time and patience the latter should triumph over the former. The confusion and lack of clarity of Anglican beliefs will clear up with study of the Orthodox faith; a foundation for this is being laid by the work of individual theologians and by the Eastern Church Association. Their custom of conservatism and slowness will also change with time and trouble. England moves slowly, but she does not stand still. National pride will not be undermined by Orthodoxy, for Orthodoxy does not seek external domination, but the resolution of human diversities. The accord of Parliament for Anglo-Orthodox moves towards unity might be gained by constant but gradual education. It might be hoped that the governing minds of England, looking at this matter with impartiality, might find it advantageous for their own nation while not at variance with advantages to our own fatherland. But if for some reason none of this takes place, the truth of Orthodoxy, thanks to effort, time, and above all the grace of God, might sway the hearts of some members and carry them forward toward unity with the Eastern Church. Even though they call this little flock of Christ a sect, it might be as a mustard seed cast on English soil.
>
> We can see good reason to hope for a positive outcome in the religious direction of the Anglicans if we consider the very similar movement in the American Episcopal Church. There the customs are less deep-rooted, there do not exist the obstacles of indissoluble links with the government and its maintenance of the clergy. Thus the Americans seem to proceed more decisively and the English, fearing their "childish rashness" (in the words of Mr. Williams), fear to be left behind.

For our part (I make so bold as to think) it would be both imprudent and sinful to remain indifferent observers of the conciliatory movement of the Anglican and American Churches toward the Orthodox Church. To help, to show our sympathy in this, to educate those searching for the light of truth—thus to level out the path approaching the Orthodox Church is an unavoidable part of our duty, and to neglect it might make dangerous enemies out of those who are at present holding out the hand of love and unity to us. Seeing the example of individual members of the Church who have unsuccessfully sought help and have thrown themselves blindfold into the depths of the Roman Church, we must beware of similar deviations by significant sections of the Anglican Church who move toward the Orthodox. In following the papists they would become our irreconcilable and uncompromising enemies. Such a hostile situation might be more disruptive in England than elsewhere, owing to the means at the disposal of the state.

What then can we do? We should enlighten those who wish it whenever circumstances and resources permit, testing them in love, indicating and easing their path towards increasing accord with us, veiling impatience and correcting in humility those plans and initiatives of theirs which seem inappropriate. To this end, apart from the activities of individuals, it would be useful to establish an unofficial society of several Orthodox priests, who would devote their energies to the study of the Anglican Church in all its aspects, the selection of Orthodox literature for translation and the writing of original works aimed at the reconciliation of Anglicans with the Orthodox.

God alone plants and nurtures vegetation. Whether it becomes productive in accordance with God's grace and wisdom, or remains unfruitful, we could comfort ourselves by saying, "We are unprofitable servants, we have done that which it was our duty to do."

These views echo those expressed by Metropolitan Philaret after his meeting with Palmer: "Hopefully the whole Anglican Church will reject its errors and be united with Orthodoxy; meanwhile we must do everything in our power to help small groups of individual converts without waiting for the conversion of the entire body of Anglicans."

In fact, by 1865, when this report was written, some of these ideas were not just mere conjecture. The Holy Synod of the Russian Church had already examined ways to nurture the seed of Orthodoxy in England, following the conversion in 1856 to the Orthodox faith of Stephen Hatherly, about whom more is written later in this chapter.

Meanwhile, in December 1865, Count Dimitri Tolstoy, the new procurator of the Holy Synod, wrote to Father Eugene Popoff saying he was consoled by the fact that "the idea of the union of the churches has not completely died out in England." He observed, however, "it can move forward only on condition that it is placed on the right path, and this path is the dogmatic one. Otherwise there will be no practical results." Metropolitan Philaret, concluding his remarks quoted at the beginning of this chapter, lamented that the Anglicans seem to be lost in a fog of Western ideas, often ascribing beliefs to the Greek Church that it does not really have. "From this it is evident, that they wish to draw people into union not through a precise interpretation of the Orthodox doctrine, but through an artificial and invented one. Is this the path to unity? Is this even the path to establishing mutual trust between two parties deliberating about unity?" By 1865 both the procurator and the metropolitan were beginning to doubt the fruitfulness of the Anglican-Orthodox contacts, which had appeared to offer so much promise when Palmer first visited Russia twenty-five years earlier. Thereafter, although subsequent developments in the Church of England seemed, from time to time, to indicate that some parts of it were moving toward Orthodoxy, for the most part, these contacts had lost their creative vigour and developed into outward civilities and barren theological discussion.

In 1867, two years after Father Wassilieff's visit to London and his report to the Holy Synod, Father Eugene received a series of questions from an unidentified Anglican layman. He felt them to be sufficiently important that he sent them to Count Dimitry Tolstoy, the procurator, to seek advice and obtain authoritative answers. The count, in turn, sent them to Metropolitan Philaret, who replied after some delay.

The questions concerned the willingness of the Russian Church to receive converts and to support a mission in England if sufficient numbers wished to become Orthodox. They also concerned the possibility of English converts using an order of service other than that of the Eastern Churches. The questions, in many ways, were quite confused and imprecise, and the metropolitan betrayed a note of exasperation in that an anonymous layman had posed the questions and yet he was expected to provide responses that could only be construed as official. He therefore provided his answers anonymously, as a guide for Father Eugene to use in providing his own replies. Although he referred, with meticulous politeness, to the "English Church" and was anxious not to cause offense to the "English hierarchy" and so on, it is interesting to note that he had not a moment's hesitation over the question of receiving converts and supporting a mission in England. His response to the questions on this theme could be summed up as, "Of course we would; why ever not?" The metropolitan devoted far more space to his response to the sixth question, in which the possibility is raised of retaining some Anglican rites and of omitting prayers to the saints. Although the other questions presuppose a willingness to embrace the fullness of Orthodoxy, if only the Russians would permit it, this question reveals an underlying confusion that, at the same time, he did not wish to relinquish Anglican beliefs completely. This is probably what the metropolitan found particularly exasperating. His response to this question included a moving and eloquent explanation of the Orthodox teaching on prayers to the saints. Here, characteristically of Philaret of Moscow, a spiritual fire shines through his external manner of extreme and almost legalistic formality.[10]

Stephen Hatherly and the Missionary Plans of Counts Alexander and Dimitry Tolstoy

As noted earlier, sowing and nurturing the seed of Orthodoxy in foreign lands was something very close to Count Alexander Petrovitch Tolstoy's heart. He was procurator of the Holy Synod from 1856 to 1862. A comparatively little-known figure of Russian Church history, Tolstoy was acutely aware of the uniqueness of Orthodoxy and he had an uncommon zeal for the conversion of non-Russians to the Orthodox faith. A decree from the Holy Synod, dated near the beginning of his tenure of office, attempted to simplify the process of receiving converts at churches outside Russia:

> Referring to cases where persons of heterodox confessions seek to be united to the Holy Orthodox Church. . . . The delays which can arise from the preliminary correspondence on this subject can cool the ardour of those seeking such union. . . . It was therefore resolved on 20 September 1858: Priests abroad may receive into communion with the Orthodox Catholic Church of the East all those seeking to be united to her from heterodox confessions on condition that the priests should observe articles 25 and 30 of the regulations (regarding instruction). They must use extreme care, particularly in those countries where renouncing the state religion is considered to be a crime, and they must carefully avoid creating the impression that they are thereby conducting general religious propaganda.

In fact, "general religious propaganda" was what the count would have wished possible. In his letters to Father Eugene Popoff, he discussed his hopes and plans at length and even encouraged the rector of the London church to work at building up a small group of English converts to Orthodoxy.[11] It seems that he was personally acquainted with Father Eugene. In one of his first letters after being appointed procurator he wrote, "Your most agreeable letter reminds me of the days we spent together visiting London and Oxford." In all probability the visit to England was in the summer of 1845, when an entry in the baptismal register records that Alexander Tolstoy, son of Peter, was the godfather at a baptism performed on June 30 of that year.

Together with other leading Russian churchmen, Tolstoy placed great hopes in William Palmer and was most disconcerted by the latter's conversion to Roman Catholicism in 1855. However, when news reached Russia of Stephen Hatherly's conversion in the following year, it appeared that all the hopes and enthusiasm that had previously focused on Palmer were then transferred to Hatherly. Count Tolstoy first learned of Hatherly's conversion to Orthodoxy in 1858 when Father Eugene Popoff sent him an article that Hatherly had written. In October 1858 he wrote to Popoff full of enthusiasm, asking what could be done to encourage and help Hatherly:

> My Dear Sir, Evgeny Ivanovich,
> Very shortly the Director of the Russian Shipping and Trade Company, Nikolai Alexandrovitch Novoselsky, will be departing for London, and he has kindly agreed to deliver this letter of mine to your Reverence. Accordingly I would humbly ask you to offer him your kind assistance where he needs it, as he is devoted to the Holy Church and is well known for the useful enterprises he has undertaken on behalf of the fatherland.
>
> I send you sincere thanks for Mr. Hatherly's article, not only on my own part, but also on behalf of all the members of the Holy Synod. Since your son[12] has assured us that the author is agreeable, this article will now be printed both in the periodical *Spiritual Talk* (*Dukhovnaya Beseda*) and as a separate booklet, and in this way the whole of Russia will come to know how we have received our firstborn from out of the Anglican Church. We will all rejoice the more in that this article will reveal to all his new brothers in the faith the fact that the dearest thing of all to his noble soul is Truth.
>
> Perhaps you would be so kind as to write and let me know whether something could not be sent to him with the blessing of the Synod, such as an icon of his patron saint, and one for his son as well, and what style of icon he would prefer (Greek or Italian), and what size; or perhaps something else? Another question: what further action could we take in England for the Orthodox Church to acquire further new members? At the end of his article Mr. Hatherly expresses certain desires and hopes in this regard.

We fully share all of these—how best to act? I shall wait impatiently to learn what you and he think about this.

I am enclosing a brochure entitled *The Reply Of An Orthodox Greek To The Jesuit Gagarin.* Here we value this little book very highly. If you place an equal value on it, it would be an excellent idea to publish it in English. I will refund the printing costs to your son or send the money on to you in some other way if you prefer.

From myself and from my wife I must convey our profound gratitude for the little task you performed on her behalf, as well as for your kindness towards us and for your prayers, in which I have great confidence and which I highly esteem.

I have the honour, Reverend Sir, to be your obedient servant, Count A. Tolstoy.

P.S. I am also sending you the Greek version of the reply to Gagarin; but I really must ask you to write and let Father Joseph know about this version; he is working in Paris on the publication of this most remarkable brochure in the French language.

7 October 1858, St. Petersburg.

Stephen Hatherly was born in Bristol in 1827 into a devout Anglican family. He had considerable musical talents, was an accomplished organist, and, in 1853, went to study music at New College, Oxford. By that time, at the age of 26, he was married and had a young son. At Oxford he came into contact with leaders of the Tractarian Movement, including Dr Pusey, who considered him a suitable candidate for the Anglican priesthood. On May 24, 1853, Pusey wrote to him:

> I see no reason why you should not follow your heart's wish and seek to be admitted to Holy Orders. You desire to help in the salvation of souls, and God, who has given you the desire will, I trust, help you. You will seek to win them by love and not to be stiff in carrying out theories, but try to adapt yourself to them, if, by God's grace you may win them. God bless you.

However, Hatherly did not take the path indicated by Dr Pusey. Over the next three years he became convinced that salvation was to be found, not in the Anglican Church, nor in the Church of Rome, but in Orthodoxy. He learned much about the Orthodox faith from John Mason Neale's writings; he later acknowledged the "variety and fullness" of the "laborious tomes of the late Dr. Neale." However, he had been influenced in his decision to embrace Orthodoxy by, among other things, his study of the Apocalypse and the Divine promises made in it to the churches of Smyrna and Philadelphia. Both churches were surviving as parts of the Orthodox Communion, while the Church of Rome was not mentioned at all. Some years later he wrote,

> I think I may say, without a moment's hesitation, that this wonderful fact, of the fulfillment of God's special promise to these Churches of Smyrna and Philadelphia, did more than any other single thing, at the time, more than twenty years ago, (when so many friends, staggered by the historical difficulties of Anglican Churchmanship, joined the Roman Communion,) to draw me into the Orthodox Church. I saw that Rome was not the only Church coming down unbroken from Apostolic times; nay, I saw more: I saw that Smyrna and Philadelphia had each its Angel or bishop in the first days of Christianity even as now, while Rome has no mention at all in the New Testament of its Angel or Bishop.

In focusing his attention on the ancient churches of the Apocalypse, Hatherly was following in the footsteps of William Palmer, who visited Philadelphia in Asia Minor in 1853. It was there that the local bishop told Palmer that he would have to be baptised if he was to be received into the Orthodox Church. Although this requirement by the Greek Church was a stumbling block to Palmer, such was not the case with Hatherly. In January 1856 he was baptised at the Greek Church in London.[13]

After his baptism, it appears that Hatherly turned to the Russian Church. Father Eugene Popoff's confession list for 1856 includes "the English citizen Stephen Hatherly, who was united to the Orthodox Church in January of this year." The following year the baptismal register includes an entry under August 15 that reads, "a son, Alexis, was born to Stephen Hatherly, who has joined the Orthodox Church." Then, in a letter written in 1858, Count Tolstoy expressed his condolences over the infant's early death.

On October 30, 1858, Tolstoy wrote again to Popoff, full of enthusiasm over Hatherly's conversion and asking how best to further the cause of Orthodoxy in England:

> How can we express our sympathy (*sochustvie*) to Hatherly and, most importantly, how can we make use of this beginning to the glory of God and his Holy Church? Many of Hatherly's fellow countrymen have shown (while he has shown more precisely and decisively than

> the others) how they are seeking the truth with a pure heart. It would be most propitious now to provide them with the means of recognizing the truth—that is to say, to publish books in which the truth would be revealed. Meanwhile, can we not begin translating the Church Service Books into English, starting with the Liturgy? In directing your attention to these questions, I would wish that they should occupy you completely. You would be rendering a great service to the Holy Church if beside you and with your participation there should appear in London even a small community of sons of the Orthodox Church. Mentally transporting myself to you in London, I cannot but feel how great was the loss of Palmer for the work which is occupying us. With complete respect and devotion, I have the honour to be, Reverend Sir, your obedient servant, Count A. Tolstoy.

Less than two weeks later, Tolstoy wrote again at length about Palmer, his regrets that Palmer failed to become Orthodox, and his hopes for Stephen Hatherly:

> I will try to track down the notes concerning Palmer's ideas which you sent me during the war, but I must nevertheless ask you to do all that you can to find them and send me a copy of them.
>
> I have never lost hope that Palmer will be united to the Orthodox Church. He sought it too zealously and too tirelessly for the Lord to refuse him His revelation and enlightenment, and leave him forever in that state of mental contradiction which his Orthodox friends observed with great sorrow (but not, I should add, without an admixture of triumphalism) in his confession written in Rome, which I am sure must be known to you. This hope of mine has been revived again at the present time as a consequence of Hatherly's conversion. I knew—and Palmer admitted it himself—that to become Orthodox in England would be rather frightening even if one was inclined in that direction by one's convictions, by virtue of the isolation which it implies. Such an unprecedented change in one's religion would entail the greatest social and moral hardship. I do not say that Hatherly's example will have abolished all these difficulties, but it must have great importance for Palmer; Hatherly's great effort of profound humility in the face of the Truth, and his bold confession of this truth before all those who have been hesitating and succumbing to temptation must have raised Palmer's spirits. If Palmer now converts to Orthodoxy (and may God grant us all to see this), what will await him in England will not be, as before, a

depressing and frightening loneliness, but a joyous and encouraging community of spirit with his great fellow countryman who has preceded him and, more than that, the calling of being an Apostle in his native land.

Please convey to Palmer, on behalf of his many true friends here—A. S. Khomiakov, T. G. Potemkina, A. N. Mouravieff and many other Orthodox, who know him either in person or by reputation, that we cannot accustom ourselves to the idea of permanent spiritual separation from him, and are continually praying to the Lord for the Divine enlightenment of his mind, "that, together with us, with one mouth and with one heart, he may glorify and exult the Most Honourable and Majestic name of the Father and the Son and the Holy Spirit." It is hard to imagine that such a precise understanding of the Orthodox Church and such a strong inclination towards it, as this noble zealot of the truth once expressed, was revealed in vain by God's Providence without a purpose. And surely a difference in one point of doctrine—a difference not yet overcome only due to difficulties in communication—cannot really be a sufficient reason to put an end to this most extraordinary purpose, and to make such exalted strivings stumble? May it not be! The time will come when, taught by God, our friend will acquire the truth and with it the quiet peace of soul and mind in the calm haven of the Catholic ["Conciliar"] and Apostolic Church, which has faithfully preserved truth and peace. O Lord, it is fitting that Thou shouldest give this unto him, for "he loveth our nation."

I have read Hatherly's note to the members of the Holy Synod, and they have come to the conclusion, which I share completely, that what is needed for the success of Orthodoxy in England is not so much establishing Orthodox churches in the coastal towns he has indicated, or in other towns for that matter, with services being held in them in Greek and Slavonic. What is needed most of all is to organize somewhere—first of all, of course, in London—Orthodox Divine Worship in the English language, and to translate into English those spiritual books from which English people could become acquainted with the very essence of our Church and, consequently, come to understand their own errors. From your letter it is evident that the Orthodox Liturgy, the Paschal Canon, the Catechism, and certain other things have already been translated. This is very valuable, because in England, of course, we can also expect to have some success among the simple people, who would be impressed by the visual impact of the church services. On the other hand, those who investigate the faith from a scholarly point of view, can be brought to salutary conclusions through studying the proofs of history in the light of true dogma.

The best thing, to start with, would be if Hatherly agreed to accept the priesthood; judging from your letters, he had been inclined towards holy orders, but was held back by his doubts about the truth of his former religion. Now that he is standing in the truth, will he wish to accept priestly orders? If he is not averse to this idea, then perhaps you will agree that it would be appropriate for him to come and see us in Petersburg to receive ordination and the sacred blessing of the hierarchs standing at the head of the Russian Church, and at the same time this would let us, his new brothers in Christ, see him face to face, and be mutually comforted in our common faith which is both his and ours. On this journey he could visit Moscow and make the acquaintance of the Metropolitan of Moscow. I earnestly hope that he would be pleased with how he was received, both here and in Moscow.

However, all this is just conjecture, and you are the only person who can judge how possible it is, as you know Mr. Hatherly personally. Then it would be possible to establish an Orthodox Church in London, where the services would be held in the English language. If all this should be possible, it will be essential to resolve the question of money—the costs of the journey, of setting up the church, and so on. I shall expect information from you about all this in due course; for the present, please let me know whether Mr. Hatherly is short of money or not, and whether it would be a good idea to send him some sort of financial assistance through you.

Be so kind as to convey to him my feeling of profound grief for his loss, which is our loss also. I will enter the name of his deceased infant Alexis for commemoration. The icons for him have been ordered from Poshekhonoff and, as soon as they are ready, they will immediately be sent on.

Is the translation into English of *Thoughts of an Orthodox Greek* going well? I humbly request you not to put this off, as I expect that this little book will create a strong impression. Father Joseph is working in Paris on translating it into French. By the way, please ensure that Palmer, on arriving in Paris, should come into contact with Father Joseph. To this end, be so good as to give Palmer something to take to him, and then write to Father Joseph asking him to pay particular attention to his dealings with Palmer. I will write to him as well.

My sincere thanks for the latest books you have sent me: *Information About Religious Sects In England* and *Household Economy* by M. M. Brewster; they are most interesting. Her Majesty the Empress is really taking a very close interest in girls' education—for those of both clerical and secular backgrounds.

With deepest respect and devotion, I remain your Reverence's most humble servant, Count A. Tolstoy.

11 November 1858, St. Petersburg.

It appears from this letter that Hatherly had written to the Holy Synod with plans to make the existing Orthodox churches in England (and possibly some new ones) into missionary centers. Tolstoy's preference was to ordain Hatherly and start a missionary church using the English language; nevertheless, he was keen to have Father Eugene's opinion because he knew both Hatherly and English conditions. Evidently Father Eugene's recommendations were not in favour of ordination. In June of 1859 the Holy Synod passed the following resolution:

> 17 June 1859. Ukaz 1315.
> The former Anglican protestant, now an Orthodox Christian, Stephen Hatherly, set out his thoughts about the means for spreading the truth of the Holy Orthodox Church in England, for which he suggested appointing missionaries in Cardiff and Hull as well as London, Manchester and Liverpool. But the rector of our church in London, Archpriest Eugene Popoff, informs us that he finds the means proposed by Hatherly for spreading the Orthodox faith in England to be impractical and unrealizable at the present time, because we cannot find a person suitable for the English character. One would first have to take a graduate of a theological academy and then train him at a church outside Russia for at least five years.
>
> Resolved: The Holy Synod, mindful of the need to train missionaries who could profitably carry out such service, orders that at our Orthodox Churches abroad, in accordance with the opinion of the member of the Holy Synod, the Most Reverend Metropolitan of St. Petersburg: clergy should be prepared for missionary service by way of additional education, and to this end graduates of the Theological Academies should be appointed to the minor clerical positions (*prichetnicheskiya mesta*) at our churches abroad, and should there continue their studies under the supervision of the local priest.

The London archives include a list of twenty-three Russian churches in foreign countries. In addition to major European cities, there were churches in Jerusalem and Japan. The priest shown as being in charge of the Japanese mission was Priest-monk Nicholas Kasatkin, chaplain to the Russian consulate in Hakodate, who later became the first bishop of the Japanese Orthodox

Church. This was the only Embassy church to become a missionary centre in the way that Count Tolstoy had hoped.

The text of the resolution itself was brief and did not give a clear indication of Father Eugene's thoughts on the matter. It is tempting to see it as an example of the classic bureaucratic tactic of vetoing a proposition by approving it in a modified form. It would be years before the students to be attached to the foreign missions gained sufficient experience and maturity to become missionary priests. Meanwhile, it is possible that Father Eugene judged Hatherly, at that stage in his life, was in need of more understanding and experience before being ready to take on such a service.

There is little information about Hatherly for the next ten years. He remained in contact with Count Alexander Tolstoy. In 1861 he sent him a copy of a work titled *Baptism, an oratoriette*, which was his thesis for the Oxford degree of doctor of music and had, in its day, earned the praise of the examining professor. On June 31 of that year, Count Tolstoy wrote to Popoff,

> When you see Mr. Hatherly, please give him my thanks for the copies he sent of his musical composition called *Baptism*. Some people are sorry about the difficult position he finds himself in as a result of the closing of the Greek church in Liverpool, and are prepared to look for some means to offer him assistance. These means, of course, cannot be very great, and it would be more appropriate, I think, to give them to Mr. Hatherly in his own country rather than in ours, where it would be difficult to find an occupation appropriate for his erudition which could be of use to the Orthodox Church. However, I would like to hear your opinion about this matter, and at the same time to receive some information as to the reasons why the Greek church in Liverpool was closed; it existed until very recently and of course it is needed there for the Greek merchants who, as is well known, live there in large numbers.

There is no indication of the activities that Hatherly engaged in or how he supported himself and his family during this period. It is known that he attended the church on Welbeck Street. Hatherly later wrote of how attached he was to the old chapel, and his name is included in the list of donors who contributed to the rebuilding of the church in 1865; he donated £5. At some point Hatherly worked as a tutor aboard the Russian frigate *Oslavya*. Apparently he traveled in Russia and, by the end of the decade, had acquired some knowledge of the Russian language. By that time he was calling himself Stephen Georgeson Hatherly, having adopted the additional forename in imitation of the Greek and Russian patronymic.

Independent of Stephen Hatherly, in 1861 a former Anglican clergyman, Athanasius Richardson, was received into the Orthodox Church in Nice by Father Joseph Wassilieff, the priest of the Embassy church in Paris. He had been staying in the south of France for his health, but after his reception into the Orthodox Church, was called upon to return to England as a missionary. From Cannes, Richardson wrote to Metropolitan Philaret of Moscow, seeking ordination. "It is already a month since I was united to the Holy Orthodox Church by the respected Father Wassilieff in Nice," he wrote, and continued, saying that God had guided him to the true Church so that his fellow countrymen could know of the true Orthodox teaching and accept him as their spiritual guide. He said he was ill with rheumatism but getting better. He asked the metropolitan to forgive his boldness in writing so directly. The letter had been sent to Father Eugene to translate. Evidently Richardson was not considered suitable for ordination at the time. Two years later he was still a layman when he presented the Empress Maria Alexandrovna with a copy of his translation into English of the Divine Liturgy of St John Chrysostom. The empress's secretary wrote to Father Eugene on February 17, 1867, about this gift from "Athanase Richardson," which included the following instructions: "If he is known to you, and if the information gathered about him shows that he is a respectable person, then thank him on behalf of her Imperial Highness for his presentation and good wishes."

The year 1868 was marked by a significant event in the history of Orthodoxy in England. For what was probably the first time since the schism of 1054, the Orthodox Divine Liturgy was celebrated in the English language. The request for this came from the Eastern Church Association, of which Father Eugene was a member. Writing to St Petersburg to seek permission, he recommended Hatherly's translation as the best of those that had been made to date. Father Eugene's son, Basil, returned to England from Russia and was ordained to the diaconate. Having been brought up in England since the age of 3, he spoke English like a native, and his father was keen to have him serve at this English liturgy as deacon. On August 24, 1868, Count Dimitry Tolstoy, who had been appointed procurator of the Holy Synod in 1865, wrote to Father Eugene to convey the Synod's formal approval:

> My Dear Sir, Evgeny Ivanovich,
> Your petition seeking permission to celebrate the Orthodox Divine Liturgy in the English language, in the church of which you are rector, at the request of the members of the Eastern Church Association, and as set out

in Your Reverence's letter of 12 August of this year, has been presented to the Holy Synod.

Seeing in this desire on the part of the members of the Association a new step in the direction of the Anglican church becoming more closely acquainted with the Church of Russia, which has faithfully preserved the dogmas of Orthodoxy, and bearing in mind that the truths, living and actively fulfilled, which are set forth in so important a service as our Divine Liturgy, cannot be without fruit for those who hear these truths in their own native tongue, the Holy Synod has permitted Your Reverence to celebrate the Divine Liturgy from time to time in the English language, selecting the most suitable translation of the Liturgy for this purpose.

I consider it my duty to inform Your Reverence of this decision of the Holy Synod, announced by the Most Reverend Metropolitan of St. Petersburg, in order that appropriate action may be taken.

Please rest assured of my deepest respect and devotion, Count Dimitry Tolstoy.

The Synod's approval was conveyed not only through this letter from the procurator but also by a decree issued in the name of the emperor. The text of this decree is as follows:

Decree of HIS IMPERIAL HIGHNESS, AUTOCRAT OF ALL RUSSIA, delivered from the first Section of the St. Petersburg Spiritual Consistory to the Rector of our Embassy Church in London, Archpriest Eugene Popoff.

By decree of His Imperial Highness, the St. Petersburg Spiritual Consistory heard the resolution of the Holy Governing Synod, dated the 23rd day of August last, No. 2598, as follows: The Holy Synod has heard the petition of the Rector of our Embassy Church in London, Archpriest Eugene Popoff, which was presented by the Procurator on 15th August of this year, and read as follows: "The members of the Eastern Church Association are constantly and insistently expressing their desire to be able at some time to hear the Divine Liturgy in their own native English language. With the appointment to our church of the Deacon Basil Popoff, who has a perfect command of spoken English, it has become very much easier to put this into practice. As for the translation of the Liturgy into English, of the many such translations which exist, the best one (in the opinion of Father Archpriest Popoff) is the translation made by the Bachelor of Music, Stephen Hatherly, who has long and constantly remained faithful to holy Orthodoxy." Resolved: Seeing in this desire on the part of the members of the Easter Church Association, that the Divine Liturgy of our Orthodox Church should be celebrated in London in English, a new step in the direction of the Anglican church becoming more closely acquainted with the Church of Russia, which has faithfully preserved the dogmas of Orthodoxy, and bearing in mind that the truths, living and actively fulfilled, which are set forth in so important a service as our Divine Liturgy, cannot be without fruit for those who hear these truths in their own native tongue, the Holy Synod has resolved: 1. To permit the Rector of our Embassy Church in London to celebrate the Divine Liturgy from time to time in the English language, selecting the most suitable translation of the Liturgy for this purpose; 2. To inform the Most Reverend Metropolitan of this decision so that appropriate instructions can be given; and 3. To request the Procurator of the Synod to bring all of the foregoing to the attention of His Highness the Sovereign Emperor and to inform the Ministry of Foreign Affairs, and also to inform Father Archpriest Popoff. The resolution of The Most Reverend Metropolitan in respect of this decree is as follows: That it should be sent to Archpriest Popoff to be carried out.

Resolved: From the three points in this decree of the Holy Synod it is clear that the task of informing the Archpriest of the London Church, Father Eugene Popoff, about the Holy Synod's decisions was entrusted to the Procurator of the Synod; therefore the Father Archpriest should be asked to report whether he has received this information, and what action has been taken in response to it. Appropriate instructions are to be sent to the Archpriest. 20th day of September, 1868.

So it was by imperial decree that the first English Liturgy was celebrated, and it was Hatherly's translation that was used. It is not known whether Hatherly approved of his text being used at the request of the Eastern Church Association, rather than for more direct missionary aims. At the time, the association was still seen by the Orthodox as a means of witnessing the truth of Orthodoxy without the compromises entailed by present-day ecumenism. By 1868, however, Hatherly had developed some more concrete plans, that is, to start an English Orthodox mission in his hometown of Wolverhampton. He and a small group of Orthodox, including the Greek vice-consul in Birmingham, had plans to purchase a disused Methodist chapel in Waterloo Road North, Wolverhampton, and convert it into an Orthodox church. The next year Hatherly set off for Russia armed with the following petition, addressed to the Holy Synod:

> To the Most Holy Governing Synod of All Russia.
> We, the undersigned, His Hellenic Majesty's vice-consul in Birmingham and other residents of Wolverhampton who are members and friends of the Orthodox Catholic Church (usually called the Greek Church), in connection with the plan to establish an Orthodox Church in Waterloo Road, Wolverhampton, for which cause Mr. Hatherly senior is departing for Russia, most humbly request the Most Holy Governing Synod of All Russia to extend its blessing, sanctification and support to this pious undertaking. On their part the undersigned promise to do everything in their power to support the work of the aforementioned Orthodox church when it is established.
> Signed: Anthony Klados, Greek Vice-consul in Birmingham, Stephen Hatherly, Bachelor of Music, George Shann, Thomas Hatherly, Anna Hatherly, Eugene Hatherly, Olga Hatherly, Frank Shann, Roland Rogers, Charles Ford, Samuel Ford, Alfred Webb, Isaac Woness, B. Woness, John Seccombe, Doctor of Medicine, Frederick Hall, George Frederick S. Hatherly.

All gave their address as Wolverhampton, except for the Greek vice-consul, who lived in Birmingham, and Dr Seccombe, who lived at King's Lynn. The vice-consul certified the authenticity of the signatures. A note in the margin read, "There are two Orthodox Christians who are unable to write: Catherine S. Hatherly and Minadora S. Hatherly." Of these twenty-one names, approximately half were members of Hatherly's family. Attached to the petition was a written offer from the trustees of the Methodist chapel to sell it for £700, subject to completion within six months. The offer was dated May 10, 1869. Details of the property were attached and indicated that it was freehold and included a house and a chapel, and that the chapel had been built in 1866.

After hearing this petition, the Synod decided, as it had done eleven years previously, to refer the matter to Father Eugene Popoff. By that time, the procurator was Count Dimitry Tolstoy and his assistant (*Tovarishch Ober-Prokurora*) was Count Yuri Tolstoy. The assistant procurator wrote to Father Eugene in a most urgent tone:

Confidential.
20 June 1869.
Dear Sir, Evgeny Ivanovich,
Mr. S. G. Hatherly, an Oxford Bachelor of Music who is known to your Reverence, has presented to the Holy Synod a translation of a petition signed by the Greek Vice Consul in Birmingham which asks for the Synod's blessing and assistance in obtaining a building, in which it is proposed to establish an Orthodox church. Together with this Mr. Hatherly has presented us with a letter and a note, accompanied by translations. Finally, in a conversation with me he told me that, if the Holy Synod should look favourably on this request, and if money can be obtained to acquire the Methodist chapel for which they are negotiating, it would be most desirable if you could be permitted to donate to them the former iconostasis of the London Embassy Church, which is in your charge. He also reports that you and the rectors of the three Greek churches in London, Liverpool (if I am not mistaken) and Bristol have agreed to visit from time to time to conduct services in Wolverhampton. Further, for the purpose of holding public worship at other times, he requests that he, Hatherly, should be ordained to the stikharion,[14] so that he could offer these prayers not as a layman, but as a cleric.

In all these requests the members of the Holy Synod saw only the confirmation of what they had already heard from you as to Mr. Hatherly's sincere zeal for our Holy Orthodox Church. They greeted this request to erect an Orthodox altar in the heart of Protestant England with rejoicing in Christ, but as wise sowers of the seed, they are concerned that the seed of Orthodoxy should not fall on stony ground, nor by the wayside, lest it should wither up or be choked by thorns. And so, before coming to any conclusive decision, the Holy Synod has entrusted me with the task of finding out from your Reverence: Is Mr. Hatherly's desire feasible? Can an Orthodox church, established in the place he proposes, anticipate success, given the conditions of English life and legislation? Will our contributing a sum of money for obtaining this property be sufficient to prevent it remaining in heterodox hands? What is the extent of the assistance expected from the Holy Synod of All Russia in this matter; to what extent will it be permitted by the local laws and, in general, what is the best method for bringing this undertaking to the desired conclusion? Concerning Hatherly himself: Is he suited for a clerical office—for being ordained to the stikharion? How much does he really know and how firm is he in Orthodox dogma? On the other hand, will this office, which is the lowest order of the clergy, be appropriate to his degree of knowledge and to his zeal for raising the banner of Orthodoxy in these parts which have departed so far from Orthodoxy?

Such are the questions, Most Reverend and much respected Father, the resolution of which the Holy Synod is entrusting to your wisdom and discretion, enlightened as you are by your experience of life, your zeal for our Holy Church and in addition by your loving, truly Christian study of the people, albeit of another faith, amongst whom you have been carrying on your sacred ministry for so many years.

I consider it superfluous to ask you to reply with haste; I am sure that you will not delay, knowing that on your reply will depend the decision of the Most Holy Synod of All Russia as well as its most respectful report to our Sovereign Emperor, to whose most August attention I shall have the honour of bringing the matters hereinbefore set forth, after his return from Moscow.

I have the honour to remain, reverend father, your most obedient servant,

Yuri Tolstoy.

Father Eugene noted at the top of this letter, "Received on 28th June and replied the same day." It is likely that his reply was generally favourable because the Holy Synod seems to have approved, in principle, the plan for the Wolverhampton mission. Two months later, Hatherly wrote to Father Eugene from Moscow indicating that he had received most of the sum needed for the new church from a private donor:

Moscow. August 19/31 1869.
My dearest Friend,
I am happy to inform you that I have met one friend whom you know very well (Mr. A. M. Polejaieff) who is wishing to make himself responsible for the first cost of our new church, and he intends that you should be his medium in transacting the business. Of course Mr. Polejaieff does not hinder others from doing what they please in the way of furnishing, decorating or maintaining the building, but the first thing is to get the building itself. You will feel as thankful at this as I feel, and thank God with me and for me.

I heard from my wife on Sunday evening. She was glad to hear from you, but she said nothing about Anna. Did you forget to tell her?

This evening I go down to Solunshkovo, for I feel a little poorly, and the ladies think I shall be better with them than staying alone in town.

I find that the *Pall Mall Gazette* copied my letter from *Moskovskiya Vedomosti* and that it was then re-copied into the *Birmingham Daily Post*, with a leading article headed "Twenty one new schismatics." Of course, everybody is now teasing my poor wife about it, so I want to get home and put her right with everybody. Please write her a line again. I did so on Sunday, but she will be comforted to hear also from you.

With best love to all, believe me, your most truly,
S. G. Hatherly.

P.S. Mr. Bisoffeky who is writing to you has kindly offered to enclose this in his letter. I find he is a very old acquaintance, and as you know is connected with *Moskovskiya Eparkhialniya Vedomosti*.

This letter touchingly gave the impression of Father Eugene as a close family friend who fully shared Hatherly's aspirations and, at the same time, provided a glimpse of a family united by a common cause. From later correspondence it is clear that Father Eugene did travel to St Petersburg to act as intermediary in these transactions. The fact that Polejaieff and other donors gave to Father Eugene but not directly to Hatherly is testament to the esteem in which the rector of the London church was held.

Hatherly made the acquaintance of Metropolitan Innocent (Veniaminoff) of Moscow,[15] who succeeded Metropolitan Philaret on the latter's death in 1867. The new metropolitan had served as a missionary priest in Siberia and was later consecrated as bishop of Alaska and the Aleutian Islands. (William Palmer was present at his consecration in 1840.) He was favourably impressed by Hatherly and publicly recommended his work to the sympathy and support of the Russians.

Despite his wish to return to England to support his wife, Hatherly remained in St Petersburg in October. The Synod had doubts as to whether Wolverhampton was the most suitable place for an Orthodox mission in England. Meanwhile Hatherly was becoming more insistent in his request for official status and possibly ordination to the priesthood. In a short, anxiously worded note to Father Eugene, Assistant Procurator Count Yuri Tolstoy wrote:

St. Petersburg. 10/22 October 1869.
Dear Sir, Evgeny Ivanovich,
On the instructions of Count D. A. Tolstoy I have the honour to ask your Reverence to be so good as to inform his Excellency in the most speedy

manner as to whether Wolverhampton, the place chosen by Mr. Hatherly, has any advantages as a place for establishing an Orthodox church other than the fact that it is near to the place of residence of Mr. Hatherly and his family. I ask your holy prayers and blessing, and with sincere respect and devotion I have the honour to remain, Reverend Sir, your most obedient servant, Yuri Tolstoy.

P.S. I will write soon in more detail about Mr. Hatherly; so as not to miss the post I will limit myself for the present to a few words. His requirements began at 700 pounds sterling and ordination to the stikharion; at the present time, besides this, he is in need of £200 for remodeling the church and the house, as a residence for himself and his family; he would like ordination to the priesthood; he says he has the right to receive an annual salary, and insists that he should be sent back to England in the name of the Holy Synod!

Despite these misgivings, the Synod eventually approved his basic plan of establishing an Orthodox church in Wolverhampton, although he was not, at that time, ordained to the priesthood. Perhaps Father Eugene had indicated that he did not think Hatherly was ready for the priesthood, or perhaps the Synod hesitated before something that could only have difficult political repercussions; again, perhaps Hatherly's insistent manner had not commended itself well to the Russians.

In England, the purchase of the chapel was consummated and work began on the conversion for Orthodox use. In two letters written in May 1870, Hatherly reported on the progress to Father Popoff.

Chapel Ash, Wolverhampton. May 1/13 1870.
Reverend and Dear Sir,
I am happy to inform you that since my return from Russia I have been enabled, through the means placed at my disposal by the liberality of Mr. Polejaieff and other friends, which I received from you in St. Petersburg, to secure the freehold of the Methodist chapel, house and land, in behalf of which I pleaded while in Russia. The cost of the property was £700, and the legal expenses amounted in addition to £12.15.10, as you have witnessed yourself by reference to the original documents. I have also, as you have testified, sedulously laboured to put the property in a state of thorough repair and have progressed considerably in giving the chapel an Orthodox character by, among other things:

1. Adding two crosses to the gables of the building, one of which is the Russian traditional eight armed cross, with crescent and stay chains;
2. Walling up the eastern doors, and making a new door in the south-west corner of the building;
3. Opening up by means of an arch the former eastern porch, and thereby forming a proper place for the iconostas and the altar;
4. Raising the floor for, and properly enclosing a soleas etc., with all of which, as before hinted, you have kindly expressed to me your satisfaction.

I am sure you will feel great pleasure in informing our warm hearted friends of the good results which have already followed from their liberality. Believe me to remain, yours very obediently, S. G. Hatherly.

P.S.

1. When you write to Moscow will you please give my most humble reverence and affectionate regard to our dear good Vladyka the Metropolitan Innocent.
2. It may be of interest to know that Mr. Polejaieff's donation of R 5,000 furnished me after discount, stamps etc. (at the bank in Wolverhampton) £589.16.1½.

This was accompanied by the following letter of the same date:

Chapel Ash, Wolverhampton. May 1/13 1870.
Reverend and Dear Sir,
The Most Holy Synod of the Russias having, as you are aware, given its blessing for the establishment of an Orthodox Temple in this town, and Christ-loving brethren in Russia having furnished the means for the acquirement of the necessary freehold property, and furthermore, the Most pious and Most gracious Lady Her Majesty the Empress of All the Russias having condescended through your instrumentality to assist materially in the same; I venture on all these grounds to solicit your influence with the proper authorities for obtaining for this new Orthodox Temple the grant and donation of the Iconostas previously in use at the Embassy Church in London, which, now that the Church in London is re-constructed, is superseded by the new and better adapted Iconostas, and which, as I happen to know, is still in your custody, though without any apparent use. I may venture to add, that having had the consolation of worshipping before

the old Iconostas during many years, my affection for it is naturally great and, moreover, it has the good fortune to suit most admirably the style and architecture of the new church building in Wolverhampton.

I beg to remain most truly yours, S. G. Hatherly.

These letters hint that Father Eugene was aware of some of the points mentioned in them. This knowledge and the fact that the letter about the iconostasis was written separately seem to indicate that they were written at Father Eugene's request to be included as part of his reports to Russia on the mission's progress. It is interesting to note Hatherly's creative approach to the building's floor plan. The first letter indicated that it was turned around completely, so as to have the altar at the east end, according to Orthodox tradition, even though this is where the entrance had been. It is not known whether the old iconostasis from London was ever placed into the opening thus formed. If Father Eugene endorsed the idea of it being donated to Wolverhampton (and it seems likely that he would have), in all probability the Synod would have agreed. However, events soon underwent a change of course that would certainly have called this into question.

In September 1870 Stephen Hatherly left for Russia again. By the end of 1871 he had been ordained to the priesthood, but his ordination took place, not in Russia, but in the Patriarchal Cathedral in Constantinople. It is not clear what brought about this change of allegiance. In a report written many years after Hatherly's death, Father Eugene Smirnoff, rector of the Embassy church from 1877 to 1922, indicated that Hatherly's second visit to Russia had not been properly authorized and so led to unpleasantness, after which he "turned to the Greek Church." Of course, because Father Smirnoff had no personal knowledge of this, his report may not have been completely accurate. It is known that Hatherly had raised the question of the priesthood in 1869 and the reaction in St Petersburg was immediately favourable.

In fact, Hatherly made two visits to Constantinople in 1871. The Anglican hierarchy took the prospect of his ordination as a serious threat and protested so vigorously to the patriarch that Hatherly returned from his first visit without being ordained. The bishops of Winchester, Ely and Carlisle, approached the patriarch directly. Hatherly wrote later:

In addition, Bishop Jackson, of London, addressed to the Turkish Ambassador a most vigorous Note, in which "difficult complications" and "serious consequences" were predicted, if every possible step was not taken to prevent my ordination in the Greek Church. Ali Pasha, the then Grand

Vizier, did not, however, share the Bishop's fears, and took no steps in the matter.[16] Bishop Wilberforce, of Winchester, fancying that his and his colleagues' labours, with the Rev. W. Denton's telegrams to the Serbian Agent at Constantinople, being certain of success, must as certainly have succeeded, wrote to the All-Holy Œcumenical Patriarch, thanking His Holiness for refusing to ordain me, and "thus preventing schism."

Nevertheless, notwithstanding the protests of the Anglican hierarchy, Hatherly was ordained to the priesthood on his second visit to Constantinople that year, on Sunday, October 8, 1871. From Constantinople he wrote a letter that was published in the *Wolverhampton Chronicle* some ten days later:

The Greek Church
Sir,
As Pastor of the Greek Church in our town of Wolverhampton, I would like to inform you that I was ordained Priest here on Sunday last, by order of His Holiness Anthimus the Sixth, Œcumenical Patriarch.

You will, I hope, pardon this mention of a comparatively private matter, in consideration of the great attention which *The Guardian* newspaper invited to it some months ago, when I first visited Constantinople for ordination. The libel trial which followed at Stafford Assizes,[17] also, in a sense, made the question public property, and pleads my apology.

A propos of *The Guardian* and its libel, may I be permitted to remark in extenuation of the Bagnalls and the Dentons, of whom I would wish to say all that is personally respectful, notwithstanding their conduct towards me, that, were our Greek Church as well assured of their churchmanship and of the validity of Protestant ordinations as they (the High Church party) are of ours, we should not have been treated to that lusty and malevolent hue and cry of "Schism" for which their organ had to pay so dearly.
I remain, Sir, very truly,

S. G. Hatherly
Constantinople, October 10 1871.

Attacks in the press, mostly ill informed as well as ill intentioned, continued, despite the verdict of the Stafford Assizes in *The Guardian* libel case mentioned here. *The Church Times*, for example, wrote of "little schisms . . . fostered by Russia for the means of political intrigue." The Eastern Church Association was outraged by Stephen Hatherly's ordination, and this compelled Father Eugene Popoff to resign from the committee. In its annual report for 1871, it reported to the members, "it is unnecessary for your Committee to state that they did everything in their power to prevent what appeared to them to give a blow to their hope of friendly relations between the Eastern and English Churches."

While these storms raged in the outside world, Father Stephen Hatherly was at last able to build up his small community of English-speaking Orthodox. These included the "twenty-one new schismatics" who signed the petition to the Russian Synod in 1869 and some others. Of the original twenty-one, the most active were Theodore Frank Shann (1850–1917) and his brother, George Vincent Shann, who published a number of liturgical translations. Dr John Thomas Seccombe, also a signatory, was Norfolk magistrate and physician and a man of some learning. Later converts included Sir Edmund and Lady Katherine Lechmere of Severn End, Worcester. The *Church Times* attacked Sir Edmund in 1877 for having "seceded to the Greek Church." Another convert was James N. W. B. Robertson, who also made some liturgical translations. The Marquis of Bute was also friendly with Hatherly and seriously considered becoming Orthodox but eventually converted to Roman Catholicism.

In the spring of 1873, a Wolverhampton solicitor handed a letter to Father Stephen. He was shocked to find that it was from Dorotheos Evelpides, the *protosynkellos* (chief secretary) to the Patriarch of Constantinople, and stated that he was "invited and ecclesiastically enjoined" to adopt the patriarch's ruling that "he should not conceive in his mind the notion of proselytizing . . . even one member of the Anglican Church, which has moreover given of late many proofs of fraternal sympathy towards our Orthodox Church." The influence of Anglican intrigues was obvious. The Eastern Church Association triumphantly published both the original Greek text and the English translation and congratulated itself on having achieved good results from the advice it had offered to the patriarch. Hatherly said he was "hopeless of unraveling the intrigue" and lamented that the letter had "scandalized the Orthodox, disquieted converts, enchanted Protestants and pleased Romanists." In short, after less than two years, the work of the new mission had been halted by patriarchal decree.

Although he had waited so long and worked so hard to achieve his goal of starting an English-language parish, Father Stephen appeared to have accepted this directive and devoted himself thereafter to pastoral work among the Greek community. Late the following year, the Wolverhampton church was let to Wesleyans, and the small group of converts carried on as best they could without a priest. Much is unclear in all of this. When Hatherly wrote to the *Wolverhampton Chronicle* that he was "pastor of the Greek Church in our town of Wolverhampton," was he using the word "Greek" as a synonym for "Orthodox," which was a fairly common usage at the time? Or had he been ordained to act as a pastor for Greeks in the neighborhood? Had the patriarch ever really wanted to support English-language missionary work? In moving away from Wolverhampton, had Hatherly acted on his own initiative or had his ecclesiastical superiors assigned him to other work? What is remarkable is that, despite everything, Father Stephen persevered in the Orthodox priesthood and in obedience to his Church authorities.

In October 1874 Hatherly delivered a lecture in the Greek Syllogos in Manchester, which was subsequently published and is his only surviving written work, representing a kind of *apologia* or explanation of his most deeply held beliefs. It is remarkable for its tone of faith and confidence, despite the trials he endured. He spoke of the troubles of the preceding seventeen months and of the attention that his High Church opponents had "directed to the Work of God, in which I had been permitted to engage in this my native England." He went on to say that, instead of being put down, "I still . . . stand erect before you, and glory in nothing more than that, in spite of all the opposition which the wealth and influence of the Protestant Episcopate could bring to bear, even upon the Turkish Government itself, to prevent my ordination, I am an Orthodox Priest, and a Greek Priest in particular." He said that the theme of his talk would be "Ancient and modern traces of God's Providential Hand in the History of the Orthodox Church." He emphasized the Greek (or "Hellenistic") nature of Orthodoxy and that the command to "go and baptize all nations" was originally given in Greek, quoting this text from St Mathews' Gospel in Greek to reinforce his point. It is not clear whether he actually adopted such a Graecophile viewpoint or whether he was simply trying to speak in language that his Greek (and undoubtedly chauvinistic) audience would find sympathetic. He also quoted contemporary Russian ecclesiastical writers, such as Mouravieff and Kireeff, and spoke of the ancient churches mentioned in the Apocalypse and of the importance of the Orthodox Church in contemporary Russian and Greek history. He said:

> Yes, it was in truth the same Church which has given me my priesthood that has preserved your national existence to this day. My obligation to it is immensely great, but your obligation to it is still greater. Had there been no Greek Church, there would be now no Greek nation. Let us then prove our gratitude by a greater and greater love to this Divine Institution to

> which we owe so much, by a more jealous guardianship of her Holy doctrine and discipline, and by our increasing zeal in all good works which she commends to our observance. . . . That truth which God first gave to our Greek Church we must hand down unimpaired, that all future generations may enjoy the privileges we enjoy, and may, in the Last Day, rise up and call us Blessed.

One has the impression that Hatherly used his audience's nationalistic fervor as a basis for encouraging greater piety and devotion to Orthodoxy, rather than proclaiming his own conversion to a kind of pro-Greek chauvinism.

This may be a far cry from the missionary zeal of Count Alexander Tolstoy, with which this review of Hatherly's activities began. If that is the case, one can draw inspiration from the count's noble sentiments and also from Hatherly's own perseverance in his faith and his priesthood, despite the attacks from Anglicans and the human failings that prevented achievement of more concrete results.

Dr Joseph Overbeck and Plans for Western Rite Orthodoxy

It is unclear why the Russian Synod cooled toward Stephen Hatherly from 1869 onward. It may have been due, in part, to the fact that during that time the Holy Synod was being approached by Dr Joseph Overbeck, who had completely different ideas as to how England should be converted to Orthodoxy. His idea was to retain Western liturgical usages but adapt them so that they expressed Orthodox doctrine and were purged of all non-Orthodox influences. He believed that would be more acceptable to Western Christians, who were becoming increasingly disillusioned with the Roman and Anglican confessions and might find the Byzantine heritage of Eastern Orthodoxy too foreign and unpalatable.

Joseph Julian Overbeck, born in Germany in 1820, graduated from the University of Bonn, where he had distinguished himself in linguistics. Ordained to the priesthood in the Roman Catholic Church, Overbeck then spent several years studying in the Vatican Library and, in 1852, made his first visit to England to meet Cardinal Wiseman, a Syriac scholar of international repute.

The proclamation in 1854 of the doctrine of the Immaculate Conception prompted Overbeck to leave the Roman Catholic Church and become a Lutheran. After resigning from the University of Bonn, he obtained a stipend from Prussian King Friedrich Wilhelm IV. He used this money to conduct Syriac studies at the British Museum. Dr Overbeck arrived in England, which was to be his new home, in 1857. The following year he married Josephine Walb, also from Bonn. After living for two years on the Prussian stipend, he accepted an appointment to teach German at the University of Oxford for £150 a year.

For seven years, Overbeck continued his studies of ancient Syriac texts by St Ephraim the Syrian, which are preserved in the British Museum and at the Bodleian Library in Oxford. Oxford University Press eventually published his translations. His own fee for the work was a mere £40. However, a recompense that was far more valuable to Dr Overbeck was his close contact with the writings of this Holy Father, which led him to examine the history and teaching of the Eastern Orthodox Church. Through his studies, he reached the conclusion that "the Orthodox Church was the only one that could claim to be the ancient Catholic and Apostolic Church of our Creed, and that all the other churches of Christendom were schismatically and heretically cut off from the Catholic and Orthodox Church."

It was not until 1869 that Overbeck was finally received into the Orthodox Church by Father Eugene Popoff in London. The following year, to his great joy, his wife and three oldest children followed his example. On that occasion, Overbeck wrote the following acknowledgment and pledge, in Latin, which was inscribed in the Memorandum Book of the Embassy church:

> Very Reverend Sir, My Lord Archpriest,
> When, one year ago, I embraced the Orthodox faith, I had no dearer wish than to bring the other members of my family into the bosom of the Orthodox Church. What I prayed for has now, at length, through the Divine mercy and grace, come to pass. My wife Catherine, my son Joseph, and my daughters, Margaret and Eugenia, were solemnly received into the Communion of the Orthodox Church on the 15th and 16th days of the current month. Furthermore, our youngest son was baptised in the Orthodox Church four years ago.
>
> Now it remains for me to render great thanks to God for the great things He has done for our benefit; at the same time we all pray together to God, that He will preserve us faithful to the Orthodox doctrines and precepts in this life, that in the other life we may be found worthy to enjoy the heavenly joy.
>
> And you also, Most Reverend Sir, and our spiritual father, to whom after God we owe everything in this work of our conversion, please be so

kind as to accept our sincere thanks. Wherefore it is our prayer that God will bless you for everything that you have done for us.

I remain, Reverend Sir, your most devoted and grateful servant,

Josephus J. Overbeck.
Reading. 20th June 1870.
To the Very Reverend Archpriest Eugene Popoff, in London.

On the occasion of Catherine Overbeck's reception into the Orthodox Church, Father Eugene celebrated the liturgy in the Embassy church in English. As noted, he received permission to do this the previous year from the Holy Synod. He also gave a sermon in English. Thereafter, Overbeck always referred to Father Eugene as his "dearest friend." In a letter written in 1869 he said that in the five years they had known each other "there never passed a single word of discord between us; we always most wonderfully agreed."

Although the Russian Church received Overbeck and his family into communion, this was not a course he thought many would be able to emulate. Overbeck set out his missionary ideas in his book *Catholic Orthodoxy and Anglo-Catholicism: A Word about Intercommunion between the English and the Orthodox Churches*, which was published in 1866. The following year he published the first issue of *The Orthodox Catholic Review*, which became the chief vehicle for expressing his ideas for the next twenty years. It seemed to Overbeck that the Church of England was likely to split apart due to its inherent contradictions, while at the same time, many within the Roman Catholic Church were experiencing doubts, as he himself had done. This intensified after 1870, when the doctrine of papal infallibility was proclaimed. Many Roman Catholics never believed this doctrine, and, in fact, some groups in Holland and Germany split away after 1870, forming the Old Catholic Church. So, Overbeck argued, it was essential to provide a spiritual home for the growing number of Western souls who were becoming aware of the errors of existing Western confessions.

As early as 1865, Overbeck wrote to Count Dimitry Tolstoy, procurator of the Russian Holy Synod, privately setting out these views. On July 17, 1865, the count wrote to Father Eugene that Overbeck's letter had been submitted for examination by the Moscow Vladyka (i.e., Metropolitan Philaret of Moscow). "Until we learn his views it is better not to mention this to the Holy Synod. Therefore please try to dissuade Overbeck from taking further steps at present, of course without cooling his Orthodox disposition . . . . Perhaps when he becomes better acquainted with the ritual side of our faith, some of his prejudices about it will be eliminated, and his religious outlook will become more mature."

Tolstoy asked Father Popoff to send him Overbeck's biography and added, "Do not suppose that I am indifferent to the intentions of Mr. Overbeck; the opposite is the case. But because the matter is so important, it requires very careful thought." Eighteen years earlier, in 1847, the metropolitan had shown himself not averse to a form of Western Rite Orthodoxy. At that time, he discussed with Khomiakov what changes the Anglicans would have to make if they were to be accepted by the Orthodox into communion. Khomiakov wrote,

> His sympathy was unexpectedly warm and strong. He listened to many things with a joyful smile and with tears in his eyes. It was even a strange emotion to behold in a man of such concentrated feelings . . . . He said "Everything that can be done without offending the Christian conscience will be done," and that was said earnestly. He said likewise that . . . every rite not implying a direct negation of a dogma would be allowed, "Unity of rites being very desirable indeed, but unity of dogma being the only *sine qua non.*"[18]

It is not known how Metropolitan Philaret reacted on this occasion or what response Overbeck eventually received to his letter. Nevertheless, despite Count Tolstoy's attitude of caution, in March 1867 Dr Overbeck began to circulate a petition publicly that was addressed to the Russian Holy Synod asking it to establish a Western Church in communion with the Eastern Orthodox Church. "We are westerns," he wrote, "and must plead an inalienable right to remain Westerns." By September 1869, he had collected 122 signatures; at that point the petition was closed and sent to the Holy Synod in St Petersburg. The Synod established a special commission under the chairmanship of the metropolitan of St Petersburg to examine the proposals. Dr Overbeck was appointed a member of this commission, and this status was confirmed in a letter from Metropolitan Isidore at the end of August 1869. The letter is a remarkable example of very formal Russian translated literally (possibly by Father Popoff) into even more formal Victorian English. Nevertheless, the letter conveyed the author's warm feelings toward a fellow believer from a far-off country.

> Dear Sir,
>
> I perceived with pleasure from your letter of the 25 July/6 August that you are willing to accept the name of member co-adjutor of the Commission

known to you, as I had proposed to you through the medium of the Arch-priest Popoff.

Confirming you as member by these presents officially, I do so with the greater pleasure that your conviction in the truth of Orthodoxy, attested by your very act of union to the Orthodox Church; your extensive knowledge evinced in your literary labours, and your experience, of which a pledge has already been given by you in your above mentioned letter,—afford us the right of expecting much from you for the success of a work equally dear to you and to us.

Your remarks, inspired by your hearty care for the benefit of this valuable work, and founded on a near and substantial acquaintance with the local position of affairs, have been received by me with the attention they deserve, and their contents have been conveyed to the other members of the Committee for investigation.

With all my heart greeting in you a new member of the Orthodox Church and an indefatigable labourer in the Lord's vineyard, and invoking the blessing of God on your good work to the glory of God, I have the honour to be your, dear Sir, ready servant,

Isidore, Metr. of Novgorod and St. Petersburg.
29 August 1869.

When Overbeck's petition arrived in St Petersburg, Stephen Hatherly had already been in Russia for several months trying to gain support for his Wolverhampton mission. It is possible that Overbeck's petition, which he began to circulate in 1867, was a stimulus to Hatherly, in that he realised Overbeck's approach was very different from his own and felt he should more actively further his own ideas. Regardless of what brought Hatherly to Russia precisely at the time Overbeck's petition was being considered by the Synod, Overbeck considered this as a threat to his work and he wrote a letter of protest, which was later published in the Russian press. "Two rival Orthodox churches," he wrote, "one with the Eastern Rite, and the other with the Western Rite—such a state of things would be utterly intolerable."

When this letter was published, Hatherly wrote to Overbeck from Moscow:

I shall not suffer your criticism to pass in silence but shall enter the warmest protest against any attempt to blend any figment of your old Popery, or any old Protestantism, with our Orthodox ritual under whatsoever name

> it may be disguised, or by whomsoever it may be proposed. As an Englishman I shall call things by their proper names, and shall hold myself free to criticise your criticism . . . your scheme will not be forwarded by attacking mine, as you will see.

Overbeck took great exception to his work being branded as "old Popery" and wrote back to Hatherly, "Your highly offensive, ungentlemanly, and eminently un-Christian lines are in my hands, a witness against you, and a stigma of the cause you mean to further by them." In conclusion he wrote that he declined to receive any additional letters from Hatherly.

Considerable insight into Overbeck's thoughts and feelings at that time and in later years can be gained from his correspondence with Olga Novikoff with whom he met in the late 1860s. Married to Lieutenant General Ivan Novikoff, rector of St Petersburg University, Madame Novikoff spent several months each year, usually in the winter, living at Claridges Hotel in London. Her father, General Kireeff, was the well-known theological writer, and she was a devoted member of the Orthodox Church, despite having become a prominent society figure both in St Petersburg and in London. After a meeting with Gladstone she realized that Anglo-Russian relations often suffered simply due to misunderstandings and ignorance, and she felt called to work at improving relations between the two countries. She became known as the "M. P. for Russia" due to her frequent correspondence with influential persons and letters to the press.

After receiving the letter from Metropolitan Isidore in which he was appointed to the Synodal Commission, Overbeck was informed that the Synod wanted Father Eugene Popoff to accompany him to Russia; however, no word came as to when the commission would meet. At that time he was employed as a professor of German at the Staff College, Camberley (then known as Cambridgetown). Consequently, he could travel to Russia only during college vacations. When January 1, 1870, came and he had not yet received an invitation, he wrote to Olga Novikoff, "*Entre nous*, is there anything going on behind the scenes? It forcibly struck me for the first time, that, in the same proportion as Hatherly's stay was prolonged, my invitation was delayed. He will start, as soon as he sees that the term of my vacations compels me to decline the invitation."

Eventually he received the official invitation. By January 9, Dr Overbeck was in Berlin waiting for Father Eugene to join him, and on January 13 they arrived in St Petersburg. The commission meeting went smoothly. Overbeck's proposals were approved in principle, and he was asked to prepare a draft of the Western Orthodox liturgy for their examination. While in Russia, he also met a number of influential people and was invited to breakfast with the Imperial family. He had a separate interview with the empress and Grand Duke Constantine, which he always remembered with "affectionate devotion." (Remember, the empress had contributed to Hatherly's Wolverhampton mission, and would, in all probability, have shown a sincere interest in Overbeck's plans as well.)

During the remainder of 1870 Dr Overbeck worked on his liturgical draft. The Synod became impatient and expected him to produce it more quickly. He wrote to Olga Novikoff, asking her to remind them that he was not, as he put it,

> an independent gentleman who devoted his whole time to the work of his choice, but a hard-worked professor, who after a toilsome day's work comes home, and, instead of taking his necessary and well-earned rest, sits again directly down and works for the Orthodox cause . . . . It would be good if our dear friends in St. Petersburg would consider this a little.

By December 1870 the 73-page draft was finally dispatched to St Petersburg. This *Liturgy of the Western Orthodox-Catholic Mass*, as Dr Overbeck called it, closely followed the Roman Catholic mass, but with certain modifications. The prayer "Holy God, Holy Mighty, Holy Immortal, have mercy upon us" was added to be recited twice in Greek and once in English, "in remembrance of our union with the Orthodox Church." References to the "merits of the saints" were dropped. A prayer was added after the words "Take, eat, this is my body, " invoking the Holy Spirit for the consecration of the Holy Gifts (which the Roman rite does not otherwise have). Holy Communion was administered from a spoon containing both the Body and Blood of Christ.

After a short wait, Dr Overbeck received his second invitation to St Petersburg, as well as the money for his fare, and he arrived shortly before the Russian Christmas. The commission met in two long sessions at the beginning of 1871 and examined his liturgy. They expressed their approval and said they were prepared to give it their full support.

The question arose as to who should be the priest for the new Western Rite church. Overbeck petitioned the Synod for restoration of his own (Roman) priesthood. Apparently he expected to be simply "reinstated" as a priest, rather than receiving ordination from an Orthodox hierarch. As he waited anxiously for news, Overbeck frequently asked

Madame Novikoff to glean some piece of information that would give him encouragement.

Dr Overbeck was distressed to learn of the initial success of Hatherly's Wolverhampton mission and even more so to learn of Hatherly's ordination to the priesthood, especially because the press tended to think they were working together. On October 17, 1871, *The Times* wrote of "Father Overbeck . . . the gentleman who has embraced the Orthodox belief, become a Greek priest, opened a Church of his denomination near Birmingham, and is now engaged in promoting a reunion between the Anglican and Roman establishments." More misunderstandings in half of a sentence are hard to imagine! Overbeck wrote a lengthy clarification to the editor, but his reply was cut down to a few lines, with emphasis on the statement, "I most strongly protest against being mixed up in any way with the Hatherly affair, since I always denounced his plan as an unlawful encroachment of the East on the West." Nevertheless he saw the attacks from the Anglican press against the idea of an Orthodox mission as a positive sign and wrote that the "cry of anger was a more hopeful sign than dull insensibility."

Overbeck was outraged and shocked when he heard of the Patriarchal decree banning Hatherly's missionary activities. He wrote to Olga Novikoff, "The only true Church, which shall be our guide to heaven, is the Orthodox Church. And this Chief Secretary to the Patriarch does forbid to receive Anglicans . . . into the Orthodox Church, and does not care that four or ten truth-seeking souls go 'to the dogs' not to say 'to the devil.'"

The Russian Synod continued to hesitate over the practical implementation of Overbeck's plans. Although they approved of a Western Rite liturgy in theory, they hoped that it could be put into practice by uniting the Old Catholics to Orthodoxy. Meanwhile Overbeck received no concrete reply from the Russian Synod on the question of the "restoration" of his priesthood or establishment of Western Rite churches.

The cooling of the Synod toward Hatherly may be explained, in part, by the alternate plans put forward by Overbeck and by the possible influence of Madame Novikoff and her family in St Petersburg circles. However, it is likely that the silence toward Overbeck was not unconnected with the political events of 1870–1871. In 1870 Russia seized on the opportunity of the Franco-Prussian War to demand a relaxation of some terms of the peace treaty that was signed at the end of the Crimean War, in particular, the so-called Black Sea Clauses that restricted Russia's right to keep naval forces in the Black Sea. British agreement was essential. Since the opening of the Suez Canal in 1869, Britain had an even greater interest in the security of the

Near East. In January 1871 a conference on the Black Sea Clauses was held in London, attended by representatives of the German, Russian, and British empires. Some may have thought that this was not an opportune time for Russia to be undermining the established Church of England by supporting Dr Overbeck; backing the Old Catholics against Rome would have been a much safer course. Only study of the Synodal archives will reveal the extent to which political pressure was brought to bear and whether other factors were involved.

From the Russian perspective, both to Father Eugene Popoff and Count Dimitry Tolstoy, the Eastern and Western Rite missionary schemes of Hatherly and Overbeck need not have appeared mutually exclusive. While they doubtless felt more disposed toward Hatherly's plan to use the familiar Eastern Orthodox services in English, they evidently appreciated the logic of using a form of worship that was closer to what Western Christians knew. Indeed, it is surprising that Overbeck's proposals were given such serious consideration by a body such as the Russian Synod, well known for its conservatism in small matters as well as larger questions of principle. The missionary cause was obviously hampered by the failure of these two equally dedicated men to agree or at least adopt an attitude of toleration toward each other's plans.

Death of Father Eugene Popoff: Father Basil Popoff as Rector

Father Eugene Popoff died in the spring of 1875, during a visit to Russia at the age of 63. His death was a severe blow to Dr Overbeck, who had always received encouragement and support from him. In fact, Father Eugene seems to have been genuinely loved and respected by everyone who came in contact with him. Father Popoff had traveled to St Petersburg in 1869 to act as intermediary in Hatherly's fund-raising, and went again in January 1870 to accompany Overbeck to the Synodal Commission on the Western Rite. He "worked like a horse" for Dr Neale, and Baron Brunnow wrote that "here he has a widespread reputation for wisdom and piety." The Synod was, in many cases, prepared to trust his judgment implicitly in matters affecting Orthodoxy in England. It is regrettable that many of the lengthy reports and articles, which he was constantly being asked to provide, have not survived; they would have given a clearer impression of his personality and his attitudes about the burning religious issues of the day. The existing information leaves the impression of someone who was always prepared to help, to act as a channel of communication, and to provide detailed factual information, yet was reluctant to express views of his own. Perhaps this is not far from the truth. A key to his personality may be the letter he wrote to Count Alexander Tolstoy over the apostasy of Countess Aponi to Roman Catholicism. Obviously very distressed, he wrote, "But for the dead there are no physicians, and so I limited myself to a brief reply: 'As it is an already accomplished fact, it remains only to leave it in the hands of Him who is our Judge and Saviour, and who alone knows the purity of our intentions.'" Father Eugene was reluctant to express his disapproval openly, sensing that this would serve no purpose to someone already committed to a course of action. Was he, as in his dealings with Anglicans such as Neale, being excessively diplomatic or was he using wise moderation and tact? With the limited information available, it is hard to know for sure. Of all the materials that survived, his reports of his visits to the Crimean War prisoners probably provide the most vivid impression of the kind and loving personality that inspired such universal love and respect.

Eight years before his death, Father Eugene recorded his wife's demise in the church register: "4/16 May 1867 at 4 o'clock Anna Iakovlevna, wife of Archpriest Popoff, died in her 51st year from a 'malignant disease of the uterus and liver.' 9/21 May buried in Kensal Green Cemetery." The unusual detail of this entry, with the cause of death given in English, seems to betray the distress Popoff must have felt at the loss of his spouse and companion of nearly thirty years.

A consolation for Father Eugene in the year of his bereavement was the ordination of his son, Basil, to the diaconate on August 26 of that same year, to assist him at the London Embassy church. Basil Evgenievitch Popoff was born in Copenhagen and grew up in England from the age of 3. In his late teens he went to St Petersburg to pursue his theological studies. As early as 1858, at the age of 21, he had met the procurator of the Holy Synod, who commented in a letter to Father Eugene that he was glad to see his son following in his footsteps and bringing good to the Church. In 1864 Basil graduated from St Petersburg Theological Academy and in December of the same year he was appointed psalm-reader for the London Embassy church. He also translated Ostroumoff's *The History of the Council of Florence* into English, which was published under the supervision of John Mason Neale. Count Alexander Tolstoy referred to this in a letter to Father Eugene dated November 8, 1860, where he wrote, "The translation of *The History of the Council of Florence* into English is, I am informed, already finished and is being copied out. I can see no reason why it should not be printed, but I would just like to know about how much it will cost." Basil Popoff's ordination to the diaconate in 1867 was made possible by a regulation of May 1, 1867, which increased the size of the London church clergy staff to one priest, one deacon, and two readers. At that time, the priest's salary was 4,000 silver roubles and the deacon's was 2,000 roubles, and the readers' salaries were 1,500 roubles each. (The priest's and readers' salaries had remained unchanged since the time of Popoff's arrival in England in 1842.) Basil's assistance in deacon's orders made it feasible to hold the Divine Liturgy in English from time to time.

In January 1874 Prince Alfred, Duke of Edinburgh, Queen Victoria's second son, married the only daughter of Alexander II of Russia, the Grand Duchess Maria Alexandrovna. The wedding took place in St Petersburg. In the spring of that year, Alexander II paid a state visit to England. He visited the Embassy church and made the customary awards of gold and diamond rings to the clergy as a sign of imperial largesse. Queen Victoria had been very apprehensive about a royal alliance with the Russian throne, both from political and religious points of view. She wrote of her fears that bearded priests with scapular crosses would take up residence in Clarence House and that the Duke of Edinburgh would be "ready to be quite a humble servant of Russia."

However, the Queen soon warmed to her new daughter-in-law, who became known in England as Princess Marie, but her fears of bearded priests in Clarence House were not totally unfounded. The Duchess of Edinburgh remained faithful to Orthodoxy and had a private chapel set up in one of the rooms in Clarence House, which was her official residence in London. Here she placed the magnificent copy of the Smolensk Icon of the Mother of God, with a gold plated *riza* (cover), that had been given to her by the peasants of the Smolensk region as a wedding present. The iconostasis was a simple screen with only the Royal Doors, the two main icons of the Saviour and the Mother of God, and the two side doors with icons of the Archangels. A semi-circular arch framing an icon of the Last Supper surmounted the Royal Doors. The arch was carved with a Slavonic inscription: "Alleluia. Thou shalt love the Lord they God with all thy heart and with all they soul and with all thy mind." Smaller arches also surmounted the other four icons of the iconostasis and carved ornamentation ran across the top. A Russian artist named Neff painted the icons themselves in the customary nineteenth-century style.

Deacon Basil Popoff was ordained to the priesthood to serve as chaplain to Princess Marie on December 5, 1874. The annual report for 1874 indicated that Father Basil was 38 at the time. He had been married but was by then a widower, with a 4-year-old son, Eugene. The report also mentioned that he had a 21-year-old brother, James (Yakov), who was doing his military service in St Petersburg, and a 31-year-old sister, Nadezhda, who lived "in her father's house." Deacon John Speransky, who had been ordained since 1848 and had served as the senior deacon in the Cathedral of Saints Peter and Paul in St Petersburg, took his place as deacon at the Embassy church.

After his father's death early in 1875, Father Basil was the only Russian priest left in London. On April 2, 1875, a directive was sent to him from Russia: "Since no one has yet been appointed to the Embassy church in London in place of Archpriest Popoff, the priest Basil Popoff, who is serving at the London house church of the Grand Duchess Maria Alexandrovna, should send all the papers of his deceased father to St Petersburg." On January 2, 1876, Father Basil Popoff was appointed rector of the Embassy church. No new priest was appointed to the Clarence House chapel; thereafter it was served by the rector of the Embassy church on occasions when the Duchess of Edinburgh was in residence.

It seems that Father Basil Popoff did not create as favourable an impression, at least among non-Russians, as his father did. An article in the *Church Review*, dated November 4, 1876, reported how two Anglican clergymen had gone to Welbeck Street on a Saturday evening and been received with great discourtesy. Apparently they were told before several witnesses that they had no right to be there and that the ambassador had given strict orders that none should be allowed in but members of the Russian Church. It was not clear to what extent the rector was involved in this rebuff. Dr Overbeck lamented in a letter to Olga Novikoff, "After old Mr Popoff's death, Basil and Naddy turned the cold shoulder on us and in fact since then the Popoffs virtually had ceased to exist for us." (Naddy would have been Father Basil's sister, Nadezhda.) Overbeck's disgruntlement went beyond matters of personality; he was still pursuing the question of his priestly orders being "reinstated." Meanwhile he had come to confession to Father Basil, expecting to be treated as a priest. The rector told him he could hear his confession if he presented himself as a layman, and wrote to St Petersburg for guidance on how to handle the matter. He was sent a directive, dated March 7, 1877, stating that Overbeck had joined the Orthodox Church as a former Protestant and so could not be considered a priest, although he was apparently calling himself "Reverend." It was suggested that if Overbeck was persistent, Father Basil should quote the rule of the Russian Church that a younger priest cannot confess an older one.

Father Basil never had the opportunity to present Overbeck with this rather roundabout explanation. On the day that it was signed in St Petersburg, Father Basil died in London, at the age of 40, having served as rector for just over a year. Prince Shouvaloff, the ambassador, arranged for Father

Eugene Smirnoff, who had been acting as chaplain to Prince Orloff to come from Brussels to conduct the funeral. He came again several times during March and April to conduct services in the Embassy church on Welbeck Street at the request of the ambassador and the Duchess of Edinburgh. Then, by a decree dated April 4, 1877, Father Eugene Smirnoff was appointed permanent rector of the London church, a position that he occupied for forty-six years.

Chapter 6

[1877–1919] Archpriest Eugene Smirnoff

The Embassy Church and Its People

Archpriest Eugene (Konstantinovich) Smirnoff is the first rector of the Russian Church in London of whom we have a photograph. The broad, strong features of his face contrast surprisingly with the fine, often barely legible handwriting of his draft correspondence and lengthy reports. Because Father Eugene Smirnoff kept extensive files that contained these rough drafts—which were presumably copied by a clerk either by hand or, in later years, on a typewriter, before being sent to their recipients—far more material has been preserved from this period than from earlier years with which to reconstruct a picture of the times and the London church.

The mid-nineteenth century was a period of great creativity in the Russian Orthodox Church through the influence of Metropolitan Philaret of Moscow and the rise of the Slavophile school of theologians. For a time, there appeared to be real striving toward Orthodoxy by parts of the Anglican Church, although by the end of the century, it was clear that little change could be expected in the Church of England. The dominant figure in the Russian Church in the late nineteenth century was probably the procurator, Constantine Pobedonostseff. An able administrator and devoted son of the Church, he was marked by extreme conservatism and caution. He maintained the policy of friendly relations with the Anglicans but privately had no hope that union could ever be attained. Father Eugene Smirnoff was in regular correspondence with Pobedonostseff and had a similar approach in his dealings with the Anglicans. However, he lacked something of his mentor's finesse and tact. As a consequence, although he made many close friends in England, he was not as universally revered as Father Eugene Popoff had been.

Russian Church authorities continued to regard the position of rector of the London Embassy church as important because of ongoing contacts with the Anglicans and a number of other matters which became part of the rector's responsibility. Sharing the Christian and family names of his two illustrious predecessors, Father Eugene Popoff and Father James Smirnove, Father Eugene Smirnoff shared many, but not all, of their personal qualities as he carried on his activities as rector.

An Anglican friend recalled, "The Rev. Father Smirnoff was endowed with a singularly beautiful voice, and possessed a very clear articulation. These, combined with his deep sense of reverence, and with the dignity of his presence gave a wonderful and impressive beauty to his rendering of the Liturgical offices of the Church. . . . His Russian was comparable with that of the best Russian Classical authors. Every letter he wrote was an example of finished Russian prose."

Prince Mestchersky, who had known Father Smirnoff for more than twenty years, recalled,

> Those who knew Father Smirnoff will feel how truly this touching parable [of the Good Shepherd] applies to one who, for more than forty years, was the loving spiritual father of his flock, the best friend of the destitute and friendless; who always had the right words of sympathy and consolation for anyone in distress or moral affliction. . . . For forty years the Russian flock in London had the blessing of such a shepherd as is described in the beautiful verses of the tenth chapter of St. John, who taught "as one having authority, and not as the scribes". . . . The Rev. E. Smirnoff undoubtedly belonged to these rare chosen ones; he was a light, not only of love, but of profound erudition: having, besides, a complete knowledge of the principal dogmas of the leading churches of Christendom, and having studied the manifold intricacies of ancient and modern philosophy, Father Smirnoff was able to grasp any questions of a theological or philosophical nature. There are few men of his erudition; he would discuss almost any questions of an abstract nature in his clear concise manner with unquestionable authority.

Although written as part of an obituary, we can surmise that the appreciation shown in these paragraphs was not entirely unfounded.

When Father Eugene Smirnoff arrived in England in 1877, he already had experience serving the Church outside Russia in an English-speaking country. After graduating from the St Petersburg Theological Academy in 1870, he was appointed church reader to the Russian Church of the Holy Trinity in New York. He was born in 1845, son of the rector of churches in Reval (now Tallinn, the capital of Estonia). He received his primary education in German before entering the St Petersburg Seminary and then the academy. In New York, he was instructor to a convert Orthodox priest, Father Nicholas Bjering, who was a Dane by birth and at first unfamiliar with the order of service of the Russian Church. In 1874, Father Eugene returned to St Petersburg, where he married Zinaida Naumoff, a clergyman's daughter. He was then twenty-nine years old, and his bride was twenty. They later had two sons: Nicholas, born in 1875, and Alexander, born in 1882. Two weeks after the wedding, Eugene Smirnoff was ordained to the priesthood by Bishop Palladius of Ladoga, acting on the instructions of Metropolitan Isidore of St Petersburg. He was appointed to the private chapel of Prince Nikolai Alekseyevitch Orloff in Brussels. On January 1, 1876, this chapel became the Brussels Embassy church, and from that point Father Eugene Smirnoff was considered a staff member of the Ministry of Foreign Affairs of the Russian Empire. In March 1877, he visited London to conduct Father Basil Popoff's funeral, and a month later he was appointed permanently to the London church. Over the years, he received all the various ecclesiastical awards of the Russian Church. In 1882 he was elevated to the rank of archpriest, and in 1901, on the occasion of the emperor's birthday, he was awarded the right to wear a mitre, which was sent to him from St Petersburg. Father Eugene also received a number of civil awards, the highest of which was the Order of St Anne, 1st degree, which he received in 1904. In 1900, he and his two sons were entered in the book of hereditary nobility. He also received decorations and stars from the rulers of Serbia, Bulgaria (the *Naroden orden za grazhdanska zasluga*), and Montenegro.

Although the London church had always been under the ecclesiastical jurisdiction of the Metropolitan of St Petersburg, there had been little regular contact with the diocesan bishop. Father Eugene Smirnoff was the first rector to maintain regular correspondence with his bishops, particularly Metropolitans Palladius (1892–1898), Anthony (1898–1912), and Vladimir (1912–1915). It was Metropolitan Palladius who had ordained Father Eugene while still a vicar bishop of the St Petersburg diocese. The letters received from him were handwritten, lengthy, and replete with the standard phrases of ecclesiastical courtesy. They were signed by the shaky hand of an old man. After his death in 1898, the letters from the new metropolitan were typed, brief, and to the point. Metropolitan Anthony Vadkovsky was a gifted hierarch and theologian who was widely mourned when his activities were cut short by his untimely death in 1912. He had visited England in 1897, while still Archbishop of Finland, to represent the Russian Church at Queen Victoria's Diamond Jubilee.[1] While in England, he celebrated two hierarchical liturgies: on one Sunday at Welbeck Street and on another Sunday in the Greek Church, in Moscow Road. A visit from a bishop was, needless to say, quite rare, and the congregation was moved by the special features of the hierarchical service. Remarkably, it was the second episcopal visit in two years. In 1895 Bishop Nicholas of the Aleutians and Alaska visited London whilst on his way back to San Francisco following an official visit to London.[2] He also celebrated services in both the Russian and Greek churches. This was in all probability the first time that a bishop officiated in the London Church of the Dormition since the departure of Metropolitan Arsenius nearly two hundred years previously. The Prince of Wales (the future Edward VII) was present in the Welbeck Street church on this occasion. In 1907, the care of the Russian churches in Europe was delegated to the Bishop of Kronstadt, one of the vicar bishops of the St Petersburg Metropolitan see. Bishop Vladimir of Kronstadt visited London at the end of November 1907 and served at the Embassy church on the feast of the Presentation of the Mother of God in the Temple.

In 1893, the Grand Duke Nicholas Alexandrovich, heir to the throne of Russia, made a state visit to England. He visited Queen Victoria at Windsor and observed a debate in the House of Commons from the Peers' Gallery. He attended a Sunday service at Welbeck Street, where he noted that the reading and singing were not of the standard he felt was required for a church in so important a capital. On returning to Russia, he commented to the procurator of the Holy Synod, Pobedonostseff, "The situation at the church in London is quite impossible; they have a decrepit deacon, a hoarse psalm-reader, and no choir. A small choir of singers should be formed there, and the deacon and psalm-reader should be replaced." These impressions resulted both from his own observations and from the complaints from his aunt, the Duchess of Edinburgh. The "decrepit deacon" was Father John Speransky, who had been in London since 1874, when the previous deacon, Father Basil Popoff, was elevated to the priesthood. By 1893 Speransky had been in London nineteen years, had been a deacon for forty-five years, and was no less than eighty-two years old. As a result of the future emperor's recommendation, he was granted an honourable retirement on a full pension. The procurator asked Father Eugene what the requirements would be for a new deacon. He replied that two factors would have to be taken into account: first, the need to conduct the services in a suitably impressive fashion, which he said was particularly important in view of the frequent visits from Anglicans, and second, the high cost of living in London. He concluded that it would therefore have to be a relatively young deacon who had a light bass or baritone voice and who was not yet burdened with a large family to support.

The recommendations for the new deacon and the new choir were not put into effect until 1897 and 1898. One may surmise that the stimulus came as a result of Archbishop Anthony's visit in the summer of 1897, when he would have noticed that the emperor's earlier recommendations had not yet been carried out. Whatever the precise chain of events, in the autumn of 1897 two new graduates of the St Petersburg Theological Academy were appointed as singers to the London church. The following year, Nikolai Alekseyevitch Preobrazhensky, who had also graduated from the academy in 1897, was ordained to the diaconate to serve in London. So, by the turn of the century, the emperor's wishes for improving the quality of the services in London had been put into practice.

Deacon Preobrazhensky served for about ten years, and Father Smirnoff commented that "he never brought discredit on the Divine Services." In 1907, he left London and the position again became vacant. Father Eugene favoured a singer named Vasily Yartseff as a candidate, but this plan was dropped after a scandal emerged involving Yartseff's landlady, who claimed to have become pregnant by him and threatened to sue the church. Eventually Deacon John Strokovsky was transferred from Prague to serve in London. Strokovsky had graduated from the Lithuanian seminary in 1902 and then studied natural sciences for two years at the Warsaw Veterinary Institute before being ordained deacon for the church in Prague in 1904. Here he taught religious instruction classes at the Orthodox church school on a voluntary basis. At the age of twenty-nine, he arrived in London in January 1908 with his twenty-three-year-old wife, Sophia Nikolaevna, and two small children: Natalia, age three, and Irina, who was one.

At first Strokovsky appeared to manage his duties well. Bishop Vladimir of Kronstadt called on him to assist at various services in Paris and at other churches in Germany and Austria during 1908, when he had just been appointed to oversee the parishes in western Europe and was making archpastoral visits. However, with the passage of time Strokovsky succumbed to the difficulties created by the high cost of living and the inadequacy of a deacon's salary for a family man. He incurred debts and began drinking, which led to further deterioration in his financial condition. By early 1914, Father Eugene had become increasingly worried about the situation; the deacon was not always sober, even during evening services, which was quite unacceptable and obvious to people attending the church. On March 5, 1914, Father Eugene wrote to Metropolitan Vladimir of St Petersburg, asking for a replacement. He said that Deacon Strokovsky could not stay in London and the sooner he went, the better. However, he preferred that Strokovsky stay until Pascha to help with the festal services, although the Ambassador, Count Benkendorff, wanted him to go at once. "I am sorry for him as an individual," wrote Father Eugene, "and for his family." He expressed hope that Strokovsky would mend his ways when removed from the stresses of life in London and that he would be given a new position in Russia. A month later Father Eugene wrote again to the metropolitan to say that Deacon Strokovsky had gone and that a collection had been held to pay off his debts; £1,600 had been raised, with a contribution from the ambassador. But it was not clear if that would have been enough.

Later that year, Smirnoff again wrote to the metropolitan that a new deacon had arrived. This was Vladimir Theokritoff, who had been a singer at the London church and had subsequently occupied positions in Biarritz and Paris. Father Smirnoff wrote of him in glowing terms, "His wonderful voice, which so disposes one to prayer, has enraptured the whole congregation." So by the beginning of the Great War, the problem of finding a suitable deacon was finally solved.

The future Russian emperor's comments after his visit in 1893, which were put into practice in 1897, also led to the establishment of a vocal quartet to sing at the services, paid for from the Imperial Treasury. The annual report for 1910 stated that the clergy of the London church had been established on May 1, 1867, at "1 priest, 1 deacon and two psalm-readers. In 1897 it was increased by Imperial command by four singers." In 1910 the annual salaries of the clergy, received from the personnel and administration department of the Ministry of Foreign Affairs, were 7,500 roubles for the rector, 3,750 roubles for the deacon, 3,000 roubles each for the psalm-readers, and 1,500 roubles each for the four singers. The first singers to be appointed, in 1897, were Konstantin Nikolaevitch Faminsky and Foka Feodorovitch Volkovsky. In 1902 Vasily Tikhonovitch Timofeyeff was appointed, and in 1908 Vladimir Theokritoff was appointed; he subsequently became the deacon. In 1912, commending Timofeyeff for the order of St Stanislas, Father Smirnoff wrote that "throughout the whole of his time of service in the London church he has shown exemplary diligence and unremitting zeal in carrying out his duties."

Father Eugene was constantly concerned that the singing should be up to standard. In the spring of 1913, for example, he wrote anxiously to the Metropolitan of St Petersburg that Faminsky was leaving for Italy and that Timofeyeff and Volkovsky had lost their voices. How were they to cope with Easter approaching, together with the likelihood of being summoned to perform ministrations for the Dowager Empress Marie Feodorovna, then living in London? He asked that a first tenor replacement be sent immediately. The male quartet would have provided a marked contrast to the singing of a single chanter, which had been heard in the church since its foundation as the Graeco-Russian Church nearly two hundred years earlier. A contemporary believer would probably consider the style of singing "monastic" in comparison with the mixed choirs common in parishes today. Of the four singers we have mentioned, Theokritoff, Timofeyeff, and Volkovsky remained in London after 1917 and were able to put their talents and theological education to the service of the Church in Exile.

It appears that psalm-readers and singers, especially if married, were not expected to be able to live on their ecclesiastical salaries alone, and most of them seem to have taken secular employment in London as well. The most distinguished of these minor clergymen was Nicolas Vasilievich Orloff, the "hoarse psalm-reader" of whom the emperor complained. If his voice was poor, he had many other talents. Orloff, who came from a clerical family, had been attached to the London church and embassy since 1869. From the beginning he had what his service record referred mysteriously to as "other special occupations" at the embassy in addition to his duties as psalm-reader. When he was first appointed, Baron Brunnow was still the ambassador and arranged for him to be paid separately for this extra work. In 1874 he was attached to the imperial suites, presumably to act as translator, when Alexander II and Empress Maria Alexandrovna paid state visits to England after their daughter's marriage to Prince Alfred. In 1884 Orloff was appointed to supervise the embassy's financial affairs, for which he was paid an additional £5 a month. In 1891 he was involved in the investigation of forged coupons of Russian government securities that were circulating in England, and he gave evidence when the case came to trial. In 1899 he became a professor of Russian at King's College London, one of the founding colleges of the University of London. In 1901 and subsequent years he was appointed to serve on the senate of the University of London and on the board of studies, which was a committee that reviewed the course syllabi and supervised instruction. He also provided the Russian government with information on the workings of the English Parliament in 1906; in 1907, Orloff was made a correspondent member of the Holy Synod's committee on Old Catholic and Anglican questions.

The greatest achievements of Orloff's distinguished academic and ecclesiastical career are probably his English translations of liturgical and other religious texts, which he began in 1897 at the request of Bishop Nicholas of Alaska. Passing through London on the way to his new missionary diocese,

Bishop Nicholas doubtless felt that Orloff's rare combination of academic and ecclesiastical experience qualified him to take on this task. The first books translated were *Elements of Christian Doctrine* (a translation of Archpriest Peter Smirnoff's *Instruction in God's Law*, a book of basic instruction in Orthodoxy), the *Horologion* (*Book of Hours*), and the *Octoechos* (Sunday services of the eight tones). They were published at the expense of the Orthodox Mission in America in 1897 and 1898, although printed in London. These were followed in 1899 by *The General Menaion*, published with the blessing of Bishop Tikhon, the future patriarch who was then the newly appointed bishop of the American diocese, and *The Ferial Menaion*, which contained services for the twelve great feast days of the Orthodox Church.

These service books would have provided sufficient material to conduct the full liturgical cycle of services for most Sundays and great feast days in the year. Although Orloff's English is somewhat obscure,[3] these books must have been a great benefit for the bishops in their vast missionary diocese. Orloff received numerous civil awards in recognition of his work, culminating in the Order of St Anne, 2nd degree, in 1906. In 1899 he received a *gramota*—an official document from the Holy Synod that expresses gratitude and calls down God's blessing upon the recipient in appreciation of his work—to mark the thirtieth anniversary of his service to the Church. On this occasion he also received an award of 500 roubles, which he donated to the Russian Red Cross Society to help victims of the famine resulting from the failed harvest in Russia that year. Orloff presented copies of his translations to various members of the Russian Imperial family, including the Empress Alexandra, who was a German convert to Orthodoxy and had been brought up speaking fluent English. She expressed her sincere gratitude, as did Queen Victoria who was presented with an advance copy of the *Horologion* in 1897 on the occasion of her Diamond Jubilee. In 1899 Orloff received a letter of appreciation from Patriarch Constantine of Constantinople, in which Constantine described his translations as "work that is pleasing to God, worthy of praise and profitable" and "while giving just praise to the unremitting labour and zeal inspired by God," expressed to him "the gratitude both of the Holy Great Church and of the Patriarch himself."

On March 5, 1903, Father Eugene reported to the ambassador, "We have received permission to attach outside the main entrance of the Church House two brass plates not more than 8 inches by 3 inches with inscriptions, on one in Russian and on the other in English, to the effect that in this house is located the Orthodox Russian Church." So the previously anonymous façade became identified to the whole world as the home of the Russian Orthodox Church in London. However, this spirit of welcome was not universally applied to all who visited the church. A report written in 1912 by a Russian traveller named Theodore Kontorshchikoff, which was sent to the Synod and then distributed to rectors of overseas churches, is somewhat disconcerting:

> In London the duty of church watchman [*storozh*] is carried out by an Englishman and Anglican, the lackey of the rector of the church. I will permit myself to say a few words about this church. It is very richly appointed and splendid, but it is too small. Further, the "regular places" in the church, with chairs set out for the more honoured parishioners and official personages, are treated as inviolable, while Orthodox people of the lower classes are pushed aside. This order, together with a strict selection of who is to be admitted to the church—those in dirty clothing and "politicals" are not admitted—causes a discontent against the church among all Orthodox of the lower classes. Admission is permitted only on days when services are held, and even then, only ten minutes before the beginning of the service.

To what extent this approach was dictated by Father Smirnoff or was due to his "lackey" seizing the initiative, we cannot be certain. This change was due, in part, to the increased size and importance of the embassy, which seems to have required that space should be set aside specifically for the ambassador and those of higher rank. Of course, the church technically was still the private chapel for the ambassador and his staff. Statistics from that period are difficult to analyse—the records of baptisms, marriages, and funerals are copies of the individual certificates issued at the time they were performed, without a convenient summary. For example, between 1900 and 1904, forty-seven weddings were performed, of which ten occurred in 1900, four in 1901, eight in 1902, eight in 1903, and seventeen in 1904. This increased level of activity was the result of there being more Russians in London on a temporary basis who sought the ministrations of the church. However, the regular congregation seems to have remained small. A book published in 1904, titled *The Religious Life of London*, gave the following statistics for a representative Sunday: "Borough of Marylebone, Russian Chapel, Welbeck St Morning: Men, 17; Women, 6; Children, 0; Total, 23."

The late nineteenth and early twentieth centuries were periods of turbulent but steadily improving Anglo-Russian relations. In England this was the era of "jingoism," of Queen Victoria's Diamond Jubilee, and of a heightened pride in the British empire among ordinary people, which led to a certain suspicion about the Russian threat on the world stage. The year 1877, when

Father Eugene Smirnoff arrived in England, had seen Russia's declaration of war on Turkey and invasion of the Balkans in support of the independence movement among the Slavic peoples. Gladstone and a significant segment of the British public were outraged by reports of the Bulgarian massacres perpetrated by the Turks in 1875. However, by 1877 Disraeli was prime minister, and he pursued a policy of protecting British imperial interests before all else. As the Russians advanced toward Constantinople, Disraeli joined other western European leaders in issuing threats and ultimatums, and in early 1878 the British fleet was anchored off Constantinople ready to counter a Russian invasion.[4] Eventually Russia and Turkey made peace at San Stefano, resulting in the creation of an independent Bulgaria and full independence for Romania, Serbia, and Montenegro. The Bulgarians felt an immense debt of gratitude to Alexander II and the Russians. Even the London Embassy church offered what assistance it could to the newly independent Orthodox Bulgaria. The archives contain a file titled "Inventory of church articles and vestments contributed in 1879 by the Russian Orthodox Church of the Imperial Embassy in London to Orthodox churches in Bulgaria."

The ambassador in London during the crisis was Count Peter Andreyevitch Shouvaloff, who succeeded Baron Brunnow in 1874. He was succeeded in turn by Prince Alexei Andreyevitch Lobanoff-Rostovsky (1879–1882), Baron Artur Pavlovitch Morengeim (1882–1884), Baron Yegor Yegorovitch Staal (1884–1902), and Count Alexander Konstantinovitch Benkendorff, who was ambassador from 1902 until World War I. After the Treaty of San Stefano in 1878, Anglo-Russian relations steadily improved. Germany's militaristic power was emerging as the principal threat to the peace of Europe, and this had the effect of drawing Britain, Russia, and France together as allies in the Triple Entente. The chief remaining bone of contention was Russian policy in Central Asia, which threatened British interests in India. However, there was little substance to these fears.[5] Count Benkendorff in particular worked hard to cement friendly relations between Britain and Russia. The count was helped in this task by being a distant relative of an earlier ambassador, Count Woronzow, whose daughter married into the English aristocracy. The son of Count Benkendorff recalls in his memoirs,

> My father had . . . been Ambassador to the Court of St James for fourteen years. During the first years, what with the close association of England with Japan, and the ensuing continuous friction culminating in the Dogger Bank[6] incident, he had had by no means an easy time, and yet it soon became apparent that he had achieved for himself an exceptional position in

the diplomatic world. The reasons for this were many, but most of them had to do with conditions which in the present day have no value whatsoever.

There was, for instance, my father's close acquaintance with King Edward and his Queen, sister of the Dowager Empress Marie of Russia, both daughters of Christian, King of Denmark. There was also the fact that sometime in the early nineteenth century an Earl of Pembroke had married the daughter of the then Russian Ambassador, Prince Simon [*sic*] Woronzow: these Woronzows were in various degrees connected with the Shuvalovs, and all the Herberts took up this relationship, however distant and vague it had become.[7] Prince Lichnovsky, the German Ambassador, was a first cousin of my father's, while the Austrian Ambassador, Count Mensdorff, claimed to be related by marriage through a minor Archduchess of Hapsburg—née Croy. Mr. Isvolsky, who had been my father's Chancellor in London, was [later] Russian Minister of Foreign Affairs.

All I have said so far should make it clear that my father had advantages exceptional even for those days, which greatly helped him to establish his status; but in his case, I think, they were enhanced by the personality of the man who had the opportunities of making use of them. Master of the technique of his calling, he was a man completely devoid of personal ambition, profoundly imbued with a sense of duty and service, and not to his own country alone, but to humanity as a whole. The more conscious was he of the obligations which the advantages I have been speaking of had given him, the more they made him independent both in his judgements and his actions.

Other senior embassy staff at the turn of the century enumerated by Maltseff in his book on Russian churches and institutions abroad include the following:

Counsellor: Sergei Dimitrievitch Sazonoff
1st Secretary: Stanislav Alfonsovitch Poklevski-Kozel
2nd Secretaries: Matvei Matianovitch Sevastopoulo and Prince Mikhail Nikolaevitch Svyatopolk-Mirsky
Military Attaché: Major General Nikolai Sergeyevitch Yermoloff
Naval Attaché: Captain (1st rank) Ivan Feodorovitch Bostrem
Agent of the Ministry of Finances: Mechislav Vladislavovitch Routkovsky
Consul General: Baron Robert Robertovitch Ungern-Shternberg
Vice Consul: Lev Andreyevitch Norgren
Attached to the consulate general: G. Osmond Kapel-Knapp

This list gives some indication of the size of the diplomatic presence in London. However, because many of the names are not Russian, it is likely that not all of even the senior officials were members of the Orthodox Church. In addition to the diplomatic staff, the number of Russians in London was growing for commercial reasons; Russia increasingly sought capital from Britain and other west European nations, both by selling Russian government bonds and by soliciting British investment in factories and other enterprises in Russia. The officials listed above include an agent of the Ministry of Finance, and church records indicate that in the 1890s there was an agency of the Russian Ministry of Finance situated at 107 Cromwell Road. Maltseff also gave details of an Anglo-Russian literary society and a Russian club that existed in London at this time:

> At one time there existed in London an Anglo-Russian Literary Society, under the presidency of Mr. Kazalet and under the protection of the Sovereign Emperor Nicholas II. The Society organized a series of public readings, but then died down.
>
> At the present time, a Committee has been established to organize a Russian club, with S. D. Sazonoff as President, A.V. Adiyasevitch as secretary, and members: N. N. Vinevitinoff, A.O. Gousakoff, V. K. Matveyeff, D. D. Morgan, M. P., B. F. Smith, and Stuart Hogg.
>
> The aims of the Russian club in London are as follows: The club has a purely social character and is completely non-political. Both Russians and English people sympathetic to its aims are accepted as members. The founders intend to found a centre for Russians living in England, and at the same time to make it possible for the English to become acquainted with Russian society. A Russian library and reading room are being organized at the club. Besides this, the organizers have made it their aim to make the Russian Club in London a useful institution for people visiting England from Russia temporarily. It is well known how difficult it is for a newly arrived Russian to orient himself in London; the club will be in a position to assist their guest members in taking their first steps in England. The club's By-Laws and the size of the annual dues are to be established at the first general meeting. Persons requiring further information are requested to address their enquiries to the temporary Honorary Secretary, Alexander Viktorovitch Aliyasevitch. The committee's temporary quarters and the Secretary's office are at: Hotel Russell, Russell Square, London, W.C.

The flock to which Father Eugene ministered was made up primarily of these embassy officials. Many officials stayed in London for a limited period, although some, such as Prince Mestchersky, whose recollections were quoted earlier, spent an extended period in the United Kingdom. Perhaps typical of the varied ministrations that Father Eugene performed was the marriage in 1905 between Gherman Alexandrovitch Scholts and Nelly Cameron, which is described in the memoirs of their daughter, Eugenie Fraser. Despite his Germanic surname, Scholts was a Russian from the Baltic provinces. He had been staying in Dundee, working for a local firm of merchants to gain business experience. There he met Nelly and, before returning to Russia, they decided to marry. Eugenie Fraser described some of the complications that arose and the advice they received from Father Smirnoff:

> There were several aspects of a Russian-Scottish marriage that had to be explained and eventually agreed upon. Letters were exchanged between the British Embassy in St. Petersburg, the head Russian Consulate in London and my grandfather's lawyer. According to the marriage laws of Russia my mother had to have the consent of her parents before any marriage could take place. By marrying my father she would automatically become a Russian subject. Any children of the marriage would likewise be Russian subjects and be baptised in the church of that country and of their father. My mother was a Presbyterian. My father belonged to the Russian Orthodox Church. In deference to his church he wrote to the Arch-Priest Father Evgeny Smirnoff, chaplain to the Russian Embassy in London. "My son," replied Father Evgeny, kindly explaining that while there was no objection to a Presbyterian service, the Orthodox Church would consider the marriage invalid unless it was solemnised in the Russian church as well. One of the important rituals in the ceremony is the crowning of the bride and bridegroom, when the two groomsmen, standing behind the couple with outstretched arms, hold the heavy golden crowns above the bridal pair and follow them as they are led by the priest three times round the lectern. The church also did not approve of any wedding taking place during the period of Lent, when the great fast of seven weeks begins around the end of February and lasts until Easter Sunday.[8]

The Presbyterian wedding was held in a church in Scotland on January 18, 1905, followed by a reception. The wedding party then boarded a train for London for what in their eyes was the "second" wedding. Eugenie Fraser continued:

> On 23 January, Nelly, by now having been married for five days, donned once again her bridal dress and veil and set off for the second marriage service to be held in the Russian church in Welbeck Street. She carried no flowers, for in the Russian Orthodox Church the bride and bridegroom stand together holding lighted candles entwined with orange blossom.
>
> The marriage rites of the Russian Church are impressive. The singing of the unseen choir deeply moving. The ritual of exchanging rings moves on to the circling round the lectern led by the priest and followed by the groomsmen holding the crowns over the heads of the bridal pair and adroitly side-stepping the train and veil. The chanting of the priests, the singing, the flickering lights of the candles and the saintly faces of the icons had a strange dreamlike effect on my mother. As they slowly moved behind the priest, the inner tension, the unaccustomed odour of the incense wafting all around her, proved too much. She was overcome and had to be taken to the vestry. Shortly after, Father Evgeny sent the deacon to enquire if "Miss Cameron" was able to proceed with the service. "Miss Cameron" pulled herself together and went back to complete the ceremony which in the eyes of the Russian Church gave her the right to be recognized as a married woman.
>
> In the afternoon, after tearful partings from the family, they embarked on another journey by train to Hull. There they had to join a ship which would carry them across the North Sea and through the Baltic to Finland.[9]

The couple lived in Russia until the early 1920s and then returned to Scotland.

Others who sought the ministrations of the London Embassy church during Father Smirnoff's time included someone of Jewish background and another who was Japanese. In 1893 Moishe Shevtel approached Father Eugene seeking baptism. He had left Moscow for the United States in 1891 when forced to close his factory. Two years later, unemployed and homesick, he hoped to return to Russia as an Orthodox Christian. He made plans to be baptised in London with his wife and children before arriving in Russia. Father Eugene felt obliged to seek permission to perform the baptism; and in his report, he pointed out that the baptism might give Shevtel the right to live in Moscow. There is no clear indication as to his religious motivation, although apparently he had considered becoming an Orthodox Christian even before leaving Russia. Unfortunately, it is unclear from the records whether his wish was fulfilled, but Father Eugene's report described the plight of this unfortunate man vividly and with compassion.

For several years Father Eugene corresponded with Archbishop Nicholas of Japan, the former priest at the Hakodate Consulate who later became an Orthodox missionary to the Japanese (see Chapter 5). In the summer of 1907, one of these Japanese converts to Orthodoxy was working in London. In a postscript to one of his letters to Archbishop Nicholas, Father Eugene noted, "During the summer our church was regularly attended by Titus Kanenari, a Japanese. . . . His zeal in attending the services can serve as an example to many Russians." In his reply the archbishop wrote, "Titus Kanenari, whom you so kindly mentioned in your letter, has been to see me, and gave me an excellent portrait of you, for which I thank you sincerely. Titus told me in most moving terms about the services in your church, of how you gave him the antidoron at the end of the Liturgy, and of all your kindness towards him. Please accept my sincere gratitude also for all of this." This was only two years after the Russo-Japanese War, yet it is apparent that unity in the Orthodox faith was of more concern than ethnic differences and past hostilities.

We have already mentioned that the chapel in Clarence House, which was set up for Maria Alexandrovna, wife of Prince Alfred, Duke of Edinburgh, was where Father Basil Popoff served as a priest before being appointed to the Embassy church on his father's death. Father Smirnoff reported that on April 13, 1879, at the request of the Grand Duchess, he performed the rite of blessing the chapel, which had just been reconstructed.[10] There is no evidence of a permanent priest being attached to this chapel after 1875, although in December 1879 Father Eugene Smirnoff wrote in a letter to the diocesan authorities in St Petersburg that "her Highness's church exists quite independently in London . . . and has its own separate clergy." Possibly the clergy referred to were psalm-readers only. In 1882 there was a reference to a reader attached to this church who married Emma Sanders, who had converted to the Orthodox faith. Otherwise, it must be assumed that Father Eugene served there occasionally and that the Grand Duchess attended services at the Embassy church. In 1901 Prince Alfred died, and Maria Alexandrovna went to live in Germany. The iconostasis was given to the Russian church in Darmstadt, which was then being built. However, the large icon of the Smolensk Mother of God with the gold riza, which had been presented to her by the peasants of the Smolensk province at the time of her marriage, was given to the London Embassy church, as was another large icon of the Myrrh-Bearing Women set in a marble frame. With assistance from the embassy, these icons were sent to Moscow for repair before being installed in places of honour in the church in Welbeck Street.

A few years after the departure of Maria Alexandrovna, another member of the Russian Imperial family took up residence in London. This was Marie Feodorovna, the Dowager Empress and consort of Alexander III, who died in 1894. Born Princess Dagmar of Denmark, she was the sister of Queen Alexandra of England, the consort of Edward VII. In childhood the sisters had been very close, and in widowhood the empress spent some of her time staying with her sister in London. In his service records, Father Eugene Smirnoff noted that on several occasions he was summoned to Buckingham Palace to perform religious ministrations. For example, on March 1, 1907, he recorded, "During the stay in London of Dowager Empress Marie Feodorovna, at her order, served, together with all the clergy, in Buckingham Palace, in the presence of the Dowager Empress and Queen Alexandra of England, a panikhida for the late Emperors Alexander II and Alexander III. Received personal expression of thanks from their Highnesses." The same is repeated under March 1, 1909, and that year the Dowager Empress attended the Paschal Matins and Liturgy at Welbeck Street. In 1910 Father Eugene was summoned to Buckingham Palace on three occasions with the other clergy: on May 25 to serve a moleben, on June 28 to serve a panikhida, and on July 22 to serve a moleben. That year Marie Feodorovna attended the Liturgy and Vespers of Pentecost in the Embassy church.

The Russian Embassy church also served the needs of other Orthodox Slavs in London. In 1898 Prince Nicholas of Montenegro attended the Liturgy and a moleben of thanksgiving; afterward he awarded the Montenegrin Order of Prince Daniel to Father Eugene and two readers, Nicolas Orloff and Constantine Veselovsky. In 1908 King Peter I of Serbia awarded Father Eugene the Order of St Savva in recognition of his help in conducting services and ministrations for the Serbian Embassy in London over the previous several years. At the time, the only other Orthodox Church in London was the Greek Church. The Greek community no longer needed recourse to the ministrations of the Russian Church, having had their own church in London since 1838. In 1879 it moved to new premises—the magnificent new Church of the Holy Wisdom (Aghia Sophia) in Moscow Road, Bayswater.

The Embassy church building underwent no substantial changes during Father Eugene Smirnoff's time in office, although he was constantly concerned with its good repair and adornment. Shortly after his arrival in 1877, he wrote to the ambassador with a list of necessary repairs: the church and narthex needed repainting, and the carpet needed cleaning, as did the chandelier, the chimneys, and the basement. A contemporary recalled that in Father Smirnoff's day the house was painted a sombre brown, which effectively concealed the delicate eighteenth-century ornamental plasterwork. In June 1886 the rector reported that substantial repairs to the building had been carried out, which had become essential as a result of London's terrible climate. The Ministry of Foreign Affairs of the Russian Empire expressed its appreciation for the fact that the repairs had been paid for out of current revenues and savings, without having to allocate funds specially for the purpose. In 1891 there was further mention of repairs performed by Fowler, the architect of the Portland Estate, which still owned the freehold of the property. In 1906 Father Smirnoff again wrote to the ambassador about the need for repairs to the house that had been built around 1770. By the late nineteenth century, it was suffering from crumbling foundations and other structural failings, which were evidently corrected.

In 1880 a new chandelier was donated for the church by a Syrian named Simeon Bustros. Ten years later, in 1890, a large mural was painted for the London church in Paris by V. V. Cheremetieff. Depicting St Paul's farewell to the presbyters of Ephesus, it was 7 feet wide and 6 feet high, set in a gold frame, and placed on the wall directly above the main entrance to the church.

Vestments, when required, were ordered from specialist suppliers in St Petersburg. Between 1900 and 1905 Father Eugene regularly corresponded with Ivan Alexeievitch Zheverzheff of 18 Troitskaya Ulitsa, St Petersburg, a vestment maker by appointment to the Imperial Court. In 1903 Zheverzheff quoted a price of 377 roubles for a set of priest's vestments in gold silk brocade, as used in the chapel of the Winter Palace, with a sample of the material enclosed. The entire set, including deacon's and readers' vestments as well as coverings for the altar table and other sanctuary coverings, would come to 1,935 roubles. The following year, he quoted 249 roubles to make sets of dark Lenten vestments out of velvet material to be supplied by Father Eugene for a priest, deacon, and two readers. It is interesting to note that most of this cost was attributable to the silver crosses, tassels, and other trimmings applied to the fabric, with only 14 roubles, 75 kopecks allowed for labor. The completed vestments were sent from St Petersburg to the embassy in the diplomatic bag; later, when the need arose, they were returned to St Petersburg by the same route for repair.

Contact with Orthodox in Other Countries

In 1908, Father Eugene Smirnoff wrote to an Anglican friend, "It is amazing how many letters I receive in my position. I correspond with people all over the world, and yet there never seems to be an end to them." In addition to his principal duties as rector of the London Embassy church and his dealings with the Anglicans, Father Eugene became involved in furthering the Orthodox Church's mission in various ways and in countries as far away as Spain and America.

Father Eugene became better known to the outside world, particularly in America, as a result of the publication of his book in 1903 titled *A Short Account of the Historical Development and Present Position of Russian Orthodox Missions*. In the preface, he explained the circumstances that led to its being written.

> During the nearly thirty-three years of my ministry in the Orthodox Churches abroad, of which I have passed twenty-six in the capacity of Superior of the Russian Church in London, representatives of both the Protestant and Roman Catholic Churches have constantly come to me with the most diverse questions respecting our Orthodox Eastern Church. As far as my knowledge and the time left free from my ministerial duties would allow, I have always endeavoured to give my questioners the fullest and most circumstantial replies.
>
> The questions proposed repeatedly referred to our missions. Moreover, I have noticed during the lengthy period of my life beyond the frontiers of Russia, that the substance of these questions has gradually taken a different form. At first I used to be asked: "Of course you have not yet any missions, any more than you had in former times?" Then: "Is it true that you have established some sort of mission in Japan?" Further on: "It seems that you have missions of some sort in Siberia?" Still further: "Could you not give us some sort of precise statistics as to the number of conversions in your missions?" And finally: "What is your opinion—would it not be better for us to close our mission in Japan, in order not to hinder the regular growth of your mission, especially as our Church aims at reunion with yours?" It is evident how the questions gradually took a different form in accordance with the spread of information concerning the working of our missions appearing on the pages of the periodical press. . . .[11]
>
> Just two years ago, a much-esteemed theological magazine, published in the United States of America, became interested in the subject of our missions, and the editor applied to the Chief Procurator of the Most Holy Synod, Mr. C. P. Pobedonostzeff, with the request to tell him of some person who could write a short article for his magazine in the English language. Mr. Pobedonostzeff was pleased to mention my name, and I gladly undertook the work proposed to me, but very soon became convinced that my task far exceeded the limits of a simple magazine article. However

much I endeavoured to shorten and condense my account, it grew of itself beyond the extent of an article, and became transformed into a separate little book. . . .[12]

The contents of my little work hardly require any explanation. At one time the enemies of Orthodoxy gave currency to the assertion that the Orthodox Eastern Church never had and has not now any missions, that she is in a state of stagnation and backwardness, and is therefore on the brink of destruction. The reader can judge for himself how far these assertions are just.[13]

In his short work of 83 pages, Father Eugene covered the history of Russia's missions, beginning with the colonist monks of ancient Russia and continuing to the establishment of the Orthodox Missionary Society by Metropolitan Innocent of Moscow (a former missionary in Alaska) in 1870. He also provided details and statistics regarding the contemporary missions in the territory of the Russian Empire as well as the four missions outside her boundaries—in China, North America, Korea, and Japan. The book was published by Rivingtons and sold for 3s. 6d. Contemporary reviews indicated that it was somewhat successful in accomplishing its declared aim—to dispel the myth that the Russian Church was moribund. It is interesting to note that the book was first published in English and only later, at the request of the procurator of the Holy Synod, translated and published in Russian at the expense of the Mouravieff Fund. In 1903 Father Eugene was asked to provide fifty copies of his book for the Universal Exhibition, to be held in 1904 in St Louis, Missouri. The following year he sent an additional fifty copies to Metropolitan Anthony of St Petersburg.

In 1896 Father Eugene published another book, which was his own translation of *The Rites for Uniting Those of Other Faiths to the Orthodox Church*. This was of particular value to several Orthodox royal houses in Europe because those of "other faiths" who were marrying into them generally had to accept the Orthodox faith. Queen Olga of Greece and her daughter, Princess Sophia, thanked him for presenting them with a copy, as did the newly crowned Emperor and Empress of Russia and the Dowager Empress Marie Feodorovna. In fact, Father Eugene helped Queen Olga of Greece by providing her with several English texts, including translations of the Liturgy and the Book of Needs (*Trebnik*) as well as a rare book titled *The Rites and Ceremonies of the Greek Church in Russia*. A letter of thanks was sent to him that read, "The Lord Himself has put this book into your hands at the very time when Her Highness, in her motherly concern, is acquainting Her Royal

Highness, the wife of the heir to the throne of Greece, with the rites of the Orthodox Church."

In the preface to this book, Father Eugene made clear his view of how Orthodoxy relates to other confessions: "[The Orthodox Church] . . . is the one true Church of Christ. . . . [T]hrough her, at some time or other, the whole of the West will, in the ecclesiastical sense of the word, be renovated." In the introduction he continued, "The Church of the West, for reasons which are well known, perverted the truth of the Church of Christ (by introducing the *Filioque* into the Symbol of Faith), and broke up the equilibrium of the Church's life as established from former times (by introducing into it the supremacy of the Pope), in consequence of which she arbitrarily, and therefore unlawfully, departed from the unity of the Church, and of her own accord placed herself outside the bounds of the one Church of Christ." He explained that the practice of the Russian Church is that Protestants are chrismated, while Roman Catholics are not, and continued, "The Russian Orthodox Church . . . has always, in the matter of the reconciliation of new members, assumed a less exacting and more indulgent attitude than the other Churches of the East." He said this was explained by the large number of Catholics and Protestants living in Russia, by contrast with other Orthodox countries. There were two translations of the services, published in 1858 and in 1866. It is interesting to note that the second one was a less demanding rite formulated specially for the reception of royal converts, specifically Mary Sophia Frederica Dagmar, Princess of Denmark, bride of the Tsarevitch, Grand Duke Alexander, which omitted a requirement for an explicit renunciation of previously held beliefs.

Assistance to Orthodox Missions in the Americas, India, and Spain

Before his ordination to the priesthood, Father Eugene had served as a church reader in New York for four years, and he maintained contact with the Orthodox Church in North America for most of his life. In 1896 Bishop Nicholas of Alaska established the missionary Brotherhood of the Nativity of the Most Holy Mother of God in New York, and he invited Father Eugene (whom he had met in London the previous year en route to America) to become an honorary member. The letter of invitation indicated that the brotherhood wished him to become a member "with a view to expressing the deepest respect for your most useful activities in furthering the cause of Orthodoxy in the midst of heterodoxy." In reply Father Eugene sent five copies of his book *The Rites for Uniting Those of Other Faiths to the Orthodox Church* and wrote, "The very fact that such a society has come into existence on the other side of the Atlantic, provides a proof of the fact that the work of Orthodoxy is beginning with God's help to obtain firm foundations in America, thanks to those who are working most zealously in its cause."

In 1908, Father Eugene received a letter from the Reverend Leonid Turkevitch[14] at the Russian Orthodox Theological Seminary at 1701 Fifth Street N.E., Minneapolis, Minnesota. He was seeking help in finding suitable textbooks for the seminary, then in its third year of existence, which held classes in English. He hoped Father Eugene would be able to help because he was faced with similar conditions, working in non-Orthodox surroundings where the main language was English. Father Eugene replied,

> I read your letter with great joy and I will attempt to fulfill your request with heartfelt readiness. I also once served in America and I have read not a little about the religious and church situation in the United States. I still continue to follow the successes of the Orthodox Church on the other side of the Atlantic with fervent interest. Her every victory in that country which is wild and alien to us in spirit gives me joy and fills me with prayerful compunction. For a long time I have been insisting on the necessity of forming in America an Orthodox clergy educated in full accord with the local conditions, in order to consolidate the successes of Orthodoxy for the future.

He concluded that he would be glad to help but would need some time to assemble a suitable collection of books and send them off.

Some years earlier, in 1890, Father Eugene had received a request to obtain information about pre-schism British Orthodox saints. He responded enthusiastically, if in his usual formal style,

> Further to the Imperial Embassy's request, I hasten to express my complete and heartfelt readiness to take on the task of gathering the information required by the Moscow Theological Society [*Mosckovskoye Obshchestvo Liubitelei Dukhovnogo Prosveshcheniya*] about the saints of the Orthodox Church who suffered and struggled to the glory of God in Britain during the first millennium A.D. As requested by the Society, I will attempt first of all to collect the information they need about the three saints they have mentioned: St Joseph of Arimathea, the Holy Apostle Simon the Zealot and the Holy Bishop Aristobulus. However, besides these saints, there were others in Britain during the first millennium; so the question arises

> as to whether the Moscow Society wishes me to gather information only about these saints, or whether it wishes me to gather information about other saints as well, and, if so, which ones?

In conclusion, Father Eugene asked the embassy to let him contact the society in Moscow directly to clear up these questions and, also, to provide him with whatever assistance he might need in consulting English specialists in the field. Unfortunately, the results of his investigations have not survived, although there is now extensive literature available about the Orthodox British saints.

A very different concern that claimed Father Eugene's attention was the situation of the Syro-Chaldean Church in India. In 1904 a member of this church was in London and approached Father Eugene to ask if the Syro-Chaldean Church could not be taken under the protection of the Russian Church. This was a matter that combined theological and ecclesiastical concerns. The Syro-Chaldeans were an ancient Monophysite group that had broken away from the Orthodox Church many centuries previously, but in the late nineteenth century the Russian Church had been actively helping to reunite some of these communities with Orthodoxy. However, the British government was constantly suspicious of Russian intentions toward India; clearly, "interference" in India by the Russian Church would be seen as a political ploy and would not be welcome. Father Eugene informed Metropolitan Anthony Vadkovsky of St Petersburg, who replied that it was not possible to send a bishop or priest to India at that time. He also noted that the Syro-Chaldean gentleman could not be ordained because he did not know the Orthodox typicon and that there were no suitable translations of the services that he could use. In a more constructive vein, he pointed out that there was an Orthodox Syro-Chaldean Church in Urmia (in Persia) with three bishops and many priests who were using Orthodox services translated into the ancient Syrian language. He suggested that the gentleman go and learn from them and that, in time, perhaps the Indian Church could be united with Orthodoxy through contact with the Church in Urmia. In conclusion, he pointed out that there was nothing to prevent him from being received into the Orthodox Church in London as an individual after proper instruction.

Perhaps one of the most surprising areas that Father Eugene Smirnoff was involved with was helping to establish an Orthodox mission in Spain. Because there was no Orthodox Church in Madrid, the secretary of the Russian Embassy there, George Kolmsin, turned to Father Eugene for spiritual guidance. Kolmsin visited Central America in the company of Spanish General Vincent Voi-Peres; while there, they both came into contact with Bishop Raphael of the Syrian Orthodox Church, who was apparently visiting the area for missionary purposes. This meeting made a strong impression on the general. After returning home, he arranged to be received into the Orthodox Church through chrismation at the Russian Church in Biarritz in April 1911.

Kolmsin and the general published a translation of the Orthodox Liturgy in Spanish and, in gratitude to Bishop Raphael, arranged for 500 copies to be sent to him in New York with the assistance of Father Smirnoff. In his cover letter, dated February 13/26, 1912, Father Eugene explained some of the circumstances to the bishop: "In the matter of his conversion to Orthodoxy and in the translation of the Liturgy the most enthusiastic part was taken by his close friend and spiritual guide, the Secretary of the Russian Imperial Mission in Madrid, George Alexandrovitch Kolmsin, a very religious and intelligent man, and my spiritual son. He has fully entrusted both himself and his disciple and godson, Vincent Voi-Peres, to my guidance. This circumstance explains my contact with him and with their work."

On May 17/30, 1912, Bishop Raphael replied[15] from the Syrian Greek-Orthodox Catholic Cathedral, 320 Pacific Street, Brooklyn, New York. He thanked Father Eugene for the promised 500 copies of the Liturgy of St John Chrysostom in Spanish, received the previous day from the Russian Cathedral in New York, which would be very useful in the Spanish-speaking countries of North and Central America. He went on to ask Smirnoff to "please inform that Apostle of Orthodoxy in the 20th Century in the heterodox west, General V. Voi-Peres, and the glorious warrior of Christ, G. A. Kolmsin, that I have written about this and about the conversion of the former to Orthodoxy through the latter, who is your spiritual son, in *Tserkovnie Vedomosti* and in my Arabic theological journal."

Apparently, General Voi-Peres was followed by some of his fellow countrymen who adopted the Orthodox faith. However, the movement was hampered by the lack of a church and a permanent priest, although the Russian priest from Biarritz visited whenever he could. In an attempt to alleviate their plight, Father Eugene appealed to Russian Foreign Minister Sazonoff, whom he had met during a visit to London. His letter, dated November 19, 1913, gives some insight into the difficulties of the Spanish mission and Father Eugene's attitude toward it:

Your Excellency,

Respected Sergei Dimitrievitch,

I will take advantage of your kind permission, which you gave me during your last stay in London, to submit a humble request to you. It does not concern me personally or my family, or even the church in London, but rather the question of Orthodoxy in Spain. In Madrid, through the efforts of G. A. Kolmsin, a small Orthodox community has been formed, which has every promise of further development. Nor is there any doubt that a movement favourable to orthodoxy is developing among the Catholics. This community and this movement should be supported and encouraged. At the present time, it is greatly to be regretted that they are deprived of direct and constant contact with the Orthodox Church. Furthermore, the Spaniards who have been received into the bosom of Orthodoxy are now like sheep who do not know, or simply do not have, their own shepherd. Sometimes the archpriest of the church in Biarritz, Nikolai Vasilievitch Popoff, visits them occasionally to minister to their religious needs, as his church is the nearest one to them. These journeys always entail expenditures which Father Popoff is absolutely unable to meet, and it would be quite wrong to impose this financial burden on the one priest who has expressed his complete readiness to concern himself with the spiritual and religious well-being of the Spaniards.

Much the best thing would be to restore the Embassy church which used to exist in Madrid in the 1860s and was later closed simply because there was not one Orthodox person working at the diplomatic mission there. At the end of 1875, the furnishings of the Madrid church were transferred to the church in Brussels, but only on condition that the Ministry of Foreign Affairs retained the right to obtain a special credit towards the cost of reestablishing a church at the Madrid Embassy if this should prove necessary. Of course, I quite understand that it will not be easy to bring this idea to fruition and that at best any action could well be delayed for a long time.

In order to resolve this problem, it would be highly desirable to dispatch a scholarly priest-monk to Madrid for a period of several months, from November to May, to attend to services and ministrations. This would entail a significant amount of expenditure, but then in our mercenary age there is absolutely nothing at all which can be accomplished without money.

If it proves impossible to arrange for this, would it not be possible to request 700 roubles a year from the Holy Synod to enable the archpriest and the psalm-reader of the church in Biarritz to go to Madrid twice a year, stay there for a whole week, and during that time conduct services and ministrations for the community there?

Of course, it is quite possible that even this plan would encounter obstacles. If so, things could be arranged even more simply on a temporary basis. You are, respected Sergei Dimitrievitch, aware that every two weeks a courier travels from Paris to Madrid and Lisbon, and he has to stay in Madrid for about a week on the return journey. The people sent from Paris as couriers on these journeys are usually minor officials or psalm-readers. Would it not be possible to send the archpriest of the Biarritz church as a courier instead of them twice a year, at the end of November and the beginning of May? While staying the week in Madrid, he could attend to ministrations and conduct services for the members of our Spanish Orthodox community. This is the most inoffensive plan, it would not burden anyone with expenses or cause anyone to incur financial loss, but it would make it possible, at least to a limited extent, to satisfy the religious needs of the Orthodox Spaniards in a correct and regular manner.

The Orthodox community in Spain came into existence in part through my own initial directions. This is why I am keenly interested in its fate, and why it is to me that they pour out all their joys and hopes, as well as their troubles and woes. I would like to help them with my whole soul and heart.

A few days ago, I received a letter from the archpriest of the church in Biarritz, Father Nikolai Vasilievitch Popoff. He is, in all respects, a fine and good shepherd, prepared to devote his strength and abilities to serving the Orthodox Spaniards, but he has absolutely no funds to travel twice a year to Madrid. He did not ask me, but rather begged me, as a fellow pastor of the Orthodox Church, to say a good word on his behalf to the Ambassador in Paris, so that he might be allowed to travel twice a year as courier to Madrid and Lisbon—at the end of November and the beginning of May, which are the times he is most free of his direct responsibilities. Unfortunately, I cannot bring myself to trouble the Ambassador in Paris about this matter, since he hardly knows me at all. It is this fact that gives me the boldness to appeal to you, respected Sergei Dimitrievitch. The situation will be quite different if you, your Excellency, would be so good as to put in a good word in favour of Father Popoff. I ask and beg you not to refuse me this request. May the Lord bless and keep you.

The records that have survived do not throw any light on the subsequent fate of this mission or whether Father Eugene's heartfelt petition met with a sympathetic response from Sazonoff. However, because his letter was dated less than a year before the outbreak of World War I, it seems likely that whatever initiatives were being considered would have succumbed to more pressing wartime priorities.

Contact with Anglicans

As rector of the London Embassy church, Father Eugene Smirnoff continued to be responsible, as his predecessor had been, for relations with the Church of England since hopes of eventual Anglo-Orthodox union had not entirely disappeared.

The history of Anglican relations with the Russian Church during this period cannot be considered without reference to William Birkbeck. He was an Anglican who travelled extensively in Russia, learned both Russian and Church Slavonic, and wrote extensively about the Orthodox Church, yet remained convinced of the Anglican "branch theory" developed a generation earlier by Neale and others. Nevertheless, Birkbeck's writings show great warmth and understanding of many aspects of the Russian Church.

Although Birkbeck's published works deal primarily with his visits to Russia and make little reference to the Russian Church in London, there are indications from his correspondence that he was in regular contact with Father Eugene Smirnoff throughout the latter part of his life. The author of Father Eugene's obituary in *The Christian East* notes, "The Very Rev. E. Smirnoff was a life-long friend of the late Mr. W. J. Birkbeck, who 'at his feet' received his knowledge of Russia and the Orthodox Church."

A relative of Birkbeck's, Sir Samuel Hoare, gave the following character sketch:

> I had in William John Birkbeck a friend and cousin who was as well qualified to advise me upon Russia and Russian affairs as any Englishman. Johnny Birkbeck, as everyone called him, was the representative of a family that has for generations been connected with banking and good works in East Anglia. Being a man of means, he had bought himself a considerable property near Norwich where he lived the life of a country gentleman. A historian by instinct rather than by training, a theologian possessing qualities that are rarely found in Englishmen, and an almost passionate enthusiast of everything Russian and Orthodox, he had equipped himself with a comprehensive knowledge of literary Russian, had made many

> visits to Russia, and numbered amongst his closest friends some of the most influential leaders in the Russian Church and State. Apart from the fact that we were cousins and neighbours, English Church politics had brought us together and many had been the efforts we had made in past years for Church Schools and the Anglo-Catholic cause. Of all my friends, none had a more curious fund of rare knowledge than this country squire, Quaker by origin, theologian by self-imposed study, who lived for the most part in Norfolk amidst pheasants and Russian icons, immigrant woodcocks and equally immigrant foreigners.

Birkbeck's first extended visit to Russia was in 1888 on the occasion of the 900th anniversary of the Baptism of Russia. His mission was to deliver the Archbishop of Canterbury's letter of greeting to the Metropolitan of Kiev. He described the festivities in glowing terms in a series of letters published in *The Guardian*. The following is a brief extract:

> Words cannot describe the beauty of the scene—the officiant surrounded by the other clergy, amidst numerous burning tapers and clouds of fragrant incense, raising the Cross on high, and blessing the people at each of these stations, and the choir meanwhile chanting various anthems and psalms and the Kyrie Eleison; while below, lit up by the rays of the setting sun, were all the gold and coloured domes of the other churches of the city, and the broad stream of the Dnieper winding its way for miles over the plain; and in the streets and windows of the houses near the church were to be seen dense crowds of worshippers, who testified to their devotion by repeatedly bowing and crossing themselves, and, when near enough, joining in the singing of the choir. . . . Many of these pilgrims had come from Siberia, and even from the shores of the Pacific, the whole way on foot, to pass a fortnight at this great centre of Russian Christianity, and when one comes to consider that it is quite a common thing for there to be 200,000 pilgrims in the year at this monastery alone, one begins to have some faint notion of the hold which the Orthodox Church has upon the Russian people.

It was in Kiev that Birkbeck first met Constantine Pobedonostseff, the procurator of the Holy Synod—an acquaintanceship that developed into a long and close friendship. Pobedonostseff and Metropolitan Platon of Kiev had both been impressed that the Church of England was the only Western church to have sent greetings to the Russian Church on the occasion of this great festival, at a time when Anglo-Russian relations were still strained (this was only ten years after the Treaty of San Stefano) and even some members of Orthodox Churches had declined to attend the festivities for political reasons. Eventually the metropolitan wrote a lengthy reply to the Archbishop of Canterbury; this gave the impetus to a new series of friendly contacts between the Anglican and Russian Orthodox Churches. Father Eugene Smirnoff delivered Metropolitan Platon's reply in London. It is possible that through this connection, Birkbeck first came into contact with Father Eugene. Athelstan Riley, Birkbeck's biographer, continued the story:

> After the visit to Kiev, Birkbeck took up the study of Russia and the Russian Church which was to remain his absorbing interest to the end. He now set to work to learn Russian and Slavonic—the old ecclesiastical language—and every year saw him in some part of the Russian Empire. In 1889, we were in Petrograd together and paid an interesting visit to Great Novgorod. By that time, he could carry on a conversation in Russian fairly well. The same year he travelled extensively in the Diocese of Archangel, in the far north of Russia, and later published a detailed account of his visit. He spoke extensively on the Orthodox Church in Anglican circles, with a view to eradicating misunderstandings and conveying something of his knowledge and enthusiasm.[16] In 1896, it was proposed to send Mandell Creighton, Bishop of Peterborough, to Russia to be present at the Emperor's coronation, and Birkbeck was the obvious choice to be his guide and assistant during the visit. Pobedonostseff ensured that they both had good places in the cathedral in the Moscow Kremlin to see the ceremony, and on their return, the bishop's descriptions so moved Queen Victoria that she wrote to him "How the Queen wishes she could have seen it!"

The following year, 1897, Archbishop William Maclagan of York resolved to visit Russia. This time it went without saying that Birkbeck would make the arrangements and act as his guide. This was a much more extensive and eventful visit. It was timed to coincide with the end of Lent, Holy Week, and Pascha. Birkbeck's detailed descriptions of the Orthodox Holy Week and Paschal services are both instructive and moving. On the day they arrived in St Petersburg, a long article was published in the Russian press, written by Father Eugene Smirnoff, to introduce the visitors to the Russian public. He began by pointing out the factors that had recently stimulated interest in Orthodoxy among Anglicans:

> The hearty reception afforded in St Petersburg last year to Bishop Wilkinson, the attendance of Bishop Nicholas of Alaska and the Aleutian Islands in St Paul's Cathedral in London in a stall during evensong, and his prayer pronounced there "for the peace of all the world, for the welfare of the holy Churches of God and for the union of all," and the presence of a representative of the English Church, in the person of the Bishop of Peterborough, Dr. Mandell Creighton (who has since been raised to the see of London), at Moscow for the solemnities of the Coronation, have aroused and strengthened to a remarkable degree the interest taken by English Churchmen in the Orthodox Church of Russia.

He went on to mention recent papal pronouncements that served to increase the Anglicans' hostility toward Rome and draw them closer to the Orthodox Church. Giving a brief biography of Archbishop Maclagan, Smirnoff wrote,

> [He] has now in the eventide of his life resolved personally to visit the land of Orthodoxy, and to experience for himself the impressions which the majesty and sanctity of the Orthodox Church will produce upon him. We cordially welcome this his good intention, and with all our hearts pray to God that He Himself, the Lord Almighty, may so direct his footsteps on our soil, that out of this small seed, as from the grain of mustard seed, a great tree may in due season spring up. . . .

Writing of Archbishop Maclagan's preaching abilities, Father Eugene referred to two occasions when he personally heard the archbishop speak at the opening of the Church Congress: at Cardiff in 1889 and at Norwich in 1895. In conclusion, he observed, "Mr. Birkbeck is accompanying him on his journey, and by reason of his knowledge of our Church and of our holy places the Archbishop could not have provided himself with a better guide. This is the tenth time Mr. Birkbeck journeys to Russia. . . ."

There were small Anglican churches in both St Petersburg and Moscow, and the Archbishop of York celebrated early services in them on most days before going on to attend the solemn festive services in the various cathedrals and monasteries of the Russian capitals. The archbishop was warmly received both in the churches and on other visits. Of particular interest was his hour-long meeting with the holy Father John of Kronstadt, who went to see the archbishop in his hotel in St Petersburg.[17]

On arrival in Moscow, the archbishop and Birkbeck were met by Father Triphon, an old London acquaintance of Birkbeck's:

> On the platform, we were met by Prince Shirinski-Shikhmatoff, Procurator of the Moscow Department of the Holy Synod, and by my old friend Father Triphon (Prince Turkestanoff), the brother-in-law of General Boutourline, who was formerly Military Attaché at the Russian Embassy in London, and has so many friends in England. Father Triphon is now a monk in priest's orders at the great Donskoi Monastery, where he has charge of an excellent school for the sons of the clergy, conducted on semi-monastic principles, somewhat analogous to our own older collegiate foundations. The Metropolitan of Moscow had placed him in attendance upon the Archbishop during his stay in Moscow, and nothing could have exceeded his kindness to us throughout our whole visit. . . . [Metropolitan Sergius of Moscow] belonging, as is well known in Russia, to the older school of Russian theologians, and deeply imbued with the traditions of the great Philaret of Moscow, of whom he was one of the most distinguished pupils, he makes no secret of his uncompromising attitude towards all Western confessions of faith. . . . And yet I have never heard of anyone coming away from one of these discussions with any feeling of irritation or resentment. His words, even when one has least agreed with them, are always well worth remembering, and leave behind them a no less pleasant impression that the gentle and kindly smile with which they are accompanied.

The archbishop and Birkbeck were greeted warmly wherever they went. On their return journey, Bishop Nicanor of Smolensk met their train at two o'clock in the morning when it stopped in Smolensk to present the archbishop with gifts, including an Orthodox episcopal omophorion, as a token of the day when union might become possible between the Anglicans and Orthodox. The friendly reception was, of course, encouraged, if not orchestrated, by Pobedonostseff, the procurator of the Holy Synod, who was committed to a policy of good relations with the Anglicans. To a certain extent, the continuing policy of cultivating an ally against the common foe of Roman Catholicism remained and, to some extent, there were still genuine hopes that ecclesiastical union might be possible. Nevertheless, a realistic understanding of the vast changes required in the Church of England before this could become a reality meant that the friendly overtures rarely went far beyond vague expressions of goodwill. In the words of Pobedonostseff's biographer, "only the golden glow remained after these visits."

While in St Petersburg, Birkbeck and the archbishop spent some hours with Archbishop Anthony Vadkovsky of Finland, whom Birkbeck described as "one of the most able Bishops and theologians of the Russian Church, who, although he is still a comparatively young man, little over fifty years of age, has already been for many years a Bishop and is a member of the Holy Synod." In fact, this was not Birkbeck's first meeting with Archbishop Anthony. In an unpublished letter written from Russia on January 8/20, 1896, he wrote, "I went to see Bishop Antonius of Finland today, he was so particularly nice, and said that he was sure more Russian bishops ought to go to England." This wish was fulfilled the following year when he was appointed to represent both the Russian Church and the Russian Empire at Queen Victoria's Diamond Jubilee.

Both the emperor in person and Pobedonostseff asked Birkbeck to look after Archbishop Anthony during his visit to England. However, when Father Eugene Smirnoff learned of the upcoming visit, he felt that he should act as host to the visiting hierarch; this thought caused Birkbeck some consternation. He felt that Smirnoff lacked the refinement necessary for the job. According to Birkbeck, Smirnoff could speak only rough and bad English and would not take the trouble to become acquainted with "the usual conventionalities of English society . . . how is one to go to see the Queen, the other royalties etc?" In another letter to Prince Galitzine, who was in charge of arrangements for the visit from the Russian side, Birkbeck noted in parentheses, "His book, although he never acknowledges it, he wrote in Russian and got *me* to translate!" Nevertheless, in a letter of a similar vein to Pobedonostseff written at about the same time, he wrote,

> I don't wish to injure him in your eyes; he is, as you know, a friend of mine, and I know his good qualities and value them. Indeed, I hate writing you this letter more than I hated writing the last on the same subject: but after what you said to me in your letter this morning, I should be abusing the confidence which I believe you have always placed in me, and your friendship which I value so dearly, if I were not to write quite plainly.

In any event, it seems, at least from published accounts, that Birkbeck's fears were groundless. The visit appeared to have gone quite smoothly. Of course, Archbishop Anthony was just one of many visitors from foreign lands who came to honour the Diamond Jubilee of the queen-empress. The country was seized with intense patriotic fervor, renewed devotion to the aged queen who had spent so many years of widowhood in near seclusion, and great pride in the achievements of the British empire. This pride became more concrete in the popular imagination as the capital filled with exotically dressed potentates from remote colonies who had come to pay tribute to the venerable empress. Such was the prevailing atmosphere when the archbishop arrived in Dover on the morning of June 17, 1897. Following is an extract from a detailed account of the visit that appeared in *The Guardian*:

> The Archbishop of Finland and Viborg, accompanied by General A.A. Kireeff, Mr. Yury Sabler, and the rest of his suite, arrived at Dover of Thursday morning, 17 June, by the Ostende boat, on his way to London to attend the commemoration of her Majesty's reign of sixty years. He was met on the pier by the Very Rev. E. Smirnoff, Chaplain to the Russian Embassy, and by Mr. W. J. Birkbeck. As this was his Grace's first visit to Great Britain several of the local clergy and others from Folkestone assembled on the Admiralty pier to greet him, amongst them being the Revs. E. G. L. Mowbray, Vicar of St Bartholomew's, Dover, T. Evans, S. F. Green, and Canon Woodward (Folkestone). The reception had to be very hastily arranged, and some who had promised to come did not do so, owing to a mistake as to the arrival of the boat. The following Address was presented to the archbishop by Mr. Mowbray:
>
> "We, representing the clergy of Dover and Folkestone, in the diocese and province of Canterbury, offer to you, Most Reverend Father in God, by Divine Providence Archbishop of Finland, greeting in the Lord.
>
> Intelligence having reached us of your gracious visit to this country on the occasion of the celebration of the sixtieth year of the reign of our most gracious Queen Victoria, and the gathering together at Lambeth of our holy fathers of the Anglican Communion, we seize the opportunity of your Grace's first landing on our shores to express to your Grace, and through your Grace to all the Holy Russian Church, our most sincere goodwill and sympathy, and we recall with gratitude and pleasure the tokens of goodwill and kindly feeling which have lately passed from time to time between our respective branches of the Holy Catholic Church, especially as shown on the occasion of the visits of his Grace the Archbishop of York and the Right Rev. Bishop of London to your Grace's country, and we pray Almighty God that your Grace's visit may tend to strengthen the hands of those, both in your Grace's country and ours, who heartily desire and endeavour to keep the unity of the Spirit in the bond of peace.
>
> "We ever remain your Grace's most faithful and devoted servants in our Lord and Saviour Jesus Christ."

The Address was read to the Archbishop in English, and translated by his chaplain, through whom he suitably replied. He shortly after proceeded to London.

News of the Archbishop's coming only reached London some twenty-four hours beforehand, so that very little time was given for making proper arrangements for receiving him with something of that cordiality which was afforded to the Archbishop of York by the Russian clergy and laity in all the towns which he recently visited in Russia. Thus it was a very impromptu gathering which assembled on one of the platforms of Victoria Station to welcome his Grace. It was, however, a very striking scene as the train drew up alongside the platform, which, at that part, was crowded with some hundreds of clergy, sisters of mercy, and laity. On stepping out of the carriage, the Archbishop, who was dressed in a black episcopal cassock with tall monastic black cowl, with his jewelled panagia and cross on his breast, was received by the Bishop of Grahamstown, the Archdeacons of London and Middlesex, the Duke of Newcastle, Lord E. Churchill, Sir Theodore Hope, Mr. Athelstan Riley, Colonel Hardy, Prebendary Montagu Villiers, the Rev. J. Storrs, and others, Professor Bevan and the Rev. L. J. Percival attending as the Bishop of London's chaplains. Several Russians were also present, including Prince Andronikoff, Professor N. Orloff, and others.

As soon as the Archbishop appeared on the platform, a small choir of boys and men from Holy Trinity, Sloane Street, sang *Is polla eti, despota.*

As the words were sung, the Archbishop, extending his hand to be kissed on every side, made his way through the kneeling crowd to the royal reception-room of the station, accompanied by his suite and Mr. Birkbeck. Here a pause was made while Colonel Welby, of the Scots Greys (the Tsar's own regiment), who was present in an official capacity at the Tsar's Coronation, read an address. . . .

In reply, his Grace spoke a few words in Russian expressive of his delight at the Christian love and kindness which had prompted them to welcome him, a stranger and a foreigner, coming in obedience to a royal command to a country unknown to him before, at the very moment of his entrance into this great city. His prayer would ever be for the glory and well-being of her Gracious Majesty the Queen, and for the closer intercourse and union of the Churches.

Thereupon the Archbishop and his party stepped into the carriages which were in waiting, and, amidst loud cheers from the crowd that filled the approach to the station, drove off to Fulham Palace, where an episcopal welcome was awaiting him.

In the afternoon the Archbishop attended a garden-party at the Palace, at which many of the Colonial Bishops were presented to him.

On Friday a reception was offered to the Archbishop at the Chapel of the Russian Embassy, Madame de Stael, wife of the Russian Ambassador, and all the members of the Embassy being present. The Archbishop was received by the Chaplain to the Embassy, the Very Rev. Eugene Smirnoff, who delivered the following address:

"My Lord Archbishop, Most Reverend Father in God,

"With peace and love we welcome your arrival in this country, and your entrance into our house of prayer.

"You have come here to bring a greeting from the Orthodox Russian Church to the Sovereign Mother of this land, her most gracious Majesty Queen Victoria, on the occasion of the completion of the sixtieth year of her reign.

"But you have come to this country as the messenger of peace and love in a still wider sense. You bring a greeting from the Orthodox Church to the Anglican Church, which a year ago honoured the coronation of our autocratic Tzar by sending her Bishop to our ancient capital. Greeting for greeting, peace and love in answer to peace and love.

"Our little church, founded in 1716 by the loving care of the great reformer (Peter the Great) of the Russian land, was raised by the thought and blessing of the ever-to-be remembered Arsenius, Archbishop of Thebes, and Exarch of Paranie, with a view to bringing the Churches nearer to each other and uniting them. The fate of nations and Churches is accomplished by extraordinarily slow means. It is only in the eyes of God that 1,000 years are as a day. It is not so with us. Nearly two centuries have elapsed since the foundation of this holy house of prayer, and it is only now that the first steps have been taken towards bringing men nearer to each other in Church matters. The former enmity is faded away and dying, and in its place peace and love are appearing; you gracious Prelate and Father in God, come from holy Russia as their messenger.

"One of the occasions for this advance was afforded by the venerable crowned Mother of this land, who during her life has gone through many trials, sent down to her from above, and who at the sorrowful news of the blessed end of our Tsar-peacemaker (Alexander III) raised to the Most High her prayers for the repose of his soul in the words and chants of our church.[18] The death of the Peacemaker breathed new life into the hearts of believers, and predisposed them to this work of peace abounding in love. . . .

"But twofold glory and unceasing honour to the Great Source of peace and love, the King of kings and Lord of lords. Unto Him be glory, honour and worship unto ages if ages. Amen."

The Archbishop briefly replied, and a short service followed, concluded by the usual "desire for many years"[19] for the Imperial Family of Russia, the Holy Synod of Russia, including the Archbishop as a member of Synod, and Queen Victoria, and all the Royal Family.

Over the next few days, Archbishop Anthony visited the Russian ambassador, Birkbeck, and the Archbishop of Canterbury, as well as Oxford and Cambridge Universities, the House of Lords, and St Paul's Cathedral. On June 23, 1897, he was present at the brief service held outside St Paul's Cathedral to give thanks for the sixtieth year of Queen Victoria's reign. Perhaps the most striking event during his stay in England was his visit to the Anglican parish church of St Barnabas's, Pimlico. He was subsequently criticised in Russia for appearing to participate in an Anglican service. However, it is reasonably clear that he did no more than bestow his archpastoral blessing on the congregation. The article in *The Guardian* recounted the event this way:

In the evening (of 19th June) he went to St Barnabas's, Pimlico. The vicar (the Rev. A. Gurney), surrounded by the clergy and choir, received him in the south porch, where the choir sang in Slavonic the *Dostoino jestj* from the Liturgy of St Chrysostom, which is always sung when an Eastern Bishop arrives in a church.

After being censed by the Vicar he gave his blessing to the choir, who greeted him with *Is polla eti, despota.* The procession then entered the church, his Grace following the Vicar, preceded by cross and candle bearers and blessing the congregation on each side as he proceeded up the nave. When he arrived at the chancel he turned to the congregation and blessed them in the usual Eastern fashion, towards the west, the south and the north. He then sat in a place prepared for him on the north side of the sanctuary, the choir again singing the salutation before mentioned. After the censing of the altar at the Magnificat the Vicar censed his Grace, who gave him the usual blessing. At the conclusion of the service the Archbishop gave the blessing to the whole congregation. He afterwards had supper with Mr. Gurney, who had invited the other clergy of the parish and Lord and Lady Halifax to meet his Grace.

The following year (1898) Archbishop Anthony was appointed Metropolitan of St Petersburg and so became the de facto primate of the Russian Orthodox Church under the Synodal system of administration. He had an ongoing interest in the Old Catholic and Anglican Churches and hoped that both could eventually be reconciled with Orthodoxy. He died in 1912 at the relatively young age of sixty-six and was greatly mourned by the entire hierarchy of the Russian Orthodox Church.

World War I

The outbreak of war in 1914 brought turmoil to every aspect of life throughout Europe. The Russian Embassy church in Welbeck Street was no exception. Now nearly seventy years old, Father Eugene Smirnoff found himself faced with new responsibilities in circles that were very different from his habitual surroundings of ambassadors, nobility, and ecclesiastical prelates. As had been the case with his predecessor, Father Eugene Popoff during the Crimean War, Father Eugene Smirnoff had to attend to the needs both of soldiers fighting on the Allied side and others taken prisoner who had been fighting for the Austro-Hungarian Empire. Initially he did his best to help these people in addition to performing his other duties. However, by 1916 he began to feel overwhelmed and appealed for help. He wrote the following letter to the Metropolitan Vladimir of St Petersburg describing the wartime situation vividly:

> Your Eminence,
>
> Since October 1914, Canadian regiments have been arriving in England, including some soldiers within their ranks who are Russians, who emigrated to Canada to find work. They numbered 28 in one regiment, 26 in another, 14 in a third, and so on. Their regiments were housed in camps to undergo their final training to be ready for combat. Beginning last February (1915) they began to be sent off to the front lines in Belgium and France. While some soldiers were still leaving, others were already returning wounded from the Continent. They were accommodated in hospitals, both government-run and private, situated throughout the kingdom of England. The Russians among the wounded were scattered by ones and twos in different hospitals in London, Cambridge, Liverpool, Dundee, Kent, Shorncliffe and on estates such as Woburn, Bartley etc. When they recovered, some of the wounded were sent back to their units and then back to the front, while others, completely unfit for military duties, were sent back to Canada, and a third group, also determined

to be unfit for active service, was left in England and assigned to work in munitions factories.

From the time they arrived from Canada until the present, our church has served the religious needs of all these Russian soldiers. When on leave, they would come to London, attend our services, and go to confession and receive Holy Communion, both before setting off for the front, and when they were here recovering from their wounds. I also had to visit many of them in hospitals. Besides this, when I visited the wounded in hospitals and convalescent camps, they constantly sought consolation, encouragement and assurance of all kinds from me. Every day I have had to write letters for them, send them Gospels and Prayer Books, spiritual literature and Russian newspapers, as well as sending them warm clothing and tobacco, looking after their financial affairs and communicating with their relatives in Russia.

Until now, thanks and glory be to God, I have so far managed to deal with all this by myself (or more precisely, together with my wife). However now it is beginning to be more than I can manage by myself, and I urgently need an assistant in the person of another priest.

Recently, new regiments have arrived in England from Canada, in which there are more than 160 Russian soldiers. An Anglican military chaplain, also from Canada, approached me to ask whether it would be possible to arrange Sunday church services for these men in the camps where they are billeted. "There are many reasons" he said "why it is not feasible to let these soldiers go to London to attend your church: they do not know the country at all, they do not have a good command of English, they could fall into all kinds of temptations among all the people there are in London, and so on."

"Permit me" I replied "to report this matter to my ecclesiastical superiors, and ask them on your behalf to send here a monastic priest, who would be able to serve the religious needs of the Russian soldiers."

"I will think about that" he replied. "I cannot give you this authorization. But in a few days the chief military chaplain will arrive here from Canada. I will talk to him about it and let you know what he says. Shouldn't we try to get an Orthodox priest from Canada?"

"I don't advise you to expect that" I replied. "In Canada there are relatively few Russian priests, and they are all dedicated to work from which it would be difficult to take them away."

"What we need" he said "Is a young man in good health, who could be sent round from one camp to another, who could adapt to the military situation, and who would get on with what needs doing."

I have not yet had any reply from this chaplain.

However, I have quite unexpectedly received a request of a similar nature from another direction.

Many prisoners of war are currently being brought to England from the Mediterranean front and most of them have been interned in special camps on the Isle of Man, which is in the northern part of the Irish Sea. The journey there from London is a long one—200 miles by train to Liverpool, then 75 miles by boat to the port of Douglas. Among the prisoners on this island there are more than 150 Ruthenes and Romanians, who consider themselves Orthodox.[20] They asked the Governor of the island to find them a priest who could conduct a service for them on the day of Pascha. The Governor then appealed to the Anglican Bishop Herbert, Bishop for North and Central Europe, and he in turn relayed this request to me.

I fully appreciate that it will be far from easy to find a solution to these last two matters, and may in fact be quite complex. However, one thing is absolutely clear, which is that a young priest-monk in good health should be sent to England as soon as possible, so that he could serve the religious needs of all these Russians who have been assembled in England—both the soldiers from Canada and the Ruthenian[21] and Romanian prisoners of war from the Mediterranean ports. He would have to be provided with an antimension,[22] a small moveable church and all the equipment needed for conducting Church Services. This is not all. He would also have to be provided with a reader who could accompany him everywhere on his journeys and help him with both the church services and in all other respects. The duties of church reader could be assumed by Father Paul Adamantoff, the deacon from Wiesbaden, who has come to England for the duration of the war, and otherwise has nothing to do. This would be most desirable in that Adamantoff, who has been living near London during the war, has already managed to learn some English. This is something that should be given serious consideration. A priest-monk sent here, and relying on the help of Adamantoff, would not be thrown as it were into a forest.

The most difficult aspect of all this will be material support. Funding will be needed for:

1. The costs of the priest-monk's journey to London
2. Living expenses for the same priest-monk in London
3. Support for Deacon Adamantoff, who receives the extremely limited stipend of the Wiesbaden church reader, as a result of which

he cannot live in London, but has found shelter together with his wife and infant daughter on a farm in the country, which would be completely impractical if he were to become involved in this very responsible work.

4. Travelling and other costs for both of them to enable them to attend to the need for conducting Church services in various parts of England.

I am daring to hope that all the costs under item 4 above should be borne by those English institutions which will benefit from the ecclesiastical ministrations to be performed by these clergymen.

In submitting the aforementioned matter to you Eminence's pastoral discernment, I am personally convinced that a positive resolution/decision is the only one possible.

Humbly asking your Eminence's Archpastoral Blessing,
I have the honour to remain your Eminence's obedient servant,
Archpriest Eugene Smirnoff.
London 3/16 March 1916.

We have no record of any reply to this letter. By 1916 Russia was showing signs of great strain from the war effort, so it is possible that the post did not get through or that the Synod was simply in no position to find help. There is certainly no indication of any new clergymen coming to England at that time. Evidently, Father Eugene attempted to handle the situation himself as best he could.

Despite these problems, Father Eugene was able to obtain help from William Birkbeck, who made his last visit to Russia in 1916. An account is preserved in the archives at Lambeth Palace:

> [Birkbeck] told us how he visited the Troitza Monastery[23] and went to buy crosses and little sacred medals at the little shops and booths there, to bring back to the Embassy priest in London, Mr. Smirnoff, to give to the Russian Canadian soldiers who go to the Embassy Chapel to make their communion before leaving for the front. Turning to the peasants who clustered around him, he told them about this and said these Canadians were under our King, but had kept to the Orthodox faith; then he told the peasants to help him choose them, and they all went into the church with him, while the priest said some prayers, all the peasants

joining in the devotions, and the crosses and medals were blest on the relics of St Sergius.

Despite the difficulties of travelling during wartime, the congregation at Welbeck Street was considerably enlarged due to military personnel. As Easter approached in 1916, Father Eugene became extremely anxious about possible overcrowding at the Easter night service, and he wrote to the Russian ambassador asking permission to change arrangements for this service. He vividly described the anticipated overcrowding and possible dangers it could cause:

> To the Imperial Russian Embassy in London
>
> I urgently and insistently request the Imperial Embassy to resolve the situation in which the Embassy Church, which is entrusted to my care, may find itself on the approaching day of Holy Pascha.
>
> In normal times the congregation at the Easter night service would number about 120 to 130 people, and even then the church and the narrow corridor leading to it would be so congested, that many people have become faint for lack of air.
>
> Now it appears that in addition to this extreme number of people, which is the most that can possibly be accommodated in the Embassy Church, we can expect some 80 soldiers and 50 servicemen from India House. I learned of this only yesterday from Lieutenant-General N. S. Ermoloff and the General Counselor of the Embassy, K. D. Nabokoff, and they also expressed their view that we should be expecting closer to 400 people in the congregation rather than 300.
>
> I strongly urge the Imperial Embassy to take all possible steps to avert an experiment of this nature. Such experiments can never be conducted without giving rise to terrible disasters. You cannot cram three or four hundred people into an area designed for just one hundred without the most terrible consequences.
>
> I am particularly concerned about this because during Easter Matins the congregation usually holds lighted candles in their hands. God forbid that due to overcrowding or lack of air there should be an accident involving fire. Then the Embassy Church will turn into a fire trap with no way out.
>
> The only possible way I can see to avert an experiment of this sort would be as follows: immediately to cancel the Easter Night Service, and instead to celebrate the Liturgy alone at the usual time of 11 o'clock in the morning.

This approach will eliminate the lighting of candles, and make it possible to regulate the admission of people to the congregation with the benefit of daylight rather then in the semi-darkness of night.

The replacement of one service by another could be announced at the earlier services as well as in the newspapers.

I consider it my duty to add that, as rector of the Embassy Church entrusted to me, and foreseeing the disaster that could happen on the night of Easter, I personally cannot take responsibility for it.

I respectfully request that you give me, if at all possible, an immediate answer, so that I can make an announcement after the evening service, which will take place between two and three o'clock this afternoon.

London
8/21 April 1916.

Again, we have no record of the ambassador's reply, but it can be assumed that in this case he would have agreed with Father Eugene's proposal. Sad though it would seem to hold the Easter service in the late morning instead of at night, this is not contrary to the typicon of Orthodox Church services. Although Father Eugene described conditions in rather lurid tones, the dangers of overcrowding were not inconsiderable.

At the same time, it became increasingly difficult to conduct the regular weekly services. The quartet of singers established in 1897 at the tsar's insistence was falling apart. The bass singer, P. Odintsoff, was a reservist; upon outbreak of hostilities in 1914, he was called up and returned to Russia. In April 1915 news came that he had been killed at the front. Another member of the quartet, Nicolas Orloff, died in December 1915 after a long life dedicated to teaching and translating liturgical texts. Salary payments became irregular while the cost of living mounted due to wartime inflation. Father Eugene noted that there were many Russians in London working at India House for the "Russian Committee." It seems most likely that this was the Russian Government Committee in London, set up to procure and ship military supplies to Russia, which at its peak employed more than 700 people. Four members of the clergy at the Embassy church found work there to supplement their irregular and inadequate church salary—Deacon Theokritoff, the reader Vasily Timofeyeff, the singer and reader Foka Volkovsky, and Mr Vydra, one of the quartet. They often were at work when services were held, with the exception of the Sunday Liturgy. Although he understood their predicament, Father Eugene was distraught by the collapse of the quartet:

> What kind of singing can we have, when one singer has been killed, another has as good as left, and a third [Timofeyeff] has lost his voice and is anxious to leave the quartet and take up the position of psalm-reader, to which he has already been appointed. It is hardly surprising that the Russian congregation—absolutely all of them—are dissatisfied with the singing and many have stopped attending our services. . . . Even Anglicans who have been attending have stopped coming. . . . They come to our church hoping to hear the singing that is the glory of all Russian churches, but leave in bitter disappointment. As rector of the church I am in tears over the complete collapse of our singing, hearing constant complaints and seeing how the Russian congregation is deserting us, not to mention the Anglicans who have recently joined us, but there is absolutely nothing that I personally can do to rectify the situation. . . . It was the Emperor's good intention [in establishing the quartet] that it should attract both Russians and those of other faiths to our church, satisfying their religious needs and filling them with comfort and joy. . . .

Nevertheless, these disruptions to the ordered life of the Embassy church were relatively minor compared with the changes that came when the Russian Empire collapsed in 1917. Hundreds of thousands of refugees fled from the Bolsheviks, taking refuge in many European cities including London.

Chapter 7

[1919–1922]
The Church in Exile

The Revolution and Civil War

In addition to other war news in 1917, the London newspapers carried reports of the growing turmoil in Russia—the February Revolution, the abdication of the emperor, and the Bolshevik coup d'état in November. From England, these events were viewed primarily in terms of their effect on the Russian war effort because the collapse of the eastern front put greater pressure on the British and Allied armies fighting in France. We are so accustomed to thinking of November 7, 1917, as the date of the Communist takeover in Russia that it is easy to overlook the fact that the Bolsheviks only gained control of Russia after a long and bloody civil war that lasted until the end of 1920.

Throughout these years of horror, famine, and bloodshed, people outside the Russian capital had little interest in the political ideals proclaimed by the opposing parties. However, one aspect of the conflict soon became crystal clear. Militant atheism was a fundamental tenet of Russian communism, and in the early years after the Revolution it was pursued in a particularly naked form. In the Bolshevik-held territories, thousands of clergymen were killed and churches were pillaged and desecrated. By contrast, the White anti-Bolshevik forces allowed freedom of religion. Thus, to take one example, when the Reds captured Tsaritsyn on the Volga, the cathedral was closed and turned into a food store. When the city was recaptured by the Whites, the church was cleaned and reopened, the priests were released from prison, and the archbishop came out of hiding and held a service of thanksgiving to celebrate the restoration of religious liberty. Many who regarded Holy Orthodoxy as the highest value in their lives saw Bolshevism as an alien force occupying Russia, whose most significant aim was its war against the Church. This war was waged not only by force of arms and the ruthlessness of Leon Trotsky's campaign of terror. It was, as Fyodor Dostoyevsky foretold,[1] waged in the hearts of men who, in exchange for promises of a better future, willingly or half willingly supported the new regime in its destruction of religious and civil liberty. The Church, however, was adorned by the many thousands now glorified as New Martyrs.

Anxious to bring Russia back into the war against Germany, the Allies sent supplies and expeditionary forces to aid the anti-Bolshevik forces. They were also concerned with guarding the large quantities of military stores that accumulated in various ports, particularly Archangel in the Far North. However, this intervention had little practical effect. Once World War I was over, the Allies were not interested in continued fighting in Russia. The exception was Winston Churchill, then minister of war under Lloyd George, who hung up a map of Russia in his office and waged a personal campaign to crush Bolshevism, which he saw as a threat to the future of civilized humanity. However, his enthusiasm evinced little sympathy in a war-weary Britain.

It was against such a background of violence and bloodshed in their own country that the Russian émigré communities and parishes abroad began to organize. The refugees arriving in London fell into roughly six groups. First, there were those who had come during the war as liaison officers in the Anglo-Russian alliance. Second, there were soldiers in the Russian army who had been fighting on the western front. Third, there were some, mostly aristocrats and members of the royal family, who were rescued from the Crimea by the Royal Navy in 1918. Fourth, there were those who came from Archangel when the British Expeditionary Force withdrew in 1919. This was probably the largest and most cohesive single group to come to London. Fifth, there were those who made their way to London at the end of 1920 after the mass evacuations of the Crimea and Southern Russia. Finally, there were small groups that managed to find their way out of Russia as late as 1921.

Generally speaking, the Home Office required evidence of support before granting visas to Russian refugees, but there were numerous exceptions, and it is far from true to say that the Russian colony in London was made up exclusively of wealthy aristocrats. For example, there was a section of the Russian Army fighting in the trenches in France; when the Revolution took place, the Allies gave them the choice of either joining the British or French army or going back to Russia.[2] Many decided to stay in the British Army. After the war, survivors had the right to return to England. Thus, many private soldiers as well as noncommissioned officers found their way to England.

Count Wladimir Kleinmichel, who later became the churchwarden and treasurer of the London parish as well as a successful banker, came to England as a penniless young man of nineteen. He escaped from Russia via Malta on a destroyer and went to England to join the North Russian Expeditionary Force going to Archangel. However, because he walked with a limp, the War Office did not accept him but he was given a work permit to stay in England.

A plan to bring the tsar to England after his abdication in 1917 came to nothing; however, his sister, the Grand Duchess Xenia Alexandrovna, was able to settle in England. In the spring of 1919, King George V arranged for the HMS *Marlborough* to be sent to Yalta, in the Crimea, to rescue members of the Imperial family from the rapidly advancing Bolshevik forces. These included the Grand Duchess Xenia, the Dowager Empress Marie of Russia, mother of the tsar, who was the sister of King George's mother, Queen Alexandra. Both were originally Danish princesses, daughters of King Christian IX of Denmark. After a short stay in England, the Dowager Empress left for Denmark, but Xenia remained in England. King George V allowed her to settle in Frogmore Cottage, a grace and favour house[3] in Windsor Great Park. She visited her mother in Denmark as often as she could until her mother's death in 1928. Later, the Grand Duchess Xenia moved to Wilderness House in the grounds of Hampton Court Palace. Until her death in 1960, she occupied a revered place in the Russian émigré community, and many émigré leaders and Church hierarchs went to England to visit her.

These tumultuous events directly impacted the Russian Embassy in London, which was located in Chesham House at the corner of Chesham Place and Lyall Street, near Sloane Square. Count Alexander Benckendorff, the highly respected ambassador who held the post for thirteen years, died suddenly of pneumonia in January 1917, just before the collapse of the Imperial regime in Russia. Constantine Nabokov, who was an uncle of the well-known writer Vladimir Nabokov, succeeded him as chargé d'affaires at the Russian Embassy in London. Many of the left-wing Russian exiles who had been living in London sought to return home as soon as possible so as to enjoy the new conditions of political freedom, which, of course, were to be short-lived. Nabokov served at various posts in the diplomatic service of the Russian Empire and was transferred to London from India at the end of 1915. He remained at his post after the tsar's abdication; with relatively liberal views, he was acceptable to the Provisional Government that took power immediately afterward. The British government was determined to keep Russia in the war and used the embassy as a channel of communication to this end. Russia's European allies regarded the change of government in Russia positively because the Provisional Government favored a democratic form of government that her allies thought would provide a sounder basis of support for the war effort. What they did not realize, however, was that the Provisional Government, which was made up of well-intentioned aristocrats and politicians, had a very tenuous grip on power and would soon be swept away by the Soviet of Workers' and Peoples' Deputies.

The British government initially did not recognize the Bolshevik regime but continued to maintain relations with the former Imperial Embassy as representing anti-Bolshevik forces. Meanwhile, the Soviets abolished ambassadors and embassies but appointed Maxim Litvinov as Peoples' Plenipotentiary in the United Kingdom. Thus, there were effectively two embassies, one recognized by the British and one recognized by the government in Petrograd. Constantine Nabokov represented the White Army governments in Siberia and Southern Russia, but he was increasingly aware of his tenuous diplomatic status. Disagreements with Admiral Alexander Vasilyevich Kolchak's government in White-held Siberia led to his dismissal in 1919. He was replaced as chargé d'affaires by Eugene Vasilievich Sablin, who had been a member of the diplomatic staff in London since 1914. Thus, Sablin took charge just as large numbers of Russian refugees began arriving in London. He tried to use his position at the embassy to help the refugees in every way possible, even though it was increasingly unclear what government in Russia, if any, he actually represented.

The Formation of the Parish in London

In the summer of 1919, it seemed probable that the White Army would be victorious in the Civil War. Moscow was encircled on all sides. In the south, General Anton Denikin reached Kursk, 250 miles from Moscow, while Admiral Kolchak was advancing from Siberia. The London Embassy was in contact with Kolchak's government in Omsk, which continued to supply it with funds in place of the Imperial government.

In 1917–1918 it finally became possible to hold a Council of the Russian Church (*Sobor*) after planning for at least ten of the previous years. Bishops, clergymen, and lay representatives travelled to Moscow from all parts of Russia, where they met in the Kremlin, often to the accompaniment of Red artillery bombardments outside the city. The greatest achievement of this council was restoration of the Patriarchate, which had been abolished by Peter the Great, with the election of Patriarch Tikhon. This was part of a reorganization of Church administration along more canonical lines, with supreme authority being vested in the Council of Bishops. At the local level, parish life was to be reorganized; a set of bylaws was developed that provided for lay members to support the parish financially and to elect a parish council and officials such as the churchwarden (*starosta*) and treasurer. In part, this reform was necessitated by the separation of church and state proclaimed by the Bolsheviks. It provided a means by which, it was hoped, the parishes could survive independently through popular support, without reference to the government of the day.

The Grand Duchess Xenia Alexandrovna, sister of slain Tsar Nicholas II, lived in England after the Russian Revolution. Photograph probably dates from the early 1920s. (Source: Sophia Goodman)

In 1919, in response to a decision of the All-Russian Church Council and in view of the increasing size of the community, it was decided to form a parish at the Embassy church in London. On September 18 a small group of laymen constituting the Parish Organization Committee met in Father Eugene Smirnoff's flat at 32 Welbeck Street. Father Eugene produced a document, dated April 7/20, 1918, that he received by post from the Bishop of Omsk few days earlier. It was titled *Decisions of the Sacred Council of the Orthodox Church of Russia Parish.* Father Eugene said that, in his view, the committee's proposals were in full accord with the decisions of the Moscow Church Council. News of the formation of the parish was to be spread as widely as possible through the Russian community in London. Applications for membership would be accepted in the church after services. Previously, money to support the church had come from the embassy. It was assumed that this would continue, but the question arose as to whether these funds would now become parish property. A leading member of the Organization Committee, Mr K. G. Goudim-Levkovitch, thought that the unique origins and function of the London Embassy church made the position clear. He said,

> The Embassy church in London has always served the needs of all Orthodox in London and not only the Embassy staff. It has fulfilled and continues to fulfill the functions of a parish church, so the funds allocated to

> it are of a different nature to those allocated to the chapels of most other institutions outside Russia, which only serve the needs of the staff of the particular institution.

A meeting of all those "zealous for the local Orthodox Church in London" was called for September 25. Forty-seven people attended the meeting, the purpose of which was to publicize and discuss the steps being taken to form the parish. The first general meeting was set for October 17. Meanwhile, the committee received some disquieting news from Eugene Sablin, the chargé d'affaires at the embassy. He said that there would be no difficulty in passing the funds over to the parish. His only concern was in obtaining the money for the church; what was done with the money was up to the parish. However, a telegram from Omsk noted that Admiral Kolchak's government would be forced to reduce the funds available for the support of embassy churches. A reply protesting this was to be drafted for approval at the general meeting.

The first general meeting of the parish was held on October 17, 1919, on the premises of the Russian National Committee. By that time 104 valid applications for membership had been received and 62 people were present at the meeting. Father Eugene announced the formation of the Orthodox Parish of the Dormition in London in accordance with the rules of the Moscow Church Council. The word "Russian" was not included in the parish's official name; evidently this was considered superfluous. The first task was to elect the Parish Council. Father Eugene, as rector of the parish, would be the chairman. The following members were elected by ballot: I. F. Burenik (churchwarden), K. E. Zamen, K. G. Goudim-Levkovitch, Count D. C. Cheremetieff, I. S. Smolenkoff, A. E. Riabchenko, F. A. Dukhovetsky, F. A. Ivanoff, A. Ya. Miller, O. A. Novikoff, S. A. Durasova, B. Fillipova, and R. Burenin. (K. E. Zamen, who also spelled his name as Conrad de Sahmen, formerly a financial agent of the Russian government, was admitted to the Orthodox Church in 1917.) The clergy of the new parish was composed of Archpriest Eugene Smirnoff (rector), Deacon Vladimir Theokritoff, and two psalm-readers, Constantine Veselovsky and Vasily Timofeyeff.

Having achieved its purpose, the organization committee made its final report at the meeting, in which it outlined the future tasks before the parish: "to care for the upkeep and splendour of the church and later, to build or acquire our own building for the church, which is now located in a leasehold building; to organize a Russian Orthodox cemetery, a parish benevolent fund, a parish school and library."

In order to avert the threatened reduction in funding, it was agreed that a telegram would be sent to the Omsk government describing the parish's situation. The text approved at the meeting ran as follows:

1. The parish now being formed at the London Embassy church is still in an embryonic state and will need time to strengthen and develop. As yet it has no funds available—these will come later as the spiritual life of the parish gathers strength. At the present time the parish cannot maintain the church out of its own funds.
2. Despite all this however, the number of parishioners at the church has vastly increased since 1914. With the arrival of refugees from Russia it continues to grow, and the present clergy are often insufficient in numbers to satisfy the ecclesiastical and spiritual needs of the parishioners. The number of church services and private services [*treby*] has grown enormously under these conditions, and a reduction in the number of clergy would have a harmful effect both on the church and the dignity of the services and on the congregation, who are now uniting themselves into a parish.

The amount required to support the church and clergy for a year was declared to be £3,725 12 s. 9d.—the same as the previous year's budget. However, it is doubtful if this communication from London was given urgent attention in Omsk. Admiral Kolchak would soon be forced to retreat to Irkutsk, 1500 miles to the east.

The Beginning of Parish Life

Thus, life at Welbeck Street was organized along new lines. The Parish Council met every Monday evening, usually in Father Eugene's flat. Very detailed minutes of these early meetings were kept, and they provide a vivid picture of developments during this formative period. There was a great enthusiasm for parish work. It was felt that the existence of parishes both in Russia and abroad would have a great regenerative effect at the "grassroots" level. "Soon Russia will be covered with a network of parishes," said one council member, "and the parish will bring us back to Moscow." Much time at the meetings was spent discussing requests for financial assistance from refugees, some of whom were arriving in England in disastrous financial circumstances. Many other matters were also discussed: it would be imperative to work together with the other emigrant groups being formed in London; religious instruction would have to

A 1938 photograph of a founding member of the London parish, Colonel Potekhin. (Source: Parishioner of the church at Emperor's Gate)

be organized for the children; promote more active participation in church services by encouraging congregational singing, beginning with the creed and "Our Father" at the Liturgy.

Anxiety over the financial situation increased during the winter of 1919–1920. Father Eugene worried that the infamous damp London fog was damaging the magnificent golden silk brocade vestments ordered during imperial days. They could no longer be sent back to Petrograd for repairs, and there was no question of buying replacements. The parish had enough money set aside for a year in advance but was uncertain how to raise funds beyond that time. In February 1920 a cheque was received from the embassy with a letter attached, warning that it may well by the last. Some were confident that if government funds ceased, the Russian colony would be able and willing to support the Church. Father Eugene was doubtful. Because most of the Russians abroad had previously been employed by the government, he reasoned that if any recognizable form of government ceased to exist, then the Russians would have to leave. He did not see the massive emigration that was already gathering momentum. Meanwhile, as a first step, minimal contributions were to be requested for various ministrations: 6d. for commemoration at the *proskomedia*, half a crown for private services such as prayers for the deceased, and 10s. for special liturgies. Poor people would not be expected to contribute. Otherwise, it was anticipated that people would pay the priest for such services according to their means and generosity and that the priest would pass the prescribed amount over to the parish, keeping the rest for himself.

After his initial enthusiasm, Father Eugene began to have doubts about the parish organization. Did it really correspond to the intentions of the Moscow Church Council? He was now seventy-three years old, hardly an age at which it is easy to adapt to new arrangements. From being a government civil servant (*chinovnik*), answerable only to the Church hierarchy and the Imperial Ministry of Foreign Affairs, he became virtually an employee of his own flock. At the weekly council meetings, he was called on to account for various matters, some purely practical and others that exceeded the competence of the laity. Thus, the reverend rector was asked to be sure to put enough incense in the censer, not to hurry during the services, to be sure to serve the Hours before the Presanctified Liturgy, and so on. Some complaints about the services showed an ignorance of the Church typicon: why had the praise to the Mother of God been omitted at the ninth kathisma at the vigil of a recent feast day? (Anyone familiar with that vigil would know that the complaint was related to the *Magnificat* that is sung at the ninth ode of the canon.) Apparently the priest failed to intone the words required to introduce this part of the service—he promised not to omit it in future!

Friction developed over the old custom of candles at confession. Before confession, the penitent would buy a candle and give it to the priest instead of lighting it. The priest would then return the candle to the candle desk in exchange for its value in money. This was accepted as a normal part of the priest's income. However, the people selling the candles felt that they had no authority from the Parish Council to buy the candles back. By this time, the salaries of all clergy were several months in arrears, and this may have been the last straw for Father Eugene. He said he was being robbed and could not live on the same diet as St Anthony (a third-century ascetic). Ultimately the council members calmed him down and resolved to find the money to make up the arrears, even if they were not forthcoming through the embassy in the usual way. There was also the question of Father Eugene's manservant, James, without whom he said he could not manage in his old age, as well as his cook, who was supposed to be an embassy employee assigned to the task of washing the church floor. The question was also raised as to whether Father Eugene should be able to occupy a flat on church property without paying for it out of his salary.

Metropolitan Evlogy, who was subsequently appointed diocesan bishop (1921–1927), described Father Eugene's difficulties:

> The rector of the Embassy Church, the aged Archpriest Eugene Smirnoff, had not experienced the Revolution, and was used to dealing with important, influential people, of serving for ambassadors; his home life was typical of the pre-war upper classes. . . . He could not understand the psychology of the emigrant masses who were pouring into London—primarily from the Archangel region, the Northern front of the Civil War—he could not understand them and just became irritated. . . .

The Embassy church was in the same building as the rector's house. Previously, funerals were not held there because Father Smirnoff's wife could not bear to have a dead body in the same building, so funerals were conducted at the cemetery instead. Now this sort of personal predilection was expected to be put aside—everything had changed. People were badgering Father Smirnoff with new demands that, from his viewpoint, were inadmissible. His agitation and suffering were sincere: he did not understand what had happened in Russia or what the Russian people had endured. At the Parish Council meetings he argued his point vehemently, and it became clear that the old rector was not able to come to terms with the new Church community. Father Smirnoff, who was not accustomed to taking notice even of requests made by his psalm-readers, was now compelled to hear out declarations and demands of these recently arrived Russian people who were so utterly unlike his previous stiffly prim and proper, well-brought-up parishioners. Nevertheless, many refugees received help and comfort from Father Eugene in their hour of need.

It should be remembered that it would take years for the provisions of the Moscow Church Council to "settle" and become fully absorbed into the life of the Orthodox Church. The original bylaws had been modified several times since 1918 at the Councils of the Church Abroad to ensure that the democratic nature of the parish was properly balanced by the authority of the diocesan bishop and the priest appointed by him. The parish was now supposed to provide full financial support and living quarters to the priest and the deacon or reader. Yet in 1919, things were still at an "experimental stage." To some, the idea of an elected Parish Council (*sovét*) seemed to have revolutionary overtones. The underlying problem was that by being cut off from their diocesan bishop in Petrograd, the parish was deprived of archpastoral guidance in the implementation of the new order of parish life.

Other changes were beginning to be felt at Welbeck Street. The church was getting very dirty from the increased numbers in the congregation. Representatives of the Vacuum Company were called in to give an estimate for cleaning the whole building with a new invention—the vacuum cleaner. Then there was the question of electric light for the church. "Electricity, with its brilliant illumination, will add to the splendour of the church," said one enthusiastic supporter. He added that all the big churches in Russia had electricity and that in his own experience in Siberia, as soon as one church had electric light, all the others in the area wanted it. After a careful study of the cost of this project, the installation went ahead.

In the summer of 1919, the Liberal prime minister, Lloyd George, ordered the withdrawal of British troops from the Archangel region in the Far North of Russia. Continued involvement there almost a year after the end of the World War had been severely criticized in the press, and it was suggested that the commander-in-chief of the Allied force in Russia, General Edmund Ironside, had exceeded his brief by engaging the Bolsheviks deep inside Russian territory. Ironside hoped to leave the Whites who remained behind in as strong a position as possible. He promised to aid those who wished to leave. In addition to the soldiers, some citizens of Archangel who anticipated reprisals at the hands of the Bolsheviks also asked to be taken to England. The British troops also wished to take furs back with them and did some last-minute bargaining for them, which they called *skolkering*, after the Russian word *skol'ko*—"how much?" The evacuation took place in an orderly fashion. On September 27, 1919, a convoy of forty-five ships sailed from Archangel for England carrying Russian refugees as well as British troops. A camp was set up at Newmarket for the refugees, among whom were two priests. A temporary church was set up there using a portable iconostasis. In time, some of these refugees made their way to London, where they augmented the congregation. One former soldier was employed by the parish to act as a doorkeeper during the services. A former parishioner recalled his family's arrival from Archangel:

> There were several people from Archangel in England—mostly in London—on business, when the Revolution started, who decided to stay and did not return home. We came in September 1919 when the Allies decided to pull out, and many emigrated then. We came by boat and nearly did not get here, as the ship called "Vedic" went aground off the Orkney Islands, but was refloated and limped into Invergordon a day late. We then proceeded overland. In 1919–1920 there were quite a few people from Archangel living in London—there must have been at least 100 families from the Archangel area.

In December 1919, the new parish received its first episcopal visit when Bishop Nicholas celebrated the Liturgy according to the episcopal rite. It seems likely that this was the Serbian Bishop Nicholas of Ochrid,[4] who studied at Oxford University and maintained contacts in England. He also studied in Russia before his ordination and had a deep love for the Russian Church and its people. Later he did much to help and encourage the Russian refugees who settled in Serbia. He is remembered as being like an Old

Testament prophet—a fiery person who concealed enormous strength within him. Doubtless his visit provided a degree of inspiration and spiritual edification to the parish as it took its first faltering steps. Bishop Nicholas told Russian exiles that if they believed in God and the power of prayer and if they really loved their fatherland, they should cry out to God day and night, praying to Him to save Russia. It is probably no coincidence that at the next council meeting after his visit, some of those present suggested that services be held daily in order to pray for Russia. Father Eugene said that this was more than he could manage and that the parish really needed a second priest. Perhaps one of the priests at Newmarket would come and join them in London.

This was achieved in February 1920 when Father Vladimir Diligensky came to London. Little is known about him except that the vestments had to be shortened to fit him. He helped Father Eugene with the services and private ministrations, especially where traveling was involved. He also attended most Parish Council meetings and received some financial support from the parish; however, he was never officially considered a member of the parish clergy.

In late February 1920 news arrived of the final defeat of the White Army in Siberia and of the death of Admiral Kolchak, who was shot by the Bolsheviks in Irkutsk on February 7. A panikhida was served for the repose of the servant of God Alexander, former supreme ruler of the White-held territories. Some Russian students at Oxford requested that a panikhida be served at the university also. Expecting that the service would attract wide attention, the Parish Council persuaded Father Eugene to go, so that he could give an address in English.

The plight of the Church in Russia and of the refugees was attracting wide sympathy in England. The Anglo-Russian Committee was formed, primarily by leading members of the Anglican Church, to provide whatever help was possible. Father Eugene blessed his parishioners to work with the committee, provided that it avoided politics and also the complex question of union between the Anglican and Orthodox churches. As a further precaution, he offered to give a talk on the Anglican Church to his parishioners.

With increased numbers of refugees, the church in Welbeck Street was becoming overcrowded on Sundays and feast days. To help alleviate this, the Anglican Bishop of London offered the Russians use of St Mary-le-Bow Church on Cheapside in London for their Sunday services. Initially the idea of celebrating in an Anglican church seemed quite wrong to Father Eugene, so the Anglicans were thanked for their kind offer and told that the matter was under consideration.

The Evacuation of Southern Russia and the Beginning of the Church Abroad

On March 8, 1920, Mr Goudim-Levkovitch reported to the Parish Council that there were as many as 200,000 Russian refugees concentrated in Constantinople, as well as large numbers in Serbia. He said that the parish should assist in resettling the refugees. Some people, including Goudim-Levkovitch and Mr Philip Ivanoff, a mining engineer who lived near Regent's Park, were planning to go help with this work on the spot, and he suggested that perhaps the Parish Council would find it desirable to give them a special mandate to take part in this work as delegates of the parish. It was agreed that the parish should take part in resolving the fate of the Russian refugees. The Council also gave Goudim-Levkovitch and Ivanoff the necessary mandate for this work as the parish's delegates, with the right to co-opt other people to help them. There was no explicitly stated plan to bring refugees back to England, but evidently these parish delegates, as people settled and with contacts in England, would propose England as a potential place of resettlement, to the extent that visas could be obtained from the Home Office.

The figure of 200,000 refugees in Constantinople was quoted on March 8, 1920, before the evacuations of Novorossiysk and the Crimea, which were to bring at least that many from southern Russia.[5] These masses of refugees leaving from ports in the south of Russia formed the basis of the Russian communities in Europe, and it was the clergy who emigrated with them who founded the Russian Church Abroad. Of interest, therefore, is the following brief discussion of these events, which were central to the experiences of the émigré community.

After the defeat of Admiral Kolchak in Siberia, the only major centre of White resistance was in Ukraine and the Caucasus, under the leadership of General Denikin. After advancing to within 250 miles of Moscow, the Whites were steadily driven back throughout the autumn and winter of 1919. Many civilians felt threatened by the Bolsheviks and crowded into the few available trains, which took them south toward the coast. Typhus was rampant. On March 17, 1920, the Soviets took Ekaterinodar, the capital of the Kuban, or Northern Caucasus. Then they threw their whole weight against the White Army as they retreated to the coast—to the port of Novorossiysk, where a small British military and naval detachment remained to guard stores. The following description of the ensuing evacuation is based on eyewitness accounts, as recalled by Richard Luckett in *The White Generals*:

> Freezing winds tore through the mountain passes, periods of thaw were terminated by appalling frosts, ice on the decks and rigging of the ships in Novorossiysk had to be chipped off each day if the vessels were to remain stable.
>
> The approach roads to the port were blocked for miles. It was not simply a case of evacuating the troops: there were thousands of families clamouring to be taken into safety. Many of these were relatives of White officers, and knew very well what treatment they might expect at the hands of the Reds. Amongst those who straggled through the mountain passes were some who had no idea where they were going, but were caught in the human tide and infected with the fear and panic which characterised the whole retreat. There were Cossacks, nomad families with their black tents, Caucasian tribesmen and families from the Caspian shores. Their route was marked by bodies, stripped naked and frozen; dead horses, mules and camels; abandoned guns, field-kitchens and vehicles, together with all the debris of an army in flight. . . . almost the whole Don Cossack Army demanded to be evacuated. . . . At the waterside the Cossacks shot their horses; starving refugees tore the corpses to pieces for food.
>
> It was not long before the Red artillery had begun to shell Novorossiysk from positions in the spurs of the mountains that rose up behind the town. With the help of the British Mission a rearguard was organised while the last stages of embarkation took place. . . . eventually it became apparent that a large number of those assembled in the port would have to be left behind. . . . Several officers shot themselves on the quay; more drowned trying to swim out to the ships. On 27 March the Reds swept into the town, and the laden ships of the British fleet set sail for the Crimea. . . . On board the Allied ships were some 50,000 Whites, many of them women, children and wounded.[6]

Although the military units that remained intact were taken to the Crimea, which became the last bastion of resistance against the Bolsheviks, many civilians were taken directly to Constantinople and ports in the Aegean.

In the chaos of Novorossiysk before it fell, one man refused to leave. This was Anthony (Khrapovitsky), the Metropolitan of Kiev, an eminent theologian and spiritual leader of the Russian Church. He was appointed to the see of Kiev in 1918 by the Moscow Church Council to replace Metropolitan Vladimir who had been shot by the Bolsheviks, becoming the first Russian New Martyr. Metropolitan Anthony refused to leave his see as the Red

Army advanced toward Kiev. However, in November 1919 he went south to Novocherkassk to attend a meeting of the Council of Bishops comprising the Supreme Church Administration of South Russia. This administration had been set up in accordance with a decree of Patriarch Tikhon which stated that where communications with the central Church administration in Moscow were disrupted, the bishops in each area who could communicate with each other should meet with the full authority of a Church Council. By the time the meeting was over, the Reds had taken Kiev. Unable to return to Kiev, Metropolitan Anthony agreed to take on temporary administration of the Kuban diocese and left for Ekaterinodar. On the way, at Taganrog, he held a solemn vigil lasting seven hours before the miraculous Kursk icon of the Mother of God, which had been brought to safety by twelve monks from Kursk before their city fell to the Bolsheviks. He stayed in Ekaterinodar for about four months under extremely difficult conditions and used his limited means to help the streams of refugees who passed through on their way to the coast. Eventually he was persuaded to move to Novorossiysk for safety. The journey of about one hundred miles took eighteen hours by train. On March 1, 1920, with the blessing of Metropolitan Anthony, the miraculous Kursk icon was taken on board the steamship *St Nicholas*, which set sail for Thessalonica.

A plot was hatched, with the aid of some Greeks, to take Metropolitan Anthony to safety. He was told that the Church of the Holy Wisdom in Constantinople had been restored for use as a church after having been a mosque for several centuries. The Greeks asked him to come on board their ship, the *Elivzis*, to celebrate a service of thanksgiving. Overjoyed at this one piece of good news in the Orthodox world, Metropolitan Anthony, who loved and admired the Greeks, readily agreed. He went aboard, the anchor was raised, and the ship set sail. However, there was no service because the "news" was a pure fabrication. Metropolitan Anthony accepted it calmly, realizing he had been saved from certain death.

The *Elivzis* docked in Piraeus, the port of Athens. From there Metropolitan Anthony went to Mt Athos, where he planned to spend the rest of his days in monastic seclusion. However, on September 5 he received a telegram from Baron Peter Nikolayevich Wrangel, asking him to return to the Crimea to assume his rightful place as chairman of the Council of Bishops of the Supreme Church Administration of South Russia, which was based in Sevastopol at that time. Baron Wrangel was undoubtedly the most competent of the White leaders, but he assumed control too late to achieve lasting results. The only territory that he held was the Crimea, where more than

250,000 troops and refugees were crowded together. Seeing that the military situation was hopeless, Baron Wrangel mounted a mass evacuation of all who wished to leave. This was very efficiently organized, in complete contrast to the chaos of Novorossiysk.

Between November 12 and 14, 1920, a throng of 145,693 people embarked in 126 ships, mostly from the large port of Sevastopol. This time Metropolitan Anthony did not protest but left together with the other bishops and the miraculous Kursk icon. Some rearguard units were taken off from Theodosia and Kerch, which, at the easternmost tip of the Crimea, is only a few miles from the Kuban, the northern part of the Caucasus, from which it is separated by a narrow strait.

From the other side of the Strait of Kerch, a young priest who had been ordained that year watched as the last ships of the Volunteer Army passed through the strait, taking with them the last hope for the overthrow of Bolshevism in Russia. Many years later, after experiencing extraordinary sufferings and signs of God's mercy, this priest left Russia and found his way to London. This was Father Michael Polsky, who later served as rector of the London parish from 1938 to 1948.

On the afternoon of November 16, 1920, this massive flotilla turned west toward Constantinople. It included Russian, British, and French warships as well as merchant vessels and passenger ships. These ships flew various flags and were filled to capacity with Russian men, women, and children, including about six thousand sick or wounded bishops and clergymen, academics, writers, intelligentsia of all professions, and representatives of all social classes. People of all different attitudes, views, and convictions were united by the common danger and the common flight from the Bolsheviks. Arriving off the coast Constantinople on November 19, 1920, some ships anchored in the Bosphorus, some were directed to other ports on the Black Sea such as Varna in Bulgaria, while many of the White Army units made their way to the Greek island of Lemnos.

Seeing the masses of refugee ships in the roadstead off Constantinople waiting to disembark their battered and demoralized passengers, Metropolitan Anthony realized that he must continue to provide archpastoral care and leadership, although he was now in the territory of the Patriarch of Constantinople. On November 19, 1920, the first session of the Supreme Church Administration of South Russia to be held abroad took place on board the ship *Grand Duke Alexander Mikhailovitch*. In Constantinople, the hierarchs were welcomed by Archbishop Anastassy of Kishinev, who was already living there. He joined the Church Administration, which now consisted of five bishops and met regularly in Constantinople for about three months with the blessing and approval of the Greek Patriarchate. In February 1921, at the invitation of the Patriarch of Serbia, Metropolitan Anthony and the Church Administration, renamed the Supreme Administration of the Russian Church Abroad, moved to Sremski Karlovtsi in Yugoslavia.

Turkey had sided with the Germans in World War I and was now under allied military occupation. Constantinople also had the air of having been overrun by a bedraggled, bewildered army of Russians who were settled temporarily in army barracks and large tents. During the next two to three years, with the help of the Allied Command, this colony gradually dispersed and settled in different countries of the Balkans and other parts of Europe. Paris became the largest centre of the emigration between the wars, with its legendary Russian taxi drivers and garage mechanics, as well as the cultural flourishing of institutions such as the Ballets Russes. Another large centre of the emigration was China, especially Manchuria, where a significant portion of the population consisted of Russian refugees from Siberia.

London attracted relatively small numbers of refugees, partly because of restrictions on visas. Nevertheless, when one considers that half a million Russian refugees fled to Europe, even a small proportion would amount to a considerable number of people. Some made their way to London with the aid of travel documents issued by the Dutch Consulate in Constantinople, which was looking after Russian interests.

The Arrival of Father John Lelioukhin

A young girl, Galina Ampenoff, who was fleeing from Russia with her parents and two older sisters, Rufina and Nonna, described the family's escape to England:

> We came in a train with the Austrian and German soldiers—war prisoners being returned home. To it was attached a carriage of Swiss subjects who were returning. Amongst them there were very few real Swiss . . . it was all made up of people trying to escape. And we also escaped among the Swiss subjects. And so we came to England. We had left all our dear ones and knew what a difficult situation they were in, and we felt quite lost. We went to church in Welbeck Street and I remember that Father Eugene was very kind and very affectionate, and we felt greatly comforted.

Galina's father, Vsevolod, subsequently became churchwarden. She later became a nun and Abbess Elisabeth of the Convent of the Annunciation in London.

The church at Welbeck Street could hold eighty to one hundred people. Crammed into the corridors and passageways in the building that gave access to the church, a maximum of two hundred could be accommodated. With the approach of Holy Week and Easter in 1920, it became obvious that something else would have to be done. The offer of St Mary-le-Bow remained open, but still Father Eugene hesitated. "In principle," he said, "there is no objection. All we need is to put up two stands with icons on, and I can open up the antimension on the altar table. If necessary you can serve anywhere. I have even served on the deck of a ship." He visited St Mary's with the Anglican Bishop of London and enthusiastically invited him to the first Orthodox service there.

Pascha was celebrated at Welbeck Street. Every piece of furniture and other superfluous items were removed from the church and corridors to gain more space. The Parish Council deliberately refrained from putting pressure on Father Eugene as to the location of the service. They reasoned that as a theological expert, he was better qualified than they to determine whether it was right to use an Anglican church or not. Nevertheless, it was likely the experience of Pascha under such cramped conditions that was the decisive factor in moving services to St Mary-le-Bow, the first of which was held on Sunday, May 8, 1920. The next service was on Pentecost, and thereafter St Mary's was used regularly on Sundays and some Great Feasts, with other services still held at Welbeck Street. By early 1921, Father Eugene reported that the Sunday congregation at St Mary-le-Bow numbered three to four hundred. The Russians were warmly welcomed by Canon Masterman, the Anglican rector of St Mary's. They paid a nominal rent but did not have exclusive use of the church, which was located in a commercial district and was still required by the Anglicans during the week. There was no iconostasis, although it was hoped that a portable one that had been brought down from Newmarket and put into storage could be used. An architect advised that this was impractical and suggested that a curtain with icons painted onto the fabric be put up. St Mary-le-Bow alleviated the problem temporarily, but it was clear that a more permanent solution had to be found.

By May 1920 the refugee camp in Newmarket was disbanded, and the last resident priest, Archpriest John Zakharievitch Lelioukhin, came to London. Father John, who was 37, had been the rector of the cathedral in Archangel. His record of service (*formulyarni spisok*), compiled for the Church Authorities Abroad in 1923, indicates that he graduated from St Petersburg Theological Academy in 1910. He was ordained to the priesthood and appointed diocesan missionary for the Don Province. He then became a teacher at the Archangel seminary, where he taught for three years, and was elevated to archpriest by Bishop Theodossy in Smolensk in April 1915. In 1918 he returned to Archangel, where he was appointed rector of the cathedral church and confirmed by the patriarch as a member of the diocesan council. In 1918 he was elected member of the municipal *duma*, or city council of Archangel. He left Archangel for England in 1919 together with a large number of refugees.

"The emigrants," wrote Metropolitan Evlogy, "grouped themselves round their own *batioushka*,[7] Father Lelioukhin, whom they had brought with them," and to whom they felt much closer than they did to Father Eugene. Father John was the victim of a profound family tragedy: his wife, Maria Nikolayevna, who evinced sympathy for communism, had stayed behind in Russia with their two small children where she gave birth to a third child in 1920. This separation took a heavy toll on Father John and appeared, according to Metropolitan Evlogy, to have dampened his pastoral spirit.

Nevertheless, the arrival of such an energetic and young but relatively experienced pastor was an immense benefit to the London parish. Despite financial pressures, the Parish Council established the position of assistant priest with a regular salary and elected Father John to fill the position.

Father John Lelioukhin soon acquired a reputation as a gifted preacher, for which he received a vote of thanks from the Council, which praised his "outstanding oratorical talents." Nevertheless, it was reported that there were complaints about sermons becoming too frequent. Father John explained that this was his duty as a pastor, that it was required by the Church canons, and that the Moscow Church Council of 1917–1918 had particularly stressed the importance of preaching. Father Eugene added that by preaching at every service, Father John was only restoring an ancient practice, not bringing in anything new. Father Eugene remained rector of the parish, but Father John soon assumed most of the burdens and responsibilities of pastoral service while remaining tactful and respectful of the aged Father rector, who, at the age of seventy-four, was hardly capable of meeting the demands imposed by the influx of refugees. Increasingly, Father John took the initiative at the council meetings, while Father Eugene briefly signified his agreement, as in the matter of sermons.

By early 1921 requests were coming in through the embassy for clergy to be sent to minister to peoples' needs in places outside London. For example, a sailor in hospital in Greenwich and a Russian convict named Leteniouk in Parkhurst Prison on the Isle of Wight had requested assistance. Father John said he realized that many Russians scattered throughout England were in need of a visit to satisfy their religious needs. He was prepared to go anywhere as long as the fare was paid, and an announcement to this effect was to be made through the embassy. He had obtained from Archbishop Seraphim of Finland an antimension for use while travelling. Father John had also obtained a folding altar table and table of preparation. With such equipment it can be assumed that he celebrated the Divine Liturgy for small groups of Orthodox faithful and also attended to private ministrations.

There was frequent discussion at the council meetings about the church choir, which was established shortly after the parish was formed. All agreed that the choir added to the beauty of the services and, as one council member put it, "attracts many English people who are captivated by the beauty and splendour of our Divine Worship." The question was, could the parish afford it? Choir members were paid a certain amount, but there was the question of their traveling costs for attending choir practices, which were held three times a week. There was undoubtedly a charitable aspect to these payments; they were not enough to live on, but for those not regularly employed, the payments supplemented their other meager sources of income. Some, however, said the choir was a luxury that the parish could not afford. Father Eugene expressed the view, based on the old Russian practice, that the only essential people required to hold a church service were a priest and a psalm-reader; everything else was a luxury. If the parishioners wanted a choir, they would have to pay for it separately. In the end, a separate fund was set up so that contributions could be earmarked for the choir. Father Lelioukhin strongly advised that the choir be preserved and improved; he obtained music by Bortniansky and other composers. And so the choir gradually improved and developed under the watchful eye of Colonel Potekhin, who did not fail to complain when the singing was not, in his view, up to scratch. "Despite the vast sums of money we pay them," he wrote in a letter to the Parish Council after the feast of the Meeting of the Lord in 1921, "at the Vigil before the last feast day they did not sing a single one of the festal *stikhiri* and, at Vespers, they sang 'O come let us worship' instead of 'O quiet light.'" The choir remained an amateur body, while the psalm-readers, who had some formal theological training in Russia, were the experts at the details of the church services.

In February 1921, it was agreed that the embassy would formally hand over the church at Welbeck Street and the church property to the parish, which would take responsibility for its upkeep and payment of taxes. By now it was obvious that no more money would be received from Russia, so they launched a serious fund-raising effort. Printed circulars were sent out on which people could indicate how much money they wished to contribute to each of four categories: (1) general church needs, (2) the choir, (3) assistance for accommodating needy members of the clergy, and (4) benevolence for helping the poor. Special appeals were also addressed to the more wealthy Russians who lived in the London area.

With the passage of time, a number of organizations were established to help the refugees in London. Many Parish Council members also sat on the committees of these organizations, and council meetings were often rescheduled to avoid conflict. The Western Bank Limited, with offices on New Broad Street in London, had three directors who were Russian: Messieurs Riabouchinsky, Groudistoff, and Rittich. They formed the Russian Relief Committee, which had a long list of applicants for financial assistance. Four women received monthly allowances of £10–£15 through Father Eugene, who cashed the cheques for them and also interceded for an increase in the amount they were given. The Relief Committee also helped pay hospital bills.

People were driven to support themselves in various ways. Some icons, which were brought by a Russian officer, were displayed for sale in Selfridge's window. At the request of the Parish Council, Father Eugene wrote a letter of protest and the icons were removed.

The opening of a Russian Labour Bureau—or labour exchange—was announced in November 1920 "due to the presence of many unemployed refugees in London." People seeking work or with any information about offers of work were asked to contact the bureau, which was located in the former Russian Consulate at 30 Bedford Square. As noted previously, a substantial amount of time at each Parish Council meeting was spent discussing requests for financial assistance. For example, Anton Ilyich Argaieff declared that he had been out of work for six months, his wife was ill, and he had four children to support. Mrs Ananieff wanted a grant to buy a sewing machine so that she could earn some money for herself. Eight pounds, ten shillings was requested to pay half the school fees for a boy named Goffman. Later, an additional £8 10s. was requested to cover the other half of this expense. Not all requests were accepted. A Baroness Korf, who had come to London to study the new art of cinematography but had let her studies lapse, was refused a request for an additional £100 and told she should move somewhere such as Serbia, where the cost of living was cheaper. However, such frivolities were rare. In November 1921 Father John reported to the diocesan authorities, "In the London parish there are many people who are completely destitute, for whom the clergy perform private services without any form of recompense."

Children particularly suffered from the effects of the Civil War and exile. Father Eugene received a list of children from an organization in Switzerland that was looking for their parents. The list was distributed among the congregation. An hour's journey from London was a school run by Mrs Clark. Twenty-nine Russian children up to age twelve were being looked after and educated at the expense of Russian benevolent institutions. Shortly after he arrived in London, Father Lelioukhin was asked to travel to the school once a week to give the children religious instruction. Father John had worked extensively with children in Russia. In 1915 he had been appointed director of church schools in the Smolensk province in central Russia. During 1916 and 1917 he organized and ran a refuge for children displaced by the war on the northwestern front. In Archangel he resumed his teaching activities as an instructor of God's Law, both in primary schools and in high schools and colleges. Thus, he responded enthusiastically to the request to teach at Mrs Clark's school and set about organizing lessons in London.

A parish house was purchased in Chiswick to provide shelter for homeless refugees. Funds for this had been solicited by Philip Ivanoff during his travels in Europe. The administration of the property was supervised by Baron Raush. The house, which was blessed on February 14, 1921, sheltered thirty-six people who paid rent sufficient to cover the costs of upkeep. It was a source of constant anxiety to the Parish Council; the house had to cover its costs because the parish had no other funds with which to subsidize a deficit. However, the occupants, who included children, could not be turned out onto the street if they did not pay the rent. One resident undertook the bookkeeping; in return, he paid only 4s. per week rent instead of the usual 6s. 6d. As a result, records were kept up to date, although the finances remained delicately balanced. By resolution of the Parish Council in April 1922, it was decided that "the house shall not be known as the poor house (*dom prizreniya*) although that is in fact what it is."

The parish register that covered the period up to 1921 consists of a file of approximately two hundred applications for membership. It is reasonable to assume that many regular or occasional members of the congregation refrained from signing up for various reasons. The new type of parish organization was unfamiliar to many people. Although there were no set membership dues, it was clear that one was expected to make a contribution, and the poorer people who looked to the parish for assistance would have felt deterred from applying to join. Among other things, applicants were asked to fill in their "rank, vocation or nature of occupation." Some left this blank; others made entries such as "nobleman," "noblewoman," "officer," "major-general," "agronomist," and "financial agent of the Russian Government."

Among those mentioned was Pavel Grigorievitch Kushakoff, member of the Standing Polar Commission of the Russian Academy of Sciences.

Other documents preserved in the church archives testify to the diverse nature of the Russian community in England. For example, there are certificates of registration under the Aliens Order for a Mr Poushkareff, a glassblower, who arrived in Rochester in 1919 and lived in Strood; for Zina Iefsioutine, a parlor maid, of Charlton; for William Platonoff, born in Kronstadt, formerly an engineer in the Baltic Fleet, now a "British munitions worker" living on Great Eastern Street, London E.C.2. A passport was issued by the Provisional Government to Mlle Parascève Boudnikoff, born in Moghileff, Russia, in 1903, now a "servant" living at a prosperous-sounding address in Pinner, Middlesex. By contrast, a passport was issued by the Imperial Administration for Claudine Engelgardt, described as "Dame Noble" (Noblewoman) of No. 3 Torgovaia, Petrograd, destination London, Grand Hotel, via Bergen. The intended stay was stamped in 1916 to be "about 1 year"; evidently the stay was unexpectedly prolonged beyond 1917. The passport belonging to Catherine Ivanovna Savitcheva showed one of the most complete records of a young refugee's journey to England from Archangel in 1919, when she was only fifteen years old. All documents testify to individual lives shattered and turned on upside down by the historical events that occurred in Russia.

The path of a Russian exile, Catherine Ivanovna Savitcheva, illustrated by passport stamps: first, the Russian authorities in Archangel, then British military control in Archangel, then disembarkation in Scotland, and, finally, issue of a ration book in London in 1919. (Source: National Archives)

The members of the parish, however, were not exclusively Russian. Before the first service in St Mary-le-Bow, the council received a letter from Dr Eugène De L'Hoste Rankin, a member of the parish, who offered his services to help English visitors by showing them to their places and answering their questions. The offer was enthusiastically accepted. Rankin, a doctor of laws and fellow of the Royal Society of Literature, then in his seventies, had been received into the Orthodox Church by Father Eugene in 1894. A few weeks later he was asked to join the Parish Council, which was concerned with the need to give the parish proper juridical status under English law and hoped to make use of Dr Rankin's expertise. This was not accomplished until the following year, with formation of the London Russian Orthodox Parish Community. Dr Rankin attempted to resign from the council on several occasions—perhaps due to problems of language or age—but each time he was persuaded to stay.

Dr Rankin was not the only non-Russian member of the congregation. In November 1920 the council received a letter (written in Russian) from a Mr Priestley, a former resident of Moscow, who was a British subject and lived in Fulham. He observed that he had never heard the Orthodox service in English. "As a British subject and devoted son of the Holy Orthodox Church," he wrote, "I would greatly desire the union of the Anglicans with the Orthodox Church. Also, as I have heard, there are Orthodox here in London who do not know the Russian language at all." He had been very moved when someone read the prayer "I believe, O Lord, and I confess . . ." in English before receiving Holy Communion. Evidently Mr Priestley could not understand Russian, and suggested that the Liturgy be celebrated once a month in English. The council discussed this seriously and told Mr Priestley that the matter was under active consideration, where it remained, being subordinated to other pressing concerns. It was not until eighteen years later that regular services were started in English by Father Nicholas Gibbes.

By contrast, most parishioners felt that they were only in London temporarily. Thus, one membership applicant, Alexander Matveyevitch Azanchevsky-Azancheyeff, senior engineer of the All Russian Union of Consumer Societies, gave his address as follows: "Temporary: 40 Albermarle Rd., Bechenham, Kent. Permanent: Sadovaya, House no. 5, Moscow."

The Parish and the Church Hierarchy

The formation of the parish in 1919 and the changes which then burst in upon the peaceful life of the Embassy church were circumstances in which a parish priest would normally turn to the diocesan bishop for clarification and confirmation of his actions. We have seen how, in its early months, the parish suffered from the lack of archpastoral direction and care. It was impossible to communicate with Petrograd—in fact the diocesan bishop, Metropolitan Benjamin, was shot by the Bolsheviks in 1922, becoming, together with Metropolitan Vladimir of Kiev, one of the first of the New Martyrs of Russia. Nevertheless, Father Eugene tried to communicate with Church authorities in Siberia. A month after formation of the parish, telegrams were sent to Irkutsk, Siberia, and Rostov-on-Don in the south of Russia to inform the hierarchy of action taken in organizing the parish. As well as the aforementioned visit by the Serbian Bishop Nicholas of Ochrid, a Greek bishop, Philaretos of Demotikes, agreed to be present at one of the services in St Mary-le-Bow in July 1920. Nevertheless, the parish had no contact with its own diocesan bishop, and Father Eugene evidently felt the need for advice and authoritative clarification, especially regarding the question whether or not it was right to celebrate the Sunday services in an Anglican church such as St Mary-le-Bow.

In July 1920, Archimandrite Sergei Dabich, the rector of the former Russian Embassy church in Athens, was in London. He had been given a temporary assignment as dean of parishes in Europe by the Church Administration of South Russia. At Father Eugene's invitation, he attended several Parish Council meetings, where he was thanked for the edifying sermons he preached while in London. Concerning the question of using an Anglican church, Archimandrite Sergei advised Father Eugene to contact the Church Administration of South Russia, which was meeting at Sevastopol in the Crimea and headed by Metropolitan Anthony (Khrapovitsky). Father Sergei sent a telegram on his behalf and, on August 30, 1920, he reported to the council that, as a special representative of the Foreign Department of the Supreme Church Administration of South Russia, he had received a telegram containing resolution number 13 that gave permission, as of August 10/23, 1920, for Orthodox Divine Services to be held in an Anglican church in London. The resolution also authorized the clergy of the Church of the Dormition to conduct these services. The authorization was signed by Anthony, Metropolitan of Kiev, and Archpriest Gregory Lomako. Father Sergei was thanked for his efforts.

For some time Father Eugene and the Parish Council had been considering that their oldest psalm-reader, Constantine Veselovsky, should be ordained deacon in recognition of his long, faithful service to the Church. However, they did not know where to turn to ask for this ordination. On September 6, 1920, the council made the following resolution:

"The authoritative figure in closest proximity to London is Metropolitan Anthony, living temporarily on Mount Athos, as a representative of the foreign department (*zagranichnoye otdeleniye*) of the South Russian Ecclesiastical Administration. The authorized representative of this administration, Father Archimandrite Sergei, who is at present in London, will be asked to contact Metropolitan Anthony by telegraph and intercede with him for permission to have C. V. Veselovsky ordained." Philip Ivanoff was about to leave London for the South of Russia and was asked to go to Sevastopol and make a personal report to the Temporary Church Administration about the situation and needs of the parish in London. He was also asked to find out where would be the best place for this ordination to be held. On September 13 Father John Lelioukhin bade Mr Ivanoff an emotional farewell and wished him a safe and speedy return. He also said that as an intellectual who worked energetically for the Church, he was sorely needed in the face of all the Church's difficulties. Father Eugene said these were his own thoughts as well. For his part, Mr Ivanoff said he saw the parish as a united family now and he was sure that the work would continue in his absence. So Ivanoff set off on his travels, but for a time nothing happened about the ordination. Thus, the London parish recognized Metropolitan Anthony and the Supreme Church Administration of South Russia, even before it left Russia and became the Supreme Administration of the Russian Church Abroad.

In February 1921, Father Eugene reported to the council that he had received a directive from the Russian Church Administration Abroad, located temporarily in Constantinople. The directive, signed by Metropolitan Anthony, explained the formation of the new administration, with the approval of the Patriarch of Constantinople, "until such time as normal and free communication with his Holiness the Patriarch of Russia should be restored." It also appointed Archbishop Evlogy, formerly Archbishop of Volhynia and Zhitomir, to be administrator of the Russian churches in Western Europe, with the status of a diocesan bishop. This appointment was later confirmed by Patriarch Tikhon. The clergy and parish organizations were directed to refer all matters to him as their diocesan bishop. It was resolved that, henceforth, he would be commemorated in church as diocesan bishop, instead of Metropolitan Benjamin. The entire text of this directive was read in church the following Sunday.

After escaping from Russia, Archbishop Evlogy had found refuge in Yugoslavia, where he accepted a position as a religious instructor in a girls' school in the small town of Bela Cerkva. A few days after he received the above-noted decree from Constantinople, Father Eugene received a handwritten letter from Archbishop Evlogy, citing the authority of the Church Administration of South Russia for his appointment as diocesan bishop and asking for information about the parish—the church, number of congregants, whether the parish was organized according to the bylaws approved by the Moscow Council, the financial situation, and so on. The reply was to be addressed as follows: "Serbie, Banat, Bela Cerkva (Blanche-Eglise), Archevêque Evloguy."

To advance the ordination of Constantine Veselovsky, the Parish Council sent Archbishop Evlogy a telegram. They hoped that the Patriarch of Constantinople might perform the ordination during an imminent visit to London. Archbishop Evlogy's reply on March 31 read: "I authorize reader Constantine Veselovsky be ordained deacon ask the Greek bishop." The Serbian Bishop Nicholas of Ochrid performed the ordination.

Archbishop Evlogy then left Bela Cerkva, also known as Blanche Eglise, for Berlin, which for a time was a focal destination for Russian emigrants in Europe. In May 1921 Archbishop Evlogy confirmed the appointment of Father Eugene Smirnoff as rector of the new parish. From Berlin he was able to make regular visits to England, the first in September 1921. After almost two years of uncertainty, the parish was assured of the canonical protection of its own diocesan bishop and of the fatherly guidance and inspiration of archpastoral visits.

Still, the parishioners valued their membership in the wider Church organization abroad, whose centre moved during 1921 from Constantinople to Sremski Karlovtsi near Belgrade. In March and April 1921 there was great excitement when Metropolitan Anthony was expected to visit London. Father John Lelioukhin received a telegram from him, giving his expected date of arrival, and the Parish Council resolved to send him £50 for travelling expenses. However, the visit did not materialize at that time.

In November 1921, a Church Council was held in Sremski Karlovtsi that included clergy and lay representatives from émigré parishes all over the world. Father John Lelioukhin attended from London and Philip Ivanoff was elected as lay representative of the parish. At the end of the council, Metropolitan Anthony addressed a pastoral letter to the flock in exile—one of many epistles in which he called the exiles to unity and repentance. The letter read:

> "By the waters of Babylon we sat down and wept, when we remembered Sion." Grief, combined with repentance, is salutary, but grief filled with despair leads to perdition. Admittedly, the majority of our refugees,

including the young and the very old, have learnt much through their sufferings. However, anyone tried by such prolonged sufferings can be overtaken by the spirit of inconsolable grief and even, God forbid, bitterness and rebellion against God. To forestall such a sin the "All-Emigration" Russian Church Council, which has met in the town of Sremski Karlovtsi on the day of St Michael and the Bodiless Powers of Heaven, is appealing to you with a word of consolation. . . .

Much good has been revealed in the lives of the Russian refugees—more than could have been expected. And the first good thing is that we have remembered God; some, who before did not know the power of prayer, have learned how to pray, while others, who prayed in their youth but later lost the habit of prayer under the weight of sinful passions and under the influence of false teachings, have again returned to the intense effort, or *podvig*, of prayer. Many, in these sad months and years of our lives, have turned to reading the Holy Scriptures, which they did not do before. . . .

Further, albeit not of their own free will, but under the pressure of necessity, how many noble women, youths and even old men who formerly led pampered lives have taken up manual labour, both in their own modest homes and working for hire in other peoples' houses, and are showing an enviable endurance and industriousness and wise humility of soul. When you see a respected mother of a family with a Count's or General's title doing the laundry with her own hands, or an officer of the Guards, who used to have 10,000 roubles a year to live on, now polishing boots or carrying sacks of coal; when you then find out that they are bearing this with equanimity and without murmuring against God for the privation which has fallen to their lot; when you see this, you are convinced that our own people has a glorious future, not only through its simple people, but also thanks to its educated society, for these people are displaying depth of soul and Christian endurance, great vitality and a great capacity for adapting to the changes which have come upon them.

We will not close our eyes to the dark side of the situation—to the fact that, succumbing to hunger and oppressed by necessity, many Russians in exile have lost the concepts of honesty and marital fidelity. . . . Falls are natural to any community which has been subjected to poverty and wanderings, but that moral uplifting which we see in the other, larger part of the emigration can come about only in a people which has a future. . . .

Only now has it been revealed that refugees from the nobility and intelligentsia had a Christian soul underneath a secular and irreligious exterior,

> that they hid in their souls, perhaps unawares, the exalted evangelical rules of humility, submission to God's providence, and a readiness to redeem their former sins through suffering. . . . Russian people, it is on you, on your inner re-birth, that the question depends as to whether the Lord will shorten the years and days of His chastisement and return to us the joy of His salvation (Psalms 50:14).

St Philip's Church

As soon as services started at St Mary-le-Bow, the parish began looking for a permanent church. St Mary's was a temporary solution to the problem of overcrowding, added to the fact that the lease at Welbeck Street only had another five and a half years to run, at which time they would be left without any place of worship. In July 1920 Father John Lelioukhin and a group of parishioners visited St Philip's Church at 188 Buckingham Palace Road, near Victoria Station. The Anglican parish there was to be closed and there was a possibility that the Russians could be given exclusive use of the building. Father John was particularly enthusiastic. They would have to bear the cost of converting the building into an Orthodox church and of repairing the structure. Regardless of its condition, they reasoned that it would be cheaper than building a church themselves. A surveyor's report showed that in fact the building was in good condition, needing only minor repairs to the roof. The report also noted that the building had a good heating system for which 2 tons of coal per month would be adequate. However, they felt that they must act quickly because other parties appeared to be interested. They immediately started collecting funds, even before negotiations were complete, so as to be in a position to act at once if and when an agreement was reached.

St Philip's stood on land that belonged to the Duke of Westminster, who objected to closure of the Anglican parish. In January 1921 the Parish Council was in the middle of a heated debate about the choir when the arrival of Athelstan Riley, "a Member of Parliament,"[8] was announced. The previous discussion was put aside and the council listened while Mr Riley explained (in English, of course) the problem with St Philip's. Because the Church of England was an Established Church,[9] he said, there was some doubt as to whether it was legal to close the parish, especially where objections were being raised. He suggested that St Philip's had no architectural merit at all; surely the Russians would rather have a church built in the seventeenth century by the famous architect Christopher Wren? In fact, he said, twelve such churches were to be demolished and the Church of England would much prefer to give them one of these. A bill would have to be passed through Parliament approving the transfer, but after that the Russian parish would have absolute title to the building. He suggested that they should look at these churches as soon as possible and decide which one they liked best. A city church would be just as central as Victoria, he said, thanks to London's excellent public transport system. Meanwhile, he assured the Russians that they could continue using the church in Cheapside on a temporary basis for as long as they wanted and at any time.

However, the Russians had their hearts set on St Philip's. After a half-hearted look at St Magnus the Martyr, near the Monument Underground station, they renewed negotiations with the Church of England. An offer to use the building temporarily while the legalities were sorted out was turned down. That would have brought no improvement to the present situation but only perpetuate the state of uncertainty. Pascha in 1921 was celebrated at St Mary-le-Bow. The midnight procession was made along Cheapside, by arrangement with the Lord Mayor of London and the City of London Police.

By June 1921 all parties agreed to hand over St Philip's to the Russians. A contract was signed that permitted their use of the building. There was much discussion about an act of Parliament being passed to transfer the title to the church to the Russians, but this never occurred and the building remained the property of the Church of England.

The interior of St Philip's Church, Buckingham Palace Road, London.

The 1922 wedding of Prince Paul Chavchavadze and Princess Nina Romanoff at St Philip's Church. Second from left, Queen Olga of Greece; fourth from left, Queen Alexandra of Great Britain. The wedding was featured on the front page of the *Daily Mirror*. (Source: British Library)

Work began immediately on preparing the church for the first service, which was announced for Sunday, September 4. Athelstan Riley launched an appeal in the *Church Times*, an Anglican newspaper, to collect money for the repairs and conversion work that yielded £250.

At this point the parish realized the need to implement the plans to establish a legal body that could hold its property. The parish bylaws, which were established in accordance with the Russian Church Council of 1917–1918, were not legally binding in England. By moving to new premises, the parish became less closely connected to the Russian Embassy, and the status of the embassy was increasingly tenuous after the collapse of the White Army, especially with regard to its ability to support the church. On August 24, 1921, a legal body was formed with the name The London Russian Orthodox Parish Community. It was considered a company limited by guarantee, which is a form of corporate organization used by some nonprofit bodies and charities. Because it is not a commercial enterprise, it does not have a share capital; however, its members provide a guarantee to contribute a nominal sum in the event the company is wound up.[10] Although in principle all members of the parish could be members of the company, they tended to regard membership as a legal formality and, since most were penniless refugees, were discouraged by the possibility of having to contribute the required guarantee amount of £2. The names, addresses, and occupations of the subscribers to the company shown in its Memorandum and Articles of Association were as follows:

Eugene Smirnoff, 32 Welbeck Street, London W1, Archpriest
Arcadi Chmutin, 59 Eastcheap, Merchant, Siberian Agricultural Union
Conrad de Sahmen, 51 Coleman Street, E.C. Merchant
Stephan Reabinin, 26 New Oxford Street, Merchant
Victor Halfter, 80 Iverna Court, Iverna Gardens, Lieutenant General
Alexander Riabtchenko, 10 Riverdale Road, Twickenham, Gentleman
Vsevolod Ampenoff, 33-35 Eastcheap, Merchant

It is interesting to note that Father Eugene's name appeared at the beginning of the list of subscribers. Despite years of service as essentially an employee of the Imperial Ministry of Foreign Affairs, he was prepared to participate in the formation of this new legal body in what to him was a foreign land.

The biggest problem in establishing the church at St Philips was obtaining an iconostasis. Father Deacon Vladimir Theokritoff was asked to investigate the possibility of obtaining one ready-made while he was traveling on the Continent. For years Father Theokritoff had been responsible for purchasing wax for the synodal candle factories in Russia. Despite the Revolution, he still made visits to Paris and other places in connection with this. (Not surprisingly, he found it difficult to get the wax into Russia. At one point he thought he would have to directly contact the Bolsheviks in order to resolve these difficulties, but the Parish Council advised him against this.) In August 1921 Father Theokritoff was due to go to Finland, so he was asked while there to ask Archbishop Seraphim of Finland about the possibility of obtaining a lightweight, portable iconostasis for London. He was given plans of St Philip's to take with him.

The first Divine Liturgy was celebrated at St Philip's on September 4, 1921, as planned. The church was not completely ready, but there could be no further delay because the first annual General Meeting of the parish had been called for that day. At the meeting new members were elected to the Parish Council including Prince Vladimir Galitzine and Mr Vsevolod Ampenoff, who had recently arrived from Russia.

Later that month, Archbishop Evlogy visited London for the first time and celebrated at St Philip's. After his move to Berlin, Archbishop Evlogy set out on his first tour of the parishes in Western Europe, which were now in his charge. London was his second stop after Paris. He recalled the visit as follows:

> I stayed in Paris about two weeks. The city astounded me with its riches, its abundance of foodstuffs (white bread!). In Berlin we had become accustomed to extreme economies in everything.
>
> For the feast of the Elevation of the Holy Cross (14/27 September) I went to London. I was accompanied by the Protodeacon Father N. Tikhomiroff, and the deacon, Father Vdovenko. When we arrived in London it suddenly occurred to Father Vdovenko that we had forgotten to bring my *mantia*. We had to send a telegram and the next day my *mantia* flew over in an aeroplane. I stayed with a former shipping agent, Mr. Volkoff, and his wife Vera Nikolayevna; they took me to their home straight from the station.
>
> [During the service at St Philip's] I advanced Deacon Theokritoff, a very good man, with an excellent voice and speaking fluent English. I made him a Protodeacon.

We have already considered the new archbishop's first impressions of the London parish—the difficulties experienced by Father Eugene and the role of Father John Lelioukhin. Concerning Father Eugene, he added, "I tried to persuade him: 'Be condescending, be kind to them, . . .' but it was hard to convince him. . . . In general it seemed to him that new life was bursting into the London parish in a stormy and disorderly fashion. . . . After staying a week in London I set off for Nice via Paris."

The church in Welbeck Street was used on occasion until the end of 1921. Some people asked to have private services there, which entailed problems of transporting vestments and other items back and forth. Naturally Father Eugene was attached to his old church and was sad to see most of the icons, sacred vessels, and other sacred objects being taken away to St Philip's. However, the parish could not afford the upkeep of two churches. At the end of the year the lease on the Welbeck Street property was transferred back to the embassy and an announcement was made to the effect that all future services would be held exclusively at St Philip's, while the clergy continued to live at Welbeck Street.

At 9:30 p.m. on January 13 (December 31 on the old calendar), when he calculated it would be midnight in Moscow, Father John Lelioukhin held the New Year moleben. The year 1922 saw a further strengthening of the parish. The Sisterhood of St Xenia was established, with responsibilities for cleaning the church, visiting the sick, and teaching children. Religious instruction continued under the direction of Father John Lelioukhin. Lessons on Saturdays had been started at St Philip's as soon as the church opened for Orthodox use. However, many children lived too far away to come to the lessons regularly. The congregation grew, and candles were ordered by the ton, made specially to the Orthodox shape and size under the expert supervision of the Father Protodeacon. Finances were still very difficult. The budget for the new year was looked at closely in terms of fixed and discretionary costs to determine where savings could be made and where there was no choice. Eugene Sablin, the former chargé d'affaires at the embassy, held a collection among his contacts at the embassies of other Orthodox countries—Bulgaria, Yugoslavia, Romania, and Greece.

The honorary patron of the newly formed sisterhood was the Grand Duchess Xenia, sister of Tsar Nicholas II, who settled in England in 1919. As an honorary patron she was primarily a source of moral support. She attended bazaars and some functions organized by the sisterhood but was not otherwise actively involved. The sisterhood was dedicated to her patron saint, St Xenia the Roman.[11]

In January 1922 Archbishop Evlogy visited again and took the chair at a meeting of the Parish Council on January 31, where all these matters were discussed. Mr Ivanoff expressed the view that the Parish Council, with its new members, comprised all the best forces of the Russian colony in London. He expressed the conviction that the current council would be immensely successful in all of its future undertakings.

On April 21, Vladyka Evlogy again presided over a Parish Council meeting. The council congratulated him on his elevation to the rank of metropolitan and said they were honored to have him present at this, the one hundredth meeting since the foundation of the parish just two and a half years ago.

There was still no iconostasis. Estimates were obtained for having one made in Germany, but this proved to be too expensive. Then, in March Father Theokritoff's earlier visit to Finland finally bore fruit; word came from Captain Sukhonik in Finland that he was able to buy the iconostasis from the chapel in the house of the former governor general in Helsinki. Finland was once a province of the Russian Empire ruled by officials sent from St Petersburg. Now that it was an independent country, there was no longer a Russian governor general, and the contents of his former official residence were being sold for nominal prices. Two thousand Finnish marks were sent to Captain Sukhonik to pay for the iconostasis, along with an additional 9,000 marks to pay for other items he had purchased from the same chapel. In return, a mass of shipping documents in the Finnish language arrived in London to be followed at last by the iconostasis, duly dismantled and crated for shipping.

When unpacked and erected in St Philip's, it proved to be not altogether suitable for the space in which it had to fit. Meanwhile the church in Welbeck Street was finally closed. In June Metropolitan Evlogy wrote, giving permission for the altar and iconostasis to be removed from the building. He suggested that the iconostasis be set up in a side chapel in St Philip's. In fact, the iconostasis, with its marble pillars and stone arches, blended far better with the existing architecture, so it was erected at the main altar in place of the wooden one from Finland. Some panels of the Finnish iconostasis, with icons of St Nicholas and St Seraphim, were placed separately in the church. It seemed that all the efforts and expenditure of bringing it over had been in vain, however this iconostasis was to prove invaluable at a later stage in the history of the parish.

On October 29, 1922, Metropolitan Evlogy consecrated the church as an Orthodox place of worship, according to the full rite (rather than the lesser rite used to bless a temporary chapel). It was consecrated in honour of the Dormition of the Most Holy Mother of God, thereby succeeding the church in Welbeck Street, which had also been dedicated to the Dormition, as the home of the Orthodox Parish of the Holy Dormition in London. The church was still commonly known, even to the Russians, as "St Philip's," and this remained its postal address.

Father Eugene remained at 32 Welbeck Street, but he was ill and rarely went out. Parish Council meetings were usually held at St Philip's in his absence. He died on January 4, 1923, at age seventy-six. He was the last chaplain of the Imperial Embassy and the first rector of the newly formed parish. At the end of his long life, after more than forty years of service at the embassy, he faced the entirely new conditions of a parish formed of refugees. One of his greatest achievements was that he had presided over this transition period, difficult though it was for him, and provided the parish's link with the Church of pre-Revolutionary Russia.

Chapter 8

[1923–1927] St Philip's Church

Parish Life: 1923–1925

In his Christmas Epistle for 1922, received early in 1923, Metropolitan Anthony wrote:

> A new year of God's goodness has begun and we are all approaching one step closer to the day of our return to the Fatherland. Which one? We have two countries, beloved—one of the land of Russia, Orthodox and God-loving, and the other is that, of which Solomon says to all peoples "and dust shall return to the earth, where it was before, and the spirit shall return to God, who gave it." (Eccl 12: 7)
>
> Almost all of us wish to return to our Russian fatherland, but do we wish to return to that other fatherland which is common to all of humanity? We do not know for certain whether we will return to Russia, but we will all return without fail our souls to God and our bodies to the earth—both those who believe in God and those who do not believe. . . .
>
> Of course, the purpose of my epistle is not to cool the love of those who will read and hear it towards their own land of Russia or to cool their desire to return. My purpose is to unite this love and this desire as strongly as possible with our preparation for what is the inevitable end of each of us. . . .
>
> It is possible, beloved, that the fulfillment of these hopes will begin and even be accomplished in the present year, 1923. But if the measure of our atonement for our sins is not yet fulfilled . . . even so, the advice given in these lines, to prepare yourselves for the two big journeys which await us, will not remain without profit.

The émigrés expected that the Communist regime would soon fall and busied themselves making plans for the future of Russia after communism. Metropolitan Anthony, whose pastoral encyclicals were regularly received from

Yugoslavia, naturally shared these hopes but thought the communist yoke would last a long time. He continually pointed to spiritual renewal as the essential prerequisite for the end of atheistic tyranny. In London, as elsewhere, the exile community still regarded the situation as temporary but had become more settled—the refugees were émigrés.

Metropolitan Evlogy came from Paris for Father Eugene's funeral and appointed Archpriest John Lelioukhin the new rector of the parish. In 1922, Metropolitan Evlogy moved from Berlin to Paris, which was becoming the centre of the emigration in Western Europe. Paris was also a more convenient base from which to visit England. The metropolitan's visits became more frequent, and a set of bishop's vestments was made by the parish's Sisterhood of St Xenia. Vladyka Evlogy established contacts with Oxford University. He arranged for a number of Russian students from Europe to study there with the aid of various stipends and subsidies; Father John helped him with these arrangements. In place of the letters from Bela Cerkva copied by hand, the parish now regularly received voluminous diocesan circulars from Paris, printed on a stencil duplicating machine.

Appeals for funds for various projects were received from other countries, which was an indication that steps were being taken elsewhere to organize church and community life. Thus, a church was being built in Berlin and a convent was being established in Bulgaria. In the small town of Wainow, formerly in Russian territory but now in East Prussia, funds were being collected for a church building and a copy of the plans was enclosed. In Czechoslovakia a group of students was publishing a "black book" (*chernaya kniga*), documenting the persecution and destruction of the churches in Soviet Russia. In Paris, the St Sergius Theological Institute was being set up. In Belgrade funds were being collected for a Russian Church in honour of the Holy Trinity. In Paris, the Brotherhood of St Photius was being established with the avowed aim of defending the Church against her enemies within and without. Details of all these projects came to 188 Buckingham Palace Road in the hope that special collections would be raised. St Philip's Church was also a centre through which friends and relatives, flung in opposite directions by the upheavals in Russia, hoped to regain contact. From as far away as Java, Indonesia, a letter came from someone looking for his childhood friend, Koublitsky, whom he had reason to believe was now in England. Koublitsky was very religious, so would surely be known at church if he were there, the letter said.

By 1923 sixteen organizations had joined forces to form the United Council of the Russian Red Cross and the Russian Charity Organization of

Great Britain. These included the Russian Relief Fund (for Great Britain), the Russian Army and Navy Ex-servicemen's Mutual Provident Association, the Russian Academic Group, the Russian Refugees' Self-help Association in Great Britain, the Self-help Association for Refugees from North Russia, and the Ladies' Section of the Russian-British Bratstvo, in addition to the Russian Orthodox Parish Church Council. Father John Lelioukhin attended meetings of the Red Cross to discuss joint fund-raising projects. In January 1924 the parish was promised 5 percent of the net proceeds of certain charitable functions. The first fruits of this arrangement soon followed—£1.18s.5d.,[1] the parish's share from a bridge and mahjong competition! Later contributions were more substantial. Arrangements were made for Russian refugees to be treated free of charge in certain hospitals. A list of these hospitals was circulated together with details of which diseases would be treated immediately under these arrangements. Treatment of some diseases was dependent on a bed being available that was not required by other patients.

The Russian Red Cross occupied a unique position among these organizations. It had a presence in London as early as 1893. In 1916 it opened an office in London to assist the wounded and prisoners of war, especially those in Germany. As such, it was registered under the War Charities Act and later known as "The Old Organization of the Russian Red Cross Society, a Charity registered under the War Charities Act 1916." By 1919 it had broadened its activities to caring for former prisoners of war and refugees. In 1920 it moved to the embassy building at Chesham House and was led for many years by Colonel Zinovieff, a former Russian officer. In a single year, 1923, the Russian Red Cross raised nearly £7,000 to help refugees. Over the years it became well known in London as a result of the bazaars and other fund-raising events it organized.

The November 4, 1922, edition of the *British Medical Journal* contained the following urgent appeal in the name of the Russian Red Cross for medical aid for Russian refugees:

> **Medical aid for Russian refugees**
> MR. D. ZINOVIEFF [Special Delegate of the Russian Red Cross for Great Britain] and Dr. B. BELILOVSKY [Medical Adviser to the Russian Red Cross] write: The Russian Red Cross Society [Old Organization] makes an urgent appeal at the present time to all kind friends and sympathisers for help for the destitute Russian refugees. These unfortunate persons, deprived of their own mother country, are scattered all over

> the world. The above society is doing its utmost to provide at least the minimum of help necessary, but is greatly handicapped by lack of funds. The majority of the Russian refugees are living in Serbia, Bulgaria, and other Balkan States. Though helped to a certain degree by the Governments of these countries, they are in a very distressed condition. One of their chief needs is medical help, for which surgical instruments are very sadly lacking. Thousands are suffering and help is urgently needed. The Russian Red Cross, therefore, pleads for assistance by donations in money or in surgical instruments—even old and used ones. Such donations will be most gratefully received at the offices of the society, Chesham House, Chesham Place, London, S.W.1.

In the 1920s the North Russian Association—*Obshchestvo Severyan* or Society of Northerners—was formed to unite those who had come from the area around Archangel. On July 6, 1926, it was incorporated under the Companies Act as a company limited by guarantee under the name of the North Russian Association Ltd. The articles of association provided that membership be limited to refugees from North Russia and Siberia, qualified either by "birth or continuous residence for a considerable period of time, or the holding in the past of public offices in or services rendered to the Northern Region of Russia (comprising the pre-war provinces of Archangel, Vologda, Viatka Perm and Olonetz) or Siberia," or alternatively by "such personal association with the territories just mentioned as in the opinion of the council shall be deemed sufficient." Artemy Ananin, whose family came from Archangel, recalled:

Young members of the North Russian Association in 1924. (Source: George Knupffer)

> The North Russian Association was formed, which carried on the social side, and most of its members belonged to the Russian Orthodox Church which was in Welbeck Street [and later at St Philip's]. I would say that the majority of the parishioners were from the Archangel District at that time. . . . The immigrants found jobs as best they could. My father found work in an office which dealt with importing timber. Several became taxi drivers, some took up farm work, one person I know did odd jobs, mostly as a shop assistant, and one of them, Mr. Vorobieff, opened his own shop, selling Russian food. Another, who had some capital, joined up with two partners and opened a billiard hall. I also knew two doctors who had connections with Archangel, who set up their practices in London.

Under the leadership of General Halfter, who was also an active member of the parish, the North Russian Association played an important part in the Russian community in London by organizing social and cultural events. Vassily Zakharov, who grew up in London during this period, described it in his book *No Snow on Their Boots* as follows:

> I cannot stress too greatly how important the North Russian Association was to our community, for it was the principal channel for keeping alive the wonderful cultural tradition of pre-revolutionary Russia. It played a major part in the formation of the children, and there were several concerts or productions every year organized just for them, the most notable being the great Christmas party soon after January 7th.

Zakharov also pointed out how the North Russian Association, to some extent, made up for the lack of a church hall at St Philip's:

> Although the church did provide a meeting place for the community, somewhere where one might meet other Russians, it really was not suitable for anything other than a brief conversation with friends after services. Indeed, I can remember the old Russian church in Buckingham Palace Road where, after the Liturgy on Sundays, one could hardly move outside the church because so many people lingered to speak to each other (one certainly could not "chat" inside the church itself!). Having a brief conversation outside in the open air, particularly when it was cold or raining, was no solution to the needs of the community. But these needs were more than met by the North Russian Association.

In a similar vein, Zakharov provided an interesting view of Easter night service from the perspective of a family friend, Ivan Stroev, who was a taxi driver:

> Our usual way to get to St. Philip's before the war was to go by bus from Kensington to Victoria and then to walk along the Buckingham Palace Road, and this used to be pretty tiring when we were kids, especially on the way back, after having had to stand in church for nearly two hours. But at Easter we went there by taxi, and this was an even greater privilege than it sounds.
>
> I have to explain that there were so many Russians attending church on Easter in the pre-war years that the police used to close off part of Buckingham Palace Road to traffic. Only taxis and some private cars were allowed, and then only to drop off (or collect) passengers. So important was the occasion, particularly if one of the Royalty were attending, that it became the custom for one particular police superintendent to ensure that all went well, although in those days this was a question not of crime but of traffic circulation. He of course knew all the taxi drivers by name. So on this occasion, when all the Russian aristocracy would arrive by taxi and chauffeur-driven cars, we too would come by taxi, all in our finest clothes.
>
> There would usually be quite a queue of cars and taxis arriving to drop everyone off, and it was the custom of the police superintendent I mentioned to stand at the side road leading to the church. I always remember that when it came for us to turn in, the superintendent just used to put his head in to the cab and say a few words to Ivan Stroev: "Lovely night for Easter, John," he would say, and then we drove further. We were always mighty impressed!
>
> After the service we would all go once again by taxi back home, and there we would have our Easter breakfast. As kids, we usually just ate little, and then went to bed, utterly exhausted. The big celebrations would take place next day, when we visited other families, or they would come to us.

Eugene Sablin continued to use the embassy at Chesham House as a centre for helping Russian refugees in London until Great Britain formally recognized the Soviet Union in 1924. Then he left the embassy building and bought a house at 27 Cromwell Road, Kensington. He called it the "Russian House," and developed it into a centre for the Russian émigré community. He lived with his family in a few of the upstairs rooms; the rest of the building was used by organisations such as the Russian Red Cross, as well as for recitals and readings by Russian literary figures.

In January 1923, during his visit for Father Eugene's funeral, Metropolitan Evlogy ordained a new priest for the parish. This was Father Vassily Tikhonovich Timofeyeff, who was the parish secretary. Now forty-six years old, he had been in London since 1902, when he graduated from St Petersburg Theological Academy. He held various posts in the embassy including that of psalm-reader in the Embassy church. During the 1919–1920 and 1920–1921 academic years, he had also been a lecturer in the history of the Russian language and Russian literature at King's College—a part of the University of London. He lived with his wife, Elizaveta Petrovna, and a daughter, Vera, who was born in 1920.

Father Vassily helped Father John with the religious instruction of children. The size of London and the limited time available reduced the effectiveness of the Saturday lessons, and so Father Vassily organized summer camps for the children where they combined recreation with instruction in their own religion, language, and culture.

Father Vassily, together with Father Vladimir Theokritoff, published an English translation of *The All-Night Vigil Service of the Russian Orthodox.* Father Vassily wrote an introduction to this in which he explained that its purpose was to provide a translation of the Vigil Service exactly as it is performed in the Russian Church in London, as a help for the many English visitors to the church. The Vigil Service, if performed without any omissions, would take all night, as the title implies. In parishes it is considerably shortened, and, in the process of abbreviating the service, many different practices have evolved. Thus, it is of interest today to have a precise record of the order of service used in 1924, which was probably due to a continuity of clergy and psalm-readers, unchanged from that of the pre-Revolutionary Embassy church. This order of service was not particularly lengthy; the service would probably have taken less than two hours.[2]

In 1923 Father Vassily was elected a member of the Committee of the Anglican and Eastern Churches Association (founded in the nineteenth century to acquaint Anglicans with Orthodoxy). In May 1929 he was accredited to the Archbishop of Canterbury as the official representative of the Russian Church in its relations with the Anglican Church and the English people generally.

For Holy Week and Pascha in 1924, Father Vassily travelled to Lille in northern France where a new parish was being established.

The third priest in London during this period was Father Constantine Vasilievich Veselovsky. He was ordained deacon in May 1921 and priest in September of the same year, at the age of seventy-one. After graduating from St Petersburg Seminary in 1870, he had served only as psalm-reader in churches outside Russia: first in Dresden, Germany, and then, from 1875, in London. Among the many medals and awards he received was a pair of gold cuff links, "with ornamentation," for participating in a service on June 20, 1893, in the presence of the heir to the throne, the Tsarevich Nicholas Alexandrovich. He was ordained chiefly in recognition for his long years of irreproachable service to the Church and for, at times, continuing to help with the singing and reading when required. Father Constantine had a son, Victor, who worked as a doctor in a hospital for tubercular patients. In November 1926, Father Constantine was raised to the rank of archpriest. He died later that year at the age of seventy-six.

Throughout this period the predominant influence in the parish was the energetic rector, Father John Lelioukhin. Abbess Elisabeth remembered the time as follows:

> Every Saturday we used to go to St. Philip's Church. We were made by the caretaker, Sergei Vasilievich, to dust all the chairs. Then Father John would come and teach us religion. He was marvellous—very kind and encouraging. He used to come to our house and often gave very edifying spiritual talks. He was greatly loved, as I remember, by all the parishioners. We loved him and trusted him.

The 1,600th Anniversary of the Council of Nicaea

The £50 sent to Metropolitan Anthony in 1921 for travelling expenses finally bore fruit in June 1925 when the Russian parish in London was blessed by a visit from the senior hierarch of the Russian Church Abroad, as well as the Patriarchs of Jerusalem and Alexandria. They went to England in connection with the Nicene celebrations that marked the 1,600th anniversary of the First Œcumenical Council held in Nicaea (present-day Turkey) in A.D. 325. In the 1920s there was still great interest within the Anglican Church in Eastern Orthodoxy. The Anglicans, therefore, organized a solemn celebration of this event in England, inviting representatives of the Eastern Orthodox Churches including the Russian Church Abroad.

Before the Revolution, when he was Archbishop of Volhynia in western Russia, Vladyka Anthony devoted much energy and love to furthering the return of Uniates and Old Believers to the Orthodox Church. His relations with the Anglicans were inspired by similar motives. During the nineteenth century and until the 1920s, there seemed to be a very real hope that the Church of England might become united with Holy Orthodoxy.

Vladyka Anthony left Belgrade on June 22, 1925, accompanied by his assistant, Priest-monk Theodossy and E. I. Makharoblidze, who was in charge of the Synodal office. They were met at Victoria Station by the London Russian clergy and a delegation from the Archbishop of Canterbury led by Canon John Douglas, who took them to their quarters in St Edward's House, a small Anglican monastery in Dean's Yard, next to Westminster Abbey. Metropolitan Evlogy and Bishop Benjamin of Sebastopol, who had also been invited to represent the Russian Church, were given accommodation there as well.

The high point of the celebrations was a service in Westminster Abbey at which Patriarchs Photios of Alexandria and Damianos of Jerusalem were present, as well as Metropolitan Germanos of Thyateira, who, as Exarch of the Œcumenical Patriarchate for Western Europe, was in charge of the Greek Church in England, and Metropolitan Anthony, Metropolitan Evlogy, Bishop Benjamin, and representatives of other Orthodox Churches. The Orthodox Nicaean-Constantinopolitan Creed was read in Greek by Patriarch Photios of Alexandria—a direct successor of St Athanasius the Great, who defended Orthodoxy at the Council of Nicaea. This made a profound impression on all present. Nevertheless, in his address, the Archbishop of Canterbury hinted that the Anglican Church had taken all possible steps toward unity but that favourable results could not be expected in the near future because the question was very complex and difficult. In several instances, Metropolitan Anthony was invited to address the Anglicans. On one occasion, when a banquet was held at a restaurant in Holborn, he addressed approximately 600 people, including virtually all the Anglican bishops and numbers of academics and politicians. Representing the government of His Majesty King George V was Sir Samuel Hoare, Minister of Aviation. In view of later developments in ecumenism, which have been severely censured by the Russian Church Abroad, this speech, presented here, is of great interest in that it shows how far this strictly Orthodox hierarch was prepared to go in reaching out a hand to the Church of England:

> Only yesterday evening I received a card bearing the message "Metropolitan Anthony is invited to reply to the address by Sir Samuel Hoare on Christian Unity."

It is far easier for me to fulfill this task than it would be if I had been asked to talk about union of the Churches. From childhood we have been accustomed to believe in one Holy Catholic and Apostolic Church, as the Fathers of the Second Œcumenical Council taught us. This Church cannot be divided, since Christ has said, "I will build my Church, and the gates of hell shall not overcome it."

It is another matter if we talk about Christian unity—that is to say, the unity firstly of individual people, religious communities and whole peoples, believing in Christ as God, and recognizing the Holy Gospel and the Holy Bible. Everyone zealous for the word of God must also free our souls from the constant intellectual striving to prove them wrong.

On the contrary, more pleasing to God is he amongst us who attempts to bring out everything which unites us together, and who will try not to reduce the number of such truths to a minimum, but to find as many points in common as possible. This relates particularly to those Christian communities and confessions which are making friendly moves towards our Church.

Let nobody think that the principle I have first stated is a concession to the liberal spirit of the times, or to confessional indifference, because the Orthodox Church has been guided by this principle in the times of the strictest application of the Œcumenical Canons, as expressed in the 95th Rule of the 6th Œcumenical Council and the 1st Canonical Rule of St. Basil the Great.

I will not quote from these canons at this point (although I have brought them with me). However, I can only report my personal view, which I published some two years ago in the Russian newspaper, *Novoye Vremya,* and this view is in full accord with the two canons I have just mentioned. If any Anglican bishop or clergyman wished to enter the Orthodox Church, then he could be received by the third rite, that is to say, without his ordination being repeated or, in other words, he could be received in his orders.

Let no one think that these last remarks are made for the purpose of propaganda—they are simply an expression of my conviction of the confessional closeness between the Anglican Church and the Orthodox Church. I have become even more convinced of this closeness over the last few months when I learnt that the religious leaders of the English nation accept the Nicene-Constantinopolitan Creed, are restoring monasticism and no longer reject the veneration of icons or the seven sacraments.

It appears that the Orthodox hierarchs were greeted with a genuine reverence wherever they went in England. In Oxford, Metropolitan Evlogy celebrated the Orthodox Liturgy in a packed church, and sick people were brought on stretchers to be blessed by the Orthodox bishop. Metropolitan Anthony and Professor Glubokovsky were received in the House of Lords, where they spoke before a special committee on church matters.

While the Russian hierarchs were in London, hierarchical services were celebrated at St Philip's. Metropolitan Evlogy served on the first Sunday and Metropolitan Anthony served on the second Sunday. The church was filled to capacity, and the congregation included many Anglicans and Roman Catholics. On the day that Metropolitan Anthony served, Patriarchs Photios of Alexandria and Damianos of Jerusalem visited the church. Metropolitan Anthony greeted them vested and descended from the episcopal throne in the centre of the church, while Metropolitan Evlogy wore the episcopal *mantia*. Metropolitan Evlogy, as local diocesan bishop, greeted the patriarchs with a speech. Patriarch Photios replied, thanking him for his kind words and observed that even in poverty the Russians found the means to adorn their churches magnificently. Such people, he said, could not disappear, but God would give them rebirth. The patriarch expressed his joy at seeing a spiritual leader at the head of the emigration—Metropolitan Anthony, who was a zealot of Orthodoxy and a most learned hierarch. Through him the patriarch conveyed his best wishes to the Russian exiles and extended his blessing to them.[3]

While in London, Metropolitan Anthony gave two lectures about Patriarch Nikon and the question of restoring the patriarchate in Russia.

The Nicene celebrations were concluded by a visit to Wales. On July 4/17, Vladyka Anthony served a panikhida in the Russian church in London for the repose of the souls of the Emperor Nicholas II and his family. After this the Russian hierarchs left London. Both Russian émigrés and English friends came to bid them farewell.

A Definitive Statement on Anglican–Orthodox Relations

One leader of the movement toward Orthodoxy in the Anglican Church was Canon John Douglas (1868–1959), one of the founders of the Anglican and Eastern Churches Association, successor to the Eastern Church Association. After the Festival of Nicaea, he was awarded a *gramota* from the president of the Synod of Bishops of the Russian Church Abroad in recognition of his efforts. This *gramota* was solemnly presented to Canon Douglas in the Russian Church in Buckingham Palace Road. On receiving it, Canon Douglas made a speech expressing his hopes for future unity.

In reply Archbishop Anastassy of the Russian Church sent Canon Douglas a letter. This letter, written with the sensitivity and tact for which Archbishop (later Metropolitan) Anastassy was renowned, is valuable in that, while it expressed fervent hopes for unity, it also pointed to some of the fundamental differences that ultimately proved irreconcilable. Archbishop Anastassy wrote:

> The noble sincerity of your speech, so characteristic of a true Englishman, is as remarkable as is the clarity and breadth of your theological approach to the matter of the union of the Churches. With your characteristic spiritual sensitivity you have understood how hard it would be for us to lay ourselves open to criticism on the grounds that we were prepared to sacrifice the precious treasury of faith which the Orthodox Church had preserved so watchfully since the time of the Apostles. The unsullied purity of her belief and the fullness of Œcumenical truth which she possesses—these are our chief boast before the whole world, and we do not want anyone to steal them away from us.
>
> If the Eastern Churches had really set out on the path of compromise as she is now being accused of doing by certain theologians of the Church of Rome, then, to begin with she would lose her authority in your eyes, for what is it that draws you to her, if not the desire to find in her dogmatic teachings and ecclesiastical practice the unsullied Apostolic Tradition?
>
> Compromise can be used only in the realm of purely worldly political relationships but in matters of the faith, as the respected Mr Riley has commented, there is no scope for bargaining.
>
> Being aware of the particular importance and responsibility of this holy work [Church union], the Russian Church has always approached it with particular caution and [has] never attempted to underestimate the importance of the dogmatic, canonical and liturgical differences which separate us from the Anglicans.
>
> If we consider the views of the entire Anglican Church, and not just those of the Anglo-Catholics, who so far constitute a minority, then the differences prove to be far more profound than many people think. When studying the official confession of the faith of the Anglican Church our theologians, from Khomiakov to Professors Sokoloff and Kerensky, have pointed out this aspect of the situation quite distinctly, as well as the lack of inner unity within the Anglican Church itself.
>
> Nevertheless, with each passing year the two Churches are increasingly drawn to one another. What, then, is it that brings them together?

Evidently there is some inner kinship, which is revealed as we become more closely acquainted.

The Protestant storm did not completely extinguish the spark of ancient patristic tradition [in the Anglican Church]. This has continued to shed its quiet, joyful light and the darkness has not extinguished it (John 1:5).

The striving of the Anglican Church to commune once again with the Unity of the Universal Church, combined with a profound and sincere disposition in her pastors and her flock—the spirit of love and humility, which inspires the best of her children—this is the basis on which the spiritual alliance between her and the Eastern Church is now being created and strengthened.

Anyone who values the truth of Orthodoxy so highly inevitably becomes akin to us in spirit.

Anyone who has such a sincere admiration for our much-suffering Russian Church, whose vesture is drenched in the blood of the martyrs, will illuminate his own spiritual state with a reflected light, which will give him the same zeal for preserving eternal spiritual truth and the same readiness to suffer for it, for like is known by the like, for we usually admire in others that which we bear as a sacred ideal in our own souls. . . .

May the God of patience and consolation grant us to attain to perfect unity of faith and love, so that there will no longer be divisions between us, but we will be united in one Spirit and in the same thoughts and with unity of soul glorify God the Father and our Lord Jesus Christ, who have called us to eternal glory (Rom 15:5; 1 Cor 1:9–10).

After 1925 Metropolitan Anthony briefly corresponded with the Archbishop of Canterbury. However, it had become clear, as Archbishop Anastassy outlined in his letter to Canon Douglas, that the differences between Orthodoxy and the main body of the Anglican Church were simply too great for the desired union to be possible.

Archbishop Seraphim of Finland

In early 1926 Father John Lelioukhin left London for Florence, Italy. It appears that Metropolitan Evlogy had the impression that he could not manage his pastoral responsibilities properly, being crushed in spirit by his heartbreaking separation from his wife and daughters.[4] The metropolitan wanted to give greater responsibility to Father Vassily Timofeyeff who was younger and spoke fluent English. Nevertheless, Father John was loved by many who were greatly saddened by his departure. Metropolitan Evlogy gave the following account:

> I hinted to Father Lelioukhin that he should ask for a transfer to another parish but his friends rose up against me. Ultimately, however, I was able to transfer him to Florence. I should have appointed Father Timofeyeff to the vacant position but, in order to impress the English, I brought Archbishop Seraphim over from Finland. He had been deprived of his see in Finland and was confined to the Konevitz Monastery.

So in 1926 Archbishop Seraphim of Finland was appointed rector of the London parish with the status of first vicar bishop in the diocese of Western Europe under the leadership of Metropolitan Evlogy. Before the Revolution, Finland had been part of the Russian Empire. Vladyka Seraphim was Bishop of Vyborg, a vicar of the Finnish archdiocese. In the summer of 1917, when Russia was still torn between different revolutionary factions, he welcomed Archbishop Anthony (the future metropolitan), who had been driven from his see in Kharkov in southern Russia, and helped him settle in the Valaam monastery. Later, he helped arrange for Vladyka Anthony to attend the All-Russian Church Council of 1917–1918 as a representative of Russian monasticism. The same year, Vladyka Seraphim was appointed ruling bishop of the Finnish diocese, the centre of which was in Vyborg, with a country residence nearby at Markovillo. Vyborg was only 100 miles from Petrograd,[5] but after the Civil War it was included in the territory of the newly formed Finnish state. So Vladyka Seraphim and his whole diocese found themselves outside the borders of Russia without actually having moved. He was raised to the rank of archbishop and given the right to autonomy in ruling his diocese by the Supreme Church authorities in Russia. Nevertheless he recognized the authority of the exile Synod in Yugoslavia and in April 1923 became a member of the Council of Bishops of the Russian Church Abroad. Living in Vyborg, he acted as a channel of communication between the clergy in Europe and Patriarch Tikhon by forwarding letters and other documents.

The Orthodox in Finland were a minority but sufficiently numerous to attract the attention of the new, independent Finnish government. They did not consider it desirable for the head of the Orthodox Church in Finland to be a bishop belonging to the Russian Orthodox Church. So in 1923 they arranged for an autonomous Finnish Orthodox Church to be set up under the Patriarchate of Constantinople.

According to Metropolitan Evlogy, Archbishop Seraphim first attempted to cooperate with the Finns. A bishop of Estonian origin was appointed to be his vicar. Then Archbishop Seraphim was given three months to learn

Finnish. When he failed to come to the examination, he was confined to the Konevitz Monastery, and the diocese was handed over to the vicar bishop.

Describing this period later in a letter to a priest in Switzerland, Archbishop Seraphim wrote:

> In 1923 more than half my diocese was taken away from me without any justification, over my protests. I fought against the forced introduction of the Gregorian ["New"] Calendar, against the autocephaly, against separation of the Finnish church from the Russian. However, I did not consider it necessary to fight against the division of my diocese, since this was a purely administrative matter, not one affecting the foundations of Church life. . . . For nine years I suffered for Orthodoxy in Finland and endured everything—banishment, oppression, mockery and exile and poverty and other privations. All this has taught me much.

Metropolitan Evlogy helped to have Archbishop Seraphim liberated from Konevitz and brought to London, where he was appointed rector of the parish.

For the first time London had its own Russian bishop, and the services of St Philip's were regularly conducted according to the episcopal rite. Young people were attracted to serve in the altar. Anatoly Vassilisin joined this team of altar boys at the age of fourteen. The chief subdeacon, who knew all the details of the pontifical service, was a former Russian naval officer whose aunt was the abbess of a convent in Russia. The second subdeacon was a young man by the name of Evgeny Mollo.

In September 1926 Archbishop Seraphim was invited to attend a meeting of the Anglican and Eastern Churches Association. The meeting was held at a country house near Willoughby in Lincolnshire on the property of Mr Hitchcock, who was a friend of William Birkbeck. At this meeting Archbishop Seraphim recommended that members of the Anglican Church study the sacred Tradition of the Orthodox Church: the canons of the Holy Apostles, of the œcumenical and local councils and the Holy Fathers, and also the works of the Holy Fathers and Teachers of the Church and the Orthodox services. Archbishop Seraphim told his audience:

> A close acquaintance with Orthodox divine Services is of particular importance, as our services are a detailed and comprehensive expression of Orthodox theology, which they express in a beautiful poetic form. They act not only on the mind but also—even more so—on the heart, in which they

will kindle a yearning towards Orthodoxy and a reverence for its truth and spiritual beauty.

Archbishop Seraphim's time in London was cut short as a result of tragic divisions brewing in the Church Abroad which prompted his move to Paris in 1928.

The Schism in Western Europe

For six years, from 1920 to 1926, the life of the exile church developed peacefully, united under the leadership of Metropolitan Anthony and the Synod in Yugoslavia. The émigré bishops in all the centres of the emigration, including North America and China, united to form a single council, or *Sobor*. Initially this council consisted of thirty-five bishops and included Metropolitan Evlogy, who was entrusted with the care of the churches in Western Europe. The unified church gained strength as a refuge for the Russian exiles in its efforts to mitigate the persecutions in Russia and in its contacts with the non-Orthodox. However, the peace of the exiled church was not to endure.

In a book such as this, one would prefer to avoid mentioning the divisions that tragically affected the life of the Russian Church after 1926. It may be that the history of some parishes could be written by concentrating on the development of the particular community and ignoring the events outside. However, the schism had such a profound and prolonged effect on the life of the London parish that a brief explanation is essential.

The first hint of impending trouble in London might have been detected at the 100th Parish Council meeting, held in April 1922. At the meeting, Metropolitan Evlogy announced that "closer ties had been established between the churches outside Russia and the main part of the Russian Church headed by the Patriarch." Future events would show whether this was an accurate assessment of the situation. It was well known that the patriarch was under constant pressure from the communist secret police. In 1921 he confirmed Metropolitan Evlogy's appointment as bishop for Western Europe, which had originally been made by the bishops of the Church Abroad. Then in May 1922 Patriarch Tikhon issued a decree disbanding the Supreme Administration of the Russian Church Abroad; this was sent by telegram to Metropolitans Anthony and Evlogy. There were grounds for believing that this was a forced response to the Russian Church Abroad's protest over persecution of the faith in Russia made in April 1922 to the Genoa Conference.[6] The wording of the telegram from Moscow was confused and imprecise. The reaction of Metropolitan Anthony and the other bishops was to comply formally with the patriarch's decree but set up a Council of Bishops and a Synod of Bishops in place of the former Supreme Administration. Because the Supreme Administration included lay representatives as well as bishops, it may have been more influenced by political considerations. The telegram from Russia appeared to confirm, albeit on a temporary basis, Metropolitan Evlogy's status in Western Europe. Nevertheless, his initial reaction was one of shock, and he said the telegram should be disregarded as obviously having been sent as a result of Soviet pressure. However, with the passage of time, he began to insist that the decree contained in this telegram was the basis of his authority, rather than the Council of Bishops of the Church Abroad, which he increasingly disregarded. Tensions mounted until 1926, after the death of Patriarch Tikhon, when Metropolitan Evlogy walked out of the annual meeting of the Council of Bishops and declared his complete independence. For this and other acts, which were considered serious breaches of the Church Canons, Metropolitan Evlogy was relieved of his duties in January 1927 and his right to celebrate Divine Services was suspended by the Russian Church Abroad.

Beyond these questions of ecclesiastical authority, which in themselves could probably have been patched up, were serious theological and political differences. The former churchwarden of the London parish, Count Kleinmichel, expressed the view that the schism was inevitable in view of several fundamental differences of outlook that existed among the émigrés. Metropolitan Evlogy found ready support among liberal theological circles and other influential émigrés. The chief bone of contention was the St Sergius Theological Institute where the faculty included renowned Christian philosophers such as Nicholas Berdyaev and Father Sergius Bulgakov. Even before the Revolution, Metropolitan Anthony was known as the leading theologian of a conservative, traditional school, and it was obvious that he would oppose some of their ideas. In fact, the Council of Bishops condemned some of Bulgakov's teaching on "Sophia," the Wisdom of God, as having no origins in Orthodox Tradition. The institute, not surprisingly, refused to submit its program of studies to the Council of Bishops for approval and avoided this problem by supporting Metropolitan Evlogy. He also found support among exiled liberal politicians who regarded Metropolitan Anthony as too reactionary. Paradoxically, one of Metropolitan Evlogy's chief supporters was Count Vladimir Kokovtseff, a former minister of the Imperial government who was an extreme conservative yet had, even before the Revolution, vehemently opposed Metropolitan Anthony, regarding his ideas as dangerous.

Perhaps the schism within the Church Abroad was the final legacy received by the Russians from Peter the Great, who deliberately tried to wipe out the conciliar (*sobornaya*) principle of church government, which sees the Council of Bishops assembled together as the supreme ecclesiastical authority, and to replace it with the authority of a single individual or with a government department. Thus, despite the restoration of a more canonical order at the Moscow Church Council of 1917–1918, many clergy abroad strove to discern the right path in telegrams received from the Soviet Union, despite the obvious pressures, and obvious control, by the communist government that determined their contents.

At that time, the "main part" of the Russian Church was no longer headed by Patriarch Tikhon who died in 1925, but by Metropolitan Sergius (Stragorodsky), one of the few senior bishops still at liberty; he agreed to cooperate fully with the communist government, in the hope of preserving some form of church organization. Thus, under government pressure, he demanded a declaration of loyalty to the Soviet state from all Russian clergy abroad. Metropolitan Evlogy and many of his clergy initially gave this declaration of loyalty, but some left him as a result of the demand. The degree of political pressure became so great that by 1930, Metropolitan Evlogy realized direct submission to Moscow had been a mistake. However, by then the schism was too firmly entrenched for him to return to the Church Abroad. So in 1930, under an interdict from the Moscow Synod as well as the Sobor of the Church Abroad, he applied to and was accepted into the jurisdiction of the Patriarch of Constantinople.

Metropolitan Anthony sought continuously to end the schism. In 1934, detecting signs of repentance, the Council of Bishops lifted the suspension over Metropolitan Evlogy and his clergy as a gesture of reconciliation. In the same year Metropolitan Evlogy went to Yugoslavia and concelebrated with the other hierarchs, but when he returned to Paris, he reverted to his previous policy.

Throughout Western Europe there were groups of clergy and believers who remained faithful to the Council of Bishops. However, the majority sided with Metropolitan Evlogy, whose episcopal seat was the Cathedral of St Alexander Nevsky in Rue Daru in Paris.

In London, several parish meetings were held about the schism. Eugene Sablin, the former diplomatic chargé d'affaires in London, sent a series of telegrams to Metropolitan Anthony in the name of the Parish Council in which he demanded that the Synod retract its decisions about Metropolitan Evlogy. Vladyka Anthony replied to these telegrams with a long and detailed letter, in which he wrote,

> Your telegrams will be reported to the Synod of Bishops at its next meeting. Nevertheless I consider it my duty to inform you that there is no authority that can rescind the Synodal decision about Metropolitan Evlogy. It can be halted only by the means indicated in the decision itself—if Metropolitan Evlogy offers repentance and submits to the Sobor of Hierarchs of the Russian Orthodox Church Abroad.

The parish was split into two almost equal parts, neither side with a clear majority. The theological problems of Father Sergius Bulgakov's teachings and the issues of canonical authority were not well understood by most parishioners in London. It appears that people took sides mainly based on their personal loyalties and political affiliations. Metropolitan Anthony was known as a strong monarchist as well as a great theologian, and most of the aristocracy sided with him and referred to the church that he headed as *sobornaya*, that is, the church led by the assembly of hierarchs. The more politically liberal refugees tended to side with Metropolitan Evlogy and referred to his church as "Patriarshaya," that is, "patriarchal" because, at least initially, he based his authority on his nomination by the late Patriarch Tikhon. Each group felt that they were "remaining" with "their" bishop and the other was starting something new. At the same time, many felt overwhelmed by this development and appealed to the church hierarchy to sort things out.

A meeting was held at the Russian House at 27 Cromwell Road on March 13, 1927, which passed the following resolution:

> The London parish sees only one way forward to maintain peace and the authority and integrity of the Russian Orthodox Church outside Russia, in unity with the All-Russian Orthodox Mother Church, headed by his Holiness the Patriarch or his lawful locum tenens:
>
> 1. To assemble at the soonest possible moment an All-Emigration [*Vsezagranichniy*] Sobor of the Orthodox Church of Russia in accord in all things with the spirit and resolutions of the Sacred Council of the Russian Orthodox Church in 1917–1918.
> 2. Until the restoration of normal church life in Russia, this All-Emigration Sobor should organize a Supreme Administration of the Orthodox Church Abroad, in accordance with the rules and resolutions of the Sacred Council of 1917–1918.
> 3. The London Parish urges the Hierarchs to summon an All-Emigration Sobor with participation of bishops, clergy and lay people, within the next six months.

4. The Russian Church Abroad should remain until the end in the bosom of the All-Russian Orthodox Church, headed by his Holiness the Patriarch or his lawful deputy, and renounce all thoughts of autocephaly or autonomy.
5. At the same time, the London Parish invites all other parishes outside Russia to join in this urgent appeal.
6. The London Parish considers the only honourable path to follow until the organization by an All-Emigration Sobor of a Supreme Church Administration of the Russian Orthodox Church Abroad is:
   a) not to discuss the canonical dispute of the hierarchs in its essence;
   b) to leave to the conscience of each clergyman all questions of canonical obedience; and
   c) to recognize as practical, until the decision of a Council, to continue the system that has developed to date of conducting services by the clergy of the London Parish.

The first five points were accepted unanimously by all present; the last point was hotly debated and passed by a narrow margin of ninety-four votes to eighty-nine.

The "system" for conducting the services referred to in this resolution was a compromise arrangement between the two groups that appears to have been unique in the history of the Russian Church outside Russia. The church property, including the right to use St Philip's Church, was legally held by the body incorporated under English law, the London Russian Orthodox Parish Community. As the schism developed, it became unclear who should conduct the services at St Philip's, and there was a risk that chaos would develop if practical matters were neglected. Under the circumstances, paying bills and taking care of the church building could be overlooked. The directors of the Parish Community were aware of their legal responsibilities and took matters into their own hands. In the spirit of the above resolution, they decided that until the church authorities resolved matters, St Philip's should be made available on alternate weeks to clergy of each group—those in obedience to the Synod in Yugoslavia and those in obedience to Metropolitan Evlogy.

This arrangement lasted for nearly thirty years. The Parish Community limited its activities to administering the property and the expenses of using St Philip's. In addition, two parish organizations were formed, each with its own Parish Council. In time, arrangements were worked out with meticulous fairness to ensure that each parish had use of the church for alternate weeks. The basic schedule was modified to ensure a fair allocation of the services for the major holy days such as Holy Week, Easter, Pentecost, and Christmas. Each parish appointed six directors to the Parish Community, and decisions over practical matters were made by consensus. This could be referred to as "sharing" the church, but it would be more accurate to say that an Anglican church was available to each parish on alternate Sundays. There was never any concelebration between the two sets of clergy, although they did share the printed music that was carefully stored at St Philip's and handed out by the verger, or watchman, to the choir director on duty that week. A budget agreement was made as to how many singers should be paid for each service, for example, at the Saturday Vigil three singers were paid 5s. each, and at the Sunday Liturgy five singers were paid 8s. each. For the Easter night service, nine singers were paid £1 each. Later it was agreed that each parish would organize and pay its own choir separately. The accounts for the Parish Community showed that each parish contributed equally and the expenses related to upkeep of the building and wages paid to the verger who looked after the church. The Parish Community kept the £500 invested in a government bond, apparently to ensure that no unpaid liabilities would have to be met by the members of the Parish Community on eventual dissolution.

In a letter written in 1927, a parishioner, Mr G. Walneff, pointed out the benefits of this shared use of the church compared with what happened elsewhere as a result of the schism:

> We can say with confidence that the resolution passed on 13th March has assured the parish of its . . . existence up to the present day, and at the same time, has made it possible for parishioners with different canonical obediences to attend Church services. What we see in parishes elsewhere in Western Europe is that as soon as one side gains predominance, the other is deprived of all Church services, sometimes even in places such as Nice, where there are two church buildings.

This division into two parishes was bitterly opposed by many members of the Parish Council, including Vsevolod P. Ampenoff and Prince Vladimir Galitzine, but was eventually accepted de facto.

Archbishop Seraphim remained the rector of the parish under the Council of Bishops, and Archpriest Nicholas Behr was sent from Paris by Metropolitan Evlogy to conduct services for the other parish. Protodeacon Vladimir Theokritoff sided with Metropolitan Evlogy as, initially, did Father Vassily Timofeyeff. In the face of the demand for a declaration of loyalty to the Soviet regime, Father Vassily realized that he had been mistaken and returned to Archbishop Seraphim after a public act of penitence.

By a synodal decision of January 1927, Archbishop Seraphim, as hierarch of considerable seniority, was appointed ruling bishop of the parishes in Western Europe in place of Metropolitan Evlogy. Initially it was left to his discretion whether to remain in London or move to Paris. However, in the autumn of 1927, he moved to Paris, which was the largest centre of emigration, and established a diocesan centre at 3 Rue Theodore de Banville in the 17th arrondissement. Father Vassily Timofeyeff also moved to Paris to assist the archbishop.

In London the unity and splendour of the previous few years were shattered. Following the death in late 1926 of Father Constantine Veselovsky and the departure of Father Vassily with the archbishop, the only clergyman who remained in London was a protodeacon of the Evlogian jurisdiction, Father Vladimir Theokritoff. For a time neither parish had a permanent priest. Father Nicholas Behr later moved to London permanently to lead the Evlogian parish. In his memoirs Metropolitan Evlogy noted that the parish in his jurisdiction in London neither flourished materially nor spiritually. This he attributed to the meekness of Father Nicholas Behr which, he said, had never been a virtue to inspire crowds.

To serve the needs of the parish under the Council of Bishops, Protopresbyter Basil (Vassily) Vinogradoff came every two weeks from Brussels. These visits were coordinated with the Sundays that St Philip's was available to the parish. Father Basil was a theologian and preacher of the highest repute who started building the Memorial Church in Brussels, erected in honor of Tsar–Martyr Nicholas II. Later in 1932, he died suddenly of a heart attack while waiting for a tram; he was not yet 60. Shortly before that he had preached a sermon that became deeply imprinted on people's minds. Preaching on the miraculous catch of fishes and also censuring those who came to church only at the end of service, he said, "I am not Chrysostom, and I do not know with what words to inspire you at the beginning of the Liturgy. While the night of your lives is yet passing, do not cast your nets in the shallows but cast out into the true deep of true joy and true wisdom."

Archbishop Seraphim proposed Archpriest Vladimir Poliakoff, then living in Belgrade, as a new permanent parish priest for London. As an alternative, he proposed Bishop Germogen,[7] also living in Serbia. The Parish Council did not feel that a bishop would be the right person because the parish no longer had the resources to conduct services in accordance with the full episcopal rite. In addition, the presence of a bishop would require a deacon, a priest, and several altar servers. Father Vladimir Poliakoff's planned arrival was delayed because of problems with his travel documents. He had a Romanian passport stamped with a residence visa for the United Kingdom. However, before he could leave Belgrade, the Romanian government cancelled his passport.[8] He could then apply for a *Nansen* passport that was issued to stateless refugees. However, with only this document, it was difficult to obtain another visa for the United Kingdom. On October 7, 1927, the Parish Council wrote to Archbishop Seraphim:

> Of the two possible priestly candidates mentioned by your Eminence, we have unanimously resolved to ask your Eminence to appoint Father Basil Vinogradoff, whom the London parish already know after his two visits here.
>
> As a priest and as a preacher Father Basil Vinogradoff has made the most favourable impression, not only on our own parishioners, but also on our opponents. We are convinced that Father Basil would not only strengthen the parish, but also attract new parishioners. We cannot hide from your Eminence the fact that the absence of a rector for two months has had the worst possible effect on the parish and all parish matters, especially as regards private services and ministrations. For these, our parishioners have had no alternative but to turn to the Evlogian clergy, and therefore only an authoritative, persistent and energetic pastor can strengthen our parish and help it grow. We all believe that Father Vinogradoff is just such a pastor. We also request that the appointment of a new rector should, if at all possible, be made without delay. Father Vinogradoff's final move here could be postponed slightly, but it is absolutely essential that he should come to conduct the services on 15th and 16th October, when we will next have use of the church.

Archpriest Basil Vinogradoff, who traveled from Brussels to London fortnightly to serve Divine Liturgy, 1926–1928. (Source: George Volossevich)

Despite this heartfelt appeal, Archbishop Seraphim decided that he could not appoint Father Basil to the London parish because there would be no one to replace him in Brussels. Despite the affection with which Father Basil was regarded, the absence of a permanent priest in London increased the tension and anxiety caused by the schism.

Chapter 9

[1928–1932] Bishop Nicholas (Karpoff)

The Arrival of Archimandrite Nicholas

The state of uncertainty stemming from the absence of a rector did not last for long. Father Vladimir Poliakoff's passport and visa problems appeared insoluble, and in November 1927 the Parish Council received a letter from Archbishop Seraphim, recommending another Russian priest from Serbia, Archimandrite Nicholas (Karpoff). In his letter, the archbishop said that Metropolitan Anthony also recommended Archimandrite Nicholas and asked the parish whether they were prepared to accept him as their new rector. He said that in view of the distance from Serbia to England, it would not be practical to send him on a temporary basis. Initially the council was hesitant to consider a different candidate; some thought that they should persist in trying to obtain permission for Father Poliakoff to come to England. However, one council member, Colonel Korotkevitch, mentioned that he had visited Serbia the previous summer and attended services officiated by Archimandrite Nicholas. He had made a strong impression both as a fine preacher and by the reverent manner with which he conducted the services. Ultimately the Parish Council accepted the proposed appointment of Father Nicholas. He was one of the most outstanding clergymen of the Russian diaspora and immediately brought peace and new life to the parish.

Orthodox Bishop of London Nicholas (Karpoff), 1929–1932. (Source: Deacon Andrew Bond)

Father Nicholas was thirty-eight years old when he arrived in England at the beginning of 1928. He had graduated from Moscow Theological Academy in 1915. He taught in theological schools in Russia and was a preacher at the monastery in Oboyan in the Kursk province. After leaving Russia, he served in various Serbian parishes in Yugoslavia (then known as the Kingdom of the Serbs, Croats, and Slovenes). Later he taught in a seminary in Bytol, where he was greatly loved by the staff and pupils. He was appointed to London at a time when the parish was still reeling from the effects of the Church schism. He dealt remarkably well with the immense problems that he faced. Through his piety and religious fervor, he quickly won the hearts of his parishioners and brought peace to parish life.

Within a short period, Archimandrite Nicholas had the honor of becoming the first Orthodox Bishop of London. This see was considered particularly important because of both the political importance of London, which provided opportunities to mitigate the persecution of the faithful in Russia, and because of the great interest in Orthodoxy that existed in some circles in England.

Metropolitan Anthony (Khrapovitsky): Impressions of Abbess Elisabeth

For the consecration of Bishop Nicholas in 1929, Metropolitan Anthony (Khrapovitsky) came to London for his second and last visit. While in London he stayed for two weeks with the family of Vsevolod Ampenoff. The following describes the impressions left by Metropolitan Anthony on the youngest daughter of the family, who later became Abbess Elisabeth of the Convent of the Annunciation in London:

> At the time when Vladyka Nicholas was ordained they brought the miraculous icon of Our Lady of Kursk to London for the first time. There were many healings—not only Russians, but English people also had healings when they came and prayed before that miraculous icon. With the icon came Archbishop Theophan of Kursk.
>
> Metropolitan Anthony first stayed at Nashdom Abbey[1] (an Anglican Monastery). He was not very happy there, so my parents asked him to stay with us, and so he stayed with us for two weeks. There were many services, many meetings, and while he stayed with us he gave long talks about different church matters. I remember particularly how he explained the great personality of Patriarch Nikon [1605–1681] who was misunderstood by his contemporaries. He explained what a right vision he had of

Russia as the symphony of the Church, on the one hand, and the Tsar, representing the state, on the other. He spoke much about spiritual life and how to prepare for it; it was with so much peace and inner joy, which gave one great encouragement. Some non-Orthodox theologians (I do not remember their names) used to send him their work for him to read and give them his opinion. What one notices in him is an immense power of the intellect—more than just intelligence—a great noble character and a very generous heart.

He had a room in our house. In that room I left a book, a description of Kiev, of all the holy places, by—if I am not mistaken—Mouravioff. He found this book and thanked me for leaving it, because it reminded him of all the time he had lived in Kiev and all the shrines and holy places. He said that I made him feel as if he were back in Kiev.

We had a dog, a Doberman pinscher called Drouzhok, and for some of our visitors he had a special dog's love. Metropolitan Anthony had very bad feet; he used to wear special boots and then change into slippers when he came home. One day he came back very tired; there had been a lecture or something and I was alone in the house. He and his assistant, Father Theodosius, were looking for his slippers. I hadn't seen them; then I said "Drouzhok!"; he had taken the Metropolitan's slippers and slept on them. He was out, he missed him, so he took his slippers. If there was anybody whom he liked very much he would go and take their shoes, put them under the cushions and sleep on them. So the Metropolitan was very touched. Drouzhok knew some tricks: if you wrote the number 2 he would bark twice, if you wrote 4 he barked four times, and so on. The Metropolitan said he was quite a genius. When he wrote to us he always sent greetings to our "genius of a dog," who had such a special love for the Metropolitan.

The thing I really want to say is that Metropolitan Anthony was clairvoyant (*yasnovidyashchi*). He had such pure crystal-blue eyes, and when you looked at him he read your soul like an open book. There was a lady—she has died now—a very difficult character, and she wanted to see him. She was with him quite a long time. When she came out she said, "If ever anybody were to tell me that there is a saint that could read one's life, I would have to believe it." He had never met her, but he had told her all her life in detail. He made a great impression on her. He gave her an *epitemia*.[2] After two years she had to go to Yugoslavia to be released from it; and she went.

And with me—he had a talk and he looked at me and said, "You are not thinking about marriage, you are thinking about monasticism." And I said "Yes." And I thought there and then to go. He says "No, the convent where you will be doesn't exist. In ten years' time you will be there." In exactly ten years' time I went there—in 1939. Mother Maria came to England [from Jerusalem] and she offered to get me a visa. I was never very strong, so I stayed mostly at home. My parents were very attached to me. Metropolitan Anthony, before he left, had a long talk with them. I never found out what he said, but when it came time for me to go they said, "We can't resist because Metropolitan Anthony said it was the will of God." It came at the worst possible time. My father was ill, my sisters were trying to find some work; there were all these difficulties but they still obeyed and they blessed me to go. That is the great spiritual courage of Metropolitan Anthony.

The Consecration of Bishop Nicholas

The consecration of Bishop Nicholas took place in London in St Philip's Church on June 30, 1929, the feast of All Saints. There was a great solemnity and outpouring of God's grace in the life of the parish. In addition to Metropolitan Anthony, the other consecrating hierarchs were Archbishop Seraphim of Western Europe, Bishop Theophan of Kursk, Bishop Tikhon of Berlin, and Bishop Simon of Kremenetz.

On handing the archpastoral staff to Bishop Nicholas, Metropolitan Anthony gave a moving address in which he called on the new bishop to extend his care not only to the Russian flock but also to English people who were drawing near to Orthodoxy. Despite the troubles that afflicted the Russian Church in both Russia and in the emigration, this great hierarch was able to combine Russian patriotism with a missionary zeal and concern for the "local inhabitants."

Most Reverend, newly endowed with grace, Bishop Nicholas!

While greeting and congratulating you today on receiving the grace of the episcopate, I consider it my duty to remind you that in earlier times our Russian bishops not only remembered the day of their consecration for their whole lives, but also kept it holy each year by intensified prayer and celebration of Divine services, combined with intercession to the saint commemorated on that day, who would be considered the special protector of that particular bishop.

The Lord has granted you to receive bishop's orders on the day not just of a single saint, but of all the saints, whom you must therefore hold all together in special veneration.

Of course, you know that the Russian people, more than all others, venerate the saints pleasing to God, surpassing in this not only all those other faiths, but all the other Orthodox people. There is not one people which has such an attitude of love tinged with compunction towards the saints as the Russian people, who revere them as their closest protectors and friends, thereby showing where their treasure is and where their heart is.

While warrior peoples revere ancient heroes, and devotees of philosophy revere famous scholars in their own field of specialization, the Russian people revere the saints, properly considering that righteousness is the field of specialization for all of mankind, in accordance with the Saviour's words: "But seek ye first the Kingdom of God and His righteousness, and all these things shall be added unto you." (Matt 6:33)

So, being called to guide the people of God, be guided in your turn by the people's example of this virtue—the love and veneration for the holy saints—because through this one shows that for oneself also spiritual perfection is dearer than anything else in the world.

A second indication from above is given to you by this day of your consecration: that in this life you should be not only a servant of God, but a Russian servant of God, sharing the highest strivings of our Russian people, its reverent love for the saints. This is not understood by the Protestants, who assert that the Russians, in venerating the saints, thereby belittle the Glory of Christ. Christ Himself, however, gave us a firm basis for this when He said "And the glory which Thou gavest me I have given them. . . ." (John 17:22)

However, while remaining a Christian and a Russian patriot you will, of course, be far from that sinful chauvinism which now afflicts all peoples calling themselves Christian, even alas, Orthodox peoples.

We can boldly assert that only the Russian people, in the person of its best representatives, is able to combine an œcumenical, universal love with patriotism, and regards these two exalted concepts not as mutually exclusive, imposing limits one on the other, but as interpenetrating and complementing each other.

An example of this wonderful combination was shown by the Lord Jesus Christ Himself, who was Himself the good Samaritan Who, while He was the Saviour of all peoples, yet remained a Jewish patriot, who lamented for Jerusalem and exclaimed, "O Jerusalem, Jerusalem, thou that killest the prophets and stonest them that are sent unto thee, how often would I have gathered thy children together, even as a hen gathereth her chickens under her wings, and ye would not!" (Matt 23:37)

The Lord has sent you the destiny of beginning your archpastoral service in the land of a people which has many enlightened sons, with a heartfelt love for our people and our faith. I have become convinced of this while spending a few days in the newly established Anglican monastery of Nashdom Abbey.

There I was consoled to observe the profound and fervent piety of the young monks and was convinced that, for them, prayer is not just an accepted ceremonial, but a profound cry of the soul, fervently striving towards God and towards spiritual purification. We are further convinced of this by the very fact of the establishment of Anglican monasteries in recent years, at a time when, in other countries, even Orthodox countries, monasteries and monasticism are rapidly declining in numbers.

So, show particular pastoral concern for those souls, mostly young, in the Anglican Church, who would wish to become acquainted more closely, and in a more heartfelt manner, with the Orthodox faith and the Orthodox Church.

Accommodate them in your pastoral heart and pray to God for the salvation both of your own Russian people and of those English people who are drawing near to the Orthodox Church, so that you also, in the measure of God's gifts to you, may be able to say "I am made all things to all men, that I might by all means save some." (1 Cor 9:22)

Bishop Nicholas outside St Philip's on the day of his consecration as a bishop, 1929. First from left, Prince George Galitzine; fourth from left, General Halfter, Parish Council Chairman; fifth from left, Prince Emanuel Galitzine. (Source: *Church Times*)

This, of course, should be the confession of every Orthodox bishop, and of you personally in particular, as one ordained for the sons of the Orthodox dispersion living in a country which is not Orthodox, but friendly towards Orthodoxy.

May you be strengthened in this holy intention by the saints pleasing to God, who are glorified today throughout the whole world. May you be strengthened in particular by the Holy Hierarch John of Tobolsk, a saint whom you, as a true Russian and a sincerely Orthodox clergyman, honour with a special reverence, and at whose canonization [in 1916] you were accounted worthy to participate. Run ceaselessly to him for the help of God's grace, while at the same time honouring all the saints of God, and may their prayers protect you from the temptations of life and from all troubles.

Parish Life Under the Leadership of Bishop Nicholas

The first problem facing the new bishop was that St Philip's Church was only available on alternate Sundays, so half the time his congregation had no church. To alleviate the situation temporarily, a chapel was set up in Prince Vladimir Galitzine's house in Chessington, about 20 miles southwest of London.[3] This was a favorite gathering place for the Russian community during the 1920s and 1930s. Mrs Sophia Goodman recalls,

> In Chessington, in Surrey, was a house which my aunt—my mother's sister—and her husband, Prince Vladimir Galitzine, rented, near where the zoo is now. She was a very pious person and knew everybody in the church, so in the summer the whole choir would come down after the service—it acted as a church hall or meeting place. Many people would go down by train to Chessington and sit around in the garden there. It was quite wild, not a proper garden. I remember sitting down at a table with about twenty people round it. There was an old colonel with one leg; he was supposed to give Russian lessons to my aunt's three sons, but on the whole he just went around and fed the chickens—that sort of thing. There was always a mixture of people, because my aunt spoke four languages. She had a great variety of friends in London, so you'd have people from the Austrian Embassy mixed up with somebody from the Russian choir who was driving a taxi somewhere in London . . . it was a real mixture, and they all got on very well. So the place had a tremendous spirit about it, and it was closely bound up with the church and with the congregation.
>
> It was a very big, rambling, tumbledown farmhouse, so there was plenty of room, and people sometimes used to stay the night. I remember, as a little girl, waking up and checking who was in the house, because people would be sleeping on the carpet and on camp beds. The bishop was often there. Bishop Nicholas baptized me, but I was too young to remember his visits. There are photographs with him always in the middle, surrounded by the children. This whole period he certainly used it as a place where people could meet and he held services there until they bought the Podvoria.

Bishop Nicholas immediately set about acquiring a church and base for the parish in a central location. It should be remembered that St Philip's was acquired through the generosity of the Anglicans, and any property the parish bought for itself would be of far more modest proportions. The bishop started a collection, to which he added some funds of his own, and a grant was obtained from the Spaulding Foundation, through contacts with the Galitzine family. Soon the freehold of a house at 14 St Dunstan's Road, in West Kensington, was purchased. Today this is considered a desirable area, expensive even by London standards; however, at the time it was bought by the parish, it represented a low-priced piece of property in a very rundown part of London. Mrs Goodman recalled,

> They bought it for just a hundred pounds,[4] but a hundred pounds was quite a substantial sum in those days—a year's salary for some people. It was in a real slum area. Along the road between Baron's Court underground station and the Podvoria, where now houses are being done up, alongside the railway. . . . I remember seeing all the children with filthy knees and sometimes no socks and shoes at all; it was really very dirty. We preferred to come in by tube, because otherwise it meant one had to walk from West Kensington, and all that area was very squalid—a really bad London slum. Nevertheless, being in West London it was reasonably central for the Russian community. Many of the Russians lived in Fulham,

Archimandrite Nicholas in Chessington with a group of parishioners at the home of Prince Vladimir Galitzine (first on left), 1928. (Source: Sophia Goodman)

> where there were two Russian shops. There was Shestakoff and another. Both were our parishioners and there was a sufficient number of people living there to use them. They had kasha and such things, but it was all on a very modest scale.

Front door of the Podvoria, St Dunstan's Road, in 1980.

Once inside the door of number 14, one was in a different world. The ground floor had been converted into a church, which Vladyka Nicholas consecrated in honor of All Saints, thereby fulfilling Metropolitan Anthony's precept to accord special veneration to the feast on which he had been ordained to the episcopate. This tiny church, beautifully converted in the ancient Russian style, impressed visitors as a holy place, an oasis in the middle of the noisy city. The rest of the house was used as the bishop's residence and also as accommodation for the monastic brotherhood started by Vladyka Nicholas. The house was small, but at least it was owned outright by the parish. Originally it was described as *Arkhiereiskoye Podvoriye*—the bishop's residence. In later years it was not always occupied by a bishop, but the name stuck, so it was known simply as the "Podvoria" or affectionately, in English, as the "Pod."

Bishop Nicholas attracted the young people of the parish to help him set up the church. Anatoly Vassilisin, then in his late teens, vividly remembered helping with the carpentry, making analoi (icon stands) and other objects. He had great admiration for Bishop Nicholas, whom he found very approachable and who inspired him to devote his time and energy to the Church. Vassilisin was the senior subdeacon and applied the experience he had gained in the days of Archbishop Seraphim. On the Sundays when the Podvoria church was used, the services were conducted according to the episcopal rite, despite the cramped conditions of the small chapel.

In his work with youth, Bishop Nicholas placed great importance on the summer camps, which were organized with the aid of the church sisterhood and held in a different location each year—Windsor, King's College, Canterbury, Ewell, Enfield, Bexhill. Forty to fifty children attended the camps, where the bishop held morning and evening services and gave religious instruction. Other subjects such as the history and geography of Russia and

Bishop Nicholas conducting the wedding of Kenneth Williams and Ariadne Ackerman at St Philip's, c. 1930. (Source: George Volossevich)

Russian literature were also taught. Yet these summer camps were intended mainly to be holidays, so the bishop also played games with the children, who all greatly loved him.

Bishop Nicholas was a natural leader and an inspired preacher. On one occasion, during a sermon about the Church schism, he is said to have become so carried away that he broke his bishop's staff. At the meeting of the Council of Bishops in 1931, Bishop Nicholas gave the following report. One is struck by its positive tone, thanking God for what had been achieved, rather than dwelling on the difficulties and hardships.

> Orthodox life in London is developing well. It is centred on the Church of the Dormition of the Most Holy Mother of God, which is situated in the building of the Anglican Church of St. Philip's. In addition a church has been opened near London, in Prince Galitzine's house. On Palm Sunday [of 1931] the church in the Podvoria was consecrated.
>
> As a bishop's residence [Podvoria] I have acquired a four-storeyed house, in which a splendid church has been established, in the ancient Russian style. The work on the inside of the church has been done by our own young people, and we have ordered an iconostasis from Paris. At the Podvoria there are two priest-monks and one hierodeacon. Church services are conducted daily according to the monastic rule [typicon], and the monks fulfill other obediences in the house. The Podvoria church is attended zealously by the congregation, on whom the monastery services and monastic order of life in the Podvoria are having a very beneficent influence.

At our parish church we have the sisterhood of St. Xenia with the Grand Duchess Xenia Alexandrovna as President; Mrs. V. N. Volkoff and Princess Meshchersky are active members.

At the present time a brotherhood of young people is being organized. One of its purposes is to give talks on religious and moral questions. These talks will be given by me and by the young people themselves. The most active members are Eugene Moloff, [George] Knupffer and [Anatoly] Vassilisin.

The last parish meeting showed that our life had passed without a deficit in the material sense, and is in fact developing with great success. Prince Galitzine was chosen as the new churchwarden, G. F. Walneff was chosen as honorary trustee, General Halfter as chairman of the Parish Council and V. P. Ampenoff as treasurer.

As we were establishing our new Podvoria, church service books were sent to us from Mount Athos; vestments and other items were acquired through the generosity and efforts of parishioners, and from Metropolitan Dionysius in Warsaw we have received some very fine sacred vessels and four icons.

Every summer we gather together about 40 to 50 Russian children, rent a house for them somewhere outside the city, and there organize a school where we teach them subjects they do not learn in the English schools, such as religious instruction and the Russian language, so that the rising generation retains its links with Russia.

Besides this, a Russian educational society is currently being organized under the presidency of the Grand Duchess Xenia Alexandrovna, which will have various divisions—lectures, artistic and so on. This society will be dedicated to questions of the study of Russian life and its creative aspects.

Interior of All Saints Chapel, Podvoria, St Dunstan's Road, c. late 1930s. (Source: Deacon Andrew Bond)

Interior of All Saints Chapel, Podvoria, St Dunstan's Road, c. 1980. (Source: Deacon Andrew Bond)

Generally speaking our life is developing calmly and quietly, with a profound conviction that we are following the right path, and with faith in God's help.

Bishop Nicholas: A Spiritual Portrait

Bishop Nicholas was a great friend of the Ampenoff family. The following recollections, recounted by the youngest daughter, Abbess Elisabeth, testify to his spiritual nature:

> In 1928 when Father Nicholas came he brought new life. He had a very joyous, encouraging personality, with a very keen sense of humour. But he was very strict and uncompromising in Church matters. At St. Philip's the altar was blessed every time before the service, due to it being shared with the Evlogian group. It was very soon after the schism. He gave talks for the adults and, separately, for the young people.
>
> My friends and I helped sew the analoi covers and other items for the church. The iconostasis was painted in Paris by Princess Lvov [a relative of Bishop Nathaniel]. The Podvoria was always spotlessly clean. The Bishop and his two assistant priests, Father Kallistos and Father Zossima, cleaned whenever they noticed "more of that London dust." Incense from Mount Athos was used in the church, and as soon as you went into the house, it was not like being in London at all—people said it was like Mount Athos.[5]

He worked hard at learning English, but found it difficult. Sometimes shopkeepers would not give him change, thinking he would not know the difference. So he would muster his few words of English and say, "Yes, I Russian, but . . . ha'penny, ha'penny!"

Every Great Feast we felt it was different; he put so much into it. He served with great concentration and intensity. I remember one occasion when he was reading the Gospels, he suddenly went very pale and stopped reading, as if all the blood had drained from his face. The colour returned and he continued reading. God alone knows what he saw or understood in those moments. Another thing that was quite remarkable about him is that he loved to serve the panikhida (memorial service for the departed). He would pray, reading the names as if they were his own mother, his father or his sister, with so much love and feeling. So that when he was buried, Metropolitan Anthony said that, as he loves so much to pray for the deceased, God had sent him such a death—quiet and peaceful.

He had a great power of prayer. Through his faith and prayers there were some wonderful healings. I know of one healing which a young woman told me about. She had a very bad inflammation of the middle ear. The doctor said she must have an operation. She had a very high temperature and atrocious pain, so bad that she could not sleep. The doctor gave her some drops. Then Bishop Nicholas came and served a moleben. He put his epitrakhilion (stole) on her head. While he was praying the pain went and she fell asleep. After an hour her mother came up to see her. The pain had gone and all the pus that was inside was coming out through her mouth and nose. When the doctor came, he said he could not explain it.

Another time, my father had an operation. Nobody knew he had an ulcer—duodenal—and after the anaesthetic he started terrible internal bleeding. The doctors decided that he was dying. It was the first week of Lent and that week I was in church. Vladyka Nicholas was there. And suddenly I felt worried about my father. So Vladyka Nicholas agreed there and then to serve a moleben to St. Panteleimon. He had a great reverence for St. Panteleimon. The doctor couldn't understand what happened. My father was actually dying, he was bleeding to death. Then it stopped.

The Death and Testament of Bishop Nicholas

Bishop Nicholas remained only three years in his see. In August 1932 he went to Yugoslavia to take part in a meeting of the Council of Bishops, after which he fell ill with appendicitis. Because of an oversight he was not operated on in time, and he died on the night of October 10/11. His last words were, "Give me a candle to hold. I am dying. I want to go away to heaven." After taking hold of the candle, Vladyka Nicholas quietly departed this life.

His funeral took place on October 12 in the Church of the Iveron Mother of God in Belgrade. It was conducted by Metropolitan Anthony, Archbishops Germogen and Theophan, and thirteen Russian and Serbian priests with three deacons. The funeral was an occasion of profound compunction and spiritual edification. During the service, Vladyka Anthony wept profusely on several occasions. Archbishop Theophan gave a sermon about the deceased bishop, and after the service Vladyka Anthony addressed the congregation:

> On behalf of the deceased I thank the Russian and Serbian clergy, who have accompanied him on his journey to the next world. I thank you also, laypeople, for having prayed so fervently. Throughout my life I have observed that, to those who love to pray for the deceased, the Lord sends a quiet and undisturbed end, and an edifying funeral. This end awaits all of us—some earlier, some later—but it comes to all without a doubt. People have gathered at this funeral not out of obligation but following the inclination of their hearts, and this has given it a spiritual beauty.

Bishop Nicholas was buried by the walls of the Iveron Church beneath an icon of the Holy Hierarch Nicholas of Myra, which is set in the outside wall of the church.

The untimely death of her first bishop undoubtedly was a tragedy of the first magnitude for the Orthodox Church in England. All the parishioners had come to love Bishop Nicholas and were very distressed. "Even the milkman," recalled Abbess Elisabeth, "when they told him that he had died, had tears in his eyes. 'What a pity,' he said, 'what a wonderful person!' All loved him. Many, many English people who had met him expressed great sorrow that he was so young, and had died."

The Anglican Canon Douglas, who was a great friend of the Russian Orthodox Church, wrote in an obituary:

> All who knew him grieve for the death of Bishop Nicholas, the priest of that part of the Russian Parish of London which holds by the Metropolitan Anthony and the Karlovic Synod of Russian Bishops in Exile. His was a sunny personality. Always eager, always enjoying life, always smiling, always loving and asking for love, even—and at times such moods swept over him in indignation—when in excited, combative anger, he was typical

of Russian monasticism in its most engaging appeal. Quite unworldly, childlike in many things, as mystic altogether, he was one of those folk to whom, as it has been said, the world owes a supreme debt just because they are so manifestly happy.

As he lay dying, Bishop Nicholas wrote the following testament to his flock in London, in his own hand:

> In the Name of the Father and of the Son and of the Holy Spirit! My dearest London flock!
>
> I am writing to you for the last time before departing into eternity. I have not the strength or the words to express my love for you. As I depart, I am taking you with me in my heart. I am thinking of you, particularly my friends the Meshcherskys, the Galitzines and the Ampenoffs and all my young flock. I bequeath to you the church and Podvoria in prayerful memory. Gather there and make intercession for me. It would be good if you were to fulfill my last request and choose Father Anatoly as your priest. Then the Podvoria would not be destroyed. Continue in love one for another.
>
> I bow to the ground before our hierarch Kyr Anthony. How glad I am that he will close my eyes and conduct my funeral. I also bow to the ground before our hierarch Archbishop Seraphim and all the members of the Church Abroad. I have tried to be useful. On all Orthodox Christians and on my brother monks and priests I invoke God's blessing.
>
> I am growing weaker. Oh to be able to do "all things" by the power of Jesus who strengthens me!
>
> Nicholas
> Orthodox Bishop of London

CHAPTER 10

[1933–1938]
Archpriest Boris Molchanoff

A New Rector Comes from France

During the remainder of 1932 and into 1933, the parish was served by Archpriest Simeon Solodovnikoff. Father Anatoly, mentioned in Bishop Nicholas's last testament, had not yet completed his theological studies and remained in Yugoslavia. The young monastic brotherhood dispersed after the death of its founder and spiritual guide; none of the monks were able to take over as the parish abbot or rector. (Later Priest-monk Kallistos became rector of the parish in Nice and Priest-monk Zossima as rector in nearby Menton.) In January 1933, the following synodal decision was reported:

> Due to the current financial difficulties in the London parish, brought on by the Depression, and the urgent need to seek funds in order to consolidate the parish's ownership of the All Saints Podvoria, the Synod of Bishops has, by a resolution dated 2/15 December (1932), authorized the Most Reverend Archbishop Seraphim to appoint, as rector of the parish, a person in priest's orders; not, however, abolishing the *cathedra* of the Bishop of London, Vicar of the Diocese of Western Europe, but considering it to be a widowed see.

The "person in priest's orders" was Father Boris Molchanoff, who was sent to England from Meudon, near Paris, by Archbishop Seraphim. Father Boris was born in St Petersburg on July 24, 1896. In 1916 he enrolled in Petrograd University, in the faculty of natural sciences. However, he was soon drafted into the Imperial Army and joined the White Army under General Nicholas Yudenitch during the Civil War. After the war he went to Paris and in 1926 entered the newly founded St Sergius Theological Institute, from which he graduated in 1928. Metropolitan Evlogy ordained him to the priesthood and assigned him to the parish in Meudon, where he served his first Liturgy on Palm Sunday in 1927.

Metropolitan Evlogy wrote the following in his memoirs (which, having been written in hindsight, must be regarded with some caution):

> The church community in Meudon was started by Fr. A. Kalashnikoff. On great feasts he used to come from Clamart and held services in a private house. He was replaced by Fr. Boris Molchanoff, a student from the Theological Institute. In Meudon there lived an engineer, Chaeff, the inventor of "Solomite," a special mixture of straw and clay suitable for light construction work or buildings of a temporary nature. Chaeff started building a church out of his "Solomite" on a plot of land which he owned. No sooner was the roof in place, than a dispute broke out between Father Molchanoff and two members of the Ladies' Committee. At the General Meeting half the members of the parish were for Father Molchanoff and half against. I did not support the priest—I spoke in favour of the Committee ladies. As a result, no sooner had the Karlovtsi schism broken out, than Father Molchanoff abandoned me and took the church builder, Chaeff, and some of the parishioners with him. The others were left without a church.

Archpriest Boris Molchanoff, rector of the London parish from 1933 to 1938. (Source: Archbishop Mark)

A 1935 advertisement for a concert organized by the North Russian Association. (Source: George Volossevich)

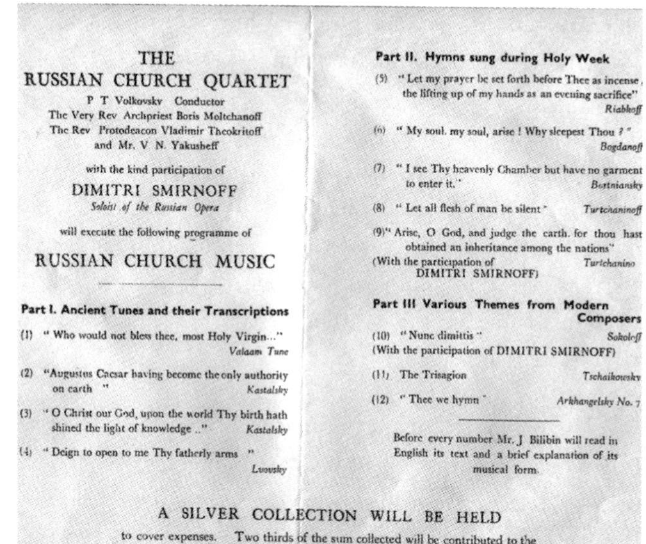

THE
RUSSIAN CHURCH QUARTET
P T Volkovsky Conductor
The Very Rev Archpriest Boris Moltchanoff
The Rev Protodeacon Vladimir Theokritoff
and Mr. V N. Yakusheff

with the kind participation of
DIMITRI SMIRNOFF
Soloist of the Russian Opera

will execute the following programme of

RUSSIAN CHURCH MUSIC

Part I. Ancient Tunes and their Transcriptions

(1) "Who would not bless thee, most Holy Virgin..." *Valaam Tune*

(2) "Augustus Caesar having become the only authority on earth" *Kastalsky*

(3) "O Christ our God, upon the world Thy birth hath shined the light of knowledge.." *Kastalsky*

(4) "Deign to open to me Thy fatherly arms" *Lvovsky*

Part II. Hymns sung during Holy Week

(5) "Let my prayer be set forth before Thee as incense, the lifting up of my hands as an evening sacrifice" *Riabkoff*

(6) "My soul, my soul, arise! Why sleepest Thou?" *Bogdanoff*

(7) "I see Thy heavenly Chamber but have no garment to enter it." *Bortniansky*

(8) "Let all flesh of man be silent" *Turtchaninoff*

(9) "Arise, O God, and judge the earth, for thou hast obtained an inheritance among the nations" (With the participation of DIMITRI SMIRNOFF) *Turtchanino*

Part III Various Themes from Modern Composers

(10) "Nunc dimittis" *Sokoloff*
(With the participation of DIMITRI SMIRNOFF)

(11) The Trisagion *Tschaikowsky*

(12) "Thee we hymn" *Arkhangelsky No. 7*

Before every number Mr. J Bilibin will read in English its text and a brief explanation of its musical form.

A SILVER COLLECTION WILL BE HELD
to cover expenses. Two thirds of the sum collected will be contributed to the London Russian Orthodox Parish Community,

A program of Russian church music, 1935. (Source: George Volossevich)

In fact, the reasons for Father Molchanoff's departure from the Evlogian jurisdiction were, as one would expect from such an idealistic and intellectual clergyman, beyond a mere dispute with the Meudon Ladies' Committee. The decisive factor was the demand that was received from Moscow that all clergymen within Metropolitan Evlogy's jurisdiction give an oath of loyalty to the Soviet Union. Father Boris wrote the following to Metropolitan Evlogy:

> I must report to your Eminence that I cannot, in good conscience, satisfy this demand, since by the very fact of my existence in the emigration I am affirming my protest against the Soviet government. I have never been involved in politics and do not plan to become involved. I do not belong to any political party. But I cannot think of pastoral service as something artificially divorced from national and social activity. I consider it my pastoral duty to fight against socialism and communism, which are violently anti-Christian doctrines, and even more so, to fight against their attempts to implement these anti-Christian principles.

On August 8, 1928, in reaction to a threat of suspension for clergy who did not give the oath, Father Boris wrote,

> I consider that unity with the Moscow Church authorities, which are unconditionally demanding recognition of the atheist Soviet government and a renunciation of all spiritual struggle against it, does not constitute

> unity with the genuine Mother Church of Russia. On the contrary, such unity would constitute the strongest affront to her radiant, much suffering person.
>
> Desiring to preserve a genuine inner spiritual unity with our suffering Russian Church, and with her most worthy hierarchs who, in internal exile and imprisonment are "rightly dividing the word of truth," I have the honour to inform your Eminence, that as of today's date I am transferring my canonical obedience to the Synod of Bishops, to whom I am submitting this decision of my conscience for their judgement and consideration.

When the day of the ultimatum arrived in August 1928, Father Boris called a general meeting of his parishioners, explained his decision, and told each to decide according to his or her conscience. Thus, the Parish of the Resurrection in Meudon became a principal centre of the Church Abroad in the Paris region.

Five years later, Archbishop Seraphim appointed the dedicated, young Father Boris to the responsible position of rector of the parish in London, after having raised him to the rank of archpriest. He arrived with his wife and three children and moved into the All Saints Podvoria at 14 St Dunstan's Road.

Abbess Elisabeth remembered Father Boris as a very serious person who warned of the apocalyptic changes that were beginning throughout the world. He had a flaming orange–red beard, but otherwise did not leave a vivid impression on his parishioners, as did his predecessor (Bishop Nicholas) and his successor (Father Michael Polsky).

George Orloff, a faithful parishioner for over half a century, wrote the following recollections of Father Boris:

> My first meeting with Father Boris Molchanoff was to seek advice on the question of freemasonry: as a young man, I received an invitation to become a Mason and in reply to my questioning the nature of the Society, and not receiving a satisfactory answer, I spoke to my mother, who suggested that I should talk to Father Boris.
>
> This was in 1936. At first he was suspicious of me and was anxious to know more about me, what were the circumstances of the masonic approach and so forth. Then suddenly he decided to be helpful and gave me on loan the manuscript of his book on the subject, which he was going to have published.

In retrospect this was a remarkable act of confidence and I read it with reverence; it was a profound thesis on the history and nature of that secret society with a surprising number of references and parallels made with the Revelation of St. John: needless to say, I never joined the Freemasons.

After I returned the manuscript our conversations became quite frequent concerning "the Subject": as we became stronger in friendship, he confided that they [the Freemasons] were largely to blame for the lack of spirituality of the times. He distrusted the Scout movement and the YMCA and Rotarians, considering these as being recruiting agencies for Freemasonry and a means of achieving a unified unchristian fellowship made up of a mix of world philosophies.

He warned against material traps such as financial loans with easy repayments. He considered that pornography was being spread, not only as a perversion of eroticism, but also through music (jazz of the 1930s), visual arts (Picasso's Post-Blue Period) and literature.

In about 1937 he was appointed to head a holiday camp of Russian émigré children in a place near Blackwater (Hampshire), from memory somewhere north of what has since become Blackbush Airport. I visited him and his family at the camp on one or two occasions, since it was not far from Basingstoke, where I was a student.

Father Boris was a noble and dedicated priest . . . and true to his vocation; he was tireless and fearless in his pursuit and exposure of iniquities of the world. Since leaving England, before World War II, he had the kindness of sending some beautiful icons to me, which we treasure. It has been a great privilege to have known Father Boris and to have been considered as his friend. I constantly mention his name in my prayers and thank God for having known him.

The London-based Urals Cossack Choir, c. 1935. (Source: George Volossevich)

Visits from Archbishop Seraphim of Western Europe

In May 1935, Father Boris attended special services of intercession for the persecuted Church in Russia that were organized by the Anglicans. Many Orthodox hierarchs were invited, including Archbishop Seraphim of Western Europe. Solemn services were also held in St Philip's by the Orthodox clergy. The following description is taken from the June 1935 edition of *Tserkovnaya Zhizn*, the official publication of the Church Abroad, printed in Yugoslavia:

> **Intercession in London for the Russian Church**
>
> On 16 May, at the initiative of the Russian Clergy and Church Aid Fund, a solemn service of prayer for the end of persecutions of the faith in the Soviet Union was held in London at the church of St. Martin-in-the-Fields. Representatives of the Russian Church Abroad were invited to be present at this service—Archbishop Anastassy of Kishinev and Khotyn, Vice-President of the Synod of Bishops, Archbishop Seraphim, ruling the Russian Orthodox Diocese of Western Europe, and the rector of the Russian Church in London, Archpriest Boris Molchanoff. Also present were representatives of the Patriarchate of Constantinople—Metropolitan Evlogy, Archimandrite Constantinides, the rector of the Greek Church in London, and Archpriest N. Behr.
>
> The large and beautiful church was filled to capacity. The service was conducted by the Archbishop of Canterbury assisted by many bishops and clergymen. The order of service was specially compiled out of Russian litanies and prayers. The Lord Mayor's Choir sang "Lord have mercy" and "With the saints give rest" [a hymn from the Orthodox funeral service]. The Orthodox hierarchs stood wearing the episcopal *mantia*. In the middle of the service, the Archbishop of Canterbury gave a moving address about the need to pray for the Russian Church and actively help her clergy. After the address a special collection was taken up. One lady sent the Archbishop of Canterbury a cheque for £1,000 for the benefit of the two Russian parishes in London.
>
> After the service, the Archbishop of Canterbury held a reception in honour of the invited representatives of the Orthodox clergy. On the following day, 17 May, in the evening, a solemn service was held in the church of St. Cyprian, the most beautiful church in London, at which all the Orthodox bishops and priests were also present.

On 19 May in the Russian Church, after the Liturgy, a service of intercession (moleben) was held for the suffering believing Russian people. The Liturgy and moleben were served by Archbishop Anastassy, Archbishop Seraphim, Protopresbyter Alexander Shabasheff (rector of the church in Brussels), Archpriest Boris Molchanoff (rector of the London church) and Deacon P. Voinov (from Paris). Many representatives of the Anglican clergy were present in their vestments. The bishop of Fulham was there as representative of the Archbishop of Canterbury. In luxuriant vestments and a mitre stood the abbot of the Anglican monastery Nashdom Abbey.

Her Imperial Highness the Grand Duchess Elena Vladimirovna and His Highness Prince Nikita Alexandrovich were present in the church.

Before the beginning of the moleben Archbishop Anastassy gave a moving address about the attitude of the Anglican Church to the persecuted Russian clergy. The church was filled to capacity. The moleben ended with proclamations of "Many Years" to: (1) Metropolitan Peter of Krutitsa (locum tenens of the Patriarchal See), His Beatitude Metropolitan Anthony and all the Russian episcopate, (2) King George V of Great Britain and his consort Queen Mary, (3) the Grand Duchesses Xenia Alexandrovna and Elena Vladimirovna and all the Russian Royal House and (4) the suffering Russian people and all those present, standing and praying.

After the moleben all the clergy served a panikhida for the repose of the murdered Sovereign, Emperor Nicholas II.

That evening the Parish Council of the London Russian Church organized a reception in honour of the visiting Russian bishops. Archpriest B. Molchanoff spoke a few words of greeting in the name of the parish.

The following day, 20 May, at the abbot's invitation, our Vladykas, accompanied by Father Protopresbyter Shabasheff and Father Archpriest Molchanoff, visited Nashdom Abbey, an Anglican monastery 19 miles from London. The abbot, Dr. Collett,[1] is one of the most remarkable people in England, charming and highly cultured.

This monastery is located in a property that used to be the country home of Prince Dolgoruki; the prince gave it the Russian name *Nash Dom* [Our House] which has been retained by the present occupants in the name Nashdom Abbey. The enormous but comfortable building, now adapted as a monastery, is located in a large rambling park surrounded by ancient lime trees—a very peaceful setting.

DECEMBER 18, 1937] THE SPHERE 511

A 700-YEAR-OLD ICON BROUGHT TO LONDON

And Other Pictures of Religious and Artistic Interest, Relating Particularly to the Orthodox Church

ONCE THIS ANCIENT ICON WAS INLAID WITH GEMS WORTH A KING'S RANSOM, to-day its frame is much less richly adorned, but as a religious relic it is beyond price. It has been brought to London from Yugoslavia

TREASURED SYMBOL OF THE ORTHODOX FAITH: Archbishop Seraphim (right), standing beside the 700-year-old icon of Our Lady of Koursk in the Russian Church in London where it is being displayed. The Archbishop has been responsible for bringing it from Yugoslavia, where it has been kept ever since Archbishop Theophan of Koursk escaped with it across the Russian border at the advent of red rule

A NEEDLEWORK MASTERPIECE: This icon is one of the treasured permanent possessions of the Russian Church in London and bears a representation of the body of Christ awaiting burial. Moscow nuns made it

The *Sphere* article showing Archpriest Boris (left) and Archbishop Seraphim (Lukianov) (right) with the Kursk icon at the Podvoria, December 1937. (Source: Sophia Goodman)

While they were in London, Archbishop Anastassy and Archbishop Seraphim visited the Grand Duchesses Xenia Alexandrovna and Elena Vladimirovna. Archbishop Seraphim visited England again in November 1937. On this occasion he brought with him the miraculous Kursk icon of the Mother of God of the Sign. The icon was brought out of southern Russia along with the departing masses of refugees who left in 1920.[2] It was treasured as a holy object by the church in exile. Periodically it was taken to different dioceses and parishes of the Russian Church Abroad throughout the world for the faithful to pour out their prayers to the Mother of God. The previous occasion it had been in England was for the episcopal consecration of Bishop Nicholas in 1929.

The October 31, 1937, edition of the newspaper *The Russian in England* contained the following announcement:

> The miraculous Kursk Icon of the Mother of God will arrive in London not on 30th October, as announced in the previous issue of this paper, but

on Friday, 12 November, as a result of delays in France. The Icon is being accompanied by his Eminence Archbishop Seraphim. While the Holy Icon is in London, services will be held as follows:

In St. Philip's Church
13 November—Vigil and Moleben (service of intercession)
14 November—Liturgy and Moleben
27 November—Vigil and Moleben
28 November—Liturgy and Moleben

In the Podvoria Church
20 November—Vigil and Moleben
21 November—Liturgy and Moleben to the Mother of God and the Archangel Michael

Private services will also be conducted in the homes of those wishing to receive the holy icon.

The archbishop also took the icon to Walsingham in Norfolk, where he blessed the proposed site of an Orthodox chapel that was to be built at this ancient English holy site. Walsingham was venerated for centuries as a place where a pious Saxon noblewoman had a vision of the Mother of God. A contemporary of the author, the Orthodox priest Father Philip Steer, describes its significance for Orthodoxy in England, "It represented perhaps one of the last flowerings of the Anglo-Saxon Church, which was still Orthodox, until it was overwhelmed and altered by the Norman Conquest in 1066." In the 1930s Anglo-Catholic circles in the Church of England began a revival of the ancient veneration of this site and invited the Russian Orthodox Church to participate in the project. The Church of England had built a large new church known as the Shrine Church, and an Orthodox chapel was to be built beside it on the south side of the main building.

The Walsingham newspaper *Our Lady's Mirror* described the archbishop's arrival as follows:

Visit of the Most Reverend Seraphim
Orthodox Eastern Archbishop in Western Europe
Friday, November 19th [1937], was a wonderful day in the history of Walsingham. Some of us had been astir at an early hour, despite the absolute downpour of rain; such a deluge as is seldom seen here; putting up flags and bunting, outlining the site where the Orthodox Eastern Chapel is to be

> built with coloured lights. . . . However, about 1:30 the sun broke through, a Spring-like afternoon took the place of gloom and wet. After a long wait the bus from London arrived and the Orthodox were greeted by peals of bells. The Archbishop, vested in his great mantle, with its long train borne by a server, wearing his golden mitre, holding his Cross, accompanied by Abbot Gibbes, who carried the Miraculous Icon of Our Lady of the Sign, together with Russian Singers and others who came with them, went in procession from the Hospice to the West Entrance of the Sanctuary.

A less colourful, but more factual account was provided by the *Church Times*:

> On Friday last, the Most Rev. Seraphim, Archbishop of the Russian Church in Western Europe, visited Walsingham and blessed the site of the chapel of the Orthodox Eastern Church, which is to be one of the new chapels in the extension of the Holy House.
>
> The Archbishop, bearing a holy icon of very ancient and historic interest, and his suite accompanying him, were received in the courtyard of the Holy House by the Rev. A. Hope-Patten, vicar of Walsingham. There were also many other priests present, and a large congregation, each of whom carried a lighted candle. The procession entered the Holy House as the Litany of our Lady was sung. Before the shrine of our Lady of Walsingham the Archbishop performed the rite of the lesser sanctification of water, placing the crucifix in the water and blessing it with holy oil. The choir of Russian singers rendered anthems and Litanies.
>
> The procession passed through the extensions until the site of the Orthodox Eastern chapel was reached. Here the Archbishop perambulated the boundaries and blessed the site, sprinkling the same with holy water.
>
> On the return of the procession to the Holy House a visit was made to the altar of the Annunciation, where the Archbishop offered the "moleben," a service of praise of our Lady, with thanksgiving and prayer. An opportunity was given to those present to venerate the holy icon, placed in a position on the altar by the Archbishop, who led such devotion.

After the service, the archbishop gave an address, which the *Dereham and Fakenham Times* reported on as follows:

> The Archbishop said, "This place has again become a holy place, and at the present time this place holds a very famous thing—the famous image of the Mother of God. The Icon appeared in Russia 700 years ago and the Russian

people by millions reverenced that image who you see before you and received from it very many miracles." He hoped they would be glorified in Walsingham, and that faithful Christians would come in many numbers to pray to the Virgin Mother and to receive from Her grace and help. . . .

It is understood that the visit of the Archbishop of the Russians in exile was the first of its kind since the Reformation. . . .

After the ceremony of blessing the site of the Orthodox Eastern Chapel a supper was held in the Hospice, adjacent to the Holy House.

A toast of the health of the Most Rev. Seraphim, Archbishop of the Russian Church in Western Europe, was submitted by Fr. A. Hope-Patten, who said that it was a great honour to have received the Archbishop and his suite at the "England's Nazareth." He wished the Archbishop and his suite every happiness.

After replying to the toast, the Archbishop submitted a toast to the "head of this house and those who dwell in it." The Archbishop said, "May God's blessing rest on them and their work."

The Vicar's speech was translated into Russian by Prince Nicholas Galitzine, who is a member of the Russian Royal family. . . .

At the conclusion of the service the Icon was placed at the entrance to the chancel and the ceremony of veneration took place. The Russian choir sang hymns of prayer and praise while the image was being venerated.

A Closer Acquaintanceship with Father Boris Through His Writings

The name of Father Boris Molchanoff is well known to many English-speaking Orthodox because a number of his articles have appeared over the years in *Orthodox Life* and other publications. While in London, Father Boris worked on his book *The Mystery of Iniquity* (*Taina Bezzakonia*), which was printed on Russian language printing presses in Harbin, China, in 1938. This work is based on the second chapter of St Paul's Epistle to the Thessalonians, which speaks of the great "falling away," or great apostasy, which will precede the coming of the antichrist and the end of the world. Interpreting this chapter in light of the commentaries of the Church Fathers and his own observations of the world, Father Boris points to three principal signs of the onset of the great apostasy: first, a falling away from the true teaching and Christian morality—evidenced by the prevailing materialism; second, political apostasy—especially the Russian Revolution with its attack on the Orthodox Church and destruction of the former way of life in Russia; and third, "religious apostasy"—the appearance of false religions that lure people away from the true Church of Christ. All of Father Boris's writing was based strictly on the Church Fathers and later respected authorities, particularly the nineteenth-century writer Bishop Ignatius (Brianchaninov). Illustrations of these basic teachings were taken from other writers and philosophers such as Vladimir Soloviev. Father Boris's pastoral experiences provided ample evidence of the prevailing materialism. After explaining the Church Fathers' condemnation of excessive attachment to the cares of this world, Father Boris continued,

> This advice of the Holy Fathers does not indicate a total condemnation of all worldly cares, of all work done to provide for oneself. The sin and danger are not in the work, but in an exclusive and total preoccupation with material concerns, while all idealistic interests and questing of the spirit are pushed aside. Nor does this mean that only wealthy people can be subjected to such temptations. These desires can be present in the very poorest people to no less a degree. Someone who is totally impoverished can be overcome by a vague attraction to wealth, which can develop into a morbid passion, recognizing nothing that will hinder its satisfaction, and thus making him ready for crimes of all kinds.
>
> Of course, God will not live in such a soul when it is devoted exclusively to material good things. We must remember that in such cases God is not so much denied as pushed out of a person's heart, by attachment to material things.

In describing the signs of the great apostasy, Father Boris drew practical conclusions for his readers:

> In pointing out the terrible signs of the present apostasy, which will culminate in the coming of Antichrist, we must refrain from any attempt to determine exactly when he is going to appear. The preparation for his coming may even develop very quickly, but it may be delayed by unexpected events. A delay in the final denouement is brought about through God's mercy for the sake of the repentance and desiring the salvation of at least a small remnant of believers. But when the saving fear of God and capacity for repentance are exhausted in the hearts of men, then all the punishments foretold by God's Judgement will quickly begin.

A later work written by Father Boris, which was reprinted in 1982 by Metropolitan Vitaly in a single volume containing both Russian and English texts, is *Understanding our Church Calendar*. This booklet explains the significance of the Church calendar with its cycle of feast days and fast periods and the complex interrelationship between the Julian calendar and the lunar calendar, which determines the dates of Pascha, as prescribed by the First Œcumenical Council, and the other feasts and fasts that depend on the date of Easter. On turning the pages of this book, one is immediately struck by the large number of numerical tables and arithmetical calculations—not what one would expect in a work of theology. Most of these were taken from the work of a Russian astronomer, E. B. Predtechensky, but rearranged and presented by Father Boris who previously studied natural sciences in Petrograd. By explaining the workings of the Church calendar in detail, Father Boris intended to quash the false impression that the Church hierarchy was only keeping to the Julian calendar, which is thirteen days behind the Western, or Gregorian, calendar, out of old-fashioned stubbornness. He wanted would-be reformers to understand that what they wanted to renounce was really a "most valuable treasure." Concerning the practical difficulties, he said,

> We will not dispute that our schoolchildren face difficulties in observing our holy days according to the old calendar. Such difficulties do exist, of course, but they should not be exaggerated. Jewish and Mahommedan children have the same difficulties as ours. However, they find ways of observing their holy days without changing their calendar. Why is it only amongst us that it seems so essential to renounce our own Julian calendar?

Father Boris is known for his ominous warnings about the coming great apostasy and antichrist. However, behind these exhortations lies the sensitive and compassionate heart of a priest devoted to his pastoral work. This is evident in the following paragraphs, taken from his article "Let Us Who Represent the Cherubim," which was a commentary on this well-known hymn of the Orthodox Liturgy:

> But what likeness do we bear to the Cherubim? We are all sinners, unable to live even a single day without sinning: then here in church we must suddenly represent the highest, sinless orders of angels.
>
> We are given an answer to this perplexity by the Word of God. It says that man was made "in His image and likeness" (Gen 1:26–27). It is this "image of God," implanted deep in the heart of each person by the Creator, which constitutes our likeness or kinship with the highest spiritual world. If we lead a life of prayer and virtue, the "image of God" burns up brightly in us like a lamp filled up with oil; when we are sinfully estranged from

God it is completely hidden in the unseen depths of the soul, but it does not utterly vanish. However much someone may sin, to whatever depths he may fall morally, the "Cherubic" heart, or centre, of the soul remains in him, languishing under heavy layers of sin. Our great writer and psychologist Dostoyevsky wrote in his *Notes from the House of the Dead* that even in prison, in the most hardened criminals, their hearts would experience radiant, lucid movements, just as if a ray of heavenly light was bursting forth from within the depths of a soul covered by the hard crust of dark crimes.

This heavenly aspect of our soul, its likeness to the Cherubim, is more valuable than all earthly values, is more valuable than the whole world. In comparison with it, all the good things of this world are worth nothing. It was in order to restore the "image of God" in fallen man that the Son of God came down from Heaven to earth, was made man, suffered and tasted death on the Cross, and triumphed in His Resurrection. . . .

If man only for one instant felt the heavenly beauty of the "image of God" in himself, if he saw, with his spiritual eyes, the "Cherubim" hidden in his own heart, then he could never forget it and become reconciled with his former sinful life. Then we would understand the words in the Gospel which say how blessed he is, who digs up the treasure hidden in the field of his heart, and how blessed is the man who, "when he had found one pearl of great price, went and sold all that he had, and bought it." (Matt 13:44–46)

But we always forget that each person, despite his sinfulness, carries this heavenly treasure, the "image of God" within himself. Here in church the servant of the altar incenses each sinner as he turns with prayer to God, censes the image of God, not made by hands, that is within these sinful people, with the same degree of respect, as when he censes the images of the saints. The Church here wishes to see in each of us, under the coarse and repugnant crust of our sins, that most valuable thing in us, which makes us akin to the angelic world. And the Church invites us, like the choir of the Cherubim, to "sing the Thrice-holy hymn to the Life-Creating Trinity."

Visit of Archbishop Nestor and Arrival of Father Nicholas Gibbes

In 1938, soon after Metropolitan Anastassy succeeded Metropolitan Anthony as leader of the Russian Church Abroad, an All-Emigration Church Sobor—an assembly of lay and clergy representatives from Russian communities all over the world—was held. Archbishop Nestor of Kamchatka came from China accompanied by his secretary, Archimandrite Nathaniel. Before the Sobor in Yugoslavia, they both paid a visit to London that lasted from before Easter to the end of July. Mrs Sophia Goodman recalled:

I remember the arrival of Archbishop Nestor and Father Nathaniel. They had a tremendous impact. I was only about seven or eight years old. I'd never noticed a priest before. It really changed my whole outlook on Church, listening to them. They visited everybody and they both preached in church, Father Nathaniel as well as Archbishop Nestor.

This was Father Nathaniel's first visit to the parish in London; later, after the war, he was to return as diocesan bishop. Before the Revolution, Archbishop Nestor had been a missionary in Kamchatka and studied the Tungusic languages, including Evenki and Koryak, spoken by the native people of that remote part of Siberia. On one occasion his Koryak parishioners presented him with a mitre made from the tusks of prehistoric mammoths preserved in the permafrost of that region, which is an interesting testimony to his wide-ranging interests and pastoral concerns. After the Revolution, he moved to neighboring Manchuria, which became a large centre of the Russian emigration. On his way to the Sobor in 1938, he made an extended stop in South India, where a large group of Indian Christians were interested in joining the Orthodox Church.

Archbishop Nestor conducted the Easter service in April1938 in London. The May 1938 edition of *The Russian in England* included this description of the service:

> The Easter Matins and Liturgy of the parish under the Council of Bishops were held this year in St. Matthew's Church in Kensington because the house chapel at the Podvoria proved to be too small for the service with a bishop. St. Matthew's Church, which the Anglicans let us use, proved to be eminently suited for Orthodox worship due to the positioning of the altar, which created the impression of an open iconostasis. The numerous mosaic depositions on the walls also harmonized with one's usual expectations of an Orthodox church.
>
> Archbishop Nestor conducted the services, assisted by the local clergy. The church was packed with both Russians and English people. During the service a special collection was made to help Russian children in the Far East, where the situation of the Russian emigration is so bad, that there have been cases of Russian children being sold into slavery. The Orthodox Church in the Far East needs funds to redeem these children from their new owners.

St. Philip's Church, where the Easter service was conducted by the rector of the Evlogian parish, Father Nicholas Behr, was also filled to capacity.

One purpose of Archbishop Nestor's visit to England was to introduce Father Nicholas Gibbes to the Orthodox faithful in England. Father Nicholas, known affectionately to the Russians as *Otyets Geeps*, had a unique background. He was an Englishman, formerly Charles Sydney Gibbes, whose father intended for him to pursue a career in the Church of England. Instead, he went to Russia to seek his fortune as a language tutor and was employed by the Imperial family to tutor their five children. He developed a warm, affectionate relationship with them and accompanied them in exile to Ekaterinburg in Siberia, where the entire family was executed by Bolshevik firing squad. Gibbes managed to escape and found his way through Siberia to China, where there was a large Russian colony. There were also English trading enterprises established in all the large ports, which made it possible for Gibbes to support himself through various commercial ventures.

Archbishop Nestor of Kamchatka with the Grand Duchess Xenia at Hampton Court, May 1938. (Source: Sophia Goodman)

Gibbes's experiences in Russia affected him profoundly, and in 1934, after much soul searching, he accepted the Orthodox faith at the age of fifty-eight. Later Archbishop Nestor of Kamchatka tonsured him a monk, gave him the name Nicholas, and ordained him to the priesthood. Father Nicholas left Manchuria to spend a year in Jerusalem with the Russian Mission before returning to England late in 1937, where he was attached to the London parish by Archbishop Seraphim, the diocesan bishop. Who better to introduce the new priest to the flock in London than Archbishop Nestor, his spiritual mentor from Manchuria? During a solemn service in London, Archbishop Nestor raised Father Nicholas to the rank of archimandrite. He was the first Englishman to receive this honour from the Russian Church. In addition to the mitre, Father Nicholas also received the right to carry a staff, similar to a bishop's staff, an honour rarely accorded to priests of this rank.

Archbishop Nestor and Archimandrite Nicholas Gibbes at the Anglican National Pilgrimage, Walsingham, May 1938. (Source: Walsingham Anglican Archives)

The Russian community revered Father Nicholas because of his association with the Imperial family. He visited the Grand Duchess Xenia at Hampton Court and Windsor on several occasions in the company of leading members of the exile community. On several occasions he was called upon to pronounce on the authenticity of the various "Anastasias"—persons claiming to be the tsar's youngest daughter on the strength of a rumour that she had escaped the fate of the rest of the family. Father Nicholas declared them all to be bogus; often he based his views on his knowledge of childhood incidents of the type that one does not easily forget in later life.

However, Father Nicholas's primary pastoral responsibilities did not concern the Russian community in London but rather the establishment of a church for English-speaking Orthodox, which was situated in a chapel in Bayswater Road. His major problem seemed to have been the lack of a choir, without which it would be impossible for his English-speaking congregation to appreciate the splendor of Orthodox worship. A number of young Russian women in Yugoslavia wanted to come to England and learn English; Father

Nicholas devised a scheme to help them travel to England and find lodging in exchange for singing in his choir. Thus, the women's choir of the twelve "Belgrade Nightingales" was formed as were the convent choirs that Father Nicholas would have heard during his year in Jerusalem. The choir director, Manya Rodzianko, managed her task very well. Other choir members were Olga Illiashevitch (d. 1987) and Sonia Kvachadze (d. c. 1990), a young lady of Georgian descent who freely admitted that she did not have much of a voice, but was covered by the others. Antonina Ananin, who eventually became the choir director at the cathedral at Emperor's Gate, joined in the choir as best she could while she looked after two small children. The choir sung the same arrangements and compositions as they had learned in Church Slavonic, but with English words substituted. According to Mrs Ananin, they did not feel any sense of deprivation over the language of worship because the music was exactly what they were used to. There is likely a lesson here for the future of English-language Orthodoxy and the need to ensure that it is not divorced from its roots.

Shortly after the church opened, World War II broke out, and the Nightingales, who planned to stay only a short time as students, were unable to return home. In 1941 Father Nicholas was asked to move to Oxford, where there was a large Orthodox community composed partly of wartime translators. It was decided that his services were more necessary in Oxford, so the church in Bayswater Road was closed. It fell to the new rector of the Russian parish in London, Father Michael Polsky, to care for the Nightingales, most of whom eventually settled in London.

During his stay in England in 1938, Archbishop Nestor visited Walsingham, as Archbishop Seraphim had done the previous year. On the Anglican feast of Whitsun (Pentecost), the archbishop attended the solemnity of the consecration of the restored Anglican shrine church. This was a major event that drew crowds of as many as 6,000 people. Although he did not officiate in full vestments, the archbishop joined in the procession, as described in *Our Lady's Mirror*:

> The little procession of the Eastern Orthodox Clergy, again headed by cross and lights, came next. First walked the Archbishop Nestor in golden mitre and splendid robes, the train of which was borne by two boys from the little Norfolk village of Gresham; another boy carried his Episcopal staff. Behind His Grace, with train also carried by servers, walked the Archimandrite Nicholas Gibbes and the Archimandrite Nathaniel, followed by Orthodox Priests.

The next day, Whit Monday, which was at that time a public holiday in England, Archbishop Nestor celebrated the Orthodox Divine Liturgy. According to the account in *Our Lady's Mirror*, "Some of the Orthodox visitors to the shrine on Whit Monday said it was the happiest day they had had since leaving Russia."

The proposed Orthodox chapel, the site for which had been blessed by Archbishop Seraphim the previous year, was never built, in part because of the turmoil caused by the Second World War already on the horizon. However, a small Orthodox chapel was constructed in a side chapel next to a staircase within the main Anglican shrine church. Father Nicholas Gibbes was actively involved in this project and designed a slightly convex iconostasis that would fit into the limited space available. It was finally consecrated at Pentecost 1944 by Archbishop Savva of the Polish Orthodox Church. At the time there was a prisoner-of-war camp at nearby Hempton, and many of the prisoners were Orthodox. The chapel, dedicated to the Mother of God of the Life-giving Spring, remains today and, although tiny, has a dramatic location, with a window overlooking the shrine's high altar.

Miraculously Renewed Icons of St Savva and St Nicholas

While in London in 1938, Archbishop Nestor celebrated the first moleben before two miraculously renewed icons that had appeared in the home of a parishioner. This phenomenon—when an icon darkened by age inexplicably regains its original bright colours—occurred in Russia at the height of the persecutions of the faithful and was seen as a sign of God's consolation. The following narrative is taken from an account by Princess Irina Galitzine (d. 1985), who witnessed the miracle:

> Before escaping from Russia a Russian lady called Apollinaria was married to a Greek by whom she had six children. However, the couple divorced and Apollinaria subsequently married a certain Henry von Hollen, a German Lutheran, who had been tutor to her children. Later Henry qualified as an engineer and then the couple escaped to England, where they lived in extreme poverty, for Henry could find no work. In desperation Apollinaria took a position as a cook in the house of the ballerina, Anna Pavlova.
>
> Back in Russia one of Apollinaria's daughters heard of the couple's plight and became furious that they should be reduced to penury and begged them to return to Moscow with the offer of a job. In a weak moment they agreed and, on their return, Henry indeed was offered a good job in Novocherkassk. Later the Soviet authorities offered him an even better job

in Siberia, but he would have to be separated from his wife. This Henry refused to do and so the Soviets made life very difficult for him.

Since Henry had previously acquired British citizenship, the couple left Russia again without much difficulty in 1932, and returned to London. Then Henry became ill with consumption. They lived in a room very near the Russian Church in Buckingham Palace Road, which played a big part in the life of Apollinaria, who was very devout. Life was very difficult, for they were very poor. Apollinaria vowed that, if Henry recovered, she would do her utmost to help the poorest pregnant woman in the parish. Eventually it happened that Henry went into hospital, and, after much persuasion and discussion with the parish priest, Father Boris Molchanoff, Apollinaria took a room in the house of a poor, but aristocratic, Russian couple,[3] where the wife was expecting a baby, and Apollinaria was indeed a great help when the baby was born.

She brought with her holy icons, and one of them had a special interest for me. I used to study it attentively, for it seemed to be very old, and there was no indication of which saint it could represent. I am very shortsighted and can only see details at a close range; all I could see was a dark figure of a monk standing in front of a very dark brown background.

I asked Apollinaria Michaelovna who was the saint in the icon and she answered that it was St. Savva the Serbian. "But how is it St. Savva the Serbian when there is no indication whatsoever on the icon?" I asked her. Then she told me the whole story of it.

"You see, we were living in Moscow after returning from London. Then his (my husband's) persecution started. They threatened him with all kinds of things, but luckily he was an English subject, and they did not dare imprison him. We passed through a hell of a time, especially at night. The Black Maria would stop at our house to frighten us and to try to make us reverse our decision. How well we understood our mistake in having left London.

"As we were English subjects we applied to return to London. We would accept any job to get back to England. I started to get ready for our departure but, as I was frightened at the crossing, I wanted to buy an icon of the holy wonder-worker, St. Nicholas. I was determined to get one at any price, but all to no avail. I could not find one anywhere. Then one day, passing a market place at Novocherkassk I saw a woman selling all kinds of household items—pots and pans, old crockery, irons, wooden spoons, old frames and knick-knacks of all descriptions. I saw what looked like an ancient icon lying on the ground amongst other things and I picked it up. 'Is it an icon of St. Nicholas, the Wonder-worker?' I asked the woman. 'How can you allow a holy icon to lie about amongst all that junk and rags?' I was determined to buy it just to be able to take it away from all that rubbish. The woman told me that the icon was not of St. Nicholas the Wonder-worker, but that it was of St. Savva the Serbian.

"I took the icon home, washed and cleaned it as best I could, but it still remained the same, just as you see it now. And, not being able to find the icon of St. Nicholas, we started on our journey back to England. God was merciful to us sinners, and at the beginning of spring, 1932, we arrived safely in London."

I listened and wondered at all these happenings; it was in the autumn of that same year, 1932, that we also escaped from the clutches of our detestable government. So, under the care of our dear Apollinaria Michaelovna, the last few weeks of my pregnancy passed. . . .

Then came the year 1938. I remember it was St. Nicholas Day (the spring one), 9th of May. It was a Sunday and I went, as usual, to visit my dear friend, Mrs. von Hollen. By this time they had changed their flat to another one in 58, Airedale Road, Chiswick. Their little flat consisted of two rooms—a very small kitchen serving them as a dining room, and a living room, slightly larger, where they slept.

For the last few weeks Apollinaria Michaelovna had been in poor health and I was unable to collect her, as usual, on my way to Church as she did not leave home, but hardly a day passed without my visiting her. She greeted me in her little kitchenette all smiles, and bursting with delight. I asked her how her health was. Was her cough any better? She said "My cough—I have no cough, it's gone—I am well, completely well. Come, come." She took me towards a corner where her icons were. "Look at them, can you see something?" I looked but did not understand what I had to see.

"Can't you see that the icon of St. Nicholas has completely changed? Do you not remember how dark that icon was when it was given to me . . . and look at it now!"

I understood that a miracle had happened—a miracle that I longed to see, about which I had heard and read in many of my holy magazines, and, there I was, standing before it and in my heart I spoke to St. Nicholas. "Why was it that I had not noticed that particular icon before?"

"I am so unobservant. I did not know or remember that particular icon at all, and so, therefore, this miracle is not mine—in other words, I am part of it." My thoughts continued; "If something happened with the other icon, of the Savva of Serbia, then that would be different, then it would be my miracle as well" and I concluded, "Oh, St. Nicholas, why have you neglected me, deprived me of that joy?"

With this I turned my face to Apollinaria Michaelovna and asked her about the icon of St. Savva. "Has it also been enlightened? May I have a look at it?"

"Oh," she answered, "It's in the adjoining room; I was in poor health and did not dust my icons for a long time. Here," she continued, passing me a clean cloth, "do be so kind as to wipe the dust from my other icons for me; I am ashamed of myself for such negligence."

Quite automatically I took the cloth, climbed on to a box that stood before the icons and started to wipe the icon of St. Savva of Serbia. To my amazement the very dark figure had completely changed. There stood a beautiful face of a monk fully visible with all the details, with an analoi nearby with an open book on it, with the written words of a prayer which I could read and a beautiful icon of our Saviour in the background with a golden halo around the Head. Everything was beautifully painted with all the details and colours. On the left-hand side of the Saint I read the inscription *St. Savva the Sanctified*. The beautiful icon had become completely renewed.

I said, "Apollinaria Michaelovna, this icon is not of St. Savva the Serbian—it is St. Savva the Sanctified."[4] At that moment she was standing below and cried "The hand, the hand, I can see his hand clearly. The miracle has happened."

This time it *was* mine as well. Oh, the mercy of God for me the sinner! We were both sharing the same great thing.

Mr. Hollen was at the time in his *kirche* where he used to spend most of his day on a Sunday. I returned home and decided to bring all my family to share that great event. Nicky [Prince Nicholas Galitzine], of course, knew as I did what the blessed icon had looked like before the transformation. We were all sharing our dear Apollinaria Michaelovna's joy. She looked radiant, all her illness had gone. We were having tea which she had prepared for us when Mr. Hollen returned home. She told him the latest news about the restoration of St. Savva the Sanctified, and he also marvelled at it.

In fact, he was the first one to notice the renovation of the icon of St. Nicholas. He was, at the time, attending the little oil lamp [lampada] before the holy icon when he heard a small cry coming from the holy icon. He looked and saw it happening—the dark layers of oil paints were falling off, and the new, bright colouring taking the place of the old. It was at that moment that he said to his wife "Look what is happening. Your holy icon is getting brighter and brighter." Apollinaria Michaelovna also heard the sound, but thought it was coming from somewhere outside the window. The renovation of St. Nicholas icon was with a noise, and that of the icon of St. Savva the Sanctified was a quiet one—at least, it seemed so to us.

Mr. Hollen, being a very learned man, was deeply impressed with all these happenings. He said, "It is something out of the order of things for all of us, and things of this sort should not pass unnoticed, but should be made public." I remember that some newspaper correspondents came and had a look at the holy icons. They heard all the details but would not make much of them, and the great event passed unnoticed, as all the greatest events do.

Very few of our Russian émigrés understood our great miracle. I remember that one of the first arrivals at the humble flat at 58, Airedale Avenue, Chiswick, W6 was His Highness Prince Andrew of Russia, the eldest son of the Grand Duchess Xenia of Russia. He came with his first wife, Princess Elsa. My children and I were all present.

A moleben in front of the icons was served by Fr. Boris together with Archbishop Nestor, who was at that time visiting London, and in the presence of Prince Andrew of Russia. Father Boris was keen to point out to Henry, who readily acknowledged that a miracle had taken place, that this was a sign, leading him to the true path of Orthodoxy, but Henry refused to be converted. However, the miracle did greatly affect the life of the friend of Apollonaria, Princess Galitzine.

Many years later, in 1965, Princess Galitzine went on a pilgrimage to Jerusalem. Her visit coincided with the return of the relics of St Savva the Sanctified to the Holy Land, after being in Venice for many centuries. St Savva, a desert father, was born in Cappadocia in 439 and founded the monastery now known as "Mar Saba" in Palestine. Thus, Apollinaria's friend received the blessing of venerating the relics of St Savva while they rested in the Holy Sepulchre, before being taken into Mar Saba where women are not admitted.

For some time it was necessary to place a dish under the icon of St Savva in order to collect the oil that exuded from it, but the phenomenon stopped as suddenly as it began. Today the icon[5] hangs in the Cathedral of the Dormition at Harvard Road, London W4.

Departure of Father Boris Molchanoff

Father Boris stayed in England for five years and departed in the summer of 1938. George Orloff's recollections describe some of the reasons for this move:

> I remember that Father Boris was worried by his poor knowledge of English. He was also worried about the publication of his book, which he finally arranged to have printed in Harbin. Last, but not least, were his worries concerning his wife's health and for the safety of his family: it appeared that she could not stand our dampness and yearned for a dry, warm climate. He acquainted me with the project of an exchange with Father Michael Polsky from Beirut, which eventually came to be.

After leaving England in 1938, Father Boris served as parish priest, first in Beirut, then in Bela Cerkva, Yugoslavia, later in Austria, and, after the war, in France. In 1956 he moved to the United States, where he was appointed assistant chancellor to the Synod of Bishops. In this capacity he carried out many difficult and important assignments, and his abilities were greatly appreciated by the Synod. At the same time, he wrote for various Church publications. Despite the onset of cardiac illness, Father Boris continued working long hours in the synodal office in New York. On August 22, 1963, he suffered a heart attack and died at the age of sixty-seven.

In 1986 Father Boris's son visited London. On the Sunday of his visit, he went to 14 St Dunstan's Road where the Liturgy was being celebrated in English. After the service the parishioners offered him hospitality in what had previously been his own home.

Chapter 11

[1938–1948] Archpriest Michael Polsky

Recollections of Melvin Mansur

In 1938 Father Boris Molchanoff left for Beirut, and Father Michael Polsky came from Beirut to London to take his place. Father Michael occupied a unique place in the Russian emigration. After suffering imprisonment at the hands of the Communists, he escaped from Russia in 1930 to bear witness in the West of what he had seen and heard. He is best known for his book *The New Martyrs of Russia*. Father Michael was warm-hearted, with an outgoing personality that drew many people closer to the Church. He also had the rare gift of inspiring hope and confidence in the dispirited.

Father Michael left the following general impressions on Melvin Mansur, an American convert to Orthodoxy, who at that time was living in London whilst working in the U.S. Navy:

> Fr. Michael Polsky was an extraordinary priest. The fact that he was ordained in the 1920s when the persecutions in Russia were at their height speaks for itself. From his own experience, he knew the evil of communism and during the war, when apologists for the system were everywhere, he never changed his views. He seldom mentioned the Soviet Union without adding either "horror," "nightmare" or "madhouse."
>
> He was a gifted preacher and his animated style riveted the attention of the congregation. His sermons abounded in apt illustrations.
>
> Father Michael was a jolly and sociable person, and his house was open to all. We young people would gather for meals at his hospitable table after the Vigil or Liturgy and listen to his never-ending flow of anecdotes and experiences. I remember his telling how after his escape from Solovki and arrival in Moscow, he was walking along the street when he was stopped by a policeman, who asked to see his documents. Of course, he had none. "I have lost them," Father Michael said, "and am on my way to the station to report the loss."

Archpriest Michael Polsky with choir director Foka Volkovsky, 1948.

"Very well," said the officer, "I will accompany you." As they went, Father Michael prayed as he had never prayed before. On their way, they came upon another policeman who was struggling to lift a drunk from the gutter. "Give me a hand with this drunk," he said to the man accompanying Father Michael. "I can't, I'm taking this priest to the station." "Oh, let him go by himself. You help me." A miracle occurred, and Father Michael walked away.

Besides his gift as a raconteur, he had the gift of wit. Once, when Foka Feodorovich[1] (bless his soul), the choirmaster, was absent, and we were having difficulty with one of the tones, Father Michael stepped out of the altar and said, "Are you singing the goat's tone?"

All who knew Father Michael remember him with affection and admiration. Eternal Memory.

The following account of Father Michael's experiences in the Soviet Union includes extracts from two of his works in which he drew on these experiences to illustrate conditions. The first of these, *The State of the Church in the Soviet Union*, was published in Jerusalem in 1931 under the name Michael the Priest. The other, *Report to the 1938 Assembly of the Russian Church Abroad*, was printed in 1938 under the name Rector of the Russian Orthodox Parish in London, Archpriest Michael Polsky. Father Michael spoke frequently of his experiences, always with a view to draw some spiritual benefit from them. To understand Father Michael as he was in London between 1938 and 1948, it is necessary to consider the various events he lived through that made him the person, and the priest, that he was.

Father Michael's Life in Russia

Father Michael was born into the family of a psalm-reader in the *stanitsa* (Cossack village) of Novo-Troitskaya in the Kuban Province. His ancestors were church readers and chanters. Father Michael's relatives on his mother's side were in the military; his uncle was a Cossack who reached the rank of general and later died in Yugoslavia as an émigré. The young Polsky graduated among the best students from his theological school and seminary in Stavropol. D. I. Bogoliuboff, an antisectarian missionary from St Petersburg who was well known for his writings, was the seminary inspector that time. He prepared young Michael for missionary activity among the many sectarians in the Caucasus at that time, including Molokani, Baptists, Adventists, Khlysti, the New Israel, and other Judaizing and paganizing sects.

With the onset of the Bolshevik Revolution, the Church in Russia entered a terrible, apocalyptic period. In 1920, in Ekaterinodar, Father Michael was ordained to the priesthood. The White Army, hopelessly outnumbered, was being evacuated. The young priest watched as the last ships carrying the Volunteer Army passed before his very eyes through the Strait of Kerch and sailed away, seeking safety abroad.

Remaining with his flock, Father Michael shared their fate of searches, robbery, and violence. In the town of Temryuk, where he was serving, he had the spiritual strength to take part in the public debates, or "disputes," that the Bolsheviks organized with the aim of discrediting religion and, as Father Michael pointed out, with the aim of revealing the truly convincing opponents of atheism. One such debate, which was held before a large gathering of people, ended with complete victory for the missionary, much to the people's joy. But the victor knew that the Bolsheviks had already decided to send him to prison. Following the advice of the dean of the town's main church, Father Michael secretly left the Caucasus, made his way to Moscow, and entered the Moscow Theological Academy, which had been moved into the city from the Lavra of the Holy Trinity and St Sergius. Before long, the academy was closed and the rector, Bishop Bartholomew, was shot. Father Michael continued his studies in secret, having private lessons with the academy professors.

He met Patriarch Tikhon and was invited to stay with His Holiness in the Holy Trinity residence. Father Polsky's wife and daughter remained in the south of Russia with relatives. In Moscow Father Michael continued to preach Christianity; he constantly spoke out against atheism in various industrial centres and always spoke to the very heart of the working class. These public speeches brought personal success to the young missionary, and he saw a triumph of Orthodoxy among the so-called proletariat. Archbishop Hilarion (Troitsky), who was in charge of missionary activity, gave Father Michael the right to speak in any church in the Moscow diocese. During his time at the Holy Trinity residence, the Church was subjected to further acts of persecution: the confiscation of Church valuables, the Living

Church movement,[2] and the arrest of Patriarch Tikhon. Father Michael concelebrated with many other clergy at the last Liturgy celebrated by the patriarch before his arrest. He wrote,

> I remember the Patriarch in the days when he was under house arrest, before he was imprisoned. I concelebrated with him at his last Liturgy in freedom (22 April 1922 o.s.) in the Bogorodskoye village church near Moscow. Late the night before he had returned from the Cheka. He had just been through a long and harsh interrogation. At home, the Patriarch said to his closest associates, who were tormented by waiting, "That was a very severe interrogation."
>
> "What will happen to you now?" asked one person anxiously. "They promised to chop off my head," replied the Patriarch in his usual good-natured way.
>
> He celebrated the Liturgy as always: there was not the slightest hint of nervousness or even tension in his prayer. Looking at him, preparing for prison and perhaps execution (this was then a serious possibility), I could not help remembering the words of Christ: "The prince of this world walketh and hath nothing in me." Let them accuse him, they will find nothing, he will be innocent. This is what I thought, and I preached on this theme at the Liturgy. As he blessed me to go out and preach the sermon the Patriarch whispered, "Just leave 'them' out of it."
>
> I knew that he wanted to spare the preacher. He was afraid not for himself, but for those around him who were risking themselves. But I do not remember that anyone, to whom it fell to preach at a Patriarchal service, kept silent about the truth in what he said. Somehow everyone, everywhere managed to say what was necessary, what corresponded to the person of the Patriarch, without giving heed to any fear.

From Moscow, Father Michael made the long journeys to the Optina and Sarov monasteries, which were then still functioning. The young priest categorically rejected the "renovationism" that the Bolsheviks were trying to introduce. Priest-monk Alexei, an elder of the hermitage of St Zossima, who was then Father Michael's spiritual guide, blessed his spiritual son for this path of struggle.

The bold missionary did not enjoy his freedom for long. In 1923 he was incarcerated in the Butyrki Prison, from which he was released after four months in the expectation that he would join the Living Church. Father Michael continued,

On the first day of my imprisonment, when I was being questioned by the GPU[3] interrogator, I was confronted by the ineradicable nature of the higher spiritual strivings in humanity and the fruitlessness of the Bolsheviks' war against them. The interrogator said, among other things, "If you only knew what harm you are causing people through religion, you would never have taken it up." I replied that I preached for the very reason that I knew that through religion I was bringing benefits both to myself and other people. When he asked what was the use of religion, I said, "If you came home and found out that your wife had been run over by a car, then the horror and senselessness of this event will leave you spiritually crushed; any kind of love or attachment will seem quite meaningless to you, as will your intelligence and your life itself. Well, we believers know that God's will is done in all things and that God's wisdom and providence guide all things, that love is eternal and not in vain, for it is eternal life."

My interrogator shuddered and became agitated. He could not think how to reply. At another interrogation, when I was already in jail, he once said to me quickly, "I am a believer myself." He was extremely lenient and entered a very mild conclusion to my case, which was quite inconsistent with the harsh verdict of the GPU, who gave me three years in the camp in Solovki. Later I found out that my interrogator had a young wife and loved her very much, so the example I had used when talking to him had hit a very sensitive spot. . . . In the third month that I was in the Butyrki jail under investigation, I underwent a spiritual crisis. The interrogation was dragging on and could have had very grave consequences, since the offences of which I was being accused carried sentences ranging from three years' imprisonment to the death penalty. My initial boldness had gone, had been dissipated, I felt a great desire for freedom, and I was seized by an unbearable sadness for my close and dear relatives. My heart became ready for anything if only I could be delivered from captivity. The poison of faintheartedness infected my entire being. Thousands of times my mind followed its special path to Golgotha, to death, along those corridors of the GPU which were so familiar, between two cold, oppressive walls, and between men who were implacably harsh and heartless, like the walls, from whom it was utterly impossible to break free with any amount of strength. But now they are calling me for interrogation, and the interrogator's first questions call forth in my heart determination, boldness, words of independence and truth. Again, you start saying things which you know will only harm you, and when the questioning is over, you feel again that you have dug your own grave and made your position worse. And once again you are beset by faintheartedness. Only in these hours is the soul visited by the knowledge that confession of the faith is a gift from above, and that in this you have nothing for which to thank yourself. And I was visited by a profound compassion for all those who had fallen, by an understanding of them and forgiveness of them. And so you thank God for His great mercy, in that you are standing firm and have not betrayed the truth.

In this fiery furnace in which we were all tried, all values were reevaluated. Very highly regarded, prominent, talented people, of whom much was expected and who could have done so much in this war with atheism, fell terribly, and lost their prestige and did much harm to the Church. Meanwhile others, both clergy and laity, who had passed unnoticed and sometimes perhaps even been indolent in ordinary times, suddenly rose up in all their strength and become true heroes and defenders of the Church. . . .

St. Peter had much love for the Saviour, but in the hour of trial he fell grievously. This eternal lesson comes vividly to mind, illustrated as it is by many new examples. Who in the clerical world does not know of the late Metropolitan Arseny Stadnitsky? His great breadth of intelligence and erudition, his powerful will, honesty and directness, his very hard, decisive unbending character, his strictness to his subordinates and to himself? This great personage, the Metropolitan of Novgorod, a member of the Synod and of the State Duma and Council, frankly admitted to me, a lowly and unknown priest, in the Butyrki prison in Moscow, where the Lord united us for a short space of time, what feelings of faintheartedness and cowardice he had suddenly experienced in the inner jail of the GPU while waiting to be shot. "I am already an old man," he said, "there is no future before me, I am a monk from my youth, finally a bishop, an example and image of Christianity and Christian boldness, yet now I just cannot help myself. I feel such a thirst for life, such a desire not to die, such grief and inner torment, such fear of death and faintheartedness—it is horrible! I struggle and cannot conquer myself. I am quite bankrupt with self-pity." Later this great man fearlessly wrote to Metropolitan Sergius from exile in Turkestan, protesting against his agreement with the atheist government, and denying that there was any possibility of compromising with it. And it was in Turkestan that he died. . . .

The government used the Living Church movement as a basis for persecuting the Orthodox, and in order to be released from prison it was necessary to declare that one would go over to the Living Church. . . . Temptations came from various directions. After months of imprisonment

I was suddenly released with the warning that my case would be decided that week—a hint that my subsequent fate would depend on me. By the mere fact that I did not go, during that week or ten days, to the Living Church people, did not seek their protection, but went to the Patriarch and even concelebrated with him, I condemned myself to years of imprisonment. Such, approximately, was the path taken by all the others. Each one of us knew that he did not have to be in jail, and that if he was there, it was through his own will.

My wife said to me during one of our sad prison visits, "Why is it that the others manage to keep out of jail?" She meant those who joined the "Living Church" but then, when the crisis had passed, returned to Orthodoxy under pressure from their own flocks; such people were of no concern to the government. "Surely you do not want me to be a dishonourable man?" "No," she said, and did not raise the question again.

Other priests were drawn into the Living Church by their wives in the hope of avoiding prison, and were then unable to leave. However, I knew of one case which worked in the opposite direction. A priest I knew was in prison for renouncing the "Living Church." He could easily have got out. But his wife, during a visit, said that she could not bear their previous life and told him, if he joined the Living Church, not to bother coming home.

From far away my mother sent a note to me in jail, which I was able to receive and read only during the period when I was temporarily released. My mother wrote to me that she blessed me to stay in prison and not to weaken in spirit, to endure everything and not to give in. I wept from joy. . . .

After four and a half months in the Butyrki prison I suddenly had a week and a half of freedom. I brought the Patriarch the greetings and respects of the imprisoned bishops and priests. Among other things, the Patriarch said to me, "It is better to stay in prison. You see I am free only on paper, but I cannot do anything. If I send a bishop to the south, he ends up in the north, if I send him to the west, he is taken eastwards." The Cheka reduced the Patriarch's activities to nothing, not even allowing the bishops he appointed to reach their dioceses, but sending them off to places of imprisonment and internal exile.

Nevertheless, that was still a happy period. The Church was strong. The Church's strength and superiority over her enemies were quite evident.

Bishops who had not reached their sees, or lasted in them only three weeks or a month, as well as those who had been in their diocese for many years but were now in exile, concentration camps and prisons, were all officially considered as belonging to their diocese and their names were commemorated in the appointed place in the services in every church of the diocese. Who now could forget them? Like the imprisoned priests, they were sent letters without number, the contents of which were beyond price; all the love of their flocks, their gratitude for their steadfastness and boldness, their reverence for the innocent suffering of their spiritual leaders were poured out in them. Between the clergy and their flocks were formed such bonds as were known only in the first centuries in the life of the Church of Christ. I do not even know if there had ever been previously, in the history of the Church the world over, cases of such a widespread and profound spiritual resurgence. Every Christian considered it his duty to write the name of his imprisoned bishop or priest on the list for commemoration of his living relatives at the Liturgy. And as the deacon commemorated them, he would read the word "imprisoned" over and over again, as he read out their names. The Church grieved for her suffering ones and prayed zealously for them. And when the bishop returned, after completing his term of imprisonment or exile—admittedly, very often this would be only for a few weeks—when he returned to his own city, then the triumphant rejoicing of the people was indescribable. They scattered flowers and their tears in his path and considered it a blessing to kiss the edge of his *riassa*.

During the week and a half that I had at liberty, I, a lowly parish priest, was so weighed down by outpourings of gratitude, love and reverence, which each parishioner hastened to display, that when I again found myself in the convicts' railway wagon and in the transit prisons on the way to Solovki, I felt I was resting and found the burden of imprisonment easier to bear than enduring undeserved veneration and love. I had never begun to imagine that my case was so valuable in the eyes of the people. But this made the Cheka very bitter. The authorities remained powerless before the Church, although it was only the moral power of the Church which could withstand their crude physical violence. . . .

I last saw the Patriarch after I came out of prison [and after his own release], when I brought him the greetings of my fellow captives. The Patriarch was good-natured and calm as before, but he looked so thin and exhausted that, when parting from him, I wept out of pity. Holding my head to his chest, the Patriarch said, "Why are you crying?" I was surprised to find myself answering, "I have a feeling that I will not see you again. . . ." Of course, as the Patriarch stood before me, I did not think he would last long, and I had an inner conviction that I would not remain at liberty for long myself. The Patriarch laughed and said, "Well, mountains won't move apart, but people are always parting. Celebrate with me tomorrow."

Among other things, when talking to the Patriarch, I repented to him of the fact that, when I was in prison, I had more than once mentally condemned him for yielding ground to the Bolsheviks. The Patriarch heartily forgave me and said that his freedom was worse than prison; he himself remembered his imprisonment as a better period. The next day I had another opportunity of concelebrating with the Patriarch in the Church of the Holy Great Martyr Anastasia by the Butyrskaya Gate. After that I was arrested and sent to Solovki, and did not see the Patriarch again. The Patriarch died. The Bolshevik government tortured him to death, burning him up on the slow fire of its satanic hatred. . . .

Father Michael was again arrested and sentenced to three years in the prison camp on Solovki. The Bolsheviks had turned this ancient monastery on an island in the Far North into a prison camp, where many bishops and clergymen were imprisoned.

Father Michael was dispatched in the same convoy as Archbishop Hilarion (Troitsky), the boldest of Patriarch Tikhon's supporters. But the White Sea was frozen and the convoy spent the winter in a transit camp on Popov Island in Kem. On January 21, 1924, came the news of Lenin's death, and the following order was sent to all the camps: at the moment when Lenin's body was lowered into the ground, all the prisoners were to line up silently on parade in their barracks at the command "Attention!" All the prisoners followed the supervisor's command, among them several clergymen. Only Archbishop Hilarion and Father Michael demonstratively remained on the top bunks. One clergyman (who later followed Metropolitan Sergius) tried to persuade them, "Get up, Lenin was still a great person and you'll really be for it if the bosses find out!"

They both remained lying down. When the siren sounded, proclaiming that Lenin's body was being lowered into his temporary grave (pending construction of the mausoleum), Archbishop Hilarion announced in a loud voice, "Just think, fathers, what is now happening in hell: Lenin himself has arrived—what a festival for the demons!" Neither the commandant nor the clerk of the barracks gave them away, so neither of the two confessors suffered for the boldness they displayed in those minutes.

In the spring, they were sent to Solovki; Father Michael, together with the other bishops and clergymen, was sent to work in a workshop at the "Philemon" fisheries, where they made fishing nets. This was officially known as "Troitsky's Workshop," from the family name of the senior person there, Archbishop Hilarion. The name also testifies to the fact that all who worked there passed through the spiritual school of Vladyka Hilarion, which did not permit compromise with communism. Father Michael wrote,

> A "Chekist," a secret collaborator with the GPU, whose job had been spying on the employees of financial institutions, was the supervisor of our convoy at the fisheries on Solovki, where I was working as a forced labourer with the other prisoners. In the workshop where we made fishing nets, he heard our spiritual conversations, started arguing with me, and finally, through God's grace, hidden from the eyes of his comrades, he received confession and Holy Communion from me.
>
> Such examples are very joyous. The soul exists and the image of God within it is indestructible, even in these half-men, half-beasts known as Chekists. As a result of this, the Bolsheviks' work of warfare against God and destruction of souls is built on sand, and even at the slightest wafting of the quiet, joyous breeze of God's grace, it collapses immediately. Of course, the greatest number of crimes and the most profound damage are those done to the souls of children. But even here, it often happens that the soul of a child who has been subjected to these evil influences melts like wax before the fire of God's love.
>
> Once on Solovki, by the doors of the cemetery church, which had been left open for the monks working as hired labourers in some of the camp workshops, I came across a little boy of six, the child of one of the administrative staff. "Where are you going, monk? There is no God, you don't need to pray, it's all a trick," he muttered, scowling at me, with a boldness rare for his age. I was stunned. Bending down to him, I said, "Dear little boy, who told you to say things like that? It is not right at all. . . . God is there and you should pray . . . where did you get all that from?" The boy was embarrassed and blushed, and the frown disappeared from his face. What could such a small creature reply? He was silent. I stroked him on the head. For him my smile was the same as anyone else's. There was nothing frightening about me, despite what his parents had probably said. . . .

While he was imprisoned on Solovki, Father Michael's twenty-eight-year-old wife died from loneliness and grief. His orphaned daughter, who had never known her father, was taken in and brought up by relatives.

In 1927, at the end of his term in the concentration camp, Father Michael was sent for three years of internal exile in the Komi Autonomous region, also in the Far North, which is populated by a tribe of Finnish origin called the Zyranians (*Zyriani*). Father Michael was dispatched together with Bishop Platon (Rudnieff), a vicar of the Moscow diocese, who later died. In exile they learned of the Declaration of Metropolitan Sergius[4] and decided not to accept his leadership of the Church. That was when Father Michael began serving in a secret church in a private apartment, using an antimension given to him by Bishop Platon. He served in this way for three years. Later, Father Michael was always careful not to reveal many details about these secret services in order to protect the identity of those still involved in similar activities in Russia.

Concerning Metropolitan Sergius, Father Michael received letters from his parishioners in Moscow asking his advice. Father Michael wrote,

> In the end people were left only with the churches of Metropolitan Sergius; there were no others left. The clergy led the people in the same direction they had followed themselves. Since the days of the Living Church, the people had been shocked and broken up into factions by their leaders, but finally the time has come, under Metropolitan Sergius, when even the Orthodox Christians do not know where to lay their heads. Nobody can put his heart into attending the churches of Metropolitan Sergius, where his name is commemorated and prayers are said for the Soviet government, but there is nowhere else to go. Not to attend these churches means being left completely without a church, without Divine Services, without religion. The majority of the believers are quite unable to take such a step. The only thing left is to follow Metropolitan Sergius, albeit with a severely compromised conscience.
>
> My parish, the church of Sts. Peter and Paul by the Preobrazhenskaya Gate in Moscow, was giving no rest to my fellow clergy, and they managed to get some letters through to me in the Zyranian region, wanting to know my attitude to Metropolitan Sergius. My position was grievous in the extreme. If I had been at home, then I would have opposed the parish to Metropolitan Sergius and suffered for it myself. My colleagues would have again have been left in peace. But under the circumstances, there was nothing else I could do except advise each parishioner separately to depart from communion with Metropolitan Sergius. But I knew that this would be beyond the strength of many, since it meant leaving their own church. So I recommended this to some, the strongest, and even to these not at once, but only when I was convinced of the firmness of their spirit. . . .

As the term of his exile drew to an end, Father Michael felt certain that he would be sentenced to another term of imprisonment and exile and, in the end, would lose his resolve and join the official Church. So he formulated a plan to flee from his place of exile. After escaping, he lived without any proper identification documents in an "illegal situation." His plan was to travel throughout Russia using false papers under the guise of a glazier or stove-setter. He carried an antimension and sacred vessels hidden in his toolbox, so that he could celebrate secret liturgies in houses where the appearance of a stove-setter or glazier belonging to the secret Church would not cause suspicion or alert the neighbors. That was 1929, the year of collectivization when hundreds of thousands of "Kulak"[5] peasant families were forcibly sent to Siberia. Some refused to go or left illegally, so the GPU put out a strict surveillance to catch these fugitives who were posing as wanderers or vagrants. This made travel particularly difficult for an "illegal" without proper papers. Father Michael wrote,

> During the period of collectivization, I had the opportunity of meeting people who were prepared for total Christian self-sacrifice. People came to me and asked whether, from the Christian point of view, it was acceptable to join a collective farm. If it was not, they feared neither prison nor death itself. I was profoundly struck by the strength of such faith and the high level of spiritual development which these Russian people had achieved. I had to say that even in the collective farm one must not betray one's faith, must not take the icons off the walls of one's house with one's own hands, must not give up going to church, but that if people refuse to join the collective farm for practical, economic reasons, then it is for these reasons that they will be suffering, not for the faith. The government can take away whatever it wants, just do not surrender your soul and your faith to it. However, neither did I constrain the consciences of those who resolved not to join the collective farm out of fear of a slavery which it was beyond their power to endure. . . .

In 1930, having reached Turkmenia, Father Michael contacted a bishop of the underground Church, who was later killed. He blessed Father Michael, as one young, bold, and strong in spirit, to cross the frontier illegally, despite the danger, in order to testify in the Western world about the real situation of the Russian Church and about the secret Church that did not accept compromises with the Bolshevik government. Father Michael wrote,

> After my escape from my place of exile, when I was travelling through Russia looking for a way of getting to the border, I stayed with a diocesan bishop, an old friend of mine from one of my places of imprisonment. Not wishing to cause him any anxiety on my behalf, or on his own, during the few hours that we spoke I did not say anything to him about my escape or that I was already being sought by the GPU. Therefore, when he learned that I did not wish to occupy my position in Moscow, the bishop offered me a position as a priest in his own diocese, at the same time pointing out in a friendly way that he would have to submit my candidacy to the GPU. I need not say how inappropriate that would have been for me in my situation! But that apart, the very idea was an absolute abomination to me. "No, I will never accept a priestly position from such hands," I said. It turned out that each time lists of candidates for vacant positions were submitted to the GPU, which then chose whoever it thought was most suitable. . . .

So Father Michael continued on his journey, sometimes on foot, sometimes as a stowaway on trains. He later recounted how one time he got off the train at a small station to look for water. A station worker he met said, "Why aren't you wearing a cassock, priest?" "How do you know that I am a priest?" "Well," came the reply, "it's obvious from the way you walk!" Father Michael did not stop to ask about the distinctive walk of a priest but hurried back to his place on the train.

Later, Father Michael often spoke of his experiences during this illegal journey to the Persian frontier. He spoke about it both to describe Soviet conditions and, more importantly, to encourage his listeners with hope in God's help and protection. These accounts are etched firmly in the minds of all those who knew him. In his own words, the following description tells how he crossed the frontier with the miraculous help of the Most Holy Mother of God. This was originally published as a footnote in a book Father Michael wrote about the veneration of the Mother of God, which also points out the ways in which Roman Catholic and Protestant teachings about Her diverge from the Orthodox. Father Michael wrote as if reluctant, in the third person, without his usual warmth, as if anxious to retain a state of spiritual sobriety.

> The author of these lines is forced to tell of his own experience, although he would not wish to, lest anyone should think more of him than he is worth. Coming to the end of a six-year period spent in places of imprisonment and exile at the hands of the Bolsheviks, and expecting to be sentenced

to another term, he ran away from his place of exile. Then, in a certain place, he received, through another person, the blessing of a bishop, who gave him the precept, among other things, of always calling on the help of the Most Holy Virgin Mary when faced with grievous circumstances. He conveyed to him the idea that it is especially pleasing to the Most Holy Virgin when people read her the "Rejoicing" brought to her by the Angel Gabriel—that is to say, when they "call Her blessed" using the wonderful angelic greeting. Then the Most Holy Virgin, receiving as it were a new blessedness from any such recollection by people of Her grace, hastens to help them with the same grace. Of course, there is generally no need to teach an Orthodox priest to pray to the Most Holy Virgin Mary, but in the given circumstances, this clear indication to him of the place of constant refuge and speedy help in danger was extremely relevant.

These dangers proved to be beyond all measure. At one point, throughout a two-day railway journey, he was utterly worn out by the constant checking of documents. Every "Chekist" who entered the carriage, after taking one look at the passengers, singled him out as a suspicious-looking type and demanded his papers. He had nothing except a small note from the militia stating that he claimed to have lost his papers. This was all he had been able to obtain for the journey. Such a document could only make him seem more suspicious.

All the people in the carriage became utterly exasperated from this hounding after one single passenger. All sighed and groaned while this questioning and badgering continued—it could easily lead to the unfortunate person being arrested and taken away. So the latter, seeing the approaching danger, said the "rejoicing," or "blessing" to the Virgin: "Virgin Mother of God, rejoice, Mary full of grace, the Lord is with Thee. Blessed art Thou among women." As soon as he began to say this prayer, the strength of the Chekists withered up, their stubbornness weakened and they "melted like wax before the fire, they vanished like smoke," retreated and left.

But the greatest trial was before this, when he had no papers. In the town of Poti, a militiaman stopped him on a bridge, demanded his papers, and took him away. The unfortunate escapee felt the ground sinking under his feet. There would not be a long investigation. In his confusion he seized on the "blessing" of the Virgin. They walked along for several minutes, and then they stopped to talk to another militiaman. "And who's that?" asked the man they had met, apparently the senior of the two, as he pointed at the arrested man. "No papers," said the militiaman. "Why have you got no papers?" he asked the arrested man. "Lost," he replied. "Oh well, off you go," came the reply.

There were many more adventures of the most terrible sort. They were crowned by his crossing the frontier from the Soviet Union into Persia, which took place on 25 March 1930 on the very day of the Annunciation of the Most Holy Mother of God. This was a wonderful sign of God's mercy through the Virgin Mary and a sign of Her glory. In the morning he was told that they would cross the frontier that day, after two weeks of waiting by the frontier in mortal danger, and after a terrible attempt the day before had failed, and he was delighted by this news. His despairing fellow travellers were amazed at his reaction. "You see, today is the day of the Annunciation of the Most Holy Virgin Mary! Can we possibly fail? Mary the Mother of God will take us across." But they would not believe him in this. However, at 11 o'clock on a brightly moonlit night, they arrived on the Persian side, passing along secret paths between the Bolsheviks' border posts. "Even a dog would not wag his tongue," as the saying goes, during that journey fraught with mortal danger.

Father Michael in London

Father Michael made his way from Persia to Jerusalem, where he venerated the holy places and made the acquaintance of Archbishop Anastassy (the future metropolitan), who was then head of the Russian Ecclesiastical Mission in Jerusalem. Father Michael was assigned to the parish in Beirut where he remained until 1938. In that year, he gave his report to the assembly of hierarchs, clergy, and laity of the Russian Church Abroad, from which quotes have been provided here. "It is with feelings of deep emotion," he said, "that I am addressing this exalted gathering today. Some years ago, I wondered whether God would judge it right for me to testify here about the sufferings of Russia from my own experiences. Now this hour has come."

Later in 1938 Father Michael moved to 14 St Dunstan's Road in London. Father Nicholas Gibbes lived in the basement of the house and continued his activities among the English-speaking Orthodox until 1941, when he moved to Oxford.

Father Michael quickly won the hearts of his new parishioners. "He was an extraordinary person," recalled Mrs Sophia Goodman. "From the very beginning he drew people to the Church through his sermons and his attitude towards everybody."

He was a person full of love, recollected Abbess Elisabeth. She had come to know Father Michael well during his first two years in London, before she departed for the Holy Land, where she went in 1940 to become a nun. She continued,

> There were many young girls whom Father Nicholas Gibbes had brought over from Yugoslavia. Father Michael cared for them, feeding them and giving them money when they needed it. He was most unmercenary. I used to help him travelling and visiting hospitals. There was one case of a man who was in hospital, injured. Father Michael talked to this man and then said, "Have you got any money?" He says "No." [Fr Michael] put his hand in his pocket and took out ten pounds—in those days ten pounds was a large sum—and gave it to him. And going back, he couldn't pay his fare, so I had to pay for him. That was always happening. In church, as he gave the blessing to make the collection, he would always be the first to put something on the plate.
>
> He also gave a course of explanation of Holy Scripture. It was well organized. The classes were held in a big hall just opposite the Podvoria, within walking distance. It was very convenient and made a beautiful auditorium. We went in the evening, and afterwards, he insisted we go to the Podvoria and had tea. It was most interesting, and to those who visited he gave a certificate that they had been to the missionary courses. I still have my certificate.
>
> His sermons in church were always clear and to the point. First he would state the title or theme of what he was going to say, then would follow the sermon itself and, at the end, in a few words, came the conclusion. That way people remembered what had been said.
>
> Father Michael was a very strong personality, but he was always radiant, always happy. He had a very keen sense of humour. There was a lady, a widow, who was always very sorry for herself. She was poor but she had a great treasure: one of the famous violins, an "Amati" I think. And she wanted to sell it. The price that she wanted to get was more than it was really worth. My family, through some connections with the musical world, tried to sell it. And they sold it for her, if I am not mistaken, it was for about six thousand pounds.[6] But she was always complaining. If you did a kind deed to her she was upset, and if you tried not to pay too much attention she would get upset; whatever happened, she was always upset. So she went to Father Michael. "I can't go on," she said, "it's no life for me. I must commit suicide." He says, "Truly you want to commit suicide?" She says, "Yes." For the first time she was happy that Father Michael took her seriously. "Are you sure? Promise?" She says, "I promise." So he put his

hand into his pocket. "Here is half a crown. Buy a very strong rope, so that you will do it properly." Then she stopped thinking about it, as she saw how ridiculous it was.

He would make fun of people who were concerned about their appearance. He would pull his hair back into a bunch behind his head and say, "There. Don't you think I have a Greek profile? Just like Socrates, a pure Greek profile!" Of course, all he had in common with Socrates was the beard; otherwise he had the coarse, peasant features of a Cossack!

Many people came to him for long talks of spiritual direction and spiritual advice.

He was a very striking personality, and I remember him recounting about when he was arrested and they brought him for questioning. He used to say, "You are cold, you are in great fear that you will not be able to stand up to the psychological, mental torture, and you pray. You answer absolutely without hesitation, boldly, and then you go back to your cell and you begin to shake. That's the difference, how God helps you, and your own weakness." There was an *irmos* which he always used to sing to prepare himself when he was going for questioning. So he had a tremendous experience of the depths of human weakness and experience of God's wonderful help when the trial comes.

After he was released from Solovki and he was on the mainland, he was living in a flat, and there he took confession of a communist. He spoke with him and he confessed. It was a proper confession. At first he said, "For me, who has killed innocent people, there is no forgiveness." But Father Michael spoke to him, he made peace with him, and gave him Holy Communion. There were two or three instances like this that he told us about.

Father Michael used to visit a young couple, the Ananins, who lived in Purley. In the afternoons of these visits, he would go to see a Russian inmate of a large mental asylum on the top of a hill nearby. This man had a long beard but was otherwise completely naked and was kept in a separate room by himself; he thought that he was Jesus Christ. Father Michael found a way of talking to him and calming him. In the end the man died of syphilis, which was believed to be the cause of his mental disorder. The Ananins used to visit Father Michael in London during the week, when it was quieter. On Sundays his house was always full of people, particularly the young. Sometimes young couples made each other's acquaintance at these gatherings, beginning friendships that ripened into courtship and marriage.

In July 1938, Father Michael gave a talk about the state of Russia and hopes for its regeneration. This account in *The Russian in England* illustrated his warm-hearted approach as well as his insight:

> A Lecture by Father Michael Polsky on the subject of "The Spiritual State of Russia" took place in the premises of the North Russian Society on 6 July. It was attended by a large audience by London standards which listened with rapt attention.
>
> Father Michael provided a scathing criticism of Marxism as interpreted by the Bolsheviks, expressing the view that the Russian people and indeed all of civilized humanity could find both spiritual consolation and the basis for a just social and state order in Christianity. Capitalism, with its semi-pagan materialism, had already outlived itself both spiritually and socially, and so people had to seek other, new ways of organizing and arranging their lives. Socialism provided a convincing criticism of capitalism, and had thereby brought about the destruction of the spiritual and material basis of the bourgeois order, but it proved incapable of positive creativity. The example of Russia showed that so-called scientific socialism brings in its wake a complete enslavement of the human personality and a terrible spiritual and material oppression.
>
> Christianity, especially in its Orthodox confession, should provide a spiritual and social synthesis[7] of the ideals that had inspired capitalism (thesis) and socialism (anti-thesis).
>
> The Russian emigration must take this to heart and then go to Russia preaching love and forgiveness rather than hatred and vengeance.
>
> The speaker expressed his bitter disappointment that many emigrant circles do not understand this truth and seek the salvation of Russia through extreme nationalism, fascism and other contemporary political doctrines, which in essence are a regurgitation of either atheist bolshevism or materialist and pagan capitalism.
>
> The speaker promised to give, in a later talk, a more detailed explanation of the idea of establishing a Christian order of state and social life in Russia after the destruction of the unnatural and ungodly rule of the Bolsheviks.
>
> The interesting and penetrating lectures by Father Michael, who had experienced Bolshevism personally, are inspiring far reaching questions, which need a profound examination of these questions in all their aspects. It is therefore regrettable that these talks are not followed by a discussion where people could join forces to express their doubts and thoughts and

thereby jointly think through and develop the postulates asserted by the speaker.

We hope that in the future Father Michael will take this wish into consideration and that his lectures will be followed by a discussion of the questions he is raising.

In July 1938 celebrations of the 950th anniversary of the Baptism of Russia by St Vladimir took place throughout the Russian emigration. People looked back to the celebrations of the 900th anniversary that were held in 1888 under very different circumstances. At the same time, celebrants looked forward to the much grander anniversary of the millennium that would occur in 1988, with the prayer and hope that Russia would again be free by then. In London, Archbishop Nestor, Father Michael Polsky, and Archimandrite Nathaniel spoke at a meeting arranged to mark this anniversary after the vigil service for the feast of St Vladimir. *The Russian in England* provided this account:

Celebration of the 950th anniversary of the baptism of Russia
On Wednesday 27 July, the Vigil Service was held in St. Philip's Church, following which there was a celebratory meeting dedicated to the baptism of Russia and the memory of the Holy Prince Vladimir.

Archpriest Michael Polsky, rector of the parish under the Council of Bishops, spoke at the meeting and depicted the high Christian ideal established by Saint Vladimir. The holy prince Vladimir provided an example of this both in his private life and when fulfilling his official functions.

Archimandrite Nathaniel gave an extremely beautiful and inspired speech in which he outlined how the good seed sown by Prince Vladimir had grown throughout the course of Russian history despite the frequent attempts by the forces of evil to stifle it.

Then Archbishop Nestor spoke and explained the plans for forming a Brotherhood of Christian Russia dedicated to Saint Vladimir. The archbishop said he planned to present this plan for confirmation by the forthcoming Bishops' Council. The task of the Brotherhood would be the spiritual healing of the Russian nation based on Christian ideals and collective prayer for the salvation of Russia. People joining the Brotherhood would be expected to recognize the spiritual authorities and submit to them, spend some time every week saying specific prayers, and help the Brotherhood materially in publishing and distributing periodicals and books.

At the end of the meeting Archbishop Nestor blessed those present and gave them specially blessed icons of Saint Vladimir.

Shortly after this event, the visit of Archbishop Nestor and Archimandrite Nathaniel to London ended, as reported in *The Russian in England*:

> On Saturday 30 July Archbishop Nestor left London for Belgrade, where he will take part in the Council (Sobor) of the Russian Church Abroad. After the end of the Council meeting, Vladyka will leave for India in order to unite a Christian community in Malabar to the Orthodox Church. Vladyka will be accompanied by Archimandrite Nathaniel, who is expected to remain in Malabar as a missionary and spiritual guide for the Indian Christians after they have newly joined the Orthodox Church.

Father Nathaniel did not remain in India but returned to Europe and joined the Monastery of St Job of Pochaev in Ladomirova, a small town in a part of Carpatho–Russia that was then part of Czechoslovakia. Archbishop Nestor returned to China and continued his archpastoral service. In 1948 he was arrested by the Chinese authorities and handed over to the Soviets who imprisoned him in the Gulag until 1956. On his release he served as a bishop in Russia until he died in 1962.

Archpriest Michael Polsky visiting the grave of Karl Marx, Highgate Cemetery, with Prince Dmitri Galitzine (left) and George Knupffer (right). (Source: Sophia Goodman)

World War II

Father Michael had been in London for little over a year when World War II broke out; in fact, he spent six of his ten years in London under wartime conditions. Many young men in the parish joined up and many were killed. The air raids brought mortal danger to the civilian population as well. Father Michael advised those who were able to move out of London for the duration. He, of course, remained at his post. He joined the local Fire Watchers and, in the company of Mstislav ("Slava") Perott, a young man who lived at 1 St Dunstan's Road, went on patrol, looking for signs of fires started by the bombs.

St Philip's Church, which was close to an important railway station, suffered bomb damage on several occasions. The following anonymous account is preserved in the church archives:

> At the beginning of the Second World War, when the air raids started, some of the sacred objects in the church which could be moved were sent to Scotland for safety with Her Imperial Highness, Grand Duchess Xenia Alexandrovna, who stayed at Balmoral for the duration. Other items were taken to the home of the churchwarden, Mr. G. F. Walneff, at 121 Castelnau Avenue, Barnes. At the end of the war all these objects were returned to the church unharmed. The house in Barnes hardly suffered any damage during the war.
>
> The air raids began in September, 1940. The church first suffered damage in the evening of 21 December, when a landmine fell on the permanent way of the railway, almost directly opposite. The force of the blast blew in some of the windows and damaged the wooden frame of the stone iconostasis; splinters of glass and metal fragments from the windows scratched some of the icons. The front door was blown in and in places the roof tiles were dislodged. Through the efforts of the Churchwarden the windows were boarded up and temporary repairs were made to the other damage. Services continued through the winter, even though there was no heating.
>
> On the night of 17 April 1941, the eve of Holy Thursday, there was more bomb damage from explosions both behind the church, in Ebury Street, and again in the same place on the railway. The church was hastily cleared of debris and that evening, when the Twelve Gospels of the Passion were being read, bowls and other containers had to be put on the floor to catch the rain water leaking through the damaged roof, which was then carried out in buckets. Most of the windows, already boarded up, had been blown in again and remained open. Again the churchwarden, assisted by a parishioner, Evgeny Samoilovich Mollo, made temporary

repairs, but the tiles on the side part of the roof had to be replaced with roofing felt, and the roof propped up with wooden supports inside. The services continued. On 15 March 1942, during the third week of Great Lent, a phosphorous incendiary bomb pierced the roof (above the icon of Our Lady of Mount Athos) and fell into the church. Fire broke out in several places but was put out with the help of some of the neighbours who were acting as Fire Watchers. The hole in the roof was patched up somehow and services continued.

On 15/28 July, 1944, on St. Vladimir's day, at about 2 p.m. (the service had finished at about 12:30) a flying bomb fell in the square behind the church. The explosion blew all the boards off the windows, completely destroyed the roof on the south side and severely damaged it on the north side, as well as removing some tiles from the central part of the roof.

In such conditions it was finally impossible to continue the services and the church was temporarily closed. Services were resumed at Christmas, 1945, after a temporary repair of the building carried out by the government. The government arranged for more extensive repairs in 1948, after the war was over.

Parishioners killed in the air raids included Princess Ekaterina Georgievna Galitzine, killed in 1940 in Holborn, and a couple named Arpezoff, whose house in West Kensington suffered a direct hit.

Of course, for Father Michael, as for many of his parishioners, the dangers of the war on the home front paled in comparison with what they had lived through in Russia. "Strange to say," wrote Princess Irina Galitzine, "we were never frightened when the sirens sounded their wailing calls at any time of day or night. It seemed that all my fears and terrors were left behind the Iron Curtain." Nevertheless, times were hard, and Father Michael's warm personality, combined with any practical help that he could offer, bolstered the morale of his flock. Mrs Sophia Goodman recalled,

People just came to him. He had these girls who had practically never been in a church before arriving from munitions factories in their trousers; he would put his arms around them and said "what did it matter?" as long as they came. . . . (In those days women did not wear trousers at all, so you can imagine elderly ladies saying things and complaining.) Very soon he persuaded them all to wear skirts.

Then there were the meals under the church. I couldn't take it because often it was brawn.[8] He only had one ration book. He'd simply open his bag around all the butchers and say, "Please, please, something . . . people . . . feed." He always got bones with a bit of meat on them or some other pieces that were "off ration." He would cook that all into a soup or make brawn with it, and so he would feed about fifteen to twenty people downstairs after the services at the Podvoria.

His English was extremely basic. By the time he left [England] he could understand fairly well, but even then he could only speak very basic English.

He had suffered so much himself, so he understood everything. I remember him telling about how he had said goodbye to his wife and daughter, how they didn't know if he was dead or alive, and how he never saw them again after he was taken off to Solovki. I remember reading his memoirs. To me, then, it was appalling because I was very young. He described how he was having a tooth removed without anaesthetic in the camps. Then, when they took it out, they found it was a good one. And on that, he escaped with a raging toothache and walked through Russia. This made a great impression on me.

I remember the incident when we were all in church and the doodle-bugs—flying bombs—were coming over. It was Sunday morning. We had heard the engine, and then it stopped. Then you would know within a few seconds whether you had been hit or somebody else. So, we heard the engine stop. Father Michael came out on to the ambo and blessed every-body . . . and then we heard the crash. That was when the Guard's Chapel near Buckingham Palace was hit.

Did he talk about politics? Yes, he did all the time. He was not pro-Nazi. He had suffered too much to support anything totalitarian although he shared the feelings of many Russians who were horrified that England was fighting on the side of the Soviets. He would say, "We're backing one devil to fight another devil."

The Home Office called him out. This came up years later, when my father [Count Wladimir Kleinmichel] went to get visas for the nuns. A man came up to him and said, "What happened to Father Michael Polsky?" My father said that he had gone to California. He said, "He was an extraordinary man. Do you know that during the war we called him here to warn him not to speak that way, that there was a war on, that he should keep his feelings to himself; he couldn't talk like that. He argued with us. Then we told him that he had to be careful because there were people informing on him. To which he said, "Oh, yes, I know who that is." "How do you know?" "He has lunch with me every Sunday!" They had never forgotten that incident.

Father Michael started classes of religious instruction and he gave us all a Bible. We were a group of 10 youngish people from about fifteen to twenty. But it did not ever get very far. We ended up talking about everyday things and how to react to them. I suppose it was quite good, although we were never taught about the Orthodox faith in a systematic way.

The most vivid incident I remember during Father Michael's time occurred just after the war—it must have been about 1947. The troubles were going on in Jerusalem, and Father Michael chose to make a statement in front of the Ampenoff family from the ambon.[9] And he said, "Now we must all give thanks that there has been an attack on the nuns in Jerusalem and our dear sister and dear friends. . . ." And then they all more or less fell down in hysterics, because they hadn't heard about it. Then he

Archbishop Savva blesses a newly married couple, Captain Colquhon Ancram and Princess Xenia Romanoff, at St Philip's Church; on the right is Archpriest Michael Polsky, 1942. (Source: Sophia Goodman)

was terribly put out because he did not expect this reaction, because the point of his announcement was to say that they were now safe. He thought it would be a very good way of breaking the news and that everybody would be thankful. I always remember that. It was something I had never seen happen in church before.

Father Michael at the christening of Peter Orloff, with Madame Nina Djakally, 1944. (Source: George Orloff)

During the war, when travelling was difficult, Father Michael went to Warrington in Lancashire to visit George Orloff (the friend of Father Boris Molchanoff) who was working there on government business. George was married to his "lovely Swiss bride," Marie Louise, and Father Michael was to baptise her into the Orthodox Church. On the train people looked with suspicion at his priestly robes and suggested that he might have weapons concealed underneath!

In 1944 he was allowed a single visit to a camp in Yorkshire where Russian prisoners of war, captured in France, were interned. Their fate is described in Chapter 12.

In Memory of Father Michael Polsky

This chapter ends with a remembrance written by Valentina Bogdan, a Cossack woman from the same *stanitsa*[10] as Father Michael. She came to England in 1946 and observed Father Michael and his relationships with people at close quarters in the immediate post-war years.

> My family—that is, my husband, myself and our ten-year-old daughter, Natasha—first met Father Michael when we were in very straightened circumstances. We came to London from Germany towards the end of 1946. My husband had been offered work in Kenya through the British Colonial Office. At that time, however, there were no regular passenger ships sailing to Kenya, and it was suggested that he go alone on a military vessel, leaving me and Natasha in England for the time being. We were

lodged in a large hotel, paid for by the Government on the understanding that the expenses would later be deducted from my husband's salary.

Although we were very happy to be out of wartorn Germany, and were lucky to receive work corresponding to my husband's qualifications in order to start a new life abroad, we could not but be worried in the face of an indefinite period of separation. My husband was concerned that I would experience difficulties in England, not knowing the language, as well as looking after a child. We decided to look for help amongst the Russian émigrés in London, and so made enquiries as to the existence of an Orthodox Church: we wanted to find lodgings with a Russian family. The church was discovered, near Victoria Station, and the next Sunday we went there, to be greeted by Father Michael Polsky. We felt a kinship with him immediately, and he lifted our spirits enormously!

After we had told him about ourselves, he understood our difficulty at once, and, in order to make our acquaintance further, he invited us to lunch after the service. There is in fact a house belonging to the Church in London, a Podvoria. Father Michael then cautioned us not to tell people that we had come out of Russia during the war. We were surprised, but heeded this strange warning.

Arriving at the Church house we found a large Russian gathering. As we later learned, Father Michael regularly invited lonely Russian people to the Podvoria. We had one course, and that was thick, meaty, Kuban-style borsch, prepared by Father Michael himself before the service. At that time meat was rationed in England, but the local butcher knew that the Father fed many of his parishioners, and helped him out with off-cuts and bones.

Most of the guests at lunch were refugees from Europe during the war: there was a member of the French Legion, a young engineer from Belgium who had escaped German captivity, and a young girl called Lenochka who was the daughter of a Leningrad professor and who had come to university in England. There were several young ladies from an institute in Serbia, who had come over to learn English, and also Volodya Miloslavsky and Alexander "Zhuk" Obolensky. There were also permanent Londoners: the Galitzine brother and sister, a lonely Russian gentleman, and a young woman, Melissa, who had escaped from Shanghai with her English husband.

As soon as they arrived, the girls set to work serving the meal, and others began asking us about ourselves. Afterwards, the whole lively company began to clear up, and Father Michael invited us up into the large reception room on the first floor above the church. First of all he explained to us that at that time England was sending back to the USSR those Russians who had escaped during the war, and so even though we had a visa and work, it was best not to reveal our origins. We might encounter over-zealous officials who would not stop to find out our credentials, but would just bundle us off to be repatriated. During the war, the British media were very sympathetic to the Soviet Army, helping in the fight against a common enemy: Hitler's Germany. This had such an effect on some people that they considered anti-Soviet feeling to be hostile.

There had even been complaints against Father Michael when his sermons touched on the crimes of the Bolsheviks against the Russian people, and since we were undoubtedly anti-Soviet, some people could take offence. He would tell us himself which people could be trusted with the truth: those who could help us, firstly, which meant the Church Council. Father Michael could promise us nothing that day, but invited us to return a few days later.

When we went back to see him, there were several members of the Church Council with him, including the Chairman, Mr. Ananin; a senior member of the sisterhood, Countess Kleinmichel; and I. P. Georgievsky. The Council asked us questions for a while, and then Father Michael revealed to us that they had suggested we should live in the Church House itself while we were waiting to go to Kenya. The Podvoria had a guest room which was empty at that time. A weight was truly "lifted from our shoulders"!

In church, I found Father Michael's services to be wonderfully moving. He had a beautiful, soft voice, and always pronounced his words clearly and with a profound sense of reverence. During his services, the people in church somehow felt that they were made a part of the priest's communion with God. After such a service, one's own personal problems seemed to diminish, strengthening a belief in the ultimate help of God.

In other ways, too, Father Michael was a true father to exiled Russians. I was told later by parishioners that during the cruel bombardment of London by the Germans, many people, especially those exiled or alone, found refuge in the Podvoria. People hoped that being "God's House" would somehow protect it, and the Father upheld this view to calm those who sought shelter.

Batioushka[11] did not distinguish between Russians and other nationals when it came to giving help, and neither did those he helped have to belong to the Russian church. I once found at his house a young Russian woman who was a non-believer. She had left Russia after marrying an Englishman, and had begun to miss her family and Russian society. She went to see the Father and asked him "Would it be possible for me to come to your house on Sundays? I am an agnostic, and can't come to church, but I miss Russian company." Father Michael gave her permission to come.

While living in Germany, we had practically run out of clothes; we had to travel light on leaving our homeland, since part of the journey was completed on foot. Natasha in particular was growing fast and out of her clothes. At that time in England clothes were bought with coupons, and Father Michael gave us not only his own ration, but also many extra coupons, saying that the parishioners wanted to help us. These people were especially generous with my husband, when he had to travel to Kenya. Although Father Michael never told us which people had donated their possessions, so that we could not even thank them, we were nevertheless embarrassed to receive such generosity. Father Michael persuaded my husband, however, that it was essential for him to be respectably dressed on the journey and in Kenya as he was on Government work, convincing him with the Russian proverb: "People meet your appearance, but take leave of your mind." One person sacrificed a good suit; another gave a pair of pyjamas: the rest of his clothes we bought with coupons.

Natasha and I lived for about four months in the Church House, and on Sundays, as I mentioned before, Father Michael always welcomed parishioners to lunch there; he chatted with them and always had a kind word for everyone. During the week, he was mostly on his own, busying himself in his room on the top floor. When visitors came to see him—which was quite often—he would meet them in the reception room on the first floor above the church. On one occasion an officer from a Soviet ship arrived (not for the first time, it seemed). Fr. Michael asked me not to let anyone in to see him while the officer was there—not even to open the front door. Their discussion lasted rather a long time. When the visitor had gone, Batioushka protested to me, saying, "He keeps asking me to give him religious and philosophical books to read, but it's a terrible shame, because he is too frightened to take them home with him, so as soon as he's read them, he throws the books into the sea—and they are not at all easy to get hold of!" In reply to the officer's complaint that it was difficult to engage the sailors in political education while the ship was in a foreign port, Father Michael suggested he organize a trip to see the tomb of Karl Marx. At the same time they would be able to see London itself, while the officer would seem to be doing his political duty, and everyone would be happy!

Fr. Michael collected engravings on religious subjects, and he had quite an impressive collection. He showed them to us one day, saying that he would donate them all to his own country, the very day it freed itself from the Bolsheviks.

Once I asked him why he came down so rarely to be with us in the evenings when friends visited us. Wasn't he lonely, being by himself all that time? "But I am not alone," he replied, "I am often praying, and prayer is talking to God and to the saints, so I am never lonely."

Unfortunately Fr. Michael had a liver complaint, and when this made him feel ill, he looked sad. If anyone said to him "You don't look well today, Father," he would reply "I'm in low spirits today," jokingly changing the Russian for low spirits *ne v dukhi* to *ne v dukhakh*, which means "not wearing perfume."

I was particularly grateful for the affectionate attention which Batioushka showed towards Natasha. My ten-year-old daughter used to spend the whole day without the company of children her own age. When we all ate together, Fr. Michael would always joke and even play games with her! Christmas was getting nearer, and he began to receive many Christmas cards, which he immediately gave to Natasha. She had never seen such pretty cards before, and carefully looked at each one, even trying to copy some of the designs. Father Michael's concern for the child was revealed also in the following way: one evening, when she was not very well, I went alone to the church at Victoria, where Batioushka asked me who was looking after Natasha. I replied that no one was with her, and that she did not mind being left alone. "You must go home at once," he said. "You should not leave a girl all alone in a big house like that." I returned home, and only later realised how wise he was to send me back! Some time after that, with the help of Mstislav Perott, his neighbour from across the road at No. 1 St Dunstan's Road, Fr. Michael arranged for Natasha to attend an English school. She had already started to learn English with her father in Germany.

Natasha also loved Father Michael very much. At Christmas time she was worried that she had no present to give him. "Why don't you draw him a Christmas card?" I suggested. She did more than that: she composed an amusing poem with illustrations about how Fr. Michael made his borsch and invited his friends round to eat it. Batioushka read the poem out at the Christmas dinner, and everyone was amused. After that incident, a Russian gentleman gave Natasha a volume of the collected works of Pushkin, inscribed "To a young Russian poetess." In March 1947 Natasha caught influenza and was coughing for a long time after. Batioushka asked Dr. B. Perott [Mstislav Perott's father] to examine her. The doctor found that she was anaemic, and that her lungs were weak; she needed a warm, dry climate, otherwise there was a danger of her developing tuberculosis. At this

Mstislav Perott as a child (left) and his father Dr Perott (right). (Source: Mstislav Perott)

conclusion, Father Michael sought help from one of the parishioners. A letter was written to the Home Office, explaining that the child's father lived in Kenya, and that the warm, dry, mountain climate was exactly suitable for her to regain her health: it was hoped that steps could be taken to send the little girl there as soon as possible. Doctor Perott's report was enclosed in the letter. Two weeks later we received tickets for the boat to Kenya.

Natasha and Father Michael kept in touch until the end of his life. His last message was in 1959 on the occasion of her marriage, when he sent her an icon of the Virgin Mary: we blessed her at the wedding with that icon. My husband and I also did not lose contact with him, as he sent us copies of books he had written, including *The Canonical State of the Russian Church Administration in the USSR and Abroad* and *The New Martyrs of Russia*.

When we returned to England, Fr. Michael had already gone to America, and Princess Galitzine told me how sad the parishioners were to see him go. Many of them went to the station to see him off, and when the train moved away, some fell to their knees in tears, asking for his blessing. I don't think he approved of this kind of emotional demonstration: he was very reserved with his own emotions and did not like others to be demonstrative, especially towards himself.

Father Michael was a true father to his parishioners!

Chapter 12

[1945–1950] The Second Wave of Emigrants

The Great Betrayal

Father Michael's move to America came at a time of great upheaval, when millions of displaced persons were being resettled in the aftermath of World War II. His successor in London, Archimandrite Vitaly, was faced with the task of caring spiritually for the "second emigration," which in England came to outnumber the old émigré community formed after the Revolution. By the time he arrived in England, however, Father Vitaly was known and respected by many of these new immigrants, not a few of whom had been his spiritual children in the displaced persons camps in Germany, where he played a very active role in saving them from forced repatriation to the Soviet Union.

The horrors of this period, many details of which were suppressed by the British government, have been described by Nicholas Bethell and, in greater detail, by Count Nikolai Tolstoy in his book *The Victims of Yalta*. Both sources go beyond the subject matter of this present study. However, these events so profoundly affected both the clergy and the flock of the post-war London parish that it is essential to consider them briefly. Of particular interest are interviews with members of the Russian community in London, which are included in Count Tolstoy's book.

In 1945, there were some 4 million Russians in the former territory of the Third Reich. About 6 million Russian prisoners of war fell into German hands, most of them soon after the invasion of Russia in 1941. The Russian prisoners of war were kept in appalling conditions; some were simply herded into open fields in the winter and left to die of exposure. This treatment, so different from that accorded to British prisoners by the Germans, was explained largely by the fact that Joseph Stalin had renounced them, stating that anyone who allowed himself to be taken captive, rather than die fighting, was a traitor. As a result, most Russian prisoners died and only about

1 million survived by May 1945. Understandably most of these "traitors" were terrified at the prospect of returning to the Soviet Union. In addition, there were the *Ostarbeiter* ("workers from the east")—Russians who were brought to Germany to work in the war industries. Some had volunteered but most were conscripts. They were treated poorly and humiliated by the Nazis, who regarded them as *Untermenschen* ("subhumans"), close to the bottom of the racial hierarchy they devised. Whenever outside the camps, these workers were required to wear a badge with the word *OST* (EAST) written on it to display their origin.

When the war ended, there were some 3 million *Ostarbeiter* in Germany. These formed the majority of the vast numbers of Russians liberated by the Allies in 1945. In addition, there were refugees who had decided to leave Soviet territory with the retreating German armies. Some were terrified of Soviet reprisals meted out to anyone "contaminated" by contact with the invaders; others, especially those in areas where the Germans had behaved with a degree of restraint, simply seized the opportunity to escape from communist rule. The populations of entire districts, particularly Cossacks from the Caucasus, piled their possessions into wagons and evacuated to the west. Finally, there were those who agreed to fight with the Germans in the hope of overthrowing communism in Russia, approximately 800,000 in all. The largest group was the Russian Army of Liberation (ROA—*Russkaya Osvoboditel'naya Armiya*), nominally led by General Andrey Vlasov, who was taken from a prisoner of war camp by the Germans and made head of this organisation. However, the ROA existed more on paper than in the field because Vlasov had very little control over the units, most of which had German officers. The Germans distrusted these brigades of Slavic *Untermenschen* and sent many to the western front after the Normandy invasions. In addition to the ROA, Cossack units were formed under the German General Helmuth von Pannwitz.

At the infamous Yalta Conference of February 1945, Winston Churchill and Franklin D. Roosevelt reached an agreement with Stalin to hand over any "Soviet Nationals" who fell into British or American hands. A Soviet National was defined as anyone who had lived in Soviet territory before September 1, 1939. Thus excluded were the old émigrés as well as inhabitants of western parts of Russia and Ukraine, which had been annexed to Poland during the Civil War. On arrival in the Soviet Union, the displaced persons were either shot or sent directly to labour camps, most in the Far North of Siberia. Alexander Solzhenitsyn described graphically the fate of many such people in his book *The Gulag Archipelago*.

One might wonder why the Soviet authorities were so determined to secure the return of these people. The explanation largely lies in the personal paranoia of Stalin, which infected the rest of the Soviet power apparatus. Another significant factor was the Soviets' genuine fear of the existence of a strong, anti-Soviet emigration or even scattered groups of exiles. As one Soviet leader observed, "That's the way we got our start!" Only thirty years previously, the émigré Russians were not "White" Russian exiles but rather various groups of Bolsheviks, Mensheviks, and anarchists who were plotting the overthrow of Imperial Russia.

When the Normandy invasion began in 1944, the prisoners who fell into Allied hands included Russians who had been sent as forced labourers to work on the fortifications, as well as Russian units in the German army. Most were taken to England and interned. A camp was set up at Kempton Park, near the famous race course on the southwestern outskirts of London, while most camps were in Yorkshire. Although this occurred before the Yalta Conference, Stalin had made clear his demands for repatriation, and prisoners were sent back to the Soviet Union by the thousands on transport ships via Archangel and Odessa.

The Soviet liaison officers in England complained about supposed interference with the Soviet prisoners by an ominous sounding organization of White Russian émigrés that was headed by the aged General Halfter and Princess Mestchersky, as well as Mr George Knupffer. In fact, their activities were restricted to showing films of the coronation of Nicholas II in towns near the camps in Yorkshire.

Father Michael Polsky was permitted a single visit to the camp at Catterick. Count Tolstoy related the following:

> In accordance with the dictates of humanity (or possibly Article 16 of the 1929 Geneva Convention), the commandant of a camp at Catterick had given permission for a priest of the Orthodox Church in London to visit the prisoners and minister to their spiritual needs. Father Michael Polsky travelled to Yorkshire, where he was surprised to find many of the Soviet citizens familiar with the Liturgy. A service was held in a large barracks hall, which was completely packed by devout prisoners. Even the forty or so Soviet-inspired officers of the "inner ring" watched curiously from the rear. About seventy of the inmates were confessed and received Holy Communion. Afterwards, Father Michael chatted on general subjects with the prisoners, and presented them with musical instruments and literary works in Russian of a non-political nature collected amongst his

> congregation. He noted the excellence of the food supplied, and was told by British officers that it was hoped the Russians would carry home with them a favourable impression of British goodwill. Following complaints from Soviet authorities, however, all further such visits were forbidden.
>
> The camp was about to have a very different visitor. On 8 September, when most of them had been prisoners for three months, the Russians met their first Soviet representative. Major-General Vasiliev, who was about to take over as head of the Soviet Military Mission, travelled to Yorkshire with a party of Soviet and British officers. . . . On the third and final day of the tour, General Vasiliev and his party called at Stadium Camp, Catterick. There things passed off smoothly, until the Commandant proudly showed off for inspection his collection of Russian literature provided for the prisoner's recreation. These were the books provided by Father Michael Polsky on his visit. Vasiliev was aghast, and offending editions of Turgenev, Aksakov, and Lermontov were hastily packed off back to Russian Church House in London. . . . In view of the supposed embarrassing allegations made by Captain Narishkin [an émigré Russian serving as interpreter], British military authorities instituted strict measures to ensure that no one holding suspected anti-Soviet views, and in particular no member of the White Russian community, should be permitted to have contact with the prisoners. No Russian books other than those supplied by the Soviet Military Mission were to be retained, and Father Michael Polsky was not to be allowed another visit.

Because of the shortage of interpreters, the army had to use the services of White Russian emigrants. One such interpreter was Prince Leonid Lieven who recounted his experiences to Count Tolstoy:

> Another . . . was an old friend of the author's, Prince Leonid Lieven. Born in Courland [now a part of Latvia], he had come to Britain and enlisted in the Royal Fusiliers. The shortage of Russian speakers in Britain at that time meant that a number of émigrés of British nationality had to be employed as duty officers in the camps. The anguish suffered by many of these Russians at being placed in the terrible position of actually arranging for their fellow countrymen to return to a fate, the nature of which they well knew, has become a memory from which few have fully recovered.
>
> It was not just that they were compatriots in whose misery they were actively assisting. As fellow Russians they conversed freely in the camps, and knew the prisoners as individuals and not as a mere mob of prisoners

> who, in the words of Churchill, Eden and Morrison, we must "get rid of as quickly as possible."
>
> Prince Lieven, who had, on account of his Russian, been seconded to Brigadier [Roy] Firebrace's Russian Liaison Group, was sent first to a camp at Oakley, near Leeds, and in October 1944 found himself in another at Thirsk. Two things struck him on arrival. First was the sight of genuine Russian peasants, bearded, simple and melancholy.
>
> However, not all were men of the people. Prince Lieven got to know well a Russian doctor, a man of considerable intelligence and integrity. . . . He knew enough about the nature of the Soviet state to guess what his fate would be if he were returned. He was nevertheless prepared, up to a point, to face that, if it really were inevitable. But, as he confessed one day to Lieven, "I do not fear death, but I am afraid of torture."
>
> Aghast, Lieven tried to persuade the Camp Commandant to arrange for the unfortunate man to be withheld from repatriation. Poles from another camp had offered to help, perhaps by certifying him as a Ukrainian from west of the Curzon Line. The Commandant, well aware that he was powerless in the matter, angrily told Lieven not to raise the matter again. "You are a White Guardist, Lieven," he snapped. "If you persist in this hopeless folly, you will find yourself under arrest." Notwithstanding this, Lieven managed to interest the Adjutant in the case, but before anything could be done, Lieven had to leave suddenly to embark on the *Duchess of Bedford* at Liverpool, and the doctor went to his fate.

Lieven sailed to Odessa on the *Duchess of Bedford*; when she arrived at her destination, he saw the prisoners being herded into a warehouse to the sounds of a sawmill and aircraft flying overhead. He guessed that the prisoners were being machine-gunned to death under cover of the noise. When he tried to alert his commanding officer, he was ignored. Lieven's guess was confirmed by other prisoners who witnessed similar events from the other side.

Thus, the Russian prisoners interned in England during the war remained almost completely insulated from the émigré community and from the Church. Those who eventually settled in England were displaced persons who had been in German territory when the war ended. Many were Cossacks who retained their identity as a separate group within the Russian community and congregation. Some fortunate survivors escaped the fate of forced repatriation, which fell to the majority of these people.

For many years, on the Sunday closest to June 1, the surviving London Cossacks held a panikhida for the victims of the "Lienz tragedy."[1] It was on that date in 1945 that mass deportations of Cossacks from the Drau Valley in Austria began. Some 30,000 Cossacks were assembled there after surrendering to the British. The men had been recruited as a cavalry division of the German army serving under General von Pannwitz, and they were accompanied by their wives and children, their domestic animals, and all of their worldly possessions. They had evacuated en masse from their home territory in the Kuban as the Red Army recaptured it. They moved hundreds of miles to the west in the hopes of delivering a blow against communism and with the avowed intention of never again falling into Stalin's clutches. Most had an almost childlike trust in the honesty and integrity of the British officers, unaware that specific orders had been issued for implementation of the Yalta agreement. On May 28, the officers were told that they were being taken to a conference with General Alexander about the future of the Cossacks; they were told they would be back in the camp that night. In fact, they were taken directly to the Soviet-occupied zone and handed over to the Red Army. Most were shot. Generals Krasnov, Shkuro, and Domanov and other senior officers were flown to Moscow immediately and incarcerated in the Lubyanka prison. They were formally sentenced to death and hanged in January 1947. Krasnov and Shkuro, like many of their subordinates, were old émigrés and therefore not subject to repatriation under the Yalta agreement.

Meanwhile, the main body of Cossacks realized that their officers were not going to return; they were informed on June 1 that they, too, were to be transported to the Soviet zone. They displayed placards with messages in broken English, such as "Better our death here than our sending in the SSSR!" and wrote petitions in a similar vein, but to no avail. In the absence of the officers, the priests in the camp assumed the leadership of the community. Early in the morning of June 1, the priests gathered all the Cossacks for an open-air service. A wooden platform on which an altar and a large cross had been erected towered above the crowd. The priests stood around the altar in brightly coloured vestments. After the Liturgy, a moleben was served and other prayers were sung. The congregation of thousands joined in the singing. With no sign of the service ending, the British started dragging people away, one by one, and loading them onto lorries and then trains to take them to the handover point. The altar table was overturned and the priests' vestments were torn. People were screaming and resisting to the last. Once inside the Soviet zone, they began the long, desolate journey to the labour camps in different parts of the Gulag Archipelago.

Commenting on these events, Nicholas Bethell wrote, "The special horror of the Lienz events was that they involved some 4,000 women and

2,500 children and were seen almost as an act of genocide, marking as they did the liquidation of a large part of the émigré Cossack nation."

A few people slipped away or hid. One survivor, Tatiana Danilewicz, hid in a cellar in the nearby village of Peggetz. She later found a home in London. Her reminiscences are presented in Chapter 14.

In other areas the British took a more lenient view, applied the definition of Soviet citizenship less strictly, and sometimes did not enquire too closely of those who said they were not Soviet.

Such was the case with some members of von Pannwitz's Cossack Cavalry Corps. George Nikolayevitch Druzhakin, a prominent member of the London Cossack community after the war, lived in Paris before the war. After the German occupation, he was called on as interpreter for the Cossack Cavalry Corps. He later recounted some of his experiences to Count Tolstoy. He was part of a convoy that had set off on May 29, 1945, for the Soviet zone. However, he was called back following receipt of last-minute orders to exclude all non-Soviet Russians; the "screening" that followed was quite perfunctory and the British officers who conducted the inquiry were evidently content not to probe very far. Major Druzhakin retained vivid, verbatim memories of the exchange. The interrogating officer came up to him and asked him where he lived before the war. When told "France," the officer asked Druzhakin a series of questions in French about the geography of the streets around the Place d'Italie where the Cossacks had lived. Able to answer these satisfactorily (because his story was true), Druzhakin was asked further where the other fellows came from. "They are all old émigrés, like me." "But what about these youngsters, some of whom cannot have been born at the time of the Revolution?"

Many were in fact youths who had fled from the Soviet Union during the war; Major Druzhakin explained that they were the younger generation of émigrés, born abroad in Yugoslavia. Fortunately the young men had picked up enough Serbian during their campaigns to convince the unsympathetic interrogator. In the end, only three of the youth admitted to being Soviet citizens, apparently through obtuseness. They were transferred to a truck in the convoy that contained all who had, under pressure, entered the trucks "voluntarily."

The interrogating officer blew a piercing blast on a whistle, and the engines of the forward lorries began to roar. As they moved off, some Cossack officers in the rear trucks raised a pitiful cry that they, too, were old émigrés. But the officer in charge yelled back that they had volunteered by entering the trucks and must go back. The agonized faces were glimpsed for a moment and then hidden as they turned on the road. Many were indeed old émigrés who were then bound for the SMERSH[2] interrogation centre at Graz and the death camps of Kemerovskaya Oblast, near Tomsk in Siberia.

The fifty officers who were released returned to the Weitensfeld camp with a mixture of emotions: jubilation at their inexplicable last-minute reprieve, lamentation for their departed comrades, and deep suspicion that they might not yet be safe. Back in the camp they received firm assurances that nothing could be done to compel their surrender to the Soviets. That night, when Major Druzhakin removed his cap, he found that the extraordinary stress he had been under had caused all of his hair to fall out. The next day the officers were taken south and brought to a camp where they found, to the astonishment of many, thousands of Russians of the old emigration. The commanding officer, Colonel Rogozhin, explained that he had extracted assurances from the British that all in that camp at Klein St Veit were safe from return to the Soviet Union. All were freed at a later date to find work and homes in the West.

The Fischbek Displaced Persons Camp

Further north in Germany were other refugee camps that held displaced persons under threat of repatriation. Two priests there, Hieromonk Vitaly (Oustinow) and Archimandrite Nathaniel (Lvov), worked day and night to save the refugees from this fate. They also worked to bring about the spiritual awakening and growth of many who had grown up under Soviet conditions and knew little of the Church or religion. As a result, bonds of intense gratitude and love were formed between the flock and their pastors.

Archimandrite Nathaniel (Lvov), at the Fischbek displaced persons camp, Germany, 1946. (Source: Archbishop Mark)

Father Vitaly, who was thirty-five years old at the time, grew up between the wars in an émigré family in Paris. After completing his studies and performing military service in France, in 1936 he entered the Monastery of St Job of Pochaev in Ladomirovo in the Carpathian Mountains of eastern Czechoslovakia. The monastery had been founded by Archimandrite Vitaly (Maximenko), formerly abbot of the Pochaev Lavra in Russia who carried on the Pochaev tradition of printing religious literature. Father Vitaly (Oustinow) was tonsured a monk in 1939 and ordained to the priesthood by Metropolitan Seraphim (Lade) of Germany in 1940. Almost immediately he was required to serve the churches in two villages on the border between Czechoslovakia and Poland—Porubki and Medvezhye. As the Red Army advanced westward in 1944, the monastery was evacuated. Father Vitaly went to Berlin where he was faced with the daunting task of ministering to Orthodox in the war-torn city and the surrounding area. Daily he visited a camp of Russian *Ostarbeiter*; there and elsewhere, he preached to, served, confessed, and gave Communion to the hundreds who were dying of starvation, tuberculosis, and other diseases. While in Berlin, he once again came into contact with Archimandrite Nathaniel (Lvov), who had been appointed dean of the cathedral in Berlin. Father Nathaniel was four years his senior and had grown up in China where he received the monastic tonsure in 1929. In 1938 he accompanied Archbishop Nestor to the Bishops' Council in Serbia and from there visited England.[3] He did not return to China but settled in the monastery of St Job in Ladomirovo, where, like Father Vitaly, he was overtaken by wartime events. He was known as an outstanding preacher with a warm, open-hearted character, combined with extensive learning in secular as well as theological subjects.

Bishop Nathaniel with Archimandrite Afanassy (Mogilev) (left) and Archimandrite Vitaly (Oustinow) (right) holding the Kursk icon at the Fischbek displaced persons camp, Germany, 1946. (Source: Archbishop Mark)

As the Red Army advanced on Berlin, Father Nathaniel and Father Vitaly fled again, as did many Russians. They established themselves near Hamburg, which subsequently surrendered to the British Army that was advancing from the west. Soon the question of repatriation was raised. The following personal account by one survivor, L. Tenson, told of their efforts to save their flock from this terrible fate:

> In the early spring of 1945, three weeks before Hamburg surrendered to the British, I fled from Berlin to Hamburg to escape the advancing Soviet armies, as the fighting had already reached the Friedrichstrasse. Before leaving Berlin I had been given the address of a hostel where I was told I would be able to stay. A week later Archimandrite Nathaniel and Hieromonk Vitaly also arrived from Berlin. Everything was so strange and uncertain that the arrival of clergymen in those troubled times was a matter of particular joy to us Russian fugitives! They immediately began Divine Services in a church made available by the British. These services were packed by multitudes of people who, by that time, had fled to Hamburg by various routes from the many camps which had earlier been set up for the *Ostarbeiter*—forced labourers brought from occupied territories to the east of Germany. Soon the British gave Archimandrite Nathaniel and Fr. Vitaly the former headquarters of Hitler's SA[4] organization to use for church services and as living quarters.
>
> After Easter the British Army started transporting Russians into the Soviet zone. The vast majority went unwillingly, with no real idea of what awaited them, but their hearts were filled with anxiety and distrust of the Soviet promises. They went only because they could see no alternative. But then the most terrible news started to come over from the other side. A few of those who had been transported managed to escape and return. They told of their experiences and some of those who were due to be transported committed suicide.
>
> Once, coming downstairs in the house where we were staying, I saw Archimandrite Nathaniel standing in the hallway and three men, who had just entered the house, approaching him. At the time it seemed to me that they were three Russian peasants. They walked briskly up to Fr. Nathaniel and went down on their knees before him. When Fr. Nathaniel asked them to get up, they did not react, but just asked him to hear them out. So, kneeling down, they told of their woes. They asked and prayed to be saved from transportation to the Soviet zone. They were from the camp at Querkamp, and scheduled for transportation at the end of May. They had hoisted a black flag and composed a petition in Russian and English, in which they firmly asked the British authorities to shoot them on the spot rather than send them back to their own country. Fr. Nathaniel

told them that he would take all possible steps to rescue them. He took their petition to the officer in charge of repatriation, Colonel James. The colonel took the petition from Fr. Nathaniel and promised to contact his headquarters about the matter and give an answer within a few days. The reply came at the beginning of June. "Nobody is to be repatriated against their will unless they are either guilty of war crimes or were Soviet citizens on 1 September 1939." This meant that any who had been Soviet citizens by 1 September 1939 were liable to be repatriated even against their will.

From the moment this reply was received from the British, Fr. Nathaniel began ceaseless efforts to rescue these people. This was very difficult, as the British military stubbornly repeated, "All the Russians must go home." After considering all the possible methods (and there were not many) of avoiding the harsh regulations, Fr. Nathaniel chose the most promising one and the next day went to see Colonel James again. He gave his word that all the 600 people were not Soviet citizens, but Polish. He explained to the English colonel that there had been about a million Russians, Ukrainians and Byelorussians in Poland before the war. He said they could not offer documentary evidence of their Polish citizenship because the Germans had confiscated all documents from the *Ostarbeiter* forced labourers, both Poles and Russians. Accordingly it would be necessary to rely on the testimony of the people themselves. In response, the colonel required a list of all the inmates of the camp at Querkamp to be made up and handed to the Polish liaison officer. If he accepted this list, said Colonel James, the British administration would have no objection to these people being transferred to the Polish camp and staying in Germany. It seemed as if all would be well, as the Polish liaison officer proved to be from the army of General Anders [Wladyslaw] and fully understood the terrible problems of the Russians. He signed the list at once and told Fr. Nathaniel that the inmates of Querkamp would be transferred to the Polish camp in a few days. Father Nathaniel and Father Vitaly went to the camp and spread the good news, which was received with boundless joy. As space became free in the camp barracks, a church had been set up. Here they immediately began celebrating the Vigil service, after which they heard the confessions of all those who wished to receive Holy Communion the next day—about 400 people. Many of the children in the camp had not been baptised, so about 30 children were baptised early the next morning before the Liturgy.

After the Liturgy, with crowds of communicants, a marriage service was held for those who had previously been unable to be married in church.

Apparently all their troubles and anxieties were behind them, but at seven o'clock that evening two men sent from the camp rushed up to Fr. Nathaniel in a state of great agitation and reported that thirty British trucks had arrived at the camp to take them away somewhere. The drivers would not say where they were taking them, but the main cause for concern was that they were due to go to the Polish camp, as Fr. Nathaniel had been informed, on 5 June, whereas now it was only 2 June. Fr. Nathaniel and Fr. Vitaly went straight to the camp and saw that the situation was very serious. They saw as many as a hundred British military police surrounding the camp, letting no one out, and thirty lorries, in to which the police were loading the inmates' belongings and forcing them to get in themselves. They really would not answer questions as to where they were taking the people. Fr. Nathaniel decided that Fr. Vitaly should stay there in the camp office by the telephone, and he would go with the people himself. If all was well, he would telephone Fr. Vitaly. If all was not well, Fr. Vitaly would hasten to Colonel James to try and rescue them all. Fr. Nathaniel did not think for a moment about what would happen to him if their terrible suspicions were justified and they were all taken to the Soviet camp. The one thought in his mind was that he must defend and save these people. In fact it was to the Soviet camp that they were taken! The gates slammed shut behind them and they all saw a large red flag with the hammer and sickle flying over the main camp office. The Soviet officer accepted the entire transport and said that they would all be sent into the Soviet zone the next morning. Fr. Nathaniel managed to find a British officer in the camp. He behaved very formally and sent his Polish liaison officer to check whether the people in question were really Polish citizens. Unfortunately the Polish officer proved to be a communist and he reported back that none of them spoke Polish and that beyond any doubt they were not Polish citizens, but Russians. The British officer finally lost all confidence, but very coldly acceded to Fr. Nathaniel's request to telephone Colonel James.

The situation was now really very bad, and that night none of the new arrivals would enter the barracks or sleep, nor did Fr. Nathaniel sleep. News came from a British officer, who said he had spoken to Colonel James, that lorries would arrive at seven o'clock to take them to the Polish camp. However, a despondent mood prevailed, the people no longer trusting anything, and were very gloomy, saying that they knew the way out, hinting at suicide. Great strength and presence of mind was needed to dissuade them from such mass killing and suicide. But with God's help Fr. Nathaniel managed to persuade them to wait until seven o'clock in the morning. At 5 a.m. Fr. Vitaly arrived. Without waiting for the telephone call from Fr. Nathaniel, he had reported the events to Colonel James, thereby saving the situation. At 7 o'clock the lorries arrived and took everyone—that is to say, all the people and Fr. Nathaniel—while Fr. Vitaly again waited by the telephone in case it turned out that they were not actually taken to the Polish camp. But they were all taken to the Polish camp at Wentorf.

Just as Fr. Nathaniel had not been afraid of entering the Soviet camp with his people, so now he was not afraid to provide all those rescued with false documents. We started work in the church with a feverish intensity. Fr. Nathaniel sat us down to work at forging the documents.... Thanks to him we had managed to obtain the requisite Polish forms and a seal, and a Polish friend showed us how to write. We wrote all night, and by morning all the camp inmates had Polish papers in their hands.

Within a few weeks there were already two thousand Russian inmates at Wentorf. In the autumn the Russians in the Polish camp were given their own camp at Fischbek, where a large church was made out of two barrack huts joined together. By the church two schools were started, Russian and Ukrainian, as well as a secondary school and pastoral theological courses, at which several future clergymen of our church studied, including Philemon Zadworny and Sergei Jefimenko, who later served as clergymen in England. A school of art and iconography was also started. The camp flourished for several years and left all its inhabitants with fond memories.

After rescuing the people from Querkamp, Fr. Nathaniel began agitating on behalf of all those threatened with forced repatriation. His reputation spread throughout the British occupation zone as a defender and helper. Many started coming to him asking for help and deliverance, and nobody went away without consolation. Those of us who were then working for the Russian Refugees Committee were constantly coming into contact with what Fr. Nathaniel had done to help people, because all those whom he rescued then turned to the Committee to receive further directions—either to stay in a camp or to depart for some other country such as America, Canada, Australia or New Zealand. I remember how Fr. Nathaniel once rescued a quartet of Soviet vocalists from repatriation. When they came to thank him, he refused to listen. Then they asked if they could sing for a Vigil service and Liturgy. "To the glory of God," Fr. Nathaniel finally gave them a reply. I was present at that Vigil and

Liturgy. The four singers sounded like a large choir, and one could hear in their voices the praise they offered to God for their rescue and salvation.

Time passed and Fr. Nathaniel, by then a bishop, was transferred to Paris. After a year or two he came to Hamburg on business and naturally went to Fischbek to visit Fr. Vitaly, who was then the priest in charge there. We—that is, several Committee workers—also went. As we approached the end of our journey and the camp came into view, its gates opened and out came a Church procession—the people were carrying the Cross, icons and banners. The car at the front of our convoy stopped and Vladyka got out. And as soon as the people saw Vladyka they bowed down, like a field of corn bowed to the ground by the wind. All were kneeling. I will never forget this sight and even now cannot write about it without great emotion.

If Kiev was the cradle of Russian Christianity, then it could perhaps be said, without too much exaggeration, that Fischbek was the cradle of the post-war Russian Church Abroad. Throughout the Western world one encountered Russians of the second emigration who found religious awakening as well as physical safety in this refugee camp. Father Vitaly subsequently led the Church Abroad as Metropolitan, and the Fischbek school also gave the Church another hierarch, Archbishop Paul of Australia. Another "graduate" of this school, Archimandrite Theodore (Golitsin), came to London as a young monk with Archbishop Paul to join Father Vitaly's monastic brotherhood where they continued the work of printing, using rudimentary equipment and much zeal in the Pochaev spirit, which they had begun at Fischbek. In 1987, after the sudden and untimely death of Archimandrite Theodore, Archbishop Paul wrote his recollections of this period under the title *In Memory of a Friend*:

Memory takes me back forty years to a Germany destroyed by war, vanquished and bleeding to death. The ruins of once flourishing, wealthy cities had to shelter not only their distraught and despondent populace, but also hundreds of thousands of refugees, belonging to different races. The victors set up special camps for these people who were known as DP's—displaced persons. I ended up in one of these camps and there met Vasya Golitsyn. This was in June of 1946. The camp was located near Hamburg and was called Fischbek.

We immediately became firm friends. We were brought together particularly by an interest in the Church and Divine Services. Services were conducted daily in the church in our camp barracks, both morning and evening. We zealously attended God's temple and did not miss a single service.

The rector of our parish, Father Archimandrite Vitaly, attracted a large group of youth to himself. We started to study the arts of the kliros—reading, singing and the order of the Divine Services. There was a great interest in these matters. We hungrily swallowed the knowledge that was offered to us, trying to assimilate the ancient science of Divine worship.

Among the diverse multitudes of camp inmates, or DP's, were many people belonging to different professions. These included several instructors from Russian seminaries and even a professor from the Kazan Theological Academy. Inspired by Father Archimandrite Vitaly and by the blessing of Vladyka Nathaniel (Lvov), our diocesan bishop, they were happy to start teaching us theology.

We all lived together in one large room of the so-called Church barracks. In the mornings, before dawn, the Midnight Office was read, and every evening, without fail, there was Small Compline with the reading of a canon. We studied in the next room. There we had breakfast, lunch and dinner. We tried to live in a monastic way. Our youthful enthusiasm drew us towards this. And so Vasya Golitsyn and I formed the firm desire to follow the monastic path. We became novices. And then, in the Great Lent of 1947, during the first week, on the Friday evening, Fr. Archimandrite Vitaly tonsured us *riassophore* monks. Brother Vasily was named Theodore in honour of the Holy Great-Martyr Theodore and I was named Paul in honour of St. Paul the Simple.

Continuing the glorious tradition of the Pochaev Lavra, and also of the Pochaev Monastery at Ladomirovo in Carpatho-Russia, Father Vitaly organized a printing works. We began to work hard at printing. The type was set by hand. With great difficulty, we managed to obtain a printing machine, the so-called *Bostonka*, which was pedal-operated. In the ruins of Hamburg we found a hot metal linotype machine which had survived by a miracle. By trading in coffee and other foodstuffs which were in short supply, we managed to order a Russian type font. We typeset and printed a book of akathists, a church bulletin and other things. We worked at a frenzied pace and this inspired us. Fr. Theodore immediately displayed his mechanical talent. Easily, with no apparent difficulty, he managed to fix the printing machine, which often misbehaved itself. He prepared the plates and did the printing. I was responsible for proofreading and worked at setting the type along with the others.

And so we lived until Fr. Archimandrite Vitaly was appointed to England as Administrator of all our Russian Orthodox parishes. When he left, Fr. Theodore and I moved to the Monastery of St. Job of Pochaev in Munich. The abbot was then Fr. Archimandrite Job (Leontiev). The brotherhood and other residents were quite numerous. In the monastery there was a well-organized printing works, and we immediately joined in the work there. The typesetting was done by hand.

In 1949, on the eve of the feast of the Dormition of the Mother of God (14/27 August), with the blessing of Metropolitan Anastassy, Bishop Nathaniel tonsured Fr. Theodore and myself into the lesser schema. After the tonsure Fr. Theodore and I spent three days in the church. I will never forget that time of grace, which drew us further together in spiritual kinship. This feeling of spiritual kinship has united us for the rest of our lives.

In the same year on the day of St. Job of Pochaev—28th August by the old calendar—on the patronal festival of our monastery, Metropolitan Anastassy ordained me hierodeacon and exactly two months later on the 28th October—on another feast of St. Job of Pochaev—Fr. Theodore was ordained to the order of hierodeacon. He also was ordained by the First Hierarch, Vladyka Metropolitan Anastassy.

In December of 1949, in accordance with a decision of the monastery's Spiritual Council, part of the brotherhood had to move to France, to found a monastery there. Fr. Theodore and I were included in this group. We moved to Ozoir-la-Ferrière, a small town near Paris where a fair number of Russians were living. We had a hard time in France. These were the difficult and, for us, hungry post-war years. Fr. Theodore and I supported ourselves by working for hire, one day at a time, in vegetable gardens belonging to the local residents. I remember how our neighbour, a warm-hearted Russian woman, who was herself experiencing the shortages, had somehow acquired two bags of artichokes and brought them to us. We cooked a whole cauldron of them at once and readily set about satisfying our appetites. Imagine how much time and patience are needed to come anywhere near filling oneself up with artichokes! In the winter we suffered particularly from the cold. Our little group was guided by Fr. Igoumen Nikodem (Nagaieff) who later became Archbishop of Richmond and Great Britain.

Soviet Interference in the Life of Russian Churches Outside Russia

In addition to its achievements through the Yalta agreement, the Soviet government touched the lives of Russians living abroad through a renewed interference in the life of the Church during the later stages of the war and in the post-war period. This came about through a revival of the Moscow Patriarchate that began in 1941. During this year as the Germans advanced into Russia, Stalin realized that he could not win the war without popular support. However, the invaders met with little resistance in some of the occupied territories; a major reason for this was that the Germans allowed churches to be re-opened. In fact, Metropolitan Sergius took the initiative to issue patriotic appeals to resist the invaders, while Stalin was still stunned by the Germans' sudden renunciation of their alliance. In turn, and doubtless in view of the spontaneous religious revival taking place on German-occupied territory, Stalin was prepared to allow the election of a new patriarch—the Patriarchal Throne had been vacant since Patriarch Tikhon died in 1925. Of the 200 bishops in Russia after the Revolution, only nine were at liberty by 1941, but in 1943, nineteen were gathered for the Patriarchal election. Metropolitan Sergius was elected. The Church Abroad did not recognize the validity of this election and felt that it included an artificially selected minority of bishops at Stalin's behest, like all other Soviet-style elections. Patriarch Sergius died the following year, and when a new election was held under similar conditions, Patriarch Alexis, who had been a close supporter of Patriarch Sergius, was elected. In Russia the clergy of the Moscow Patriarchate tried as best they could to serve the needs of the faithful people; however, on missions abroad, they were often forced to foster Soviet diplomatic interests.

As the war drew to a close, the Moscow Patriarchate attempted to use the new conditions affecting the Church in the Soviet Union to gain greater influence among émigré Russians, on the grounds that the regime had changed and there was nothing to prevent full unity with the Mother Church. This policy found a ready response from some older émigrés, who succumbed to a great wave of nostalgia for their homeland under the influence of wartime events. A vivid example of this psychology is shown by none other than Metropolitan Evlogy.[5] Then an old man afflicted by impaired hearing, he spent most of his days in his apartment in the Rue Daru in Paris, sitting in an armchair with an enormous hearing trumpet inserted in one ear and resting on a small table beside him. He was grief-stricken when he heard the news of one Russian town after another falling to the advancing Germans in 1940–1941 and imagined the suffering and destruction that would affect those areas, which he knew well from his early days of episcopal service. In the same way, he rejoiced when the tide turned after the battle of Stalingrad (1942–1943) and the Russians reclaimed the lost territory. He started reading

Leo Tolstoy's *War and Peace*; in his mind, the Soviet generals merged with Kutuzoff and Bagration, the heroes of 1812. At the same time came news of the changed conditions of the Church and the restoration of the Moscow Patriarchate. In 1942 he said, "Now Russian blood is flowing in rivers, washing away the terrible sins of the revolutionary years. . . ." Of his feelings in 1944, his biographer, Tatiana Manukhina, wrote, "Vladyka received the news of the end of persecutions, then of the Sobor and election of a Patriarch as the joyful news of spiritual victory, linked to the victory on the field of battle, as a sign that the Russian people was forgiven."

Metropolitan Evlogy did not wait for the arrival of patriarchal representatives. As soon as the Allies liberated Paris in August 1944, he went directly to the Soviet diplomatic mission in Paris to enter into communion with the Moscow Patriarchate. This was soon achieved, and the suspension from Moscow of fifteen years earlier was not formally rescinded but simply forgotten. In September 1945 a representative of the Patriarchate, Metropolitan Nikolai of Krutitsa, concelebrated with Metropolitan Evlogy in the cathedral in Rue Daru. Metropolitan Evlogy was appointed exarch of the Patriarchate. Tatiana Manukhina wrote:

> Vladyka's striving to return to the bosom of the Russian Mother Church, and the steps taken to accomplish it, did not exhaust his patriotic desires. This was not enough for Vladyka, his plans extended further—to return to Russia, there to find his final resting place. And to return not alone, but with his entire émigré flock, to lead a kind of migration, like the grandiose caravan including children, servants and animals which he led from Galicia into Russia during the Great War.[6]

Commenting on this, Archbishop Nikon (Rklitsky) of the Russian Church Abroad wrote, "At the end of June 1946 Metropolitan Evlogy died, not having managed to accomplish his last terrible plan—to return to Soviet Russia together with his flock." On Metropolitan Evlogy's grave, in accordance with the instructions he left before his death, a tombstone was erected bearing the inscription, "God be merciful to me, a sinner."

The fundamental fallacy of his position was, of course, that there was no change in Stalin's aims or policies toward the Church and that the abatement of persecution was only superficial. The triumphant advance of the Red Army served only to extend the Soviet tyranny across half of Europe. After Metropolitan Evlogy's death, part of his flock followed his example, but the majority remained with the Œcumenical Patriarchate.

Perhaps more surprising and shocking than the changed allegiance of Metropolitan Evlogy (who had been under the Moscow Patriarchate from 1927 to 1930) was the fact that his former rival, Metropolitan Seraphim (Loukianoff), the former Archbishop of Finland, followed his example. Seraphim (Loukianoff) later led the parish in London and, after the schism of 1927, was appointed bishop of Western Europe under the Sobor of the Russian Church Abroad. After Metropolitan Evlogy's death, Seraphim (Loukianoff) was appointed exarch in Europe for the Moscow Patriarchate. This caused great confusion. In the chaos of the immediate post-war period, people did not know if the Russian Church Abroad still existed; they could not believe that Metropolitan Anastassy and the Synod had survived the war in Yugoslavia. In fact, at the time of the German surrender, Metropolitan Anastassy and the Synodal headquarters were located in two railway carriages that were shunted from Karlsbad to Munich; one carriage was filled with a stock of Church service books that had been printed in Ladimirova. Gradually the Synod was reestablished in Munich and the service books were distributed to the many refugee camp churches that were being set up. Metropolitan Anastassy visited many of the camps. The venerable, ascetic metropolitan, whose name, Anastassy, means "resurrection," made a strong impression on the displaced persons, many of whom were coming into close contact with their own Orthodox Church for the first time. Almost universally, it was the old émigrés who succumbed to the new nostalgia for the Soviet Union, while the displaced persons had a deep suspicion of any organisation, ecclesiastical or other, that they perceived to be connected with the Soviet Union.

In London a certain amount of realignment also took place under these influences. After the election of Patriarch Sergius, Father Michael Polsky was summoned to the British Home Office and told that because the Soviet Union was an ally, it was considered highly desirable that he accept the leadership of the Moscow Patriarchate (in Great Britain), rather than remain in the jurisdiction of a bishop who lived in occupied France and a Synod in occupied Yugoslavia. From what is known of Father Michael, it is evident that the civil servants "backed the wrong horse." Probably within the entire Church Abroad, there was not a single priest less likely to accede to this demand. However, in 1945 the London parish in Metropolitan Evlogy's jurisdiction applied to join the Moscow Patriarchate. Its rector was Father Vladimir Theokritoff, the former protodeacon, who was ordained to the priesthood in 1939, shortly before the death of Father Nicholas Behr.

In June 1945 a delegation from Moscow, led by Metropolitan Nikolai of Krutitsa, arrived in London. Initially the visit was shrouded in secrecy;

some Russian émigrés were told that he had come to develop contacts with Anglicans and that he would have no time to see them. Nicholas Zernov, a life-long supporter of the Evlogian/Patriarchal parish in London, described his great desire to meet the metropolitan to learn about the life of the Church in Russia. He noted the great difficulties he encountered in making contact with the delegation, whose time, he felt, was being wasted by the Anglicans on matters of secondary importance. At other times, the delegates were summoned unexpectedly to the Soviet consulate and thus unable to keep appointments. Zernov also described his meeting with Protopresbyter Nicholas Kolchinsky, one of the delegates, who had been a friend of the Zernov family, years before:

> Father Nicholas was unrecognizable—he had changed so much over the twenty-five years—years of Stalin's terror. In 1920 he was 30 years old, [and] he had been burning with faith and his fire caught all those with whom he came into contact. Now he was like an extinguished volcano. As before, we were confronted by an exceptional man, strong willed and intelligent, but now he was shut in by an impenetrable shield. All the time he was in England, Father Nicholas never said a single word about what he had experienced during the Stalinist years, and he did not ask us much himself. . . .

Zernov's impressions of Metropolitan Nikolai were particularly revealing:

> Meeting the delegation from Moscow was my first attempt at making contact with the official representatives of the Church from the Soviet Union. The impressions I then received were repeated on numerous subsequent occasions: they behaved like people under constant surveillance by some unseen eyes. An impenetrable wall divided them from people belonging to the free world. . . . It was clear that the leading role belonged to Metropolitan Nikolai. He created the impression of a man of genuine faith and devotion to Orthodoxy, but at the same time it was clear that it was he who maintained contact with the NKVD, which was closely and unremittingly following the delegates' every step. The more we came to know him, the stronger grew the feeling that he was doomed.[7]

Zernov had no illusions about the conditions of the Moscow Patriarchate but supported it out of feelings of solidarity with the believers in the Soviet Union. However, it is clear from his vivid description why many Russians living in the free world felt unable to accept the leadership of a hierarchy that was not free to speak or act.

Although it disapproved of some of the Patriarchate's policies and found voluntary submission to it by those living in the free world difficult to comprehend, the Church Abroad regarded the situation with deep compassion. In his description of the terrible pressures to which Church leaders in Russia were subjected, Father Michael Polsky wrote,

> Even Archbishop Hilarion could not describe in greater detail all the deceptions, lies, brazenness, disgusting pretences and hypocrisy, the provocative attacks and other baseness of the government agents. When conversation touched on the relations between the government and the Church administration, he said this: "No, my friends . . . you see, you have to actually be in the situation at least for a while otherwise you can't describe it. . . ." Looking at us as we listened, and, as it were, asking us whether we believed him or not, he added, "You are face to face . . . with Satan himself."

Chapter 13

[1948–1951] Archimandrite Vitaly (Oustinow)

Departure of Father Michael Polsky

When World War II ended in May 1945, Father Michael Polsky was still the priest in charge of the London parish. During most of the war, England had been cut off from continental Europe, and the parish was temporarily placed under the jurisdiction of Archbishop Vitaly (Maximenko) in New York.[1] In September 1945 the Parish Council held a meeting, with Father Michael Polsky presiding. After council members reviewed the news of recent developments in the Russian Orthodox Church, including the submission of some parishes and bishops to the Moscow Patriarchate, they resolved that the parish would remain under the jurisdiction of the Russian Church Abroad. At the next meeting in October they resolved that the parish would remain directly under the diocesan jurisdiction of Archbishop Vitaly of New York. However, in the spring of 1946, Metropolitan Anastassy convened an assembly of the bishops of the Russian Church Abroad in Munich to begin reorganizing Church life in the aftermath of the war. This council decided to consecrate Archimandrite Nathaniel (Lvov) as the new ruling bishop of the European parishes, with the title of Bishop of Brussels and Western Europe. His Episcopal consecration took place on March 10, 1946. Nathaniel (Lvov) was known for his service in the cathedral in Berlin in the final period of the war and for his fearless efforts in rescuing Russian displaced persons from repatriation to the Soviet Union. At the Parish Council meeting in London in May 1946, Father Michael announced that he had received a decree from Metropolitan Anastassy stating that the parish should commemorate the Holy Orthodox patriarchs, Metropolitan Anastassy as primate of the Russian Church Abroad, and Bishop Nathaniel as diocesan bishop at all services. In November 1946 Father Michael received a letter from Archbishop Vitaly in New York stating that the parish should not turn its temporary attachment to the church in America, which was the result of wartime conditions,

Archimandrite Vitaly at All Saints Podvoria Chapel, 1950. (Source: Deacon Andrew Bond)

into a permanent departure from the European diocese of the Church. After reading the letter, Father Michael affirmed that there was never any intention to leave the European diocese and noted that he would reply in this vein to Archbishop Vitaly.

As early as April 1946, as displaced persons began to settle both in London and in other parts of the country, Father Michael spoke of the need to find an assistant priest to help him look after the growing number of parishioners. Archbishop Savva of the Polish Orthodox Church offered to send one of his priests, Father Nicholas Krawchenko, to help out temporarily. Accommodation for an assistant priest could be provided at the Podvoria, but only limited funds were available to pay a salary. A priest in Switzerland, Father Igor Troyanoff, might also be able to move to London. Several members of the Parish Council received very positive reports about him, and he seemed to be the best candidate for assistant priest. However, by April 1947, he had not made up his mind as to whether or not he should move to London.

In June 1947 Bishop Nathaniel made his eagerly awaited first visit to England as diocesan bishop. He had been to England in 1938 when he accompanied Archbishop Nestor. Before the bishop arrived, Father Michael suggested that the parish make a special collection because the bishop was extremely short of money; he needed new clothes and a new pair of shoes and he urgently needed to visit a dentist because his teeth were in terrible condition. In addition, he needed £17 for his travelling expenses. The council agreed to make a special collection among the parishioners for Bishop Nathaniel's needs and to pay the £17 directly from church funds.

Bishop Nathaniel explained the situation of displaced persons (DPs) in Germany and Austria. The British government had decided to allow some of them to come to England to work because there was a shortage of manpower after the war. He said that, naturally, the responsibility for their spiritual well-being would fall to "our" parish—that is to say, the parish of the Russian Church Abroad. Father Michael needed help, the bishop said, and he recommended Archimandrite Vitaly (Oustinow)[2] as an assistant priest, rather than Father Igor Troyanoff. He said Archimandrite Vitaly had worked with

Archbishop Savva with Starosta Prince Vladimir Galitzine (left) and Prince Andrei Alexandrovich Romanoff (right). (Source: Sophia Goodman)

him in Germany, and many of the refugees already knew and trusted him. In addition, he spoke excellent English and, being a monk, would not need to support a family, as would Father Igor. The Parish Council accepted the bishop's offer; they resolved to make a room ready for Father Vitaly in the Podvoria and to pay him a salary of £2 per week.

At the council meeting on September 2, Father Michael announced that Archimandrite Vitaly had received his visa permitting him to leave Berlin and come to England and that he would be in London in a week or so. There were also about five priests who would be coming to England as refugee workers. After they fulfilled their work commitments, it was felt that these priests might also be able to help Father Vitaly in his work with the refugees in England. On September 23, Father Michael reported that Archimandrite Vitaly had not yet left Germany because he had no way to pay the fare. The council resolved to find someone who planned to travel to the British-occupied zone in Germany and could take the money because postal and other communications with Germany were very problematic at that time. Father Michael also warned that once Father Vitaly arrived and began visiting displaced persons, they would need to collect funds to support those activities. The parish was encouraged to set up a benevolent fund and seek support from the Russian Refugees Relief Association.

Evidently Father Vitaly made his way to England over the next two months. The Parish Council meeting on November 19, 1947, was the first one he attended. The minutes indicate that the chairman of the council was the rector, Mitred[3] Archpriest Michael Polsky, and the members of the council were Archimandrite Vitaly, Mrs V. I. Ampenoff, Mr A. S. Ananin, Count W. P. Kleinmichel, N. M. Perott, T. D. Pesiakoff, and F. F. Volkovsky, the secretary. Mr Volkovsky thanked the council for their efforts made in celebrating his fiftieth anniversary of service in the Russian Church in London. He had arrived from Russia in 1897 to take up a position as psalm-reader at the Imperial Embassy church and remained at that post, despite the changes and tribulations of the intervening period. Then Archimandrite Vitaly explained his plans for visiting the workers, conducting services, and telling them about the Orthodox faith. He also said that there were things these people might be happy to do to help the Church, such as making Russian wooden toys that could be sold at the Christmas bazaar. Because the council expected many of these DP workers to go to London for the Christmas celebrations and because it was not the parish's turn to use St Philip's Church, the decision was made to hold the service in St Cuthbert's Church, Philbeach Gardens, near Earl's Court. This was the church that the Anglican vicar promised they could use in case of need for Russian Christmas. At the December 18, 1947, meeting, Father Michael told the council what Archimandrite Vitaly had achieved; he was in the process of organizing two parishes, one in Preston and the other in York. Then Father Vitaly spoke of the difficulties and hindrances he was encountering. The DPs were scattered throughout England and it was often difficult dealing with the local authorities when trying to help the DP workers. He wanted to set up machinery to print spiritual literature for these DPs, but it would cost a lot of money. He had to go back to Germany for a short visit and he hoped to discuss the situation with Metropolitan Anastassy while he was there. At the meeting on January 29, 1948, it was noted that Archimandrite Vitaly was still in Germany but was expected back any day.

The next meeting was on March 30, 1948. Mitred Archpriest Michael Polsky presided and Archimandrite Vitaly was present. The minutes began with a statement that Father Michael had been transferred to San Francisco and would be leaving on Friday, April 2. This evidently came as a great shock to the parishioners; Father Vitaly initially came to help Father Michael, not to replace him. It seems likely that Father Michael's reassignment was part of a concerted effort by the hierarchy of the Russian Church Abroad to send more priests to North and South America and Australia, where many of the refugees were moving. In economic terms, these parts of the world were more promising than war-torn Europe and they were farther away from Soviet-occupied territory. As the Red Army advanced, many countries such as Serbia, Poland, and Czechoslovakia, which had been havens of refuge after the Russian Revolution, fell into Soviet hands. At that point it was far from clear if Western Europe would be a safe place for Russian refugees to settle. San Francisco was also a place where large numbers of refugees from Harbin and other parts of China were settling as these areas also fell under communist control. Evidently it was felt that Father Michael would be valuable as a pastor there. Perhaps the good relations he established with Archbishop Vitaly (Maximenko) of New York during the war contributed to his being asked to move to America. Father Michael served in San Francisco until his death in 1960.

During their time together in England, Archimandrite Vitaly (Oustinow) developed the greatest respect for Father Michael Polsky and continued to speak of him in glowing terms until the end of his life. Father Michael took Father Vitaly all over London on foot to show him the city and told him of his experiences in Russia and reasons for his continued loyalty to the Russian Church Abroad. In a later review of Father Michael's book *The Situation of the Church in Soviet Russia*, he wrote,

> And now I . . . address him, as a living person, for in the Lord all live, and say "May the Lord save you for all your labours. . . . May the Lord receive you, dear Father Michael, into His Heavenly Kingdom, where there is neither sickness, not sorrow, nor sighing, but life everlasting.

At the council meeting in March 1948, the treasurer Count Kleinmichel gave Father Michael a cheque for £100, a sum which had been collected from the parishioners. The council had received 150 copies of his book *The Canonical Status of the Supreme Church Administration in the USSR and Abroad* that were to be distributed to members of the council and the parish. The parish also bought Father Michael's radio for £5. There was also further discussion about how Archimandrite Vitaly would manage as the only priest in London. Rather than bring four monastic novices to England, as had been planned, the council proposed applying to the Home Office for a visa for a priest, Father Sergei Schukin, and two novices instead of four.

In early April 1948, a large group of parishioners gathered at Waterloo Station to see Father Michael off on the boat–train to Southampton, many of them in tears as they asked for his final blessing before his departure.

Father Sergei Schukin, first rector of the Bradford parish, 1949–1952. Photo dated 1963. (Source: Ioann Suscenko)

Pastor of Displaced Persons

At Christmas, 1948, Archimandrite Vitaly addressed the following appeal to the older generation of émigrés living in England:

This year the Lord has placed a great responsibility before our parish. Its ranks, which had been thinned through the passage of time and as a consequence of the different paths in life taken by some of its members, have now been swollen by thousands of new parishioners, who have brought the aroma of our own country with them from our distant fatherland. They put their hope in us who are well versed in the way of life in Western Europe, hoping that we will help them to find their bearings and familiarize themselves with their new life.

Now the concern of our Church must extend to the most distant towns and villages in England; London will have to become the centre for our countless Orthodox compatriots dispersed throughout Great Britain. Our four priests are constantly travelling in order, at least partially, to feed the dispersed flock of Christ and satisfy its spiritual hunger. There is a desperate need to create houses of prayer and Orthodox community centres. These are the great responsibilities which the Lord has placed before us, while rewarding us with the rich field, ripening for the harvest, which requires so much care and work.

We must all join in this work of the Church: some by offering words of kindness and advice, others by taking on specific responsibilities and all, by making such financial contributions as are within their means. Anyone who remains aloof from this holy work will lose a great spiritual treasure, for he will be depriving himself of the riches of the Church's new experience, that of uniting the old and new emigrations under the one dome of the Church. During the long years of our refugee life, the Lord has helped us to preserve the garment of Christ in purity; our community has always trodden the paths of God, not bowing the knee to any human values, and for this the

> Lord has given us in addition outward piety, an ordered Church life and services according to the Church typicon, as well as the whole culture of the Church. Our new parishioners have been deprived of all this, but they in their turn will bring us a childlike simplicity, a freshness of religious feeling and popular wisdom. They are now filling our churches in Western Europe by the thousands—and only our churches, thereby bearing witness to the fact that we were right, having chosen this path which is without compromise and therefore hard, even grievous. Let us be watchful and filled with holy anger against all injustice and falsehood in the Church, for the people have brought to us the true voice of our millions-strong nation.

Beginning in 1947 and throughout 1948, European Voluntary Workers arrived in England by the boatload—some 60,000 people, including between 8,000 and 10,000 Russians—recruited from among mostly East Europeans to help alleviate the labour shortage in the United Kingdom when the war ended. However, the experience of mass unemployment that occurred in the 1930s was fresh in people's minds, so immigration was closely controlled. Officials from the Ministry of Labour and personnel officers from private companies went to Germany to recruit from the DP camps. After landing at ports such as Southampton, Hull, Harwich, and Dover, the Voluntary Workers received railway tickets to London where they were met at the railway station by officials of the Ministry of Labour. Large signs were erected to sort them by their nationality—Polish, Russian, Lithuanian, and Yugoslavian. On their arrival, they were already under contract to work in a specific location, and reception committees were set up to ensure that the DPs found their way to the right place with a minimum of delay.

Ministry officials faced daunting problems of language and culture in dealing with these large numbers of East European emigrants. Where the Russian contingent was concerned, they sought the assistance of the old émigré community through the Russian Red Cross. Hence was born the Russian Refugees Relief Association in Great Britain. Led by representatives of the old emigration—Prince Vladimir Galitzine, Count Bennigsen, Barbara Volkoff-Muromtsev, Lev Rabenek—the association sought to help the new immigrants, not just as translators but also by offering practical help and moral support in every way possible.

When the DPs arrived in London, they were met by representatives of the Refugees Relief Association, who stood alongside the ministry officials to interpret and offer advice and ensure that relatives and friends were able to stay together, rather than being sent to different parts of the country. There were very few family groups because they had either been conscripted into the Soviet army or taken as forced workers to Germany. Family life had been torn apart by five years of warfare and destruction. Many were single, while others had left wives and families behind in Soviet Russia with no hope of ever seeing them again. Most men were sent to the north of England, where they were needed to work in factories, mines, and quarries and on farms; women were given jobs in the textile industry and hospitals, particularly those for tubercular and mental patients. Single men were often given accommodation in "hostels," which were similar to the German refugee camps they had lived in. After Germany, their first impression of England was one of prosperity, despite the rationing and relatively frugal regime in the hostels. Many workers felt a sense of immense relief at no longer having to worry about day-to-day survival. Those sent to work on farms were astounded to find that the normal working day was only eight hours.

Not all passed through London or came into contact with the Refugees Relief Association. Some were asked at the port of disembarkation to choose between farm and factory work and then despatched to the appropriate location. The Cossacks preferred to form their own groups to preserve their separate identity.

Galina von Meck, who came to England from Germany in 1948, wrote,

> Young girls, with the help of the Salvation Army, found jobs as home helps in England: some were happy, many were not. According to my knowledge, it is the men who went to work on farms in England for war widows who had the best deal. Quite a few of them married these widows.
>
> I remember an amusing conversation about crops and such matters between two "English" farmers on a Sunday, after the Liturgy in our Russian Church in London—"English" farmers now, who had brought their new little Englishmen and English daughters to the service, to receive the sacraments of the Russian Church.
>
> Unfortunately, many of the D.P.'s still had to experience the humiliation of being branded the Untermenschen, which the Germans had started and which somehow appeared again in the attitude of the other Europeans towards people from the east, even after the war, when they volunteered for work.

Most new immigrants were concentrated in or near northern industrial cities such as Bradford, Manchester, Preston, and Nottingham. For most, it was unrealistic to hope to find work in London. However, some old émigrés had established businesses in the London area and hired their own compatriots exclusively to fill their vacancies. Others worked in hospitals in or near London. They often found the old émigrés strangely "de-Russified" and were, at the same time, amazed to find that some had become infected by a nostalgic longing for Russia that found expression in a "pro-Soviet" mentality, or at least a desire to view the Soviet Union in favourable light. (Most of these people belonged to the parish of the Moscow Patriarchate.)

The question of national identity was a thorny one among the immigrant masses. For this reason, it is hard to be precise about numbers, although the figure of 10,000 Russians has been widely accepted. But who was a "Russian"? Many came from the western territories of Byelorussia and Ukraine who considered themselves Russian, while others were adamant that they were Ukrainian or, to a lesser extent, Byelorussian. The Russian Church Abroad went to great lengths to avoid offending such national sensitivities. For example, they used the word "Orthodox" instead of "Russian" wherever possible. The Church felt it was important to guard such people from the allure of the Ukrainian Autocephalous Church, a body widely regarded as non-canonical because its first bishops were priests who "consecrated" themselves in a completely unprecedented manner.

During 1948 and 1949 a Russian-language newspaper, *Rossianin*, was published in London. Subsidized by the personal funds of a young, idealistic Russian patriot, Prince Valerian Obolensky, the intent was to create an atmosphere of unity and mutual support within the community. The very name *Rossianin* means "a person from Russia" (who could be of any nationality).

Another factor that clouded the issue of national identity was the lurking fear of repatriation, which made many new immigrants afraid to identify themselves as Russian. Many claimed to be Poles, some with justification if they had lived in Polish territory. This was one factor that contributed to the flourishing of the Polish Orthodox Church in London after the war.[4] The community was headed by Archbishop Savva until his death in 1949 and then by Bishop Matthew of Wilno who died in 1985. When ties with communist-controlled Poland were severed, the Polish Church placed itself under the protection of the Œcumenical Patriarchate. It remained separate from the Russian Church Abroad, but relations were reasonably friendly and cooperative. The funeral of Archbishop Savva in 1949 was a solemn event that united Orthodox of all jurisdictions. Photographs of the funeral show the procession of Orthodox clergy and people through the grim streets of post-war London as they accompanied the coffin from the Polish Church of St Matthew in Warwick Road to

Archbishop Savva in the uniform of a Polish Army chaplain. (Source: Douglas Papers, Lambeth Palace Library)

Bishop James (Virvos) of Apamaea, accompanied by Bishop Nathaniel and Protodeacon Nicholas Jakimowicz, at the funeral of Archbishop Savva in the West London Polish Orthodox Church, 1949. (Source: Deacon Andrew Bond)

the archbishop's last resting place in Brompton Cemetery. These photos are particularly evocative of the contrasts in the lives of the new Orthodox immigrants at that time.

The sense of insecurity that the refugee workers felt even after they had lived in England for several years is illustrated by the following article from the October 15, 1950, edition of the *Sunday Dispatch:*

Soviet Embassy woos refugees

The Soviet Government, acting through its London Embassy, is trying to break up the anti-Communist refugee groups of its nationals in Britain.

In the past few weeks, the Russians in London have launched a great "Come back to Russia" campaign, offering free travel, food, free baggage transport, and educational facilities, in an effort to attract back the tens of thousands of Soviet citizens who work in British industry here . . . in some cases at wage rates as high as £15 a week. No questions are to be asked as to why they did not return home earlier. Consular officials have even visited hospitals to try to talk sick Ukrainians into going home.

The initial drive is directed mainly at men, but women who have married Britons are promised that if they go back they will not be prosecuted for marrying a foreigner. Home Office officials are watching the campaign.

Hundreds shocked
The Soviet Embassy is addressing letters to their nationals which prove that the Soviets possess elaborate details about the refugees working in Britain. Much of the information has been supplied by the few Russians who have returned to Russia in the past two years, taking with them lists of names and home towns of their former friends. Hundreds of men who thought their identities were unknown to the Soviet authorities have been shocked to find that so much is known about them. They are worried about their families in Russia.

At a private hostel at Bletchley, Buckinghamshire, numbers of Latvians and Ukrainians received "Come back to Russia" letters, following the disappearance of a Ukrainian named Kevalenko from the camp. He was taken out of Britain on a Russian vessel and was next heard of from his home town, Kirovograd. The manager of the hostel said last night: This propaganda has been sent back, marked "Worthless rubbish."

Footnote: There are 40,000 Ukrainian, 35,000 Baltic and 16,000 Polish displaced persons in Britain.

The majority of new immigrants who joined the Russian Church Abroad identified closely with the new priest, Archimandrite Vitaly, who was transferred to London from the Fischbek camp in 1948, after most of its

Bishop James leading the coffin of Archbishop Savva on its way to Brompton Cemetery. To the right of Bishop James is Bishop Nathaniel; to the left are Hierodeacon Paul and Bishop Matthew of Wilno. Protodeacon Nikolai precedes the bishops, and ahead of the procession is Archimandrite Vitaly behind a group of clergy. (Source: Ioann Suscenko)

inmates had been resettled. However, the old émigrés who had grown accustomed to Father Michael Polsky found the change somewhat of a shock. The refugee camps and the expatriation issue were outside their immediate experience and initially this seemed to hinder development of a common understanding and outlook. Nevertheless, the initial misgivings were soon dispersed. The new priest seemed to be burning with spiritual and pastoral zeal, and this kindled a more intense spiritual life in his parishioners. The complete cycle of services was celebrated daily at the Podvoria, as in the days of Bishop Nicholas, beginning at 5 a.m. with Nocturnes (*polunoshchnitsa*), which was regularly attended by some parishioners before they went to work. People were impressed by the fact that Father Vitaly spoke good English, that he had acquired an old pre-war car (at that time it was still the exception to own a car in England), and, in general, by his organisational abilities, which were essential because of the increased size and wide dispersion of the community. For example, people long remembered the Paschal meal, held after the midnight service to break the fast; it was held in an old air-raid shelter in Clapham, and a fleet of double-decker buses was hired to transport the congregation. "It was fireworks," recalled Abbess Elisabeth, who visited London from the Holy Land for three months during 1950. "If someone didn't come for the evening service, he would get straight in the car and go round to see the family. 'What is wrong? Are you ill?' The Podvoria was like a beehive full of activity and bursting at the seams with spiritual energy."

Archimandrite Vitaly's greatest concern was for the Voluntary Workers who lived in the camps and hostels in the north of England. He travelled extensively in his old car, an Austin Seven, to visit them and conduct services. He worked closely with the Refugees Relief Association, which helped to identify the places where services were needed and to gather people together before the priest arrived. In the hostels, a room was set aside as a chapel, and on Sundays when there was no service, prayers were read by laypeople. Before the great feast days, representatives of the Refugees Relief Association toured the camps and invited people to London for the church services; 700 to 800 people attended these festal services at St Philip's. Because St Philip's was a large Anglican church, when the pews were removed it was easily able to hold this number of people. Again, the Refugees Relief Association helped to arrange overnight accommodations with Russian families for visitors from the north.

The demands on the clergy were immense. After having felt relief upon leaving Germany, people became demoralized due to the dreary living conditions, thoughts of loved ones left behind in Soviet Russia, the haunting fear of repatriation, and, at best, a poor command of the local language. With his fluency in English, Father Vitaly offered practical help as well as spiritual support, and this strengthened the bonds of love and gratitude between the pastor and his flock.

It soon became clear to Father Vitaly that more clergy were needed to minister to all these people and that properly established parishes needed to be set up in the north of England. It had always been accepted that the parish in London would serve the needs of Orthodox scattered throughout England, not just those in London. However, some of the old London émigrés disapproved of the idea of actually having a church "up north" because it was a departure from established practice.

Father Vitaly reported the situation to the Synod of Bishops, which still held its meetings in Munich. In reply he received a directive in June 1948 to "take energetic steps to bring more Orthodox clergy into England." The result was the arrival later that year of Father Nicholas Popoff and Father Sergei Schukin, who established parishes in Manchester and Bradford, respectively. During a visit to Bradford in 1948, Archimandrite Vitaly found a deacon, Father John Logvinenko, among the refugee workers. Because he had all the required canonical documents to confirm his status as a deacon, he was asked to join the clergy of the United Kingdom Deanery. Before long, Father Logvinenko moved to London to help with the church services and the work of Father Vitaly's brotherhood.

The diocesan bishop, Bishop Nathaniel of Brussels and Western Europe, was well known to many of the new immigrants for his work in the German DP camps, and his visits to England were eagerly awaited. Some older émigrés remembered his visit to England in 1938. He was a remarkable preacher; his talks revealed the truth of Orthodoxy to many people for whom it had previously been something quite unknown and incomprehensible. The following account, which was taken from *Church Life*, the official publication of the Russian Church Abroad, told of his visit to the United Kingdom Deanery in 1950:

> On 12 January 1950 a meeting of clergy and laity belonging to the United Kingdom Deanery of the Russian Church Abroad was held in the presence of the Right Reverend Bishop Nathaniel, diocesan bishop of the Diocese of Western Europe. The priest in charge of the Deanery, Archimandrite Vitaly, gave a report in which he said that there were now as many as ten thousand faithful in his Deanery. He outlined plans

to expand the publication, *Orthodox Review*, and to set up a workshop for making candles. The meeting resolved to organize a lay brotherhood dedicated to the Protection of the Most Holy Mother of God and, in general, to take energetic measures to strengthen the spiritual life of the Orthodox, so as to prevent further development of the feeling of moral depression which was making itself felt. Bishop Nathaniel gave a report on the subject of *Our Jurisdictional Allegiance*. It was resolved to form separate groups of Byelorussians within the parishes[5] and to commemorate, together with the other bishops, one of the Bishops of the Byelorussian Church who were in the jurisdiction of the Russian Church Abroad.

In London the Right Reverend Bishop Nathaniel gave a talk on the situation of the Russian Church Abroad. He then visited Ireland, where he celebrated the Divine Liturgy for the local parish.

The Bradford and Manchester parishes were founded with the blessing and active support of Bishop Nathaniel. Father Nicholas Popoff later described the beginning of the parish in Manchester:

> By a decree of the Right Reverend Bishop Nathaniel, in January 1950 I was appointed to Manchester to organize an Orthodox parish. During my first five months in Manchester, with the help of Archimandrite Vitaly, I organized a parish community numbering forty souls. On the day of the Holy Apostle Peter and Paul [29 June], the Right Reverend Bishop Nathaniel officiated at the Divine Liturgy held in an Anglican church, concelebrating with Archimandrite Vitaly and myself, with Deacon John Logvinenko assisting. The congregation numbered about 150 of our Orthodox people, most of whom had come from the surrounding towns and cities. After an inspired sermon, Vladyka Nathaniel announced that he was establishing a parish in Manchester dedicated to the Protecting Veil of the Mother of God. For three years after that, services were conducted in Anglican churches. We did not always feel at ease here and feared to abuse the Anglicans' hospitality. We resolved to create our own sacred corner to be able to pray in our own Orthodox church.

A house church at 64 Clarence Road, Longsight, Manchester, was opened on June 7, 1953, on the feast of All the Saints of Russia.

In London, Father Vitaly was building up his monastic brotherhood. He brought Hierodeacons Theodore and Paul, whom he had tonsured, from France to join him. "The plan to start a monastery in France came to nothing," wrote Archbishop Paul. "Too many insurmountable difficulties stood in the way, so Father Archimandrite Vitaly brought us over to join him in London." Father Paul spent a short time in Yorkshire, where he helped Father Sergei Schukin in the Bradford parish. He recalled this period as follows:

> Towards the end of 1950 Father Archimandrite Vitaly sent me to Yorkshire to study in an Anglican seminary at Mirfield. There I spent only two months, after which I was forced to return to London due to ill health. Every Saturday, while staying at Mirfield, I used to take the bus to Bradford. The rector of the parish there at that time was that most remarkable pastor, Father Sergei Schukin. There was not a proper church there, but a very small house chapel, which was located in a house bought specially for the purpose. There was also a small flat in the house, where Father Sergei lived with his daughter and son-in-law, and that is also where I stayed. The Vigil service was served in the evening in the house church. Not many people came. The Sunday Liturgy was held in a large school hall, which the school authorities put at our disposal for the day. We arrived there at 8 o'clock in the morning. We had to erect the portable iconostasis, the altar table and the table of preparation, put up the icon stands with icons on them, the candle stands and so on. This was a substantial amount of work. We began the Liturgy at 11 a.m. The congregation completely filled the hall. People came from various places including Leeds. When the service was over everything had to be packed away again and put into a storeroom, also put at our disposal by the school. There was a Russian library in the church house, and many of the congregation went there to borrow books, to sit and talk. On Sundays we were never able to sit down for lunch before four in the afternoon.

Father Vitaly had collected funds to buy this first church house in Bradford from people scattered over a wide area and it was intended to become a centre around which they could be united. However, it was evidently too small and in 1951 a larger house was acquired which could be converted into a church big enough to hold the congregation. Count Kleinmichel, the Treasurer of the London parish, helped raise funds for this purchase through appealing to various non-Russian benefactors of the Church and part of the sum was financed directly by the parish in London.

Concerning his time in London, Archbishop Paul wrote,

> In London we moved into the Church House, which was known as the Podvoria. Father Vitaly already had a printing works and we zealously set about the typesetting and printing. It was there that we printed the first edition of *Orthodox Review* [*Pravolslavnoye Obozreniye*] [which was later published in Canada]. Father Theodore printed with great enthusiasm, not knowing what it was to be tired and forgetting everything else in the world in his zeal. On more than one occasion Father Archimandrite Vitaly had to restrain his enthusiasm. More than thirty years have passed since then. Two or three years ago I visited the Podvoria. How we burned with inspiration in those days! In that little house, under incredibly cramped conditions, we not only had our own living quarters (there were eight of us), but also found room for the printing machinery and candle-making workshop. In the same building was a house chapel where we held daily services. But the cramped conditions did not trouble us at all. We simply did not notice them.

The Russian Church continued to attract the attention of English visitors. With his fluent command of English, Father Vitaly offered them a clear, intelligent explanation of the truths of Holy Orthodoxy, and with the passage of time, fifteen English people accepted the Orthodox faith and became members of the London parish. These included Gerald Palmer, a former member of Parliament, who became well known as a translator of ancient patristic texts. The London clergy were also joined by a priest of English origin, Priest-monk Lazarus (Moore), who had previously been an Anglican clergyman. In 1932 he was received into the Orthodox Church in Serbia by Metropolitan Anthony (Khrapovitsky), first hierarch of the Russian Church Abroad, professed as a monk in the Milkovo Monastery in Serbia, and ordained to the Orthodox priesthood. Thereafter, he served in Jerusalem and worked closely with Sisters Mary (Robinson) and Martha (Sprott), also English converts to Orthodoxy who established the convent at Gethsemane and a school in Bethany. Apparently Father Lazarus left Palestine due to the Arab–Israeli war that broke out in 1948. In June 1949, Archimandrite Vitaly told the Parish Council that Father Lazarus would be returning to England and described him as a "substantial spiritual force" ("крупная духовная сила"). He anticipated that Father Lazarus would help in three ways: by improving contacts with the English and the Anglican Church, by undertaking missionary work among English people, and by giving religious instruction to children of Russian parishioners who did not speak Russian. Father Vitaly entrusted Father Lazarus with the task of celebrating the Divine Liturgy in English every Saturday. However, these services were poorly attended and soon ended. Some converts preferred the Slavonic worship to which they had already grown accustomed, while others lacked the zeal or the opportunity to attend church on Saturday as well as Sunday.

The eight occupants of the Podvoria mentioned by Archbishop Paul included a married priest, Father Nicholas Uspensky, who went to London via a long and tortuous path, as described in the following excerpt from the book by Archpriest Michael Protopopov,

> Father Nicholas Uspensky came from Kostroma. In 1909 he was enrolled at the Soligalichsky Theological School and then went on to study at the Theological Seminary in Kostroma. In 1913, he married Vera Alexeevna Rabkova, the daughter of a church reader, and was ordained that same December to the diaconate by the Right Reverend Eugene, Bishop of Kostroma and Galich. Fr Nicholas had served the Church for but a short time when the Revolution broke out and, in the purges of the clergy, the Bolsheviks arrested him under Article 58 for treason and anti-Soviet propaganda. The deacon was sentenced to nine years imprisonment in the concentration camps and at one time worked as a slave labourer on the Moscow-Volga canal. After being released, he did not return home, but settled in the Orel Region and worked on flower farms. With the invasion of the Wehrmacht, Fr Nicholas and his family were sent to Germany to work as *Ostarbeiters* until the end of the war.
>
> On 23 June 1946, Fr Nicholas was ordained a priest by Bishop Nathaniel Lvov of Hamburg and sent to serve the Russian community in London. There he celebrated at the Bishop's Chapel in Baron Court and, in addition to his pastoral duties, he was personal chaplain to Her Imperial Highness the Grand Duchess Xenia Alexandrovna Romanoff, sister of the martyred Tsar Nicholas II. The Grand Duchess lived at Hampton Court Palace and Fr Nicholas would often spend time with her and the family. When Fr Nicholas made plans to migrate to Australia, the Grand Duchess presented him with an icon belonging to the murdered Royal Family, found in Ekaterinburg and which was partially burnt by the campfire at the Four Brothers Mine, where the Bolsheviks attempted to dispose of their victims. Xenia Alexandrovna also gave her confessor a knitted rug which covered the knees of the Tsarevitch whilst he suffered the effects of haemophilia and which she held sacred as a personal relic of her murdered nephew.

Fr Nicholas Uspensky came to Australia in 1951 and was the parish priest at St Seraphim's Church in Brisbane. He died in 1980.

Recollections of Paul Uspensky

Father Nicholas's son, Paul, wrote the following description of church life in London during this period:

> With the arrival of Father Archimandrite Vitaly in London in 1947, church life was transformed. Everything changed—everything took on a new air. The full cycle of Divine Services was served every day: in the morning—the Midnight Office, Matins and Liturgy, and in the evening—Vespers with Akathist. The old London émigrés were not particularly impressed. People said that too much oil was being used in the icon lamps and that other church requirements were costing too much, but the energetic Father Archimandrite could not be dissuaded and he held his line firmly. The rest of his brotherhood had to be got out of Germany. All his printing machinery had to be brought over and the printing works, which was like a favourite child to him, had to be started up again. All had to be accommodated in the small house where there was also a house church—and it was not particularly easy to fit us all in. The Father Deacon had to set up his bed in the *trapeza* [dining room] in the evenings and put it away again in the mornings. In time, though, everything settled down.
>
> Father Hierodeacon Paul (later Archbishop of Australia and New Zealand, d. 1993), Father Hierodeacon Theodore, Father Deacon John, the priest Father Nicholas Uspensky with his wife and children, and John, who worked with us, were the trusted helpers of the Father Archimandrite. Later priest-monk George from the Evlogian jurisdiction in Paris came and joined the brotherhood. Our life imitated to some extent the life of the first Christians. Admittedly, unlike them, we did not give away our property or bring money from the sale to the feet of the Apostle Peter; we had nothing to bring, as we were homeless and impoverished. We could only offer our labour and our love to the Church and the Father Archimandrite.
>
> The garage intended for a car was turned into a printing works. Here the printing presses and composing tables were set up and the typesetters worked at enormous desks, setting entire pages of spiritual literature by hand. Due to lack of space, Deacon John set up his carpenter's bench under the open sky in the miniature yard behind the house. When he was free from church services, he banged away with his hammer, like a woodpecker,

perhaps making an icon lamp or constructing something out of wood for the church. Matushka Vera's obedience was the kitchen. Her feet hurt her badly but, often standing on one foot, she regularly cooked for the whole brotherhood without complaint. Seeing that the work was too much for her, Father Archimandrite decided to reduce her workload and appointed each person in turn to wash the dishes after trapeza. To give an example, over matushka's protests, he did the washing himself the first day. That was as far as it went—the next day matushka was back at the sink, until after a while Father Archimandrite gave the same order again and washed the dishes himself. Again this order remained unfulfilled—not out of laziness, but because everyone was over-worked.

Every second Sunday, when the Liturgy was celebrated at the Podvoria, the congregation stayed to lunch. Only half the people would fit round the large table in the dining room at any one time, so they ate in two sittings. This brought the parishioners together: they came to know one another and exchanged views. Gradually the parish came to love the Father Archimandrite and all tried to help him as best they could. Tatiana Pavlovna Gherken, Larissa Alexandrovna and others, imitating the myrrh-bearing women of ancient times, helped by reading from the kliros and doing good works, depriving themselves of essentials as well as looking after sick people in their own homes for weeks at a time. On Sunday evenings young people met in the large room in the basement. Father Archimandrite gave talks which were listened to eagerly and with close attention. Father Nicholas would read something lighter, and then, in a relaxed atmosphere over a cup of tea, they asked questions and we exchanged views.

With the beginning of the Great Lent there were more church services, everybody had more work to do, and by the time Holy Week came round, it was more than anyone could manage. In order to get the church magazine out for Pascha the typesetters worked almost through the night, sometimes falling asleep over their work just before dawn. Father Archimandrite would be rushing around in his small, aged car to get the printing paper, or rolling up his sleeves to set a page of type, his hands covered in printer's ink, or giving instruction elsewhere in the house. Soon it would be the Resurrection of Christ and joy must be brought to all. After the Paschal Liturgy, the Father Archimandrite gave his flock the traditional greeting with red eggs, although at that time, just after the war, eggs were rationed and each person received coupons for one egg a week, so they were very hard to obtain. Almost all the parishioners came to the Podvoria for the traditional meal at which the fast is broken and the little house turned into a beehive. All the narrow corridors and stairways were filled with people and it was impossible to move between the kitchen and the second and third floors. The hubbub of conversation filled the whole building and a human chain passed plates of food up to the very top of the house and returned them again when they were empty. By dawn people were beginning to disperse, but anyone who had no transport stayed behind and it was amusing to see some self-important lady, satiated with spiritual and bodily food, fallen asleep over the table or in a corner.

Soon the summer holidays came round, the school term was over and the long awaited time of recreation approached. Father Archimandrite took the trouble to ensure that our youth used this time sensibly. A visit for three days to Mrs. Legat[6] in the country was arranged well in advance. This was a large ballet school, located in an enormous country house with a hundred rooms and all conveniences, surrounded by shady pathways and bordered by flowerbeds in a quiet spot beside a lake, well away from the turbulent "sea of life," and made an ideal place for a holiday. Everyone went who could possibly manage to either by train or by bus, and five of us lads went by bicycle. It was raining, we were almost there, but then we got lost. The main party had already arrived and we managed to get through to them by telephone to utter a cry for help, which soon came. One of the large reception rooms had been turned into a church through the efforts of the new arrivals. The Vigil service was conducted in an orderly and prayerful fashion. Looking at the strictly calm and concentrated face of the Father Archimandrite predisposed us to prayer as well. Father Deacon John, whom we called "blue-beard" because he had a long, spade-shaped beard like a merchant in old Russia, pronounced the petitions so simply and fervently in his unaffected bass voice, while to the side of the room an improvised choir, directed by a young man named Vanya, sang simply, but in a most heartfelt manner.

The first rays of the sun glistened on the flowers, wet with dew, peered in through the window of our makeshift church, the birds were already glorifying their Creator in their own language; the morning was beginning to assert itself. How could one sleep through the early Liturgy? Everyone was up, everyone hastened to pray. The Hours and the Liturgy proceeded with such concentration and such a festive spirit that we did not notice how the time was passing.

Strengthened with an appetizing and plentiful breakfast provided by the ladies, we all amused ourselves as we wished. Some sat by a lilac bush and read, some walked along the pathways deep in conversation, while a few of us lads sailed peacefully on the lake in a rubber boat. But what is this? Something fell with a plop into the water beside the boat. A minute later a potato whistled by and hit the side of the boat; we were being attacked! The battle soon heated up. A potato flew at us from the shore; we resisted in desperation and hit out at it—the "enemy." With great difficulty we managed to sit it out and go over to the counter-attack. It was amusing to see the potato projectile ricochet off the back of the Father Archimandrite while the Deacon, muttering in his beard, hid in the bushes. Nature, the fresh air, tranquillity, evening and morning services, and innocent mischief, these strengthened us before our return to the bustle of London.

After the First World War a part of the cultured stratum of émigré society had come to London. In church you could often see a count, princes and members of the merchant classes, while on the outskirts of the city, at Hampton Court Palace, modestly lived the Grand Duchess Xenia Alexandrovna, sister of the martyred Emperor. Our clergy often visited her. Besides our clergy in London there was the Polish Orthodox Church, which was headed by Vladyka Savva with his own clergy, but it did not join forces with our Church and, as far as I know, it was not very numerous.

Archimandrite Vitaly in the All Saints Podvoria Chapel. (Source: Deacon Andrew Bond)

The *Orthodox Review*

The *Orthodox Review* (*Pravoslavnoye Obozreniye*) was the name of Archimandrite Vitaly's monthly publication. It was a pastoral journal that effectively supplemented the sermons and other spiritual talks given in church. It contained news items that affected the Church both in England and elsewhere, commentary on political events, and commentary on events that affected the lives of the faithful. Information was always presented with a view to placing these events in an Orthodox perspective, based on the teachings of the Church Fathers. The pages of this journal leave an impression of intense creative activity directed toward building a church community that was part, as it were, of a family spread throughout the world, to which it was linked by the loved and respected diocesan bishop, Bishop Nathaniel.

Following are some articles, news items, and announcements taken from the journal that give a clear impression of the development of the Russian Church in England during this period. The first article was an appeal addressed to the new immigrants:

> [Christmas 1950]
>
> **Appeal**
>
> **Dear brothers and sisters!**
>
> Words do not suffice to express our praise for the fact that, out of the land of terror, oppression and slavery, you have brought faith in God, burning like an inextinguishable vigil lamp in your hearts. The countless churches which you constructed with your own hands in Germany, both in the camps and in the cities, will remain as an undying memorial to your faithfulness to the Orthodox Church. This was the wonderful period of your spiritual flowering, and, as such, will always remain in your memory, for then your prayers in the Church, after thirty years of unheard-of persecution, flew up before the throne of God, like a bird escaped from the hunter's snare. Your souls bathed in the abundant waves of grace which the Lord, as a generous Father, sent down upon us.
>
> But now our life has turned to a new page; we have left Germany behind and been dispersed throughout the whole world and a new task now stands before you. You were able to preserve the Faith under persecution; you must now preserve it in freedom and plenty. The Lord has not led you out of slavery and captivity in order for you to hurl yourselves at the vain good things of this earth and put your hearts—your whole soul—into food, clothing, houses and other cheap, transient human values. May

we not succumb to such a fall, to such ingratitude! Is it that long since the Soviet agents of the NKVD were after our heads? If the Lord sees that satiety and freedom are harmful to us and that we turn aside from His good will and have exchanged our birthright for a mess of pottage, then God is mighty to be able to cast us again into suffering, to put chains on us once again and cover us with sores. The whole world can now see that our country is growing faint from torments at the hands of blasphemers, haters of mankind, and monstrous individuals such as the world has not seen before. Who, if not you, can testify before all peoples about the holy Russian martyrs; and who better can tear the mask off the tormentors, so that all peoples can see that the countenance of Satan himself, the murderer is brazenly and cynically peering out from behind their faces. Perhaps our testimony can sober those peoples who are deluded and intoxicated by the sweet wine of communism. And what shall we call ourselves if we spurn all these great responsibilities and instead begin to crawl along the ground, and say, together with the foolish man in the Gospel, "My soul, thou hast much goods laid up for many years; take thine ease, eat, drink and be merry." But God said to him, "Thou fool, in this night thy soul shall be required of thee." (Luke 12:19-20)

Standing now at the threshold of the new year, as well as of a new period in our lives, I express my whole-hearted wish for you to preserve faith in God and faithfulness to the suffering Orthodox Church of Russia, and to be truthful and zealous witnesses to God's truth.

Archimandrite Vitaly

[Christmas 1948]

Chronicle of Church Life

Father Nicholas Popoff has arrived in England. He has already conducted services several times in Bradford and once in Mansfield, where he is now living. Father Nicholas is known to many of our Orthodox DP's for his zealous work for the Church in Germany, where he was living near Brunswick.

Father Sergei Schukin is also due to arrive here with his children before long, from the camp at Fischbek, which we all know. All Orthodox will be informed where he is to live.

For the New Year a small calendar is to be published in Russian, containing all the information essential for those living in England. Price 2 shillings. All income will go towards the needs of the Church.

On Mondays at 7 p.m. talks on spiritual topics are given for adults in the Church House.

After Orthodox Christmas, lessons for children will be given twice a week in the Church House.

Early in 1949 there will be a deanery meeting of all clergy in canonical obedience to the Chairman of the Synod of Bishops, Metropolitan Anastassy.

For the first time in England a Russian printing press has been started by the Orthodox press in London. It prints exclusively to satisfy the needs of the parishioners.

Announcements

In the Podvoria, where Archimandrite Vitaly is living, there is a large Russian library, consisting of 5,000 volumes. Up to four books at a time can be ordered from the provinces. Another four books will be sent immediately [when] they are returned. Price 5 shillings per month plus postage.

Subscribe to the only Russian newspaper published weekly in England. Order from *Rossanin* 119 Adelaide Road, London NW3.

[Lent 1949]

Holy places in England

We wish to bring to the attention of all our Orthodox people the fact that in England there are places, as there were in our own land in times gone by, which are chosen by God, to which one can go to strengthen oneself spiritually, pray and prepare oneself. In the county of Norfolk, in the village of Walsingham, in about the eleventh century, when the whole of England was an Orthodox country, there was an appearance of the Mother of God and to this day there is a spring of healing water on the place where she appeared. Very soon news of this event spread round the whole of the then Orthodox world and pilgrims started travelling there in the thousands from England and northern Europe. A large monastery gradually came into existence there and every Christian considered it his duty to visit it once a year. . . . Inside the main church there is an Orthodox chapel with an Orthodox priest, Father Dmitrie Naidanovich, permanently in residence. We earnestly recommend all Orthodox to contact Father Dmitrie, who will give you all the information you require. . . . In the monastery there are hundreds of small particles of the relics of Orthodox saints—holy hierarchs, martyrs and monastic saints. Be certain to ask to venerate them, and to take some of the holy water away with you. Visiting this shrine will be particularly convenient for those Orthodox who are living in camps in Norfolk, since the public transport in the area is very good.

[Lent 1949]

Advertisements

Easter cards: 4 shillings per dozen. Available from the editor or from Pesiakoff's Second-hand shop, 78 Earl's Court Road, W8.

Buy your men's suits and shirts at Bourne and Tant Ltd. Russian spoken.

[Lent 1949]

Chronicle of Church Life

1. On 24th and 25th February a meeting of all clergy serving foreign workers in England was held in Dorchester College. It was attended by Archbishop Savva, Archimandrite Vitaly, Archpriest Miloje Nikolich and representatives of other Orthodox and Protestant churches, but not by Catholics or Uniates. This meeting was sponsored by an organisation known as Christian Reconstruction in Europe. It was attended in an advisory capacity by officials from the Ministry of Labour, the Department of Agriculture and Trade, and the Home Office. The chairmen of the meeting were the Reverends Dekin, Aineson and Foster. Three sessions were held at which many different questions concerning the life and welfare of the foreign workers was discussed. The ministry spokesmen asked the clergy to explain to their flocks that the British government had never taken a favourable view of the way the foreign workers had to live, crowded together in camps, and would be taking all possible steps to ensure that the workers could lead the life of British subjects at the earliest opportunity. Meanwhile, any of the workers who found accommodation privately would immediately be able to leave the camp. It was resolved that the church representatives would meet regularly to discuss matters of current concern with the secretary of the British Council of Churches.
2. In June an exhibition of iconography of the old and new schools is to take place in a gallery of one of the museums. Schools of iconography and individual icon painters will be represented in the exhibition. For full information ask the editors of *Orthodox Review* or Mr. A.A. Agapeyeff, Campden, Glos., England.

3. The Parish Council of the London Russian Orthodox Church requests all those wishing to come to London for Easter and take part in the meal after the night service to register immediately. The charge of twelve shillings and sixpence includes accommodation for the night of 23rd–24th April. The deadline for registration is the fifth Sunday of Lent.

[Lent 1949]

Message to all those working in mental hospitals

Of all those who have come to work in England, you are bearing the heaviest burden. Looking at your efforts we, clergymen, sorrow for you in our souls, and so you should regard this message to you as a sincere desire to help you bear your cross. We are convinced that we will be able to lighten your burden if we open your mental and spiritual eyes to the significance of your work, by giving you some spiritual advice.

During the first days that you work among these unfortunate people, you easily and simply draw a clear boundary between your own sanity and their madness. However, as you spend more time amid the sea of insanity, your soul soon becomes weary from the constant effort it has to make, both consciously and unconsciously, to correct the abnormality of the mental patients against the normality of your own mind. Your soul is drained of strength, and this strength cannot be made good by either vitamins or good food. This is when the second period of trial begins for you: your soul begins to be invaded at first unnoticeably, then more persistently and boldly, with doubting thoughts: "Why am I normal, while these thousands are not normal?"

The Orthodox Church has many centuries of experience and calls all these phenomena "possession." Admittedly, the Church does not dispute the fact that mental illness can afflict both people who are in perfect physical health, without any bodily disorders, as well as people whose nervous system has become paralysed to such an extent that it permits the other, base world to invade their souls. . . .

Holy Scripture helps us to understand the reasons for these terrible illnesses. Some are seized by the forces of darkness by God's permission, because the Lord sees that they would use their mind for their own perdition. Others the Lord allows to fall into this infirmity in order to turn them away from some terrible sin, according to Saint Paul "to deliver this man to Satan for the destruction of the flesh, that his spirit may be saved in the day of the Lord Jesus." (1Cor 5:5)

Living alone among the mass of possessed people, you should remember that the only "norm" on earth is Christ, and the closer you are to Christ, the more perfectly normal you will be. Then it will not be your own small, vacillating normality that you oppose to the insanity which surrounds you, but the normality of Christ and of God. Yours is no ordinary work; the Lord has sent you to engage in a great task, that of struggle with the unseen powers of darkness. While being in the body, with all its infirmities, you are forced to struggle against the unseen spirits, which are not subject to the limitations of the flesh. So be attentive to yourselves and to your souls. Pray and unfailingly observe all the Church's fasts; go frequently to confession and Holy Communion.

Be warned that if you do not observe these precepts, you yourselves will slide gradually into insanity.

Believe in God's providence, believe that the Lord has sent you to do this work, in order that you should think more deeply about life and enter on the path of the Christian struggle; otherwise change your job, give it up, for "this kind never comes out except by prayer and fasting." (Matt 17:21)

I wish to share these thoughts with you, observing the life you have to lead, sorrowing with your sorrows, and having a sincere desire to help you.

Archimandrite Vitaly

[August 1949]

A. Zemlev

We print below one chapter from *Land Of Willows* by A. Zemlev, a writer among the new emigrants from the Soviet Union, who is now living in England. He is known to some readers here through his literary readings at the Podvoria. . . .

[1950, no. 17]

Chronicle of Church Life

At the beginning of January, Bishop Nathaniel will visit our deanery and will serve in London and the provinces. A meeting of our clergy is due to take place during his visit.

On the 14 December, in Warwick, a diocesan meeting of Anglican clergymen took place with the Bishop of Coventry in the chair. Father Archimandrite Vitaly, the Dean of the Russian Orthodox parishes in England, gave a report on the displaced persons. In a few sentences the Father Archimandrite outlined the horrors of Soviet life, from which God's Providence had delivered many of the DP's now living in England. "However, despite his outward prosperity, the soul of the new immigrant is still uneasy and anxious, and finds little joy in life," and this, according to the speaker, was due to two main causes. Firstly, the DP's know communism, not through books and newspapers, but through their own bitter experience and they are very disturbed to see the childishly naive attitude of the western world to this evil, of apocalyptic proportions, which has started playing games with them. The second factor undermining the new immigrants' peace of soul was their limited freedom to work. The Anglican clergy listened to the speaker with great interest.

Talks are being given on spiritual topics at 6 p.m. on Sundays at the All Saints Podvoria, after Vespers and the *Akathist* to the Mother of God. These talks are arousing great interest among the young people.

[Pascha 1950]

Chronicle of the Bradford Parish

On 25 February [1950] a young woman of 24, named B., a refugee from the Soviet Union, was baptised in the parish church. She had not been baptised in childhood as her father was serving in the Red Army and her mother was a teacher in a Soviet school. But then it happened through God's will that her father was killed in the first few months of the war and her mother died in Kiev during the German occupation. Being, despite everything, a religious woman, she left to her sixteen-year-old daughter, as her last testament, the wish that she should be baptised by an Orthodox priest. However, immediately after her mother's death, B. was sent to work in Germany. After the end of the war she did not wish to return to the Soviet Union but was living in one of the D.P. camps in Austria where there was no Orthodox priest. In England she was also far from a church until 1949, when she started attending the church in Bradford. After studying the teachings of the Orthodox Church, she was baptised and became an Orthodox member of the parish.

From the beginning of the Great Lent, the rector of the Bradford parish has intensified his excursions to the hostels of Yorkshire, so that the Orthodox could confess and receive Holy Communion. On 24–25 February a service was held in a camp for miners in the town of Castleford; on March 10–11 there were services in the camp at Hawden Hall, near Keighley and on 18–19 March in the camp for families in Priory Road, near Hull: in this camp almost all the Orthodox received Holy Communion—17 adults and about 39 children of all ages.

At the General Meeting of the parish held on 26 March the half-yearly financial accounts were presented and a new Churchwarden was elected. P. N. Klimoff was elected to fill this post. He assumed his duties from 1st April.

The Parish Council of the Bradford parish is organizing a festal meal after the Paschal service for the parishioners and visiting members of the congregation at 8 shillings per head. This sum includes accommodation for the night for those unable to stay with friends in Bradford.

[August 1949]

Pushkin abroad

The smallest parish of the Russian Orthodox Church Abroad in northern Europe is situated in Ireland. This little community consists of some thirty people, scattered throughout various towns and villages, and despite the fact that Orthodox services are held there only two or three times a year, the handful of Russian people zealously holds on to the Church and keeps to their Russianness with a touching steadfastness.

During our last visit to this community, after the Divine Liturgy, we were taken into the interior of the island to a small hamlet in order to take Holy Communion to an elderly woman who was sick. The Russian family which had invited us leads a quiet, country life and ekes out part of its modest living by taking in students and young officers to teach them the Russian language. The householders managed to combine in themselves a profound thoughtfulness and an intense degree of practical help which is so essential in country life. I will cite only one, most important, thought from our conversation with them. As one of their young boarders was leaving for home after completing his Russian course, when he came to bid them farewell, he said, "Before I came here I used to look *at* things; now I have understood that one must look *within* them, at what is behind them."

Such testimony from a young foreigner concerning the properties of our language is a consolation which Divine Providence is sending to us, in order to help us see the meaning of our often-thorny path in exile.

The dispersion of the Russian people has a profound purpose. Following the footsteps of the Jews, who had renounced Christ and been scattered abroad, and following after them, the Russians have borne the Orthodox cross on their weak shoulders and carried it to all the ends of the earth. But Orthodoxy is being received slowly; it enters the soul in minute doses. We have not conducted missionary work in the sense in which it is understood by the Roman Catholics: we do not organize missionary camps, public debates, youth societies. The reasons for this apparent inactivity must be sought in the very understanding of missionary work by the Orthodox Church. The transition to Orthodoxy—that is to say, the rite of being united to the Church—has always been regarded by us as the final act of the soul of the converted person, as the crown with which the Church crowns, in so visible a fashion, the inward acceptance of the Orthodox culture, which he has achieved slowly and freely, and now finally brought to completion. . . .

Now, at a time when the public opinion of the whole world is so riveted by the Russian tragedy, Pushkin[7] has provided a sort of invisible narthex, or entrance, to the Church for catechumens of all nations—the "narthex" being formed of Russian culture, in which the light of Christ shines. Already there are many non-Russians who have entered this narthex but not remained there, not become stuck there, but have gone on to enter the church itself and even the altar.

But for those who have lost their spiritual riches, who have gone after "other gods," who have been Orthodox but now ceased to be, Pushkin does not have this Orthodox spiritual authority. How deeply mistaken are those who, desiring to retain their Russianness while living here, outside Russia, and not to be dissolved into the mass of non-Russians, insist emphatically on the culture of Pushkin alone. Such people have not fully considered the implications of these ideas; they have not understood Pushkin. May God be merciful to them.

Archimandrite Vitaly

Visit of Metropolitan Anastassy and the Miraculous Kursk Icon

The following description of the remarkable tour of the miraculous Kursk icon through England appeared in *Church Life*, the official publication of the Russian Church Abroad:

On the Thursday before the feast of Pentecost, 25 May 1950, the Chairman of the Synod of Bishops of the Russian Orthodox Church Abroad, the Most Reverend Metropolitan Anastassy, taking with him that most holy object of the Russian diaspora, the miraculous Kursk Icon of the Mother of God, and accompanied by Archimandrite Job, departed via Belgium for England, in order to visit the Orthodox flock there. This flock has grown significantly in numbers over recent years and has long been awaiting this visit, which was an occasion of great joy.

They were met on the way in Brussels by a group of faithful from the local parish, headed by Archpriest Victor Ilienko, who had come specially to the station to greet the First Hierarch and venerate the sacred icon.

On the day of Pentecost the First Hierarch celebrated the Divine Liturgy in London in the spacious church of Saint Philip, near Buckingham Palace. The church was filled absolutely to capacity, both by the old Russian residents of London and by former DP's, who had moved to England to work. With deep faith and compunction all venerated this most sacred Russian icon and came up to receive the blessing of the First Hierarch.

The Most Reverend Metropolitan made visits to the head of the Anglican Church, the Archbishop of Canterbury, and to the Grand Duchess Xenia Alexandrovna, sister of the murdered Emperor.

On the second day of Pentecost the Metropolitan celebrated in the Podvoria church which is in the care of the Dean of the churches in England, Archimandrite Vitaly.

On the third day the Right Reverend Bishop Nathaniel of Brussels and Western Europe came to London to venerate the sacred icon and meet the Metropolitan.

On Wednesday 18/31 May there was a well-attended meeting of members of the London parish, convened at the initiative of the Church sisterhood. A moleben was held before the miraculous icon, after which the hierarchs gave a spiritual talk.

On Saturday 21 May/3 June the Most Reverend Metropolitan Anastassy attended a specially convened meeting of the Russian Refugees Aid Committee. When he arrived, in the company of Bishop Nathaniel, the Most Reverend Metropolitan was met in the Conservative Club meeting hall by members of the Committee. After prayer, the President of the Society, Prince Galitzine, and the Secretary, Count Bennigsen, greeted the Metropolitan, expressing their joy at having with them a hierarch who had done so much to rescue so many Russian people and who had been able to show the zeal of Christian Russia to those of other lands. In his reply Metropolitan Anastassy pointed to the importance of the Refugees Aid Society for the Russian cause in Europe as a whole and touched on the times just experienced when everything Russian was under threat, when the inhabitants and public opinion of the West had been unable to distinguish the persecutors from their victims. The First Hierarch noted with satisfaction how the awareness of western people was growing.

As an illustration, he quoted from a speech made recently in this respect over the radio by Monsignor Fulton Sheen, a professor of the Roman Catholic university in Washington. Metropolitan Anastassy expressed his profound gratitude towards him for such love and understanding of the Russian situation. He gave his blessing to the Refugees Aid Society to continue its work of rescuing Russian people who had broken free from the chains of slavery in their own country.

The same day, 21 May/3 June, Metropolitan Anastassy departed for Bradford where the miraculous icon and the First Hierarch were greeted by the rector, Father Sergei Schukin, with all the parishioners of his church of Saint Nicholas. On Sunday 4 June the Divine Liturgy was concelebrated there by the Metropolitan together with Archimandrites Job and Vitaly, and Father Sergei Schukin with Protodeacon Sergei Tchertkoff. Faithful from Manchester and all the nearby settlements of Russian workers also gathered at this service. On the Monday the Metropolitan returned to London with the holy icon

During the night from Monday 5 June to Tuesday 6 June a full Vigil service was served at the All Saints Podvoria Church in London, strictly according to the typicon. The service lasted from 8 p.m. until 12.30 a.m. When the Vigil ended, lives of the saints were read to many of the congregation who stayed in the church, a moleben with an akathist was served, and the rule of prayer before Holy Communion was read. Then at 5.30 a.m. the Divine Liturgy began. On Tuesday the Most Reverend Metropolitan Anastassy and Archimandrite Job took the miraculous icon back to Munich by way of Brussels.[8]

Consecration as Bishop and Departure for Brazil

In 1950 and 1951 many people in England were turning their attention to Britain's former colonies, particularly the Dominion of Canada and the Dominion of Australia, as places of greater opportunity. These countries were readily accepting immigrants, and many British people applied. Not surprisingly, many of the DPs, who had no roots in England, thought of emigration as their three-year contracts came to an end. Particularly younger people saw greater opportunities overseas for the establishment of a stable family life. Others wanted to move farther from the borders of the Soviet Union.

Thus, many new immigrants left for Australia, Canada, and, to a lesser extent, the United States and South America. The Christmas 1950 issue of the *Orthodox Review*, for example, contained the following announcements:

The Butkovskys, Nikolskys, M. Evseyenko . . . and the Udalovskys have arrived at the distant shores of Australia. They greet all their friends in England and send best wishes for Christmas and the New Year.

The editors of *Orthodox Review* ask all the Orthodox dispersed throughout Great Britain to let them know the addresses of their friends and relatives who have left to live in America, Australia, Canada and other places, so that we will not lose our spiritual ties with them, but will still be able to supply them with spiritual literature, completely free of charge. Some clergymen have emigrated also, either due to the dictates of personal circumstances, or in response to specific directives from the Synod of Bishops.

June 29/July 12, 1951, the feast of Saints Peter and Paul, was an occasion of great spiritual solemnity for the London parish, but, at the same time, an occasion of great sadness. It was on this day that Archimandrite Vitaly was consecrated bishop—but not as bishop of the parishes in England. He had been appointed Bishop of Montevideo and, as such, would be a vicar bishop to Archbishop Theodossy of Sao Paolo and Brazil.

Father Vitaly had not anticipated this turn of events and initially was opposed to accepting episcopal consecration. Church life was flourishing in the United Kingdom Deanery. Plans were in place to buy another house in St Dunstan's Road, just across the street, that would alleviate the overcrowding of the Podvoria. There was even a plan to relocate the headquarters of the Holy Synod of the Russian Church Abroad from Munich to Oxford, where a suitable building belonging to one of the Oxford colleges was for sale. Father Vitaly called a meeting of his monastic brotherhood and, with their support, resolved that he would categorically refuse to be consecrated bishop. However, as he recounted, he was convinced to change his mind by an unexpected meeting. Late one evening he was called to take Holy Communion to a dying man who lived near Tunbridge Wells in Kent. He drove in the dark for a long time and got lost because many of the signposts that were removed during the war had not been replaced. He eventually found the house, heard the man's confession, and gave him Holy Communion. As he was leaving, the dying man called him back, looked intently at him, and said that he had had a dream of three bishops sitting down and saying to each other that it was time for Archimandrite Vitaly to become a bishop. Father Vitaly was stunned because the telegram had only arrived that morning and the man could not possibly have known about it. He decided it was the will of God and he could not refuse, notwithstanding the disruption of the parish life he had organized in England.

Initially there was no indication of who would replace Father Vitaly as rector in London. Meanwhile, Priest-monk Lazarus left for America and Father Nicholas Uspensky departed for Australia. So, Father Vitaly was left alone in London with three deacons (Hierodeacon Theodore, Hierodeacon Paul, and Deacon Philemon Zadworny). The daily services at the Podvoria came to a halt and, during the Great Lent, Father Vitaly turned for assistance to the clergy of the Serbian Church.

During this unsettled period, the parish lost its deeply loved and respected choir director, Foka Feodorovich Volkovsky, who died on March 16, 1951. He had served in London for fifty-four years, first as a singer in the Embassy church, then as psalm-reader, and finally as choir director.

The situation eased when Bishop Nathaniel came to London at the end of Lent and remained to celebrate the Holy Week and Pascha services, which took place that year in St Philip's. It seemed likely that Bishop Nathaniel would remain in London and take over leadership of the parish.

The consecration of Father Vitaly took place in St Philip's Church. The consecrating hierarchs were Bishop Nathaniel and Bishop Leonty of Geneva, and the service was concelebrated by all clergy of the Russian parishes in England as well as visiting clergy from France and Belgium. A reception was given afterward that was attended by the Anglican Bishop of Kensington.

On the evening before the consecration, at the service of "nomination" (*narecheniye*) Archimandrite Vitaly, according to custom, gave the following address in which he outlined his understanding of the episcopal office:

> Most Reverend Bishops!
> It is with feelings of fear, trembling and deep reverence that I am approaching the sacrament of episcopal consecration. When I cast my mind back over the host of archpastors, both those who have departed into eternity and those who are still living, who have been adorned with learning, wisdom, piety and the greatest and highest ecclesiastical culture, which only the Russian Empire at the very zenith of its glory could give them,[9] when I reflect that I am now to enter their ranks and receive their Apostolic mantle[10] upon my shoulders, my soul is struck with fear—with the fear that, by the very fact of entering this sacred assembly, I am debasing the level of their episcopal calling.
>
> Further, fear penetrates my entire being because this augmented grace cannot be contained in an impure vessel, while I, in addition to the corrupted human nature which I have naturally inherited, have shown a sinful determination to add, through my own will, the sins and passions

which I have acquired. I now better understand the Holy Prophet David when he said "From thy face whither shall I flee?" It seems to me that this is also how it will be at the end of the present age, when the Lord Himself will approach the earth, and all that is sinful and passionate will shudder and tremble at His approach, and will be made manifest with such force that each person will truly seek a fissure in the earth in which to hide, if it is possible, from the Eye of Him Who sees all things.

The Lord is calling me to serve His Holy Church in Apostolic orders. But in what conditions is the Church now living? Is it in the ancient Roman Empire, which was able with its hand of iron to forge all the peoples of the world into a single whole—peoples who received the joyful message of the Christian teaching with a child-like simplicity of soul and did not oppose the grace of God? No. The world in which the Orthodox Church now lives in such lowliness has lost its spiritual virginity. False teachers and false "christs" have overrun every place under the sun and have told each people about Christ in accordance with their false teachings, so that only the name of the Saviour remains—and this name is used to cover an invented Christ. In our zeal we would almost be justified in exclaiming, "It would be better for them to know nothing at all about Christ, for it is easier to teach something for the first time than to re-teach it."

Is the Lord calling me to archpastoral service in a world which is ruled by a pious ruler anointed by God? No. There is no longer one holding the sceptre, "he who withholds" is no more, and after him there is hardly a single ruler left who considers those things to be evil, which are considered evil by the Orthodox Church. Deprived of such powerful support from the secular authorities, the bishop often, with pain in his heart, has to be an impotent witness while wizards and sorcerers plunder the flock of Christ, destroy these "little ones," for the mighty hand of God's Anointed One is not there to oppose them.

Although the whole world is divided into two camps, nevertheless the same cosmopolitan strivings are at work in both. The frontiers between peoples are being erased, national values are perishing, turning the different peoples into a single mass. Yet we are confronted by a strange paradox: there was much more love in the world than there is now, when so much malice and ill-will has entered in to the outward unity of peoples.

Many hasty minds would wish to submit the Orthodox Church also to this dangerous tendency, and in submitting to it, certain large parts of the Church are abandoning their native Mother Church and are hurling themselves like meteorites into the abyss, vanishing completely from the heavenly vault of Orthodoxy.

I confess with my whole soul that one cannot leave one's own Mother Church, unless it is by growing out of it through sanctity as St. Nicholas, for example, grew to such an extent that our Russian people has always venerated and loved him as if he were their own Russian saint. Nevertheless, is it really possible to grow out of one's own Church, without first casting off one's earthly shell?

So these are the difficulties facing the Orthodox Russian Church Abroad. And such is the path of episcopal service, a path of bearing one's cross, on which I am setting out. I will need much help, and especially I will need the augmented grace of God, the grace of wisdom and intelligence, which can help me to find in my soul such a wide range of spiritual qualities, from extreme condescension to unhesitating martyrdom. Pray for me, most reverend bishops, and you also, Christ-loving Orthodox people, that the Lord would fill me with these spiritual riches. This is a task for all. Amen.

After the consecration, when handing the archpastoral staff to newly consecrated Bishop Vitaly of Montevideo, Bishop Nathaniel addressed his new brother bishop with the customary words of counsel. "Today the Holy Church has raised you up to the highest level which can be attained in the whole world," he began. "On the day of the Holy Apostles Peter and Paul, the Church has made you an apostle—a bishop—a supreme representative of the Church, a prince and a repository of the Church, as the Holy Hieromartyr Cyprian of Carthage said, 'where the bishop is, there is the Church.'" He then went on and described the exalted nature of the episcopal office according to the teachings of the Church Fathers:

Does this mean, that there is really nobody and nothing which can deliver a blow to one following this sacred calling and that there are no falls or even attacks which can affect the person arrayed in this sacred office?

Alas, no. There is one person in the world who cannot only strike out at the person bearing the Christ-like orders of the hierarchy, but can also cast him down from the heights, make him the most miserable and despised creature—salt that has lost its savour, dust and ashes.

This is the person himself who bears this sacred calling. Only he can debase himself, cast himself down from the heights. Nobody and nothing else in the world can do this.

But he can do so himself. Created in the image and likeness of God, with full power over the realm of his spirit and his heart, man always, in all circumstances and in any vocation, preserves this, his terrible and great property of inner freedom, and the exalted office of bishop does not limit this freedom in the slightest degree. Following the calling of bishop, just as any other calling, man remains man—the author of his own fate, the director of his own heart, which can incline to the right or to the left, to good or to evil.

How blessed is he if it inclines towards good! The angels will accompany him on this path. And he, the archpastor, the successor of the Apostles imbued with the fullness of their power, will lead thousands of souls in his flock after him along the path of salvation. He will become a guiding star to which, especially in our times which are so full of darkness, thousands, hundreds of thousands or perhaps even millions of souls thirsting for the light will be drawn. This we know to a small degree from experience.

But woe to him if he slips; if, imitating him who was also in the choir of the Apostles but then became a traitor, he betrays his exalted calling. Truly it would be better for him not to have been born.

Vladyka, hierarch of God, Vitaly! We live in terrible times. The whole world has risen up against God, against the Church of God. We are surrounded on all sides by the hatred of him who has been the enemy from the beginning and of his human servants. They will arm themselves against you with all the strength with which they hate Christ and the Church, inasmuch as you, from this minute, have become the repository of the Church in the fullest and most perfect sense. They will exploit every weakness, your every unsure step, every faltering.

But if this great service is so awesome, so full of dangers, then perhaps it would be better not accept it, to flee from it as from a terrible abyss?

Many even who were strong in spirit have fled.

But they fled from the episcopate at a time when it was not only exalted to the greatest heights spiritually, but also surrounded by outward splendour, and so attracted thousands of the most worthy candidates, and when a large proportion of the million-strong masses of mankind awaited only a sign from the Church of Christ in order to obey her.

But is it possible to flee now, when the Church is left with only a small handful of people, when it has so few to serve it, so few people active, when there are so terrifyingly many who have betrayed her and are now betraying her; but also at a time when the fields of human souls are whiter than ever for harvest and have ripened for what may be the most responsible harvest—the last harvest of all?

However much your heart may tremble, however much it may fear this awesome and exalted lot, you have done right in not fleeing, but submissively bowing beneath the yoke of this Christ-like service.

If you do not betray Christ, Christ will never betray you. Furthermore, in moments when you fall, in hours of weakness, in order to overcome, then you can say to Him with boldness, "I have abandoned Thee, abandon me not. Go forth to seek me, raise me up unto Thy pastures, and unite me unto the sheep of Thy chosen flock."

With Christ there is an unconquerable force, at which all His enemies fear and tremble. As a symbol of this power, you are given this archpastoral staff. Receive it, arm yourself with it in the great warfare for our beloved Lord, who is hated and persecuted by the world; shepherd His sheep which are entrusted to you, and may all the enemies of God be driven away from beneath your feet.

All Saints Podvoria chapel, 1951. Seated left to right: Bishop Leonty of Geneva, Bishop Nathaniel, and the newly consecrated Bishop Vitaly. Standing: Father Sergei Schukin (fourth from left), Protodeacon John Logvinenko (sixth from left), and Hierodeacon Paul (seventh from left). (Source: Deacon Andrew Bond)

St Philip's Church, 1951. Bishop Vitaly (left) and Bishop Nathaniel (right). Behind the bishops: Hierodeacon Paul (left) and Protodeacon John (right). (Source: Archbishop Mark)

Thus inspired, the new bishop prepared for his departure, together with his monastic brotherhood and some of the printing equipment. After celebrating several Sunday services in London, they set sail and arrived in the Brazilian port of Santos on August 23. They were then taken immediately to Sao Paolo, to meet Archbishop Theodossy. Before long Bishop Vitaly organized a new monastery in Villa Alpina, a suburb of Sao Paolo. In 1955 Bishop Vitaly and the monastery were moved to Canada by decision of the Holy Synod; first to Edmonton and then, in 1958, to Montreal. In 1986 Archbishop Vitaly was elected first hierarch of the Russian Church Abroad; he served in that capacity as metropolitan until he retired in 2001. The London parish was as stunned by Bishop Vitaly's departure in 1951 as it was by his arrival in 1948. His time in England created such a strong impression on the parish that it is surprising to find that he was only there for three years. He sowed many seeds, both in London and in the north of England, but the duty of watering and nurturing them would fall upon his successors.

CHAPTER 14

[1951–1959] Archbishop Nikodem: The Preston Diocese

Bishop Nathaniel of Preston and The Hague

As Bishop Vitaly sailed for Brazil, Bishop Nathaniel remained in London temporarily as the head of the parish. A period of great social upheaval continued while tens of thousands of refugees resettled in different parts of the world in the aftermath of World War II. At the same time, the Russian Church Abroad received an influx of new clergy; the Synod of Bishops was faced with the task of ensuring that the clergy who were distributed among the various dioceses throughout the world matched the concentration of parishioners. It was this consideration that dictated the transfer of Bishop Vitaly to Brazil and also prompted reorganization of the Diocese of Western Europe, which was implemented at a meeting of the Synod in December 1950. On that occasion the life of the parishes in England was directly affected by events in places as far away as China, which had been taken over by a communist regime in 1949.

In 1950 the synodal headquarters moved from Munich to New York. That year also marked the death of Metropolitan Seraphim (Lade) of Germany, a senior hierarch who enjoyed wide respect. At the same time, Archbishop John (Maximovitch) of Shanghai, a bishop renowned for his ascetic life and pastoral gifts, was forced to leave China as a result of the communist seizure of power. He helped most of his flock emigrate and assisted some to obtain visas to the United States. Many more went to Australia. The Synod made use of Archbishop John's abilities and his immense authority as an ascetic and a man of prayer to unite the life of the Church in Western Europe. At the same time, he retained responsibility for the remnants of the Russian Mission to China and the few parishes of the Shanghai diocese that remained outside mainland China.

At its meeting on December 15, 1950, the Synod made the following resolution:

> To appoint Archbishop John of Shanghai as representative of the Synod of Bishops in Western Europe. . . . To divide the Diocese of Western Europe into two dioceses, entrusting the principal, continental part of the previous diocese (France, Switzerland, Belgium and Luxembourg) to Archbishop John, who should assume the title of Bishop of Brussels and Western Europe. The parishes in England and Holland are to be entrusted to Bishop Nathaniel, who should assume the title of Bishop of Preston and The Hague.

Thus the parishes in England became known as the Preston Diocese until 1957, when the name was again changed. Preston is a city in Lancashire, north of Manchester, where a large concentration of Russian workers lived after the war. Services were held in rented premises by visiting clergy. No permanent parish was ever established there. Preston was used in preference to London because of the convention whereby the title Bishop of London was only used by the Anglican incumbent. (Evidently this was not appreciated by Bishop Nicholas, who was consecrated as Orthodox Bishop of London in 1929.) Preston was a centre of Orthodox life and perhaps the only city that had a Russian Church community but no Anglican bishop.

So, in accordance with the synodal decision, Bishop Nathaniel took up residence in London (which is approximately halfway between Preston and The Hague) in the spring of 1951. After Bishop Vitaly departed in August

Clergy at Walsingham, 1951: (left to right) Deacon Sergei Jefimenko, Father George Moisseyevsky, Father Ambrose (Pogodin), and Bishop Nathaniel (far right). (Source: Antonina Ananin)

of that year, Bishop Nathaniel became rector of the London parish, assisted by Father George Moisseyevsky and two newly ordained deacons, Fathers Philemon Zadworny and Sergei Jefimenko.

Using the printing presses and the equipment that had been left behind, Bishop Nathaniel resumed the work of printing spiritual literature. By the end of the year, the first edition of a new magazine was ready, *Orthodox Messenger (Pravoslavni Vestnik)—Publication of the London Diocese of the Russian Church Abroad.* It began with the following message from the editor:

> On 1st January new style, during the holy days which precede the Nativity, we are publishing the first edition of our church magazine, *Orthodox Messenger*, thereby reestablishing our printing work for the church in London after a short interruption. In character and general direction our journal will be a continuation of the *Orthodox Review* which was published here for several years by Archimandrite (now Bishop) Vitaly. He is planning to continue publishing his journal under the same name in Brazil, where he has now gone to serve the Church. For our part we will attempt, under this new title, to give our parishioners some words of instruction from the Church—something which is always needed, but especially in our evil, confusing times.

In addition to his warm, open-hearted character, Bishop Nathaniel was distinguished by a breadth of learning in both secular and theological subjects. This enabled him to understand the doubts and concerns of contemporary people, and he strove to lead them back to the Church by showing that only through Orthodoxy could they fulfill their highest ideals. Many of his apologetic writings were directed toward new immigrants who came from the Soviet Union knowing very little about God or the Church. Many of these writings were reprinted in special editions for distribution within the Soviet Union. Here, as an example, is a talk that was based on the Church's prayer *Lord, have mercy*.

> All the Orthodox Church's services are shot through with a prayerful cry: *Kyrie eleison*—Lord, have mercy!
>
> This is man's most ancient prayer. Church tradition tells us that when our forefathers sinned and were expelled from Paradise, they sat "opposite Paradise" and began their blessed path of repentance, which made possible the salvation of the human race, with precisely this penitential cry of the soul: "Have mercy!" "O Merciful One, have mercy on me who am fallen!"

The most sacred Old Testament compositions, the Psalms and prophecies, incessantly repeat the words "have mercy." "Have mercy upon me, O God, according to Thy great mercy" (Psalm 50). "Pray unto God, that he will have mercy on us," says the prophet Malachi (1: 9).

The first prayer to be heard in the first temple of the true God to be built on earth was, "O Lord God, hearken and have mercy!" (1 Kgs 8:30)

This is the first prayer that an Orthodox child learns, and it is also the last prayer which the waning consciousness of a dying man repeats just before death.

And if, on calm days, in the quagmire of ordinary, everyday life, the words "Lord, have mercy" are very often repeated indifferently, as a familiar refrain learnt by rote, still, in moments of either danger, or torment, or the burning awareness of the depth of the abyss into which one has fallen—then this brief cry of prayer suddenly becomes filled with the most profound meaning and power. And, like a man condemned to death standing before the judge, in whose glance he can read the last hope of pardon, and like someone dangerously ill imploring the doctor who can save him, so the human soul begins to cry out to Almighty God: "Lord, have mercy!"

Many inspired and most vivid prayers have been composed by humanity. But when death looks into one's eyes, or when the unbearable fire of shame burns the soul, then man cannot find the strength in himself to repeat the calm words of these prayers, but in place of all other forms of prayer he cries out, "Lord, have mercy," and in these three words he finds the absolute basis of all prayerful petitions.

And when, beyond all hope, it appears that this cry has been heard, when the Merciful Hand turns away the danger of death that seemed inevitable, or leads the soul out of a blind alley which seemed to have no way out, then the soul which has been saved will come to love this most brief prayer, "Lord, have mercy," with a strong, unwavering love. Now it will begin to repeat it calmly and lucidly, in all the luminous and the dark, the grievous and the joyful moments of its life.

This is why the Orthodox Church services are so filled with the refrain "Lord, have mercy!" Metropolitan Anthony [Khrapovitsky] teaches that Orthodoxy is preeminently a religion of repentance, and he also teaches that it is the sanctuary of the whole of humanity, and that everything that is truly good, valuable and right in the world, wherever it may be found, belongs essentially to the Orthodox Church. And so, of course, here, in the Orthodox temple, in Orthodox prayer, in the appropriate place, in a prayer which is repeated a countless number of times, we should expect to find humanity's most fundamental form of prayer—"Lord, have mercy," both as the cry of a soul which sees itself on the verge of perdition, and as the calm, joyful and grateful repetition of the prayer which has brought salvation.

Both individuals, entire peoples and the whole of humanity have already stood many times on the brink of destruction, and have been saved from it many times by God's merciful Hand. How then, are we not to repeat "Lord, have mercy" a great multitude of times? How can we not repeat these words, whose salutary power we have witnessed, when destruction in a hitherto unheard-of measure has drawn near to humanity, has taken forms which can clearly be perceived and persistently stare us in the face?

Undoubtedly, we can foretell that this, the first prayer of the human race, first pronounced by the lips of our forefathers after they had sinned, in that bitter hour of their expulsion from Paradise, will also be the last prayer to come from human lips, when human history comes to an end at the sound of the Archangel's trumpet. In the trembling of the last few minutes before the end, human souls will have neither the strength nor the time for other prayers besides this, the briefest and most unfathomably profound one: "Lord, have mercy, spare and have mercy!"

On September 24, 1951, the Synod resolved "to transfer Abbot Nikodem from Geneva to London, to help Bishop Nathaniel, at the same time advancing him to the rank of archimandrite." However, when Archimandrite Nikodem arrived in London on January 18, 1952, he found Bishop Nathaniel packing his bags to leave. Bishop Nathaniel had been in England since the previous spring. However, he had not obtained the necessary permit to live permanently in the United Kingdom, and so was required to leave until this could be arranged. He planned to go to the Monastery of St Job in Munich, and on February 4, 1952, the Synod gave him a two-month leave of absence from his diocese for this purpose. Temporary administration of the Preston Diocese was entrusted to Archimandrite Nikodem in the capacity of diocesan administrator reporting directly to the Synod of Bishops. Earlier, on January 21, the parishes in Holland had been returned to the Diocese of Western Europe, so Archimandrite Nikodem's responsibilities were confined to England.

Bishop Nathaniel never returned to live permanently in the United Kingdom. His energies were needed to a greater degree in Germany, where there were many more Russian refugees than in England. In November 1952 the Synod gave him the additional responsibility of organizing a diocese in North Africa where there were many Russian emigrants at the time but very few clergy. In March 1952 Father Archimandrite Nikodem told those at the annual meeting of the London parish that Bishop Nathaniel would be coming for a visit during the fifth week of Lent to celebrate the Lenten and Paschal services and to wind up his affairs in the diocese. He stayed until June 22 and later made two short visits, each of two weeks' duration, in October and December 1952. Although he was no longer commemorated in church as diocesan bishop, the peoples' attachment to him was such that a special petition was added to one of the litanies at each liturgy to pray for him, invoking God's help in his labours in a new country and new diocese.

Vladyka Nathaniel expressed his affection for London in the following poem, which he wrote—in English—during his first visit to London in July 1938. To compose a poem in a foreign language is no easy feat; even if the metre breaks down in places, his thoughts and feelings are clear:

To London

During days and months of endless peregrination,
In various countries swept by many storms,
I learnt to love you, jewel of Great Britain,
You, the huge city built above the banks of Father Thames!

I learnt to love the emerald green of parks and gardens.
The endless maze of countless roads and streets.
The sea of faces knowing how to keep,
Everywhere and in all circumstances their calm and dignified air!

I learnt to love London because during so many troubled years
London alone knew how to keep the tenets of goodness.
Kindness towards everybody, merriment and freedom:
An unbroken legacy of years now past.

But most of all I love you for the remembrance still found here.
Of those days unfortunately gone for ever.
When the religion of Christ ruled the world.
And His Cross was a sign for men.

Archimandrite Nathaniel

Archimandrite Nikodem: Life Before Coming to England

Although he came originally to assist the bishop, Archimandrite Nikodem remained as diocesan administrator. A period of greater stability in the life of the parish and diocese ensued, characteristic of a pattern that was observed around the world as displaced persons put down roots in their new countries. As priest, and later as bishop and then archbishop, he remained at his post in London for almost twenty-five years, until his death in 1976. This is all the more remarkable because he was already sixty-eight years old when he first arrived in England, well past retirement age in secular professions.

Vladyka Nikodem, whose secular name had been Nikolai Vasilievitch Nagaieff, was always reluctant to speak of his life before he accepted the monastic tonsure. When asked if he had any photographs or souvenirs, he replied that he had burnt them before he became a monk. Yugoslavia, where he lived before the war, was full of Russian émigrés who clung zealously to ranks and titles. Once someone was introduced to Nikolai Vasilievitch, who was at the time a modest piano teacher. He asked Nikolai Vasilievitch's surname and was told "Nagaieff." "Not the General Nagaieff?" replied the astounded acquaintance. "Yes, it's true, I used to be a general," replied Nikolai Vasilievitch. In old Russia the rank of general carried immense social status, but Nikolai Vasilievitch was already immersed in spiritual life, with thoughts of becoming a monk.

Nikolai Vasilievitch was born on April 28, 1883, in Abo (now called Turku), Finland, which was at that time part of the Russian Empire. He was born into a large, traditional family of the Russian nobility. As a young man, Nikolai Vasilievitch studied at the First Cadet Corps in St Petersburg and at St Paul's Military Academy, from which he graduated with the rank of sergeant-major. Then he was promoted to the Second Battalion of the Infantry Guards, which was stationed at Tsarskoye Selo to guard the residence of the Emperor Nicholas II. Second Lieutenant Nagaieff frequently came into contact with the emperor in the officers' mess and in later life remembered these encounters with affection.

In 1910 he graduated from the Academy of the General Staff and was entrusted with command of a company. When war broke out in 1914, he went into battle with his regiment and was seriously wounded in the leg. He was sent to the rear to recover in a hospital that was organized by the Empress Alexandra, where the empress herself tended his wounds. After recuperating, he returned to the front and later received the Cross of St George and other medals for distinguished service.

Nikolai Vasilievitch had a musical ear and a talent for playing the piano, which he turned to his advantage during evenings spent in the officers' mess. Although he was not particularly anxious to drink with his fellow officers or join in their long, noisy conversations, he remained popular by playing the piano for them for hours at a time. Nevertheless, he was not unsociable and hoped to marry; he achieved this shortly before the Revolution when he married his childhood friend, Countess Vera Sollogub.

During the Civil War he was an officer on the general staff of General Wrangel in the south of Russia. After the Civil War he was evacuated, first to Constantinople and then to Yugoslavia, where eventually his wife joined him. Conditions were very difficult. His wife was stricken with heart disease and became completely incapacitated. He gave music lessons to support himself and his wife and, at the same time, looked after her as if she were a child. After she died he devoted himself completely to the life of the Church and became an active member of the Brotherhood of St Seraphim of Sarov. The brotherhood met in Belgrade under the direction of the hierarchs of the Russian Church Abroad and were devoted to the study of the tradition of the Orthodox Church.

In 1954, on the eve of his consecration as bishop, Archimandrite Nikodem gave an address in which, according to custom, he recalled with gratitude the spiritual influences that had affected the earlier years of his life:

> The spiritual task—that of serving the Church at the present critical moment in her life—which has now fallen to me, was not indicated either through birth into a clerical family or through my education. However, as far as I can remember, I was always drawn to God's temple from my earliest years, even before I acquired a conscious attitude towards prayer. My soul gained an affinity with the atmosphere of the Church. Later, during adolescence and after I entered the military school, my spiritual education was greatly assisted by the talks given by our instructor in God's Law, Archpriest Basil Preobrazhensky, who subsequently became a vicar bishop of the Moscow Diocese, and of whom I have preserved grateful memories.
>
> However, the life and influence of the environment in which I grew up and began my independent life did not always provide favourable conditions in which the seed sown by this good shepherd could speedily bear fruit. "Thorns sprang up and choked them" (Matt 8:7). Still years had to pass, spent in the service of the Tsar and the Fatherland in the military profession. I had to pass through the stormy years of war and revolution, to see peoples' sufferings at close quarters and experience such suffering

myself, to stand before the very face of death, to feel through this the nothingness of the values of earthly life, before the Lord called me to the service of His Church and poured out His grace in a living torrent.

The first days when I entered into the life of the Church are unforgettable. Unforgettable also is the group which surrounded me in those days, a group of people seeking the city which is on high, and bound together by God's grace into a spiritual closeness which is rare in the life of lay-people—the Brotherhood of St. Seraphim! Many servants of the Church joined in its life and work for the Church and made their small contributions, like the widow's mite, out of the talents God had given them. It also owed much to the fervent zeal of its leader, Peter Sergeyevitch Lopoukhin. In spiritual proximity to him, and with his help, during that period I acquired an understanding of the Church and the life of the Church, which I was later destined to preach to others.

Participation in the brotherhood brought me into close contact with the most outstanding hierarchs of our time: His Beatitude Metropolitan Anthony, who ordained me to the first ecclesiastical degree, that of reader, and blessed me to serve the Church. The wisdom and kindness of this hierarch of God are forever imprinted on my heart. The brotherhood also brought me close to Archbishop Theophan of Poltava, with whom I later corresponded and from whom I later received much advice taken from the inspired writings of the Holy Fathers. It also brought me into contact with a number of future archpastors, including you, Most Reverend Vladyka,[1] my present father and teacher. For a long time you were living at too great a distance[2] for me to be able to borrow oil from your lamp; I had only the image of your life in Christ before me.

For a number of years I visited the famous and memorable Milkovo Monastery in Serbia, where I came to know some of the brotherhood as well as the unforgettable abbot, Schema-archimandrite Amvrossy, and where I came to know the spirit and order of monastic life. There I was protected by the caring hand of Archimandrite Tikhon, now Archbishop, who helped me overcome my uncertainties and strengthened my resolve. After him, my teacher of spiritual life and true elder was Schema-archimandrite Kirik, who for many years had been the spiritual father of St. Panteleimon's monastery on Mount Athos. He was a zealous instructor in piety for many who turned to him for advice during the time that he was in Serbia.

When the Most Reverend Metropolitan Anastassy was elected to lead our Church, through him God's voice was directed towards me, calling me to receive holy orders.[3] And so, from the grace-bestowing hands of the First Hierarch I received both the monastic tonsure and ordination to the priesthood [in 1943]. My spiritual father at the tonsure and guide on my first steps in the monastic life was Archimandrite Averky. The path of my service passed in various obediences: life in the field as a military chaplain and the hardships of battle conditions during the last war [1944–1945]; helping to build a monastic community in Munich and staying there for three years as a spiritual father[4] [1945–1949]; pastoral work in France near Paris[5] [1949–1951]; in Geneva, and finally London, where I have administered the Preston Diocese for two years.

Development of the Parish and Diocese Under Archimandrite Nikodem

When Archimandrite Nikodem arrived in England at the age of sixty-eight with little knowledge of English—although he gradually learned what he called "bazaar language," sufficient for shopping and basic practical needs—he was at an obvious disadvantage compared with his predecessors. This contrast was illustrated by the following amusing incident related by a young parishioner who opened the door at 14 St Dunstan's Road to an official from the Gas Board. "You mean you speak Hinglish?" said the visitor in amazement. He said he had been trying to get into the house for three weeks to repair a leaking pipe. "Now your Mr Oustino, he was alright, and your Mr Levovo was all right too, although I must say, he left something to be desired," continued the visitor, coming somewhere close to the surnames of Bishops Vitaly and Nathaniel, "but this lot . . . all I ever get out of them is 'No-milk-today-thank-you-very-much,' and they shut the door before I can get another word in."

Archimandrite Nikodem (Nagaieff), 1953. (Source: Antonina Ananin)

Among his parishioners, Father Nikodem—later Vladyka Nikodem—was a controversial figure. He remained first and foremost a monk, and there were many among his congregation who never fully appreciated his deep spiritual qualities, but saw him as a withdrawn, reserved clergyman who nevertheless was respected for how beautifully he celebrated the services. For example, one parishioner wrote,

> I was not close to Vladyka Nikodem because at the beginning I was still quite young, and although I did not know that he was a military man in his secular life, I felt an overpowering military authority in his presence and did not feel free to chat as I and most other young people did with his predecessors. . . . His sermons in the church were very touching and deeply emotional for us. He often recalled Holy Russia and church life there.

However, another former parishioner who established a closer relationship said that he "possessed a gift of eldership, as can be confirmed by those who were his spiritual children." This individual recalled the advice he received from Vladyka Nikodem as he set out on the path of monastic life:

> God does not reveal His mysteries immediately. The training in the spiritual life is a slow and gradual process, during which many mistakes occur. Thus we glimpse how God's mysteries were revealed to him [Vladyka Nikodem], not through book-learning and theology courses, but by struggling in piety.
>
> For the monastic Vladyka taught a complete renunciation of the world, although his advice was always tempered with a wise discretion. He once told the story of a monk of the desert who had a pet rooster, which woke him each morning. The monk was very attached to his pet; but one morning the devil sought to snare him by this attachment. The rooster, rather this time the devil, came to his cell door and scratched and crowed, and made such a din that it was obvious something was wrong. The monk hurried out, without guarding himself with the cross or prayer, to see what was up. The rooster, by running a short distance and then anxiously turning back from time to time, gave the monk to understand that he should follow him. The monk did so. And the rooster led him high up into a mountain, and it was only when he was led into impassable places and trapped over a chasm, that the "rooster" disappeared, revealing its true identity. Perhaps for some, just a quaint story; but in it Vladyka was trying to impart some teaching: the need for unattachedness to any thing of this world, the need for attentiveness, and of always turning to the Saviour—these are the lessons which Vladyka wanted to impart. But he was not fanatical or extreme in his preaching of separation from worldly interests. "Renunciation not of life itself in the world, but of its dark side is necessary," he wrote. He realized also that only to the extent that one separated oneself from concern with that dark side did one become enlightened: "You want to entrust yourself to Father X," he wrote, "but he, you write,

> doesn't give you any spiritual guidance. This means that he does not possess [*lit.* bear on himself] the gift of eldership." Vladyka then explained that this was because this father was involved in various concerns and enterprises, and he concluded: "But eldership requires separation from worldly concerns and a whole life of prayer."

Such were the ideals that inspired Vladyka Nikodem. One could rightly say that his greatest gift was as a spiritual father of individual parishioners rather than as a leader of the Church community, although his service as leader of the parish and diocese was certainly zealous and irreproachable. His other great gift, which was more widely appreciated, was the great reverence with which he celebrated the Divine Services.

The following passage, taken from a talk he gave in 1954, gives a glimpse of how he experienced the Divine Services—as a real contact with the spiritual world:

> What was it that guided the Divinely-wise Fathers of the Church when they put together the order of the services and introduced it into the Church typicon? In its earthly images and actions the Church on earth reflects that which genuinely exists in the Heavenly sphere, that which was revealed in part in the visions granted to the prophets and, especially, to that seer of Divine Mysteries, the Apostle John the Theologian, and is imprinted in the Apocalypse. It is from there, from this life of the Heavenly realm, that our priestly exclamations and the arrangement of the holy altar are taken. All these things therefore are established by God. This is why the Orthodox services have so great a power to influence the soul of the believer, as well as attracting the heterodox solely by the power of their Divine grace. Thus our Church order of life reproduces and makes manifest that which really exists in the realm of spiritual being.
>
> An echo of the angelic hymns of praise is repeated on earth by the frail lips of mortals, while rays of the Unwaning Light find their reflection in the darkened minds and hearts of men.

When Archimandrite Nikodem arrived in England at the beginning of 1952, he found three fully organized parishes with their own priests and churches—London, Bradford, and Manchester.[6] In London Father Nikodem had an assistant, Father George Moisseyevsky. Together they served the London parish and also travelled frequently to serve the needs of scattered groups of faithful throughout England. The largest communities were in Preston and Oldham.

In May 1952 Father Sergei Schukin left Bradford for Canada, and Father George Moisseyevsky moved to Bradford to take his place. Priest-monk Ambrose (Pogodin) was sent from France to be assistant priest in London. When Father Moisseyevsky left for Brazil later that year,[7] Father Amvrossy moved to Bradford in his place. Because of the constant travelling, Father Nikodem needed an assistant in London and so he appealed to Metropolitan Anastassy for help. As a result, Father George Cheremetieff was sent from Germany. Father George remained in London until his death in 1971. Together with Father Nikodem they formed an almost ideal partnership, complementing each other's qualities and enjoying close mutual confidence. Father George remained Vladyka Nikodem's father-confessor until the end of his life.

Father George was a descendant from the aristocratic Cheremetieff family, known in pre-Revolutionary Russia for its great wealth. He served as a recruiting officer for a Cavalier Guards regiment. This brought him into constant contact with various types of people throughout Russia and gave him great insight into human nature. Between the wars he lived in Paris, and after World War II he worked with refugee organizations, trying to save people from forced repatriation. He was based in the Fischbek camp. He acquired such tact in dealing with people that displaced persons felt that he was one of them, although he came from a very different background. He provided them great comfort. The people in the camp persuaded him to become a priest, thereby renouncing his status as Count Cheremetieff of the Russian nobility. He spoke fluent English, French, German, and Polish and even some Georgian. On occasion he heard confessions in all of these languages and had a book with the prayers for before and after confession written in several languages. He always found a way to peoples' hearts, overcoming initial hostility with a sense of humour. He recounted an incident during one of his train journeys to serve the provincial parishes. Some passengers laughed at him and asked

Father George Cheremetieff conducting the wedding of George and Liubov Volossevich in 1953 at St Philip's. (Source: George Volossevich)

his name. "Father George," he replied. They then tried to quote the passage in the Gospel that says, "Call no man your father." Instead of starting a theological argument, he said, "Well then, don't call me 'Father,' call me 'Dad.'" The young passengers then started laughing with Father George and, as the train trip went on, they became good friends.

Father George's health was not good, even when he arrived in England. He had a weak heart and a hunchbacked appearance that grew more pronounced as he grew older. Tatiana Danilewicz recalled,

> When Father George Cheremetieff first appeared in St. Philip's Church at Victoria, I thought to myself, "How could they have sent such an ugly-looking priest to the capital?" This thought was truly a sin.
>
> Serving the provincial parishes as well as London, Father George used to stay in Nottingham with some good friends of mine, whom I had known in the refugee camps in Austria. Once, while visiting this family, I made Father George's acquaintance and realized how deceptive appearances can be, especially as people become older.
>
> A good shepherd and a man with a quite unusual cast of soul, he did not take pride in his descent from one of the famous families of old Russia; on the contrary, he preferred not to mention it. He was descended from Count Boris Petrovich Cheremetieff, who had been a collaborator with Peter the Great and Commander-in-Chief at the Battle of Poltava. As Count George Alexandrovich Cheremetieff, [Father George] had belonged to an elite Life-Guard regiment, led a highly cultured life, with a command of several languages, surrounded by luxury in his youth. Now, in London, as modest Father George, he did not demand anything for himself. At first he found lodgings behind a curtain in a corner of an upstairs corridor, then in a dismal basement room, and then he acted as a kind of stoker for the furnace at the Podvoria.
>
> During the lifetime of the Grand Duchess Xenia Alexandrovna he was her spiritual father and, unselfish and decrepit, he brought consolation and reassurance to ordinary lay people.

In 1953 four clergymen and two parishes of the Polish Orthodox Church in England joined the Russian Church Abroad. This came as a consequence of the death of their bishop, Archbishop Savva, a few years earlier. Of these clergymen, one (Father Nicholas Makarewicz) soon left England and another (Father Vladimir Petruczyk) died the following year. This left Father John Sawicz and Protodeacon Nicholas Jakimowicz, who joined the clergy of the

London parish. This expansion of the clergy was more than offset by the addition of two parishes, one in Nottingham and the other in Leeds, both of which needed to be served by visiting clergymen. Neither parish had its own premises; both used side-chapels of Anglican churches that were set up as Orthodox churches with a small iconostasis. In addition, ties were established with Father Anthony Gramatins, a priest of the Latvian Orthodox Church, who served a flock of refugees that formed after the annexation of Latvia to the Soviet Union during the war. These people were scattered throughout the United Kingdom. Sometimes he served at the Russian church in London, adding prayers in Latvian for his parishioners. At other times he served in the provincial parishes of the Church Abroad, tending to the needs both of the Russians and the Latvians living in the area. Father Nicholas Hindo of the Estonian Orthodox Church also established ties with the Russian Diocese.

Meanwhile, the parishes at Bradford and, particularly, Manchester remained the principal centres of church life in the north of England. George Druzhakin, a member of the London Cossack community, described a visit to the Manchester parish in 1955:

> On Sunday 7 August I had the good fortune to visit the Russian Orthodox Church in Manchester. Father Nicholas Popoff was serving. The church was full, with people standing in the corridor. Children were being lifted up by their young mothers and their grandmothers to kiss the holy icons. Some of them tried to light their own candles, although they could barely reach the candle stands. The children behaved magnificently in church, while the very small ones made themselves at home on the floor, "praying" and amusing themselves in their own special language, which would be understood only by the Almighty and, of course, their own mothers. They were all taken up to receive Holy Communion—an example worthy of praise and imitation. After the service Father Nicholas invited us all into a nearby hall where the Parish Council had organized a celebration of the Day of Russian Culture.

Thus, within two years of Archimandrite Nikodem's arrival, the Preston Diocese had grown considerably, with the addition of new parishes and clergymen and acquisition of the church house in Manchester. At that time, it far exceeded the scale of church organization that existed before the war. Nevertheless, Archimandrite Nikodem's primary responsibility remained the parish in London. Every year, in accordance with established practice, he gave a report at the annual parish meeting. He outlined events that affected the parish during the past year, voiced concern over problems facing the parish and the Church as a whole, and imparted words of instruction. These carefully prepared annual reports preserved in the Church archives provide authentic and accurate information about the period. In his first such report given in 1952, he mentioned by name some of the most active members of the parish and concluded,

> Having in the parish so many valued workers devoted to the Church, both mentioned and unmentioned, we feel assured for the future of our London parish, which is one of the chief pillars of our Church faithful to the Council of Bishops. However stormy may be the sea through which our ecclesiastical ship is sailing, we have, in the person of our most active parishioners, a trusty crew, which has already proved its devotion to that one true path for the Church—the path of the Russian Church Abroad, faithful to the Council of Bishops and led by the Most Reverend Metropolitan Anastassy.

He referred, first, to the churchwarden—Count Wladimir Petrovitch Kleinmichel—whom he called a "resolute fighter for the interests of our Conciliar Church and a careful manager of the parish's material resources." (Count Kleinmichel had taken on the responsibilities of churchwarden in addition to those of treasurer, which he had borne since the 1930s.) Father Nikodem went on to mention the secretary of the Parish Council, Alexei Stepanovitch Ananin, and George Dimitrievitch Pesiakoff, whom he called the "chief architect of the Podvoria building." This was perhaps a rather grandiloquent title. In fact, Mr Pesiakoff ran a small building firm and willingly undertook all kinds of repairs and redecorations at 14 St Dunstan's Road. The rector also mentioned Valeria Ivanovna Ampenoff, head of the parish sisterhood, and Alexandra Petrovna Albrecht, who looked after the Podvoria church and made new vestments, as well as Tatiana Pavlovna Guerken-Glovatsky, a doctor who helped him as a secretary dealing with his English-language correspondence. In addition, Father Nikodem thanked the members of the choir and the many others who, with no official position in the parish, helped with the singing and reading during services as well as with maintaining the church, often to the detriment of their own material well-being.

At the same time, Father Nikodem pointed out the shortcomings of parish life as he found it, with the hope of achieving a gradual improvement. Having lived in many European cities, he was immediately struck by the immense size of London. He felt the size impeded the growth of the parish as a cohesive community. The most serious problem that he noted was the lack of properly organized religious instruction for children, which led them to drift away from the church. He appealed for people to come forward and help with this work. However, it was not until three years after his arrival in England that a solution to this problem was found with the arrival of nuns from Palestine.[8] He also encouraged the formation of a ladies auxiliary committee to help the poor and sick and ensure that isolated people received the ministrations of the clergy in case of sickness or other needs.

Grand Duchess Xenia, sister of the tsar, was among the faithful in the care of the Russian Church Abroad. Then in her eighties, she was unable to go to London to attend church, but she had a tiny house-chapel in her apartment in Hampton Court Palace, where Archimandrite Nikodem visited her. He wrote,

> Our church has the honour of caring spiritually for the members of the Russian Imperial House living in England, the senior of whom is the Grand Duchess Xenia Alexandrovna, the sister of the Tsar-Martyr Nicholas II. . . . Her faith, her deep humility and Christian attitude to life reflect the same basic characteristics of the late Tsar-Martyr and the best representatives of the Imperial House.
>
> Every year, in Pascha week, we celebrate the Divine Liturgy, together with some of the hymns from Paschal Matins, sung most expertly by three members of our church choir. The Grand Duchess always asks for the same three people to come, as she has come to know them well. After the service and the Easter meal which follows, she engages the singers in friendly conversation.
>
> Many members of the Grand Duchess's family come to Hampton Court for these Easter services, where they receive confession and Holy Communion. This year [1957] Prince Nikita Alexandrovich came from America with his wife. In addition, there were Prince Andrew, Princess Irina and the Grand Duchess's grandson, Prince Alexander Nikitich, who acts as a reader and subdeacon during the services. Besides this, the services are held there at other times during the year, the Grand Duchess receives Holy Communion at least once a month, and more often when she is feeling unwell. Communion is taken to her by Father George Cheremetieff, who visits her regularly.

When he arrived in England, Archimandrite Nikodem was determined to maintain the daily cycle of monastic services at the Podvoria, which had been started by Bishop Nicholas and then revived by Archimandrite Vitaly. Father Nikodem posed the question to his parishioners, "Do we need this more complete daily cycle of services which, in pre-Revolutionary Russia, was not restricted to monasteries, but was also applied in many parish churches?" He went on to reply, "Our experience of these daily services has shown that they satisfy the spiritual needs of a number of members of the parish who seek to lead a more intensive spiritual life. The fact that there are such people must bring joy to the Christian heart, and we must do all that we can to help them." Daily services would also be attended by people from provincial towns who went to London during the week for various reasons, but had no Orthodox church in their own area, and also those who had jobs that required them to work on Sundays. However, the following year Father Nikodem admitted that conducting the complete cycle of services every day was not practical, especially as many in the regular congregation had left to live overseas. Since the death of Mr Volkovsky two years earlier, the parish did not have a *psalomshchik* of the old school—that is, a layman with a thorough knowledge of the Church typicon who could lead the reading and singing of any service. For the first and fourth weeks of Great Lent, Father Amvrossy from Bradford joined the London community so that the complete Lenten services could be held.

In April 1954, on a Sunday after Easter that was dedicated to the memory of the paralytic healed in the pool of Bethesda (John 1:1–15), Father Nikodem led a pilgrimage to the holy site of Walsingham. Both Archimandrite Vitaly and Archbishop Nestor had encouraged the Orthodox to venerate this shrine where a miraculous appearance of the Mother of God occurred in 1061, at the time of the separation of the Orthodox and Roman Catholic Churches.

A group of parishioners left London at 8:00 a.m. in a hired bus and arrived at Walsingham at 11:00 a.m. Father Nikodem and Priest-monk Amvrossy, together with Deacon Sergei Jefimenko, celebrated the Divine Liturgy in the tiny Orthodox chapel located in the shrine building. The group was joined by about fifty Russians from Cambridge. Almost all the pilgrims received Holy Communion. In his sermon on the paralytic, Father Nikodem spoke of the spiritual paralysis that is the result of remaining in sin and of the means for healing this paralysis, one of which was making pilgrimages to holy places. Then the pilgrims went to the miraculous spring and drank the holy water; some also washed their faces with the water. After a short rest, the akathist to the Mother of God was sung, together with the canon to the Life-giving Spring (from the Matins of the Friday of Pascha week) to which the chapel was dedicated. In the words of Archimandrite Nikodem, "Many of the pilgrims were granted clearly to feel the grace of this holy place, and departed with compunction in their souls."

They were all anxious to make this pilgrimage a regular feature of parish life, and it was repeated almost every year thereafter. After Father Nikodem had become a bishop, one pilgrim recalled, "I particularly remember one pilgrimage to Walsingham led by Vladyka. We sang hymns to the Mother of God throughout the whole journey, which prepared us spiritually. After we arrived, the Vigil service began at 6:00 p.m. and ended at 1:00 in the morning, after which Vladyka continued hearing confessions until 2:00 a.m."

Living in what was for him still a foreign country, surrounded by people of a strange culture and religion, Archimandrite Nikodem placed a high value on maintaining spiritual links with other Orthodox communities in England. At the 1953 annual meeting of the parish, he observed,

> The unity of the Church of Christ, which consists of a number of separate national churches, demands that we should maintain brotherly bonds in Christ with these other churches: oneness of thought in matters of the faith, communion in prayer, mutual help and co-operation in gathering Christ's harvest. This is the purpose of the Association of Orthodox Clergy in England which has representatives from all the national Orthodox Churches. Its work at present is concentrated on protecting the interests of the Orthodox clergy in England. Our closest ties are with the Serbian Orthodox Church.

In the previous year, Archimandrite Nikodem had concelebrated with Serbian clergy at the blessing of a new church in the presence of King Peter II of Yugoslavia, who was now living in exile in Western Europe. The church was blessed by Bishop Nicholas of Ochrid, who had conducted services for the London parish on several occasions in the past.[9] During Lent in 1953 Archimandrite Nikodem was asked by Father Miloje Nikolich, the administrator of the Serbian Church in England, to hear the confessions of all the Serbian clergy when they came to London for a diocesan conference. Father Nikodem joined them for the Presanctified Liturgy and for a meal afterwards.

In 1953 the Association of Orthodox Clergy in England organized the first "Pan-Orthodox" celebration of the Divine Liturgy, at which clergy from all the Orthodox Churches in England concelebrated. The service was held on November 29 in the Serbian Church. Archbishop Athenagoras of the Greek Church was the senior celebrant; the second bishop was Bishop

Matthew of the Polish Church. Archimandrite Nikodem, who was one of the concelebrating clergy, commented that somehow the service lacked the splendour of the Russian hierarchical Liturgy, being conducted principally according to the Greek ritual.

The next year's Pan-Orthodox service was held at St Philip's with recently ordained Bishop Nikodem amongst those serving. Describing the sense of oneness he wrote,

> On 14/27 December, in our church of the Holy Dormition [St. Philip's], an event took place which is a rare occurrence in our days when all kinds of divisions are so common—a celebration of the Liturgy by the united clergy of the Orthodox Churches: The Russian Church Abroad, the Serbian, Greek, Polish, Romanian, Latvian and Estonian Churches. The service was led by three bishops: Archbishop Athenagoras, myself and Bishop Matthew. The Anglican Bishop of Gibraltar and the Dean of Westminster Abbey were present as guests.
>
> This service was intended to show the unity of Œcumenical (worldwide) Orthodoxy, which is outwardly fragmented into national churches, but inwardly united through communion in prayer in the One Organism—the Body of Christ. Together with the clergy participating in the service, the whole multitude of people who had gathered, Orthodox of all nationalities, were also united together in prayer. There were also many English people in the church, and some of them were following the service using Orthodox prayer books in English.
>
> The exclamations and litanies were mingled together in various languages, with Greek and English predominating, so as to be understood by the maximum number of people. Our choir responded in the same languages, and generally the result was very impressive. The service proceeded with great outward solemnity and made a deep impression on many of those present.

These accounts testify to the complete mutual acceptance and intercommunion which existed in the 1950s between the Russian Church Abroad and other Orthodox Churches. The Russian Church Abroad was accepted without difficulty as being the legitimate representative of the Russian Church in the United Kingdom.

From his earliest days in England, Father Nikodem had a strong sense of the Church's mission to the non-Orthodox among whom the Russians were dispersed. He took what steps he could to help and encourage the

English converts he found in the parish, despite his very limited knowledge of English. His work with English converts is described further in Chapter 15.

On June 2, 1953, Archimandrite Nikodem attended the coronation of Her Majesty Queen Elizabeth II in Westminster Abbey. He had been invited as the head of the Russian Orthodox Church in Exile in England, and felt it to be a great honour. He kept his invitation as well as the book outlining the order of the ceremony and other mementoes of the occasion for the rest of his life. Among these papers is a sheet of instructions for entering and leaving the Abbey, which had to be followed to the letter. On the bottom of this sheet written in pencil is a phrase that he must have worked hard to memorize to explain himself as the other diplomats and aristocracy were whisked away in their limousines: "I go to the Underground station on foot." On the next Sunday, he served a moleben in St Philip's Church invoking God's blessing on Her Majesty's new reign.

Russian London in the 1950s

Many of the more active parishioners also took leading roles in other Russian organizations in London, which served as focal points for community life and through which help was offered to less fortunate compatriots. Throughout the 1950s and 1960s the Russian Red Cross continued to be active in helping refugees. In 1948 it had been obliged to change its name because it was no longer affiliated with the International Red Cross. Although renamed the Russian Benevolent Society 1917, in Russian circles it continued to be known simply as the "Red Cross." One if its main functions was providing housing for poor and elderly refugees. In 1931 it acquired a house at 16 The Avenue, Bedford Park, London W4. Later, other houses were acquired also in the Chiswick area: 25 Abinger Road; 50, 56, and 58 Woodstock Road; and Nicholas House at 26 Blenheim Road. However, in the early 1950s the most prominent Russian organization in London was still the Russian Refugees Relief Association in Great Britain. Under the continued leadership of Prince Vladimir Galitzine and Count Bennigsen, it began to take on new tasks. As the need to help new immigrants in matters of day-to-day survival diminished, the association developed into a centre that could help them retain connections with their Russian friends and culture.

Through the efforts of Count Bennigsen, two houses were purchased in the Earl's Court area, at 49 Penywern Road and 19 Warwick Road, for a total cost of £11,000. This was financed partly through private fund-raising among the Russian community and English charities, by a mortgage loan of some

£4,000, and by a loan from the British Council for Aid to Refugees. These houses were used to provide accommodation for homeless refugees—in particular, for a group of old people who had been brought over from a refugee camp in Kellerberg in Austria. The association established headquarters at 49 Penywern Road, where its office was open daily from 3:00 to 5:00 p.m. and where the weekly *Bulletin* was printed. Here also there was a club known as *Russki Ochag* ("Russian Centre" or more literally, "Russian Hearth"), where literary meetings and discussions were held.

Obviously commitment to repaying the mortgage loans and taking care of the elderly refugees was substantial in financial terms. In August 1952 a financial crisis was developing. After studying the half-yearly accounts, Count Bennigsen appealed for wider support from the Russian community:

> We must not forget that the Russian Centre is our common heritage. Throughout the year hundreds of visitors have stayed in the house, while many more come on Saturdays and Sundays to sit and talk, the Association's library is constantly acquiring new books, which it would be hard to find elsewhere; we have evening meetings, entertainments and concerts, and of course the *Bulletin* is printed in the house.

After suggesting that a solution could always be found by selling the properties to an English charity on condition that the old people would still be cared for, he continued:

A group of residents outside the Russian Refugees Relief Association home in Penywern Road, London, ca. 1950s. (Source: London Parish Archive)

> But then it will no longer be a "Russian" centre, and everything Russian will gradually disappear—the meetings, the lectures, the opportunity of staying overnight, the printing of the *Bulletin*, even the Russian cooking! To avoid this happening we must work long and hard and, dear friends, we need the help of each one of you.

By 1954 the immediate crisis had passed and the Association was managing to break even. By then the Count had retired and his place as secretary had been taken by Lev Rabenek. In the spring of that year the Association mourned the death of its President, Prince Vladimir Galitzine. "Perhaps many people could have carried out the functions of President," wrote Rabenek, "but it would be hard to find another President who would be a real father and friend to all. To find a place in peoples' hearts, one must first of all bear goodness and love in one's own heart. The Prince was endowed with these qualities by the Lord God in abundance, and he showed his warmth and kindness to all with whom he came into contact."

Giving his annual report in the middle of 1955, Lev Rabenek was able to report that the financial situation had become more stable. In his review of the work of the association, he noted that local authorities were taking an interest in the old peoples' homes: no more than two people were to be allowed per room (previously some rooms had been shared by three occupants) and a member of staff had to live permanently on the premises. This meant that there would be less spare rooms to let out commercially to help cover costs. He reported that between twenty-three and twenty-five people had eaten every day in the centre's dining room at an average cost of only £24 per week—"good, nourishing Russian food, while at Easter the pascha and kulich [special foods for the celebration of Pascha] were of a quality recalling Moscow in the old days." During 1954 the association's office received 1,503 letters (an average of six per working day) and sent out about 1,000 replies, in addition to circulars and other internal correspondence. One hundred parcels containing food, clothing, vitamins, and other supplies had been sent out to the needy, including some who were still living in refugee camps in Germany. The library and reading room were open on Saturday and Sunday evenings from 4:00 to 8:00 p.m. During the year, 244 new books had been acquired through the efforts of Mr A. L. Usovsky, the librarian, who devoted much of his free time to organizing the library and rebinding the books.

The *Bulletin* was retaining its circulation. Started in 1949 when the newspaper *Rossianin* ceased publication, it came out weekly and consisted of eight foolscap-size (8½ × 14 inch) pages printed on a stencil duplicator, although with a professionally printed title page. Its pages were filled with news stories from the national press, with particular emphasis on events in the Soviet Union. The paper's coverage of events in Great Britain included the doings of royalty, whose titles were solemnly translated into Russian—thus the Duke of Edinburgh became *Gertzog Edinbourgski*, the Duchess of Gloucester became *Gertzoginya Glosterskaya*, and so on.

At first, this Russian-language news service was a matter of vital necessity because new immigrants were unable to read the English newspapers. With the passage of time, the emphasis changed to include comment on world affairs from a specifically Russian viewpoint and "practical" articles on topics such as opening a bank account, buying a house, and drawing up a will. On this last subject, a reader complained to the editor, "You say I should leave everything to my wife, but what is the use of this advice if I am living here in England, while my wife is in Siberia?" Many had left relatives behind in the Soviet Union, and while Western journalists developed the science of "Kremlinology" to try to ascertain who was in control in Moscow, displaced persons watched tensely as news of Stalin's death in 1952 filtered through. Had he been murdered? Who would now take control? And, most importantly, how would this affect the lives of ordinary people?

In addition, the *Bulletin* contained notices and reports of events within the Russian community. The back page carried a list of church services for the forthcoming Sunday. The Russian Orthodox Church Abroad was listed first with its different parishes, followed by the Orthodox Church of Poland. The latter was led by Bishop Matthew of Wilno (Vilnius) and had a church in Warwick Road, Earls Court, as well as one in Nottingham. There was no reference to the church of the Moscow Patriarchate, as presumably this did not interest the new immigrants. Every issue contained an advertisement from Baratchevsky's Bookshop at 26 Tottenham Street (just north of Oxford Street)—the only Russian-language bookshop in London.

From time to time, announcements appeared under the heading *Rozysk* (Search), or "Missing Persons," where people separated during wartime upheavals were still trying to make contact with relatives or friends.

The Russian Centre was probably best known for its evening gatherings, organized by the association's cultural and educational department. In 1954 it organized twenty-four literary evenings, nine dances, and two theatrical performances. Tickets were sold by the centre at Baratchevsky's Bookshop and at Mr Pesiakoff's secondhand shop. In a June 1955 article titled "Theatrical Spring," a contributor to the *Bulletin* described with anticipation the new season. "This year, spring has come not only in nature, but also in the social life of Russian London," he wrote. "Now all our theatrical talents have been united under the roof of the Refugees Relief Association, and this is also our springtime! Strange things are happening at No. 49 Penywern Road. Eugene Brey is there, discussing a future performance with Vera Charova . . . " and he went on to name various émigré literati who were offering their contributions. In autumn of the same year, a play by A. N. Ostrovsky was performed in Russian at a theatre in Little Titchfield Street, near Shaftesbury Avenue in London's theatre district. More often, performances were held in smaller premises, such as St Mary Abbot's Hall.

Especially popular at the Russian Centre were poetry and prose readings by Boris Ranevsky, formerly of the Maly Theatre in Moscow. For an evening's entertainment, he would select little-known works that revealed something exceptional about a poet's personality, or passages from a novel that conveyed an impression of the entire work in the space of a single evening.

The émigré world abounded in political parties and quasi-literary organizations of all kinds. According to one estimate, there were as many as fifteen such parties in Europe after the war. Some of the larger ones, such as the National Alliance of Russian Solidarists (NTS), had representatives in England. From Brussels, General Alexei Archangelsky sent out appeals for unity in the name of the Council of the Russian Exile Army, countersigned by General Alexander Onoprienko, the organization's representative in England. It saw itself as the heir and successor of the Imperial and White Armies, and called upon people to remember significant anniversary dates and so draw strength and inspiration to continue the "struggle for RUSSIA." One such appeal stated, "The hour is approaching when the fate of our Fatherland will be decided. . . . In this final struggle, undoubtedly all the living forces of our country will take part, and so victory will be ensured." Usually the only result of such appeals was the offering of prayers for the fallen. In November of each year, for example, a panikhida was held at the All Saints Podvoria occasioned by three anniversaries: the "October" Revolution on November 7, the beginning of Vlasov's "Liberation Movement" (during World War II) on November 14, and the establishment of the Volunteer Army (during the Civil War) on November 15. Prayers were also said for all those who died violent deaths since the time of the Revolution.

In pre-Revolutionary days, Cossacks had formed independent, regional communities whose loyalty to the tsars was tempered by a measure of autonomy. Each area elected its own leader, or ataman. Under communism this was no longer possible, but the tradition was carried on in exile. Thus in

1954 the respected wartime leader, General V. Naumenko, was reelected ataman of the Kuban Cossacks in New York by 1,400 former inhabitants of the Kuban, now living in different parts of the free world. In the same year, election of a new ataman of the Don Cossacks, based in Paris, was started but halted temporarily amid accusations of irregularities. Meanwhile, Cossacks living in any particular city joined together to form a single *stanitsa* (as their villages in Russia had been called), irrespective of whether they were from the Don, Kuban, or other areas. Each *stanitsa* was led by a local ataman. Thus, in London there was a *stanitsa* named after the Tsarevich Alexis, while Cossacks in the Manchester and Oldham areas formed a *stanitsa* dedicated to two heroes, Atamans Kaledin and Babitch. The ataman in London was Colonel A. I. Kudinoff, with a leading part in his community played by George Druzhakin, whose wartime experiences were described earlier in Chapter 12. Cossack celebrations were noisy, nostalgic affairs: "All the toasts which were proposed resounded with deep love for our distant but unforgettable fatherland" ran one description. Yet when the interests of the Church were in jeopardy, it was often the Cossacks who proved most steadfast in her defence.

June 1955 marked the tenth anniversary of the Lienz tragedy of forced repatriation. To mark the occasion, a meeting was held in the Russian Centre at 49 Penywern Road. At the time, the government of the United Kingdom was still keeping the affair very quiet, long before the books by Count Nikolai Tolstoy and Nicholas Bethell. The meeting's purpose was to honour the victims and ensure that, at least within the Russian community, the full story would be known. The London ataman, Colonel Kudinoff, wrote to Tatiana Danilewicz,

> I hope you have not forgotten about your talk on the "Cossacks' Golgotha"—their journey from the Don to Lienz. I have obtained a map of Europe on which you can demonstrate the complete itinerary of the historic exodus of the Cossacks from their homeland. The plan of the meeting is more or less as follows: (1) *Litya*—short service for the dead—served by Father George, with "memory eternal" [sung] for the victims; (2) opening of the meeting and my talk; (3) your report; (4) close of the meeting.

While observing this anniversary of the repatriations that had occurred ten years earlier, refugees were only too aware of the Soviet government's continued interest in them. The previous year, in October 1954, a wave of panic had spread through the émigré community after a couple from Preston, the Rudakoffs, had been spirited away to the Soviet Union under mysterious circumstances. They had come to London for medical treatment and, finding that there was no free room at the Russian Centre, eventually located some old friends from Preston where they stayed the night. The next day they went out, saying they were going to the doctor, but five hours later Mr Rudakoff telephoned from the Soviet Embassy to say they were going back home to Russia.

The next morning Mrs Rudakoff went back to the friends' house, accompanied by an embassy official, to collect their overnight bag. Two weeks later, the Embassy announced that the Rudakoffs had expressed a desire to return to Russia and would be in Leningrad the next day. However, according to press reports, other refugees who had known them in Preston described them both as committed anticommunists, having suffered in the Siberian concentration camps of Kolyma, and said they were certain that the Rudakoffs were being taken back to prison.

The incident was widely reported in the British press. There was some speculation that the Rudakoffs could have been Soviet agents, but this was felt to be inconsistent with the fact that they had abandoned all their possessions in Preston and left, at the beginning of the Russian winter, with only a single suitcase of light clothing. Then again, why had they spent so long looking for accommodations on arrival in London? Everything pointed to a forced abduction, perhaps aided by blackmail. The *Sunday Express* commented, "Even now, here, in British homes, Russian refugees, who know both the terror of the concentration camps and visits by the secret police, grow cold with fear whenever there is a knock at the door."

In an attempt to stem a wave of panic, Count Bennigsen appealed to refugees in an open letter published in the *Bulletin* of the Refugees Relief Association. While admitting that Soviet government representatives in Great Britain had initiated a campaign aimed at refugees from Russia, he took pains to point out that this campaign could only be one of persuasion. Forced abduction, he said, would be too dangerous for them, and if the Rudakoffs had even hinted to the British immigration officer as they left that all was not well, they would have been detained at the port. In a general election year there was also widespread feeling that, with a change of government, Russians might all be handed back to the Soviets, just as in 1945. Count Bennigsen stated categorically that this would not happen—that it was just one further example of propaganda by the Soviets. The greatest danger, he said, was from agents who tried to strike up acquaintance with refugees in public places and persuade them that they would be better off going "home."

The following year, questions were asked in the House of Commons. Lord Robert Vansittart publicly asked the Home Secretary what steps were being taken to protect honest citizens against interference of this nature, which was increasingly being accompanied by an element of blackmail based on fears for relatives still living in the Soviet Union. Victims of such approaches were advised to contact the police immediately, either directly or through refugee organizations. After a while, several such agents, or "headhunters" (more literally, "skull hunters") as they were called by the Russians, were caught and expelled from the United Kingdom.

Meanwhile, Soviet leader Nikolai Bulganin announced an amnesty for all who wished to return to the Soviet Union. However, this was widely understood as a deception, the third phase of the "headhunting" mission of the Soviet Ministry of Internal Affairs (the MVD). One emigrant wrote,

> Whose heart does not tremble at the alluring prospect of going back home; each of us has an irresistible longing to go back, to hold our dear ones close to us . . . to kiss the ground where we have walked since early childhood, and in which our ancestors lie buried. But, alas, at the present time this is not possible. We cannot believe the Bolsheviks, whose banners bear the terrible inscription, "The end justifies the means. . . ." Here they are trying to fulfill the precepts of Lenin, who said that the emigration represented a great danger to them and that it should be broken up and destroyed.

For some Russians who had been caught up in the turmoil of wartime and arrived in England without strong anticommunist convictions, it was relatively easy to decide to return. However, many who remained relied on their Orthodox faith for the moral determination to resist the deceptive promises and threats that were issued from the other side of the Iron Curtain.

At times the Orthodox Church seemed like just one more voice among many clamouring for immigrants' attention. The community life that developed in the Russian colony in London was certainly influenced by the life of the Orthodox Church, but was not fully integrated into it. For example, Saturday evening meetings at the Russian Centre were cancelled for the first and third weeks of Lent, and no dances at all were held until after Easter. Still, on an ordinary Saturday evening the Refugees Relief Association did not hesitate to organize social gatherings and entertainments in accordance with the normal custom in Western countries, although the Orthodox Church regards Saturday evening as the beginning of Sunday, marked by the celebration of the Vigil service in church.

Archimandrite Nikodem desired to bring the life of the Russian community closer to the Church—to convince people that the Orthodox Church was immeasurably more precious than all other aspects of the heritage they had brought with them, representing the very heart and inspiration of Russian culture since the days of St Vladimir. With this in mind, in 1954 he revived the celebration of the Day of Russian Culture held on or close to the feast of St Vladimir (July 15/28). On this occasion, Archbishop John came and gave the opening talk about the significance of St Vladimir in Russian history, which was followed by a concert, poetry readings, and tea in the usual Russian style. "There can be no doubt as to the usefulness of gatherings like this," commented Father Nikodem. "The Russian emigration in London is usually far too variegated and uncoordinated."

Another hub of the Russian community at this time was the so-called Embassy or Russian House at 5 Brechin Place in Kensington. This was not an embassy at all, but had been the residence of the former chargé d'affaires at the Imperial Embassy, Eugene Sablin. After his death in 1949, his wife remained living there for a number of years, and continued to welcome Russians to gather and treat it as a community centre. It had a number of spacious reception rooms hung with portraits of tsars and emperors, including a particularly imposing floor-to-ceiling portrait of Catherine the Great. On Sunday afternoons, Archimandrite Nikodem went there to meet the people and give spiritual talks. One regular visitor recalls,

> He would speak on spiritual subjects, such as the Gospels and their interpretation, life beyond the grave, the orders of Holy Angels, and the Divine Services. He had an excellent memory and hardly ever glanced at the notes he had on the table in front of him, which made the talks particularly vivid and interesting.

He tried to persuade the Russian community not to concentrate its hopes in the world of émigré politics but to look for guidance primarily from the Church and its leaders (such as Metropolitan Anastassy and Archbishop John) who, he said, "more truly reflect the ideals of the nationalistic emigration and better understand Russian national interests." He said,

> Christ, the Head of the Church, Who said, "My Kingdom is not of this world," has for all eternity defined the path of the Church as one which is outside the aims of party politics, lest by serving these aims the Church should become a tool of politics. But the Lord also gives us the key to a

> well-ordered life of society and of the state. "Seek first the Kingdom of Heaven," He says, "and all these things (that is to say, all that we need for earthly life) will be added unto you." In these words the Lord promises His almighty help in the ordering of our earthly life, if we only we will seek the life of Heaven. This applies equally to the destiny of an individual person and to the destiny of whole peoples and states.

Such an other-worldly approach was not always appreciated; other clergymen were prepared to lend their support to political groups, particularly those of the monarchist variety. Archimandrite Nikodem had been brought up to serve "Faith, Tsar, and Fatherland" but in the emigration he had come to concentrate his hopes on faith alone. He unhesitatingly spoke of Emperor Nicholas II as the "Tsar-Martyr," and hoped for the speedy glorification of the Royal Martyrs as saints (which did not occur until 1981, after his death). Canonization effectively lifted the tsar's memory above the political realm, which accorded fully with the feelings of Father Nikodem.

Impressions of a Visit to St Philip's by Timothy Ware

Despite competing influences in the lives of the émigrés, St Philip's Church in Buckingham Palace Road remained an important focal point in the life of London's Russian community. The very existence of the church provided a manifestation of Orthodox Christianity in the centre of London, and the clergy were fully occupied serving the needs of their Russian parishioners. In the summer of 1952, Timothy Ware, then a seventeen-year-old pupil from nearby Westminster School, visited St Philips's Church, where the parish continued to hold its services. He has since become one of the best known writers explaining the Orthodox faith, so these early yet spirited impressions are of particular interest:

> I can remember exactly when my personal journey to Orthodoxy began. It happened quite unexpectedly one Saturday afternoon in the summer of 1952, when I was seventeen. I was walking along Buckingham Palace Road, close to Victoria Station in central London, when I passed a nineteenth-century Gothic church, large and somewhat dilapidated, that I had never noticed before. There was no proper notice-board outside it—public relations have never been the strong point of Orthodoxy in the Western world!—but I recall that there was a brass plate which simply said "Russian Church."

As I entered St Philip's—for that was the name of the church—at first I thought that it was entirely empty. Outside in the street there had been brilliant sunshine, but inside it was cool, cavernous and dark. As my eyes grew accustomed to the gloom, the first thing that caught my attention was an absence. There were no pews, no chairs in neat rows; in front of me stretched a wide and vacant expanse of polished floor.

Then I realized that the church was not altogether empty. Scattered in the nave and aisles there were a few worshipers, most of them elderly. Along the walls there were icons, with flickering lamps in front of them, and at the east end there were burning candles in front of the icon screen. Somewhere out of sight a choir was singing. After a while a deacon came out from the sanctuary and went round the church censing the icons and the people, and I noticed that his brocade vestment was old and slightly torn.

My initial impression of an absence was now replaced, with a sudden rush, by an overwhelming sense of presence. I felt that the church, so far from being empty, was full—full of countless unseen worshipers, surrounding me on every side. Intuitively I realized that we, the visible congregation, were part of a much larger whole, and that as we prayed we were being taken up into an action far greater than ourselves, into an undivided, all-embracing celebration that united time and eternity, things below with things above.

Years later, with a strange shock of recognition, I came across the story of St Vladimir's conversion, recorded in the Russian Primary Chronicle. Returning to Kiev, the Russian envoys told the Prince about the Divine Liturgy which they had attended in Constantinople. "We knew not whether we were in heaven or on earth," they said. "For on earth there is no such splendour or such beauty, and we are at a loss how to describe it. We only know that God dwells there among men. . . . For we cannot forget that beauty." I started with amazement as I read those words, for such exactly had been my own experience at the Russian Vigil Service in St Philip's, Buckingham Palace Road. The outward setting lacked the splendour of tenth-century Byzantium, but like St Vladimir's emissaries I too had encountered "heaven on earth." I too had felt the immediacy of the celestial Liturgy, the closeness of the angels and the saints, the uncreated beauty of God's Kingdom. "Now the powers of heaven worship with us invisibly" (The Liturgy of the Presanctified Gifts).

Before the service had ended, I left the church; and as I emerged I was struck by two things. First, I found that I had no idea how long I had been inside. It might have been only twenty minutes, it might have been

> two hours; I could not say. I had been existing on a level at which clock-time was unimportant. Secondly, as I stepped out on the pavement the roar of the London traffic engulfed me all at once like a huge wave. The sound must have been audible within the church, but I had not noticed it. I had been in another world where time and traffic had no meaning; a world that was more real—I would almost say more solid—than that of twentieth-century London to which I now abruptly returned.
>
> Everything at the Vigil Service was in Slavonic, and so with my conscious brain I could understand not a single word. Yet, as I left the church, I said to myself with a clear sense of conviction: This is where I belong; I have come home. Sometimes it happens—is it not curious?—that, before we have learnt anything in detail about a person, place or subject, we know with certainty: This is the person that I shall love, this is the place where I need to go, this is the subject that, above all others, I must spend my life exploring. From the moment of attending that service at St Philip's, Buckingham Palace Road, I felt deep in my heart that I was marked out for the Orthodox Church.[10]

It was not until 1958, at the age of twenty-four, that Timothy Ware became a member of the Orthodox Church, which in the 1950s was a very unusual step for an Englishman to take. After leaving Westminster School, he studied Greek and Latin at Oxford University and then took another two years of theology. He decided to join the Greek Orthodox Church rather than the Russian Church, partly because the Greek language and culture was more familiar to him, and partly because he had come to know people in both the Russian Church Abroad and the Patriarchal jurisdiction, and did not wish to take sides on the jurisdictional issue. He was received into the Orthodox Church by Bishop James (Virvos) of Apamaea, an assistant bishop of the Greek Orthodox Church in England. Bishop James, however, advised him to turn to Father George Cheremetieff of the Russian Church Abroad as his spiritual father.

In 1966 Timothy Ware was tonsured a monk at the Monastery of St John the Theologian in Patmos (Greece), receiving the monastic name Kallistos, and the following year he was ordained to the priesthood. He continued his teaching work at Oxford University as Spalding Lecturer in Eastern Orthodox Studies until his retirement in 2001. In 1982 he was consecrated a bishop of the Greek Orthodox Church, being raised to the rank of metropolitan in 2007. He is best known for his book *The Orthodox Church,* widely considered the best introduction to Orthodoxy in the English language.

Metropolitan Kallistos became one of the most eloquent representatives of the Orthodox Church in England. Considering how much he has written and spoken about Orthodoxy over the years, it is interesting that his inspiration came from an experience of utter silence and inner stillness experienced at St Philips in Buckingham Palace Road.

Arrival of the Nuns from Palestine

In March 1954, Archimandrite Nikodem told his parishioners about plans for a new convent to be established in London:

> I must now explain an extremely important development affecting our Church life. There is a plan for establishing a convent in London by the well-known Abbess Elisabeth (Ampenoff) and the young sisters of her community, who are Arabs. At present they are staying in France, at the Lesna Convent, near Paris. If they establish themselves near our Podvoria, that will allow us to have an excellent choir for the weekday services and some feast days, which would attract a larger congregation. On the other hand, if they move to some other part of London and open a separate church of their own there, this will help to resolve the problem of keeping many of our congregation who do not come to the Podvoria—either due to distance or to the cramped conditions—on the Sundays when we do not have St. Philip's at our disposal. The question of starting a convent is still at the stage of collecting funds, and I fervently appeal to you to participate in this, both through your own personal donations and by encouraging others to contribute.

The nuns had been forced to leave Palestine during the Arab–Israeli war of 1948. They were led by Abbess Elisabeth, whose recollections have been cited in previous chapters. As Metropolitan Anthony foretold when he blessed young Galina Ampenoff for the monastic path in 1929, ten years afterward she left for the Holy Land to become a nun. She joined the Convent of the Resurrection of Christ in Bethany, where the abbess was Mother Maria (Robinson), a Scotswoman who had joined the Russian Orthodox Church.[11] The principal work of the Bethany community was (and still is) running a school, in which most of the pupils come from Orthodox Arab families. Besides the usual school subjects, they are taught Russian and Church Slavonic, Russian church singing, and some understanding of the order of the Divine Services. Some students acquire such a love of the Russian Church that they are moved to enter one of the Russian convents in the Holy Land after they finish their education. Galina Ampenoff worked in this school and within a few years of her arrival she received the monastic tonsure with the name Elisabeth, in honour of the Holy Righteous Elisabeth, mother of St John the Baptist.

In 1945 Metropolitan Anastassy appointed her abbess of the convent at Ein Karim. In Russian this place is called *Gornaya*—the equivalent of "hill country" in the English text of St Luke's Gospel, "And Mary arose in those days, and went into the hill country." It is the place where Mary greeted her cousin Elizabeth and where, "when Elisabeth heard the greeting of Mary, that the babe leaped in her womb; and Elisabeth was filled with the Holy Spirit" (Luke 1:39–41). Many of the sisters at Ein Karim were Arabs who had been taught by Abbess Elisabeth in the school at Bethany. After a short teacher training course, some of them in turn became teachers at the school as part of their monastic obedience. The head of the Russian Mission in Jerusalem at that time was Archimandrite Anthony (Sinkevitch),[12] who was the convent's spiritual father. In addition to instructing the nuns in the spiritual life, he also taught them many of the intricacies of the Church typicon.

Mother Elisabeth became abbess at a time of growing unrest in Palestine. This passage from an obituary throws some light on how she experienced this crucial moment in her life:

> Years later Matushka told me of the panic which seized her before her monastic tonsure and appointment as abbess. She was being tonsured only five years after arriving in the convent, at the relatively young age of 37, and she felt convinced this was only because of Metropolitan Anastassy's decision to appoint her abbess. And the appointment, she felt, was due not to her spiritual qualities, but to the need to have someone from a reliable White Russian émigré family, at a time when the Soviet government was using the Moscow Patriarchate in an attempt to gain influence amidst the confusion of the post-war years; she felt quite unprepared to be a spiritual leader of a convent. Named Galina Vsevolodovna Ampenoff in the world, she had fled the Russian Revolution as a young girl and settled with her parents in London. Metropolitan Anthony (Khrapovitsky) had visited the family in 1929 and foretold Galina's monastic path, although it would be some ten years before she left for the Holy Land, in 1940, amidst the uncertainties of the wartime period, and not knowing whether she would ever see England or her family again. Over those ten years her love for her native Orthodox Church grew and she became convinced that it offered more than the world, with all its

> glitter and excitement, could ever provide. She recalled taking the underground train to church after work on the eve of a great feast day. Her heart would be bursting with compassion for the other people on the train, who would be unable to share in the grace of the Orthodox celebration. "But you cannot stand up and start preaching in the underground," she said, "Or can you? At least, I didn't think so," leaving the thought unfinished. The paths of God's providence are unfathomable. As she awaited the tonsure, with prayer and God's help she overcame the panic, remembering the Saviour's words in the Garden of Gethsemane (the tonsure was to take place in the Gethsemane Convent): "Father, if Thou be willing, remove this cup from Me: nevertheless not my will, but Thine, be done." She went forward, receiving the new name of Elisabeth, in honour of the mother of St. John the Baptist.

Faithful to their monastic vows, the sisters remained in their convent, despite the riots and terrorism which developed in 1948 into war between Arabs and Israelis. At this time the Soviet Union supported Israel (a policy which was dramatically reversed a few years later). Soviet armoured divisions were sent to reinforce the Israeli troops. When Abbess Elisabeth saw Soviet tanks in the distance approaching the convent, she realized, in the thick of gunfire and artillery bombardments, that the time had come to flee. The Soviet soldiers occupied Ein Karim, and before long representatives of the Moscow Patriarchate were sent from Russia to take charge of the convent.

Some of the nuns settled in other convents in the Holy Land. Six novices stayed with the abbess through four years of wandering during which they endured poverty, hunger, and illness. One of them gave up the struggle and returned to her family in the Holy Land. The others eventually found temporary refuge in the Lesna Convent, then situated at Fourqueux, near Paris. The search for a permanent home continued. The ascetic, authoritative figure of Archbishop John put an end to the indecision. After one of the services in France, he called Mother Elisabeth to the front of the church and said, "God blesses you to be Abbess of the Convent of the Annunciation in London." So, London it would be, and the not-yet-existent convent would be dedicated to the Annunciation.

The nuns arrived in London on June 16, 1954. An old friend of Mother Elisabeth, Dr Tatiana Pavlovna Guerken, came to their help. She had taken over the lease on 5 Brechin Place, the former community centre or "Embassy," when Mrs Sablin remarried some years after the death of her husband Eugene Sablin, former chargé d'affaires at the Imperial Russian Embassy, in 1949. Dr Guerken used part of the building for her medical practice. She invited Abbess Elisabeth and the sisters to stay there as long as necessary until they found a permanent home. Count Kleinmichel made several visits to the Home Office to obtain visas. On the day that he was finally successful, some of the nuns met him in Cromwell Road and, when he told them the news, they sang a hymn of thanksgiving there in the street. "So I just took off my bowler hat and stood there," the Count said later as he recalled the incident, "while the passers-by stared incredulously."

An Orthodox chapel was previously located at 5 Brechin Place, which the nuns set about restoring as quickly as possible so that their daily services could proceed without interruption. Father George Cheremetieff gave them a particularly warm welcome and travelled, in his hunchbacked fashion, on the Underground to buy icon-lamps and other items they needed for the church.

On July 22/August 4, 1954, the feast of St Mary Magdalene, Archbishop John consecrated the church and celebrated the first Liturgy there. Father George Cheremetieff also served on that occasion, although he could not serve at the convent regularly because of his other commitments. Also present that day was Father John Sawicz, who had recently joined the Russian Church Abroad from the Polish Church. Before ordination he was an officer in the Polish Army and, during wartime upheavals, he had spent time in Palestine where he became acquainted with the convent at Ein Karim. After the service Archbishop John gave an address in which he explained that the convent's primary mission was to teach children—by opening a school and by helping them grow up close to the Church. As he called down God's blessing on this important work, Father John Sawicz quite unexpectedly stepped forward and said, "And bless me to be their priest!" Everyone present was astonished, partly because this was entirely unexpected and partly because it was far from clear whether a clergyman was available to serve regularly at the convent. Archbishop John gave his blessing and from then until his death thirteen years later, Father John served all the Sunday and feast day services. The Saturday school for children—religious instruction and Russian language—was started immediately. Archimandrite Nikodem rejoiced that this task, which had caused him so much anxiety, was now receiving such expert attention from nuns who had all been prepared for this work in the Holy Land.

Meanwhile, Mother Elisabeth looked for a suitable house where the convent could be established permanently and initiated a fund-raising campaign to finance its purchase.[13]

Archbishop John (Maximovitch) in England

Between 1953 and 1962, the parishes of the Russian Church Abroad in the United Kingdom had the good fortune to be under the spiritual leadership of Archbishop John. In 1950 he was appointed Bishop of Western Europe and in 1952 he was given a "watching brief" over the Preston Diocese which was nevertheless to remain in direct submission to the Synod of Bishops until the appointment of a new bishop. This did not prevent Archimandrite Nikodem from reporting that "We have been brought into the area of the Most Reverend Archbishop John's pastoral concern, and now receive most valuable guidance from him in questions of Church life, and so we entrust ourselves to his prayerful concern for us." At the Bishops' Council of 1953, the Preston Diocese was incorporated into the Diocese of Western Europe, and so Archbishop John became the ruling hierarch.

Archbishop John was a strict ascetic in the spirit of the ancient desert fathers, a clairvoyant spiritual father, and a healer and miracle worker. In the nineteenth century, people had asked St Seraphim of Sarov why there were no longer great ascetics as in the days of the desert fathers, and St Seraphim answered that there was no reason other than peoples' lack of zeal, because the gifts of the Holy Spirit were the same and everyone has the same potential for sanctity buried within them. St Seraphim, of course, shone as an example of such gifts in his own time. In the twentieth century, many who met Archbishop John felt that his loving, saintly personality opened a window into the heavenly world and exemplified the dogmatic truth of Orthodoxy, particularly the rightness of the canonical position of the Russian Church Abroad, which he defended vehemently amid the jurisdictional confusion of the Russian diaspora.

Archbishop John was also a fervent supporter of missionary endeavours. Wherever he lived, he learned the local language, celebrated Divine Services in it, and ordained local clergymen. While living in France, he encouraged the veneration of Western saints who predated the eleventh-century schism of the Western Church from Orthodoxy. Through his efforts a number of these saints were added to the calendar of saints of the Russian Church Abroad.

"If you wish to see a living saint, go to Bitol [then in the Kingdom of Yugoslavia], to Father John," said the Serbian Bishop Nicholas of Ochrid during the 1930s. While Father John was still a teacher at the Serbian seminary of St John the Theologian in Bitol, it was discovered that he stayed up all night praying, sleeping only for an hour or two on the floor before the icons. In 1934 he was consecrated Bishop of Shanghai, where he remained until forced to leave after the communist seizure of power in 1949. When appointed to the Diocese of Western Europe, he first established his see near Versailles and later in Paris at 19 Rue Claude-Lorrain in the 16th arrondissement, where a house church was established dedicated to All Saints of Russia (literally, "all saints who have shone forth in the Russian land"). Visitors to this church testify that it still emanates a special air of sanctity, as if sealed by the prayers of the holy archbishop.

In Paris, as previously in China and Yugoslavia, Vladyka John's reputation spread. A Roman Catholic priest told his congregation, "You demand proofs, you say that now there are neither miracles nor saints. Why should I give you theoretical proofs, when today there walks in the streets of Paris a saint—Saint Jean Nus Pieds (Saint John the Barefoot)." The priest was referring to the archbishop's habit of giving away his shoes to poor people and going barefoot. Needless to say, behaviour such as this shocked many people who expected their bishops to be more dignified and presentable. It is important to remember that after several decades during which his memory has been surrounded by almost universal veneration, crowned by his glorification as a saint in 1994,[14] that in his lifetime there were many pious believers who thought that Archbishop John was a disgrace: dishevelled, bent over, with a speech impediment that sometimes made him hard to understand in any language, his firmness of will taken for sheer stubbornness, and his daily celebration of the entire cycle of Divine Services being regarded by some as a needless eccentricity. Much has been written about Archbishop John, especially his service in China and America, and about miraculous healings and other help people received from him after his death in 1966. Considered briefly here are only the occasions when he visited England.

Archbishop John (Maximovitch) of Western Europe with Abbess Elisabeth (Ampenoff) at the Convent of the Annunciation in north London, ca. 1960. (Source: Ioann Suscenko)

His first appearance in England was on June 19, 1953. Archimandrite Nikodem commented, "The visit and celebration of Divine Services by Vladyka John, who is well known for his extraordinary ascetic life, was the cause of great spiritual edification among our more zealous parishioners." He celebrated three Sunday services at St Philip's as well as daily services at the Podvoria. He also visited Bradford and Manchester. Accompanied by Father Nikodem, he visited parishioners and old peoples' homes, taking a copy of the miraculous Kursk icon with him wherever he went. He carried the icon in a bag hung round his neck, which he took out to conduct services of intercession in the houses he visited. Archbishop John was known either personally or by reputation to many of the Serbian clergy and so he happily accepted the invitation to lead the celebration of the Serbian national festival—*Vidov Dan*—in Cheltenham. He also ordained a Serbian deacon to the priesthood at one of the services in St Philip's.

While in charge of the parishes in England, Archbishop John provided the parish's Sisterhood of St Xenia with a formal written constitution. This document, treasured in the sisterhood archives, demonstrated that Vladyka John was intensely practical and logical in matters of Church organization as well as being a man of prayer. At the top, typed in the same manner as the rest of the document, it said, "Approved, with my hand-written notations, Archbishop John." Among the annotated passages is the clause saying that "any Russian Orthodox woman" can be a member. The word "Russian" is underlined and marked with a question mark. Evidently he did not agree that membership of any parish organization should be limited to people who were of Russian origin—and possibly that was not the intent of whoever originally drafted it, since the term "Russian Orthodox" can refer to any member of the Russian Orthodox Church. Most of this constitution pertained to organizational matters, such as meetings and membership dues, which broadly paralleled the organization of the parish itself. The constitution specified that the principal functions of the sisterhood were taking care of the church, looking after the vestments, and visiting the sick.

When asked if he would like to visit Westminster Abbey, Archbishop John replied, "What for? There is nothing holy there." He did, however, travel to Farley Castle in Berkshire in order to pray before the miraculous Kazan Icon of the Mother of God. Farley Castle was the home of an art collector who had recently purchased the icon.[15]

Archbishop John usually visited London once a year coinciding with the patronal festival of the Dormition (August 15/28), although there were other visits also, depending on circumstances. In 1956, a plan was made for a pilgrimage to Lewes (in Sussex) to pray at the common grave where many

Russian prisoners of war were buried. These prisoners had been taken captive during the Crimean War, which ended in 1856, exactly one hundred years previously. Many died in captivity from influenza and pneumonia, and a monument was erected there in 1877 at the request of Tsar Alexander II. The Russian community in London was alerted to the existence of this grave through comment in the national press following the visit of Nikita Khrushchev and Nikolai Bulganin to Karl Marx's grave in Highgate Cemetery earlier that year.

A bus was hired to take the pilgrims and the archbishop, but on the morning they were due to leave the trip had to be cancelled. The grave was in a cemetery attached to an Anglican church, and the vicar sent a telegram saying he could not permit the panikhida to be held. Under the headline "White Russian pilgrimage ends in fiasco," the *Sussex Express* reported, "Of course it would be quite untrue to say that immigrants, whoever they may be, are not entitled to pray at their compatriots' graves. But when an Archbishop is involved, it will be understood that more than three days' notice is required." When discussions were held with responsible officials to try to resolve the problem, the source of the difficulty became clear. Because they had already been in contact with the Soviet Embassy to obtain funds to have the monument restored, a high profile pilgrimage led by an archbishop of the "White" Russian Church Abroad could have placed them in an embarrassing position. A number of laypeople, nevertheless, went individually to pray at the graves. Writing in the Paris émigré journal *Vozrozhdeniye* (*Rebirth*), Tatiana Danilewicz asked, "Does this need any further commentary? It presents a fairly clear picture of the situation in which the Orthodox Church finds itself, not just here, but everywhere outside Russia, and also of the situation of the Russian emigration in England."

This incident involved Archbishop John in his official capacity as head of the Diocese of Western Europe, and he did not visit England often enough to become well known as an individual to many members of the parish. Such information as has been preserved comes from the nuns of the Convent of the Annunciation, with whom Vladyka John established particularly close spiritual ties. The very establishment of the convent in London was, as has been said, entirely due to his initiative and blessing. While the convent was situated at Brechin Place, Vladyka usually stayed there during his visits to London. This was at first viewed with some consternation, as his ascetic routine with full daily services was seen as disruptive. Following the ancient ascetic discipline of not eating (except for Holy Communion and prosphora in church) until the ninth hour—3:00 p.m.—he would not normally eat breakfast or lunch and then, engrossed in pastoral visits and other activities, he did not eat until very late in the evening. Expecting to celebrate the Liturgy and receive Holy Communion the next day as well, he could not eat after midnight, so a meal had to be fit in hurriedly at times such as 11:00 or 11:30 p.m. Nevertheless, not wishing to interrupt the established order of the young community, when in London he ate at the normal times with the sisters and did not expect to be fed in the middle of the night.

He also showed condescension regarding services, permitting some abbreviations and celebration of weekday Matins in the evening[16] in view of the large number of different obediences required of the nuns. Vladyka John normally celebrated the full cycle of services daily wherever he happened to be, and inspired in many an appreciation of their sanctifying power on the human soul. Abbess Elisabeth and the sisters, who learned the details of the monastic typicon in the Holy Land, revered Vladyka for his knowledge and love of the typicon, while he rejoiced that they had preserved certain rare monastic chants and other ancient traditions.

When the nuns eventually found a house where the convent could be permanently established, the house and church were blessed in due order. In addition to these "official" blessings, the house received a special blessing from the prayers of the holy archbishop occasioned by a broken furnace. When he arrived on one of his first visits, he found that problems with the central heating system caused the house to be partially flooded with boiling water. The worst of it flowed into the kitchen where the prosphora were being prepared. Mercifully, no one was injured. Vladyka asked for the *Trebnik (Book of Needs)*, which contains many prayers for special occasions and prayers relating to matters of practical necessity. He asked for holy water and a candle and read the prayers "over the furnace" from the *Trebnik*. Then he told the nuns to put up an icon of the "Unburned Bush"[17] over the furnace and blessed it with holy water. He asked where the gas and electricity meters were and blessed them as well. The nuns thought he had finished; they went to their cells, but he stayed up all night praying, sprinkling the house with holy water, and, barefoot as he often was, blessing the house outside and blessing the pillar box on the corner from which he would be sending out his voluminous correspondence while staying in London. Although remaining in their cells, the nuns hardly slept either, and from then on they had a special sense of the holy archbishop's prayerful protection, which they felt would guard them from spiritual as well as practical disasters. Mother Seraphima, one of the five Arab nuns at the convent, recalled,

> We felt he loved the Arabs as a nation. We did not feel it made any difference that we were not Russian. He just seemed to accept that we came from the Holy Land and were Arabs. Once I went with Matushka [Mother Elisabeth] to Belgium. We thought we might establish the convent there, before we thought of England. He asked us to come to the Memorial Church in Brussels, where he was celebrating the Rite of Orthodoxy (on the first Sunday in Lent) for the first time after he arrived in Europe. He said some litanies which he had learned from us and the prayer "Look down from Heaven, O Lord," in Arabic. People turned to look at one another and said, "Is he saying it in Chinese?" "No," I said, "he's saying it in Arabic . . . for my sake."

One of Archbishop John's most remarkable gifts was that of clairvoyance. He would answer questions that people had only formulated in their minds without having put them into words, or which they had decided to ask but then forgotten. He often knew immediately of the misfortunes of people far away, and prayed for them either privately or publicly, long before news of their troubles had otherwise become known. Abbess Elisabeth experienced this personally when in 1965 she had an accident resulting in a broken leg. Within a short time there was a telephone call from America. It was Archbishop John asking how she was. He could not possibly have known by ordinary means. He also possessed a type of spiritual contact in times of trouble that defied time and space. Abbess Elisabeth recalled, "He said, 'If you write, don't expect an answer, but I will pray for you,' and I always knew when he had received the letter, because I could feel he was praying for us." She continued,

> Ordinary people understood that he was not an ordinary man. On one occasion while he was staying with us, a priest died in France, Archimandrite Sergei. Early in the morning we had to drive him to catch the ferry. We had to take a taxi, and as Vladyka was getting out, the driver, a young man, said, "I would love to have the blessing of this man," and he blessed him. Then he said "Who is this person?" I answered, "It is our Archbishop." He said, "He is a holy person, something radiates from him."
>
> On another occasion he had been visiting Count Kleinmichel. The Count took him to Golders Green Underground station and asked permission to go down to the platform to make sure he [Vladyka] found the right train. When he came back the ticket collector said, "Sir, may I ask you something?" He said, "Yes, what is it?" "Who is that extraordinary person

I saw?" He answered, "It is our bishop." Then the ticket collector said, "I am a Baptist. When I see a holy man, I know it. This man is a very holy person."

Archbishop John hands the pastoral staff to newly consecrated Bishop Nikodem at Brussels Memorial Church, 1954. Standing behind Archbishop John are (left to right) Archbishop Alexander of Germany, Bishop Leonty of Geneva, and Archbishop Philothei of Northern Germany. (Source: Antonina Ananin)

In 1962 Archbishop John was transferred from Western Europe to San Francisco. It would be hard to exaggerate the significance of his influence on the Russian Church Abroad throughout the post-war period up to his death in 1966, and even after his death. Having a very strong and intensely spiritual presence in all the places where he served—China, Europe, and America—he exemplified St Paul's teaching "Do you not know that a little leaven leavens the whole lump?" (1 Cor 5:6). His legacy to the Church Abroad was her new metropolitan: Bishop Philaret, the youngest of the bishops, was quite unexpectedly elected to replace Metropolitan Anastassy when he retired in 1965, entirely due to the prompting and influence of Archbishop John. Although Vladyka John's visits to England were relatively brief, it was thanks to him that the parishes in England received a bishop of their own.

Consecration of Archimandrite Nikodem as Bishop of Preston

After his first visit to England in 1953, when Archibishop John held only a "watching brief" over the parishes in England, he made a report to the Synod and then to the meeting of the full Council of Bishops held later that year. As a result, on October 21, 1953, the Council resolved,

1. To establish in England a vicarial see of the Diocese of Western Europe, the title of the vicar bishop to be specially discussed by the Synod of Bishops, after receiving full information as to what name would be most suitable in accordance with local conditions.

2. To appoint Archimandrite Nikodem Nagaieff as vicar bishop in England, his consecration as bishop to be performed at such a time and place as may be considered appropriate by the Most Reverend Archbishop John.

The consecration took place the following year on July 18, 1954, when all the European bishops were assembled in Brussels for their annual conference. Despite the proviso about reconsidering the name of the see, the new bishop was initially consecrated as Bishop of Preston. The following description, written by a member of the London parish, captured something of the awesome majesty of the occasion:

Solemnity of Episcopal Consecration in Brussels

The magnificent memorial church in Brussels, built in memory of the Tsar-Martyr Nicholas II, was filled with an atmosphere of expectancy and spiritual watchfulness. People had gathered from all over Europe and were kindly given accommodation by the Brussels parishioners. The hierarchs of the Russian Church Abroad had also assembled from different parts of Europe: Archbishop John (Maximovitch) from France, Bishop Leonty from Geneva, and Archbishops Alexander and Philothei from Germany. From England came Archimandrite Nikodem, whose impending consecration as bishop was the cause of the solemnities.

On Saturday 4/17 July a Liturgy for the departed followed by a panikhida were served for the repose of the Tsar Nicholas and his family, that being the anniversary of their death. The service went on until 2 p.m. After a short break, at 5 p.m. the congregation reassembled in the church, augmented by newly arrived clergy and laity, including spiritual children of Archimandrite Nikodem.

After the conclusion of Small Vespers, the bishops came out into the middle of the church. The senior priest present, Archimandrite Anthony (Bartochevitch) and Protodeacon Sergei Tchertkoff returned to the altar and accompanied Archimandrite Nikodem into the middle of the church. The Protodeacon then announced: "Reverend Father, Archimandrite Nikodem! The Synod of Bishops of the Russian Church Abroad blesses your holiness to be bishop of the city, saved by God, of Preston." Archimandrite Nikodem humbly, calmly, but with a firm voice replied, "Inasmuch as the Synod of Bishops has judged me worthy of this service, I give thanks, I accept, and I say nothing against it." He made a prostration to all.

Then followed a service of intercession to the Holy Spirit, served and sung by the bishops alone, to pray for the future bishop, who stood with bowed head, absorbed in prayer. After the dismissal and "Many Years" the bishops sat down and the person who had been nominated to receive episcopal orders gave the traditional address in which, in accordance with custom, he gave a brief account of his life hitherto, thanking all those who had influenced him on his spiritual path.[18] He then went on to describe his perception of the bishop's responsibilities:

"Now, by God's will, I am called, through being chosen by the Council of Bishops, to that highest service in the Church, which is known as the Apostolic service. Conscious of my sinfulness and spiritual infirmity I stand on the threshold of this service. What can give me the resolve not to turn aside from this post for which I have been chosen? Only that which has guided me in all the preceding stages of my life in the Church: an absolute obedience to the Church in the person of her hierarchy, irrespective of the weakness of spirit which I feel and my unpreparedness. Now, as I accept this exalted obedience which is now laid upon me, hoping only in the Divine Grace, 'which always heals infirmities and makes good that which is lacking,' I must account to you, Godly-wise archpastors, and before the Church, for how I understand the service now before me, and what will guide me on this path.

"The great Apostle Paul speaks exhaustively about it in his exhortation to the presbyters of Ephesus. With fear I heed the voice of this great teacher. He expresses his idea in words which are brief but rich in meaning: 'Take heed therefore unto yourselves, and to all the flock, over which the Holy Ghost hath made you overseers,[19] to feed the Church of God, which He hath purchased with his own blood' (Acts 20:28).

"Here the Apostle of the Gentiles reminds us that the bishop is not given the power of authority by any earthly authority, that he is not only an outward guardian of the rules and laws of the Church, but that he is the instrument of the Holy Spirit, receiving from above not only the authority, but also the strength to achieve success. Therefore it is with the words 'Take heed to yourselves' that he begins his address.

" 'Be vigilant,' it is as if he were saying, 'first of all over your own heart, you, who are the guardians of God's House! Do not yield to slumber, lest it should be plundered! Watch over the purity of your thoughts, feelings and desires! May you be illumined by the law and words of Christ! May your soul strive towards this exalted service.' But in order to comprehend them, the bishop's mind must be lucid, his heart pure, his thoughts and desires spiritual, his life far from the impurities of the world. As one 'sent forth to minister for them who shall be heirs of salvation' (Heb 1:14), he must watch over himself more than anyone else, so as not to seek 'his own,' but that which is of God and of his neighbour. 'Be thou an example to the believers in word, in conversation, in love, in spirit, in faith, in purity' (1 Tim 4:12), the Apostle advises his disciple Timothy, as it were developing these thoughts, when appointing him to the episcopal service.

"Take heed also 'to your own flock,' continues the Apostle. 'Feed the flock with wholesome nourishment, preserve it from the heresies and schisms which have multiplied beyond measure at the present time, seek the lost sheep gone astray in the mountains, and, imitating you, Chief Pastor, take it upon your shoulders and bring it unto the Heavenly Father.'[20] Great is the number of these sheep now wandering along stray paths outside the Church. At times it is hard to heal them and bring them back into Her bosom. How many there are among them who have no wish at all to hear or accept 'sound doctrine,' but 'turn away their ears from the truth, and shall be turned unto fables' (2 Tim 4: 3–4), as had even begun to happen during the times of the Apostles.

"Bringing his counsels to an end, the Apostle indicates the means both for strengthening oneself for the ascetic struggle and inspiring oneself with zeal for this service. He says that the Church, for which we are called to struggle, has been 'purchased by Christ with His own blood.' What do our small efforts signify in the face of His intense effort? Before the great love of Christ, what do our small sacrifices mean, our abilities, our labours and griefs—all that we can bring as a gift to the Chief Pastor? But if the Christian path is everywhere sown with grief, then even more will this apply to those who have taken on the protection and care of the flock of Christ.

"The days we are living through are a period marked by a special intensity of evil, diabolical forces. The prince of this world is building his traps not only through evil-intentioned and foolish people, but sometimes even through people who are supposedly zealous for the Church. The nets of the enemy are widely spread in order to trap the servant of God; in order to debase God's work to the level of the works of the hands of men; in order to make the servants of God into salt which has lost its savour. To avert the confusion, the minutes of faintheartedness which can come upon him, the Apostle has given his counsel, left as a testament to his disciple: 'Do thou therefore endure all evils (hardness) as a good soldier of Jesus Christ' (2 Tim 2:3).

"Help me then. Most Reverend Bishops; in the words of the Apostle who was granted to see the hidden mysteries, you are the 'angels' of the Churches. Help me through your prayers and Divinely wise counsels in the service which is before me, so that, in the day and hour when the Lord calls me to give an account of my deeds, I should not hear the words spoken to the angel of the Church of Sardis: 'I have not found thy works perfect before God' (Rev 3:2)."

The very appearance of the newly nominated bishop, humble, meek but wise, spoke of his love for the Lord, of his boundless devotion to the will of God and of his obedience to His Church. His words were spoken with conviction and it was evident that each word was carefully considered and deeply felt. Those present in church listened with compunction and rapt attention, fearing to miss a single word. When he had finished his address, he came up to receive Archbishop John's blessing, and then Archbishop John gave him the cross to kiss and sprinkled him with holy water. So ended the office of the "nomination" [*narecheniye*] of the new bishop. It was followed by the Vigil service, conducted with great solemnity.

The next day the bishops were greeted and vested in the centre of the church, where they were joined by the other concelebrating clergy: Archimandrite Anthony, Archpriest John Grigor-Klochko, Fathers Chedomir Ostoich and Slavko Niketitch, Priest-monk James and Protodeacon Sergei Tchertkoff. Archimandrite Nikodem was led out to the bishops in the centre of the church as the Protodeacon exclaimed, "Archimandrite Nikodem, beloved of God, chosen and confirmed, is brought forth for the laying on of hands as Bishop of Preston." Archbishop John addressed him: "For what cause hast thou come, and what dost thou request from us?" And the appointed bishop replied: "The laying on of hands unto the grace of the episcopate, Most Reverend Bishops." "How dost thou believe?" Archbishop John asked him. He then recited the creed, "I believe in One God, Father Almighty . . ." followed by a more extended confession of the faith. In a firm, clear and calm voice, the nominated bishop gave his oath to keep all the canons and traditions of the Church and to uphold peace in the Church. He signed his confession of faith and handed it to Archbishop John, who blessed him saying, "May the Grace of the Holy Spirit be with you."

The solemn rites of the episcopal Liturgy then proceeded as usual until the singing of "Holy God, Holy Mighty. . . ." Here Father Nikodem was led out through the north door of the iconostasis and back through the Royal Doors into the altar, where he knelt down before the altar table. In their left hands the bishops held the opened Gospel book over him, while placing their right hands on his head. So was accomplished the mystery of the laying on of hands, while Archbishop John read the most important prayers: "Let us all pray, that the Grace of the All-Holy Spirit may come upon him. . . ." While the choir sang *"Kyrie Eleison,"* he continued the prayer:

"Do Thou, O Lord, make even this man, who is being endowed with the episcopal grace, to be an imitator of Thee, the true Shepherd, who laid down Thy life for thy sheep; a guide of the blind, the light of those in darkness, an instructor of the foolish, teacher of babes, a light unto the world; that having made perfect the souls entrusted unto him in the present life, he may stand unashamed before Thy throne, and receive that great reward, which Thou hast prepared for those who have suffered for the preaching of Thy Gospel."

There was a complete stillness in the church. The Grace of the Holy Spirit descended on the new bishop, and the people could feel the power and glory of God. The inexplicable compunction, joy and solemnity of this moment seized the attention of the congregation. The priest's vestments were removed from the new bishop. Archbishop John solemnly held out the items of the bishop's vestments through the Royal Doors one by one, each time exclaiming *"Axio"* ("He is worthy"), which was taken up by the clergy in the altar and then by the choir and people. When the new bishop was vested, he received a brotherly embrace from his new brother-bishops, who put him in the place of honour, to the right of Archbishop John, and he continued the service as a bishop.

After the Gospel reading, Bishop Nikodem blessed the people for the first time with the dikyrion and trikyrion. The liturgy continued, the choir sang magnificently, and one could have wished for this wonderful service to continue forever. But soon the Holy Gifts were brought out for Communion and then the prayer before the ambo was read in Dutch by Priest-monk James, a Dutchman; Archbishop Alexander gave a moving sermon, and the Liturgy was over. The bishops removed their vestments in the altar. The new bishop was vested in the *mantia* and led out onto the ambo, where Archbishop John awaited him, in order to hand him the archpastoral staff. Before doing so, he addressed the new bishop, according to custom, greeting him warmly and speaking with great fervour about the episcopal service which awaited him, about the honour and difficulty of this service, and about the work of Bishop Nikodem himself. Archbishop John's face was suffused with love and his eyes shone with an unearthly joy. Bishop Nikodem received the staff and gave his first blessing to the people—one which is revered as being imbued with a special grace. *"Is polla eti, despota,"* thundered from the choir. The new bishop held the cross and the people greeted him as they came up to venerate it with joyful, compunctionate faces. Everything earthly had been forgotten and it was as if their faces also reflected that same grace, which had reposed on the new bishop, whose own face expressed such spiritual joy and love.

Still, this unforgettable spiritual festival was not entirely over. The bishops all remained in Brussels for their annual conference of European bishops (being a partial meeting of the Sobor of Bishops). Services were held daily; some of the bishops sang as a choir, while others officiated. The first day after his consecration, Bishop Nikodem officiated as the chief celebrant at the Liturgy.

The following Sunday he was invited to Meudon, near Paris, where he had established ties with the parish during his earlier period of service in France. Here he concelebrated with the local clergy including Father Boris Molchanoff, who had been the first priest of the Meudon parish before moving to England in the 1930s. Then he visited the Lesna convent at Fourqueux, with which he also had close spiritual ties both from his time in France and from Yugoslavia, where the convent had been situated before the war. From there he returned to England, taking with him, as he himself said, a feeling of profound gratitude to the Russian inhabitants of Brussels and a feeling of spiritual kinship with them, and from England he sent his archpastoral blessing to the clergy and parishioners of both Brussels and Meudon.

Back in England, the new bishop resumed his pastoral duties with renewed vigour, strengthened by the power of divine grace conferred by the consecration. Archbishop John remained the diocesan bishop, while Bishop Nikodem was a vicar (or suffragan) bishop, accountable to the diocesan bishop but still endowed with the fullness of episcopal grace. The solemnity with which the Orthodox Church surrounds the services conducted by its hierarchs is only an outward expression of the immense reverence it has for the episcopate: the bishop is the "icon of Christ," and, in the words of one ancient Church Father, St Ignatius of Antioch, "Where the bishop is, there is the Church." The local Church community surrounding its bishop constitutes the local Church, possessed of the fullness of Divine Grace. Now led by their own bishop, the Russian parishes achieved their proper form of ecclesiastical organization. Reflecting on this, the new bishop wrote, "I think it will be obvious that this has raised the prestige of the Russian Church Abroad in England, and also that the more solemnly conducted services, which bring out the symbolism of Orthodox Divine worship more clearly, contribute to a more profound understanding of the services by the congregation."

As a bishop of the Orthodox Church, Vladyka Nikodem's responsibilities at times extended beyond the confines of his own Russian Church. Thus, in 1955 he was invited to Birmingham by the Serbian community to lead the celebration of *Vidov Dan*—the feast of St Vitus—a great national festival which falls in June. In 1958 he was invited to assist in the consecration of a Serbian Orthodox Church in Birmingham. He also took part in the annual conferences of European bishops of the Russian Church Abroad that were convened by Archbishop John at the Lesna Convent in France and elsewhere on the Continent. In October 1957 he went to Geneva, where he assisted at the consecration of Archimandrite Anthony (Bartochevitch) as Bishop of Geneva.

On October 30, 1957, the Synod resolved, "On the basis of the information provided by the Most Reverend Archbishop John, to change the title of the Right Reverend Bishop of Preston, Nikodem, giving him the new title of Bishop of Richmond." This reflected the fact that by 1957 there was no longer a parish in Preston. Many of the parishioners had moved away, while others who considered themselves Ukrainians had joined the Ukrainian autocephalous Church.[21] Richmond was chosen as the nearest place outside London to the bishop's residence at 14 St Dunstan's Road.

In the autumn of 1954, shortly after his consecration, the new bishop travelled north to Manchester to celebrate the patronal festival of the Protection of the Most Holy Mother of God, and then went on to nearby Oldham, where he was greeted by the Cossack community. A reporter in the *Bulletin* of the Refugees Relief Association wrote,

> On Sunday 17 October the Cossack Stanitsa named in honour of Atamans Kaledin and Babitch celebrated its annual festival. Bishop Nikodem, the head of the Orthodox Church in England, was present, accompanied by the rector of the Church of the Holy Protection in Manchester, Father Nicholas Popoff. After a moleben, Vladyka gave a short speech, in which he spoke warmly of the Cossacks' historical service to the Tsars and to Russia, and also of their heroic struggle against communism. After some traditional songs of the Don, Kuban and Terek Cossacks, V. V. Dombrovsky, the Ataman of the local stanitsa, greeted Vladyka, who had graced the Cossack festival with his presence. V. V. Dombrovsky called forth a warm response when he noted that in days gone by our respected Vladyka had

led us into battle against communism with a sword in his hands, and now he was leading us, holding the Holy Cross . . . Valerian Vasilievitch's speech was interrupted by a thunderous *Ura*[22] in honour of Vladyka.

This boisterous approbation from his Cossack parishioners, the more restrained greetings he would have received from the Grand Duchess Xenia at Hampton Court, the increased solemnity of the episcopal services and, most importantly, the inner strength conferred in the sacrament of episcopal consecration—all testified to the spiritual gifts poured out on the new bishop and the diocese through the laying on of hands in Brussels Memorial Church. In the Orthodox spiritual tradition, however, it is understood that times of spiritual joy are sent to strengthen believing people before greater trials which lie ahead. Just over a year after the new bishop's consecration, the parish faced grave difficulties over the question of the church building.

Wanderings in the Wilderness

The arrangements for sharing St Philip's Church continued into the early 1950s along the same lines established when the schism took place in 1927. The fact that this abnormal situation had lasted so long amazed many Orthodox people outside the United Kingdom who learned of it. The parish church, although impressive, was only available on alternate weeks. This tended to exacerbate the effects of the schism, while at the same time leading to a lack of respect for the Church hierarchy among some people who simply went to St Philip's every Sunday, irrespective of who was officiating. Archimandrite Vitaly had found the arrangement particularly unacceptable for a number of reasons. First, the influx of new parishioners meant that the Podvoria church could not possibly hold them all on the days when St Philip's was occupied by the other parish. Second, because the parish that had been under Metropolitan Evlogy's jurisdiction was currently under the jurisdiction of the Moscow Patriarchate, it was thought to be even more heavily compromised for being directly influenced by the Soviet government.

Nevertheless, in his determination to find a separate church, Archimandrite Vitaly was constrained by the same two problems that faced the parish in the 1920s and 1930s: firstly, the wide dispersion of parishioners throughout a large city necessitating a single church in a central location (the community was not numerous enough to warrant establishment of small parishes in different parts of the city, as happened in Paris in the early days of the emigration), and secondly, the high cost of land in central London, which meant that the parish could not buy or erect a building of its own unaided. Hence the parish turned for help again, as in the 1920s, to the Church of England. The "established" or state church—led by the reigning monarch of Great Britain—had at its disposal a substantial national heritage of property, not all of which was needed to satisfy the religious requirements of its own community. Accordingly, Archimandrite Vitaly began negotiations with the Church of England, aided by Count Kleinmichel, who continued working on this matter after Father Vitaly's departure for Brazil.

By 1955 it seemed that success was achieved. At the annual parish meeting in March of that year, Bishop Nikodem told his parishioners,

> Last year we did not have St. Philip's church available to us for the great feasts of Christmas and Pascha [it being the turn of the other parish], but God sent us the magnificent Anglican church of All Saints in Ennismore Gardens, where we celebrated these services with great solemnity. This church, as most of you already know, is due to be made available to us on a permanent basis. . . . Count Kleinmichel will give you full details of the situation as it stands at present.

However, the course of events soon underwent a radical change. In the same year came news that St Philip's was to be demolished to make way for an expansion of Victoria Coach Station. In fact, the coach station had been partially opened for some time and was causing disruption to the services in St Philip's. Thus, at Pascha in 1955, the service of nocturnes preceding Easter Matins was disturbed by shouts from drunken football supporters making their way to their buses to return home after an important match played that day. The noise mounted until just before midnight when the procession came out of the church, whereupon the crowd suddenly hushed. As the congregation processed round the courtyard and pavement in front of the church, carrying their banners and icons, and singing "Thy Resurrection, O Christ our Saviour," they found themselves being stared at by hundreds of football supporters, wearing their woollen hats displaying their team colours, obviously very drunk, and with an expression of utter bewilderment on their faces, as if they thought that their last hour had struck. Perhaps through their drunken haze they had at least some perception of the Glory of God, which is present in His holy temple.

The site on which the church stood was to be turned into a car park. The Russian community was horrified at such a strange hierarchy of values, which placed transport above the worship of God. Despite discussions about transfer of legal ownership that took place in the 1920s, the building remained the property of the Church of England, so the decision had to be accepted. As far as Count Kleinmichel and his co-workers were concerned, however, there appeared to be no great cause for alarm, since the Church Abroad had already been promised the use of All Saint's, Ennismore Gardens—there remained only a few legal formalities to be completed. When the documents were presented for signature, however, he was informed of a change: the church would only be made available under conditions of shared usage, as before. With the demolition of St Philip's, it was no longer feasible to give the Church Abroad a separate building.

All the efforts of so many years to obtain a separate church had been wiped out—in the name of a bus station. Bishop Nikodem called an Extraordinary General Meeting of the parish, which took place in St Philip's church hall on January 2/15, 1956, the feast of St Seraphim of Sarov. After a moleben to St Seraphim, Bishop Nikodem opened the meeting. The question before the parish was whether to accept or reject the offer for shared use of the new church. If rejected, the parish would be left only with two small house chapels—the Podvoria and the convent church in Brechin Place. The Count explained how the situation had arisen and a letter was read from Father George Cheremetieff who was absent due to illness.

Before the meeting, the parish had received letters from clergymen from around the world with whom it had ties from earlier associations. The most authoritative voice was undoubtedly that of Protopresbyter Michael Polsky (the former rector), who wrote from San Francisco,

> Enough of this hesitation, this compromise and appeasement! This is not the time for such things. We should nurture in ourselves a feeling of revulsion towards lies and untruth, not try to repress these feelings, and the members of the Church Abroad should be educated in a spirit of faithfulness towards their own Church. The London community has gone through trials like this before, but now at last you have been given the right to make a choice, and you should hold on to that right. May God help you!

Bishop Averky of the Holy Trinity Monastery at Jordanville, New York, who had known Bishop Nikodem in Yugoslavia, retained close ties with him through correspondence. He wrote, "All of us here were quite amazed to learn that such an unnatural state of 'coexistence' has lasted for so many years in London. We are all convinced that now, under the leadership of Vladyka Nikodem, you will put an end to this abnormal situation. It would be better to depart into the catacombs."

Also from America, Archimandrite Constantine, editor of the newspaper *Pravoslavnaya Rus (Orthodox Russia)*, wrote:

> Glory to God that there are people of sufficient zeal to lift up their voices against this compromise—a position that is particularly difficult in a country where the main religious body has adopted a stance of friendliness towards the Moscow Patriarchate. Of course, this cannot remain a purely local event; it will be valued in accordance with its merits by the Church and the Orthodox people wherever they may be. It is not we who save the Church, but the Church which saves us. May God help the General Meeting to come to a unanimous decision based on a correct ecclesiastical understanding, otherwise this will be a grievous date in the history of our Church, which may God forbid.

Many parishioners who lived outside London came for the meeting, which was attended by some 30 percent of registered members. It was suggested that the shared use of All Saints at Ennismore Gardens would be only temporary until such time as another church could be found for the parish of the Moscow Patriarchate. However, many parishioners of the Church Abroad viewed this with grave reservations. It had already taken years to find even this one church, and by now the climate of public opinion in England and within the Anglican Church was changing as the Cold War period of the early 1950s gave way to "peaceful coexistence." An Anglican Church delegation had visited Moscow and Dr Hewlett Johnson was gaining notoriety as the "Red Dean" of Canterbury. If shared use were to be accepted, even on a temporary basis, it might be hard for the "White" Russian Church Abroad to extricate itself from the situation. Still, some older émigrés initially favoured such an arrangement.

Most displaced persons and Cossacks took a different view. As described earlier, most schisms and divisions in the Church outside Russia were attributable, in one way or another, to the interference of the Soviet government in the life of the Church within Russia. From the canonical standpoint of the Church Abroad, the London "Patriarchal" parish appeared to be using the newly reconstituted Moscow Patriarchate to legitimize the old schism of 1927. With their instinctive abhorrence of anything even remotely connected with the Soviet regime, the new immigrants felt that this regime was reaching out through the activities of the Moscow Patriarchate abroad to interfere with and compromise their Holy of Holies, the one treasure that remained to them—the Orthodox Church. They felt that the shared arrangement would be "coexistence" of a kind, and they wanted no part of it.

A heated debate ensued. Some people seized on the opportunity to make stirring patriotic speeches, thereby increasing the tension but contributing little of value. Most kept to the point. The Cossacks in particular spoke fervently of the need for the parish to have a church of its own, and to spare no effort or expense to achieve this.

When the vote was taken, the offer for shared use was rejected by an overwhelming majority of 245 votes to 15. Within minutes, a small mountain of pound notes grew on the table in front of Bishop Nikodem. The diocesan journal, edited by Bishop Leonty of Geneva, commented,

> The whole meeting proceeded with great animation and enthusiasm, which shows that the London parish has not lost the traits which have always characterized it in the past—its clear awareness of the rightness of our holy Church Abroad and its firm confession of her truth. . . . Those present exchanged joyful greetings: "Glory to God, truth has conquered!" "Let God arise and let His enemies be scattered!" They then turned in prayer to St. Seraphim of Sarov to ask for help in their labours which lay ahead.

Afterwards, Father George wrote to a parishioner, "I am feeling ill, with one sickness running into the next one, so that my heart is growing tired from the struggle—and now at the same time has come the struggle for the purity of our church, to separate it from the 'Soviet' parish. The Lord blessed us and, despite some strong opposition, through the voice of simple people, He granted us to achieve this victory."

Not long after this meeting the demolition contractors moved in at 188 Buckingham Palace Road. "Having lived through more than one of the catastrophes of this century," wrote Tatiana Danilewicz, "I was profoundly affected by the destruction of our magnificent church in London, with its old icons, sanctified by the prayer of generations with, I would say, its atmosphere of old Russia, where I had found myself a secluded corner within the spacious church. As one entered, one wanted to forget all the vanities of this earth."

The icons and other interior furnishings were divided between the two parishes. The marble iconostasis from Welbeck Street was transported to Ennismore Gardens where the former Anglican church of All Saints was soon converted for use by the parish of the Moscow Patriarchate. At the end of 1956, Metropolitan Nikolai of Krutitsa[23] came from the Soviet Union for the consecration. The Russian Church Abroad, whose London parish at the time was far larger, had no alternative but to put its share of the holy objects into storage against the day when it found a church of its own.

The division of the church property was not formalized until the following year. On November 6, 1957, an Extraordinary General Meeting was held of the London Russian Orthodox Parish Community—the legal body established in 1921 to hold the property of the parish. After the schism took place in 1927, the Parish Community became the vehicle for organizing the shared use of St Philip's Church. The church's demolition warranted the end of this arrangement, but by this time each parish had organized itself as a charitable trust.[24] Out of the Extraordinary General Meeting in 1957 emerged the resolution that the property of the Parish Community be divided into three parts. The first part consisted of the archives of the Russian Church in London from its inception in 1713 up to the schism of 1927 as well as the extensive parish library. These were transferred to the trustees of the two parishes jointly, and "deposited in such place or places . . . as the Trustees shall jointly decide upon." Thus the archives were deposited in the Public Record Office (now the National Archives) and the library was donated to the London School of Slavonic and East European Studies.[25] The remaining property was divided into two substantially equal parts and transferred to the trustees of each parish.

Meanwhile, services continued in the beautiful but tiny church at the Podvoria at 14 St Dunstan's Road. Only the existence of another house church—that of the Convent of the Annunciation in Brechin Place—saved the parish from disaster. The convent had been holding services early in the morning, following the practice in the Holy Land, but at the request of Bishop Nikodem, the service time was changed to 10:00 a.m. on Sundays and feast days to be more convenient for members of the parish. As in the matter of religious education, people came to appreciate the providential significance of the convent's establishment in a central location in London. Brechin Place in South Kensington was on the western side of the city, convenient for the main centre of the Russian colony and close to the Gloucester Road Underground station. Some of the parishioners began attending services at the convent regularly and, growing accustomed to the monastic singing, remained members of the congregation there for years. Nevertheless, even the two small churches combined were hopelessly inadequate to meet the needs of the parish.

In June 1956 Archbishop John came specifically to address the annual parish meeting on the question of finding a new church, although his advice and encouragement did not immediately change the situation. Exactly one year later, Bishop Nikodem told the parishioners,

> Almost one and a half years have passed since the London parish lost its leading position among the parishes in our Diocese of Western Europe. This grievous situation has inevitably caused great distress both to us, the clergy, and to all the active members of the parish throughout the whole of this period. It weighs on our hearts like a heavy stone.

His primary concern, as an archpastor responsible for the care of human souls, was that there was simply nowhere for many of his flock to attend church. He estimated that about half of his congregation had thus lost contact with the Church or, as he put it, "been forced to cease being cared for by their own Russian Church." Only at Christmas and Easter were some of these people seen again, when large Anglican churches were borrowed for the festive services from sympathetic Anglican clergymen.

Lengthy correspondence with the Church of England was initiated in the hope of finding their own church, but in the end the answer was the same as before: "Why not share with the Moscow Patriarchate?" Convinced that a completely independent solution was necessary, the Parish Council set up a special committee composed of people experienced in construction as well as the purchase and letting of real property. Bishop Nikodem pointed to the example of Church life in America, where many parishes and churches were being established through individual initiative based on privately raised funds. Closer to home, in Paris the small parish faithful to the Russian Church Abroad had recently acquired a church of its own after a period when it had been forced to rent a lock-up garage for church services. The modest scale of some of these undertakings was not important, said Bishop Nikodem, probably echoing the advice received from Archbishop John; the important thing was the burning spirit and love for the Church which the Russian exile communities were manifesting.

Various proposals were put forward. Alexei Ananin, the parish secretary, drew up plans for building a new church in traditional Russian style. This was obviously the ideal solution, but also the most expensive. Count Kleinmichel, Mr V. B. Freshville, and others, including the bishop, looked at numerous buildings with the possibility of buying or leasing either an unused church or a house that could be converted. Bishop Nikodem felt that the most realistic proposal was to extend the Podvoria church—presumably by building onto the rear of the house. He reckoned that the floor space could be approximately doubled, increasing the capacity to 150, which was the average Sunday congregation at St Philip's before it was demolished. Nevertheless, it would still be inadequate for the large numbers attending the great feast days.

Bishop Nikodem during Pascha at St Mark's Anglican Church, 1957. (Source: Dmitri Schtipakin)

Celebrating Pascha at St Mark's Anglican Church, 1957: choir director A. A. Khaltygin (first from left), Barbara Freshville (fourth from left), and Dmitri Schtipakin (seventh from left). (Source: Dmitri Schtipakin)

St Mark's Church—the chapel attached to Chelsea College in Fulham Road—was borrowed in 1957 for Christmas and Easter as well as for the last three days of Holy Week. The church was set back from the street in the college grounds, making it possible to hold the Easter midnight procession with great solemnity while processing round the church in accordance with tradition. (Buildings in London are often so close together that this is not possible.) Organizing these services in Anglican churches took a substantial amount of effort because everything necessary for an Orthodox service, including icons and a portable iconostasis, had to be transported and set up on site, and then removed afterwards. These were not ordinary services either, but those of Holy Week when the winding sheet and tomb are placed in the middle of the church, and the church itself is adorned to suit the solemn and festive occasion. Here the indefatigable Mr Pesiakoff came to the fore to organize transportation. Vladyka Nikodem took comfort at the impressive numbers who attended these services, reflecting that they still retained their fundamental allegiance to the Russian Church Abroad.

Meanwhile, Bishop Nikodem strove to impress on the regular Sunday congregation the vital importance of making the best possible use of the little church they had at the Podvoria. Any disturbance during the service would be particularly noticeable and would disrupt the prayerful atmosphere, so it was more important than ever to stand and pray quietly and reverently so that anyone who entered would be "filled with a feeling of reverence and feel the church's prayerful atmosphere." He encouraged those who were able to do so to avail themselves of the services held on saints' days during the week, when overcrowding was not a problem. True to his approach of always looking at the inner spiritual side of parish life as well as its external side, he encouraged his parishioners to derive spiritual profit from the situation. In 1957 Bishop Nikodem said,

> For the sake of the Lord and of the common prayer which is pleasing to Him, we must endure the crowding and stuffiness of our little church, which is felt particularly during the summer. We must not forget that life in accordance with the Gospel, the work of the salvation of the soul, is a work achieved through the intense Christian spiritual effort, or *podvig*. The principal component of this intense effort—which is also the means towards achieving success in other aspects of it—is prayer, and, in first place, the common prayer of the Church. When we exert our spirit in prayer, we often cease to feel physical tiredness. And only then will prayer bring forth its true fruit, which is compunction of heart.

Chapter 15

[1959–1976] Archbishop Nikodem: Emperor's Gate

Opening of the New Church at Emperor's Gate

As the search for a new church continued throughout 1956 and 1957, the situation began to seem hopeless. Then, in 1958, a suitable building was found in Emperor's Gate, a quiet square in Kensington near the Gloucester Road Underground station. The Victorian Gothic-style church was built in the nineteenth century by Scottish Presbyterians. It had been closed for worship for more than thirty years after having been sold to the Anglican parish of St Stephen, which rented it out commercially to store furniture while the parish used the basement as a church hall. It was not available for sale, but after some negotiation—conducted primarily by the churchwarden, Count Kleinmichel, and the parish secretary, Alexei Ananin—a twenty-year lease on the building was taken out by the parish. This leasehold arrangement was far from ideal but under the circumstances it represented a considerable achievement.

After being used for storage for so many years, the church interior was extremely dirty and in need of repair. The extensive cleaning and refurbishment would be expensive, so Count Kleinmichel began a fund-raising campaign. Following the example of people he knew who did postal[1] fund-raising appeals for charitable causes, he launched an appeal addressed to brokers in the City of London[2] with whom he had ongoing business contacts. Gerald Palmer,[3] an English convert to Orthodoxy who belonged to the parish, agreed to make a donation to match whatever the parish was able to raise, thereby doubling the sum collected. In this way, about £300,000 was collected, which in the late 1950s was a very substantial sum. This was more money than was needed for refurbishing the church, so Count Kleinmichel invested the rest for the benefit of the parish.

Despite the dilapidated condition of the building, the floor plan lent itself well to adaptation as an Orthodox church. It was rectangular with a narrower apse at one end where the altar could be located. It also had a gallery which could be used as a choir loft. There were no obtrusive organ pipes or stained glass windows in the sanctuary, as there had been at St Philip's. Work began under the direction of S. V. Kadloubovsky, an architect who was a member of the Parish Council. The floor in the apse and part of the east end was raised for the altar and ambo (*soleas*).[4] A small area was partitioned off to form a vestry. The ornamented railing round the edge of the gallery was regilded. A large icon of the Pokrov—the Mother of God holding out Her protecting veil over the church—was painted by Dmitri Schtipakin, a member of the parish, for placement on the wall above the sanctuary. Work proceeded hurriedly. The blessing of the new church was scheduled for the Sunday before Orthodox Christmas.

The church in Emperor's Gate, ca. 1958. (Source: Antonina Ananin)

Iconostasis at the church in Emperor's Gate. (Source: Antonina Ananin)

Interior view of Emperor's Gate, showing the Pokrov icon in the apse that was painted by Dmitri Schtipakin. (Source: Dmitri Schtipakin)

By the time the icons and other sacred objects from St Philip's were retrieved from storage, there was very little time left. Some of these items were seriously in need of cleaning and repair before they could be installed in the new church. At this pressing moment, many parishioners—and others who had rarely been seen in church before—came forward to help. At last the labours of Captain Sukhonik bore fruit, decades after he bought the iconostasis from the governor-general's residence in Helsinki for the parish in 1922. Although it had not been used at St. Philip's, this iconostasis fit perfectly into the space available. Two other large icons from St Philip's were erected at either side of the *soleas*, thus helping to separate it from the rest of the church. On the left was a large icon of St Nicholas in traditional style, which had been purchased in 1938 to mark the twentieth anniversary of the death of Emperor Nicholas II. On the right was placed an icon of the Mother of God called "Self-written" (*Sampopisavshayasya*) which had been a gift from hermits on Mt Athos to the Embassy church in 1901. Two icons donated to Embassy church by the Grand Duchess Maria Alexandrovna in the previous century[5] were also erected: the magnificent Smolensk Icon of the Mother of God—positioned at the east end over the high place in the altar, yet visible throughout the church—and an icon of the appearance of the angels to the Myrrh-bearing Women in a marble frame, which was set up by the main door of the church. Large icons were hung on the walls in the spaces between the pointed, neo-Gothic windows. Through intensive effort, the church was ready by the appointed day.

The consecration[6] of the Cathedral church was performed on January 4, 1959, by the diocesan bishop, Archbishop John. The clergy and parishioners cherished the blessing of their church by a hierarch so renowned for his personal sanctity; they believed it left the imprint of an especially prayerful atmosphere that was always felt in the building. Archbishop John was assisted by the parish rector Bishop Nikodem and by the other clergy of the parish, Abbot Ambrose (Pogodin) and Father George Cheremetieff.

Bishop Nikodem blesses the people at Emperor's Gate, ca. 1965. At left is Subdeacon Ivan Georgievsky and at right is Reader Mstislav Perott. In the altar is Protodeacon Nikolai. (Source: George Knupffer)

Father George Cheremetieff conducts the wedding of Prince Dmitri Galitzine and Patricia Wingfield in 1966 at Emperor's Gate. (Source: Deacon Andrew Bond)

Also concelebrating were Archpriest Miloje Nikolich, administrator of the Serbian Church in England, as well as Protopresbyter Anthony Gramatins of the Latvian Church and Archpriest Nicholas Hindo of the Estonian Church.

The great rejoicing on this occasion was compared by some people to the joy of Pascha. Many had tears in their eyes as the blessing and first Liturgy in the new church proceeded. The years of "wandering in the wilderness" were over and, for the first time since 1927, the parish had a church of its own. Apart from the limitations of the twenty-year lease, this was more satisfactory than the situation that had prevailed at St Philip's where the church was only available on alternate Sundays. The "stubbornness" of the Cossacks, as well as the patience and prayer of the bishop, had been rewarded.

Commenting on this joyous achievement, Bishop Nikodem said, "Now that we have acquired and converted this magnificent church, the restricted, semiparalysed state of our parish, which lasted for three years, has come to an end. Now we can set out on a broader path of Church life. Great is God's mercy shown to the London parish, and we must thank God for it without ceasing. Not only must we thank Him, but we must always strive in every way to be worthy of this mercy."

Bishop Nikodem regarded the opening of the new church as an event of more than just local significance:

> The great assembly of clergymen serving on the day our church was consecrated, the magnificent singing of the choir under the direction of A. A. Khaltygin, who made great efforts to improve the standard of the singing during the period leading up to the opening of the new church—all this added to the spiritual beauty of this festival, which was an exceptional event in the life of the London parish. It was a triumphant celebration, not just for our own parish or even for the Russian Church Abroad as a whole. We must not forget our position as fighters against the evil of atheism and the materialistic principles of life which are embracing contemporary humanity. This confrontation will be more effectual, the greater our zeal in living our life in the Church. An intense, unseen war is taking place in the world on the spiritual battlefield. And, whether we are aware of it or not, we are taking part in this warfare.

The zeal inspired by this new home can be seen in a parishioner's description of the first patronal festival held in the Emperor's Gate church later that year:

> For the first time since acquiring its Cathedral church, the London parish solemnly celebrated its patronal festival on the day of the Dormition of the Most Holy Mother of God (15/28 August). Attendance has increased markedly since the church was opened. Many new faces are seen at the services. The beauty of the iconostasis, the grandeur of the icons and generally radiant appearance of the church are attracting wide attention, not only from Russians, but also from English people. . . . Today, on the day of the patronal festival, the church is looking particularly splendid. Enormous bouquets and garlands of flowers adorn the ambo and soleas. . . . The gilded railings round the ambo and the balconies reflect the candle light and shine as if the church were flooded with a sea of fire. . . . The excellent acoustics add clarity to the exclamations of the clergy and the singing of the choir. Although it was a working day and in the summer holiday period, the church was full. During the Little Entrance Bishop Nikodem elevated Father George Cheremetieff to the rank of archpriest. The great feast day, coming at the end of a fast period, drew nearly half the congregation to the chalice of Holy Communion.

The remainder of this chapter considers the development of parish life at Emperor's Gate and some of the more remarkable individuals in the parish, as well as other societal currents and events affecting church life in London as it developed under the prayerful guidance of His Grace, Bishop Nikodem, until his death in 1976.

Development of Parish Life at Emperor's Gate

Bishop Nikodem gave thanks to God as he saw the congregation growing to include not only those who had drifted away over the past three years, but many new faces as well. He attributed this in part to the "beauty and grandeur" of the church, which was large enough to conduct services properly according to the episcopal rite. On an ordinary Sunday, the bishop was assisted by at least one of the two priests (Father George Cheremetieff and Father Ambrose (Pogodin)) and Protodeacon Nicholas Jakimowicz, Deacon Sergei Jefimenko, and a whole team of altar servers, led by the acting subdeacons Ivan Georgievsky and Mstislav Perott. Vladyka Nikodem was particularly pleased to see a younger generation of altar servers—teenagers such as Misha and Alyosha Knupffer, and others younger still. Bishop Nikodem determined to take full advantage of the new church premises to foster the parish's development, both spiritually and as a community. Turning his attention to the choir, he expressed his gratitude and appreciation, noting that it had expanded and improved in the new church. He said that the "exultant, prayerful singing" was drawing new members to the congregation. Nevertheless, he attempted to guide the choir toward a more prayerful style of singing. The choirmaster, A. A. Khaltygin, was a qualified musician; besides directing the church choir, he also gave secular concerts under the name of "Captain Strelsky." He did not, however, possess the theological and spiritual background that characterized his predecessor, Foka Feodorovitch Volkovsky (d. 1951), who was one of the last *psalomshchiki* of the old school. Guidance of this nature now had to be provided by the clergy—in as tactful a way as possible. Thus, in his 1961 report to the parish meeting, Bishop Nikodem said,

> The singing of the choir is a very important element of Orthodox Divine Worship; it is something to which we have to pay close attention. On the singing depend both the external side of the service—its beauty and splendour—and also the creation of a prayerful inner disposition in the congregation. Therefore, while expressing gratitude to the choirmaster, A. A. Khaltygin, and all of our choir for their labours and efforts, I must also encourage them to achieve greater perfection by moving towards a more religious, ecclesiastical style of singing; such a style is marked by greater restraint and the absence of the affectations

> of secular singing. . . . On the one hand, the singing in church must satisfy the outward side of the service, giving it, as it were, the magnificence and strength of the heavenly hosts, while on the other hand, through the tenderness of the melody and a corresponding approach to its execution, it must assist all those praying to become inwardly immersed in prayer and the Divine stillness and quiet.

Bishop Nikodem at Emperor's Gate, holding the miraculously self-renewing icon of St Sabbas the Sanctified, ca. 1966.[7] (Source: Archimandrite Alexis)

Like most pastors and archpastors of the exile Church, Bishop Nikodem called on his flock to receive Holy Communion more frequently. He discouraged the view held commonly by many people in Russia before the Revolution that approaching the sacraments once a year was adequate, whereas he wanted them to see this as the bare minimum. In 1960 he noted that all registered members of the parish had received Holy Communion at least once during the year, while many were coming more frequently and there were some adult communicants at almost every Sunday liturgy. Bishop Nikodem called on the congregation to arrive punctually and to draw closer to the altar to participate more fully in the sacred rites:

> Standing by the doorway, as if in the narthex—the porch, which is reserved for those still preparing for baptism—does not accord with the dignity of the believers. One thereby distances oneself from the altar and close contact with the clergy. Many forget that we do not come to God's temple for our individual, private prayer; it is not simply a question of being present at the services, but the congregation participates in it in complete unity with the servants of the altar.

Adornment of the new church continued after it was opened, as carpets and other essential items were donated through individuals' generosity. In 1962 a set of icons of the twelve great feast days was acquired, painted at the Lesna Convent in France by Mother Flaviana, a nun who was well known for her skill in the art of traditional iconography. She even used the old egg-tempera paints rather than the acrylics of many modern icon painters. The icons of the great feast days, if painted in the traditional style, express between them the whole Orthodox theology of redemption. It is considered particularly important, therefore, that icons of these feasts are well executed. Bishop Nikodem had great personal respect for Mother Flaviana, whom he had known in Yugoslavia when the Lesna Convent was located there. He admired her spiritual qualities as well as her technical skill—two essential characteristics in a good iconographer. The icons that she painted are regarded as a particular blessing to the parish.

Although the new church was greatly appreciated, some parishioners missed the little Podvoria church that felt saturated with the prayers of so many years and where many found peace and consolation amid the old icons and simpler singing of the smaller choir. In response, Bishop Nikodem agreed to use the Podvoria for the saints' days which fell during the week, reserving the Emperor's Gate "Sobor"[8] for Sundays and greater feast days, when extra capacity was required. Another icon ordered in 1962 from Mother Flaviana was that of All Saints to grace the Podvoria.

Besides the church itself, the parish also drew immense benefit from the church hall in the crypt of the building as a community gathering place. At first, meals were held only on special feast days, but at the encouragement of Bishop Nikodem, the sisterhood began providing a light meal and cup of tea every Sunday after the service. This new venture—not possible at St Philip's because there was no meeting hall attached to the church—was highly valued by the congregation, since there were then no other community centres where Russians could meet socially. The Russian Centre at 49 Penywern Road, Earls Court, had been forced to close, unable to make ends meet in the face of rising costs. Bishop Nikodem saw it as providential that the church provided such a meeting place, which also offered informal contact with the clergy. Hoping it would develop into a centre for Christian education and enlightenment, he often gave spiritual talks on Sunday afternoons, or invited others to do so.

The new church facilities enabled the long-awaited reorganization of the parish library—making use of Archimandrite Vitaly's collection of books from ten years earlier as the foundation of a subscription lending service. In 1960 the bishop announced that all the books had been transported from the Podvoria to Emperor's Gate through the efforts of Mr T. A. Volokevitch and were in the process of being catalogued and evaluated for suitability (the library having been received as a private donation and not yet thoroughly examined). This work was completed the following year but the results were disappointing in the extreme. Most of the books turned out to be novels translated from foreign languages into Russian, while others were by Soviet authors expressing anti-Christian ideas. Even the basics of Russian classical literature were missing. In time, some classical literary works were acquired and a section of books on religious subjects was added to the collection. Most of the books were curiously arranged at the bottom of a seldom used spiral staircase leading from the choir loft to the basement. Others were kept in glass-fronted bookcases in the church hall. The library was open after the Sunday service and was another factor that helped to unite the community. Meanwhile, books of a purely religious character as well as icons and crosses were sold in the church by a member of the sisterhood.

In his annual reports, Bishop Nikodem always thanked the more active parishioners for their work. In the first place, he mentioned Count Kleinmichel, who continued to act as both churchwarden (*starosta*) and treasurer. From its very inception, the London parish of the Dormition had been characterized by a strong lay organization. Count Kleinmichel continued this tradition by being *starosta* in the old Russian sense of an elected community leader rather than merely a "churchwarden." At the same time, he used his position and experience as a senior employee of a London merchant bank, Kleinwort Benson, to look after the church's financial affairs. In 1959 his wife, Countess Maria Georgievna Kleinmichel, was elected head of the sisterhood after the retirement of Valeria Ampenoff. The sisterhood's responsibilities had grown to include not only looking after the church and making vestments, but also raising funds to help pay for converting the church building and the increased costs of rental and upkeep. To this end bazaars were organized several times a year; the Easter Bazaar was organized by the sisterhood and a Christmas Bazaar was sponsored by the Russian Red Cross, at which the sisterhood had a stall. Other parishioners mentioned by the bishop included Tatiana Kharalampievna Philipova, an elderly

Churchwarden and treasurer for more than forty years, Count Wladimir Kleinmichel is shown hard at work on the accounts, ca. 1960. (Source: Sophia Goodman)

In 1961 Count Kleinmichel was awarded Commander (CVO) rank in the Royal Victorian Order by Her Majesty Queen Elizabeth II in recognition of services to the royal family. Shown outside Buckingham Palace with his wife, Countess Maria Kleinmichel (right), and his sister, Sophia Wolcough (left). (Source: Sophia Goodman)

woman of great piety who looked after the church, lighting the icon lamps and extinguishing candles that had burnt low. Known affectionately as "Babushka Tatiana," she continued this work until she was well over ninety years old. The bishop also thanked Dmitri Krasnopolsky, the watchman: "Like the angel by the gates of Eden, he guards our church and all the sacred items inside from damage and robbery."

The first solemn event held in the church at Emperor's Gate was the funeral of the Grand Duchess Xenia Alexandrovna, who died on April 20, 1960. She died shortly after receiving Holy Communion from the hands of her spiritual father, Father George Cheremetieff. Preceding the funeral, the Liturgy for the departed was conducted each day in her private chapel at Hampton Court by different members of the Cathedral clergy. Archbishop John came from France for the funeral, which was attended by representatives of the British royal family and many foreign royal houses as well as the grand duchess's two sons and their families. The church was filled to capacity. There was hardly enough room for all the wreaths and flowers which were sent. Because it took place the week after Easter (April 4/17 in 1960), the funeral featured many Paschal hymns and reflected the joy of the resurrection more than the sadness of death. After the service, the coffin was flown to the south of France for burial next to the grand duchess's husband, the Grand Duke Alexander Mikhailovitch.

The parish suffered a severe blow in 1961 when Father George Cheremetieff was injured in a traffic accident. He survived but the injuries were serious and he always walked with a stick afterwards. For a long time he was completely unable to conduct church services; thereafter he served occasionally but was officially considered retired.

Serving as assistant priest for a time was the brilliant but erratic Father Ambrose (Pogodin), who was also an accomplished pianist. He had been in England since 1953 and served in various parishes including Bradford and Nottingham, but was based at the Cathedral church in London for most of this period. He pursued his pastoral duties energetically. On one occasion he served the Paschal service for a Serbian parish in Cardiff. In August 1956 he was transferred to Australia to act as secretary to Bishop Sava (Raevsky), but he returned to England less than a year later in May 1957. In 1964 he left England permanently after receiving an appointment to the Russian parish in Rome. He did not stay there long, and left shortly for the United States where he transferred to the jurisdiction of the American Metropolia.

Father Ambrose was a prolific writer with a penetrating theological mind. The London parish archives contain a copy of his manuscript titled "The Dogma of Redemption—An Investigation of Eastern and Western Understandings of the Dogma of Redemption and Various Questions Connected with This Dogma." This work is a summary and further exploration of the ideas of Metropolitan Anthony (Khrapovitsky) on the subject. In 1955, at the behest of the Holy Synod, he composed a service in honour of St Augustine of Hippo. This request was prompted by Archbishop John (Maximovitch) who was very interested in reviving the veneration of early Western saints by the Orthodox Church. Father Ambrose's books include *St Mark of Ephesus and the Florentine Union*, published by Holy Trinity Monastery in the United States. He also undertook a translation from Greek into Russian of some newly discovered homilies by St Macarius the Great, which along with many of his other writings were published in Canada by Metropolitan Vitaly, who saw them as being of great value even though their author no longer belonged to the Russian Church Abroad.

For a year after the departure of Father Ambrose, Bishop Nikodem managed by himself. Then, at the beginning of Great Lent in 1965, Father Nicholas Troitsky moved to London. Father Nicholas had lived in Yugoslavia before World War II and his wife was Serbian. He had been a lay member of the parish in Leeds and earned his living as a gardener while preparing for the priesthood under the bishop's guidance. After being ordained by Bishop Nikodem in 1960 at the age of fifty-five, he served as priest to the two parishes in Leeds and Nottingham. He and his wife moved into the basement flat at the Podvoria that had been vacated by Father Ambrose. After his wife's death in 1971, Father Nicholas received the monastic tonsure with the name Nicanor. In 1988 he became spiritual father of the Convent of the Annunciation.

A church was opened in the grounds of a Russian old people's home at Barton-on-Sea in Hampshire on the south coast of England in 1962. Most of the home's residents came from China (from where the last Russian émigrés left in the early 1960s); some came from a refugee camp in Trieste in northern Italy after the war. Bishop Nikodem went by train every month to celebrate the Liturgy there one day during the week. Some residents gathered in the church daily to read prayers and sing akathists.

In August 1962, Archbishop John celebrated at the patronal festival of the Dormition in London for the last time before he was transferred to San Francisco later that year. Bishop Anthony (Bartochevitch) was appointed diocesan bishop and the centre of the Diocese of Western Europe was transferred from Paris to Geneva. On February 13, 1964, the Synod of Bishops ruled that the parishes in England should form a separate diocese because Geneva was too

Bishop Nikodem at the Kazan Chapel, Barton-on-Sea, 1961, with residents of the British Council for Refugees Home and Antonina Ananin (fourth from left). (Source: Antonina Ananin)

far from London for regular contact to be feasible (in the days before air travel became commonplace). Bishop Nikodem was confirmed as the diocesan bishop with the title Bishop of Richmond and Great Britain.

Bishop Nikodem at the Kazan Chapel, Barton-on-Sea, 1962. (Source: Antonina Ananin)

That same year on June 24/July 7, the feast of the Nativity of St John the Baptist, Bishop Nikodem held the first diocesan congress—a meeting of all the clergymen of the diocese. In addition to the London clergy, these included Father Philemon Zadworny from Bradford and Archpriest Nicholas Popoff from Manchester, who had been awarded the right to wear a mitre earlier that year in recognition of his fifty years in the priesthood.

A few years later, the Russian Church Abroad found itself in a dilemma when approached by some groups of anticommunist Serbian exiles who did not wish to belong to the Serbian Patriarchal Church. The Russian Church Abroad had never considered that the Serbian Church was controlled by the communist government of Yugoslavia in the same way that the Church in Russia was controlled by the Soviet government. In England, as elsewhere, the Russian Church Abroad enjoyed good relations with the clergy of the Serbian Church. So in 1967, the Bishops' Council resolved that "the Russian Orthodox Church Abroad will always render spiritual help to its brothers, the Orthodox Serbs," while at the same time "refraining from interference in the affairs of the Serbian Orthodox Church."

Acting in the spirit of this resolution, in 1968 Bishop Nikodem accepted a celibate Serbian priest into the Diocese of Richmond and Great Britain. He tonsured him a monk with the monastic name Victor, and shortly thereafter raised him to the rank of archimandrite. Speaking good Russian and English as well as Serbian, Father Victor (Jankovich) helped in the parish and diocese in addition to caring for a number of Serbs who had turned to the Russian Church Abroad. Perhaps as a result of the rapidity of his ecclesiastical advancement, Father Victor somehow never gained the complete confidence of the London Russian parish. The following year he left for America, where he was appointed rector of the parish in St Petersburg, Florida, in Archbishop Nikon's diocese.[9] After his departure from England, there remained a Serbian community in Northampton which looked to the Russian Church Abroad for spiritual care, and the duty of visiting this parish fell to Father Nicholas Troitsky who had a fluent command of Serbian.

Marked by exceptional solemnity that drew widespread attention and national media coverage was the 1965 visit of Metropolitan Philaret (Voznesensky), newly elected Primate of the Russian Church Abroad. He brought with him the miraculous Kursk icon of the Mother of God. It was the first time the icon had travelled to the United Kingdom since 1950, the year the Synod moved from Europe to New York. Metropolitan Philaret was elected to lead the Church Abroad in 1964 after Metropolitan Anastassy, who was more than ninety years old, finally retired despite the protests of his fellow bishops. At the age of sixty-one, Metropolitan Philaret was the youngest of the bishops and was virtually unknown in the Russian emigration because he had left communist China only a few years previously. He had been consecrated as vicar bishop of Brisbane in Australia and

Metropolitan Philaret and Count Kleinmichel alight from the boat train at Waterloo Station, 1965. On the left is Archdeacon Gelassy who carries the Kursk icon. (Source: Michael Knupffer)

Bishop Nikodem (right) welcomes Metropolitan Philaret at Waterloo Station, 1965. Second from left is Archdeacon Gelassy, and to his right is George Knupffer. (Source: Michael Knupffer)

attended the 1964 Bishop's Council in that capacity, only to find himself elected to fill the post of First Hierarch. His election was greatly influenced by Archbishop John (Maximovitch), and others soon began to appreciate the special spiritual qualities of the new metropolitan. The year after his election he set off on a tour of all the different dioceses in the Russian Church Abroad.

Metropolitan Philaret crossed the Atlantic by ship with Archdeacon Gelassy, who carried the miraculous icon. They were met on Friday, August 20, at Southampton by Count Kleinmichel, who accompanied them back to London on the boat train. Welcoming them on the platform at Waterloo Station were Bishop Nikodem and the London clergy, Abbess Elisabeth and the nuns from the convent, and a group of parishioners. Bishop Nikodem entered the railway carriage to greet the metropolitan. Alighting from the train, he was faced by press photographers and television film crews as well as amateur photographers from the parish. Reporters bombarded him with questions until he got into the car that was waiting to take him to the Podvoria, where the two small rooms at the top of the building had been prepared for him and Archdeacon Gelassy.

Services in the provincial parishes were cancelled that Saturday and Sunday, as clergy led groups of their parishioners to London to join in the service with the metropolitan. Father Nicholas Popoff from Manchester described Metropolitan Philaret's first entrance into the Cathedral on Saturday:

At 6 p.m. in the Cathedral Church of the Dormition of the Mother of God, the parishioners prepared to greet their First Hierarch and the miraculous icon of the Mother of God. This meeting was uncommonly solemn and triumphant. The whole mass of people stood with lighted candles. The church resounded to the exultant singing of the troparion, *As an invincible rampart. . . .*[10] Many were moved to tears by the solemn beauty of the occasion as the Metropolitan entered the church preceded by Archdeacon Gelassy bearing the icon of the Mother of God. Vladyka looked lovingly at the people who had hitherto been unknown to him. The Spirit of love and peace—God's Spirit—wafted through the church.

On Sunday, the solemn vesting of the hierarchs in the centre of the church was filmed and later shown on television. Photographs also appeared in several newspapers with articles about the metropolitan and the Kursk icon. The congregation listened attentively as it came to appreciate for the first time the new metropolitan's great gift—that of a preacher with an intimate knowledge of the Gospels and the patristic commentaries on them. Father Popoff wrote,

> All were abundantly filled with the desire to see their First Hierarch, or Primate, to pray together with him, to receive his blessing and hear his Godly-wise counsels, for the avoidance of sin and the salvation of their souls. . . . The Metropolitan's sermon at the end of the Liturgy was heard with rapt attention; it was delivered in simple words which everyone could understand. These were not the words of human wisdom, but were a manifestation of the Spirit and God's power. As in all the Metropolitan's serving and preaching, there was a complete absence of any artificiality or contrived emotion.

Following weekend services at Emperor's Gate, on Monday Metropolitan Philaret celebrated at the Convent of the Annunciation. He was joined there by clergy of the Greek Church (including Hierodeacon Kallistos (Ware), secretary to Archbishop Athenagoras) and Archpriest Miloje Nikolich of the Serbian Church. Over the next three days, services were held daily at the Podvoria. The metropolitan celebrated again on the Thursday at the Podvoria, before he left. Between services Father Nicholas Troitsky took the miraculous Kursk icon to bless the homes of parishioners, to the old people's homes, and also to people in hospital, including the choirmaster, Mr Khaltygin, who was recovering from an operation for cancer. (Antonina V. Ananin directed the choir in his place for some months, including during the festivities for the metropolitan's visit.) Meanwhile, the metropolitan met some of the parishioners personally. Some offered to take him on a tour of London's famous buildings.

From London, Metropolitan Philaret proceeded to Brussels and Munich. The clergy and many parishioners came to see him off at the station. Father Nicholas Popoff wrote,

> Having received their final blessing from the First Hierarch, all those present sang the troparion, *As an invincible rampart* . . . and, as the train moved off, *Eis polla, eti despota*. . . . The Vladyka Metropolitan stood at the window and, with a kindly, radiant smile on his face, he blessed everyone as he departed, leaving behind him happy, unforgettable memories in the souls of the faithful.

Commenting on the metropolitan's visit, Bishop Nikodem said,

> The days of his services, which were so full of grace and inspiration, in our churches—both the Cathedral and the Podvoria—brought a ray of light into our prayerful experience. . . . Personal contact and communion in prayer with our First Hierarch—an outstanding personality amidst our hierarchy—has left a profound impression on the soul of each member of the parish, as well as many who do not belong to it. We felt that he was, as it were, the very image of one of the holy hierarchs of ancient, holy Russia.

Establishment of the Convent of the Annunciation in Willesden

The same year in which the Cathedral opened at Emperor's Gate, the Convent of the Annunciation was able to purchase a suitable property. Although funds had been collected over the past five years, they were still far from sufficient. Father George Cheremetieff was particularly concerned that the convent should be established properly. "He prayed so much that we should find a house," recalled Abbess Elisabeth, "and it was through his prayers and help that we eventually succeeded." Father George introduced them to Serbian priest Father Nikolich, who had connections with the Inter-Church Aid and Refugee Service. The president of this organization invited them to submit a detailed memorandum. Before long they were informed that, as they were Palestinian refugees and had never received any financial assistance from any other organization, they were eligible for a grant of £5,000.

On the feast of the Nativity of the Mother of God (September 8/21) the abbess and Sister Susanna set off to look at a property suggested by the estate agents—a detached house at 26 Brondesbury Park in Willesden, in the northern suburbs of London. On the way, they prayed for guidance as to whether it would be pleasing to God to settle there. When they arrived, the owner of the house, who had no connection at all with the Russian Church, unexpectedly presented them with an old Russian icon. It was an icon of that feast day—the Nativity of the Mother of God. Interpreted as a sign from the Mother of God, they purchased the house to be the convent's new home.

With the legal formalities completed, the first day that the sisters entered the house they found in the loft six more old Russian icons of the Mother of God. They were covered with dirt and all but one were damaged by deeply embedded nails. Without understanding where these icons came from, or who had damaged them in such a blasphemous fashion, the nuns took this as an additional sign of God's blessing. Because the house was very dilapidated,

Metropolitan Philaret arrives at the Convent of the Annunciation in north London during his 1965 visit. From left to right, Archpriest Nicholas Popoff (from Manchester), Parasceva Timofeevna, Valeria Ivanovna Ampenoff (Abbess Elisabeth's mother), Tony James, and Abbess Elisabeth. (Source: Michael Knupfer)

builders were called in to make some fundamental repairs. Without any special knowledge of such matters, some of the sisters would take the bus from Brechin Place every day to supervise the work. From France, Archbishop John (Maximovitch) offered some practical advice: "The sisters are from the Holy Land, so they must have good heating." After moving in, the nuns continued cleaning and painting. Their primary concern was having a convent church—an important factor in choosing this house was that its living room was large enough to be converted into a church. This was completed in three days of working without a break so that daily monastic services could continue.

Metropolitan Philaret holds aloft the Kursk icon at the convent in front of Bishop Nikodem (first from left), Archpriest Nicholas (third from left), Father Nicholas Troitsky (fifth from left), and Michael Knupffer (sixth from left). (Source: Michael Knupffer)

The first Liturgy in the convent church was celebrated by Bishop Nikodem on the Sunday of the Publican and the Pharisee in 1960. On the feast day of the Annunciation that year, Bishop Nikodem celebrated there and at the same time blessed the house. The blessing of the church, however, was performed by Archbishop John later that year on the feast of St Mary Magdalene, the anniversary of the establishment of the convent in London in 1954. In addition, there was the "unofficial" blessing performed by Archbishop John at the time of the broken furnace when he prayed over the house all night, blessing it inside and out with holy water.[11]

The seven icons found in the house were cleaned and placed in the church. With the passage of time, many other icons and other sacred objects were donated to the convent. A large number of relics were also sent as a blessing from Archbishop Anthony of Los Angeles, who had been the convent's spiritual father in the Holy Land. The church has always impressed visitors with its warmth and sparkling cleanness, being of chief importance in the lives of the nuns.

Once settled in the new house, the nuns continued the life they had at Brechin Place. The following description of the convent's activities was written in 1968:

The Convent's internal mission consists of bringing the daily life of the parishioners and their children closer to the Church. Its external mission consists of a continual witness before all of the truth of our Holy Orthodox Faith and of the persecution of our Church in the Soviet Union. . . .

All the services prescribed by the monastic typicon are held in the Convent—daily, morning and evening—together with the commemoration of the living and the departed, and the traditions of the Russian monasteries in the Holy Land are lovingly preserved.

Within a month of their arrival in England in 1954, with the blessing of Bishop Nikodem, the sisters opened their school where religious instruction and Russian language are taught to the children every Saturday during the school year up to the present day. The boys are taught to serve in the altar, while the girls are taught church singing and reading and the order of service. The Convent seeks to inspire the children with a love of piety, at the same time protecting them from the materialism of the world around them. Every year the pupils of the Convent school attend the traditional Christmas party (or "yolka") at the Cathedral of the Dormition. They sing *Kolyadki* (Christmas songs), recite Russian poetry and act out parts of plays by authors such as Gogol and Chekhov.

Besides its work with children, the Convent arranges spiritual talks in both Russian and English, as well as talks about the Holy Land illustrated with colour slides. The Mother Abbess gives extensive, detailed instruction to people who have decided to accept the Holy Orthodox Faith. Fourteen people have been prepared in this way over the years, including both adults and children. . . .

People of various religious confessions turn to the Convent both personally and by correspondence for advice and spiritual edification or consolation. Contact has been established in this way with many people, both in England and abroad. The Abbess, together with one of the sisters, visits sick and lonely people in London and the provinces. Sometimes they accompany the priest when he takes Holy Communion to people who are seriously ill and dying.

Several times a year Abbess Elisabeth is invited by Anglican parishes to give talks about the Convent, about the Russian Orthodox Church and about the persecution of believers in the Soviet Union. Such invitations sometimes come from places far outside London; on one occasion a talk was given to a group of students at Cambridge University. Two years ago the sisters gave a concert of Russian Church singing in a Roman Catholic convent near London. This was preceded by a talk about Orthodox worship and church singing given by Mother Elisabeth, and translations of the hymns being sung were handed out. The nuns were deeply moved and thanked the sisters wholeheartedly, saying that the singing had been a revelation and an inspiration to them. On parting, the aged abbess said that they had much to learn from the Orthodox.

Many find refuge and spiritual consolation at the Convent where, far from earthly vanities, they can prepare for confession and Holy Communion and rest their souls. Many pilgrims come to the Convent at Christmas and, especially, at Pascha. The Convent also distributes spiritual literature in Russian and English.

The sisters carry out in turn all the usual monastic obediences. As they are few in number, each has to take on several duties at once: the daily services (reading and singing on the kliros), looking after the house, working in the garden and vegetable garden, baking prosphoras, looking after visitors, teaching the children and so on. Besides this the sisters must still find time to earn their living by taking in sewing from two shops. As this work is irregular and poorly paid, they have taken a two-year course in book-binding and are now taking in work of this nature. . . . And so, with God's help, after overcoming various difficulties, on the day of St. Mary Magdalene [1968], the Convent will begin its fifteenth year in England.

Ecumenism and Mission

The Exile Church's mission to the surrounding world—in particular, its relationships with other religions as well as with the other Orthodox jurisdictions in the United Kingdom—was as much a feature of the church's life in the 1950s as it was a century earlier, although the hope of any union between the Church of England and Orthodoxy had faded after the 1920s.

Given the importance of these matters in the Orthodox world, the written opinions and missionary endeavors of Bishop Nikodem provide special enlightenment. In the 1950s, he attended the diocesan conferences in Europe at which Archbishop John presided. There is no indication that he ever attended the meetings of the full Council of Bishops in America, even after he became diocesan bishop in 1964; however he sent a written report to each Sobor and remained in contact with the other bishops through correspondence. His views properly reflected the "conciliar" (*sobornoye*) consciousness of the Assembly of Hierarchs in reaction to developments within the Orthodox world. At the same time, his attitudes were formulated in the light of the theological instruction he received in Yugoslavia from Metropolitan Anthony and other outstanding hierarchs of the Church Abroad.

From his earliest days in England, Bishop Nikodem maintained friendly contacts with representatives of the Church of England. Thus, in his report for 1954, he noted,

> In accordance with the established tradition in England, we, the Russian clergy, as well as clergy of other Orthodox Churches, are invited to take part in the church festivities of the Anglicans—of course, without any kind of concelebration with them, as this is forbidden by the canons. One such occasion was a service in St. Paul's Cathedral on 20 October last year, when our presence was particularly noted by the Archbishop of Canterbury.

In December 1954, an Anglican bishop was invited to the festive Pan-Orthodox Liturgy held in St Philip's. Commenting on this, Bishop Nikodem told his parishioners,

> Bishop Thomas Cresco of the Anglican Church addressed the concelebrating clergy and people in a long speech, which concentrated on the question of the unity of Christians among themselves which, he said, should be based on a common striving towards the higher world and be inspired by feelings of Christian love. He emphasized the friendly relations which already existed between the Orthodox and Anglican clergy. We will not now discuss in detail the question of the preaching of Christian unity originating from non-Orthodox sources. However I consider it my duty to point out that the seeking after this unity, which now exists in the world, cannot be resolved from the side of us, the Orthodox, in any other way than on the basis of the Orthodox doctrine of the Church; otherwise we will be betraying Orthodoxy and apostatize from it. Unfortunately, many Russian Orthodox people among us do not understand this at all.

As the ecumenical movement gathered momentum during the 1950s and 1960s, the Russian Church Abroad found itself in an increasingly isolated position by adhering to this traditional view of the relations between Orthodoxy and other confessions. During the 1950s, it cautiously sent observers to meetings of the World Council of Churches (WCC), while the Moscow Patriarchate condemned the council. Then in 1961, in a sudden change of direction, the Patriarchate sent representatives to the New Delhi assembly of the WCC and became a full member. Increasingly, the Patriarchate came to

Outside the Cathedral church at Emperor's Gate, 1968: (left to right) Father Mark Meyrick, Archimandrite Victor (Jankovich), (unidentified), Bishop Nikodem, Father Nicholas Troitsky, Brother Angus Pobjoy, and Mr Krasnopolsky. (Source: Antonina Ananin)

be recognized as the official voice of the Russian Church by non-Orthodox and other Orthodox Churches, both in England and overseas. In contrast to the prevailing situation in the 1950s, it was the Patriarchal clergy who were invited to the Pan-Orthodox services and gatherings in England. At the same time, some Orthodox hierarchs, including the Patriarch of Constantinople, Athenagoras, were expressing extreme ecumenical views which tended to ignore the need for unity of dogmatic truth. In 1965 Metropolitan Philaret wrote the first of his "Sorrowful Epistles" addressed to the heads of the autocephalous churches in protest against the lifting of the Orthodox anathemas proclaimed against the Roman Catholic heresies in 1054. At their 1967 Sobor, the bishops of the Russian Church Abroad recognized that they had an important responsibility to the Orthodox world to protest these doctrinal innovations.

Bishop Nikodem's address to the annual parish meeting in July 1968 dealt extensively with these questions, which he clearly felt were so important that he discussed them before speaking about the year's events in the parish:

> Reporting on our Church life over the past year at this Annual General Meeting, I consider it essential first to give a brief review of developments in the other Churches and other Christian confessions which surround us, examining them from the Orthodox point of view. We must then consider the overall position and spiritual path of our Russian Church Abroad, of which our parish and the Diocese of Great Britain are but small parts. Our Church life cannot be considered in isolation from the life of the Russian Church Abroad taken as a whole.

If we focus our attention on what is happening in the religious life of the world, we see that the so-called "Ecumenical Movement" is forging ahead with rapid strides. Much has been said and written about this movement. It is not something new. What has now happened is that it has taken on a much wider scope, while its basic idea has become distorted. Before the Revolution, attempts were made by the Russian Church on many occasions to establish closer contacts with the Anglican Church and the Old Catholics who, it then seemed, were already close to us both in spirit and in doctrine. Here it was envisaged that they would enter into the body (*sostav*) of Orthodoxy.

To this end theological conferences were organized, doctrinal questions were discussed and a basis for unity was sought. However, despite the good will which existed on the part of the Russian Church, no constructive results were achieved. The reason for this is the difference in the very nature of religious life between Orthodoxy and the western confessions, which makes religious unity impossible.

The Russian people themselves have always been very tolerant towards those of other confessions and faiths. In Russia they all enjoyed complete civil freedom and the protection of the law. In St. Petersburg, the former capital, in the centre of the city, on the Nevsky Prospekt, stood a large Roman Catholic church. Tolerance of other religions went so far that even a Buddhist temple was due to be constructed in St. Petersburg (near the building known as Peter the Great's House). Fortunately, that dream never came to fruition. The Revolution prevented it.

If the present movement towards the union of Christians has as its aim, as is being written, the struggle for the preservation of peace[12] between states, then the falsehood of this argument is perfectly obvious. Can the Christian Churches have any voice at all, when religion is persecuted in communist countries and when the clergy in these countries are in a state of submission and are used by the regime for propaganda purposes? But that is not all. These countries themselves, at the behest of the ruling communist party, are secretly supporting warfare[13] on the territory of those states which are scheduled to be swallowed up by communism.

In the same ecumenical spirit, and proceeding from the very heart of it as personified by an Orthodox Patriarch, there is now a plan to call an Œcumenical Council (*Vselensky Sobor*). Earlier Councils were, of course, called in order to refute false doctrines, or heresies, and to confirm and strengthen the true teachings of the Church. Even now, a distorted teaching about the Dogma of the Church is being spread, and this is in need of refutation. But this is not what is envisaged. A completely different aim is being pursued by those organizing the Council—not the refutation of errors regarding the Orthodox doctrine of the Church, but the introduction of a new error by establishing the unity of all Christian confessions: that is to say, the abolition of Orthodoxy and the creation of a new kind of neo-Christianity.

We must also consider the fact that a great deal of attention is now being paid to the Roman Catholic Church in this movement—a Church which is now, after the Vatican Council, in a state of inner disorganization. Thus, at the initiative of the Serbian Patriarchate, a Pan-Orthodox centre is being established in collaboration with the Roman Catholics. The place chosen for this is Ampleforth Abbey in the north of England. As an initial step, the Orthodox Liturgy has already been celebrated in this Roman Catholic Abbey. This Pan-Orthodox centre is being organized, on the Catholic side, by the Cardinal Archbishop of Westminster and, on the Orthodox side, by the Greek Archbishop Athenagoras and Metropolitan Anthony (Bloom) of the Moscow Patriarchate. Archpriest Vladimir Rodzianko and his wife are in residence in the college which is attached to the Abbey.[14]

Such, in brief, is the picture of the life which surrounds us. Our Russian Church Abroad follows its own path, neither blending with it nor, on the other hand, remaining indifferent. . . .

In its inner life, our Church follows its historical Russian path, without entering into any associations or compromised agreements which are dubious from the point of view of Orthodoxy. Our ideals on this path are the regeneration and upholding of the life of Holy Russia. In this lies the entire meaning of the existence of our Church beyond the frontiers of Russia. In this we must see God's special Divine Providence. This is the reason why the Lord has led us out of our Fatherland, which is crushed by atheistic communism. Our path is difficult, and many temptations lie on it. Our Church is small in numbers. But we must not forget that we are not alone. In Russia there is a secret Church, with which we are in ideological and spiritual unity.

What is this secret, or "catacomb" Church? While our Church Abroad continues in relative prosperity, the "Secret Church" languishes both physically and spiritually in the jail which all of Russia has become. In torments and perpetual anxiety, it keeps faith with the testament of Holy Russia. A characteristic feature is that it is composed predominantly of young people. Otherwise, it could not exist under such conditions of strict conspiracy. But neither can we exclude from membership in the True Russian Church

> those many old women and grandmothers who fill the few open churches of the Patriarchate. Crying out to the Lord, they pray their own personal prayer, knowing who the officiating clergy are, and distinguishing the true pastors from the hired actors. The churches are dear to these old people as repositories of many holy objects and relics, and sometimes miraculous icons, and as being sanctified by the prayer of generations. They also bring children to the churches for baptism and teach the children the faith and prayers.
>
> So, there are two parts of the one True Russian Church. We of the Russian Church Abroad constitute one of these parts. I have had the opportunity to tell many of those present—at one of our meetings after the Liturgy—about some little-known facts, which testify to the spiritual rebirth of the Russian people which is currently taking place. Our people who visit the Soviet Union have seen with their own eyes to what extent some of the Russian people have preserved their fine spiritual qualities and to what extent the behaviour of many Russians—especially the women—is superior to the moral state which is observed in the western countries. All this is also a pledge of the rebirth of our people.

On the subject of ecumenism, Vladyka Nikodem wrote in his report to the 1971 Bishops' Council,

> In England the ecumenical movement continues to develop. Special joint prayer services are organized and literature is distributed. Attempts are also being made to draw our Church into this movement. For this purpose we are constantly being sent invitations to ecumenical services. On our part all this is being decisively rejected, and we do not have any contact with this or involvement in it at all. The clergy under my jurisdiction are fully aware that the ecumenical movement constitutes a violation (*narushenie*) of the Dogma of the Church.

However, Bishop Nikodem's attitude toward the surrounding world was not limited to a sterile condemnation of the ecumenical movement. He shared Metropolitan Anastassy's conviction that God had allowed Russian exiles to be scattered throughout the world in order to bear witness to the truth of Orthodoxy before all peoples. He expressed this idea very strongly, for example, in a sermon delivered in 1956 on the anniversary of the murder of the Imperial family, in which he stressed the redemptive value of the sufferings of oppression and exile being borne by the Russian people:

> It is a terrible punishment which the Russian people have now been enduring for almost forty years. We do not know whether God's justice had been fulfilled, whether the period established by God to receive the repentance of the Russian people has been completed. Are we, the sons of this people, coming to the end of our wanderings in the spiritual wilderness of the contemporary world . . . ? Are we, the sons of this people, who have passed through the often harsh school of exile, ready to become a new Israel, and enter into a Russian land renewed by sufferings and by the blood of the martyrs? Have we fulfilled the mission laid upon us by God—that of preserving, outside the borders of Russia, the Truth of Orthodoxy and the pious way of life of Holy Russia, and of revealing it to the world? It is not for satiety and prosperity, not for outward glory, that the Lord is leading our people along the path leading to their rebirth. All this will simply be added unto them, as will deliverance from the bloody tyranny which oppresses them, when they begin to walk firmly along the path of their vocation as a God-bearing people (*Narod-Bogonosets*).

From his very first year in England, Bishop Nikodem felt the need for an active missionary presence. He particularly admired the work of Father Lazarus (Moore), an English convert to Orthodoxy who had been among the London clergy during Archimandrite Vitaly's time, and again for several months during 1952. In 1953 the bishop told the annual parish meeting,

> At the end of May [1952] Father Archimandrite Lazarus arrived from America. He occupied a special position in the parish. He did not become a member of the permanent clergy here, since he had been designated for a special task—missionary work in India[15]—and he was only here temporarily while making preparations to move out there. Father Lazarus did not stay at the Podvoria but only came for the services. His departure was delayed, and this gave him the opportunity of devoting some time to a task which is very important in the Church of Christ. Being himself a native-born Englishman, Father Lazarus spread the light of Holy Orthodoxy among his own countrymen. This grafting on of new children of the Church through baptism of people who had formerly professed other faiths is a joyful event not only in itself, in that it is a great and triumphant Church solemnity, but also, because those who have been united to Orthodoxy usually prove to be particularly zealous Christians, participating wholeheartedly in the Church services, and they in turn help to spread the preaching of Orthodoxy. For the group of English Orthodox, which

has increased in numbers, we now regularly have services in English on Saturdays, in which they take part through singing and reading. (Thanks to Father Lazarus we have also been able to have Liturgies almost every day at the Podvoria. . . .)

When Father Lazarus finally departed, just before Christmas [of 1952], we felt that it was imperative to have a priest in our parish able to devote a sufficient amount of time to missionary work in order to continue this work of attracting people to Orthodoxy which Father Lazarus had begun. Our First Hierarch, Metropolitan Anastassy, places great importance on this. This responsibility has been assumed by Father George Cheremetieff, who now celebrates the Liturgy in English on Saturdays; however, his activities have so far of necessity been limited to the spiritual care of English people who have already accepted Orthodoxy. He is unable to do more at present due to his many other duties as a parish priest and as secretary of the diocesan administration.

That Father George shared the bishop's missionary ideals is evident from the following words written to a parishioner in 1956:

You see, now we live in a time when the material world appears to be triumphant. But at the same time the peoples of the whole world are afraid, and they are hopefully awaiting the spiritual message which must give regeneration in Christ to a world now rotting in materialism. I believe that only Russia is capable of saying this word: not the Russian people, but Holy Russia. This is why she has been sent these terrible and bloody sufferings.

Archbishop John, the ruling bishop of the diocese, was well known for his missionary zeal, which must have influenced Bishop Nikodem and Father George. Archbishop John's visits to England were likely too brief to produce many direct fruits of this nature, although we do know that on the feast of the Annunciation in 1955 he baptized an eighteen-year-old girl into the Orthodox Church at the convent in Brechin Place.

Commenting on the last Paschal services to be held in St Philip's before it was demolished, Bishop Nikodem observed,

English people were present in greater numbers than usual—people who valued the beauty and inner spiritual strength of Orthodox Divine Worship. In general, interest in Orthodoxy is growing and from time to time

> English people come to us to find out more about Orthodoxy. This should remind us of the missionary significance of the existence of the Russian Church in the diaspora, or dispersion of Russian people, and places upon us an obligation to help them as far as our strength and resources permit. During the past year three such people were united to the Orthodox Church. The existing group of English people who have accepted Orthodoxy includes the brother and sister G. and E. Palmer,[16] who have contributed greatly to our Church life.

The bishop repeated such thoughts from year to year, particularly when commenting on specific aspects of the Church's missionary presence. Thus, on several occasions in the early 1960s parts of the Sunday Liturgy at Emperor's Gate were sung in English by a choir known as the Wooldridge Singers, made up of about twenty-five English students. The director of this choir was Orthodox but many of the choir members were not. Vladyka Nikodem expressed the hope that at least some of them would be brought to Orthodoxy through their participation in the services. In 1961 this choir sung in Cambridge when the Liturgy was celebrated there in English by Father Nicholas Troitsky, who was rector of the parish in Leeds. The service was attended by some three hundred students from the university, who had invited Father Nicholas for the purpose of learning more about Orthodoxy.

At the annual parish meeting in 1963, Bishop Nikodem reviewed the modest missionary endeavours undertaken since the time of his appointment to England. By then Father George Cheremetieff was virtually retired due to his accident and the English services were celebrated by Archimandrite Ambrose (Pogodin). The bishop said,

> The role of our Church outside Russia goes beyond preserving the spirit of true Orthodoxy and following the testament of Holy Russia, to encompass the task of drawing towards Orthodoxy (but without employing aggressive missionary tactics) those belonging to other faiths which had in the past fallen away from unity with the Church. It should be noted that these people come to us of their own accord, seeking the truth and moved by the Holy Spirit. This clearly shows how wrong is the path of "ecumenism," which entails the unity of various confessions while denying the "One, Holy, Catholic and Apostolic Church." As many as thirty people have been united to Orthodoxy between 1952 and the present. They have not all remained here—some have moved away, including

two Anglican clergymen who became Orthodox and then moved to America. Nevertheless, a group has been formed, for whom the Liturgy is celebrated in English from time to time in the Podvoria church by Archimandrite Ambrose.

These earlier, sporadic attempts at missionary work acquired more definite form on April 24, 1966, when Bishop Nikodem ordained an English convert, Mark Meyrick, to the priesthood. With the bishop's blessing, Father Mark had prepared for ordination under the guidance of Father Lazarus (Moore) in India. Bishop Nikodem reported to the 1966 parish meeting,

> Among those who have been united to Orthodoxy, most of whom are spiritually receptive young people, there are some inspired with the desire to serve the Church in sacred orders. In response to this, I have ordained Father Mark Meyrick to the priesthood. This new clergyman comes to us at a time of great need, especially now that Father George Cheremetieff is virtually retired. This was our first ordination of an English priest and was a joyous and festive occasion. Four Anglican priests were present at the ordination as well as a large number of the new priest's relatives and friends.

Father Mark was able to undertake a number of projects that were close to the heart of Bishop Nikodem. Shortly after his ordination he formed a

St Seraphim's Church, Walsingham, 1968. Note the former railway platform at the right side of the church. (Source: Michael Knupffer)

brotherhood under the patronage of St Seraphim of Sarov to engage in missionary work. It was as a member of a brotherhood dedicated to the same saint that Bishop Nikodem began his service to the Church in Yugoslavia before World War II. The Brotherhood of St Seraphim was conceived along similar lines, as a lay (nonmonastic) brotherhood devoted to furthering the Church's mission; such groups existed in Russia in the few years of relative freedom that followed the Moscow Church Council of 1917–1918. The brotherhood started with some half dozen members who devoted themselves to the study and preaching of Orthodoxy and the printing of spiritual literature, including a monthly magazine called *Orthodox Chronicle* and leaflets on various aspects of Orthodox teaching. Father Mark and two other members also set about creating a permanent centre for brotherhood activities in Walsingham. This provided a stimulus to carry on the tradition of pilgrimages from the Russian parish in London to this holy place, several of which Bishop Nikodem led during his early years in England.

The Brotherhood of St Seraphim established itself in a converted railway station acquired on a lease from British Railways after the closure of the Walsingham branch line. The platform was enclosed to provide living quarters and the booking hall was converted into a church. The interior of the church was adorned with icons painted by Father Mark, and an onion-shaped dome was erected on the roof. Soon it became difficult to recognize the former railway station. The church was blessed by Bishop Nikodem in 1967. The following year the bishop led a pilgrimage to Walsingham from London, which he described in these words:

> Representatives of the Russian Church first paid attention to this holy place before the war, when a small Orthodox chapel was set up within the Anglican shrine church and pilgrimages of Orthodox people began. We now make these pilgrimages annually, with the help of our brotherhood community which has been founded there. We served the Vigil service in the little shrine chapel and then heard the pilgrims' confessions. In the morning, we celebrated the Liturgy in the brotherhood church and then all the pilgrims went in a procession to the shrine. Here we held an akathist to the Mother of God and then partook of the water from the miraculous spring.
>
> In connection with this pilgrimage we must mention the activities of our St Seraphim Brotherhood. Through the labours of Father Mark and his assistants, a small building has been converted into a skete [small monastery], with a small church surmounted by a dome, all of which has a very

> splendid appearance. A monastic way of life has been established. A large vegetable garden has been planted and there is also an iconography studio and a printing press which is used to publish a magazine. The Liturgy is celebrated in English for visitors—mostly Greek and English people. News of the brotherhood's existence has spread in the neighbourhood and aroused the interest of pious people. Here and there Father Mark finds young English people who are interested in Orthodoxy and instructs them further in the faith. We wish Father Mark and his helpers further success in their God-pleasing work.

While running the missionary centre in Walsingham, Norfolk, Father Mark continued to take an active part in the life of the London parish for several years. Once a month he celebrated the Liturgy in English in the Podvoria church, twice a month he assisted at the Cathedral services at Emperor's Gate, and once a month he served the parish in Nottingham. Inevitably, some parishioners were shocked at the idea of a non-Russian being ordained to the priesthood of the Russian Church, even seeing it as proof that the bishop was losing his faculties in his old age. Nevertheless, such reactions were rare, perhaps surprisingly so. Most parishioners soon warmed to Father Mark's friendly, down-to-earth character. The flurry of new activities brought a feeling of new life to the parish, even if they were all in English. Father Mark

Procession to the Shrine Church in Walsingham, 1968. Father Nicholas Troitsky carries the Holy Gospel; at his left is Michael Knupffer and at his right is George Knupffer. Carrying a banner to the right is Prince Dmitri Galitzine. (Source: Michael Knupffer)

Pilgrimage to Walsingham, 1968. George Knupffer (first from left); Princess Irina Galitzine (second from left), Princess Mary Galitzine (fourth from left, behind); Father Nicholas Troitsky, Antonina Ananin, Bishop Nikodem, Winifred Mary Morcher, Prince Dmitri Galitzine, Father Mark Meyrick, Princess Patricia Galitzine, Princess Irina Galitzine, and Michael Knupffer. (Source: Michael Knupffer)

set about learning Russian but never progressed beyond the basics; however he learned Church Slavonic well enough to participate in the services and conduct private services for people when requested. Five years after his ordination, a sufficient number of people had converted to Orthodoxy in the Walsingham area to necessitate the establishment of a parish situated at the brotherhood church to provide regular Sunday services. At that point Father Mark came to London much less frequently and ceased to have an extensive involvement in the Russian parish, although he continued to celebrate the monthly English Liturgies.

There is no doubt that Bishop Nikodem was held in high regard by English converts despite the language barrier. The following tribute, which appeared in the *Orthodox Chronicle* when he was raised to the rank of Archbishop in 1968, illustrates this esteem:

> We open this month's magazine by sending our heartfelt congratulations to Vladyka Nikodem, who on returning to London after celebrating the festival of our Holy Mother's Protection with his parish in Manchester, found a letter from the Synod in New York informing him that he had been raised to the rank of Archbishop. *TON DESPOTIN KAI ARKHIEREA IMON, KYRIE FYLATTE. EIS POLLA ETI DESPOTA!*[17] Vladyka Nikodem is a true monk, and has always shunned publicity, preferring to

live simply; even now he is resisting those who wish to make a great fuss of his new honour. However, it is certainly indicative of his character that, though he is not fluent in English (as the other three Orthodox bishops in this country are), he has gathered round him a group of English converts for whom he is undoubtedly their true father in Christ. At times Vladyka is a strict father, warning us of our own hot-headedness, and showing us how far we fall short of the perfection to which Christ calls us; but when we are prepared to step down from the high horse of our arrogance, we see in him a loving father.

The lack of a common language inevitably restricted how much the converts could learn from their bishop and how well he could pass on his experience of Orthodox Tradition. It also limited the extent to which the new Brotherhood of St Seraphim could share in the spiritual heritage of the brotherhood of the same name to which Vladyka Nikodem had belonged in Yugoslavia. Turning the pages of the *Orthodox Chronicle*, one finds many articles of great interest—some written by Father Lazarus (Moore), others reprinted from American publications or written by members of the brotherhood. However, one searches in vain for translations of articles by Archbishop Nikodem; his sermons and other instructive writings on the spiritual life gathered dust in the church archives. This was probably because the bishop always preached without reference to any notes, so the editors were likely unaware that he had ever written anything that could be translated for their readers' edification. Meanwhile, alongside more substantial materials, readers were treated to contributed articles in a slightly lighter vein: "Is this [the Orthodox Church] a haven for crackpots? Or is it a welcoming home for those who are tired of the half-truths in Western Christendom?" asked one author in the June 1969 issue, and then replied, "The answer cannot be in doubt."

Despite these difficulties, Father Mark Meyrick and his Brotherhood of St Seraphim made a substantial contribution to knowledge and awareness of Orthodoxy among English-speaking people. Archbishop Nikodem's influence in this progress was not always appreciated. The bishop's caution in advancing the English-speaking mission was often mistaken for an attitude of grudging acceptance, while many of the English Orthodox remained unaware of the extent to which this work coincided with his most deeply cherished ideals. He did not think of it as a separate department of Church activity, but as an integral part of the Church's inner mission—that of spiritualizing the life of her existing children. In 1966 he said,

> Of course the principal task facing us in our parish life is not so much the attraction of new members from the surrounding population, as [it is] ensuring our own spiritual growth in faithfulness to the Tradition of the Russian Church. Our missionary work then flows from this as a natural consequence. This idea is in the spirit of St. Seraphim's dictum, "Acquire a peaceful spirit and thousands around you will be saved."

Archbishop Nikon's Visit to England

Especially fervent supplications were offered to the Mother of God in 1968 when the miraculous Kursk icon of the Mother of God was brought to the ancient English shrine of Walsingham by Archbishop Nikon (Rklitsky), the vice-chairman of the Synod of Bishops. Archbishop Nikon,[18] accompanied by Archpriest Boris Kritsky, the guardian of the miraculous icon, was taking the Kursk icon to European parishes with the goal of including on his itinerary many of the smaller parishes which Metropolitan Philaret had been unable to visit three years earlier. Hence he visited the Brotherhood of St Seraphim and, after learning more about the history of the shrine, he served two unscheduled molebens in the Orthodox shrine chapel and by the holy spring. In preparation for this visit, the May 1968 issue of the *Orthodox Chronicle* carried an article on the history of the miraculous icon. The following month's issue contained a description of the visit, which observed,

> Perhaps the most beautiful service of the whole visit was the Divine Liturgy at which the two bishops concelebrated with Archimandrite Kallistos, Archpriest George and Father Deacon Sergei, at the Convent of the Annunciation in Willesden. . . . The chapel was full and overflowed into the hall and porch; but it was not the richness of the ceremony, nor the beautiful singing which gave the service its special beauty: it was the sense of knowledge of the infinitely more glorious joy of heaven.

The clergy and parishioners all felt inspired and encouraged by the archbishop's friendly interest and practical advice about various questions of Church life. On returning to America, Archbishop Nikon wrote a description of his European tour, which imparts a vivid impression of the life of the Russian Church Abroad in England during this period. The following extract from his account describes some of the people, places, and events he encountered:

On 31 May/13 June 1968, the day of the Holy Apostle Hermes and the Holy Martyr Hermias, with the blessing of our First Hierarch, Metropolitan Philaret, and after he had served a moleben (service of intercession) at our Synod Cathedral [in New York], Father Boris Kritsky and I commenced our journey by air which was to take us with the Miraculous Icon to Europe, to visit our parishes, homes for the elderly and children's summer camps, all of which had earnestly requested this visit.

Our route included England; our first stop—London. Thoughts came to mind about the long-standing relations between our homeland, Russia, and England. There were times of rivalry, in other times, friendly alliances, close family ties between monarchs; sometimes there were also wars. In present days when our homeland has lost its greatness and is governed by an international clique of communist brigands, a large number of émigrés have found an hospitable shelter in England. They have founded a religious centre and have educated a new generation of English Orthodox Christians of Russian parenthood. The church also attracts the attention of English people and the Anglican Church.

While travelling at great speed over the ocean there is time for reflection. Some historical facts about this great country, which has had its share of difficulties in recent years come to mind.

London is first mentioned in the year 61 AD when it was a Roman military camp. . . .

Today there is deep interest in the Holy Orthodox faith in England; however the young and energetic representatives of the Moscow Patriarchate cleverly obscure the minds of English people.

On June 14 at 8 a.m. (local time), having crossed the Atlantic in seven hours, we approached London over British soil covered by a thin cloud of fog, through which we could see green pastures, farms, villages and houses built in the old English style.

At London airport we were met by His Grace Bishop Nikodem, the clergy, Mother Elisabeth and the sisters from the Convent, and members of the parish, all of whom had come to greet the Holy Icon. We were given a very warm reception, followed by a moleben held at the Podvoria (Church House) in St Dunstan's Road, in a crowded church. The Cathedral clergy includes Archimandrite Victor (Yankovich), a Serb who has mastered both the English and Russian languages, Father Nikolai Troitsky, Father Mark Meyrick, who is English, Protodeacon Nikolai Jakimowicz and Deacon Sergei Jefimenko. The housekeeping at the Podvoria is run by the Sisterhood and a very diligent worker,

Mrs. Antonina Vladimirovna Ananin. On the evening of the day of our arrival, a Friday, the Holy Icon visited the Convent of the Annunciation for a Vigil service and, on the following morning, the Divine Liturgy. We served together with Bishop Nikodem, Archimandrite Kallistos (Ware)—an Englishman in the Greek Church and author of a wonderful book on the Holy Orthodox faith and a lecturer at Oxford University—Father George Cheremetieff, who is greatly respected and has retired due to ill-health, Father Boris Kritsky and Deacon Sergei Jefimenko. The Convent was crowded with both Russian and English worshippers. The service in the presence of the Miraculous Icon of the Mother of God, and the meal afterwards in the refectory, passed as one radiant and joyful festival, with tears of compunction and thanksgiving to God for the spiritual happiness. In my sermon I spoke of the rebirth of the soul through venerating the Mother of God and so coming to partake of the virtues over which She reigns.

The Convent of the Annunciation excels in its educational efforts on two levels. On the one hand, the Abbess and all the nuns, having become acquainted with the English way of life and language, are successful in bringing the Holy Orthodox Faith to English people; on the other, they teach religion and the Russian language to Russian children, whose achievements were demonstrated to us after lunch. The children read poetry and acted in short scenes to a greatly appreciative audience. After thanking Abbess Elisabeth and the sisters for their blessed labours, I went on to explain to those that were there that the best path in life which Russian girls and widows could choose for themselves would be to become "brides of Christ." I said that they would make themselves worthy of the goodwill and blessing of the Mother of God if they chose the blessed path of monasticism and so help this wonderful centre of Holy Orthodoxy in England to grow and strengthen.

On the evening of that day His Grace Bishop Nikodem and I served the Vigil service at the Cathedral of the Dormition, and the Divine Liturgy on Sunday, followed by a moleben before the Holy Icon. The choir, under the direction of A. A. Khaltygin, sang beautifully. Later, during the meal after the service, the choir master movingly recalled how, during the previous visit of the Miraculous Icon three years ago, when he had just undergone a dangerous operation, he had felt the beneficial power of Divine Grace present in the icon of the Mother of God, after which he completely recovered from his illness. After the meal we returned to the Cathedral and I gave a talk about the Russian Orthodox Church in Exile. I explained the importance of our Church as it had been understood by her great leaders, their Beatitudes Metropolitan Anthony and Metropolitan Anastassy, its importance for the whole of Russia in preserving the Russian Orthodox faith inviolate. I spoke of our present First Hierarch and his election four years ago and of each of the main centres of our Church—the Synod of Bishops, Holy Trinity Monastery, Novo-Diveyevo Convent, and St Vladimir Memorial Church. I spoke about life in other parishes, particularly in Canada and on the west coast of America. People listened with great interest and appreciation, saying that they were hearing many of these things for the first time.

On Monday, 17 June, after the Liturgy at the bishop's Podvoria, we were driven around London with the speed of a film show. We saw from the car the cathedrals, Westminster Abbey, the River Thames, the royal palaces, museums, parks and main streets, on our way to a lunch invitation by the wonderful couple, Kornely Kornelyevich and Valeria Nikolaevna Pekhovsky. K. K. is a Cossack, V. N. is an Orthodox English lady who speaks Russian and has come to love the Holy Orthodox Faith. Financially they are well off and they are a great support to our parish. Someone in church told us that they will do anything they are asked for the church without a moment's hesitation. In the evening we were the guests of the churchwarden of long standing, Count V. P. Kleinmichel, and his wife, Countess Maria Grigoryevna Kleinmichel.

After a moleben and moving farewells, on the next day (Tuesday 18 June) we made our way into the English hinterland. Our driver was a remarkable young man, Misha Knupffer, who has just completed his education and was a link between the bishop and the English Orthodox believers. First, we visited an English Orthodox skete dedicated to Saint Seraphim of Sarov, run by a celibate priest, Father Mark Meyrick. Father Mark came to the Orthodox Faith through the teaching of Archimandrite Lazarus (who now works for our Church in India) with whom he spent some time. Several young English novices live in the skete in Walsingham, Norfolk, near an historic holy place of England: a spring on the site of an apparition of the Mother of God, prior to the Great Schism.

We were warmly greeted by the young novices who were leading the hard life of a small monastery starting out with meagre material resources. We were also greeted by Anglican clergy from the well-established church by the Holy Well. Together with the young people we prayed fervently before the sacred icon. Later I spoke to them through our excellent interpreter, Misha, about the essence of monasticism, the Holy Orthodox Faith, and the Mother of God. After spending several hours with them we continued our journey to the parish of St Nicholas in the industrial city of Bradford. The journey took us much longer than we expected, and instead of arriving at 6 o'clock in the evening, we arrived at 10 o'clock at night. Nonetheless, most of the members of the parish were waiting patiently for us and greeted us with great joy. Father Philemon Zadworny serves this parish with great diligence. We served a moleben at this late hour, and then we were taken to where we were to spend the night, the house of the churchwarden, I. A. Sid. Mrs. Sid is English of Italian extraction and strong Catholic background. She has now adopted the Orthodox Faith, has profound knowledge of it, sings diligently in the choir, bakes the prosphora, and is a convinced follower of the Orthodox Faith.

After the Divine Liturgy and a moleben, we left Bradford the next day to visit another industrial city, Leeds. It should be noted that this whole region is famous for its woollen textile industry. There are numerous factories with blast furnaces which let out thick, black smoke, enveloping all houses and buildings, and giving Bradford and Leeds a dejected, gloomy appearance. There are many Slav workers in these cities, including Russians. Our church in Leeds is housed in an Anglican church and does not have a permanent priest. Services are held once a month by our priest from London, and the church is taken care of by Antonina Robertovna Eller, the Churchwarden, who accompanied us on our visit to the church.

From Leeds our path lay towards Manchester, another industrial centre. Our church is well-established here, with a church house, and a permanent priest. The parish is served by Archpriest Father Nikolai Popoff, a well-educated and diligent priest, a graduate of the Tauride Seminary [St Petersburg], whose rector was Bishop Mikhail Gribanovsky.[19] After the Vigil service that evening, and Divine Liturgy and moleben on the next day, attended by all the parishioners of this church, we continued our journey on 20 June to Belgium.

Altogether, we had spent seven days with the Miraculous Icon in England. We left impressed by the great strength of the Holy Orthodox faith, which has already struck deep roots here. Nevertheless, there is a pressing need to reinforce the ageing clergy with younger forces, to whom great prospects lie open for undertaking missionary work. Our diocesan administration, led by His Grace Bishop Nikodem, a venerable archpastor, who commands authority and respect, both in Russian and English circles, works zealously, despite being hampered by the prominent activity of the representatives of the Moscow Patriarchate. Our church needs well-prepared young workers to whom a wide field of activity lies open.

Galina von Meck

Within two years of Archbishop Nikon's visit, there were signs that his wishes for the Diocese of Great Britain would be fulfilled: a young seminary graduate returned from America to offer his services to the Church in England and two more young men from the diocese began their studies at the same American seminary. Hopeful signs were also coming from the fruitful work of Father Mark and the Brotherhood of St Seraphim. Meanwhile, the process of Tradition—the handing down of Orthodoxy from one generation to another—proceeded steadily by way of formal instruction from the clergy and through the Divine Services as well as informal contacts of all kinds between younger and older members of the parish. One of the older parishioners who inspired particular respect in the younger people, and to whom many of them felt particularly close, was Galina Nikolaeyevna von Meck, who was the daughter of a railway magnate in pre-Revolutionary Russia and a grandniece of Tchaikovsky.

Galina von Meck's life story had much in common with that of many of the congregation at Emperor's Gate, but her unique literary gifts distinguished her accounts of her experiences and the living faith that enabled her to endure them and profit from them. The first volume of her autobiography, *As I Remember Them*, was published in English in 1973. This was the culmination of many years of work. Brief extracts appeared in the *Orthodox Chronicle* during the 1960s. The following obituary, which appeared in the *Times* of London upon her death on April 9, 1985, captured remarkably well the essence of her life and personality:

Galina von Meck, author and prominent London parish member, ca. 1960s. (Source: London Parish Archive)

> Galina von Meck, who died on April 9 at the age of 93, was Tchaikovsky's great-niece and the granddaughter of his patroness Nadezhda von Meck.

Born in Moscow on October 13 1891, the fourth child of Nadezhda's son Nikolay and Tchaikovsky's niece Anna Davydova, she grew up in prosperous circumstances—the von Mecks had made a fortune out of the development of Russia's railway system—but came to know hardship, imprisonment and exile, all of which she bore with formidable courage.

As a small child, she had one brief encounter with her grandmother, recounted in her autobiography *As I Remember Them* (1973). Her childhood was spent as a member of a well-to-do Moscow family dividing its time between artistic and business city life and summers on their estate in the Ukraine.

Though Tchaikovsky died before she was old enough to remember him, she retained vivid and entertaining memories of the other members of his family and of his musical friends such as Taneyev. On a visit to England in 1912 she met her first husband, Noel Perrott, but he failed to settle into Russian life and the marriage ended in divorce.

At first sympathetic to the ideals of the Revolution, she found the realities disillusioning. She was arrested trying to help a prisoner escape across the frontier: there followed years of hardship in the Lubyanka and in Siberian camps, where she made a second marriage with a fellow prisoner, Dmitry Orlovsky, who later disappeared. She was not released until 1935; later she managed to make her way to Germany and finally to England.

Not until late in her long life did she begin to make use of her remarkable literary and linguistic gifts. Her autobiography is a fascinating account, told with toughness, generosity and humour, of a life in whose most appalling moments she always managed to find interest and moral reward. Her unswerving Orthodox faith sustained her throughout all her privations.

She translated a large book of *Tchaikovsky's Letters to his Family* (1981), and had completed another volume of her autobiography and was working on the three volumes of Tchaikovsky's letters to her grandmother.

Her courage and her salty wit, and her enormous charm and kindness, made her a friend of many English musicians as well as to fellow-exiles. It was appropriate that her 90th birthday party should have united English friends, her family and visiting Soviet musicians.

Her tiny London flat retained an old Muscovite atmosphere, and she herself, though quick to defend the young and much in the modern world, carried with her something of the dignified old Russia that remained so sharply etched on her memory.

As I Remember Them and the second (unpublished) volume of her memoirs, titled *Farewell To Russia*, describe honestly, without resorting to stereotypes, a vast range of human experience: the upper middle-class world of pre-Revolutionary Russia in which she grew up, the turmoil of the Revolution, the nightmare of Stalin's regime, and the chaos of Germany in the final stages of World War II. Running like a thread through all her writings is the strong, simple Orthodox faith that sustained her. Especially interesting is that she was not always "religious" in the conventional sense of the word—for example, attending all the church services or knowing all the details of church ritual and canons. One recalls the words of Father Michael Polsky quoted previously: "In this fiery furnace in which we were all tried, all values were reevaluated."

The seeds of this faith were sown during her childhood, surrounded by the influences of Holy Russia. At home, for example, the children took turns reading the daily prayers. "Even if our parents had friends at the house for the evening, one, if not both of them, would always come up and pray with us," she wrote. In the von Mecks' country house near Kiev, special loaves of bread were baked and kept ready to give to pilgrims on their way to the Russian shrines and to the Holy Land:

> When they passed by our estate they were welcome to stay the night and have a plateful of hot soup with a large piece of meat in it. If it was summer, they slept on the grass behind the house near the kitchen. We children used to talk to them. They told us all about the holy places they had been to, and the wonders and miracles they had heard about or seen.

Galina told the story of one of her own pilgrimages:

> When I was ten years old, during the last days of Holy Week, I asked my mother if I could go to the monastery of Saint Sergius[20] (now called Zagorsk) to attend the services. This was to show off before my brothers who were always teasing me about being too devout.
>
> Mother summoned her personal maid, Elizabeth Ivanova, and asked her to chaperone me. On Thursday morning of Holy Week, I took all the money out of my piggy bank and went off to the station. We took two third-class tickets and boarded the train for the monastery, which is about forty kilometers from Moscow.
>
> We arrived at the old fashioned pilgrims' rest house and an old monk took us into a small room with two high beds covered in pillows and quilts. The little window faced the courtyard and gardens of the monastery. In

the corner burned the votive light of an icon. There was an old washstand which had a little reservoir of water in the top of it. To get the water to spout out of the tap, you had to press a pedal at the foot of the washstand. After, the water ran through a hole into a bucket.

In the pilgrim's refectory we ate some potatoes, onions and mushroom soup. Then we went to the Cathedral for the evening vespers. The Passions of Our Lord were being read. They are read according to the Gospel, divided into twelve parts with the hymns and prayers sung in between. The monks sang—two choirs on each side of the altar—with a beautiful tenor voice, and chanting at the beginning of every verse. The Cathedral was absolutely full and all of the worshippers stood for three hours with burning candles.

The next morning Elizabeth and I took a rickety cab and went round all the other parts of the monastery and its annexe. Later we attended a service in the middle of the day when our Lord's shroud is brought out of the altar into the middle of the church. At ten o'clock it was time to go to the long night service of the lamentation.

Elizabeth refused to go—she was too tired. She called the old monk and asked him to take me to the church. He took me and placed me on the steps to the left of the altar where I could see everything without being squashed by the other people.

By the time the service started the Cathedral was so full that we could not move. Whenever the Deacon had to come out (swinging the heavy golden incense burner) the crowd had to make way like a wave. The service lasted for hours. I returned to my home feeling really penitent.

At about this age, young Galina first underwent a kind of inner crisis, marked by capricious behavior and recurrent nightmares. The way she overcame it reflects wise advice that she must have received: "To stop myself from dreaming at night I used to do what monks do when they are assailed by temptation. I got out of bed, and, standing before the holy icon in the corner of the room, I made genuflection after genuflection, prostrating myself thirty times or more. Exhausted, I crept back to bed and went instantly to sleep."

Later, at the age of eighteen, she went on a pilgrimage to Sarov and the shrine of St Seraphim. When the saint was glorified in 1903, Galina's father had been president of the railway company which brought the tsar and his family to Sarov. Her father's description of that journey and the solemnities in Sarov prompted Galina to make her own journey to Sarov six years later. Galina described how she endured a severe spiritual ordeal during this trip:

> . . . insidiously, a total emptiness spread through me. Outwardly I continued to be my normal self. I talked and laughed with my cousin and together we went round the monastery, seeing all the places as is the custom for pilgrims. But as the day went on, the horror which was attacking me increased hourly. Actually, the word "horror" is not the right one; and what seemed to be happening to me was a complete spiritual disintegration.

This warfare continued for four days, during which Galina went to confession and Holy Communion. It was miraculously relieved at St Seraphim's "Far" Hermitage, the hut where the saint lived in the depths of the forest:

> As we had not completed our full pilgrimage, we went off after breakfast to the so-called "Far-off Retreat," the little house of Saint Seraphim in the forest, several kilometers away. Here the Saint lived with the animals of the wild, and here he prayed, kneeling on a large stone on which over the long years his knees had worn grooves.
>
> At each "station" on this pilgrimage, I stopped to pray, but still I was not free. At last the narrow footpath through the beautiful pine forest brought us to Saint Seraphim's hut. The door was open and in the far corner of the sunlit log room, praying before the icons, stood a tall monk with a snowy mane of hair and a long white beard. I was the first to step into the hut. The monk turned round and before I had said the usual words of greeting, he stretched out his arms, came over to me, and took my hands in his, and said in a ringing voice "Come in, come in, my child, be welcome. I have been expecting you!" I fell down on my knees next to him and for the first time in those terrible three days I wept and I could pray.
>
> For a long time I stayed like that, crying and praying, with the old priest beside me. Then I got up, received his blessing and went out into the forest. Olga was a real friend. She never asked me what was wrong.
>
> The fragrance of the pines heated by the hot sun was in the air. Now and again we heard a woodpecker hard at work and the grasshoppers were singing merrily around us. We started on our journey back home.
>
> This was not the end of my dreadful experience.
>
> First came the long tiring miles in a rickety carriage and it was late, or rather early morning, when we reached the railway station and our own private railway coach. Olga went to bed, but I stayed awake, for the same feeling was sweeping over me again. Now I could fight it though, and I stayed awake all through the early hours of the morning and prayed and fought. Our coach was attached to the fast Moscow train and that same day, in the evening, we were back in our country place, Voskresenskoie.

> It was only some time later that I told my mother about my experience. It took me many years to sweep clean this grey corner of my soul and to conquer fear that it might return.

Galina emerged from this experience with a renewed and strengthened faith, which was tried further after the Revolution. When Galina's father was arrested, she collected some forty thousand signatures from railway workers for a petition demanding his release. Galina's father was arrested on six occasions, and, in 1928, he was shot by the Bolsheviks.

After her own arrest in 1923, before being tried and sentenced, Galina was imprisoned in a filthy, crowded cell with male criminals. To avoid being eaten alive by the lice, the men would remove all their clothes every day and kill all the lice concealed in them. "Every louse was met with appropriate invectives and the idea was to 'pop' them loudly to be sure they were dead." After several days of mounting discomfort, Galina was persuaded by the men to follow their example. They all scrupulously refrained from watching her as she did this.

Even under such circumstances, Galina Nikolaevna found the time to pray:

> October came. The weather was warm, there were few rainy days and when night came the deep blue of the heaven was covered with a multitude of stars. On quiet and windless nights the shutters on our windows were never closed until late, so I made it a habit to pray under the window. As soon as the men saw me on my knees on the bench, all noise, talking, blasphemy and swearing would stop. A hush came down upon the cell which lasted sometimes until well after I had finished and had turned back to them again. If, by chance, a newcomer tried to say something rude during those minutes he would be stopped at once: "Shut up, she is praying," I heard them say.
>
> With the arrival of our new guest, the old Jew, the same thing was repeated for him. Our hours of prayer did not coincide, but nobody grumbled about it. His daughter had brought him his tallith and he used to roll himself in it, tie the phylactery on his forehead and say his prayers in the darkest corner of the cell, on the boards.
>
> We had long conversations with him about life and the difference in our religious beliefs. Only one thing he would not agree to, that was to strip to get rid of the lice.

A few months later, in a prison in Kiev, Galina had a moving encounter with an unnamed bishop who was about to be executed. Such brief but heartfelt references to her faith give her autobiography its special character, not as a "religious book" per se but as one that testifies to a deep, living faith, manifesting itself in the midst of the cares and horrors of this life.

Galina was sent east, along railway lines built by her father, to a camp at Mariinsk in western Siberia where she was assigned to farm work. Fellow captives included a group of nuns from a nearby convent. She described how, even here, they managed to celebrate the feast of Christ's resurrection:

> Easter was coming but we were not supposed to think of it. The political and cultural commissar went from one farm to another, giving anti-religious talks, to teach us to work harder and to praise the rulers who had given us the opportunity to "rehabilitate" ourselves.
>
> My little office, which had originally been a shed for new-born calves, stood away from other farm buildings with its back to the woods and thickets, and small pools of marshy waters. The thicket continued for a few miles towards the railway line and there was, at least so I was told, a secret path through it leading to the little town of Mariinsk. The woods were taboo and the path was rarely used, but the wood creatures knew it well, and this woody and marshy land was a real game preserve.
>
> On Good Friday, as I was walking over the yard towards my quarters, one of the women came running towards me. She stopped me from going into the house and whispered that there was a man behind the big barn, a tall grey-haired man who had come all the way from Mariinsk to see me. I went to the barn as fast as I could without attracting attention and found Mr. Fedorov waiting there with a large basket. He and his wife had prepared the traditional food that we have at Easter to break the fast after returning in the early morning from the night service and the Liturgy.
>
> Mr. Fedorov risked much when he had walked from Mariinsk through the thickets and marshy land along the secret path. He had to go back at once, before the moon went down. . . . A minute later, when Mr. Fedorov disappeared completely and passing clouds covered the moon for an instant, I might have believed it had all been a dream, if I had not been holding a large and heavy basket.
>
> I hoped to be free on Easter night, but I had not reckoned with the cunning of our political leaders. All the administrators and clerks of the estate were summoned to headquarters on that very special Saturday night and it was impossible to refuse such an invitation. As usual, Kravchenko went off first on horseback. Two foremen and I followed in a sledge. Not much was said on the way. When we arrived at the "club" as it was called, we were

obliged to sit in a stifling atmosphere for at least three hours, listening to the usual political humbug. After which some of the prisoners danced and sang. It was so late when it all came to an end that I did not even manage to wish a curt good night to anybody before going back to the farm.

A lovely surprise was awaiting on my return. Our half of the cottage was lit up by four candles in bottles, supplied by my friend Martha Meckay. The table was laid with all the good things that had been brought to me by Mr. Fedorov. To hide the bright light shining out of the windows, Martha had covered them with several layers of sacking. When I came in all the women were there and the nuns chanted the whole of the Easter night service for us. Afterwards all of us, including the children, sat down to the feast. I said all of us, but one was absent—Maroussia the bandit. She had volunteered to keep Kravchenko company and prevent him from paying us a surprise visit.

However, our supper did not last very long. When Maroussia returned, she found the house hushed and quite. She also found a large plate filled with food which had been left for her.

I could not sleep. My thoughts were of home. My mother was nearly seventy. Her three years' banishment was coming to an end at the beginning of June. I wondered if the authorities would let her return to Moscow or if at the last moment they would prolong her exile. My thoughts were interrupted by the noise of horses outside and men's voices, then heavy boots tramped through the cold passage and two tall figures in military coats came in. Our oil lamp was not burning, so it was too dark to see who they were. I heard my neighbour whisper, "O Lord, save us! What do they want?" The intruders started to strike matches as they walked along the row of sleeping women. When they turned to go over to the other side, they collided with the bench and swore profusely. "Drunk," I thought. "Surely there are enough prostitutes on the other farms to satisfy them."

There was a pause during which the men stood and swayed, unsure of themselves and wondering what to do next, then they groped their way out, got on their horses and rode away. A loud sigh of relief came from all sides. As the darkness turned to the grey light of dawn we went to sleep at last.

Easter Sunday was just like any ordinary day. The only difference was that we were more homesick than ever.

Although Galina Nikolaevna was released from this imprisonment, she was arrested again as Stalin's purges gathered momentum. She was sentenced to spend five years in a concentration camp for "unproved espionage on behalf of England and the U.S.A."

While in the Lubyanka prison in Moscow, for a time Galina found herself in the same cell as a distant cousin, Natasha Andreyev, the widow of a popular St Petersburg priest who had been killed soon after the Revolution. She wrote,

> In those days I remembered much of the music I had heard in my life, and, in a very low voice, for my cousin's benefit, I used to sing all the concertos, symphonies, piano pieces and so on that I could remember. And at night, when I crept under the bedclothes and was alone with my thoughts, I used to recite the whole Liturgy which—apart from the silent prayers of the priest—I reconstructed gradually from memory. It was then that I really understood the deep significance of the Liturgy.

Galina was released from the Gulag in May 1934 but experienced many ordeals after this that circumscribed her liberty. At the onset of World War II, she was living in the small town of Maloyaroslavets, about 100 kilometers southwest of Moscow. The town was occupied by the Germans, but on the verge of its being retaken by the Red Army, Galina left together with many of the local inhabitants, fearing Soviet reprisals against anyone who had been in contact with the German invaders. *As I Remember Them* ends with an account of how she made her way west on a horse-drawn sledge together with her mother and two small children, her nephew Vasily and niece Elena.

In her unpublished sequel, *Farewell to Russia*, Galina recounted her further trials as she made her way across Poland to Berlin and eventually, after the Nazi defeat, to England. She crossed the frontier into Poland together with her infant great-niece, Elena, as a passenger in a military truck.

> Then, on the third day, when we had driven on for some time after our mid-day rest, we reached what looked, from afar, like a cluster of cottages, lost in the infinite snowy white plain. Three houses with only a few miserable trees, bent and misshapen from the nearly incessant winds.
>
> "This is the frontier point with Poland." said my driver. "We have to report here. . . ." I climbed out of the truck and, carrying the sleeping child in my arms, went into the cottage expecting to undergo another of the everlasting gruelling questionings that had been my lot so often. In the smaller room, behind the office, a young SS officer was standing at a large, very empty desk. He greeted me and asked me to sit down.

Twice before in my life I had heard the confessions of men in a position where they had the power of life and death over their fellow men: one who believed, when he sent them to their deaths, that he was doing so out of political convictions, realizing too late that it had only been a desire for revenge: the other, solely to protect his own skin. But now, here, I was confronted with a third confession.

I sat down and wondered what was coming. In my arms Elena slept peacefully on. Then suddenly, the young officer said, "Tell me, must one destroy the Jews?" And before I could say anything, he went on, "I have killed many, quite sure, at least I thought I was, that I was right! But now I do not know anymore. Here, alone, lost in this vastness I have to face myself, and it looks quite different. The few soldiers who are with me, I cannot talk to. Tell me, what must I do? I was a murderer, wasn't I?"

The child in my arms stirred but did not wake.

"Yes," I said, "It was murder, and you know it. I can suggest only two ways out. One—to ask to be transferred to the front and get killed, but this will be the coward's way out. You can do better. Help and save where you have until now destroyed. You will not be able, at least it will be practically impossible for you to get out of the SS, and so much the better because, as an SS man, you can do more than an ordinary person. Save where you can and, if in the end you are caught and have to pay for it, this will be the real atonement."

He said nothing in reply and we sat facing each other over the desk, the child still peacefully asleep.

Silently the young officer signed my documents and passed them over to me. I took them and thanked him, rose and went out. There was no *Auf wiedersehen*. We both knew our meeting was final.

Galina was plunged into the horror and confusion of the dying days of the Third Reich. She described the sense of disorientation in leaving what was, despite everything, her native land, and the oasis of peace she found in the Russian Church in Berlin, despite the continual air raids:

Whatever had happened to me in Russia, however hard, heartless and cruel some people were, I knew them, I could not help understanding them and the process of their thinking. So, even when I felt utterly lonely and forsaken, in prison and the camps, we at least spoke the same language.

It was when I crossed the frontier into Western Europe that I really felt an utter stranger and in the years from 1942 to at least 1952 a stranger

I stayed, in spite of meeting and being helped by kind people. It was as if I was never really myself any more, existing in a shell that did not belong to me. It took me many years to rid myself of this feeling. My Russian kaftan had not been made by a Western tailor, and the Western coat did not fit me properly.

I think this barrier was also very much one of language. Oh, yes, I spoke German fluently, and English even better, but the difference was there, even when perfectly translated, in the "nuance," sometimes quite slight but colouring the meaning of a word or a phrase. . . .

Just imagine a long film, a whole epic, Tolstoy's *War and Peace* being torn to shreds, with all the characters, consecutive actions, beginnings and endings being mixed up, facts misplaced, etc. etc. That is how Europe appeared to me during the Second World War. . . .

And this conflicting chaos was not something in documents or on paper, but a gruelling multitude of humans who were pushed to and fro, moved from place to place, who fought for their ideas and personal existence, sometimes succumbed, hungered, froze, worked hard, and all for the sake of Hope. Hope that all would be well, hope that the war would come to an end and that real peace and happiness were, in the near future, in store for them . . . and . . . last, but not quite least, the old Russian émigrés who hoped for the liberation of their country from the Bolsheviks was imminent—almost a fait accompli—and all would be as before.

Whatever was going on outside, in our little church on the Nachodstrasse, the services went on as usual without any interruption. True, quite often the church would be almost empty, especially during the week, and I too did not go very often, buffeted as I was from place to place and bombed around the town.

One particular Sunday in 1944, only a few women were in church, when another woman came in with a little flock of children—German orphans who were mothered and looked after by her. She was a Russian woman who had collected these waifs after their parents had been killed in the raids, and had adopted them. I understand that the authorities were sympathetic and helped. Anyway, here they all were at the service.

Suddenly the sirens sounded and a few minutes later the bombs started crashing down. Like sheep, the poor children swerved in a tight little crowd from one side of the church to the other, silently, too frightened even to cry, until their guardian had to take them down to the basement. At the altar, though, all was calm and serene. Just for a moment the priest, who was intoning a prayer when the sirens howled, faltered

> and then went on as before. "May the mercies of our great Lord and Saviour Jesus Christ be with you all" came the words from the altar. "Amen," responded the reader. . . . And the service continued as if nothing was happening to us or outside, or to the building itself which shuddered with shock waves.
>
> There was not much left of the streets around us when we came out. The children climbed up out of the basement a bit subdued, but recovered very quickly and chattered away as they disappeared around the next corner of what had been a street.

When Galina found work in Lodz, a town in occupied Poland, she witnessed the treatment of Jewish civilians:

> I found the work at the Repatriation Centre very hard. But worst of all, the road to the office went past a Jewish internment camp. Although surrounded by a high fence with barbed wire at the top, one could see, in spite of it, the people there—their pale, bloated, starving faces. They moved about slowly, around and over little plots of land, digging out or planting the few vegetables that were to supplement their starvation diet. I can see them now, wrapped up in all the old coats and shawls they possessed, ghosts of the grey winter landscape. This was January, 1945. And I could not help them! I had to accept it, for the sake of my children, caught as I was by secret calumny, about which there was no way to fight openly and fairly.

After the German surrender, Galina made her way to Rosenheim in Bavaria, which was in the American zone of occupation where she managed to make contact with her daughter Anne. She also made contact with Metropolitan Anastassy, Primate of the Russian Church Abroad, who had arrived in Bavaria via a circuitous and perilous route from Belgrade in the final days of the war.

> From the very first day of my life in Bavaria I did everything possible to get in touch with my daughter Anne, who was at the time with her husband at the British Embassy in Cairo. As I had not been able, as yet, to do it through official channels, when two more American soldiers came looking for schnapps, I explained my connections with England and asked if they would post a letter from me to my daughter, which they agreed to do. . . .

In 1947 all we needed for our church was given to us by the head of our church, the Metropolitan Anastassy of Moscow,[21] who was then in Munich. How he escaped death at the hands of the Soviets and throughout the war I do not know enough about to say here.

I went to see the Metropolitan on behalf of a young couple who wanted to marry. The young man was not an Orthodox and special permission had to be obtained for them to be married by an Orthodox priest. The Metropolitan's secretary at first bluntly refused to announce me. I insisted and said I would not leave without first having received the blessing of the Old Gentleman. At last the secretary went in to tell the Metropolitan that I was there and returned at once, all smiles, I was even ushered in with some pomp. My meeting with the Metropolitan was short, but he remembered me: "Come in, Galia," he said. "Be welcome, the daughter of a martyr of the Russian Revolution." And he also remembered how, as a bishop, he had presided at our examinations at the boarding school where I had studied. He too had never given in to Soviet persecution.

Eventually Galina made contact with her daughter, who managed to arrange visas for her and Elena to move to England. In this final extract, she described the journey north to the North Sea port of Bremerhaven and final embarkation for British shores:

It was comfortable for us, privileged passengers on the train; outside things at every station were more than tragic; faces appeared at our windows, begging for any scraps of food we could spare—the starving people of north Germany.

I can still, in my mind's eye, see through the wide window of our compartment the two emaciated girls' faces and the tall ashen-faced young man. If he had ever been proud before, now he was not ashamed to beg—beg in the most humiliating way. Through the open window Elena gave him the food we had with us for our lunch.

That night, arrived in Bremerhaven, we were taken to some small barracks near the sea, from where we would be shipped to England. The child was not very well but the calm reception here and the kind attention towards her made her relax. We had to wait until the next day, a dull twenty-four hours. The following day, again not feeling well, Elena did not say much. I wondered what was coming next. The people responsible for us now were polite but without much display of feelings. We had, though, one pleasant companion—a German officer who had a British wife and two cousins in England. He had not seen them since the beginning of the war. Now, allowed to join his family, he too, like us, wondered what the future was going to bring.

At last, the following evening, we were brought to the ship which was going to take us to England. To my great pleasure the ship looked new, clean and the double cabin we got was comfortable and warm.

I tucked Elena up on one of the bunks and stretched out on the opposite one. It was very quiet. I could hear the lapping of the water against the side of the ship. Then came the familiar sounds of a ship leaving its moorings, the sounds and light vibration of the engines, and then the louder swish of water as we began to move away from the shore. The child was fast asleep. Rocked by the light waves of a calm sea which seemed to welcome us, I too went to sleep. All my fears left behind, we moved towards the shores of what became with the years a true home for both of us. We came to England in January, 1948.

Gerald Palmer

At about the same time as Galina von Meck and her great-niece Elena arrived in England, Gerald Palmer was setting off to Greece on a spiritual quest which eventually led him to join the Orthodox Church. After the consecration of the Cathedral at Emperor's Gate in 1959, among all those who contributed to the acquisition and conversion of the building, one person—Gerald Palmer—was singled out for special gratitude. Pointing out that all the work had been done for the glory of God and that the names of all who had laboured and made donations would be commemorated at the Divine Liturgy in perpetuity, Bishop Nikodem said in his 1959 report, "Perhaps in time we will also erect a commemorative plaque. . . . Meanwhile, immediately after the consecration of the church, our principal benefactor, Mr. Palmer, was presented with a special icon as a blessing."

Gerald Eustace Howell Palmer was related to the Palmer family of Huntley & Palmer, the biscuit manufacturers. Gerald had come to Orthodoxy by an unusual path. During World War II he had been the Conservative Member of Parliament (MP) for Winchester, while at the same time performing active service in the army. Sometimes Gerald took his seat in the House of Commons having arrived straight from the front, still in his battledress. Like many Conservative MPs, however, Gerald lost his seat in the 1945 general election, and, like many of his former colleagues, he took up farming and forestry as an alternative to politics. This complete change of pace after strenuous wartime activity offered the opportunity to ponder the profound questions which had long been simmering within him—questions about eternity and the ultimate meaning of life. After some time, still with no conviction about the dogmatic truths of Christianity, Gerald heard of a holy man, an elder or "staretz" in the Russian tradition of spiritual guides. This was Father Nikon, a hermit who was living on Holy Mt Athos. As soon as it was possible to travel to Greece after the Communist uprising there subsided in 1949, Gerald Palmer set off for Mt Athos.

Gerald Palmer, translator of patristic texts and benefactor of the London parish, ca. 1970s. (Source: Elizabeth Palmer)

Athos, called the Holy Mountain, is a monastic republic occupying a mountainous peninsula in northern Greece, northeast of Thessalonica. It is covered with monasteries, both large and small, which have preserved an unbroken spiritual tradition going back to Byzantine times. From here the monastic ideal spread to Russia, and, in turn, thousands of monks came from Russia to seek salvation on the Holy Mountain. The Russian Revolution and increasing secularization of life in Greece led to a marked decline in the monastic life on Holy Mt Athos in the 1940s and 1950s; often, only a few monks would be caring for a monastery built to hold hundreds of monks.[22]

Gerald Palmer was one of the first visitors to Mt Athos after the end of the Greek civil war. Father Nikon, whom he sought, lived in Karoulia, a particularly inaccessible area peopled by hermits who lived in caves hewn into the face of vertical cliffs. Gerald recalled climbing up to the caves, with a guide to show him the path, supported only by chains set into the rock. At their first meeting, Father Nikon told him that this was the first lesson—to realize the precariousness of everything in this life and to put one's trust wholly and completely in God. Father Nikon was a hieroschemamonk—a priest-monk who had taken the strictest monastic vows, known also as the Great Schema. In secular life Father Nikon had a distinguished military career, even serving as aide-de-camp to the tsar. When his military service ended, he left for the Holy Mountain to embrace the monastic life, and, after many years, received a blessing to live as a hermit. Thanks to his wide education, Father Nikon spoke perfect English, and thus was able to explain to Gerald much about Orthodoxy and the Orthodox spiritual tradition. He explained that the writings of the ancient Holy Fathers "are accessible only in the light of genuine, primordial Christianity, devoid of any human considerations, additions and alterations, with integrity and purity from the times of the Holy Apostles."[23]

After returning to England, Gerald Palmer went to see Father Archimandrite Vitaly at St Philip's Church in Buckingham Palace Road and told him of his desire to enter the Orthodox Church. Despite Father Vitaly's varied experiences in war-torn Europe, this was the first time that he had been approached by a prospective convert. His reaction was one of apparent surprise: "Oh! Really? Why do you want to be Orthodox?" Gerald understood that his motives and sincerity were being tested, and this impressed him. After a period of instruction, he was united to the Holy Orthodox Church in 1949 by Archimandrite Vitaly, who gave him the Orthodox name George in honour of the Holy Great-Martyr George who is commemorated in the Church on April 23. Two years later, in 1951, Gerald's sister, Elizabeth, was also received into the Church by Father Vitaly. Their contribution to the Church in Exile would be recognized in 1956 when Bishop Nikodem referred to "the brother and sister G. and E. Palmer" when he spoke on the Church's mission to spread the knowledge of Orthodoxy.

The lofty ideals which brought Gerald into Orthodoxy did not make him feel that he was above taking an active part in the practical aspects of church life. After the demolition of St Philip's, Gerald exhibited keen interest in locating a new church as well as becoming a main benefactor when the church at Emperor's Gate was found.

Palmer's chief work in the Orthodox Church, however, was the translation of early patristic texts, in particular the collection known as *The Philokalia* or, in Russian, *Dobrotoliubiye*. So important a place do these translations occupy among English-speaking Orthodox today, it is hard to imagine a time when these Holy Fathers were simply not accessible at all in English. Gerald's interest in them began before his first visit to Mt Athos, when he was one of a small group of people who began studying these writings about the Jesus Prayer, the prayer of the heart, and the war with the passions. The precepts of *The Philokalia* were practised in the Orthodox Church for centuries, leading those who followed them to closer union with God. Before each meeting, a rough translation of the texts to be studied would be provided by a Russian lady, Mrs Evgeniya Kadloubovsky, working from the *Dobrotoliubiye.* The search for a living representative of the Tradition embodied in *The Philokalia* was what led Gerald to Mt Athos and Father Nikon.

Father Nikon encouraged him to continue with this work of translation. So they proceeded much as before: Mrs Kadloubovsky provided a first draft translation, Gerald corrected the English, and then they discussed the precise meaning of various words and phrases before agreeing on the final text. Through regular visits to the Holy Mountain, Gerald remained in close contact with Father Nikon, who helped select texts for the first book in English, most of which were taken from the fifth volume of the *Dobrotoliubiye.* Father Nikon wrote the foreword to the book that was published in 1951 under the title *Writings from the Philokalia on Prayer of the Heart.* Accepting the manuscript for publication, Faber and Faber commented that it was probably not a book which would sell immediately in large quantities, but that it would probably continue to sell steadily over the years to come. This has proved to be the case. Bishop Kallistos (Ware) of Diokleia described how the publication developed:

> A pioneer role in the transmission of the *Philokalia* to the West has been played by Britain. In the early 1950s a selection of material, translated from the Russian *Dobrotoliubiye* of St Theophan, appeared under the editorship of the Russian Orthodox Evgeniya Kadloubovsky and the English Orthodox Gerald Palmer. Two volumes were issued: *Writings from the Philokalia on Prayer of the Heart* in 1951, and *Early Fathers from the Philokalia* in 1954. These enjoyed an unexpected success: *Writings from the Philokalia* was hailed by a leading Roman Catholic journal, *The Catholic Herald*, as "one of the most important spiritual treatises ever to be translated into English," and both volumes have been frequently reprinted.
>
> It is interesting to note that the publishers of the English *Philokalia*, Faber and Faber, would never have accepted the work but for the support given by [the poet] T. S. Eliot, who was one of the directors of the firm. So favourably impressed was he by the teachings of the *Philokalia* that he insisted in its publication by Fabers, even though he in common with the other directors expected that it would incur a serious financial loss. In fact it proved an outstanding commercial success. "We have never lost money on an Orthodox book," a member of Fabers said to me not long ago. The late Philip Sherrard told me that one day, when in the library of George Seferis, he noticed a copy of the English volume *Writings from the Philokalia* on the shelves; taking it down, he found that it had been sent to Seferis

> by Eliot, with the inscription in Greek 'τὰ σὰ ἐκ τῶν σῶν' ["Thine own of thine own"]. I do not know if Seferis actually read the book, but I am reasonably sure that Eliot had done so with some care.[24]

The Philokalia, and particularly the fifth volume of the Russian text from which the selections in *Writings from the Philokalia* were mostly taken, represents some of the most advanced writings in the Orthodox spiritual tradition. They have been compared to a university education, while simpler writings such as those on the lives of the saints and the writings of St John Chrysostom, for example, correspond more to the primary and secondary school of spiritual life. The English translation of *The Philokalia* has been criticized on the grounds that it offers little practical value in terms of day-to-day guidance for the majority of contemporary Orthodox, and, indeed, may lead people into delusion if they read it in the wrong spirit. This, however, overlooks the book's immense significance in today's non-Orthodox world where it can open peoples' eyes to the spiritual depths of Orthodox Christianity that otherwise they might never suspect. In fact, the breathing of the Holy Spirit in the Church, guiding people on the path of real sanctity, is what provides the spiritual underpinning of all the traditions, rites, and dogmatic formulations of the Orthodox Church. The value of the writings of the Holy Fathers to a wider audience is given in the introduction to the *Dobrotoliubiye* written by St Theophan the Recluse, in which he says "descriptions of various manifestations of spiritual life, contained in the holy fathers, may be a gift even to all Christians in general. They give everyone to understand, that if he has not yet had experiences contained in such descriptions, it means that his established mode of life . . . is not the final perfection, above which there is nothing to wish for and nowhere to go."

Gerald Palmer and Evgeniya Kadloubovsky worked together in a similar fashion on the second volume of extracts published in 1954 titled *Early Fathers from the Philokalia*. This book comprised a broader cross section of writings, including many from the earlier, less "advanced" volumes of the *Dobrotoliubiye*. They also translated *The Meaning of Icons* by Leonid Ouspensky and Vladimir Lossky.[25] Elizabeth Palmer, Gerald's sister, worked with Mrs Kadloubovsky on *The Art of Prayer: An Orthodox Anthology*, a collection of writings on the Jesus Prayer compiled in the early twentieth century by Igoumen Chariton, abbot of the Valaam Monastery in northern Russia.[26]

In the introduction to the 1954 edition of *Early Fathers from the Philokalia,* the translators note,

> The only final solution to the problem of making the treasures contained in the *Philokalia* available to the West in a form as rich and as wisely balanced as the original is for someone with the necessary qualities of scholarship, understanding and endurance, to undertake to translate the whole from the original Greek itself. We can only hope that this work will one day be achieved; it might well be one of the greatest single contributions to perpetuating in the West what is highest in the Christian tradition.[27]

Toward the end of the 1960s this project for making a complete translation of *The Philokalia* was initiated in earnest. It was an immense undertaking, and Gerald Palmer's role was primarily that of inspiring and coordinating the team of scholars who worked on it. An editorial committee was formed, composed of Gerald Palmer, Philip Sherrard,[28] and the then Archimandrite Kallistos (Ware). The translations themselves were done by different people who reported to the committee. Bishop Kallistos described the outcome of this project:

> In 1979 a new English rendering commenced publication. This second version contains not just a selection from the Greek *Philokalia* but all the works included there; and it is based not upon the Russian version of Theophan but upon the original Greek, using modern critical editions where these are available. This integral English translation is now approaching completion: the fifth and final volume is in preparation. Like its two-volume predecessor, the new translation has appealed to a surprisingly large English-speaking readership, and the earlier volumes have been regularly reprinted. From the correspondence that the English editors have received, it is clear that the circulation of the English *Philokalia* has not been limited to members of the Orthodox Church, or indeed to the Christian world; it is appreciated also by followers of other faiths and it has proved attractive to "seekers" who do not yet belong to any religious tradition. In this way the translation is performing an important missionary function.[29]

Gerald Palmer remained close in spirit to the Holy Mountain for the rest of his life. He visited almost every year, sometimes going to spend Holy Week and Pascha with Father Nikon in his tiny church hewn out of rock. After Father Nikon's death in 1963, Palmer continued his visits to the Holy Mountain, turning for guidance to Father Nikon's successors in Karoulia and the Monastery of Stavronikita. After the departure of Archimandrite Vitaly, Gerald's spiritual father in England was Father George Cheremetieff.

Both Gerald and his sister, Elizabeth, developed a deep respect and love for Father George. Gerald in turn was able to help him when Father George became ill and needed to convalesce somewhere quiet in the country.

It was also due, in part, to Father George that Gerald embarked on his other great work in the Church, which was iconography. While remaining a member of the parish at Emperor's Gate, Gerald Palmer attended services at the Convent of the Annunciation from time to time. For some years after moving to the house in Willesden, the convent church had only a temporary iconostasis with reproduction icons hung upon it. The abbess had approached five different iconographers, all of whom said they were too busy to commit to such a large project. On one occasion when Gerald was visiting the convent in the company of Father George, discussion turned to the problem of the iconostasis. Knowing that Gerald was an amateur artist and liked painting landscapes, Father George suddenly turned to him and said, "Gerald, why don't you paint it?" Gerald was shocked at the idea, being well aware of the difference in essence and technique between iconography and landscape painting. He hesitated until a Greek monk visiting from the United States finally convinced him, saying, "Gerald, I bless you to paint for the Convent." Gerald received his first instruction in icon painting from Mother Flaviana[30] of the Lesna Convent in France, where he and his sister were regular visitors. Abbess Elisabeth recalled,

> So, Gerald started fasting, prayer, and reading about icons. First we had to choose the icons. We always consulted together. Sometimes we agreed, sometimes disagreed, but in the end we came to full agreement. We decided to choose the 13th/14th centuries. And then we chose the originals from which to draw and he started. He would get up in the morning and, after his prayers, he would close himself in the painting studio. Nobody had to disturb him unless there was an emergency. At one o'clock he came out for lunch and then he went into his ordinary life. (He had wonderful staff who were Catholics, believers, and helped him to keep the fast days.) So he worked and he worked, until he finished all of the iconostasis and the other icons. The last one he painted was of the Last Judgement.

Gerald's involvement with the icons helped to establish increasingly close ties with the convent, which became his principal place of worship, especially after Father George started conducting services there regularly. Mother Elisabeth described this special relationship:

> In the Convent church he had his regular place. And even the children who were in front of him never disturbed him. Nothing distracted him from prayer. He had great belief in God's plan, that the Convent is in God's plan. He was a great friend, in practical things as well as in spiritual things. You could discuss everything with him. If ever we had any difficulties, he was always there to encourage and support. He had a great faith in God's Providence and, in particular, he believed strongly that God had a special purpose in bringing us to England and allowing the Convent to be established here. Every year he visited Father Nikon on Mount Athos. He knew that we cannot go to Mount Athos, so during one of his visits he painted a view overlooking the sea. It still hangs in the visitors' room at the Convent.

I had the good fortune to meet Gerald Palmer on a number of occasions. My few brief discussions with him were of particular significance because the path by which I came to Orthodoxy was similar to the one that he had followed.

I first met him in the summer of 1969 when I was travelling in Europe as a student. Strongly drawn toward Orthodoxy, I determined to visit the Lesna Convent at Provemont in Normandy. After a sleepless night spent standing on a crowded train, I boarded a bus from Paris that went deep into the Normandy countryside and, despite having detailed directions, I missed the stop and had to walk several miles back from the village of Etrepagny. I arrived at the convent just as the Vigil service was beginning. Unlike Vigil services that I had attended in parish churches, there seemed to be no particular interest in drawing this one to a close. When it finally ended, I was approached by one of the nuns, who said, "As you are from England, perhaps you would like to meet Mr. Palmer." I recognized the name as I was familiar with the translations of *The Philokalia*, particularly the first volume on the Prayer of the Heart, which had made a profound impression on me.

By way of conversation, I asked if he was related to the "Palmer" of "Palmer and Kadloubovsky." He confirmed that he was the "Palmer," but it was Madame Kadloubovsky who did the translation and he only checked the English. As we spoke about the books and Orthodoxy in general, I was immediately struck by the contrast between Gerald's very upper-class English mannerisms and the utterly "un-British" and other-worldly content of what he was saying. Emboldened by curiosity, I asked what I knew even then to be an injudicious question: was he able to put these teachings into practise himself? His reply was typical: "Oh, well, of course what one does oneself is of no interest." He suggested that, instead, I should talk to

Father George Cheremetieff with whom he was travelling and whom I had previously noticed leaning on his walking stick during the Vigil service. Gerald urged me to speak to Father George, as it might well be the last opportunity that I would have. Among other things, Father George told me that Orthodoxy was really very simple, "although some theologians try to make a complicated system out of it." This thought meant little to me at the time, but it has stuck in my mind and become a guiding principle ever since.

When work started on translating *The Philokalia* from the original Greek, Gerald Palmer went to America to contact various people who he hoped could contribute to the project. He also wished to visit Father George's grandson, then a newly ordained priest in Rochester, New York, who had been ordained to the priesthood on the feast of the Entrance of the Mother of God into the Temple on November 21/December 4, 1971. While in New York State, Gerald came to the Holy Trinity Monastery and Seminary where I was studying. He gave a talk to the students in which he spoke about his visits to Mt Athos, about Father Nikon, and about his translation work. One of the other students asked which of the ancient Holy Fathers he liked the best, to which he replied without hesitation, "St Isaac the Syrian." He also visited the iconography studios and the little cemetery church where frescoes were being painted by Igoumen Alipy, one of the monastery's expert iconographers.

Gerald Palmer died on February 7, 1984, at the age of seventy-nine. Abbess Elisabeth recalled his last days:

> When he was dying I went to see him. He said, "Matushka, don't worry, the Convent will go on." When he knew that he was dying, that he was ready, he asked to be buried in the shirt in which Father Nikon had been submerged in the Holy River Jordan. He wanted to have a funeral service in the Convent as simple as possible and as humble as possible, with no speeches, and this was all arranged through instructions he had given his executor, despite the wishes of some relatives and friends to make it a pompous occasion.

As a memorial to her brother, Elizabeth Palmer shared this brief description of Mt Athos that he evidently wrote while staying at the Tower in Ouranoupolis, which is on the border between the Holy Athonite Republic and Greece.

Silence over Mount Athos

It was towards midday on the sixth of August, 1968, that the motor-boat from Daphni stopped at the *arsana* of Simono-Petra. No one else had landed so, after a friendly greeting from a monk on the jetty, I started climbing alone up the steep path as the motor-boat went on down the coast. After some twenty minutes or so, I reached the point where the path from Grigoriou joins the track from the right. Here, at the junction, there is a small shrine with a Cross and stone seats under the shade of a roof; the open sides of the little building give wide views over the sea to the next peninsula. Having reverenced the Cross, I sat down in the shade and looked out across the sea, listening to the silence.

All was still.

Immediately I felt that now at last I was back on the Holy Mountain, and thanked God for once again giving me this immediate privilege.

All was still.

This stillness—this silence—is everywhere, pervades all, is the very essence of the Holy Mountain. The distant sound of a motor-boat serves only to punctuate the intensity of the quietness; a lizard's sudden rustling among dry leaves, a frog flopping into a fountain are loud and startling sounds, but merely emphasize the immense stillness. Often as one walks over the great stretches of wild country, which form much of this sacred ground, following paths where "every stone breathes prayers" (a phrase of Father Nikon's) it is impossible to hear a sound of any kind. Even in the monastery churches, where the silence is, as it were, made more profound by the darkness, by the beauty and by the sacred quality of the place, it seems that the reading and chanting of priests and monks in the endless rhythm of their daily and nightly ritual is no more than a thin fringe of a limitless ocean of silence.

But this stillness, this silence, is far other than a mere absence of sound. It has a positive quality, a quality of fullness, of plenitude, of the eternal Peace which is there reflected in the Veil of the Mother of God, enshrouding and protecting the Holy Mountain, offering inner silence, peace of heart, to those who dwell there and to those who come with openness of heart to seek this blessing.

May many be blessed to guard there this peace or to bear it away as a lasting gift of grace.

The Tower
August 1968

Father George Cheremetieff as Convent Priest

After the accident in 1961 that left him with limited mobility, Father George officially retired from parish work although people continued to turn to him for advice and confession. When Father John Sawicz, their chaplain, died in 1967, the convent was left without a priest. Father George, who had established a bond of mutual respect with the abbess and sisters almost from the very first day of their arrival in England, asked the bishop's blessing to serve at the convent. As the convent was small and had no steps, either at the entrance or within the convent church, it was less physically demanding on him than any church where he had served previously. So, with his walking stick in his left hand and the censer in his right, he resumed regular celebration of divine services, devoting his last reserves of strength to serving God and His flock. The following spiritual portrait of Father George in the last years of his life was written by Abbess Elisabeth after his death at age eighty-four on May 12, 1971:

> It is hard to write briefly about Father George Cheremetieff in that he was a man richly gifted by God and one who had, moreover, made profitable use of the talents entrusted to him.
>
> He received a broad education on sound foundations and graduated in the Faculty of History and Philology at St Petersburg University. He then decided, of his own accord, to enter the Army, enlisting in the Regiment of the Cavalier Guards. His period of training recruits gave him the chance to meet people from many of the varied provinces of Mother Russia. His dexterity in communicating with people and going straight to their hearts evoked their love, not only among officers, but also among the lower ranks, who in gratitude gave him a painted triptych with a moving inscription on its reverse side.
>
> His living faith in God, his deep love for his Mother Country, loyal devotion to his Sovereign, confidence in the resurrection of Holy Russia, a rare knowledge of the history of the Fatherland, and not only of Russian but European literature, made him interesting and instructive in conversation.
>
> He used to show friends his little notebooks in which, even in his younger years and, later, as a brilliant officer, he entered everything that interested or stirred him; already, at that time, they contained extracts from the *Dobrotoliubiye* (*Philokalia*) on prayer and spiritual attainment.
>
> Following the death of our former priest, Father George was for five years our spiritual guide; and in that time we came to know him still better and to

value him as a rare spiritual shepherd. Father George loved and knew how to pray and to entreat with prayer, warmly, from the heart and with singleness of mind. Invariably benevolent, painstakingly well-mannered, cheerful, he knew how to support and to console and, when it was needful, he could also give instruction sternly. Being quite disinterested, he was unconcernedly capable of giving to someone in need literally the last thing he possessed. With his aristocratic origin, he was, at the same time, possessed of a rare modesty; for all of us he was an example of humility and Christian love.

For him, a soul was precious, no matter whether the person was cultured or an ignoramus, rich and famous or a simple pauper, old or young, a fellow countryman or a native of another country; he could approach each person with full attention and give something luminous, something unforgettable, as people often remarked, even those who had only once chanced to meet him.

His excellent knowledge of languages made it possible for non-Russians as well as Russians to benefit from his spiritual direction. Without hesitation and in their due order he conducted services for different people in their own languages, and likewise he worked on translations of spiritual texts into English.

Despite the weakness of old age and chronic ill health, Father George's self-denial overcame these disabilities and he assiduously celebrated the services in the Convent, visited the sick and the dying, everywhere bringing with him peace and comfort.

The services, thanks to his prayerfulness and to his musical and perfect ear, went in complete harmony with the Convent choir. He prayed for people by name with great warmth and fervour. One needed only to see his list of hundreds of names of the living, the sick, the sorrowing, of those suffering persecution and exile, as also of the dead, starting with past Sovereigns, soldiers, clergy and by name all those tormented to death by powers hostile to God, together with friends, relatives and those whom he had actually buried or for whom he had read the burial service in the event of their not having an Orthodox burial.

The last time that Father George officiated at the Convent was on the Sunday of the Triumph of Orthodoxy. On the eve of the service about fifty people came to confession, and all of them were deeply moved by his spiritual directions. Who could foresee that it was for the last time? Father George fell ill, was in hospital, and afterwards for six weeks stayed with a friend in the country where he was prepared for a beautiful departure.

Archpriest George Cheremetieff, priest of the Cathedral and, subsequently, priest of the Convent of the Annunciation, ca. 1970.

From Gerald Palmer's home in Berkshire where he was staying, Father George wrote to a friend on May 2,

> Dear Tatiana Nikolaevna, Truly Christ is Risen! I am very touched by your kind greeting. Thank you so much. I have been in hospital for two weeks and now I am quietly convalescing and gathering strength with

Mr. Palmer, who has so very kindly given me shelter. I hope, if the Lord wills and I live, to return to London on 10 May. I do not know if I will still be able to serve. I hope in the mercy of God.

Abbess Elisabeth's account continued:

Only a few days before Mid-Pentecost he returned to London. In his last days he often repeated that he was tired and had become old, but even so, one did not believe that his end was so near. He was comforted by the fact that, despite his infirmities, he could still look after himself and was a burden to nobody. He often said to me, "Matushka, death is not frightening but dying is difficult!"

And the Lord called him to Himself swiftly and without pain. At Mid-Pentecost, in the evening, I was at his house with my Assistant Nun and he was happy at having come home and that he had succeeded in putting his papers, belongings and correspondence in order. On our taking leave, he said, "If it be God's Will and I am alive, I will conduct the service with you on Sunday." He came with us to the steps at the front door of the house and blessed us several times like a loving father until we were out of his sight. Not more than three-quarters of an hour later we had returned to the Convent; suddenly, there was a telephone call: it had happened, Father George had died. He had been found dead on the floor of his room.

We were the last to receive his beloved blessings, and the first to be honoured to bring prayers for the peace of his luminous soul beside his remains. On the third day his body was brought to the Convent for the funeral Liturgy and panikhida. Although it was a working day many devout persons came, even some who were not Orthodox, but all were devoted to Father George. One felt in Church a genuine grief, yet at the same time, a luminous and peaceful rejoicing for him in his death.

The burial service was in the Cathedral, performed by a throng of clergy, four priests and two deacons, presided over by Vladyka Archbishop Nikodem. The singing was by the choir of the Sisters [of the Convent] in accordance with Father George's wishes, and it created a specially prayerful mood. The leave-taking by all those who loved Father George attracted many people wishing to bestow the last honours of grateful love. One who came from the background of DP's said, "I had to come and pray and ask pardon from Father George, for he taught me how to struggle against sins."

> In the cemetery there were many people. His grave was smothered with flowers, crosses, garlands and touching little bouquets. Simple, self-forgetting, with love for all, Archpriest George, filled with years of fruitful spiritual harvesting, quietly departed to the Lord, leaving behind him his own luminous memory. Without doubt, many souls, even embittered persons, were given peace and were spiritually the better for having met on their way Father George.

In accordance with a request made in his will, Father George was buried in Gunnersbury Cemetery in a plot that had been purchased by the convent. At the time, the area was completely empty—he was the first to be buried there. Afterwards, however, many people asked to buy a plot near Father George, and so now there are many Russian graves in that cemetery.

Something of Father George's character is reflected in the following letter written in the 1950s, in which he offered a word of comfort and encouragement to a sick and lonely refugee living in London. Simple and warm-hearted as his words are, they are based firmly on the patristic teaching that patient endurance of afflictions is akin to martyrdom:

At the grave of Archpriest George Cheremetieff in 1971: at the back, Gerald Palmer (left) and Count Kleinmichel (right), Abbess Elisabeth (wearing pectoral cross), and behind her, Rufina Ampenoff. (Source: Sophia Goodman)

I have received your sad letter, and how I would like to lighten your sufferings and comfort you. I can imagine how painful your infirmity must be. . . .

We who are here (outside our much suffering country), that is to say, those who still live by faith in the Resurrection, who have not bowed the knee before Baal—even here we are subjected to illnesses, bitter disappointments, family upsets, and often feel ourselves completely alone in this "civilized" world.

When such misfortunes are unleashed upon us, then we must ask the Lord for strength to endure them patiently; but at the same time, in the measure of our failing strength, we must also rejoice that the Lord considers us worthy, through our suffering, to take part in the purification of Russia, in order to make her worthy to deliver the message, which must awake the slumbering conscience of the world.

By enduring our sufferings patiently, we enter of our free will into the sacrifice of those who are suffering there (in Russia) and of those who, through their death as martyrs, have cleared and purified one more overgrown field in the Lord's vineyard in Holy Russia.

From the bottom of my heart I wish you a speedy recovery and strength in your continuing life as a worker in the Russian cause. Here also we serve this cause and work for it. May the merciful God and the Most Pure Mother and Saint Nicholas the Wonderworker protect you.

With heartfelt and friendly greetings, Yours, Fr. George Cheremetieff.

Then he added a poem by Apollon Nikolaevich Maikoff[31]

Do not say, there's no salvation
Or that you're worn away by grief
When night is dark, the stars shine brighter
The worse your grief, the nearer God.

While still mourning the death of Father George, the sisters of the Convent of the Annunciation were granted the spiritual consolation of receiving the monastic tonsure in 1971. Although they had been leading the monastic life for some twenty years, the five Arab sisters were still novices, not having taken monastic vows. Deferring the tonsure until the age of about forty has long been a common practice in Russian convents, including those in the Holy Land. In 1971, Archbishop Anthony (Sinkevitch) of Los Angeles was required to fly to Jerusalem to testify in a legal case. Previously the archbishop had been head of the Russian Ecclesiastical Mission in Jerusalem and as such had been the convent's spiritual father when it was still there. On his way to Jerusalem he stopped in London. The nuns had not seen him for twenty years. He told them to prepare for the monastic tonsure that, God willing, he would perform on his return journey. A few weeks later, the sisters took their full monastic vows, receiving new names which, according to custom, began with the same letter of the alphabet as their secular names: thus Susanna became Seraphima, Vera became Vassilia, and so on.

Archbishop Nikodem was unable to appoint another priest to the convent permanently owing to the shortage of clergy. In 1972 a solution was found when the Synod granted stavropegic status—placing the convent under the direct jurisdiction of the metropolitan as president of the Synod of Bishops. Metropolitan Philaret undertook to find a new priest, which was achieved later that year when Father John Stukacz came from Australia. In practice, the convent's new status did not alter its role within the London Russian church community. The Saturday School and other activities continued as before. The advantage was that now Metropolitan Philaret made annual visits to London. To establish closer contact with the European dioceses, he spent several weeks each summer at the Lesna Convent in France. From there he crossed from Dieppe to Newhaven and came to London to serve at the convent and at Emperor's Gate. He also gave talks to young people on

Litya for the slain Russian Royal Family at the Cenotaph, Whitehall, 1968. (Source: George Knupffer)

At the Cenotaph litya in 1968, at front (left to right): Father Mark Meyrick, Archimandrite Victor (Jankovich), Bishop Nikodem, and Father Nicholas. Behind the bishop (left to right): Antonina Ananin, George Knupffer, Count Kleinmichel, and Countess Kleinmichel. (Source: George Knupffer)

At the Cenotaph litya in 1968 (left to right): Tamara Labarnova, Olga Mackellar, Valerie Holmes, Olga Illyashevich, Countess Olga Bobrinskoy, Matushka Antonina Mitrofanovna Jeffimenko, and Antonina Ananin (conducting). Behind the countess to the right is Count Nikolai Tolstoy. (Source: George Knupffer)

the topics that were closest to his heart—such as the Gospels as interpreted by the Church Fathers, the sufferings of Christ, and *The Dogma of Redemption* by Metropolitan Anthony (Khrapovitsky), which Metropolitan Philaret expounded in light of the teachings contained in it.

The Last Years of Archbishop Nikodem

The fiftieth anniversary of the murder of Emperor Nicholas II and the Imperial family occurred in 1968. Mindful that the Royal Martyrs had never received a proper funeral, the Synod of Bishops ordered a full funeral service for them to be held in all cathedral churches on July 17, the anniversary of their death.

In London, a short litya for the departed was also held on the previous Sunday at the Cenotaph in Whitehall—a monument and centre of national remembrance erected in honour of those who had fallen in World War I. Traffic was halted and the area cleared by the police, and Londoners were confronted with the unusual sight of a Russian Orthodox bishop and clergy praying for their departed sovereign in the very heart of London, in the shadow of the Home Office and Foreign Office buildings and within sight of the Houses of Parliament and Westminster Abbey. The service drew a large crowd of worshippers, both Russian and non-Russian. Accompanied by the singing of "Memory Eternal," a wreath was laid at the Cenotaph by Prince Andrei Alexandrovitch Romanoff, the eldest son of the late Grand Duchess Xenia, as representative of the Russian Royal Family. Wreaths were also laid by Count W. Kleinmichel, representing the London parish, and by a member of the Royal Stuart Society, which felt sympathy for the plight of the murdered Russian tsar, perhaps seeing a parallel between the dethroned Stuart[32] and Romanoff dynasties.

Archbishop Nikodem, ca. 1970. (Source: Archbishop Nikodem)

In October 1968, shortly after Archbishop Nikon returned to America from his visit to England with the miraculous Kursk icon, Vladyka Nikodem received a letter from the Synod, notifying him of his elevation to the rank of archbishop. This honour came to him in his declining years. More than ten years earlier at the age of seventy-four, Vladyka Nikodem had alluded to the difficulties that both he and Father George experienced fulfilling their pastoral duties with old age *approaching*! By the end of the 1960s, however, the effects of age were making themselves truly felt. Exhausted after a service, Archbishop Nikodem would return home by taxi. The route passed Brompton Cemetery, where he had bought himself a plot years earlier. He would bless the cemetery from the taxi and say, "Ah, Brompton, it will soon be time for the journey to Brompton."

With his strength failing, the archbishop took great consolation in having the opportunity at last, in answer to many prayers, to ordain a new young clergyman for the diocese. In 1970, John Suscenko, the son of a Bradford parishioner, returned from America after completing the five-year course at the Holy Trinity Seminary at Jordanville, New York. His arrival back in England had been preceded by a glowing report from the seminary rector regarding his graduating thesis on the subject of the ecclesiology of St Basil the Great. Vladyka Nikodem greeted him in the Podvoria church, vested himself, and immediately began a moleben of thanksgiving. After the service ended, Vladyka Nikodem addressed John on the importance of the pastoral work that lay before him, while two parishioners unloaded the ordinand's cabin trunk packed with theological books he brought back with him from America. Within a year he had married and been ordained to the diaconate, and then on January 2, 1972, the Sunday before Orthodox Christmas, he was ordained to the priesthood. Travelling to church by the Underground on that momentous day, Father John found himself in the same railway carriage as the archbishop who, at the age of eighty-eight, was still using public transport in fulfillment of his duties without pausing to reflect that an archbishop in pre-Revolutionary Russia would have travelled in far greater style.

After the ordination, Archbishop Nikodem addressed the new priest with a few heartfelt words of instruction:

> Reverend Father John, this is a great day for you, perhaps the greatest day of your whole life. You have been preparing for this day for five years, studying theology and strengthening your spirit through constant participation in the church services. These years were not easy for you, and there came a time when you began to waver in your resolve to continue your preparations for service to the Church but, through God's Grace, you overcame this temptation and graduated from the seminary as a Bachelor of Theology. In the service which is now before you, you must not hope in your own strength, but remember that the Grace of the Holy Spirit has descended upon you, and will guide you in your pastoral

> service. In this activity you must be guided by that love for your flock which is imparted in the sacrament of Holy Orders, as was taught by our great hierarch, His Beatitude Metropolitan (Khrapovitsky). Your ordination is taking place on the day when we celebrate the memory of that great pastor of All-Russia, Saint John of Kronstadt, whose image you should always keep before your mental gaze. Your flock will be all those who turn to you for confession, those whom you visit when they are sick, and all those who turn to you in their perplexity with various questions. In conclusion, let me repeat to you, that success in pastoral work will depend on the love and compassion which you display towards your flock, while persevering in the intense spiritual struggle, or podvig, of constant prayer for yourself and for your flock. May the Lord help you, through the prayers of the whole Church, which are offered during the sacrament of your ordination.

In these few simple words, Archbishop Nikodem expressed the essence of his own ideals for pastoral service that he learned at the feet of Metropolitan Anthony in Yugoslavia more than thirty years before.

Father John Suscenko was appointed as a member of the Cathedral clergy and also served the provincial parishes when required. He started a Russian-language newsletter called *Tserkovna Byulleten* (*Church Bulletin*). In October 1972, an article in this newsletter described Father John's first visit to the Manchester parish for its patronal festival of the Protection of the Mother of God. Its author commented, "It was encouraging to see the young priest and his matushka helping him. Orthodoxy in England is far from dying out." After the deaths of Father Philemon Zadworny (1971) and Father Nicholas Popoff (1973), the burden of helping to serve the provincial parishes (on a rotational basis) increasingly fell on the shoulders of Father John Suscenko.

Archbishop Nikodem's ninetieth birthday in 1973 was observed with special celebrations held by the Cathedral parish on his nameday, the feast of Saints Spyridon and Nikodem, the prosphora bakers of the Kiev Caves, which falls on October 31/November 13. One parishioner wrote,

> During his last years his greatest grief was his badly failing eyesight, and his greatest joy to live to the next Sunday or Great Feast in order to celebrate the Divine Liturgy, which he knew by heart. How he loved to serve and how prayerfully he celebrated! No one hearing his voice and his clear pronunciation would have guessed at his advanced age.

His physical frailty revealed the extent of his burning zeal and reverence as a servant of the altar. Nearly blind, he could no longer read the service books, but it became apparent that he knew many of the Gospel readings, all the audible prayers, and all the "'secret" prayers of the Divine Liturgy by heart. He even knew the long prayer in the Liturgy of St Basil the Great, which is only celebrated ten times a year; he did not trust his memory for this, however, so before each service he recited the prayers while someone else followed the text to check for mistakes. He was always word perfect.

Inevitably, some people criticized the old bishop, particularly members of more prosperous parishes outside the United Kingdom. Visitors to America, for example, heard unkind comments along the lines of "What kind of a bishop have you got over there? He can't see, he can't hear, he can hardly sign his name. How can he administer a diocese like that? He's obviously a stubborn old man—he ought to resign." In fact, Vladyka Nikodem realized that nothing would be gained by his resignation, as a shortage of clergy throughout the Russian diaspora meant that there was no one to replace him. So he remained at his post, offering the bloodless sacrifice "on behalf of each person and all things."

In 1975 he appealed to the Synod, not for the first time, to send just one more clergyman to help him in the diocese, which had gained three new communities—Guildford, Devon, and Belfast. In each of these places, small groups appealed to the archbishop to form a parish, but all that could be provided were services conducted on an irregular basis by visiting clergymen. The published minutes of the Synod meeting on November 12, 1975, simply recorded: "Resolved: to express gratitude to the Most Reverend Archbishop Nikodem for the steps taken towards organizing three new communities in the Diocese of Great Britain." There was no indication that another priest could be sent. Indeed, what priest would be willing to exchange the expansiveness of North America for a city of narrow, terraced houses, of vast crowds and endless delays, where parishes subsisted on annual membership dues of half a crown?

Vladyka Nikodem reported all these matters to the annual parish meeting in June 1976, which was to be his last. His report that year covered a wide range of topics. He reiterated the hierarchy's condemnation of ecumenism necessitated by the publication in England of a document that shocked many Orthodox believers throughout the world, the *Thyateira Confession*. This was written by the head of the Greek Orthodox Church in Great Britain, Archbishop Athenagoras. Vladyka Nikodem said that it was written in the spirit of ecumenism and expressed a "complete distortion of Orthodox doctrine and new dogma of adaptation to the times, while departing from the teachings of the Church of Christ." In retrospect, this strange document appears to have caused embarrassment to the Greek Orthodox Church and did not receive particular attention after the author's death in 1979.

In his review of the development of parish life, Archbishop Nikodem pointed out that Father John was holding regular meetings for the young people of the diocese. Talks on religious and cultural topics were being given every week at Father John's home in Acton, with Russian and English being used on alternate weeks. "These meetings are always very lively and have been a great success, both for the young people and the adults. May God's blessing rest upon this new activity."

Vladyka ended his report with what is probably his last recorded piece of instruction and can be considered his last testament to his people:

> In conclusion I wish to say that we must always remember the meaning of our mission, our being sent and dispersed throughout the world, which is to strive to preserve the life of Holy Russia. This places upon us an obligation to stand firm in our Orthodoxy, to preserve its doctrine and rites pure and unsullied and to guard the freedom and independence of our Church from any outside influences. The Church is our great and only heritage outside Russia, our homeland, the support and consolation of our life in exile. Let us preserve it and work to ensure its prosperity and well-being, with each person helping the Church by his personal efforts in the measure of his abilities. And may the Lord help us all.

Over the last years of Archibishop Nikodem's life, there were some Sundays when he was not well enough to serve and even a few short spells in hospital, from which he always recovered remarkably quickly. People grew accustomed to the fact that theirs was the oldest bishop of the Russian Orthodox Church Abroad, and carried on as if this would continue indefinitely. However, as one parishioner wrote, "We should long ago have anticipated the inevitable." On September 26, 1976, Archbishop Nikodem celebrated the Vigil for the Elevation of the Holy Cross—the autumn feast day that resonates with experiences of Passiontide and Pascha, preaching the power of the Cross of Christ, a power derived from suffering. Archbishop Nikodem began to feel quite unwell, but used his last ounce of strength to perform the rite of the Elevation of the Holy Cross at the end of the Vigil, as always using the Holy Cross belonging to the Kleinmichel family that contains a fragment of the True Cross of Christ. He raised up the Holy Cross to all four points of the compass, extending his last blessing to his flock, to his diocese, and to the whole world. As the people came up to venerate the cross, he blessed them all individually. Then, in a state of near collapse, and feeling pains in the back of his head, Vladyka Nikodem was taken home to the Podvoria.

The following account of Archbishop Nikodem's last days appeared in a church publication in America shortly after his death. It was written by one of his spiritual children, Antonina V. Ananin, who nursed him during this period:

> On the next day Vladyka was unable to celebrate the Divine Liturgy. Doctors were called; they diagnosed shingles. Vladyka's face became swollen and painful, and he had difficulty in swallowing. Nevertheless, he did not wish to enter hospital. He had resolved earlier not to go into hospital in the event of a serious illness, as he wished to die in his own cell. Throughout his final illness, which lasted three weeks, he was nursed by a devoted parishioner, who also read prayers for him every morning and evening, very slowly and quietly, according to his wish. Vladyka received the Holy Communion and the Service of Holy Unction was performed by Father Nicanor and Father John. While he lay in bed, Vladyka continued to say the Jesus Prayer with a chotki (prayer rope). When people came to see him, he blessed them, although often he could not open his eyes due to the swellings on his face, which were particularly bad around the eyes. He would repeat, "The blessing of the Lord be upon you, always, now and ever, and unto the ages of ages" as if he could see his whole flock before him. The itching on his face became particularly bad at night, and so he sang hymns and prayers at the top of his voice to distract himself from the pain: "Virgin Mother of God, rejoice . . . ," "Blessed be the Kingdom of the Father and of the Son and of the Holy Spirit . . . ," and other parts of the divine services.
>
> During the last three nights of his life, Vladyka portentously named various people who recently had died, as if he were already entering communion with the other world. "Averky!" he said, pointing upwards to the clouds, and then, "Nikon showed everyone the path to take!" naming Archbishop Averky who had died on 13 April 1976 and Archbishop Nikon, who had died on 4 September the same year. The he added, "God is calling all to appear before His presence; everyone must remember this. And now, I have reached Brompton [the cemetery where he was laid to rest]." A little later he added, "I saw Arapov." Afterwards it transpired that a Mr. Arapov had died that night. He prayed "O Confessors of God . . ."

thinking, doubtless, of the Russian New Martyrs and Confessors; an account of the sufferings of some clergymen in the Soviet concentration camp had just been read to him and had moved him to tears. (In fact, one of his last acts before his final illness had been to compose a report to the Council of Bishops, urging speedy glorification of the New Martyrs.)

When asked if he needed anything, Vladyka appeared humble and grateful, but, as he grew weaker, he could not express himself, except by singing the Cherubic Hymn from the Liturgy: "Let us who mystically represent the Cherubim now lay aside all the cares of this life." It was clear what he wished to say: that the time had now come to lay aside all the cares of this life and trust completely in God, "that we may receive the King of all," [so the Hymn continues], "Who comes invisibly borne aloft by ranks of angels. Alleluia, alleluia, alleluia."

Archimandrite Nicanor again brought Holy Communion to Vladyka and read the last rites—the "prayers for the departure of the soul from the body." Oxygen was administered from a cylinder kept in the room. The breathing became easier and he slept. Then he became agitated, as if he had seen something terrifying. Those with him remembered how he had explained the Church's teaching that evil spirits try to frighten the soul at the moment of its departure from the body, and said, "Vladyka, be at rest. Remember, your Angel. He is with you; he will guard you." This brought him peace again.

When Saturday evening came, after the Vigil at Emperor's Gate, people came to see Vladyka, prostrated and asked forgiveness. He was very moved.

Eventually they all left. I said prayers and looked at Vladyka's beloved face, so kind and so gentle, and I remembered so much—how good he was, how noble, and sometimes strict. I took my prayer book and thought I would read him the akathist to Our Lady. Suddenly I noticed that his breathing had changed. There was a pause and I started giving him oxygen again. He opened his eyes. Vladyka looked so quiet. He made a sign that he did not want more oxygen and moved the mask away. He looked up, gave a deep breath, and, with his last breath, his soul left his body. I held his hand; I felt that our beloved Vladyka was no more with us in this world. I realized then that the body is only a shell. I felt I should look up, as if I could find Vladyka there. At the same time there was a mysterious feeling of a mystical presence in the air. Father Nicanor confirmed that Vladyka had passed away and started preparing the body.

So Vladyka Nikodem quietly and peacefully passed away on the feast of Saint Hierotheos, Bishop of Athens, at two o'clock, early in the morning of the day of Resurrection, Sunday. Later in the day the faithful gathered at his bedside and sang the first panikhida, holding beeswax candles that Vladyka had specially laid by for that purpose.

His body was vested in white vestments, as he had requested in his will, and the familiar triangular *panagia*,[33] which he had received from Bishop Nathaniel right at the beginning of his episcopal service, was placed on him.

The funeral was held the following Thursday, presided over by Archbishop Anthony of Geneva. People came from all over England; the Cathedral was as full as at Pascha. Clergy concelebrating included Archimandrite Nicanor Troitsky, Father Mark Meyrick from Walsingham, Father John Suscenko, Father Alexander Troubikoff from France; Father Vladimir Rodzianko and Father Milenko Zebic of the Serbian Patriarchate, Protodeacon Peter Figurek from Geneva, and Deacon Sergei Jefimenko. Although it was a weekday, 25 people came to sing and the whole service proceeded smoothly and prayerfully, even though there had not even been time for a choir practice beforehand. The hymns were sung alternately by the choir and by the clergy gathered in the centre of the church around the coffin, which was draped with the red, white and blue Russian flag and with Vladyka's episcopal *mantia*.

At the end of the funeral service Archbishop Anthony gave the address, speaking with warmth and love about the life of Archbishop Nikodem. He said that death, as such, exists only for the body, but the soul of the departed Vladyka was invisibly present and praying together with the congregation. At about two o'clock on a cold, wet, October day the clergy, choir and people accompanied Archbishop Nikodem to his final resting place in Brompton Cemetery. "We were seized with a feeling of great loss and desolation," writes one parishioner, "and the grey sky and the rain highlighted our feeling of grief." After a few short prayers, the coffin, surmounted by a cross made of white flowers brought from the Convent of the Annunciation, was lowered into the grave to the singing of "Memory Eternal." Father John Suscenko gave an address in English at the graveside.

One of the congregation reported,

Significantly, many of the mourners who made the effort to travel to the funeral were non-Russian, for Vladyka was a spiritual example; his very mode of life was grounded in the life of constant prayer, of stillness and peace of heart. This example of true Orthodox spirituality fired the zeal of many non-Russians who saw in Vladyka's life a model of the Life Eternal which they also seek.

In America, a young priestmonk, Father Alexis (Pobjoy), who had previously been a member of the Brotherhood of St Seraphim in Walsingham and had received spiritual guidance from Vladyka as he set out on his monastic path, wrote the following tribute when he learned of Archbishop Nikodem's death and the details of the last days of his life:

> We are instructed by the Apostle: "Remember them which have the rule over you, who have spoken unto the word of God: and observing the result of their conduct, imitate their faith" (Heb 13:7). May God grant us strength that we may now imitate his faith. Those of us who knew Vladyka know of his steadfast witness to Orthodoxy . . . and have witnessed also his standing in prayer in the divine services, and have seen how he served at the holy altar with reverence and piety. Although Vladyka was a man that had to be sought out (for he would never put himself forward), he was undoubtedly one also that possessed a gift of eldership as can be confirmed by those who were his spiritual children. But even for those who did not know him, there is an example and model to be found in the very sketchiest outline of his life: that a man of such extreme old age should continue to celebrate the services and administer a diocese with such steadfastness and resolve is in itself a witness to his faith. He was burdened by old age; he lived in a foreign country with few of his own people, and those poor and scattered far and wide. Vladyka was a noble contestant and one that finished his course nobly also, reaching forward only to the crown of his victory. He who fled the glory and honour of man will now have eternal glory and honour bestowed upon him by the Saviour. We ask all Orthodox Christians to remember Vladyka in their prayers . . . and we hope that in return, through his prayers, our Saviour will send down his blessings upon Vladyka's diocese and upon us all, and that He will grant us also to end our days in good confession of the Faith, in piety and in peace. Amen. So be it.

The funeral service and Archbishop Anthony's sermon were recorded and later broadcast by the BBC to the Soviet Union together with a commentary about Vladyka's life, including his early priesthood that was

Interment of Archbishop Nikodem at Brompton Cemetery, October 21, 1976. In foreground: Archbishop Anthony of Geneva (left) and Archimandrite Nicanor (right). (Source: London Parish Archive)

devoted to the tsar-martyr and Holy Russia, and his later years of service to the Church. Thus, those in Russia who heard the broadcast learned about the reticent, monastic archpastor who, despite long years living in the emigration, had such abiding love for the land of his birth, who wept over the sufferings of her faithful children, and who prayed fervently for her spiritual regeneration.

Chapter 16

[1976–1989] The Last Years at Emperor's Gate

Archimandrite Alexis as Diocesan Administrator

For forty days the diocese of Great Britain mourned the passing of her archpastor, Archbishop Nikodem. A tombstone was erected in the shape of the traditional three-barred Russian Orthodox cross. Flowers were placed regularly on the lovingly tended grave. A visitor to Brompton cemetery could find it easily and, if in doubt, the cemetery keeper would point it out. "Russian Archbishop? Oh yes, the one with all the flowers on it—over there."

Archbishop Anthony of Geneva was appointed temporarily to administer the diocese. A magazine devoted to Orthodox Church matters carried the headline "New Russian Archbishop for London" and included a brief biography of the Most Reverend Anthony (Bartochevitch). Nevertheless, it was forced to admit, "He will continue to reside in Geneva." Immediately after Archbishop Nikodem's funeral, he appointed the senior priest, Archimandrite Nicanor, as dean of the parishes in England. On the following Sunday, he ordained Afanasy Sytnik to the diaconate. He was a pious man in his seventies living in the church house in Manchester where he would serve as a deacon when a priest was able to visit the parish. However, because Archbishop Anthony already had a very large and widely dispersed diocese, he felt unable to give due care to Great Britain as well, and reported as much to the Synod in New York.

At the time, the Synod was attempting to fill key posts in the Church and appealed to monasteries to relinquish a few of their brotherhood to be ordained as priests to occupy these positions. The abbot of Holy Transfiguration Monastery in Boston responded that they had a priest-monk of English origin, Father Alexis. He had been a member of the Brotherhood of St Seraphim in Walsingham, but left in 1970 to study at Holy Trinity Seminary in Jordanville, New York. Seeking a stricter monastic life, a year later he joined Holy Transfiguration Monastery. This Greek monastery was then under the jurisdiction of the Russian Church Abroad, and used English extensively in its liturgical and community life. Here Father Alexis completed the novitiate, receiving the monastic tonsure in 1975 and ordination to the priesthood in 1976. The abbot felt a certain hesitation when he accepted Father Alexis into his brotherhood, knowing that Archbishop Nikodem had fervently hoped that Father Alexis would return to England as a priest.

Archimandrite Alexis (Pobjoy) at Emperor's Gate, 1980, with Nicolas Mabin (left) and Paul Kolatai (right). (Source: Christopher Birchall)

After becoming acquainted with Father Alexis, the bishops sent him back to England with a synodal decree of appointment as administrator of the Diocese of Great Britain reporting directly to Metropolitan Philaret, chairman of the Synod. On his way, he presented himself at the Synodal Cathedral of the Icon of Our Lady of the Sign in New York to be elevated to the rank of archimandrite. Father Alexis had deep reverence for the late Archbishop Nikodem and, despite spending six years in a Greek-American monastery, he retained a strong affection for the Russian church in general and for the London parish in particular as the first Orthodox parish to which he belonged. Father Alexis had a good understanding of Russian but limited conversational abilities in any language other than English. After a short period in New York spent learning how to celebrate the services in Church Slavonic, Archimandrite Alexis returned to his native England in the summer of 1977, trusting in the prayers of the late Archbishop Nikodem to help him.

Metropolitan Philaret came to London for the patronal festival of the Dormition on August 15/28, 1977, and a solemn hierarchical service was held at which Archimandrite Alexis was installed as rector of the parish and administrator of the diocese.

In addition to Father Alexis, the diocesan clergy at the time consisted of three other priests. Archimandrite Nicanor and Father John Suscenko had recently been joined by Father Yves Dubois, a Belgian convert to Orthodoxy who had joined the Russian Church Abroad from the Patriarchate of Moscow. Services were organized on a rotating basis, with Father Alexis and Father John taking turns to visit the parishes in Manchester, Bradford, and Nottingham on Sundays, and the smaller parishes in Dublin, Ireland, and Barton-on-Sea (in Hampshire) during the week. Father Yves served primarily at the Convent of the Annunciation but also had a small house chapel in his Chiswick home where some services were conducted.

Father Nicholas Couriss (ca. 1972), a Dublin parishioner who was ordained to the priesthood in 1967 and served the Dublin parish until he died in 1977. (Source: Nicolas Mabin)

The most immediate issue facing the London parish was the impending end of the lease on the Cathedral at Emperor's Gate. The parish's understanding was that the lease taken out in 1958 was for twenty-one years, with a legally binding right to buy the freehold of the building on expiration of the lease in 1979. However, on closer examination it turned out that the lease was not for the full twenty-one years, but just for twenty years and eleven months. Also, the Fidelity Trust acting on behalf of the Anglican parish of St Stephen's, Gloucester Road, was unwilling to sell the freehold. Thus, the parish's position was precarious, with no certainty of tenure after 1979. Archimandrite Alexis launched an appeal for funds to be able to acquire another church and so establish itself on a more permanent basis. So began a series of fund-raising efforts and searches for suitable properties that continued for more than a decade. In the meantime, the parish paid its monthly rent, even after the lease expired, and remained at Emperor's Gate without knowing how long they would be able to stay. These earthly concerns were exacerbated by the deteriorating health of Count Kleinmichel, who had been the churchwarden and treasurer for the past forty years.

Once established as rector of the parish, Father Alexis soon recognized a need to hold more services in English. Many younger parishioners had grown up in England and had a poor grasp of Russian, and were even less familiar with Church Slavonic. The pastoral need to serve the native English congregation was also growing. Introducing a substantial amount of English into the services at Emperor's Gate, however, would not be well received by the predominantly Russian congregation. In Archbishop Nikodem's time, a regular monthly Sunday Liturgy in English was held in the Podvoria in St Dunstan's Road; Father Alexis decided to make these services more frequent. Eventually, in 1980, the Synod gave permission to open a separate English-language parish based at the Podvoria. This new parish was dedicated to St Gregory the Great, the bishop of Rome who had sent St Augustine to England to preach to the heathen Anglo-Saxon tribes in the sixth century. The English Liturgy was served here three Sundays out of four, with Archimandrite Alexis and Father Yves celebrating on alternate weeks. On the fourth Sunday the parish of St Gregory gathered for the service of Matins without a priest. The singing and reading at these services was led by Daniel Toyne, a convert to Orthodoxy who later became the parish priest of the Greek Orthodox Church of the Resurrection in Singapore. Father Alexis began publishing a newsletter for St Gregory's parish called the *Shepherd*.

An initiative linked to the ancient roots of the church in England began when Father Alexis learned of the existence of the relics of St Edward, king and martyr, who was assassinated at Corfe Castle, Dorset, in 979, before the Western Church had separated from the Orthodox East. These relics had been enshrined at Shaftesbury Abbey in Dorset until the dissolution of the monasteries under Henry VIII in the sixteenth century, at which point they were hidden away to save them from destruction. They were discovered in 1931 by John Wilson-Claridge during an archeological dig in the ruins of Shaftesbury Abbey. Mr Wilson-Claridge sought to have the relics reverently enshrined, but found that none of the major religious bodies in England were interested. Father Alexis contacted him, and Mr Wilson-Claridge agreed to give the relics to the Russian Orthodox Church Abroad on condition of their proper enshrinement. The Synod of the Russian Church Abroad gave its blessing for this in March 1979. The bishops were impressed by the similarities between the life and murder of St Edward and the life and murder of the Russian passion-bearers, Saints Boris and Gleb.

In 1980, Mr Wilson-Claridge visited England from Malta, where he was then living, and met Father Alexis. He expressed the desire that a church be purchased and consecrated expressly as a shrine for the relics. At first

A group of St Gregory's parishioners outside 14 St Dunstan's Road, 1982. (Source: Archimandrite Alexis)

this seemed to be an insurmountable obstacle. However, a suitable church was found surprisingly quickly. It was located in Brookwood Cemetery, in Surrey, just over thirty minutes by train from London. This large cemetery was established in the late Victorian era to provide burial places after many churchyards, especially in London, became full. Brookwood had a special branch railway line so that the deceased could be brought by train directly to the cemetery. By the 1970s, the railway station and cemetery church were no longer in use as funerals were more commonly conducted in parish churches or funeral homes rather than at the cemetery itself, and so they were being sold. It happened that a substantial number of Orthodox people lived in the nearby city of Guildford, so that a shrine established at Brookwood could serve as a parish centre. Also, land adjoining the church could be used as an Orthodox cemetery, which is always difficult to establish in a crowded city.

Father Alexis began negotiations with the cemetery owners to buy the church and outbuildings. The King Edward Orthodox Trust was set up to raise funds for the shrine and to administer it. There were many obstacles in the way of fulfilling this plan, both in terms of financial resources and time commitments. Nevertheless, Father Alexis's hopes for the future of Orthodoxy in England increasingly began to centre on Brookwood Cemetery.

Bishop Constantine

Archimandrite Alexis had initially been appointed as the administrator of the diocese reporting directly to the metropolitan in New York. In 1981, however, the Synod decided it might be better if the Diocese of Great Britain had a bishop to administer it, leaving Father Alexis to concentrate on missionary endeavours and on building the shrine church for the relics of St Edward. Their choice settled on Bishop Constantine, who had most recently served in Australia but was then living in retirement in the same Boston monastery where Father Alexis had received his monastic tonsure. Bishop Constantine visited London in the summer of 1981 and met the parishioners and Parish Council of the Emperor's Gate Cathedral. Subsequently, the council petitioned the Synod for Bishop Constantine's appointment to the diocese. He was subsequently confirmed as Bishop of Richmond and Great Britain at the Sobor held in November 1981, the same meeting at which the bishops glorified the New Martyrs of Russia. Bishop Constantine arrived in England to take up his new appointment in December 1981.

Born in St Petersburg in 1907 as Emmanuel Jesensky, Bishop Constantine was seventy-four years old when he moved to London. His father had worked in the Imperial Chancery in St Petersburg, and after the revolution was arrested by the Bolsheviks and shot. His mother, on receiving this news, died of a heart attack, leaving eleven-year-old Emmanuel an orphan. His nanny took him to Riga in Latvia, where his grandmother had property, to escape the terror of the Russian Revolution. There he finished school and worked in a pharmacy. At the same time he studied iconography under the masterful Old Rite iconographer Pimen Sofronov. In 1928, the future New Martyr Archbishop John (Pommers) of Riga (+1934) blessed him to enter the Riga seminary. He graduated in 1930 and went to Paris, where he continued his studies and obtained his doctorate at the St Sergius Theological Institute. In 1932 Metropolitan Evlogy of Paris ordained him to the priesthood and sent him to the Church of St Vladimir in Berlin. He served there for two years as second priest before being assigned rector of the Church of St Alexis Metropolitan of Moscow in Leipzig.

In 1938, Father Emmanuel and his parish left the Paris jurisdiction of Metropolitan Evlogy and joined the Russian Orthodox Church Abroad. That same year he was sent as a delegate to the second Pan-Diaspora Council held in Serbia. At the beginning of World War II he began to study medicine at Berlin University.

During the war years he witnessed some horrific events that he was never able to forget. Due to ill health, he moved in 1945 to Bad Hartzburg where he lived during the American occupation. In 1949 he went to the United States and served as a priest in various parishes on the East Coast. Father Emmanuel was tonsured a monk in October 1967 by Archbishop Averky at Holy Trinity Monastery, Jordanville, New York, and given the name Constantine. Two months later, on the feast of the Kursk icon of the Sign, he was consecrated Bishop of Brisbane. He served in Australia until he retired to the monastery in Boston in 1979.

On arrival in England, Bishop Constantine immediately took great interest in missionary endeavours and made it clear he wanted to serve the English-speaking flock as well as the Russians. He was perhaps the first Russian resident of the Podvoria to enquire about the history of St Dunstan, a tenth-century contemporary of St Edward, after whom the road on which the Podvoria was named. Bishop Constantine expressed his wish to officiate at the English-language liturgies for St Gregory's parish once a month, even though it meant having some of the English texts written out in Russian letters so that he could be sure he was pronouncing them properly.

Father Alexis moved permanently to Brookwood, accompanied by his assistant, Brother Timothy Fisher, on March 18, 1982. Before they left the Podvoria, Bishop Constantine served a moleben and blessed the good intent of their undertaking. The buildings at Brookwood were not yet ready for habitation, so they stayed in an old caravan on the site. Publication of the *Shepherd* continued at Brookwood without interruption. On April 3, 1982, the nearest Saturday to the day of the martyrdom of St Edward the Martyr, Bishop Constantine arrived at Brookwood, along with some

Bishop Constantine (Jesensky) of Richmond and Great Britain, ca. 1983. (Source: Valentina Turner-Udalcova)

At Emperor's Gate, 1984 (left to right): Nicolas Mabin, Protodeacon Christopher Birchall, Bishop Constantine, Fyodor Yankovitch, and Alexander Suscenko. (Source: London Parish Archive)

parishioners from London, to celebrate the first Liturgy in what was to be St Edward's church. Although the purchase of the property was not yet complete, the cemetery owners allowed the church to be used for occasional services. Two large icon prints from Mt Athos were framed and mounted on trestles to serve as a temporary iconostasis. The service was conducted mainly in English with some Slavonic added, with the Creed and the Lord's Prayer being sung in both languages. The church building was not in very good condition. During his sermon, noticing that some of the windows had been vandalized during the church's period of disuse, Bishop Constantine recalled the destruction that came upon the churches of his homeland when the people there turned away from the fundamentals of an Orthodox Christian life. He called upon the English converts to take heed from Russia's bitter experience, and to place repentance and ascetic struggle as the foundation of their mission.

Four months later, in early August 1982, the King Edward Orthodox Trust completed the purchase of the property at Brookwood. After exploring various avenues of financing and receiving some unexpectedly large donations, the Trust obtained a loan from the Midland Bank to fund the balance of the purchase price. Extensive restoration of the church and conversion of the former mortuary chapel next to the church into living quarters was done over time as funds permitted.

In September 1984, Bishop Gregory, the secretary of the Synod, came from New York representing Metropolitan Philaret at the solemn presentation of St Edward's relics to the brotherhood by John Wilson-Claridge. However, the relics remained only briefly at Brookwood. John Wilson-Claridge's brother, Geoffrey, claimed ownership of the relics and wanted to have them returned to Shaftesbury, despite the fact that no church there was interested in providing a shrine for them. This dispute was pursued through the courts, and the High Court ordered that the relics be kept in a bank vault pending the outcome of the case, or at least until such time as an adequate security system could be installed in the church at Brookwood. Thus the relics remained at the Midland Bank in Woking until judgment was granted in 1988 permitting the brotherhood to accept the relics.

In London, the English-language parish of St Gregory continued for a while after the establishment of the St Edward Brotherhood, but eventually it was disbanded as a separate parish. Some of its members attended services at Brookwood, while others attended the Cathedral at Emperor's Gate. Before long, the regime of a monthly English-language Liturgy was reinstated at the Podvoria.

Soon after the arrival of Bishop Constantine, Abbot Seraphim (Scuratov) transferred from the Serbian Church to join the clergy of the Russian Church Abroad. He lived in Birmingham, where he had a small chapel dedicated to St Seraphim of Sarov, but travelled to London quite often to assist with services. Sometimes he served at the Cathedral to allow Father John Suscenko to visit provincial parishes; other times he served at the Convent of the Annunciation, and once a month it was his duty to conduct the Liturgy in English at the Podvoria. In 1982 Father Yves moved to Bath, where he opened a chapel and missionary centre.

Also not long after Bishop Constantine's arrival, the parish suffered the sad loss of their longtime churchwarden, Count Kleinmichel. He died on May 17, 1982, just after joining his daughter and son-in-law in celebration of their silver wedding anniversary. He was found later the same evening—he had met a peaceful end, lying in bed and saying his prayers. The following account of the funeral appeared in the *Shepherd*:

> Recently the Russian Orthodox community in London lost one of her most faithful sons, when Count Vladimir Petrovich Kleinmichel fell asleep in the Lord. He had served on the Parish Council of the Emperor's Gate Church for over fifty years, and for many years had been both churchwarden and parish treasurer. His funeral was conducted

> by Bishop Constantine, assisted by Archimandrite Nicanor, Archimandrite Alexis and Father John. Abbess Elisabeth and some of the nuns from the Annunciation Convent were among the many that came to pay their respects. After the service, this humble and hardworking servant of the Church was laid to rest at Gunnersbury Cemetery. We ask readers to remember the newly departed servant of God Vladimir in their prayers.

Another memorable event of this period was a diocesan pilgrimage to St Albans on a Saturday in August 1982. Members of the Emperor's Gate parish, regular visitors to the Convent of the Annunciation, and people from Brookwood united to make a pilgrimage to the shrine of Britain's first martyr, St Alban. A temporary altar was set up just east of the shrine, which marks the place where the martyr was slain and where his relics were kept prior to the Reformation. Parishioners from London brought everything necessary for an episcopal service. His Grace Bishop Constantine was greeted at the west door of St Albans Cathedral by the dean, the Very Reverend Peter Moore. Bishop Constantine was then vested in his episcopal *mantia* and walked in procession through the vast nave of the cathedral to the temporary altar while the singing of the Russian choir echoed from the vaulted ceiling. The shrine faces westward behind the choir and rood screen, hidden from view when one enters the west door. Here, according to the usual rite, Bishop Constantine venerated the icons and was vested for the Liturgy. The bishop was assisted at the Liturgy by Archimandrite Alexis, and the choir from Emperor's Gate sang. The service was conducted partly in Slavonic and partly in English. Also present were Bishop Kallistos (Ware) of Diokleia and two other clergymen of the Greek Orthodox Church. At the end of the Liturgy, Bishop Constantine preached a brief sermon on the significance of martyrdom, and then the faithful gathered around the tomb for a short service of intercession to St Alban. After refreshments, the dean took all the Orthodox clergy to see the newly built library, and afterward for a quiet talk at his nearby home.

The Russian Dissident Movement

For the Easter night service on May 8, 1983, the Cathedral at Emperor's Gate was visited by the Russian writer Alexander Solzhenitsyn. After being expelled from the Soviet Union in 1974, he had taken up residence in the American state of Vermont, and he came from there to London to accept the Templeton Prize for Progress in Religion. At the Cathedral he was received as an honoured guest, and people were encouraged that he had specifically chosen to visit the church then known as the Russian Orthodox Church in Exile. He carried the main festal icon of the resurrection of Christ in the Easter procession.

Alexander Solzhenitsyn carries the icon of the Resurrection in a Paschal procession at Emperor's Gate, 1983. (Source: The *Times*)

Two days later, Solzhenitsyn went to Buckingham Palace to receive the prize, and then to the Guildhall, where he gave a memorable address in which he accurately assessed many of the ills of the modern world. He showed how the failings of both communism and capitalism had their roots in the same cause—the passionate nature of fallen, sinful humanity. He also expressed the view that communism was doomed to failure:

> It is true that millions of our countrymen have been corrupted and spiritually devastated by an officially imposed atheism, yet there remain many millions of believers. . . . The awareness of God in my country has attained great acuteness and profundity. It is here that we see the dawn of hope: for no matter how formidably Communism bristles with tanks and rockets, no matter what successes it attains in seizing the planet, it is doomed never to vanquish Christianity.

In the early 1980s, such a view was widely thought to be utopian, since most people in the West assumed that the communist grip was invincible. However, this was also a period of awakening, of a growing dissident movement in the Soviet Union, inspired in large measure by the *samizdat* writings of Solzhenitsyn.[1] In Russian émigré circles also, there were now people beginning to work actively to hasten the end of the Soviet regime. One such family, who were also devoted parishioners of the Cathedral at Emperor's Gate, were the Millers—Boris, Kyra, and

Moleben served outside the Soviet Embassy in 1983 for the release from imprisonment of Irina Ratushinskaya: Andrew Bond (first from left), Valerie Holmes (fifth from left); Ludmilla Purvis (making sign of Cross, eighth from left), Father John Suscenko, Choir Director Antonina Ananin, Father Yves Dubois, and George Miller. (Source: Lillia Miller)

their son George. Boris Miller had grown up in Serbia, and later moved to Chile where he met and married Kyra Kurakin, a descendent of Count Kurakin who had been Russian Ambassador to England in the time of Peter the Great. Their eldest son, George, was born in Santiago in 1955. In 1959 the family moved to Frankfurt and soon after moved again to England, where George attended Bromley Grammar School and then Queen Mary College, London, where he studied economics. George was warm-hearted, outgoing, and cheerful, quite the opposite of the stereotype of the exiled counterrevolutionary. While many other parishioners at Emperor's Gate were supportive of the Millers' activities, and particularly of the Association for a Free Russia that George founded in the early 1980s, they were generally unaware of the wide scope and creative energy involved. After George's untimely death from heart failure in November 2009, obituaries in many English newspapers—including the *Times*, the *Guardian*, the *Independent,* and the *Daily Telegraph*—detailed his international impact:

> Intellectual and visionary, liberal and anti-Communist, George Miller inspired a generation of Conservative activists in the 1980s, when the Soviet Union seemed impregnable. His operations were so extensive that

few of his associates knew the full picture. . . . For Miller the demise of Soviet Communism was an absolute certainty, provided that the West remained strong. . . . A pillar of the Russian Orthodox Church, he was mystical, spiritual, selfless and humane. A hero of our times. (*Independent*, November 26, 2009)

While western foreign and defense policies focused on containment and détente, George created the Association for a Free Russia, which distributed *Help Free Russia* leaflets, shocking western diplomacy. In 1980 he co-authored a Bow Group paper, *Prelude to Freedom*. He worked at the Institute of European Defense and Strategic Studies, introducing newly released dissidents such as Vladimir Bukovsky to the UK media and politicians. Working with Simon Clark in the mid-80s, he edited *Soviet Labour Review*, publicising the nascent Soviet trade union movement. (*Guardian*, February 12, 2010)

Shortly after the Soviet invasion in 1979, Miller-Kurakin travelled to Afghanistan and Pakistan to obtain first-hand evidence of poison gas being used against Afghan fighters. . . . He produced educational material in Russian for Russian captives of Afghan groups, and urged the mujahedeen not to kill them. He later brought an Afghan delegation to an international youth conference which was organized in Jamaica in opposition to a Soviet-inspired equivalent held in Cuba, making sure that the travel agent did not direct delegates through Moscow, even if this was the cheapest route. (*Daily Telegraph*, December 3, 2009)

A very good man. I remember sitting in the basement of the Russian Orthodox Church in Exile with him, stuffing and addressing envelopes with *samizdat* leaflets and sending them behind the Iron Curtain. His mother was a real lady. (Letter to the editor of the *Daily Telegraph*, December 3, 2009)

George Miller, a prominent parishioner and activist on behalf of Russian dissidents, at his wedding in 1986. (Source: Lillia Miller)

George was buried in the Orthodox section of Brookwood cemetery, next to the grave of his mother, Kyra.

Bishop Mark of Berlin, Germany, and Great Britain

Bishop Constantine remained in the see of Richmond and Great Britain for just over four years. The damp English climate did not agree with him and his health gradually deteriorated. In particular, he suffered from a devastating form of anaemia, a heart condition, and bad arthritis. One of the last initiatives he undertook was to bless the establishment of the *Anchor*, an English-language newsletter for the Cathedral Parish. The first issue appeared in late 1985 and publication continued until 1990. Edited by Nicolas Mabin, it provided a valuable means of communication during the period of uncertainty over the future of the church building.

In January 1986, Bishop Constantine travelled to New York to attend a Bishops' Council of the Russian Church Abroad. The purpose of the council meeting was to elect a new metropolitan after the revered Metropolitan Philaret died on November 21, 1985. Archbishop Vitaly of Montreal and Canada was elected as the new metropolitan. At this council meeting, seventy-eight-year-old Bishop Constantine said he felt unable to continue as diocesan bishop in England due to old age and ill health. He asked to be allowed to retire, and this request was granted. After the meeting, he returned to England and remained for over a year as a retired bishop while making arrangements to settle permanently in the United States.[2]

At the same Bishops' Council, Bishop Mark (Arndt) of Germany was appointed administrator of the Diocese of Great Britain, becoming Bishop of Berlin, Germany, and Great Britain. This came as a surprise to many, since the parishes of the Russian Church Abroad in England never previously had direct contact with those in Germany. At various times in the past, England had been part of the Diocese of Western Europe, based first in Paris, then in Brussels, and finally in Geneva. The decision in 1986 was based on practical considerations. Archbishop Anthony of Geneva was already responsible for a large diocese and, although he could speak Russian and French, he spoke no English. Bishop Mark was considerably younger and fluent in many languages, including English.

Nevertheless, Archbishop Anthony of Geneva accompanied Bishop Mark on his first visit to the Church in London, on March 9, 1986, to introduce him to his new flock. Both bishops concelebrated the Liturgy together with the Cathedral clergy in the presence of Bishop Constantine, who did not officiate that day due to ill health. This service took place on the Sunday one week before the beginning of Lent, when the Epistle reading ends with the words "you are the seal of my apostleship in the Lord" (1 Cor 9:2), words providentially fitting for the occasion of a bishop taking up the apostolic ministry in a new diocese. The parish newsletter, the *Anchor*, commented,

> With great affection Archbishop Anthony spoke from the ambon to the congregation about the retirement of Vladyka Constantine and the appointment of Bishop Mark. Bishop Constantine delivered a moving address in which he warmly commended his successor, and all present were touched by the evident spirit of love which encompassed the occasion.

Bishop Mark (Arndt) outside Emperor's Gate Cathedral, soon after becoming responsible for the care of the Diocese of Great Britain in 1986. (Source: Christopher Birchall)

Bishop Mark became the new diocesan bishop and rector of the Cathedral parish in London. The Diocese of Great Britain effectively became his second diocese. He continued to live in his monastery in Munich, but remained actively involved in all aspects of the life of the Church in his British diocese. He established a pattern of visiting England at least three times a year: for the feast of Theophany in January, on the first Sunday after Easter, and for the patronal festival of the Dormition in August. However, when other occasions warranted it, he made additional visits.

When he was appointed to the see of Richmond and Great Britain, Vladyka Mark had been a bishop for just over five years. At the time of his episcopal consecration in 1980, he was the only bishop of non-Russian origin in the Russian Church Abroad. Born Michael Arndt in 1941, he grew up in Germany in the town of Chemnitz in Saxony. His parents were both musicians. After the war, Chemnitz was in Soviet-occupied East Germany and was renamed Karl-Marx-Stadt. In 1954, after the Berlin uprising the year before, the entire Arndt family fled to West Germany and settled in Frankfurt am Main. As a university student, Michael Arndt became an ardent linguist studying Russian, Serbo-Croat, Slovak, Czech, and Macedonian as well as English. His doctoral thesis was in the field of ancient Russian literature. These academic studies brought him into contact with Russian émigré circles and, eventually, with the Russian Orthodox Church. He was received into the Orthodox Church in 1964. After graduating, Dr Arndt became a teacher of linguistics and in 1969 was appointed to a managerial post in the European Division of the University of Maryland, based in Heidelberg. He was responsible for supervising 180 teachers in eleven countries. During this period, he came into frequent contact with Americans and developed his practical knowledge of English. Dr Arndt was also a member of the board of editors of the Russian émigré journal *Grani.* In 1973 he enrolled in the theological faculty of the Serbian Orthodox Church in Belgrade, and during his visits to Yugoslavia he established close contacts with the renowned Serbian theologian and ascetic Father Justin Popovic.

In 1975 Dr Arndt decided to enter the monastic life and was tonsured by Bishop Paul of Stuttgart,[3] receiving the monastic name of Mark in honour of the fifth-century Egyptian ascetic St Mark the Faster. He was ordained to the priesthood the following year and appointed deputy rector of the church in Wiesbaden. In 1980 when Bishop Paul was transferred to Australia, Father Mark was chosen to replace him, and he was consecrated as Bishop of Munich and Southern Germany, and assigned as assistant to Archbishop Philothei of Berlin and Germany. As a condition of accepting the episcopacy, Bishop Mark insisted that he would live in the Monastery of St Job of Pochaev in Munich rather than in Stuttgart as his predecessor had. In fact, Bishop Mark revived the monastery and instituted a full cycle of daily services following the typicon of Mt Athos. In his address before his consecration at the Synodal Cathedral in New York, the future bishop spoke of the contrast between the lofty spiritual ideals of Orthodoxy and the practical reality of a priest entrusted with care of several parishes, who may spend more time travelling than he can devote to his parishioners once he has arrived.

> Do we not forget, or rather, are we not forced under such circumstances to forget, about what places Holy Orthodoxy immeasurably higher than all religions and ideologies calling themselves Christian—that is to say, about building the Kingdom of God in oneself and in one's parishioners, about acquiring experience and practice in the inner unseen warfare?

He also spoke of the need to strengthen parish life so that people motivated to seek spiritual healing—perhaps baptized Orthodox Christians who had drifted far from the Church—would find in the parish "a manifestation of the living Body of Christ."

The new bishop found many practical issues to be addressed when he arrived in England, most importantly the precarious tenure of the Cathedral at Emperor's Gate. By 1986 the lease had expired and the parish was paying rent on a month-to-month basis. Under the circumstances, maintenance expenditures were kept to a minimum. After his first service in London, Bishop Mark was seen staring up into the murky rafters supporting the church roof, when Archbishop Anthony, known for his dry "English-style" sense of humour, came and joined his younger colleague, commenting, "Yes, I expect you'll be spending more time over here than at home!" Over the next few years, Bishop Mark paid visits to the Bishop of London and other senior clergymen of the Church of England to see if another church might be available to buy or lease. At one point there was a suggestion that the parish might be able to use St Botolph's in Aldersgate in the City of London. At first Bishop Mark was enthusiastic, pointing out the potential for missionary witness by having a church in the middle of the bustling financial district. However, it later transpired that it would not be possible to erect an iconostasis and the Church of England would still want to use the building during the week, only making it available on Sundays when the City of London is virtually deserted. Before long, the new bishop came to the conclusion that the Church of England was under no obligation to help the Russian Orthodox Church, and the parish should focus on finding a parcel of land where it could build a church of its own.

Being fluent in both Russian and English, as well as several other languages, Bishop Mark was able to communicate easily with all members of the congregation, both older Russian people who were more comfortable speaking Russian, and younger people and English converts who communicated more readily in English. Before long he had visited all the parishes and communities in Great Britain, as well as St Edward's Monastery in Brookwood. While Bishop Mark as diocesan bishop was the rector of the Cathedral, Father John Suscenko as parish priest was primarily responsible for conducting services and performing other ministrations. Abbot Seraphim continued to travel from Birmingham to London quite often which allowed Father John to visit the

Bishop Mark (Arndt) officiates at the Emperor's Gate Cathedral, 1987. (Source: Christopher Birchall)

parishes in Bradford and Manchester. Father Seraphim also conducted the monthly English Liturgy at the Podvoria in St Dunstan's Road, which was now preceded by a Vigil service in English on the Saturday evenings before the English Liturgy. Archimandrite Nicanor now officiated primarily at the Convent of the Annunciation. Because he had difficulty walking due to a pinched nerve, the convent chapel which had no steps was easier for him to manage, as was the case in the past for Father George Cheremetieff. In 1987 Abbess Elisabeth had appealed to Holy Trinity Monastery in Jordanville to send a priest to help with the Holy Week and Easter services. The priest sent was Abbot Flor,[4] who was a very reserved but warm-hearted individual, a true monk. His annual visits to England to serve at the convent at Easter became a fixture of church life for years to come. Later, Father Flor was able to combine these visits with a journey to Slovakia to visit his relatives.

In June 1986 the newly elected Metropolitan Vitaly paid a visit to England. He received a warm welcome, especially from people who remembered him from his time as parish priest in London and diocesan administrator between 1947 and 1951. They also knew of his efforts to rescue refugees from forced repatriation to the Soviet Union in the aftermath of World War II. On the Sunday of All Saints, which is a week after Pentecost, he concelebrated the Liturgy in the Cathedral at Emperor's Gate with Bishop Mark and the retired Bishop Constantine. That evening he attended a meeting of the London Cathedral Parish Council. Bishop Mark thanked him for coming and noted that it was most unusual for a metropolitan to come to a Parish Council meeting but Vladyka Mark had invited the metropolitan as the best way to help him understand the current problems facing the London parish and the diocese as a whole. The meeting proceeded in a warm and constructive atmosphere, helped by Metropolitan Vitaly's memories of his time in England.

Bishop Mark's appointment to head the diocese in England was especially welcomed by the Miller family, who knew him in Germany before he became a bishop. Before taking monastic vows, the former Dr Arndt had been active in Russian émigré circles and knew many of the dissidents who lived in or visited Germany. During the second half of the 1980s, the Association for a Free Russia carried on its activities, sometimes but not always using the church hall in the basement of the Cathedral to host guest speakers. Thus, in April 1986, Count Nikolai Tolstoy, a prominent member of the parish and a well-known author, gave a talk in connection with the launch of his latest book, *The Minister and the Massacres*. In January 1987, Irina Ratushinskaya spoke in the crypt at Emperor's Gate about her experience in Soviet concentration camps, where she had been imprisoned because of her Orthodox faith.[5] She was allowed to come to the West for medical treatment; but deciding not to return, she accepted a teaching post at Cornell University in America. In November 1987, a talk was given by Dr Anatoli Koryagin, a leading figure in the Soviet human rights movement who spoke about his resistance to the KGB and his experience during seven years of imprisonment and five years in internal exile. While in captivity, Dr Koryagin was converted to Orthodox Christianity by Father Gleb Yakunin. After leaving the Soviet Union, Dr Koryagin was baptized by Archbishop Anthony of Geneva. In November 1989, the speaker at the association's meeting in the church crypt was Vladimir Vilde, visiting from the Soviet Union. He represented a current of thought that supported the ideal of monarchy—an anointed sovereign at the head of an Orthodox Christian society. Nevertheless, he thought this ideal was not currently attainable as people were not ready to accept it. He demonstrated extensive knowledge of the Holy Scriptures and the Church Fathers. In discussion after the talk, Mr Vilde's ideas were compared with those of the Soviet Academician F. Shipounov, an ecologist with a profound Christian faith, whose speech delivered in the Central House of Artists in Moscow in March of that year had recently been published by Metropolitan Vitaly in Canada. Thus the association, which included members of the parish, continued to actively study contemporary developments in the Soviet Union and hope—not without foundation—for the fall of the atheist regime sometime in the not too distant future.

Metropolitan Vitaly (Oustinow) officiates at the Convent of the Annunciation, 1988. (Source: Christopher Birchall)

Amid the continual search for a new church, two events stood out in the second half of the 1980s. The first of these was the visit of the miraculous Iveron Icon of the Mother of God. This icon came from Mt Athos and hung in the room of a Chilean convert to Orthodoxy, Jose Muñoz, who was living in Montreal not far from Metropolitan Vitaly. One morning Jose awoke to find a stream of fragrant holy oil flowing miraculously from the icon. The oil continued to flow for a long time thereafter. Since 1982 the icon had been taken to churches of the Russian Church Abroad all over the world. In 1987 Bishop Mark arranged for it to be brought to England from Paris by Father Michael Artsymovitch of Meudon, and met at Charing Cross Station on Monday, February 16. An article in the *Anchor* reported,

> That evening, a service of intercession was held in front of the icon combined with an akathist—a hymn in praise of the Iveron Icon of the Mother of God. The entire akathist was sung, with the refrain at the end of each stanza, "Rejoice, O Gracious Gate-keeper, opening unto the faithful the gates of paradise." This refrain was originally composed in honour of the Portaitissa Icon which stands at the gates of the Iveron Monastery on Mount Athos. But here it took on a new meaning as the faithful saw with their own eyes the streams of oil flowing from the icon and collecting in the deep channel carved in the base of the frame, and smelt the wonderful, heavenly fragrance which filled the Cathedral.

During the ensuing week, the icon was taken to parishes in Nottingham, Manchester, Bradford, and Birmingham, as well as St Edward's Monastery and the Convent of the Annunciation. On Saturday Bishop Mark arrived and another service of intercession with an akathist was held. By this time, news of the icon's presence in London had spread and there were far more people present than at Monday's service and even more at the Liturgy on the following day.

The reality of the miraculous appearance of sacred oil from the icon was beyond doubt. Sceptical people had examined it and concluded that there was no natural explanation. The bishops of the Russian Church Abroad were all sober-minded people who were well aware of the dangers of spiritual delusion, and none more so than the Primate, Metropolitan Vitaly. Miraculous healings were recorded when people were anointed with the holy oil, but it was generally thought that the greater miracle was the outpouring of heartfelt prayer that united so many people round the holy icon.[6]

The other significant event in this period was the celebration in 1988 of the Millennium of Russian Christianity. St Vladimir had baptized the populace of Kiev in 988, and in 1888 on the 900th anniversary of that baptism there had been large-scale celebrations throughout the Russian Empire. The bishops of the Russian Church Abroad thought it their duty to organize a fitting celebration of the millennium of the baptism as it was far from clear what celebrations, if any, would be permitted in the Soviet Union. Every diocese and parish throughout the world made plans for a celebration that

Bishop Mark presides at a moleben at Emperor's Gate to mark the 1,000th anniversary of the Baptism of Russia, 1988. On his right (right to left): Nicolas Mabin, Archimandrite Arseny, Igoumen Seraphim, Father Nikolai Artemoff, and Protodeacon Christopher Birchall. On the bishop's left (left to right): Subdeacon Prince Dmitri Galitzine, Alan Mackellar, Fyodor Yankovitch, Archimandrite Alexis, Father John Suscenko, and George Miller. (Source: Christopher Birchall)

Choir director Antonina Ananin conducts the Cathedral Choir at Emperor's Gate at the celebration for the Millennium of Russian Christianity, 1988. Left to right: Kyra Miller, Margareta Dunkov, Pamela (surname unknown), and Ludmilla Purvis. (Source: *The Anchor*, November 11, 1988)

Churchwarden Sophia Goodman (daughter of Count Kleinmichel) speaks at the banquet in London marking the 1,000th anniversary of the Baptism of Russia, 1988. (Source: *Anchor*, November 11, 1988)

would be edifying and inspiring. In London it was decided to hold the celebration on July 17, the day on which the Church commemorates Tsar-Martyr Nicholas and his family. The following account is taken from the parish newsletter, the *Anchor*:

The celebration of the Millennium of Christianity in Russia in London took place over the weekend of 16/17 July, 1988. The festivities commenced with the celebration of the All-Night Vigil Service at the Cathedral of the Dormition, Emperor's Gate, London SW7, and continued with a celebration of the Hierarchical Divine Liturgy on the morning of the feast of the Holy Royal Martyrs of Russia. The spiritual atmosphere was significantly enhanced by the excellence of the choir, led by its choir-director, Mrs. A. V. Ananin. The Cathedral was crowded with believers and visitors and was reminiscent of Pascha. His Grace Bishop Mark of Berlin, Germany, and Great Britain presided. Serving with him, in addition to the Cathedral clergy, were Archimandrite Arseny, chaplain of the Lesna Convent in France; Archimandrite Alexis, superior of the Monastery of Saint Edward, Brookwood; Father Nikolai Artemoff from the Russian Orthodox Church in Munich; and Deacon Elias Jones from Suffolk. Visitors included Archimandrite David of the Monastery of Saint Seraphim, Walsingham, Archpriest John Piekarsky of the Byelorussian Orthodox Church, Archpriest Alexander Cherney of the Latvian Orthodox Church, and Dean Peter Moore (who represented the Anglican Bishop of London) of Saint Alban's Abbey. During the Divine Liturgy many people received Holy Communion. Vladyka Mark preached the sermon in Russian and in English. Then there was a service of Thanksgiving in praise of the Lord God for His mercy towards the Russian people. The Sunday morning services lasted some four hours in all.

Nearly 250 members of the congregation then transferred by coach and cars to the College of Saint Mark and Saint John in King's Road, London SW10, where a festal meal was served. This was followed by an excellent lecture which was delivered in English by Father Nikolai Artemoff, entitled *The Spiritual Path of Russia in 1,000 Years*, especially stressing the place of prayer within the history of Russia. The day finished with an informal reception.

The celebrations were considered by all to have been an enormous success, giving all members of the London Russian Orthodox Church in Exile a spiritual uplift and a particular encouragement during these difficult days when the threat of being evicted from our Cathedral has not disappeared. It was particularly heartening to see a visible demonstration of the vitality of the community, a point not lost on distinguished Anglican visitors nor on the mayor of Kensington, who was kind enough to join the Russian Orthodox Church in Exile for her celebrations.

Leaving Emperor's Gate

In the spring of 1988 it became known that the Fidelity Trust, acting on behalf of the Anglican parish of St Stephen's, Gloucester Road, was preparing a planning application involving demolition of the church at Emperor's Gate and building a block of flats in its place. This plan to completely redevelop the site provoked a storm of protest, not just from the Russian parish but also from the surrounding community. Emperor's Gate is a quiet Victorian

Outside the Cathedral at Emperor's Gate, 1988. (Source: Christopher Birchall)

cul-de-sac, ending in a green with houses built all round it. The church was part of the local landscape, and the residents had come to regard the midnight procession at Orthodox Easter with affection rather than annoyance. The day before the planning application was due to be heard, it was withdrawn by the Fidelity Trust. Nevertheless, it was clear that the trust intended to find a way to exploit the commercial value of the property, and the Russian parish considered this as no more than a reprieve.

Early the following year, a more modest planning application was submitted, which would keep the structure of the church building intact but would redevelop the interior to provide drawing studio offices on the upper level, with a meeting hall, playschool, and caretaker's flat at basement level. Because the outward appearance of Emperor's Gate would remain as before, this plan would not affect the surrounding residents nearly as much as the previous one. The application was heard by the planning committee early in May 1989 at the Kensington and Chelsea Town Hall. Some parish members stood outside with banners and placards inscribed "Save our Church." The planning committee asked the applicants about the fate of the Russian church and was told that the Russians had been offered alternative accommodation, which was not strictly accurate. True, there had been various discussions over the years, but none had led to anything concrete. The application was approved and the event was reported in the *Evening Standard* for May 3, 1989, as follows:

> Russian exiles are facing banishment once again—this time from their own church. Their prayers fell on deaf ears as Kensington and Chelsea Council planners gave the go-ahead last night for their church to be turned into offices.
>
> The Russian Orthodox Cathedral in Emperor's Gate, Kensington, is owned by the Church of England, and the lease . . . expired in 1981 [sic]. Since then, London's Russian community has worshipped at the 100-year-old building on borrowed time.
>
> The Church of England failed last year in a bid to turn it into flats. But last night its plan to install offices, a meeting hall and caretaker's flat was successful. Planners voted eight-to-five in favour. Before the meeting, 200 Orthodox church members, including actor Richard Marner—Colonel Strohm in the TV comedy series *'Allo, 'Allo*—and Count Andrei Tolstoy, great cousin of author Leo Tolstoy, prayed for success at a service outside Kensington and Chelsea Town Hall.
>
> The 1500-strong congregation many now have to hold services in Hyde Park, said Father John Suscenko.

The day after the planners' decision, the Russian parish was served with an eviction order. Initially, the parish was to vacate the building by the end of October, but later this was extended to the end of January 1990. In January, Bishop Mark came to celebrate the services for Theophany and to preside at the parish's annual general meeting and at a meeting of the Parish Council where future plans were discussed, including the immediate practicalities of moving out of the church.

On January 28, 1990, the Divine Liturgy was celebrated at Emperor's Gate Cathedral for the last time. As instructed by Bishop Mark, after the Liturgy the celebrant, Father John Suscenko, conducted a service of intercession to the Mother of God, ending with a procession into the street with the cross, banners, and icons. Many of the congregation wept as the final service drew to a close and they took their leave of the church which had been the centre of their lives for thirty years.

During the following week, a succession of large removal vans from Bishop's Removals and Storage arrived at Emperor's Gate to take away the iconostasis, icons, and other holy objects to be stored against the day when the parish would again have proper church premises. On February 3, 1990, the *Daily Telegraph* reported on the eviction:

> **MP's anger as Russian Church evicted**
>
> MP's criticized the Church of England yesterday for its "failure" to find an alternative place of worship for the Russian Orthodox Church in Exile which has been evicted from its London headquarters.
>
> Nearly 100 Russian exiles attended the last service on Sunday at their cathedral at Emperor's Gate, Kensington, where they had worshipped for 30 years. Their departure follows a long-running battle with the church's owners, a trust with strong Church of England links, over its decision to convert part of the building into offices. More than 50 MP's led by Mr. Edward Leigh, Conservative member for Gainsborough and Horncastle, have tabled an early day motion regretting the fact that no other suitable premises has been offered.
>
> Mrs. Sophia Goodman, churchwarden, whose parents fled to England in 1920, said: "We have nowhere else to go. We are negotiating for a piece of land in London on which to build a church, but these things take a long time and can fall through. It seems quite ridiculous with the number of unused churches in central London that the diocese of London could not provide us with some sort of church. We are not after anything beautiful, just something with blank walls where we can put our icons."

> Mrs. Goodman claimed that members of the Russian Church had been given assurances that a suitable building would be found. Archdeacon Derek Hayward, secretary of the diocese, said the Church had no duty to offer an alternative.

The parish announced that on a temporary basis all services would be held at the Podvoria in Barons Court, which was far too small for the needs of the Sunday congregation. One consequence of this was that the monthly English-language services were suspended. Two additional services were added, however: on Wednesdays at 7:00 p.m. was an akathist to the Mother of God, and on Saturdays at 5:00 p.m. was a moleben to the New Martyrs of Russia to ask for God's help in finding a larger church.

The 1990 Good Friday and Easter services were held in the Anglican Church of St Sepulchre, Holborn, in order to accommodate the extra people who always attend these special services. The parish newsletter, the *Anchor*, commented,

> The rector and verger were most helpful in allowing their splendid 15th century church to be transformed into the appearance of an Orthodox church. The splendid acoustics and the lofty spaciousness of the church, dedicated appropriately enough to the Grave of the Lord, allowed the services to proceed with dignity and beauty.

Chapter 17

[1990–2009] Building the New Cathedral at Harvard Road

Moving to Harvard Road

After years of fruitless investigation into the purchase of an existing church building, the parish was coming to the conclusion that the best solution would be to build its own. Providentially in November 1989, just before the departure from Emperor's Gate, the parish was visited by a priest from Australia, Father Michael Protopopov, who had been called as a witness in a court case being heard in London.[1] In Australia Father Michael had been involved in building several churches, and in his sermon he shared some of these experiences. At the time it may have seemed like a standard sermon for a parish with an accommodation problem, but in hindsight his "fibrocement" sermon predicted much of what was to happen:

> Dear Brothers and Sisters, I am told that a very important task is now before you—that of building your own church. We have said special prayers for this today during the Divine Liturgy, and although I come from very far away, from Australia, which is twenty-four hours' journey away by air, I joined in those special prayers with my whole heart. This is very important, because a church is not just a place people come to, to look at beautiful icons and adornments: a church—God's Temple—should be the heart of each person. When someone comes into the church, he should purify his heart spiritually—put aside all earthly things, in order to approach God. With all my heart I hope that next time I come to London, if there is a next time, I will be able to pray with you in a real Orthodox church with a golden dome and a cross on the top.
>
> During the years I have been a priest, I have been involved in the building of three churches, and now we are starting to build a fourth one. From experience I can tell you this: the building of a church always starts with all kinds of doubts—"Should we build or not?"—"Will it turn out well

or badly?"—"Who is doing the building anyway?"—"That group of people is in charge of the building—Oh well, they're communists!"—and all kinds of nonsense like that. However, I can tell you this from experience (and, now, you are planning to build, I would like to share my small experience with you). Everything is possible, if only there is faith in God, hope in God, and if, following the precept of our forefathers, we put hope in God, but don't spare ourselves. God will give you the strength, God will give you the inspiration, but the hands that build the church must be yours. So to just sit back and wait for things to happen would be a sin. It is essential to begin to do something.

I can tell you this. In the town of Perth, in Australia, there are about as many Russians as there are here—about a hundred families. Of course, compared to the vast size of London, this is nothing, but still, God will help you, as he is helping the people in Perth. In Perth the parish did not even have a church to pray in like this one we are in today. The church was just a barrack, a very simple building, and the roof was made of a material we have in Australia known as fibro-cement (and what that is made of, I really couldn't tell you). It lasted for years and years, but in the end, the building became quite unusable, and we had to pull it down. We began to build a new church. And this is what happened. As soon as the foundation stone was laid, all those who had been against building changed their minds and supported it. Money which we thought would never be available was donated from many different sources. . . . Money was collected from far afield. People helped, who one would never have imagined would be interested. And the same will happen with you. As soon as you make a start, other people will respond and help you. . . .

The Lord will fill you with the Holy Spirit, and you will find that it is easy to build the new church, if you are building it as a place where your spiritual life will take place. Again I congratulate you with your undertaking this great project and wish you success with all my heart.

As Mrs Goodman commented to the *Daily Telegraph* after their eviction from Emperor's Gate, negotiations were in progress for a piece of land in London. At the time, however, so many ideas and possible plans had failed that it was hard to be very confident. Count Andrei Tolstoy-Miloslavsky described how those negotiations eventually proved successful:

We considered all areas of London but decided in the end to concentrate on the Chiswick area because of the communications and the Russian old people's home nearby. It was a very long search and in the end I left our brief with an estate agent in Chiswick. The brief was a house with substantial land with the potential for planning permission for a church. Eventually (probably after 9 months) they contacted us and said there was a house by the motorway and railway line for sale. It was very unusual to find a house with such a big garden in a fairly central part of London. It also had the advantage that the land already had planning permission to build one or two houses. It was owned by two spinster sisters. One wanted to sell but the other did not. We liked the land and house and said we would wait as long as they wanted to make up their minds. I think it was almost a year later that they agreed.

The offer on 57 Harvard Road, London, W4, was formally made in December 1989, shortly after Father Michael Protopopov's "fibro-cement" sermon, and the transaction became final at the end of May 1990. The purchase price of £460,000 exhausted all the funds the parish had available in its building fund. Although this did not immediately provide a new church, it provided new hope and enthusiasm to proceed further.

Four days after the completion of the purchase, a working party of some twenty parishioners spent a day chopping wood, clearing gutters, and generally tidying up the property. A parish picnic was held on the site after Vespers on Pentecost Sunday. More than seventy people took part despite pouring rain. The picnic was preceded by prayers appointed for the occasion of taking up residence in a new house.

A few weeks later, the miraculous Kursk icon of the Mother of God was brought to England and was used in blessing the site at Harvard Road. Initially it was brought to the Podvoria on July 1, 1990, where a service of intercession was held. Some of the parishioners noted that the icon had arrived in London on the eve of the feast of the Apostle Jude, the Brother of the Lord. On this day twenty-four years earlier, Archbishop John (Maximovitch) fell asleep in the Lord. It was Archbishop John who had presided at the blessing of the church at Emperor's Gate in 1959, at which he prophetically reminded the London parishioners that they must not be content with using a converted Protestant chapel; rather, it was their solemn duty to build an Orthodox church.

The holy icon was brought to Harvard Road on Sunday, July 8, after the Divine Liturgy, where it was met with great solemnity and taken in procession around the property. An open-air service of intercession was held before the icon in the place where it was hoped the sanctuary of the new church

Blessing the site at 57 Harvard Road with the Kursk icon, 1990. (Source: London Parish Archive)

would eventually be located. Afterwards the sisterhood provided a festal meal in the garden; this time the day was sunny.

The Parish Council's first priority after purchasing the property was to secure the house from vandalism and squatters. To this end, they allowed some newly arrived visitors from the Soviet Union to live there rent-free as caretakers. The house needed extensive renovation, including new electrical wiring, central heating, and new plumbing, which was supervised by a member of the Parish Council, George Volossevich.

The Parish Council met to discuss the way forward. The building fund had been completely exhausted to meet the purchase price of the property. It was estimated that approximately £750,000 would be needed to build a new church. With the blessing of Bishop Mark, a fund-raising committee, which later became the Building Committee, was established, led by Father John Suscenko. Other members of the committee were Gregory Wolcough (chairman), Count Andrei Tolstoy-Miloslavsky (secretary), Prince Dmitri Galitzine, George Miller, and Nicolas Mabin, all of whom were members of the Parish Council. At this time, the council began to consider the idea of building a temporary chapel next to the house.

Bishop Mark recommended that the new church be built in the fifteenth-century Pskov style. This traditional form of architecture, while at the same time being simple and modest, can harmonize well with existing buildings in a city. Count Andrei Tolstoy was charged with seeking advice in Russia. About this time, the church in London was visited by a Russian actor, Vasily Livanov, famous for his role as Sherlock Holmes in a Russian theatrical adaptation of the English detective stories. Livanov became interested in the building project and introduced Andrei Tolstoy to Savely Yamshchikov, a distinguished art historian and icon restorer. "I was recommended by Savely Yamshchikov," Tolstoy recalled, "a very well-respected restorer and art historian, to seek the advice of the Pskov-based church architect-restorer, Mikhail Ivanovich Semeonov." Both Yamshchikov and Semeonov had worked for years on restoring works of religious significance under the Soviet regime. After World War II, the Communist government felt the need to recover the heritage that had been partly destroyed under the early years of Bolshevism and subsequently during the war. Yamshchikov was primarily an art restorer, working mainly on icons but also other paintings. Semeonov, however, worked mainly on restoration of church buildings. In 1956 he was invited to Pskov to work on restoration of the Pskov Caves Monastery, which had been severely damaged during the war. He became a close friend of the abbot, Archimandrite Alipy, and, indeed, received Holy Communion at the monastery. Semeonov spent eighteen years working on this project and then continued his restoration work throughout the region. It is said that there is hardly a single church in Pskov where he has not made some contribution, working alongside simple labourers and understanding the way the churches were built, what materials were used, and the logic of how all fitted together into a harmonious whole. Andrei Tolstoy visited Mikhail Semeonov in Pskov on several occasions in the early 1990s. Semeonov became very enthusiastic about the idea of building a new church in London based on the architecture he knew and loved, and expressed willingness to help when the time came to start work on the project.

Meanwhile, services continued at the Podvoria, which was overcrowded and stuffy; people stood in the corridor and on the staircase, and some even outside the front door. Many thought twice about attending church under such conditions. Therefore enthusiasm about the new property remained high and, whenever possible, people would arrange events, such as a reception after a baptism, at the house at Harvard Road that provided more space but also an opportunity to envision the future firsthand.

In May 1991 the Parish Council met under the chairmanship of Vladyka Mark, by now raised to the rank of archbishop by the Holy Synod. The Parish Council had recently sold a house that had been bequeathed to the parish and expected to receive the proceeds the following month. This influx of funds made it possible to move ahead with building a hall adjacent to the house on Harvard Road to use as a temporary church. They could afford to build something much bigger than the existing Podvoria chapel, which was essentially a tiny living room in a small house, and thereby relieve the immediate problem of overcrowding. Later, this extension could be used as a church hall once a permanent church was built. The first-floor flat in the house would also be refurbished and become the priest's residence. At this point the council envisaged all this work being completed by the end of the year. The property at 57 Harvard Road could then become the centre of parish life.

The Building Committee and then the Parish Council also reviewed proposals for building the new cathedral. The council unanimously approved the Building Committee's proposal to build a church in the Pskov style, with a single dome and a belfry. The planned floor area would be about 240 square metres, which would be only slightly less than the old cathedral at Emperor's Gate. Fund-raising would begin in earnest once the architectural plans had been drawn up and planning permission obtained.

At its meeting in May 1991, the Parish Council noted that the parish newsletter, the *Anchor*, had ceased publication. It was agreed that the diocesan journal, *Vestnik*, published in Munich would in the future include coverage of church events in England as well as Germany.

While in London, Archbishop Mark held numerous meetings with parishioners both as individuals and in groups. On Sunday, May 5, the churchwarden, Mrs Goodman, invited a large group of parishioners to her home so that they could speak directly with their archpastor. Later that same evening, the archbishop invited about thirty young people to the Podvoria to talk about unity in the Church (*sobornost*) and its importance in our Christian life, after which there was a long discussion. Not surprisingly, any serious topic about the innermost nature of the Church of Christ often led to discussion about the concrete situation of the parish in London and the building plans.

The Parish Council engaged Mikhail Mandrigin of the architectural firm Fitzroy Robinson International to submit a planning application for "demolition of outbuildings and erection of new church, extension to existing house for use as parish hall and conversion of existing house into 2 flats." The application was submitted on December 2, 1991, and approved on March 24, 1992. Shortly thereafter a local newspaper, the *Brentford, Chiswick and Isleworth Times*, quoted the churchwarden,

> Finding the money is the only problem now. We have a couple of properties that we can sell but we are hanging onto them at the moment due to

> the recession. We are pinning our hopes on starting work in a couple of years' time when we can get a better price for our properties in Hammersmith and Acton. We are also planning a fund-raising campaign.

A preliminary budget showed that the parish would need to raise a further £500,000 to complete the project.

November 1992 also marked a change in the life of the parish when a new parish priest was appointed to replace Father John Suscenko. Following a visit to the Ukraine, Father John withdrew from involvement with the parish and, indeed, from serving as a parish priest. For a period of several months, a young priest from Germany, Father Joseph Vovniuk, served the parish temporarily. Finally, Father Vadim Zakrevsky arrived in November 1992 to take up the permanent position of parish priest in London. He came from Ukraine with his wife, Natalya, and two sons. By this time the refurbishment of the first-floor flat at Harvard Road was complete and the young family was able to move in. On November 9, Archbishop Mark travelled to London to introduce Father Vadim to the Parish Council and, on the following Sunday, November 15, the archbishop and Father Vadim concelebrated the Liturgy in the Podvoria chapel. After the Liturgy, the sisterhood arranged a reception at the house in Chiswick so that individual parishioners could meet their new priest and his family.

Thereafter Father Vadim served three Sundays out of four in London, while on the fourth Sunday Abbot Seraphim from Birmingham came and served in London so that Father Vadim could visit the parish in Bradford. Father Seraphim also was responsible for services in Manchester and Bradford, as well as the Convent of the Annunciation.

At the Podvoria, 1993: Father Vadim Zakrevsky, priest of the parish 1992–2007, with (left to right) son Igor, Matushka Natalya, and son Roman. (Source: Christopher Birchall)

Construction of the church hall to be used as a temporary church at 57 Harvard Road, 1993. (Source: Christopher Birchall)

One year later at its meeting on July 6, 1993, chaired by Archbishop Mark, the Parish Council resolved to sign a contract for building the extension to the church house. Once started, work proceeded without interruption and was finished by December. Finally, four years after leaving Emperor's Gate, the iconostasis and some of the icons from the old cathedral were brought out of storage and erected in the newly built hall that became the temporary church, while another large room on the ground floor of the existing house was used for meals and other gatherings. Although the dimensions of the new premises were much more modest than the spacious Victorian-Gothic building in Kensington, it was still a great consolation to parishioners that the atmosphere of the old cathedral could be somewhat recreated in Chiswick. For the feast of Theophany in January 1994, Archbishop Mark came to London and blessed the new temporary church and presided at the services, which included the Great Blessing of the Waters. At this service, Archbishop Mark ordained two parishioners, both of non-Russian origin, to the rank of church reader. He also presented those who had worked hardest for the new church—Sophia Goodman, George Volossevich, and Andrew Neyman—with commendatory scrolls.

Later that year, on October 30, 1994, Archbishop Mark ordained an English-speaking convert of Canadian origin, Thomas Hardy, to the priesthood. Father Thomas Hardy had converted to Orthodoxy a few years previously after retiring from the Anglican ministry. Before retirement, he was occupied every Sunday with his duties at the Anglican Church of St Augustine in Lillie Road, Fulham. He became well known in the London parish, however, after years of regularly attending the Saturday evening Vigil services and singing in the choir. During this time he acquired a deep knowledge of and love for the Orthodox services. After retirement, he continued to attend Orthodox services and eventually decided that he would follow the dictates of his heart and conscience, and join the Orthodox Church. He expected to continue attending the services and praying just as he had for so many years, but now as a baptized member of the Church he loved. Before long, the archbishop approached him and asked if he would consider accepting ordination as an Orthodox priest. This had certainly not been his plan, but in the end he agreed. The bishop viewed this as a natural progression for someone who had been devoted to the Church for so long and appointed him as second priest of the parish to assist Father Vadim, entrusting him with pastoral care for the English-speaking part of the parish.

A very significant event in the life of the Russian Church Abroad occurred in July 1994, when Archbishop John of Shanghai was glorified as a saint. Archbishop John had been the ruling hierarch of the Diocese of Western Europe for twelve years, from 1950 to 1962. His visits to England in the 1950s made a great impression as his personal sanctity was evident to all.[2] When Archbishop John died in 1964, he was buried in the cathedral of the Russian Orthodox Church Outside Russia in San Francisco. A firm conviction grew among the hierarchy and people of the Russian Church Abroad that he was a saint and should be formally recognised as such. The glorification took place in San Francisco on June 19/July 2, 1994. In view of his significance for the Church as a whole and for England in particular, the London parish organized a day-long conference to honour his memory and help people learn more about him. With the passage of time there were fewer people who remembered Vladyka John through personal contact or who had heard of him directly from people who knew him. St John was part of the heritage of the Russian Church Abroad that people newly arrived from Russia were keen to learn more about. Some ninety people from different parts of the country attended the conference to hear the principal speaker, Archpriest Constantine Feoderoff from the Kursk Hermitage in Mahopac outside New York City. Father Constantine was an inspiring speaker and people left with a renewed sense of closeness to this great saint. In particular they resolved to turn to him in prayer for success in building a new church in London, something that he had personally hoped and prayed would one day happen.

After moving to Harvard Road, progress toward building the new cathedral ground to a halt for two reasons. First, money was insufficient because so much was spent acquiring the property and building the hall. Second, and

Inside the temporary church at Harvard Road, 1998: (left to right) Father Thomas Hardy, Father Vadim Zakrevsky, churchwarden Gregory Wolcough, choir director Antonina Ananin, and Father Peter Holodny. (Source: Christopher Birchall)

perhaps more significantly, nobody in the parish was capable of managing the building project.

To address the shortage of funds, the parish considered selling the Podvoria. There were two opposing views about this in the parish. Some felt that the house was a holy place sanctified by generations of prayers since it was established in 1931. People were still alive who cherished the memory of Bishop Nicholas who organized the purchase of the property and blessed the house chapel as a place of worship. People remembered his last testament in which he had written,

> I bequeath to you the church and Podvoria in prayerful memory. Gather there and make intercession for me. It would be good if you were to fulfill my last request and choose Father Anatoly as your priest. Then the Podvoria would not be destroyed. Continue in love one for another.

Others felt that this testament should be understood in the context of the times, when the parish was extremely poor and debt was incurred in building the Podvoria; if the parish did not stick together, it would be lost and they would have no church at all. Were he alive today, people speculated, Bishop Nicholas would have been overjoyed at the prospect of building a large cathedral in traditional style—a project that would have been unthinkable in the 1930s. This group argued that the parish simply could not afford to keep two buildings, especially as the site at Harvard Road provided not only church premises but also living accommodations for the clergy.

Seeing that the parish was divided over this issue, Archbishop Mark sought guidance from the Holy Synod. At its meeting in New York on May 10, 1995, the Synod decided that if Archbishop Mark submitted a resolution from a general meeting of the parish or from the Diocesan Council in favour of selling the property, then the Synod would consider the matter further. On June 25, 1995, an Extraordinary General Meeting of the parish was convened at which the matter was discussed and put to a vote. By majority vote, the parish resolved to sell the Podvoria. The bishops discussed it again at the next Synod meeting on September 5, 1995, and noted, "A minority group of the parishioners in London have come out against the sale. The majority opinion of the parishioners is that their arguments are unconvincing. At a Parish Meeting, the majority voted for the sale." The bishops then resolved,

> To confirm the decision of the aforementioned General Parish Meeting of the Dormition Cathedral of 25th June, regarding the sale of the Episcopal Podvoria in St Dunstan's Road, London, with the purpose of applying the proceeds to the building of a new church. . . . To propose to those who desire to safeguard this property for church purposes to buy the house themselves.

Subsequently, the house was sold to an outside party on the open market for approximately £250,000. Although only a fraction of the eventual cost of the new church, this sum made a substantial difference in furthering the project.

Architectural Design and Fund-Raising

Sophia Goodman, the churchwarden, recalled standing in church one day wondering how they would find someone to manage the construction. Then her old friend, Tanya, walked in accompanied by a tall and impressive gentleman—Tanya's husband, Nicholas Yellachich, who was a civil engineer. After talking with him, Mrs Goodman concluded that he was the very person they needed. She then introduced him to Archbishop Mark, and so Nicholas Yellachich was appointed chairman of the Building Committee.

Nicholas Yellachich was born and grew up in Shanghai, where he knew Archbishop John (Maximovitch). Later he became an Australian citizen, and married Tatiana (Tanya), daughter of Natalie Sowells who was a pillar of the Emperor's Gate parish. Nicholas and Tanya met at a British trade fair in Moscow in the early 1960s. Before they married, Tanya's mother enquired of Archbishop John of Shanghai about the Yellachich family. Nicholas and Tanya were married in the cathedral at Emperor's Gate in 1963. Nicholas was a civil engineer who worked mostly in the area of petroleum exploration and production. The couple had lived in many countries over twenty-seven years but returned to settle down in the United Kingdom in about 1991. Their daughter was married in the temporary church in the hall at Harvard Road.

Nicholas had a close friend, Douglas Norwood, who was an architect. His firm, Douglas Norwood and Associates, had more than thirty years' experience in the design, construction, and restoration of listed and historic buildings. Andrei Tolstoy, also on the Building Committee, realised that they could benefit from the expertise of Mikhail Semeonov, the church restorer and architectural expert. In 1996 Andrei arranged for Mikhail Semeonov to come to England to consult on the design. Mikhail had long meetings with Douglas Norwood, where he explained many intricate features of Pskov church architecture and provided detailed architectural drawings.

Both Semeonov and his colleague in Pskov, the icon restorer Savely Yamshchikov, had gradually come to appreciate the riches and faith of the Orthodox Church through their work on very old yet timeless works of art created for the glory of God. A better known individual who followed this same path was the writer Vladimir Soloukhin, who studied icons and wrote about them as early as the 1960s, and later gained greater influence during the perestroika period when large numbers of people began to turn their backs on atheist ideology. Soloukhin spoke of the Russian people's "unseverable roots" (непресекаемые корни) in Orthodoxy that led them eventually to throw off the yoke of atheistic communism. Such an "organic return" to Orthodox roots, influenced by the physical presence in everyday life of centuries-old icons and church buildings, is something beyond the experience of those in the West who live in very different surroundings. So it is particularly interesting that, just at this time when Orthodoxy was reviving in Russia, the church building project in London participated in this resurgence through the dedication and expertise of Mikhail Semeonov, who helped an English architect design an authentic Orthodox church building in direct continuity with the hallowed traditions of mediaeval Pskov.

One aspect unique to Pskov church architecture was the acoustic design. High up on each of the four walls was a series of what appeared to be holes. In fact, these were hollow clay pipes, known as *golosniki*—from the Russian word *golos* for "voice." In English they could be called resonators or "voice pots." Their purpose was to prevent the scattering of sound waves that can cause echoes in a large building, making church reading and singing unintelligible. Apparently, their significance had been forgotten, even in the Pskov region. In some churches they were filled in because of the dust that tended to accumulate in them. In other cases, there were arguments as to whether they really had any effect on the acoustics, and a theory even developed that they were inserted only to alleviate the pressure from the massive stonework in the walls. Semeonov brought two *golosniki* with him to London where they were examined by Dr A. J. Pretlove, an expert at the acoustics department of the University of Reading, who then advised on how to create a similar effect in the church being built in London.

Tragically, on October 16, 1996, soon after his return to Russia, Mikhail Semeonov was killed in a road accident. His name was inscribed in the book of perpetual commemoration at the Pskov Caves Monastery, which he had devoted a large part of his life to restoring.

Douglas Norwood recalled Mikhail Semeonov's visit:

> We have very fond memories of Mikhail when he spent time in our office at the inception stage of the church design. It was very distressing to hear of his tragic death in a road accident shortly after his return to Russia.
>
> Mikhail arrived with Nicholas Yellachich who drove them both from London to our small village of Inkpen in West Berkshire. Nicholas acted as translator for the three days that Mikhail was here.
>
> Our initial impression of Mikhail was his splendid snowy beard like that of a Russian patriarch. The profusion of the beard was in stark contrast to the precision of his brand new brown corduroy suit, which we suspect had been bought especially for the occasion of his visit to the UK.
>
> His modest, gentle, self-deprecating manner was endearing but hid an incisive mind capable of the painstaking work of accurately surveying the religious buildings of the region. He explained that each survey took many months to take measurements and prepare record drawings of each building, which then had to be submitted to the relevant authority for approval before any reconstruction could begin.
>
> He brought with him elegant handmade portfolios, tied with tapes, with a beautifully lettered Cyrillic title block on each cover listing the contents. He opened them one by one to reveal a quantity of meticulous hand drawn survey sheets of his historic little churches. Because there are no precise right angles in any of these simple peasant-built stone structures, every point on the plans, sections and elevations had to be obtained by

precise triangulation and even individual blocks of stone were numbered. The drawings were all Mikhail's own original pencil drawings, about A3 in size, and we asked, through Nicholas, whether we might make copies of them. Mikhail was puzzled at first but then astonished that we had a photocopier there in our office and that making copies would take only minutes. He seemed out of touch with modern technology and we wondered about the conditions in which he had been working in Russia. He was fascinated by our simple disposable "fine line" pens and we gave him a few to take home.

The extraordinary discovery of "voice pots" on Mikhail's surveys caused us to embark on new research involving Reading University. We knew about Helmholtz resonators used in modern concert halls such as the Royal Festival Hall, but we had no idea that these devices had been incorporated into Russian churches for hundreds of years. We subsequently discovered that these sound resonators were known to the ancient Greeks and described by the ancient Roman architect Vitruvius. On Mikhail's surveys we found the metre-thick walls had rows of circles high up below the vaulted ceiling. When we asked what they were, Mikhail answered in a matter of fact manner, that they were voice pots. "What are voice pots?" we asked, and discovered that the circles were the open ends of clay water pots placed on their sides in the wall with the neck of the pot flush with the face of the wall. The pots were used to reduce undesirable low frequency sounds. Incorporating a resonator tuned to the problem frequency was done by selecting a suitably sized pot, which reduced the unwanted frequency, thereby allowing the voice of the priest to be heard more clearly against the sounds echoing off the surrounding walls.

Current UK building regulations and economics would not allow us to replicate heavy stone construction today but, by modifying the voids inside the hollow concrete blocks that formed the inner wall face of the Chiswick church, and fitting carefully calculated sleeves into circular holes cut in the face of the blocks, the acoustic effect could be replicated.

An interesting source of information about the church's architectural plans is an application for funding that was made to the Millennium Commission in 1996. The Millennium Commission was set up by the government to fund buildings, community projects, and environmental schemes to celebrate the approaching millennium of 2000. The commission's funding came from the UK National Lottery, and its objective was to promote projects of enduring value that could make Britain a better place in the next millennium. It seemed to the parish that the church building project was ideally suited, and a detailed application was drawn up to apply for funding. Although the application was turned down, the carefully prepared document is very informative despite its slightly promotional tone, as the following extracts show:

> The appointment of the foremost expert in his field in Russia will ensure that the Cathedral retains intangible and authentic elements and references to ensure that the traditions are maintained for a building that will be the first of its kind to be built in England to celebrate the coming of the Millennium.
>
> The geometry, acoustics, details and finishes of the 15th Century Pskov churches, combined with the ancient liturgy and ceremony of the Orthodox faith draw on unique references which are translated to fit the materials, techniques and standards that apply in the UK at the end of the 20th Century. Tradition demands deep window and door reveals, small windows, a centrally supported drum and cupola, vaulted ceiling, carved gilded and painted iconostasis, interior surfaces decorated with icon frescoes, acoustics designed for the unaccompanied voices of the priest and the choir, the control of light to increase as the Mass progresses, control of temperature and humidity to protect ancient icons and works of art. Initial design work for the project has been carried out by the British designers in collaboration with Michael Ivanovich Semeonov of the Pskov Church Restoration Atelier.
>
> The following consultants have been appointed for the project:
>
> - Architect: Douglas Norwood Associates, Inkpen, Berks.
> - Acoustic Consultant: Dr A. J. Pretlove, University of Reading
> - Mechanical and Electrical Engineering Consultant: Upton Associates, High Wycombe
> - Structural Engineer SES (Abingdon) Ltd., Abingdon
>
> Detailed planning permission was obtained by Fitzroy Robinson Partnership when the application was submitted for the Hall. Fitzroy Robinson have confirmed in writing their agreement to the appointment of the present architect for the detailed design of the Church and the addition of a storey above the Hall.
>
> The Cathedral planned for the site is based on the 15th century Pskov design. The main church hall will be 203 m sq.; there will also be a Crypt which will be 194 m sq. and a choir gallery of 47 m sq.

> The Pskov church is simple in form: The main body of the church is a cube with a Narthex at the entrance at the West end; the Sanctuary and Vestry at the East end are divided from the Nave by the Iconostasis. The internal arrangement of the ceiling is in the form of a dome with a drum supported on the apex with the characteristic onion shaped cupola above the drum. Eight slit windows are built into the drum. An open belfry is situated above the entrance to the Cathedral in which six bells will hang.
>
> The acoustic qualities of the Pskov Churches have, since the 15th Century, been enhanced by the incorporation of resonators into each of the vertical walls below the cross vaults.
>
> Nicholas Yellachich is Chairman of Building Committee. The Fund Raising Committee is chaired by Count Andrei Tolstoy assisted by Prince Dmitri Galitzine.
>
> To ensure a high quality of Architecture, the selection of the Consulting and Executive Architect was critical. The principal objective is to build the Cathedral based on the 15th Century Pskov Style. To this end a specialist Russian practice, the Pskov Church Restoration Atelier, was selected. The Russian consultant has over forty years' experience in the survey and restoration of Churches in the Pskov region. Copies of valuable detailed drawings have been provided, which enables us to design a Cathedral that reflects the traditions and qualities of the style using unique historical references.
>
> The English architectural practice of Douglas Norwood and Associates has had over 30 years' experience in design, construction and restoration of Listed and Historic Buildings, Churches, Mosques, Embassies and State Buildings, as well as the design, construction and reconstruction of furniture and fittings where extensive knowledge and experience and attention to detail is essential for the sympathetic design and detailing of interior fittings and finishes. Norwood Associates are experienced planning consultants, who understand the environmental issues and the concerns of planning authorities and communities. The project is modest in environmental terms and environmental matters have been dealt with and agreed at detailed planning stage with the community and the local authority.

The total cost shown in the detailed budget presented to the Millennium Commission was £1,278,700, of which the parish sought £700,000 from the commission. When the application was rejected, the parish prepared its own fund-raising appeal, supported by the detailed costing provided by the quantity surveyor engaged by the architects. The appeal was broken into three phases that could, if necessary, be completed separately:

Phase 1: Foundations, structural frame, walls, etc.	510,000
Phase 2: Internal walls, vaulted ceilings and fittings	300,000
Phase 3: External finishes, cupola and cross, bells	295,000
Total:	£1,105,000

This sum did not include the cost of a new iconostasis nor that of ceiling and wall frescoes, which could be completed over time after the building was finished.

Of the £510,000 required for phase one, £370,000 was already in hand (including the proceeds from the sale of the Podvoria), so that only another £140,000 would be needed before construction could begin. Parish leaders recognized the importance of starting construction, as experience elsewhere proved that it is much easier to raise money when people see something actually being done. However, they also felt it was essential to the viability of the first phase to obtain the remaining one-quarter of the necessary funding before embarking. The appeal sent out in 1997 was well prepared, accompanied by drawings and photographs of the architectural model of the proposed new church, as well as forms required to claim tax relief on donations.

On April 3, 1997, a revised planning application was submitted to the London Borough of Hounslow, providing full details of the plans, which now included a crypt and a gallery for the choir. The parish thought the addition of a crypt, or lower church, with a separate altar was important for services with a smaller group of people when the large space of the upper church would be unnecessary. Also, in the Orthodox Church only one Liturgy per day can be celebrated at a particular altar, so a crypt would be useful if two services were required, such as an early morning service or a separate service in English. In the event, at the Hounslow Borough Planning Committee meeting on June 24, the revised plans were passed by only a narrow margin of six votes to five, with the five Muslim councillors abstaining. There was concern that if the building contained two churches rather than one, an influx of people into the neighbourhood might be much greater than originally envisaged. Therefore, the formal approval, or deed, issued on November 6, 1997, included a long list of conditions. The nave (upper church) and crypt (lower church) were not to be used at the same time for any purpose. A detailed schedule was provided of when the bells could be rung. For example: Sundays no earlier than 09:55 for 5 minutes; at 11:00, 12 rings of a bell (during the Creed at the Liturgy); Saturdays at 17:25 for 5 minutes; Easter Saturday no later than 23:50 for 10 minutes; and so on. Some flexibility was allowed: "All the times shown . . . are subject to variations due to the length of the Gospels, the pace of the Choir's responses, the length of the Hymns and Psalms and the Sermon, the variations shall not be more than 45 minutes from the times shown." Sound insulation against internally generated noise (excluding the ringing of church bells) was to be provided "so that there is no increase in the background noise measured at ground level 3.5 m from the facade of the nearest residential property outside the site."

A landscape management plan was to be submitted for approval by the borough council, which had to meet stringent conditions regarding tree conservation: no tree was to be "topped or lopped other than in accordance with the approved plans or particulars," and "any topping or lopping approved shall be carried out in accordance with British Standard [3998 (Tree Work)] or any other BS replacing."

Before any topping or lopping could occur, however, it was necessary to engage a contractor to carry out the building plans. Nicholas Yellachich and Douglas Norwood made a short list of three firms, and settled on Grist Building Services Ltd. from Southampton, which was a family-owned business specializing in projects up to £3 million in size. Yellachich and Norwood inspected three projects that the firm had recently built, and the projects' clients were all very satisfied with the firm's work.

Building the New Church

With approval from the Borough of Hounslow in hand, the parish was finally in a position to begin construction work. On Tuesday, November 25, 1997, Archbishop Mark, accompanied by Hieromonk Avraamy and Hierodeacon Euthymius, travelled from Munich to England to conduct the rite of laying the foundation stone of the new church. By this time, the builders had completed the excavations and laid the concrete foundation slab. Below where the altar of the lower church would be erected, a cavity was cut into the concrete for the foundation stone to be placed and cemented in during the rite which was to follow.

In the evening, Archbishop Mark presided at a meeting of the parish trustees at which the inevitable questions arose of how much money was available to pay for the construction work in progress and how much more was needed to complete the building. The parish and trustees had agreed with the building firm to divide the entire project into several phases, allowing for work to be halted between phases if necessary while more money was collected. It was hoped that this approach would allow the parish to make use of the crypt in the foreseeable future because the temporary church in the church hall was becoming overcrowded.

On Thursday, November 14/27 (the feast of the Apostle Philip), Archbishop Mark celebrated the Divine Liturgy in the temporary church together with Fathers Vadim Zakrevsky and Thomas Hardy, as well as Hieromonk Avraamy, Hierodeacon Andronik (a London-born Russian living in San Francisco), and Hierodeacon Euthymius. All the clergymen who officiated wore new vestments donated specially for the occasion. After the Liturgy, there was a short break during which the archbishop gave an interview to journalists from BBC Television. He also welcomed Bishop Kallistos (Ware) of the Greek Orthodox Church, who came from Oxford.

At exactly 12:30 p.m., the royal doors in the iconostasis were opened, and the bishop together with the priests and deacons processed to the place where the foundation stone of the new church was to be laid. The clergy were joined by the rector of the Serbian Church in London, Father Milun Kostic, who also took part in the service of laying the foundation stone. Archbishop Mark was in full liturgical vestments and on his head carried a discos which held the holy relics that were to be placed in the foundation stone. The priests carried the Gospel and cross, together with the water and oil which were to be blessed, while the deacons carried candles and censers. The choir led the procession, singing the troparion for the feast of the Dormition of the Mother of God, which had been the dedication feast of the Russian church in London for the past three hundred years. The procession went down a metal stairway into the excavated area where the concrete foundation was covered by a large tarpaulin, and proceeded toward the apse of the church, stopping where the altar steps would be. All the liturgical items were placed on a table, and Vladyka gave the blessing for the beginning of the Rite of the Foundation of a Church. First the holy water and oil were blessed and then the places for the cross and the foundation stone were blessed. The holy relics were placed in a small casket, and the archbishop read aloud the inscription stating that the relics were those of the holy martyrs Benedict and Haralampos, and a martyr whose name was not known from the Lavra of St Sabbas in the Holy Land. He then inserted the casket into the foundation stone. Father Vadim then read aloud in Russian the text on the paper to be inserted together with the relics:

> In the name of the Father and of the Son and of the Holy Spirit, this church is founded in the honour and memory of the Dormition of the Most Holy Mother of God, in God's city of London, during the primacy of the Most

> Reverend Vitaly, Metropolitan of New York and Eastern America, and during the sacred episcopate of the Most Reverend Mark, Archbishop of Berlin, Germany and Great Britain, in the year 7506 from the creation of the world, 1997 from the Nativity in the flesh of God the Word, and the year 1010 from the Baptism of Russia, on the day of the Holy Apostle Philip, in the month of November, on the 14th [27th] day.

Father Thomas Hardy read the same text in English, and then the paper with this inscription was placed into the foundation stone. Archbishop Mark took a trowel and cemented the foundation stone to the concrete foundation. After that, Vladyka blessed all four sides of the church and finally read the prayer at the founding of a church while all knelt. In his sermon after the service, translated into English by a parishioner, Vladyka Mark spoke about the importance of a church building for sanctifying mankind, and of the harmony that we must create in ourselves in order for the holiness of God's temple to be established in our hearts. The archbishop pointed out that many of the congregation in England had awaited this moment for decades and had now been deemed worthy of this moment of triumphant celebration through their prayers—and donations. He thanked all those present for their support, which was especially important at this critical juncture in the building project.

Afterwards there was a reception in the church hall, during which Archbishop Mark took the opportunity to talk to Bishop Kallistos, the mayor of Hounslow, a delegation from the embassy of the Russian Federation, and people from the press. The managing director of Grist Building Services presented the archbishop with a silver trowel inscribed in memory of the day when the foundation was laid. This was probably the most memorable event that had occurred in the life of the London parish for many decades. One parishioner, who had only recently joined the parish, promised to make the first payment that was due to the building firm, in the amount of £50,000. At the same time, one of the oldest women in the parish handed Vladyka a long-promised cheque for £30,000, which she had been saving for decades from her modest means to go toward the building of the church.[3] Many parishioners made donations that day, both large and small. In his sermon, Archbishop Mark also pointed out that there were now plenty of opportunities for people to contribute their own work while others made financial donations, but the most important motivation was love for God and His Church. He said the construction project was a challenge that offered current parishioners the opportunity to establish a spiritual and cultural homeland for their children and generations to come. The same evening, Archbishop Mark attended a lecture by Dr Nicholas Fennel about St Elijah's Russian Skete on Holy Mount Athos. This talk was arranged in central London by the Friends of Mt Athos. Here the archbishop met Bishop Kallistos for the second time that day.

The rest of the construction started soon afterwards. By the end of January 1998, the entrance to the crypt was clearly visible above ground level. By autumn, the outline of a traditional Russian church, with its tall, majestic arches reaching upward, began to emerge behind the scaffolding and other accoutrements of a modern building site. In mid-November, Archbishop Mark visited and, together with Father Vadim and Nicholas Yellachich, climbed onto the roof of the church to see for himself how the work was progressing. By this time, the vaulting that was to support the cupola was already in place. It seemed that all the outside work should be finished before the onset of winter. However, funds were running short. The bishop presided at meetings of both the Parish Council and the trust, at which the treasurer, Vitaly Matafonov, explained that they were about £200,000 short of the sum needed to complete this phase of the project. Thus, it seemed unlikely that the lower church would be usable before the following Easter. However, a loan of $250,000 was arranged from the Synod in New York and a contribution of £80,000 was received from the Gerald Palmer Ealing Trust, which allowed work to continue.

With construction in full swing, the general contractor, Grist Building Services, suddenly declared bankruptcy. This long-established family business had tried to expand too quickly under the influence of recently appointed directors. The liquidators made a claim against the parish for more than £74,000, but because the work was unfinished, the claim was rebuffed successfully with the help of the quantity surveyors. Nicholas Yellachich was able to organize a team from among the Russian community in London to work at the site on a daily basis. The roof was closed in by the spring of 1999, and the parish received permission from Hounslow Council to hold its first service in the upper church on the eve of Lazarus Saturday. Nicholas Yellachich recalled how, at the beginning of the first Vigil service, the setting sun shone through the open west door, directly and exactly onto Father Vadim, whose silhouette was thrown onto the eastern wall; it seemed like a blessing. The walls were bare breeze block and the floor was covered with hessian to reduce the amount of construction dust.

Holy Week and Easter services were held in the new, spacious cathedral, and for the first time in the history of the parish, it was possible to have

Early stages of construction of the Cathedral at Harvard Road, 1998. (Source: Christopher Birchall)

the midnight Easter procession going round the outside of the church in the traditional way. The iconostasis and other icons and church fittings were removed from the temporary church and set up in the new cathedral. At this point, the old iconostasis from the former cathedral at Emperor's Gate was still being used. The extension built on the house was converted to its intended purpose as a church hall, and the first event held there was the Easter breakfast (*rozgoveniye*) held after the end of the night service.

Sergei Grigorieff, a contributor to *Vestnik*, the diocesan journal, described this first Easter service in the new church:

> The first service in the Cathedral of the Dormition of the Mother of God in the British capital took place on the eve of Lazarus Saturday. This is the first Russian Orthodox church to be built in this country; it was built with

Construction of the Cathedral at Harvard Road, 1998. (Source: Nicholas Yellachich)

record speed and opened its doors to the faithful just before Easter. This magnificent building constructed strictly in accordance with the Pskov style, now adorns the London district of Chiswick in the final year before the second millennium of the Nativity of Christ. Is this not symbolic?

The new church, built to hold 400 people, stands next to the old church house, which accommodated the temporary church holding barely 100 parishioners. The building has been paid for entirely by donations—from the Russian diaspora in Britain as well as from organisations and private individuals, including people from Russia. The cupola and cross will crown the top of the cathedral on 27 August, which is the eve of the patronal festival—the Dormition of the Most Holy Mother of God.

Meanwhile there is a great deal left to be done. The parish priest, Father Vadim Zakrevsky, is working day and night. However, we must note that he has a large number of helpers. Building the church has inspired many people to take an interest and participate—and not just the members of the parish, but many of the Russian (and non-Russian) inhabitants of London. About fifty parishioners, including children, helped to carry the church furnishings and fittings from the temporary church in the house into the new church. Vitaly Matafonov the parish treasurer, who works at a bank, turned out to be a talented carpenter. Thanks to his work, the former iconostasis was extended to accommodate the large icons that were brought out of storage by Nicholas Yellachich. Victoria Khativada, Lioubov Ogurok and Victoria Wolcough organized a major cleanup in both the old and the new premises, while Vitaly Plamadialov, Alexander Ivanov and Sergei Zashchitin nailed, fitted and arranged everything in the new church.

The Easter service in the upper church gathered more than 500 people, even at a conservative estimate. People came from as far away as Ireland, Scotland and Liverpool. The pathways round the cathedral could not accommodate all the people wishing to join in the procession. The old church hall was also put to good use. Here the parish sisterhood, led by the priest's wife, Natalia, laid on a festal meal for 170 people. Although the upper church still needs to have the interior finishing work done, it is planned to hold all the festal services there. Other services and private ministrations will take place in the lower church, which is to be consecrated in honour of the Royal Martyrs. A small side chapel with the baptistery is to be consecrated in honour of All Saints. More and more Orthodox people in Great Britain are showing their wish to get married and baptize their children in the new cathedral of the Russian Orthodox Church Outside Russia.

Two weeks after Easter, on the Sunday of the Myrrh-bearing Women, Archbishop Mark came to conduct his first service in the new church. After the service, he presented Nicholas Yellachich with a commendatory scroll from the Holy Synod as a sign of gratitude to him and the parish for the vast amount of work involved in building the new church.

At this point the cupola and cross had not yet been installed on top of the church. Work on these continued through the summer of 1999. Just before the patronal festival of the Dormition in August of that year, individual segments of the steel framework for the cupola were brought to the site and attached together, forming a skeleton in the traditional Russian onion shape. Preformed fiberglass segments of the dome itself were attached to the framework and then some 2,000 blue tiles of fired, anodized aluminium were attached to this surface, with gold stars on top of the blue tiles at regular intervals. Douglas Norwood recalled,

> Unfortunately the original builders of the church went bankrupt leaving much of the work unfinished, and Nicholas Yellachich and I decided to have the dome and cross made without a main contractor, so that at least the church would begin to look finished. Although the bell tower at the west end remains unbuilt, thanks to Mikhail Semeonov's splendid reference details, the dome and cross give the church a semblance of completeness. Site labour to fix the blue tiles, each row of which was made to fit the circumference exactly at each course, was conscientiously and enthusiastically provided by a small group of the congregation recently arrived from Russia.

The construction of the cupola using aluminium tiles is unique. When fully assembled, but before the cross was installed on top, it measured 5.8 metres in diameter and 5.7 metres high—nearly the height of an ordinary two-storey house. It was easier to appreciate its size while it was still on the ground than when it was installed on top of the church. Its total cost of £75,000 was covered by a donation from Alexander Zhukov, a wealthy Russian gentleman who did not live in London but who wished to contribute to this inspiring project.

The cross atop the cupola was gilded by a firm based in Windsor that works for Her Majesty the Queen and is well known for its regilding of the Albert Memorial in London. It was paid for by a donation from Natalie Sowells, Nicholas Yellachich's mother-in-law.

By late October 1999, the dome was finished. Raising the cupola and cross on a newly built Russian Orthodox church is always an important ceremony.

The drum to support the cupola is added to the cathedral, 1999. (Source: Nicholas Yellachich)

While it represents the completion of the exterior construction and marks the point when the church building takes on its proper appearance and proportions, the cupola and cross strikingly proclaim the inner glory of Christ's church to the world. On Saturday, October 30, 1999, Archbishop Mark celebrated the Liturgy assisted by the seven priests of the Diocese of Great Britain. Abbess Seraphima and the sisters of the Convent of the Annunciation were also present, along with other visiting clergy and monastics. At the end of the Liturgy, the archbishop chose this auspicious moment to announce the establishment of a deanery for the English-language parishes in the United Kingdom and Ireland.

When the Liturgy was over, all the clergy and people went outside for the service of the blessing of the cross and cupola. The cupola itself, resplendent with its blue enamel tiles and gold stars, was still on a stand on the ground. To reach the top of the dome where the cross was now attached, Archbishop Mark, together with Father Vadim Zakrevsky and one of the altar boys carrying a container of holy water, climbed up the scaffolding that was erected

The cupola while still on the ground best shows its size as nearly the height of a two-storey house, 1999. (Source: Nicholas Yellachich)

The cupola is ready to be installed above the roof of the cathedral, 1999. (Source: Nicholas Yellachich)

beside it. Meanwhile Father Thomas Hardy read the prayer of blessing in English. On drawing level with the cross on top of the cupola, Archbishop Mark blessed it and the whole cupola with holy water. He climbed back down the ladder and gave a short address about the meaning of the cross for Christians, especially those living in London where with God's help they were building the city's first real Russian Orthodox church. At this point Archbishop Gregorios of the Greek Archdiocese of Thyateira and Great Britain arrived, together with a Serbian priest and people from other parishes in England.

After unvesting inside the church, Archbishop Mark invited everyone into the parish hall for refreshments. Here he welcomed Archbishop Gregorios, the mayor of Hounslow, and other officials. He also expressed gratitude to Douglas Norwood, the architect, for his love for this church, which had inspired him to stay up night after night working out details such as the positioning of each individual tile on the cupola. Vladyka presented him with a set of china bearing depictions of the Baptism of Russia, St Vladimir, and St Olga.

When everything was nearly ready to lift the cupola onto the supporting drum, everyone went outside and stood in the road beside the church, which had been blocked off by the police. Traffic police were also present on the M4 motorway which passes very close to Harvard Road, ensuring that the traffic slowed down as it passed by. The church and dome are clearly visible from the motorway, and there was a risk that drivers would be distracted and perhaps cause an accident when they saw a large dome, complete with a gold Russian cross on top, being lifted high up in the air above the tree line. As the crane lifted the cupola, the choir sang the troparion of the Dormition and the Great Doxology. Almost everyone living in the nearby houses came out into the street to watch the elevation of the dome. The cupola slowly drew closer to the drum, and many people, including the two bishops, had tears in their eyes as the crane operator gently and skillfully lowered it into place on top of the drum atop the church roof. The Greek archbishop congratulated Vladyka Mark, and many shared their joy with each other on bringing to fruition this great and long-awaited event in the life of the Orthodox Church in England, something which many thought they would never live to see.

Abbess Seraphima remarked to Vladyka Mark that they had at last fulfilled the guidance of the holy Archbishop John of Shanghai, who had told the churchwarden in the 1950s that it was time to stop wandering about as refugees and put down roots by erecting our own church. On this day, everyone felt that Vladyka John's hopes had been realized. At the end of the reception, Archbishop Mark personally thanked all those who had worked on the final phase of constructing the dome. People stayed together for a long time in the church hall, sharing their impressions of this momentous day in the life of the parish.

Since then, the impressive blue and gold dome has been clearly visible from the M4 motorway, which is the main route into central London from Heathrow Airport.

Convent of the Annunciation: Repose of Abbesses Elisabeth and Seraphima

Representing the Convent of the Annunciation at the dome-raising solemnities was its new superior, Abbess Seraphima, who had succeeded Abbess Elisabeth earlier in 1999.

For decades, the life of the convent continued in its unalterable rhythm of daily services and Saturday church school lessons. In 1995 a solemn celebration was held for the fiftieth anniversary of Mother Elisabeth's monastic tonsure. As Abbess Elisabeth grew older, the sisters of the convent devoted more time to taking care of her needs and nursing her through a succession of illnesses. Mother Seraphima, the oldest nun, took the lead in organizing care for the abbess. Despite physical frailty, however, the abbess's mind remained clear. Visitors always received a word of wise advice and consolation. The following description is characteristic:

> My most memorable visit to the convent was the last one, in October of 1998. Seeing Matushka swathed in her monastic robes, surrounded by the loving care of the sisters, one at first failed to notice that her body was shrivelled and shrunken through various illnesses to the point that there was almost nothing left. Yet in conversation she was far from being like an old lady, in fact her mind remained sharp and clear to the end; proof enough, if such were needed, of the existence of the human soul independently of the body. We spoke of Archbishop John (Maximovitch). She recalled their first meeting in Versailles, near Paris. She had been warned to expect severity and strange words, and found only love, warmth and the radiant smile of his that she always spoke of. He put an absurd amount of sugar in her tea, saying that the sisters had been through torments and now the Lord would reward them. She recalled the look on his face as he entered a church: he was really entering another world, greeting his friends, the saints, and just looking at him, one felt transported also into that world. We spoke of Gerald Palmer, an English member of Parliament who had converted to Orthodoxy after visits to Mount Athos, and later became a great supporter

of the convent. She spoke of his study of the Jesus prayer, of visiting his house in the countryside and sitting quietly on the terrace, realizing that he was praying and beginning to pray also. We spoke of the beauty and prayerful depth of the icons in the convent church which he had painted, particularly the icon of Our Lord, in front of which the Mother Abbess would sit in her abbess's seat, immediately in front of the choir desk where the nuns sing the daily church services. (Years ago she wrote to a young novice at Jordanville: "Just forget everything else, immerse yourself in the monastic services, let them be everything to you.") . . . Moments of experiencing a complete oneness of mind with this shrunken, ninety-year-old woman were combined with a realization that here was someone now very close to the other world. Her accounts of Archbishop John, for example, some of which I had heard previously, had a greater spiritual force and clarity than ever before. . . . I regretted only that I had never written after the visit to thank Matushka. "Never mind," said one of the nuns when I telephoned to offer my condolences, "She knows." And, without wishing to pass judgment, either for good or for ill, one feels that she does.

Abbess Elisabeth in 1995 at the Convent of the Annunciation on the fiftieth anniversary of her tonsure as a monastic. (Source: Sisters of the convent)

The mother abbess died less than four months after this visit, on February 3, 1999. The following is from an account written shortly afterwards of her last moments in this world:

Mother Elisabeth had lived the monastic discipline for almost sixty years. . . . The sisters report that on the day of her passing, she rose earlier than usual and insisted on going early to the convent chapel. There she made a special point of venerating all of the many relics individually and praying before each of the icons. . . . She received Holy Communion in the early evening, and was fully in charge of all her faculties, telling the sisters to prepare a table for the Holy Gifts, and when anointed with oil from the shrine of St John of Shanghai, she carefully turned her hands to be anointed on both sides. To within minutes of her end, she was receiving those who came to see her, assuring them of her prayers and her care for their souls. At the last, she sighed deeply twice, looked up and exclaimed "Angeli"—the Angels!—and so gave up her soul.

Parallels can be drawn between Abbess Elisabeth's passing and the repose of Archbishop Nikodem in 1976. He also died at home in his monastic cell, and, just before his death, spoke in a way that made clear his contact with the spiritual realm. Archbishop Mark came for the funeral, and the congregation filled the chapel and the hall, and overflowed onto the stairway and into the rooms of the convent. Mother Elisabeth was interred at Gunnersbury Cemetery. Archbishop Mark gave the following address at her funeral:

> "Precious in the sight of the Lord is the death of His saints."
> The Lord teaches us to begin our lives from death, because this is the ultimate destination of our life. A man's death brings everything to the same level, everything is directed towards this goal, because it is only the beginning of real life. That small portion of our existence which we spend on this earth as visitors, as travellers, as strangers and wanderers, is only a preparation for that day when we will take up our abode in the dwellings of the Lord. And not one of us standing here has lived in accordance with these words of Holy Scripture as has our departed Matushka, Abbess Elisabeth. She was persecuted throughout her life. Her life began with the exodus from Russia. She migrated over many of the continents of the world. She was first appointed to her duties as abbess in the Holy Land and was expelled from there by harsh godless hands. Finally after passing through many, many new stages of life she reached this land. And here, even on the last day of her life, she showed how much she loved the House of the Lord, how much her heart was devoted to dwell in the House of God and behold the beauty of the Lord. She truly beheld it as we know, many of us who are standing here, and many dispersed throughout the world, who were nourished by her words, her counsel, and her prayers. For us, dear brothers and sisters, today is a day of tears. If we shed our tears, as is quite natural, we should still remember that we are grieving for ourselves. We are grieving that we have lost a precious and dear person. But in reality, this is a day of joy, which is why we stand before God's altar in bright coloured vestments, because this is the entry of all of us into life eternal. We are become partakers in her ascetic struggles and, as she prayed for us, while yet here with us, while alive in this world, so we can be assured that she will continue to pray for us and will have more strength and boldness before the Throne of God.

So let us not be saddened, dear brothers and sisters, on this day, but on the contrary, let us receive with thanksgiving God's gift which He has given to us in the person of Matushka Elisabeth, who led us by the hand and listened to all our grief and difficulties, laying them at the altar of God all her life. Now she will be praying for us directly before God's altar, and we know that we not only have a great intercessor, but we now have still more love, more meekness and patience, because she gave us an example of all these things, she gave us an example of Christian life which we should follow faithfully in our lives henceforth. As we leave this church let us take with us this conviction, that only in the House of God can we abide in true love. Amen.

Mother Seraphima was appointed to succeed Mother Elisabeth as superior of the convent. Archbishop Mark came to install her as abbess in April 1999, but first went to Gunnersbury Cemetery where he met the nuns from the convent and there celebrated a panikhida at the grave of Abbess Elisabeth. The following day, the archbishop celebrated the Liturgy at the convent. At the Little Entrance of the Liturgy, the deacon lead Mother Seraphima up to the bishop, and he read over her the Prayer at the Appointment of an Abbess, after which he invested her with the golden cross that had belonged to Abbess Elisabeth. Then, at the end of the Liturgy, Vladyka entrusted her with the abbess's staff, and said that Abbess Seraphima now had before her the great task of preserving the oasis of prayer and spiritual enlightenment that had been created by the late Abbess Elisabeth.

Mother Seraphima had long been effectively the deputy of Mother Elisabeth, so her appointment as the next abbess seemed quite natural. Unfortunately, having only recently buried her superior and mentor, Abbess Seraphima succumbed to cancer and died just over a year later, on August 15, 2000. Archbishop Mark came for the funeral and Bishop Kallistos (Ware), a longtime friend of the convent, attended the funeral and gave an address. Abbess Seraphima was also buried in Gunnersbury Cemetery. On September 23, 2000, a service was held to mark the fortieth day of her death, and a booklet titled *The Cup of Christ* was distributed to those present. This was a translation of an essay on the meaning of suffering written by St Ignatius (Brianchaninov), a well-known Russian spiritual writer. Mother Seraphima had been the principal chauffeur for the convent, and she kept a copy in the car, which she read while waiting for those whom she had taken to various appointments. After she died, the sisters found her well-worn copy in the car, and decided to have copies printed in her memory.

Following the untimely death of Abbess Seraphima, Mother Vikentia was chosen to be the superior. On the Sunday of All Saints in June 2001, Archbishop Mark celebrated the Liturgy at the convent and, during the service, he invested Mother Vikentia with a gold cross by order of the Holy Synod. The archbishop expressed the hope that she would continue to guide the sisters in her characteristic spirit of meekness and humility, but also not shy away from strictness if warranted. He exhorted the other sisters to show obedience to their mother superior and live together in the spirit of mutual love, which imbues everyone with the power of the Holy Trinity.

Water Damage and Interior Finishing of the Lower Church

Despite the enthusiasm and genuine spiritual rejoicing occasioned by the installation of the cupola, a substantial amount of work and difficulties lay ahead. While the basic structure and outer shell of the building had been completed—a substantial achievement in itself—all the interior finishing work remained to be done. Besides this, there were deficiencies inherited from the bankrupt construction firm, the most serious of which was a lack of proper waterproofing in the basement. When the parish held services in the upper church during Holy Week in 1999, the plan was to use it only during the festal period ending with the feast of Pentecost. During that period the lower church was to be made useable, and services were to be held there for as long as it took to complete all the interior finishing of the upper church. Services were held in the lower church for a time, but soon a persistent dampness became obvious. Services were moved back to the upper church while this

Interior of the lower church at Harvard Road, 2003. (Source: Christopher Birchall)

problem was investigated. In fact, all services were held in the upper church for the next three years despite its bare concrete block walls. Although the church in Chiswick was new, the contrast of its majestic proportions and the rough, unfinished interior suggested an unplanned solidarity with experiences in Russia at the time. While churches were being slowly restored there, services would be held in formerly magnificent buildings whose insides were gaunt and dilapidated from decades of use as warehouses or neglect during Soviet times.

As soon as heavy rainfall began in the autumn of 1999, the lower church suffered severe water damage and became completely unusable. Failure of the waterproofing or "tanking" of the reinforced concrete walls was traced to the original contractors neglecting to fill in the dowel holes properly. Water seeped in, resulting in large areas of standing water and extensive damage to the internal fixtures and fittings.

The deficiency causing the water damage was first noticed in the winter of 1998, when Nicholas Yellachich and Douglas Norwood were inspecting the church basement. The walls at this level were made of monolith concrete—a single slab made by pouring liquid concrete between two temporary supporting walls known as the formwork. Metal rods, or dowels, about an inch in diameter, are used to keep the spacing within the formwork even so that the concrete wall will be straight. The dowels are greased so that they can be removed once the concrete has set. This obviously leaves a large number of holes that must be filled in, a vital step that the builders omitted. It was raining when the tour of inspection took place, and water was pouring into the basement through the unfilled dowel holes and then leaking through the brick wall that lined the inside of the concrete wall. The building firm assured the parish that this would be rectified, but it was in dire financial straits at the time and declared bankruptcy shortly afterwards, leaving the problem unfixed and hidden behind the inner brick wall.

When water reappeared in the winter of 1999, it was clear that nothing had been done. With the building firm in bankruptcy, recourse was no longer possible. At about this time, Nicholas Yellachich resigned as chairman of the Building Committee. He had become involved in an overseas engineering project, and in light of other family commitments, he no longer felt able to devote sufficient time and attention to the church building project, especially considering the complications that had arisen just as the construction phase should have been drawing to a close.

Fortunately, there was another member of the Parish Council, Pavel Lisitsin, who was able to step in and take over management of the building project. He had been a member of the council since 1998, but initially was preoccupied with his business and not actively involved other than by making generous financial donations. Pavel had been baptised in Moscow at the age of twenty and then moved to England in 1994 where he set up business as an oil trader. He grew closer to the life of the parish after having one of his daughters baptised at Harvard Road in 1996, when the temporary church in the church hall was still being used. In 2001 he retired from his business activities, and when Nicholas Yellachich resigned, Pavel Lisitsin stepped into the breach. As it turned out, Pavel's "retirement" only lasted a few years, but during this period he was able to devote all his energies to getting the church finished. First, he approached the archbishop with a plan to start on the frescoes in the upper church. This was appealing because frescoes were objects of beauty and edification, and highly visible to the congregation. However, Vladyka Mark pointed out that this was premature, as the dampness rising from the basement, as well as leaks that had appeared in the roof, would soon damage anything painted on the walls. The first priority must be to remedy the structural problems, starting with the leaky basement.

After researching the issue, Pavel Lisitsin engaged a specialist contractor, Advanced Preservations. Even these professionals found the situation particularly challenging. They eventually installed specially designed membranes from John Newton & Company over the walls to divert any continuing seepage to the base drain, rather than try to plug up all potential areas of leakage. In its report on the work, the Newton company concluded,

> The church was able to retain its intricate features with Newton meshed membranes being installed to the intricate window reveals, which, once completed by the Russian craftsmen, could not be distinguished from the original detailing pre-flood. The combination of products used ensured that all water ingress was successfully moved to the pumping system for removal out of the property. This very specific design overcame the very specific problems afflicting this property.

These extensive repairs were completed in February 2003 at a cost of approximately £250,000.

When remediation of the water damage was complete, Pavel Lisitsin hired workers and craftsmen to make the lower church fit for worship. A new iconostasis was made to fit the space available. The exceptionally fine icons for it were painted by Dimitry Hartung, an expert iconographer living in Munich. The cost of the iconostasis was covered by a substantial donation from Michael Watford (known in Russian circles as Mikhail Vatford), who was an old friend and former business colleague of Pavel Lisitsin. When the lower church reached a state where it could be used, although not entirely finished, Archbishop Mark came from Germany to conduct the lesser consecration, or blessing of the church. Beforehand, he sent out this invitation to the event:

> Dear Brothers and Sisters in Christ,
> Through God's immeasurable mercy and upon the prayers of the Most Holy Mother of God, the Holy New Martyrs and all the Saints of Russia and the Holy Orthodox Church our parish has been able to complete the Lower (crypt) church, while much work remains to be done on the Upper (main) church. We rejoice in the Lord and give thanks to all those countless faithful and friends of our Church who—through their fervent prayers and their donations both of financial kind and in form of the work of their own hands—have been and still continue to be instrumental in this great effort. We know that many parishioners who lived in London in the past and have passed away are with us in their prayers. We trust that all those faithful and friends of our church who live in this country and in many other places of our diaspora rejoice with us upon this great event. We hope that you will also be able to join us and pray and give thanks to God on this wonderful day. In order to give thanks to God for the work accomplished and ask for His help and the prayers of the Mother of God and all the Saints to support us in finishing the remainder, we invite you to be present for the service of the smaller consecration of the Lower Church on Thursday 16 October 2003 at the Cathedral of the Dormition of the Most Holy Mother of God and the Holy Royal Martyrs of Russia at 57 Harvard Road, Chiswick, London W4 4ED.

The service consisted mainly of the rite for the Lesser Blessing of the Waters, after which the church was sprinkled with holy water. Prayers were read, dedicating the crypt to the Holy Royal Martyrs of Russia as originally planned. Parts of the service were broadcast on television in the Russian Federation. Concelebrating were Archimandrite Alexis from Brookwood, Father Vadim Zakrevsky, Archpriest Peter Holodny, Father Thomas Hardy, and Father Peter Baulk. Guests included Archbishop Gregorios of Thyateira and Great Britain, and Bishop Basil of Sergievo from the Moscow Patriarchal Cathedral in London. The choir was directed by the new choir director Anna Kobrina, and everyone found the singing to be particularly uplifting.

The iconostasis and Pokrov icon from Emperor's Gate installed in the upper church of the newly built Cathedral at Harvard Road, 2001. (Source: Christopher Birchall)

Subsequently, work proceeded on finishing the interior of the lower church, including painting frescoes and construction of the baptistery at the left side of the church, which contains a font recessed into the floor that is large enough to baptise an adult by full immersion. Eventually, in May 2005 everything was ready and it was time to perform the full consecration of the lower church.

Metropolitan Laurus, the First Hierarch of the Russian Orthodox Church Abroad, came for the occasion and presided at the services on Sunday, May 29. Archbishop Mark, Archbishop Kyrill of San Francisco and Western America, Bishop Agapit of Stuttgart, and Bishop Michael of Boston joined the metropolitan who led the five-hour ceremonies. Ten priests, including Protopresbyter Milun Kostic of the Serbian Orthodox parish in London, concelebrated at the Divine Liturgy with two deacons. During the Little Entrance, Father Thomas Hardy was elevated to the rank of archpriest. At the end of the Liturgy, the metropolitan preached on the Gospel of the Samaritan woman and the missionary duty of the Russian diaspora, with Archpriest Alexander Lebedev providing a translation into English. At the very end of the service, Archbishop Anatoly of Kerch and Archpriest Michael Gogoleff from the Patriarchal church at Ennismore Gardens joined the assembly and dined with the Harvard Road clergy and faithful.

Reconciliation with the Moscow Patriarchate

As the building of the new church neared completion, much had changed in the Orthodox world since the parish had been forced to move out of the cathedral at Emperor's Gate in 1989. The fall of the Communist regime in Russia impelled the Russian Church Abroad to reassess its relationship with the Church in Russia. This was a complex process because of both the time that had elapsed since the Revolution and the immensity of the suffering and destruction wrought in the name of communism.

Russian churches, such as the London Embassy church, had existed outside the boundaries of Russia for hundreds of years before the Revolution. This emigration comprised a significant part of the Russian people, and in their distress they rallied around the Orthodox Church. The Russian Church in Exile initially maintained contact with the Church in Russia, especially during the lifetime of Patriarch Tikhon (d. 1925). Such contact became impossible as the Soviet government put increasing pressure on Church leaders and extracted a declaration of loyalty from Metropolitan Sergius, who was the deputy locum tenens of the Patriarchal Throne. The bishops of the Russian Church Abroad stayed their course, maintaining an independent church administration without reference to the dictates of a hierarchy in Russia that they knew was not free.

Nevertheless, the Russian Church Abroad clearly upheld the view that this situation was temporary, to last as long as God would permit Bolshevik rule to continue in Russia. Writing in the 1960s, Archbishop John (Maximovitch) drew historical parallels with the Serbian and Greek Orthodox Churches. He pointed out that in the seventeenth and eighteenth centuries the Serbian Patriarchs Arsenius III and Arsenius IV, fleeing persecution from the Ottoman Empire, settled with their flocks in Hungary and maintained their separate church administration without submitting to the patriarchs in Serbia enslaved by Turkish oppressors. Archbishop John also drew a parallel with the situation in the Greek Church in the nineteenth century. Once Greece became independent of the Ottoman Empire in the 1830s, an independent Greek Church was established, although the territory of Greece had always belonged to the Patriarchate of Constantinople. The patriarchs, under Turkish pressure, did not recognize the Church of Greece for about thirty years. This was regarded as a temporary measure at first, as long as Constantinople remained in Turkish hands.

In the mid-1980s, members of the Russian Orthodox Church Abroad watched with interest as Communist Russia seemed to be crumbling. Could the hated regime really be coming to an end, or was this just a period of remission, a deceptive respite before a renewed onslaught? In 1988, as solemn celebrations were held in Kiev to mark the Millennium of Russian Christianity, people within the Soviet Union began to speak openly of venerating the New Martyrs of Russia. The same year, television programmes were shown in England about the life of the Church in Russia, including an interview with a young priest serving an inner-city parish. In his small apartment was an icon of St John of Kronstadt, who had been canonized by the Russian Church Abroad in 1964, but was particularly hated by the Soviet government because he foretold the catastrophe that was to come through the Revolution. All this would have been impossible only a few years before. Then, in 1989, the fall of the Berlin Wall marked a decisive turning point, possible only because Mikhail Gorbachev, general secretary of the Communist Party of the Soviet Union, refused to use force to prop up the East German regime. But still, what was really happening? Who was Gorbachev, where had he come from, who had appointed him, and what was his real mission? Following the euphoria of 1989 were two years of uneasiness. Former satellite countries in Eastern Europe began to assert their independence, but what of the Soviet Union itself?

At this unstable juncture the bishops of the Russian Church Abroad felt compelled to help Orthodox believers in Russia. Unsure of how long this period of relative freedom would last, the Church should make the most of the opportunity that existed. At the Council of Bishops in 1990, the Russian Orthodox Church Abroad announced that it had secretly consecrated a bishop in Russia in 1983 to minister to the faithful who felt unable to accept the leadership of the Moscow Patriarchate. The bishops' view then was that their mission should be to continue in the same line, and accept into communion people who wished to be part of a free Russian Orthodox Church. In the West, some members of the Russian Church Abroad felt a new sense of purpose belonging to a Church that was finally in a position to respond openly and practically to the situation in Russia. However, even at this early stage, there were those who thought that the Church Abroad should have been more open to the official Church, which was beginning to climb out from under the oppression that had almost suffocated it. In 1990, following the death of Patriarch Pimen, a Sobor was held in Moscow that elected a new patriarch, Alexis II, the former Metropolitan of Tallinn. The Russian Church Abroad initially viewed this with great caution, not knowing if positive changes were really occurring. The Soviet Union's system of government supervision of bishops and church affairs still existed, although seemingly with far less interference than before.

Disturbing news came from Russia in August 1991 when a group of hard-line communists and KGB officers attempted to displace Gorbachev and reinstate a Communist dictatorship. The unrest and violence led many Russian émigrés to think the brief window of freedom was closing. However, the conspirators could not muster enough support and Gorbachev regained control with the support of Boris Yeltsin. In December 1991, the Soviet Union was officially dissolved leaving great uncertainty.[4] The new government of the Russian Federation did not command universal trust, and the Church's relationship with the Yeltsin regime seemed unclear. Nevertheless, by the second half of the 1990s, contacts between bishops of the Russian Church Abroad and individual hierarchs of the Moscow Patriarchate became more frequent. In addition, some bishops, such as Archbishop Laurus and Archbishop Anthony of San Francisco, went to Russia incognito, dressed as simple monks, to visit churches and pray with the people, judging for themselves what had survived of the Church in Russia. They came back convinced that, whatever issues were yet to be resolved, this was fundamentally the same Church that they had always belonged to.

A turning point came in 2000 when the Moscow Patriarchate resolved to glorify the New Martyrs and Confessors who had suffered under the Communist yoke. One of the most revered bishops of the Russian Church Abroad, Archbishop Anthony of San Francisco, was seriously ill with cancer and knew his end was approaching. On August 19, 2000, at the end of the last Liturgy he celebrated in his earthly life, he gave a sermon full of compassion and cautious optimism about the Church in Russia. In it he said,

> Present day Russia is poised between radiant hope and utter darkness. She could rise from the dead or irredeemably perish. Tomorrow, the Moscow Patriarchate is going to glorify the Royal Martyrs. It is going to glorify them as passion-bearers. Patriarch Alexis has stated that they will be glorified specifically because of the Christian way in which they met their deaths. But even that is good, it is the first step. We have glorified the Royal Martyrs for their pious lives as well as for their martyrs' deaths. But we must welcome this initial step taken by the Moscow Patriarchate. There is still much that divides us, but this first step gives us hope. Despite everything, we must embrace this step.

At its council meeting later in 2000, the Synod of the Russian Church Abroad formally expressed its encouragement at the changes taking place in Russia. Specifically, it noted that the code of moral principles adopted by the

Moscow Patriarchate at its Sobor the previous August rejected subservience of the Church to a hostile government. This effectively renounced the position taken by Metropolitan Sergius in his infamous declaration of loyalty to the Soviet regime in 1927.

As the first decade of the new millennium progressed, a process of formal dialogue between the Russian Church Abroad and the Moscow Patriarchate was started. The Synod of each church appointed a ROCOR Commission,[5] led by a bishop and consisting of some twelve members. Archbishop Mark of Berlin, Germany, and Great Britain led the Commission of the Church Abroad, while that of the Moscow Patriarchate was led by Archbishop Innocent of Korsun, administrator of the Patriarchal parishes in Western Europe. Each Commission received instructions from, and reported back to, its own Synod. Metropolitan Laurus often gave detailed instructions to the Commission representing the Russian Church Abroad before its meetings. The Commissions met both separately and together. The main points under discussion were the relationship between church and state, especially in times of persecution; the canonization of the New Martyrs; participation in the ecumenical movement; and the future status of the Church Abroad in a united Russian Church, if all the other points could be resolved. In total, the Commissions held eight joint meetings, which took place alternately within Russia and outside Russia. Father Alexander Lebedev, secretary of the Russian Orthodox Church Outside Russia Commission, described the challenges and rewards of these meetings:

> As regards the actual negotiations, it is important to note that all the members of the Commissions take a very active part in the discussions during our joint meetings, with each side expressing and defending the hallowed positions of their respective hierarchies. In the process of working out the joint documents, each phrase, and sometimes even every word, is scrupulously debated, until an acceptable formulation is found. The discussions are completely frank, sometimes debate becomes heated and we seem to be reaching a deadlock. The two chairmen then use their influence to ensure that the debate returns to a calm and peaceful discussion of the question at hand.
>
> During the first joint meetings there was a sense that to a certain extent, we did not understand one another or that there were differences in terminology, since some Russian expressions are understood differently in the Russian diaspora than they are in Russia itself. However, as we continued working together, these differences gradually began to disappear,

> and all the members of the Commissions were filled with a sense of awe, as we began to understand the importance of the obedience that had been entrusted to us by our respective hierarchies. They began to feel that what they were doing was not the work of their own hands, but God's work. The members of the Commission ask all of you for your holy prayers as we continue our work, in full awareness of our responsibility before the Lord God, that they should bear in their work for healing the wounds of division, with the aim of strengthening the spiritual rebirth of the Russian people, and for the good of the Holy and One Russian Church.

This passage was taken from a talk Father Alexander gave at a church assembly held in San Francisco in May 2006, at which clergy and lay people from all over the world were invited to discuss the future path of the Russian Church Abroad. Another speaker at this conference was Father Nikolay Savchenko, then a priest in St Petersburg under the jurisdiction of the Russian Church Abroad, who later left Russia to become parish priest at the London Cathedral parish of the Russian Orthodox Church Abroad. He spoke on "Restoration of Eucharistic Communion and Overcoming Divisions in the History of the Church." Father Nikolay was also a consultant to the Russian Church Abroad's Commission in the reunification negotiations described earlier.

From time to time on visits to England, Archbishop Mark explained the basis for the negotiations and gave details of their progress. For example, at Brookwood on February 12, 2006, at celebrations for the abbot's thirtieth anniversary in the priesthood, Vladyka Mark emphasized that there was no intention of changing the life of the Russian Church Abroad:

> In the present situation, now that the communist regime has fallen, the canonical basis for our Church is uncertain, since it was given to us at a time when meaningful contact with the Church in Russia was impossible. After emphasizing for 80 years that we are a part of the Russian Church, we must hold to this, and address the tasks that are before us. . . . It is everyone's hope that the life of our church will continue in the way that it has naturally developed so far. This is also the desire of our partners in negotiations in the Moscow Patriarchate.

The negotiations for union finally reached fruition on the feast of the Ascension in May 2007. At a solemn service in the Church of Christ the Saviour in Moscow, Patriarch Alexis and Metropolitan Laurus signed the document establishing eucharistic communion, and then proceeded to concelebrate a triumphant Liturgy in which many bishops and clergy of both the Church Abroad and the Moscow Patriarchate participated.

It was agreed that the Russian Church Abroad would retain a large measure of autonomy and its existing structure and institutions, with its Synod in New York and dioceses throughout the world. It continues as an autonomous church within the jurisdiction of the Patriarchate of Moscow, with the patriarch being commemorated at church services as leader of the Church. The bishops of the Church Abroad would also participate in meetings of the bishops' councils of the entire Russian Orthodox Church.

This change had a significant effect on church life in many parts of the diaspora. The distrust and rivalry that existed between parishes of the Moscow Patriarchate and those of the Church Abroad began to be replaced by friendly cooperation. In many places, including London, this process had already begun to develop before the eucharistic union of 2007. For example, the invitation to Archbishop Anatoly and Bishop Basil of the Moscow Patriarchate to be honoured guests at the lesser consecration of the lower church at Harvard Road in October 2003 would have been unthinkable only a few years previously.

Perhaps inevitably, there were some who felt unable to accept the union. In England, these included the nuns of the Convent of the Annunciation in London as well as the brothers of St Edward's Monastery in Brookwood. Sadly, at this point both of these monastic houses ceased to be part of the Russian Orthodox Church Abroad.

Since the shared use of St Philip's Church came to an end in 1954, the two Russian Orthodox parishes in London led completely separate lives. The Church of the Moscow Patriarchate developed under the leadership of Metropolitan Anthony (Bloom), who was a well-known writer and speaker. He grew up in France, and spoke English with a mixed Russian and French accent. He came from a White Russian émigré family, and had belonged to the Moscow Patriarchate since his youth, long before the postwar wave of enthusiasm for this jurisdiction.[6] Not being a Soviet citizen sent from Russia, he enjoyed a rare degree of independence in his ministry despite being subject to a Church administration based in a country controlled by an atheist regime. He became widely respected in the Soviet Union, where he was known as Antony Sourozhsky after the name of his titular see in the Crimea. He visited Russia for official church meetings and used the opportunity to preach and meet with believing people. His London parish based in

Kensington ministered to English converts and to descendants of the earlier wave of refugees. By 2003, he was in poor health and was looking for a successor to lead his diocese.

After the dialogue between the Russian Church Abroad and the Moscow Patriarchate began, Archbishop Mark had several meetings with Metropolitan Anthony during his visits to England. The main purpose was to get to know the local people who had been treated with deep suspicion for so long. In March and April of 2002, meetings were held to discuss pastoral care of Russians living in Dublin because at different times both Father Vadim Zakrevsky and clergy from the Patriarchal Cathedral visited to conduct services there. This concrete issue led to discussion of other topics and better mutual understanding on a personal level.

In February 2003, Metropolitan Anthony was diagnosed with cancer, and Archbishop Mark visited him in April while he was recuperating after an operation. Despite treatment, Metropolitan Anthony died on August 4, 2003. He was eventually succeeded by Bishop Elisey (Ganaba) in 2007 as ruling bishop of the Moscow Patriarchate's Diocese of Sourozh, which has parishes in Great Britain and Ireland.

Archbishop Anatoly, by then in his mid-seventies, remained as an assistant bishop. Before coming to England in 1990, he had a long and difficult life serving the Church in the Soviet Union as well as five years in Damascus as the representative of the Patriarch of Moscow to the Patriarch of Antioch. He enjoyed the love and respect of parishioners in both Russian Church jurisdictions in Britain. In August 2004 on the feast of the Dormition, he visited the church at Harvard Road to venerate the miraculous Kursk icon of the Mother of God, which had been brought to London for the patronal feast day. After the service Archbishop Anatoly gave a short talk, introducing himself and recounting some episodes from his life as a priest and archpastor. He also pointed out that it was in front of the Kursk icon during an earlier visit that he first met Archbishop Mark, and that since then they had become firm friends.

As noted above, eucharistic communion between the Russian Church Abroad and the Moscow Patriarchate was established at the feast of the Ascension in May 2007. The first concelebration between hierarchs of the two jurisdictions in England took place on Sunday, August 26, 2007, two days before the feast of the Dormition, when Archbishop Mark and Bishop Elisey served together at the church in Harvard Road. Since then, such concelebrations have become regular occurrences on major feast days. Thus, the two Russian parishes in London began to work together with the distinct architectural styles of their church buildings and differing traditions becoming a source of mutual enrichment rather than continuing rivalry.

At the feast of the Dormition in 2007, it was announced that Father Vadim Zakrevsky would be leaving the parish after a tenure of nearly fifteen years as parish priest. Archbishop Mark thanked him for his energy and hard work over this period. He had taken on the parish at an exceptionally difficult juncture, when there was no proper church building and the services were held in the small house chapel at St Dunstan's Road. After the move to Harvard Road, Father Vadim had devoted much energy to the building project and settling the parish in its new location. Father Vadim transferred to the London parish of the Moscow Patriarchate, and continued his priestly service as a clergyman of the Patriarchal Cathedral. His immediate replacement in the Harvard Road cathedral was Father Yaroslav Belikow from San Francisco.

Finishing the Upper Church: Installing the New Iconostasis

Once the lower church was fully consecrated in 2005, most of the services were held there and work began in earnest to finish the upper church. Although the exterior was done, the interior would require another few years to complete. Outstanding items included electrical wiring, heating, and the fire alarm system. Finishing included plastering the walls, woodwork on the ceilings, the dome and arched areas in the altar, the inside of the main cupola and dome, and marble flooring. Other fittings included six solid oak doors and frames, vestry doors, cupboards and stairs, choir balustrades, and finishing the choir space. Major church furnishings included the main altar table, the table of *proskimidi* (preparation), a reliquary box, lecterns, icon stands, and benches.

By the following summer, work was progressing on plastering the vaulted arches and the contours of the future interior were beginning to emerge. When he visited for the patronal feast of the lower church in July 2006, Archbishop Mark was able to see the progress being made and show it to his guest, Archbishop Anatoly of the Moscow Patriarchate. Finally the clergy, including the two archbishops, were supplied with hard hats and given a tour of the work under way, being taken up right into the central dome to inspect the details. This work continued throughout 2006.

The annual report for 2006 filed with the Charity Commission notes that "without the very substantial financial donations made by [the] Lisitsin family, the Parish would not be able to successfully finalize decoration of the Cathedral." At the annual general meeting of the parish in 2004, Pavel Lisitsin had been nominated a *ktitor* of the parish. *Ktitor* is a Greek word meaning "founder" that was adopted into Russian as part of the Byzantine heritage of the Russian Orthodox Church. A *ktitor* is usually someone who has made a very substantial contribution to building a church or monastery and remains a member of the Parish Council ex officio without further reelection. In the case of Pavel Lisitsin, this status reflected the gratitude felt toward him for his efforts and generosity, but it also helped ensure that the parish would be able to draw on his skills and energy for years to come.[7]

Within the walls of the now thoroughly dry crypt church, the life of the parish settled down to a normal rhythm. The Parish Council hired a watchman so that the church could be open every day during daylight hours. They felt that the church building itself filled a missionary function and should be accessible to people, Orthodox or not, who wanted to see it, look at the icons, light a candle, and pray. Too often, Orthodox churches in the West are closed outside service times in order to secure the icons and other church furnishings. In Russia since the fall of communism, churches in larger cities are increasingly kept open all the time, often with a priest on duty to help answer peoples' questions.

During the 1990s, more and more Russians began settling in London. By the time the Harvard Road Cathedral was open for worship, there were far more people in the congregation than had been expected at the planning stage—in fact, at one point there were fears that it might even be too big. As older people retired from their duties in the parish and passed away, there was an enthusiastic newer generation ready to learn the many facets of running a parish.

Antonina Vladimirovna Ananin, formerly Archbishop Nikodem's secretary, who had directed the choir for decades, gradually became less involved due to advancing age, especially after her husband died in 1998. In June 2006 she died in Poole, Dorset, which had been her family home since 1951. Her increasing incapacity meant that, living so far from an Orthodox church, she deeply felt her isolation from the services. During her last illness, she was given some recordings of church music to listen to in hospital, and visitors reported that she was overwhelmed by the sheer joy of hearing them. Her funeral was conducted in Poole, and she was laid to rest with her late husband. The celebrants were Archimandrite Alexis, Father Vadim Zakrevsky, and Hieromonk Avraamy, one of her godsons who was visiting from Poland.[8] The choir from the London Cathedral parish sang at the funeral service, and people felt that her soul would have rejoiced to hear their compunctionate singing. The singing at her funeral was led by the new choir director, Anna Kobrina, who arrived in London from Russia in 2001. Unlike Antonina Ananin, Anna Kobrina is a professional musician with a degree in church music from St Petersburg Theological Academy. Nevertheless, people have remarked on the similarity of spirit in the singing under the two choir directors who never knew each other.

June 2006 also marked the eightieth birthday of Father Thomas Hardy. The celebrations held to mark the occasion showed a rare outpouring of warmth and love from a mainly Russian parish for a clergyman who, while able to officiate in Church Slavonic, did not speak a word of Russian. Archbishop Mark presided at the Divine Liturgy, assisted by Archimandrite Alexis, Father Vadim Zakrevsky, Father Thomas Hardy, and Father Andrew Phillips. At the end of the service, the archbishop congratulated Father Thomas on his birthday and presented him with an icon donated by the parishioners and his spiritual children. Father Peter Baulk from Brookwood and Archpriest Nikolai Florinschi, who was visiting from Kishinev, also came for the festal meal after the service. More congratulations were addressed to Father Thomas, all expressing the great love of the parishioners for him and their gratitude for his spiritual solicitude. Archbishop Mark spoke of his unusual path toward the Orthodox priesthood starting as an Anglican vicar. As an Orthodox priest, he became a much loved spiritual father of both English and Russian parishioners. Father Vadim thanked him personally for the help he and his family received from him as their own spiritual father. Then Pavel Lisitsin, speaking on behalf of the parishioners, thanked Father Thomas for the fact that he constantly "radiates serenity and peace." The children from the Saturday church school put on a short concert all in English in his honour, with instrumental music, songs, and poems. A picture collage of his ministry was inscribed "To Father Thomas: Many Happy Returns."

Providentially, as Father Thomas was growing older, a native English priest, Father Peter Baulk, joined the clergy of the Cathedral at Harvard Road. In fact, Father Peter was ordained to the priesthood in 1994 by Archbishop Mark the day before Father Thomas was ordained. Father Peter, although not a monastic, was originally attached to St Edward's Monastery at Brookwood. After much prayerful reflection following the union with the Moscow Patriarchate in 2007, he joined the Cathedral clergy in London. Besides ministering to the English-speaking parishioners, he has taken charge of the entire parish on occasion when a Russian-speaking priest was not available. In 2008 he was appointed to act as chairman of the Parish Council at the monthly meetings, unless the archbishop is present, and subsequently he was elevated to the rank of archpriest. In 2009 he was chosen as clergy representative for the Diocese of Great Britain to attend the Sobor of the Russian Orthodox Church held in Moscow to elect a new patriarch following the death of Patriarch Alexis II. While serving as a priest, Father

Peter has continued to work at his secular profession for a company making electrical instruments near his home in Borehamwood, Hertfordshire.

The Russian Red Cross, which has played such a prominent role in helping Russian refugees since the time of the Revolution, continues in its mission "to promote in the United Kingdom the welfare and relief of aged, sick, poor and otherwise needy refugees from the area which was formerly the Russian Empire, and their families." In the 1970s it began selling houses it owned in Chiswick as there was less need to provide subsidized housing. Currently it devotes itself to assisting asylum seekers from former Soviet territories including Russia, Georgia, Uzbekistan, and Azerbaijan.

By Easter of 2007, all the plastering work on the interior walls and vaulted ceiling of the upper church was finished, so the Holy Week and Easter services were held in the upper church for the first time since the interior work began. As a temporary measure, a wooden iconostasis was constructed and the beautiful old icons from the former Podvoria were inserted into it.

The next step was to order a new iconostasis from Russia. In early 2007, Stanislav Kondrashov came forward and offered to pay the entire cost. This, however, brought to a head the need to resolve an issue that emerged following reconciliation of the Russian Orthodox Church Abroad with the Moscow Patriarchate. Both the Patriarchal Cathedral at Ennismore Gardens and the Cathedral of the Russian Church Abroad at Harvard Road were dedicated to the Dormition of the Most Holy Mother of God. This was no accident, since both parishes derived their origins from the prerevolutionary Imperial Embassy church that was dedicated to the Dormition. It would certainly be possible to have two Russian churches in London with the same dedication. In Moscow, for example, there are many churches dedicated to St Nicholas, which are distinguished by the names of the streets where they are situated. (The same applies in London where Anglican churches are distinguished in this way—St Giles Cripplegate and St Giles-in-the-Fields, for example.) However, this was felt not to be the ideal solution. Because Harvard Road and Ennismore Gardens are the only Russian churches in London, having the same dedication might impede the goal of fostering closer cooperation between the two parishes, which in turn might undermine the Church's newly achieved global unity. For example, it would be difficult to observe the pious custom of visiting neighbouring parishes on their patronal festivals as a way to strengthen unity in Christ and in the chalice of Holy Communion. As the church at Ennismore Gardens had been consecrated some time ago and the Harvard Road church awaited full consecration, there was still flexibility regarding its final dedication. The possibility of changing the church's dedication was raised at the annual general meeting in May 2008, as reported in the diocesan journal:

> Archbishop Mark suggested consecrating our church in honour of one of the other feasts of the Mother of God. However, Vladyka first wanted to hear the views of the oldest members of the parish about this—would such a rededication be too great a disturbance in the life and history of the parish? Once they had said that this would not be the case, two possibilities were discussed—the church could be dedicated to the Protection of the Most Holy Mother of God, or to the Nativity of the Mother of God. Since Archbishop Mark already had several churches under his care in Germany dedicated to the Protection, the meeting resolved to dedicate the church in honour of the Nativity of the Most Holy Mother of God.

This feast is celebrated on September 8/21, roughly three weeks after the feast of the Dormition. The archbishop referred the matter to the Holy Synod in New York for confirmation, and received the direction that the change should be made at the time of the full consecration but continue in the interim to be dedicated to the Dormition.

Resolution of this issue cleared the way to order the new iconostasis, since an icon of a church's patronal feast day occupies a prominent place on it. The next point to be decided was the style of the new iconostasis, which would have to harmonize with the architecture of the cathedral. Archbishop Mark, Father Euphemius Logvinov from Munich, and the new parish priest in London, Archpriest Yaroslav Belikow, travelled to several churches and monasteries in Russia to see for themselves the craftsmanship and style of the iconographers of the Palekh and Moscow schools. Eventually they concluded that the School of Iconography at the Moscow Theological Academy should paint the icons for the new London church. Graduates and students of the school carried out all the work required under the supervision of the school's principal, Abbot Luke (Golovkov), and the school's iconography teachers. They based their work on the Moscow style of the fifteenth and sixteenth centuries. They decided on a three-tier iconostasis—a lower tier, a full-length *Deisis* tier, and a festal tier—in accordance with fifteenth-century Russian iconographical traditions.

The lower, principal tier includes the two main icons of Christ the Saviour and the Mother of God on either side of the royal doors. Above this is the *Deisis* ("Intercession") tier centred on the *Deisis* icon depicting Christ seated

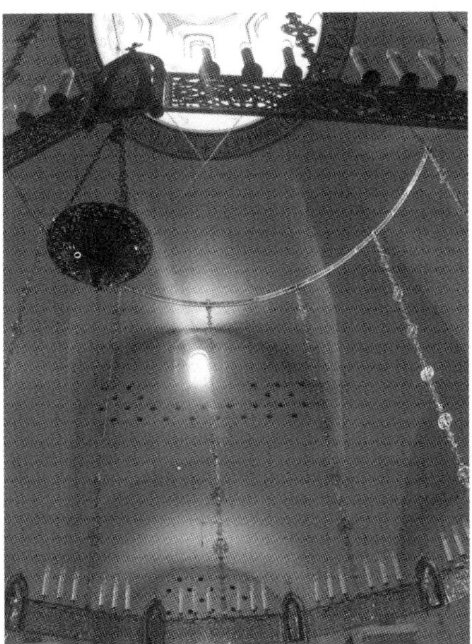

Looking toward the cupola from inside the Cathedral at Harvard Road, 2010. (Source: Christopher Birchall)

The cupola and drum above the Cathedral at Harvard Road rise above the church house. (Source: Christopher Birchall)

The new iconostasis at the Cathedral at Harvard Road, installed in 2009. (Source: Christopher Birchall)

on a throne with the Mother of God and St John the Baptist on either side, interceding for the world before Him. At the top is the festal tier, made up of eighteen icons depicting events connected with the principal feast days of the Church.

The icons in the lower tier of this iconostasis have a number of special features. On the right-hand side, next to the icon of the Saviour, the south door has a traditional icon of the prophet Daniel in the lions' den. To the right of the south door is an icon of St John of Shanghai and St Jonah of Hankow (also known as St Jonah of Manchuria). Next to this is the patronal icon of the Nativity of the Mother of God and the last icon on the right-hand side is of St Seraphim of Sarov.

On the left-hand side of the lower tier, next to the icon of the Most Holy Mother of God, the north door has an icon of the Good Thief. Next to it is the icon "In Thee rejoices," a complex composition of several figures, derived from the ancient hymn to the Most Blessed Lady and Birthgiver of God. To the left of these is an icon of the Royal Martyrs and St John of Kronstadt. The lower tier of the iconostasis intentionally emphasizes Russian saints, especially saints who were glorified in the twentieth century. Both the Royal Martyrs and the Righteous John of Kronstadt were first canonised by the Church Outside Russia, which expressed the hopes and aspirations of all Russian Orthodox, even during Soviet times when this was not yet possible in Russia itself.

The carved wooden decorations of the iconostasis were left ungilded so that worshippers' attention would not be distracted from the main focus, which should be the icons themselves.

Despite the enthusiasm with which he had devoted himself to the parish and to the design of the new iconostasis, Father Yaroslav Belikow was unable to stay in London for family reasons, so in the summer of 2008 he returned to America. Father Peter Baulk administered the parish temporarily until October 2008 when Father Nikolay Savchenko came from St Petersburg with his family to become parish priest in London. Father Nikolay was ordained in Russia by a bishop of the Russian Church Abroad at a time when the Church Abroad was still opening parishes of its own in Russia. He became well known as a prolific writer and theologian, and as noted previously, was appointed as a consultant to the Commission on Discussions with the Moscow Patriarchate. Despite regretting the loss of Father Yaroslav after such a short stay, the London parish was delighted to welcome such a prominent theologian as its new priest.

Work on the new icons continued at the school of iconography in Moscow throughout 2008 and into 2009. By August 2009 they were ready to be despatched to England. On August 30 all the vestments and sacred vessels were moved to the lower church where services were held for the next two months. The following day, a team of parishioners dismantled the temporary iconostasis, and the day after, a team of carpenters and builders arrived to construct the framework for the new 20-foot-high iconostasis. The new icons, packed into thirty-six packing cases, arrived from Moscow via Heathrow airport on September 3. Installing them into their correct places and making the doors for the iconostasis continued into October.

The large chandelier, ordered at the same time as the iconostasis, was despatched from Moscow on October 30 and arrived in London a few days later. In the shape of a large corona, the chandelier's diameter extends across almost the entire width of the church. It incorporates both electric lights and traditional oil lamps. Scaffolding was erected so that it could be suspended from the ceiling, and the electrical installation was completed.

Metropolitan Hilarion, the First Hierarch of the Russian Orthodox Church Abroad, was invited for the blessing of the new iconostasis and chandelier set for Saturday, November 14, 2009. Teams of parishioners worked for days getting everything ready, and some worked through Friday night completing the final details such as hanging the lamps in front of the icons on the iconostasis and putting the lamps back into the chandelier. Metropolitan Hilarion's visit was meticulously scheduled through the efforts of Father Peter Baulk. In the space of a few days he was taken to visit all the churches of the Russian Church Abroad in England—St Elizabeth's church in Wallasey (near Liverpool), whose parish priest is Father Paul Elliott; the church of Our Lady, the Joy of All Who Sorrow, in Mettingham, Suffolk; and the church of St John of Shanghai in Colchester, whose parish priest is Father Andrew Phillips. In addition, he visited St Albans, where he venerated the relics of St Alban; Oxford, where he met with Metropolitan Kallistos (Ware); and Lambeth Palace, where he paid a courtesy visit to Dr Rowan Williams, the Archbishop of Canterbury.

Four bishops—Metropolitan Hilarion, Archbishop Mark, and Bishop Elisey, and Archbishop Anatoly from the Patriarchal Church—concelebrated the Liturgy at the Cathedral in Harvard Road. Among the large number of other officiating clergymen from the Russian, Greek, and Serbian churches was Abbot Luke (Golovkov) from the Trinity St Sergius Lavra, who had supervised the painting of all the icons. What Archbishop Mark referred to in his address as Harvard Road's "little flock" was augmented on this occasion not only by ecclesiastical and civil dignitaries, but by guests from Russia, many parishioners from the Patriarchal Cathedral at Ennismore Gardens, the Oxford parish of St Nicholas, and the two parishes of the Russian Church Abroad in Wallasey and Colchester. At the end of the Liturgy, the metropolitan blessed the magnificent new iconostasis and the new chandelier.

Afterwards guests were invited to lunch in a marquee set up on the church grounds. During the meal, the customary speeches of congratulation were exchanged, with the Metropolitan and Bishop Elisey showing special courtesy to the non-Russian guests by speaking in English. Archbishop Anatoly spoke of the spiritual significance of the blessing of an iconostasis. Father Nikolay Savchenko moved many of those present by mentioning the great struggle endured by the parishioners of earlier generations (whom he did not know personally, being a recent immigrant from the Russian Federation).

The solemnity of blessing the iconostasis was only one step on the way toward the full consecration of the Cathedral. At the time of writing in December 2011, work yet to be completed before the consecration takes place

The Cathedral at Harvard Road, showing where the belfry will be built above the west doors. (Source: Christopher Birchall)

includes adding the belfry over the porch in accordance with the original architectural design, as well as painting iconographic frescoes on the inside walls. Outside, the fence will be replaced by a low brick wall and ornamental metal railing and gates, which are expected to improve the Cathedral's appearance from the street and encourage people to explore the inner beauty of the new church and the worship that is conducted there.

When he arrived in England in 1713, Archimandrite Gennadius could not have known that the church he started would endure for another three hundred years, providing a spiritual haven for Russian refugees and other emigrants, as well as English people who have embraced Orthodoxy. Even as recently as 1988, the parish faced an uncertain future, and it would have been hard to imagine that twenty-three years later it would be preparing for the consecration of a newly built cathedral. The history of the parish continues to develop as part of the Church of Christ for the glory of God and for the salvation of mankind, thankful for the blessings bestowed on its home in the city of London.

APPENDIX 1

Guidance from Metropolitan Philaret of Moscow Regarding English Converts to Orthodoxy

Letter from Count Dimitry Tolstoy to E. I. Popov Enclosing the Memorandum from Metropolitan Philaret

Dear Sir, Evgeny Ivanovitch,
With this I am sending you a copy of some replies given by the Metropolitan of Moscow in response to enquiries made by certain members of the Anglican Church about being united with the Orthodox Church. I would most humbly ask you to carry out the Metropolitan's promise contained therein. I would ask you not to be offended by the Metropolitan's negative tone shown in the accompanying notes, which may seem evasive at times. I am convinced that when this work becomes more developed—and here your collaboration is essential—the Metropolitan will take a more sympathetic attitude to it. On my part I cannot agree with the opinion that a layman has no right to appeal to the Holy Synod on such subjects, for everyone can appeal to the highest Church authority for clarification of Church matters. There is no doubt that the note which you will compose will provide the groundwork for the further development of this work, and will speed it up considerably. Repeating my sincere gratitude for the interesting information you have sent, I have the honour to be, Your obedient servant,

Count Dimitry Tolstoy
July 7, 1867

Text of Memorandum from the Most Reverend Metropolitan of Moscow to the Chief Procurator of the Holy Synod (28 June 1867, No. 269)

With your Excellency's memorandum of 29 March of this year, No. 1678, there were forwarded to me seven ecclesiastical questions posed by a layman of the English church, and my opinion about them was requested. The questions concern the communion of the English Church with the Orthodox, but approach it in an uneven way. A layman is posing questions which cannot be answered by a layman, but only by a priest, or even a bishop. If, in posing his questions, a layman should say something disagreeable to his English Church or even to the Orthodox Church, this will be on his head alone; the English hierarchy will remain in peace and quiet. But if, in answering these questions, an Orthodox bishop should say something disagreeable to the English church, then this will be a stumbling stone on the path of peace between the churches, because the opinion of a bishop can be taken as the official opinion of the Church. It is easy for a layman to assume responsibility for questions relating to the Church; but it is not so easy for an Orthodox bishop to take responsibility for answering questions, among which there are some new ones, which have not yet been resolved by the Orthodox Church. This has made me pause. It would have been more appropriate for Father Archpriest Eugene to have composed his own replies in draft form and then, if he felt it necessary, to have sent them to Russia to seek further advice. He should also have provided us with information about the first prayer book of Edward VI mentioned in question 6. But when the Most Reverend Bishop Nektary informed me that your Excellency wished to remind me of your desire to receive an answer, I compelled myself to write the replies which are enclosed herewith. It would not be propitious at this time to make these replies public in printed form, nor is this what was intended. Therefore, if your Excellency should see fit to convey these replies to Father Archpriest Eugene, I would propose the following conditions for this:

1. The Father Archpriest will not reveal the name of the writer.
2. He should paraphrase or read to the person posing the questions whatever he finds necessary, or even all of the notes enclosed, and say: "This is how I or another priest could answer your questions." It would not be appropriate to require an official answer to them at the desire of a single layman. It would also not be appropriate to make publicly available in print someone's private opinion about questions which await examination and resolution by the Hierarchy.

Questions

Posed by a member of the English Church, a layman by his own admission, and views on these matters, provided to satisfy him as far as possible.

Question 1

If a layman, baptised and confirmed in the established Church of England, were to apply to you to be admitted into full communion with the Greek Church, would you be obliged to receive him, even if it might seem to you that it would be better for him to remain in the English Church?

Reply

To reply to this question, one first has to understand it. But the question posed here is not readily comprehensible (*ne-udobo-ponyaten*) and therefore it is necessary to pose the following question in return: Under what circumstances could a priest of the Orthodox Church, believing in its Apostolic dignity and purity, suppose that it would be better for a member of the English Church to remain in it rather than unite himself to the Orthodox Church? Until this second question is resolved, an Orthodox priest of the Catholic Eastern Church can assume that the question originally posed does not exist; and that consequently it does not require an answer.

Question 2

If such a layman were to be received, would it be necessary to give him baptism and confirmation, conditionally or unconditionally?

Reply

A member of the Anglican Church, who has definitely received a baptism in the name of the Father, and of the Son, and of the Holy Spirit, even though it be by effusion (pouring), can, in accordance with the rule accepted in the Church of Russia (which the Church of Constantinople considers to be a form of condescension), be received into the Orthodox Church without a new baptism, but the sacrament of chrismation must be administered to him, because confirmation, in the teaching of the Anglican Church, is not a sacrament.

Question 3

Let us suppose that an Anglican priest came to you in the same way. Would his ordination then be recognized, and would he then be permitted to serve as a priest after the Greek rite? If not, could he again receive ordination (reordination) in Russia or Constantinople? And after that, could he be given a mission in England?

Reply

The question as to whether an Anglican priest can be received into the Orthodox Church as an actual priest awaits the decision of a Church Council, because it has not yet been clarified whether the unbroken Apostolic Succession of hierarchical ordination exists in the Anglican Church, and also because the Anglican Church does not acknowledge ordination as a sacrament, although it recognizes the power of grace in it. But while this question remains unresolved, a priest of this church can be ordained as an Orthodox priest, if he is not lacking in the qualities required of a priest by the rules of the Church.

The question as to whether such a person could be given a mission in England is not capable of resolution when posed in such an indefinite way. For this it is necessary to have more definite circumstances in mind.

Question 4

Let us suppose that people should turn to you in such large numbers that neither your Russian church in Welbeck Street, nor the Greek church in London Wall were big enough for them all to attend services, and that in this event they built a church for themselves. Would one of your bishops then consecrate this church, would he permit Divine Services to be held in it, and would he appoint a priest specially for this church?

Reply

To this fourth question, as to the first one, one must reply with another question. Why is it possible to doubt that an Orthodox bishop would consecrate, or permit to be consecrated, a church built by Orthodox people, or newly converted Orthodox, who desired to have in it an Orthodox priest and Divine Services following the order of the Orthodox Church, and to unite themselves into a parish under its auspices?

Question 5

Could an Anglican layman, properly received into the Orthodox Church, be ordained priest, in Russia or in Constantinople, and if he could, under what conditions?

Reply

A layman from the Anglican Church, properly united to the Orthodox Church, can be ordained a priest, on condition that his character and intentions must be in accord with the requirements of the Apostolic Canons and the rules of the Church.

Question 6

Will it be required absolutely, as a *sine qua non*, to celebrate the Greek Liturgy in full? Could not certain parts from the English Liturgy also be permitted?

Could not a national Liturgy, following, for example, the first prayer book of Edward VI, be permitted for use by English congregations? Will the direct invocation (*directa invocatio*) of the saints be required, as a *sine qua non*, in conducting public worship?

Reply

Here, under a single number, we have not one question, but many, which are in part incapable of being resolved, due to their imprecise nature.

In the Orthodox Church the word "Liturgy" is understood to mean specifically that service at which the sacrament of the Eucharist is accomplished. It must be assumed that here also the questions about the Liturgy refer to it in this sense. And if it is established in the Church that the Liturgy is to be celebrated not by a layman, but by a special member of the Church, who has received a special consecration and grace for this, and who is even entrusted with offering certain prayers secretly, and not in the hearing of the lay people, then would it not be more proper, more appropriate, more in accordance with the subject, and more lawful for a priest to ask questions about the Liturgy, consider them and enter into agreements about them, than for a layman?

The Orthodox Church has received the order of the Divine Liturgy from the early Church and from the holy hierarchs of antiquity, and she preserves it without any change; she naturally has the right and obligation to require that those who are united to her from other confessions should also keep to this order of service.

Could certain limitations to this rule be permitted in relation to certain nonessential parts of the Liturgy? One can only answer this question given a precise indication of which parts are involved, and then the answer must be given by a Church Council, because a single bishop does not have the right to make changes in the Liturgy.

To the question as to whether the whole national Liturgy from the first prayer book of Edward VI can be permitted, the gentleman posing the question has already given his own answer, when he asked if certain parts of the Anglican Liturgy can be permitted. This latter question itself presupposes the very idea that it would be inappropriate to permit this Liturgy.

After reverently hearing the expressions "The Liturgy of St Basil the Great" and "The Liturgy of St John Chrysostom" it would be hard for an Orthodox ear to come to terms with expressions such as "The National Liturgy," "The Liturgy from the First Prayer Book of Edward VI."

Will direct invocation (*directa invocatio*) of the saints be required? Here, the expression *directa invocatio* is apparently used for precision, but the result is the contrary. It does not facilitate a precise understanding of the thoughts of the gentleman posing the question. *Directa invocatio*, direct invocation, presupposes that there is such a thing as *indirecta invocation*—an indirect, or oblique invocation of the saints. And since the gentleman posing the question wishes not to admit only direct invocation of the saints, then must we not conclude that he admits indirect invocation—calling, in some way, indirectly upon the saints?

Does he not perhaps think that it is acceptable to say in prayer "Have mercy upon us, Christ our God, through the prayers of the saints" but that it is unacceptable to say to the saints "Pray unto Christ our God for us"? But if the first is acceptable, why would the second be unacceptable?

The Orthodox Church looks with sorrow on those not belonging to her who reject the invocation of the saints, since they are depriving themselves of spiritual help which is of no small importance. But to receive such people into her communion would mean bringing contradiction into her midst, and opening a path for foreign opinions to weaken and change her ancient, true and salutary tradition. Would the gentleman posing the question say that such an action would be in accord with the requirements of the truth, prudence and reasonable care?

If we had seen how the Apostle Peter prayed and raised Tabitha from the dead, would we not be inspired, when feeling the need of spiritual help, to say to him "Pray also for us"? Why can we not also say this to him now, when he is at a higher level of closeness to God?

According to the Creed we believe in "One Church." Is it only the earthly Church in which we believe? According to the Apostle's teaching, faith relates to things not seen. Is it not therefore more characteristic of faith that it should relate to the One Church of Christians, both those struggling on earth and the perfected righteous ones in the heavens? In that case, what can hinder the communion of those on earth with those in heaven? We are commanded to love one another and pray for one another; where is it said to the saints in heaven "Do not love your brothers on earth and do not wish them good things from God" or, what is the same thing, "Do not pray for them"?

In the book of the Prophet Zechariah (1:12–13) it is written "Then the Angel of the Lord answered and said, O Lord of hosts, how long will you not have mercy on Jerusalem . . . ?" Here you see the angel is praying for Jerusalem. "And the Lord answered the angel who talked to me, with good and comforting." You see, the angel's prayer is accepted.

In the book of the Prophet Jeremiah (15:1) it is written, "Then the Lord said to me, 'Even if Moses and Samuel stood before Me, My mind would not be favorable toward this people.'" This was said in a specific instance, when the Jews had, through their iniquities, made themselves incapable of accepting mercy. Consequently, in different circumstances, the Lord would permit Moses and Samuel to stand before Him in prayer, and their prayer would be accepted unto mercy, just as He accepted and fulfilled their prayers during their earthly life.

Do not reprove the Orthodox Church for the fact that her prayerful love is widespread, and is not limited to the earth, but extends from the earth to heaven, and from heaven embraces the earth.

"The one mediator between God and man is Christ Jesus, who gave Himself as a deliverance for all." But the prayers both of earth and of heaven reach out to Him, and to His intercession before His Father.

Question 7

Let us suppose that the number of such congregations grew significantly; is it possible to hope that they would not be left without a missionary bishop?

Reply

When there is an abundant harvest, then we will pray to the Lord of the harvest that He would send His workers to His harvest, and He will arrange what is propitious for it. But it is premature to make arrangements for an abundant harvest, when the work of sowing the seed is still before us.

APPENDIX 2

Persons Mentioned Glorified as Saints

Chapter Where Mentioned	Name and Title in Earthly Life	Known as Saint	Date Glorified by Russian Orthodox Church Abroad (unless otherwise noted)
5	Metropolitan Philaret (Drozdov) of Moscow	Holy Hierarch Philaret, Metropolitan of Moscow	2001
4, 5, 6	Priest-monk Nicholas Kasatkin (later Archbishop of Japan)	Holy Hierarch Nicholas, Enlightener of Japan	1994
6	Grand Duke Nicholas Alexandrovitch, heir to the throne of Russia (later Emperor Nicholas II of Russia)	Holy Royal Martyr Nicholas	1981
6	Empress Alexandra of Russia	Holy Royal Martyr Alexandra	1981
6	Bishop Raphael (Hawaweeny) of the Orthodox Church of Antioch	Holy Hierarch Raphael of Brooklyn	2000 (Glorified by Orthodox Church in America)
5, 6	Metropolitan Innocent (Veniaminov) of Moscow	Holy Hierarch Innocent of Moscow	1994

6	Metropolitan Vladimir (Bogoyavlensky) of St Petersburg (later Metropolitan of Kiev)	Holy New Martyr Vladimir, Metropolitan of Kiev	1981
7	Bishop Nicholas (Velimirovic) of Ochrid	Holy Hierarch Nikolai, Bishop of Ochrid and Zicha	2003 (Glorified by the Serbian Orthodox Church)
7	Patriarch Tikhon of Moscow and all Russia	Holy Hierarch and Confessor Tikhon, Patriarch of Moscow	1981
10, 11	Bishop Ignatius (Brianchaninov)	Holy Hierarch Ignatius, Bishop of the Caucasus	2001
11	Archbishop Hilarion (Troitsky)	Holy Hierarch and New Martyr Hilarion	1981
11	Bishop Platon (Rudnieff)	Holy Hierarch and New Martyr Platon	1981
14, 15, 17	Archbishop John (Maximovitch) of Shanghai, later Archbishop of Brussels and Western Europe, later Archbishop of San Francisco and Western America	Holy Hierarch and Wonder Worker John of Shanghai and San Francisco	1994

APPENDIX 3

List of Bishops and Priests of the London Russian Orthodox Church

Bishops and priests who served the London Russian Orthodox Church are listed in order of their dates of service. Dates of birth and death are given in italics where known.

Archimandrite Gennadios, 1716–1737: First priest of the Græco-Russian Church *(d. 1737-2-3)*

Priest-monk Bartholomew (Cassanno), 1726–1746: Priest of the Græco-Russian Church *(1697–1746)*

Priest-monk John (Yastrembsky), 1737: Rector of the Embassy Church

Archpriest Antipa Martemianoff, 1747–1749: Rector of the Embassy Church

Priest Stephen Ivanovsky, 1749–1765: Rector of the Embassy Church *(d. 1765-2-13)*

Priest-monk Jeremias, 1765–1766: Priest of the Embassy Church

Priest-monk Gennadius, 1765–1766: Priest of the Embassy Church

Priest-monk Ephrem Diakovsky, 1766–1767: Rector of the Embassy Church

Archpriest Andrew Samborsky, 1769–1780: Rector of the Embassy Church *(1732-8-12 to 1815-10-17)*

Priest James Smirnove, 1780–1840: Rector of the Embassy Church *(1754 to 1840-4-28)*

Priest-monk Niphont, 1837–1842: Priest of the Embassy Church

Archpriest Eugene Popoff, 1842–1875: Rector of the Embassy Church *(1813–1875)*

Priest Basil Popoff, 1874–1877: Rector of the Embassy Church *(1836 to 1877-3-7)*

Archpriest Eugene Smirnoff, 1877–1923: Last rector of the Embassy Church; first rector of the parish *(1845 to 1923-1-4)*

Archpriest John Lelioukhin, 1919–1926: Rector of the parish *(b. 1883)*

Archpriest Constantine Veselovsky, 1921–1926: Priest of the parish *(1850–1926)*

Metropolitan Evlogy (Georgievsky) of Paris and Western Europe, 1921–1927: First diocesan bishop for Western Europe which included London and Great Britain *(1868-4-10 to 1946-4-8)*

Archpriest Vasily Timofeyeff, 1923–1926: Priest of the parish *(b. 1877)*

Metropolitan Seraphim (Lukianov) of Paris and Western Europe, 1926–1927: Archbishop in London (title: Archbishop of Finland); 1927–1929: rector of the London parish; 1932–1946: diocesan bishop for Western Europe (including London and Great Britain); retired 1949 *(1879-8-28 to 1959-2-18)*

Bishop Nicholas (Karpoff), 1928–1932: Rector of the parish; 1929–1932: Bishop of London *(1890 to 1932-10-11)*

Archpriest Simeon Solodovnikoff, 1932–1933: Priest in London *(1883-2-1 to 1939-3-20)*

Archpriest Boris Molchanoff, 1933–1938: Rector of the parish *(1896-7-24 to 1963-8-22)*

Archimandrite Nicholas (Gibbes), 1938–1941: Priest of the parish *(1876-1-19 to 1963-3-24)*

Archpriest Michael Polsky, 1938–1948: Rector of the parish *(1891-11-6 to 1960-5-12)*

Archimandrite Lazarus (Moore), 1948–1950: Priest of the parish *(1902-10-18 to 1992-11-27)*

Priest Nicholas Uspensky, 1946–1951: Priest of the parish *(d. 1980)*

Archimandrite Vitaly (Oustinow), 1948–1951: Rector of the parish; later Bishop of Montevideo; later Bishop of Edmonton and Western Canada; later Archbishop of Montreal and Canada; later Metropolitan of New York and Eastern America, and Primate of the Russian Orthodox Church Abroad *(1910-3-18 to 2006-9-25)*

Archbishop Nathaniel (Lvov) of Vienna and Austria, 1951: Rector of the parish; as Bishop of Preston and The Hague, diocesan bishop for Western Europe (including London and Great Britain); later Archbishop of Vienna and Austria *(1906 to 1986-11-10)*

Priest-monk George Moisseyevsky, 1949–1952: Priest of the parish

Archpriest George Cheremetieff, 1952–1961: Priest of the parish; retired 1961; 1967–1971: priest of the Convent of the Annunciation *(1887 to 1971-5-12)*

Archimandrite Ambrose (Pogodin), 1952–1964: Priest of the parish *(1925-7-10 to 2004-10-20)*

Archbishop Nikodem (Nagaieff) of Richmond and Great Britain, 1952–1976: Rector of the parish; from 1954, bishop; from 1964, bishop for the diocese in Great Britain; from 1968, archbishop *(1883-4-28 to 1976-10-17)*

Archpriest John Sawicz, 1953–1967: Priest of the parish; later priest of the Convent of the Annunciation *(d.1967)*

Saint John the Wonderworker of Shanghai and San Francisco, 1953–1962: Archbishop of Brussels and Western Europe (including London and Great Britain); later Archbishop of San Francisco and Western America; glorified in 1994 *(1896-6-4 to 1966-7-2)*

Archbishop Anthony (Bartochevitch) of Geneva and Western Europe, 1962–1964 and again 1976–1981: Diocesan bishop for London and Great Britain *(1910-11-30 to 1993-10-2)*

Archimandrite Nicanor (Troitsky), 1965–1996: Priest of the parish *(1905-4-14 to 1996-4-26)*

Priest Mark Meyrick, 1966–ca. 1971: Priest of the parish; later, after monastic tonsure, Archimandrite David *(1930-3-6 to 1993-12-8)*

Archimandrite Victor (Jankovich), 1968–1969: Priest of the parish *(1929-4-25 to 1987-1-24)*

Archpriest John Suscenko, 1972–1992: Priest of the parish *(b. 1949-6-5)*

Archimandrite Alexis (Pobjoy), 1977–1981: Rector of the parish *(b. 1946-9-26)*

Bishop Constantine (Jesensky) of Richmond and Great Britain, 1981–1986: Rector of the parish; diocesan bishop for London and Great Britain *(1907-5-30 to 1996-5-31)*

Archbishop Mark (Arndt) of Berlin, Germany, and Great Britain, 1986–: Rector of the parish; diocesan bishop for London and Great Britain *(b. 1941-1-29)*

Archpriest Vadim Zakrevsky, 1992–2007: Priest of the parish *(b. 1961-7-23)*

Archpriest Thomas Hardy, 1994–: Priest of the parish *(b. 1926-6-15)*

Archpriest Yaroslav Belikow, 2007–2008: Priest of the parish *(b. 1962-5-2)*

Archpriest Peter Baulk, 2007–: Priest of the parish *(b. 1949-4-13)*

Priest Nikolay Savchenko, 2008–2010: Priest of the parish *(b. 1972-11-1)*

Archpriest Vladimir Vilgerts, 2010–: Deputy rector of the parish *(b. 1959-11-4)*

APPENDIX 4

Ecclesiastical Ranks in the Orthodox Church

This table explains the various ecclesiastical ranks mentioned in the text. In the Orthodox Church, there are three major orders: bishop, priest, and deacon. Normally parish priests and deacons are married, while the bishops are chosen from clergymen who have taken monastic vows. The ranks within the hierarchy are given in descending order of seniority.

Order	**Monastic Clergy**	**Married Clergy**
Bishop	Patriarch Metropolitan Archbishop Bishop (In the Greek Orthodox Church, archbishop is senior to metropolitan.)	
Priest	Archimandrite Abbot (or *Igoumen*) Hieromonk (or Priest-monk)	Protopresbyter Archpriest Priest
Deacon	Archdeacon Hierodeacon	Protodeacon Deacon
Minor Orders	Subdeacon Reader	Subdeacon Reader

NOTES

Chapter 1

1. The oldest Russian church in western Europe was established in Stockholm, Sweden, in 1641. (http://www.sweden.orthodoxy.ru/old/Engelska/index.htm)

2. In addition to the annual reports, in 1916 Father Eugene wrote a special report to the Ministry of Foreign Affairs of the Russian Empire that provides much more extensive information about the church's history.

3. Some information in these archives is reflected in the work of Archpriest Alexei Maltseff, rector of the Russian Embassy church in Berlin, who wrote a book in the early years of the last century titled *Russian Churches and Other Institutions Abroad*.

4. This points to 1713 as the year of his arrival because he departed in 1716.

5. Steven Runciman, *The Great Church in Captivity: A Study of the Patriarchate of Constantinople from the Eve of the Turkish Conquest to the Greek War of Independence* (Cambridge: Cambridge University Press, 1968), 311.

6. Runciman, 311.

7. Runciman, 311.

8. Runciman, 312.

9. The church building's original location in Soho is within the city of Westminster, which is a distinct entity from the adjacent city of London.

10. This was not long after the "Popish Plot" of 1678 when anything even remotely reminiscent of Roman Catholicism was considered suspicious.

11. In a report written in 1916, Father Eugene Smirnoff indicated that Metropolitan Arsenius and the clergymen from Alexandria were forced to leave England because the Anglican church leadership objected to them receiving converts and supporting the Non-Jurors. In his account, James Senyavich, a member of the Russian diplomatic mission in London,

arranged for Archimandrite Gennadius and his nephew Bartholomew Cassanno to return to London and establish a house chapel where regular services would be held. Senyavich emphasized that in Russia Anglicans were allowed to have their own churches and he argued that the same rights should apply to the Orthodox in England. The nearby presence of Peter the Great in Holland at the time doubtless added weight to this argument.

12. That is, Greek Orthodox. In the eighteenth century Greeks still referred to themselves using the ancient Byzantine word *Romaikos* (here rendered by the translator as "Romaic"), which literally means Roman, based on the view that Byzantium was the New Rome. It has less chauvinistic connotations than the modern word *Ellenikos* (i.e., *Greek*), which was not used until the nineteenth century.

13. The London church's Russian connections date from 1716 although Metropolitan Arsenius had been conducting services in London since the time of his arrival in 1713. The third Russian Orthodox church to be established in western Europe was the Berlin Embassy chapel, started in 1718. This was of a less permanent nature than that of the church in London. It was considered to be the ambassador's private chapel; when he moved, the church was packed up and moved with him.

14. Runciman, 312.

Chapter 2

1. A decree issued in Constantinople in 1755, which was to be strictly applied by most Greek clergymen, later required that all those converting from other faiths receive an Orthodox baptism. In receiving converts by chrismation (anointing) alone, Archimandrite Gennadius, in the 1730s, was following an earlier practice that permitted this in certain circumstances.

2. This icon was preserved for years in the Cathedral at Emperor's Gate. Robbers stole the icon in the early 1970s together with other valuables. The parishioners felt the loss of this icon acutely; this event is even more tragic when one considers its historical background.

3. In fact, Ludwell had three daughters—Hannah, Frances, and Lucy—although two had died by the time Woronzow wrote his letter in 1791.

4. The close similarity in names between Philip Ludwell, from Virginia, and Philip Lodvill, Peter Paradise's father-in-law, has led to some confusion, especially because the names are virtually indistinguishable when transliterated into Russian. In fact, Dr Shepperson ascribes the translation of Peter Moghila's *Orthodox Confession* to Lodvill. The version of events

given here is the one that seems most probable; that is, that the translation was made by Ludwell, who converted to Orthodoxy, rather than Lodvill, who was an Anglican clergyman.

5. Theotokis was also known for his writings on physics and mathematics. He later became Archbishop of Kherson, a see in the south of Russia (now Ukraine) with an extensive Greek population.

6. The title is of interest because it uses the word "*aglinskogo*" for "English" instead of the contemporary "*angliski*," which became more common beginning in the nineteenth century.

Chapter 3

1. This spelling of Father James's surname has been retained because it is the spelling he used during his lifetime. The name in the original Russian spelling is the same as that of Father Eugene Smirnoff, who was rector of the Embassy church later in the nineteenth century. The two "Smirnoffs" were not related. Father James's family name was actually Linitsky. After being recruited to serve in London, during the journey from Kharkov to St Petersburg, he and his three colleagues were advised to change their surnames because of an alleged prejudice among certain Russian officials against Ukrainians.

2. In pre-decimal currency, the "s" stood for a shilling that was made up of 12 pence. The abbreviation "d" is for pence, so 3d is 3 pence.

3. A candidate for ordination in the Orthodox Church must have an Orthodox spouse.

4. In prerevolutionary Russia each parish maintained a list of people who had been to confession and received Holy Communion each year.

5. This is the contemporary spelling, as opposed to the modern "Guildford."

6. See Chapter 2, "The Ludwell and Paradise Families," pages 18–22.

7. It was at precisely this point in history that Lord North wrote his Ode to the Russian Empress Catherine the Great (see page 37), in which he appealed to her not to abandon the Greeks. Perhaps it is not coincidental that he presented a signed copy of it to Father James Smirnove, who had helped to foster the Russian political and military cause.

8. Gleb Struve, "John Paradise: Friend of Doctor Johnson, American Citizen and Russian 'Agent,'" *Virginia Magazine of History and Biography* 57:4 (October 1949), 355–75.

9. These marks of ecclesiastical distinction were probably awarded in recognition of his diplomatic endeavours as well as his priestly service. Father

James Smirnove is believed to be the first priest in the history of the Russian Church to be awarded the right to wear a pectoral cross. Later, the custom was extended to all priests serving outside Russia and then, during the reign of Nicholas II, to all priests of the Russian Church in general. The pectoral cross is now considered a distinguishing mark of a Russian Orthodox priest, as it is not worn by all priests of the other Orthodox Churches.

10. One of the four "quarter days" when the rates, or property taxes, fell due.

11. In his 1916 report, Father Eugene Smirnoff gave a different account. He indicated that the original lease on 32 Welbeck Street had been signed in 1786, which is when the church moved there from Clifford Street. He said it was subsequently renewed in 1822, 1857, and 1892 and that he had handled the renewal in 1892. He also said that the church received favourable terms because the lease was concluded directly with the Duke of Portland's Estate Office, rather than being a sublease. This does not appear consistent with Count Woronzow's letter, which was preserved in the church records. It is possible that Father Eugene misunderstood the records he saw at the time of renewing the lease in 1892.

12. According to the records of the cemetery company, his daughters Sophia (d. 1852), Elizabeth (d. 1869), and Catherine (d. 1872) were buried in the same grave. The plot is No. 2491/23, near the main gates.

Chapter 4

1. Peter the Great abolished the Patriarchate and replaced it with the Holy Governing Synod, which was composed of selected senior bishops and priests, but effectively headed by a lay official who reported to the emperor, known as the procurator of the Holy Synod. Officially he was simply the emperor's personal representative to the Synod; he sat at a separate table at meetings and had no vote. However, in practice, he virtually controlled the proceedings. This was contrary to the canonical order of the Church, which should be ruled by a council of bishops, without secular state interference, and headed by a senior bishop elected by the other bishops. Nevertheless, this form of church administration was considered valid in that the Eastern Patriarchs had given it their blessing and maintained communion with the Russian Church. It lasted until the Moscow Church Council of 1917/18, which restored the Patriarchate.

2. Priest-monk Nicholas Kasatkin was subsequently glorified as a saint in 1970.

3. See more on this in Chapter 5, "The Death of Father Eugene Popoff" (pages 143–147).

4. Also like Brunnow, Nesselrode was a Protestant, having been baptised as an Anglican. His daughter, Helen, however, became Orthodox and married a Russian nationalist, M. P. Khreptovich. In1857 and again in 1858, four years before her father's death, Helen is listed as having received confession and Holy Communion at the London Embassy Church: "Countess Elena Karlovna Khreptovich, née Nesselrode."

5. The confession list for 1857 includes the following entry: "Countess Anna Alexandrovna Aponi, née Countess Benkendorff."

6. The term favoured in the 1840s was *prichotnik* (cleric) in place of the earlier *psalomshchik* and *tserkovnik*. The duties, however, remained the same: reading and singing at the church services and general care of the church.

7. This is an error as England and France declared war at the end of March 1854.

8. The Aland Islands are now Finnish territory, situated between the coasts of Sweden and Finland.

9. Subsequent references to the prisoners' families are understandable in light of the fact that an entire garrison had been captured rather than soldiers from the front line.

10. In Russian this would be a play on words: *prazdnik* = holiday or church festival (and a day off) and *prazdniy* = idle.

11. From the copy of the report (written in French), which is preserved in the church archives, it is not clear to whom it was addressed. It is possible that, despite the closure of the embassy and the consulate, there were still some Russian government representatives in England to whom the British authorities had in this case complained. Alternatively, it was possibly written as a direct response to a representative of the British government.

12. This would have been for a memorial service to mark the first anniversary of the death of Nicholas I. He died on March 2, 1855, by the Western calendar; Father Popoff is giving old-style dates. In February and March 1856 the peace treaty was being negotiated in Paris, involving the presence of many high-ranking persons from Russia as well as the other belligerent countries.

13. The year of the consecration is given as 1865 in Father Popoff's notes in the church memorandum book and is consistent with the *Illustrated London News* article that appeared in April of that year. The annual

report for 1874, the last written by Father Eugene Popoff, noted that the rebuilding took place in 1863, 1864, and 1865. Later annual reports, however, give the year of consecration as 1866. It must be presumed that this is an error. Evidently finishing work and payment of bills continued into 1866, which is how the confusion arose.

14. Apparently this would only have been the lesser rite of consecration because a bishop normally performs a full consecration. Apart from the difficulty of bringing a bishop to London, it may have been thought inappropriate to use the full rite for a church built on land that was only leased.

15. The article is unsigned, but Father Popoff attributes its authorship to Thomson in his report of June 5/17, 1866, where he gives the Russian translation (probably his own work) for the first time.

16. Presumably these had been removed by the British from Orthodox churches in Bomarsund when the city was captured during the Crimean War (see Chapter 4 "The Crimean War Prisoners," pages 69–81).

Chapter 5

1. "If a man has once seen London," Khomiakov wrote in an article in a Moscow newspaper, "then, as far as living cities are concerned, there remains nothing for him to see except Moscow . . . . We wandered about London for two days on end: and everywhere we met with the same movement, the same swarming life in the streets. The third day after our arrival was Sunday, and accordingly we went in the morning to the service at our Embassy chapel. The streets were almost empty, only here and there a few people were hurrying along the pavement, late for church. About two hours afterwards we returned. There was still no traffic in the streets: one met with nothing but people on foot, on whose faces there was an expression of thoughtfulness: they were on their way back from church. A similar silence continued all day. This is the way Sunday is kept in London . . . . I could not help rejoicing over the high moral tone of national inclination, over this nobility of the human soul."

2. *General Introduction* is Part I of *A History of the Holy Eastern Church*. Part III *(Patriarchate of Antioch)* was published posthumously as a separate volume in 1873.

3. The Reverend George Williams was a close associate of Neale's. He finished the second part of the *History of the Holy Eastern Church,* on the Patriarchate of Antioch, from notes that Neale left at the time of his death. Williams was also responsible for unearthing and publishing the correspondence of the Non-Jurors (see Chapter 2).

4. This is a question that no Orthodox theologian will approach without trepidation, touching as it does on the relationship between the three Persons of the Holy Trinity. The traditional Orthodox teaching, enshrined in the Nicaean Creed, is that the Holy Spirit "proceeds from the Father." To this the Church of Rome added the words "and the Son" (in Latin, *Filioque*). Orthodox writers have explained how this one alteration of such an important article of faith has had repercussions on the entire theology, spirituality, and understanding of the Western Church. Other Orthodox simply shudder at the thought of altering the teaching on so sacred a matter, especially as additions to the creed were specifically forbidden by the Second Œcumenical Council. Theological debate in the nineteenth century fully recognized the importance of this question. Many Anglo-Catholics, such as Pusey, were not prepared to abandon the *Filioque* and saw this as a major stumbling block to reunion.

5. This was a case involving the Reverend George Cornelius Gorham, an Anglican clergyman with radical views and whose theology was considered suspect by his bishop, himself an Anglo-Catholic. Gorham appealed to the Privy Council against a decision of the Anglican ecclesiastical court and was confirmed by the Privy Council in his appointment to a parish near Exeter. The case was felt to have dealt a severe blow to the High Church party in that it confirmed the supremacy of the Crown in matters of faith and also gave legal status to the wide variety of belief within the Church of England. It was the first of a series of such cases in the nineteenth century.

6. Philaret Amphiteatroff, Metropolitan of Kiev.

7. The metropolitan's views on church matters have been preserved mostly in the form of summaries of opinions he expressed verbally in reported speech as recorded by a secretary. Several volumes of these "opinions" have been published. This extract is translated from a handwritten copy, preserved in the London church archives.

8. Arthur Stanley (1815–1881) was Dean of Westminster and an influential nineteenth-century clergyman of the Church of England. In the controversies as to whether the Church of England should be *High Church* (Anglo-Catholic) or *Low Church* (Protestant), Stanley adopted an intermediate position known as *Broad Church*, which maintained that the Church of England should have room for people of opposing views.

9. Father Wassilieff was instrumental in helping a learned French Roman Catholic priest, the Abbé Guettée, join the Orthodox Church in 1861. Together they published a journal about the Orthodox faith, *L'Union*

Chrétienne, that had a wide circulation for a number of years. Guettée is also known today for his books *The Papacy* and *The Dogmatical Teaching of the Orthodox Church.* In Orthodoxy Guettée took the name Vladimir. He became a priest of the Russian Orthodox Church and was attached to the Russian Embassy Church in Paris.

10. The complete text of Metropolitan Philaret's guidance on English converts to Orthodoxy can be found in Appendix 1.

11. In reading this correspondence, it seems strange for a respected archpriest with many years of service to the Church to be receiving directions from the procurator, who was, after all, a layman. Still, giving such directions in a spirit of zeal for Orthodoxy is an example of the Synodal system working at its best—in sharp contrast to the interference in church life by communist officials in the twentieth century, or even by anticlerical bureaucrats in the eighteenth century.

12. Basil Popoff, by now about twenty years old, who was then pursuing his theological studies in St Petersburg, and evidently acted as his father's messenger.

13. According to Metropolitan Kallistos (Ware), Hatherly was received at the Greek Church in London through baptism. This appears to be correct because there is no record of his reception in the records of the Russian Church, although he is mentioned in the 1856 confession list. According to Overbeck, Hatherly later protested about another convert, Athanasius Richardson, being received into the Orthodox Church in Nice by Father Wassilieff by chrismation alone. This implies that Hatherly must have been received by baptism. In the mid-nineteenth century, this was the practice of the Greek Church but not of the Russian Church.

14. That is, ordained to the minor order of reader.

15. Metropolitan Innocent (Veniaminoff) was glorified as a saint by the Moscow Patriarchate in 1977 and by the Russian Orthodox Church Outside Russia in 1994.

16. Ali Pasha is reported to have said, "Let the Patriarch make all the Englishmen priests if he likes."

17. In July 1871, *The Guardian* published some correspondence accusing Hatherly of attempting to create a schism in the church in Wolverhampton. Hatherly brought a legal action for libel against the publishers of the newspaper at the Stafford Assizes (a law court). The jury gave a verdict in Hatherly's favour. Damages awarded were 40 shillings plus costs.

Summarized from Joseph Irving, *Supplement to the Annals of our Time from February 28, 1871 to March 19, 1874* (Macmillan and Co., 1875), 33.

18. A Latin expression meaning essential condition.

Chapter 6

1. See "Contact with Anglicans" section of this chapter.
2. http://www.holy-trinity.org/history/1895/12.01.call.html
3. The first hymn in the book, from Vespers of Tone 1, begins, "Accept our vespertine prayers, O Holy Lord, and grant us the remission of sins, for Thou alone hast made manifest to the world the resurrection." It seems Orloff was unconcerned that the word *vespertine* does not appear in any dictionary of the English language, having been invented by him to fit the Slavonic and Greek. Most of the text is fairly comprehensible, although rather heavy. However, there are some bizarre passages. Take, for example, the following Theotokion of the 6th Ode of the Sunday Canon for tone 7: "Of thine ineffable, all-spotless for our sake bringing forth the manner—who of men, O Virgin-God's Bride, is able to explain?" The translator is overlooking the fact that because English is not an inflected language, it is essential to adhere to the standard word order so as to convey the sense. Orloff's *Horologion* and *Octoechos* have since been superseded by more easily comprehensible translations, but his *General Menaion* remains in use to this day by English-speaking Orthodox who regard it with a mixture of reverence and frustration. The *General Menaion* is not one of the ancient Orthodox liturgical books but was compiled relatively recently and provides "common" services for different types of saints, which can be used when the complete twelve-volume Menaion is not available.
4. It was at this point that the word *jingoism* was born in a music hall song:
We don't want to fight, but by jingo if we do
We've got the ships, we've got the men, we've got the money too.
We've fought the Bear before, and, while we're Britons true,
The Russian shall not have Constantinople.

5. Emperor Nicholas II is reported to have observed that all he had to do to paralyse British policy was to send a telegram mobilizing his forces in Russian Turkestan.

6. In the autumn of 1904, Russian naval vessels, on their way from the Baltic to fight the Japanese in the disastrous battle of Tsushima, mistakenly opened fire on the British fishing fleet on the Dogger Bank in the North

Sea. It is thanks to Count Benkendorff's efforts that a crisis in Anglo-Russian relations was averted over this incident.

7. For more about Count Simeon Woronzow, see Chapter 3 sections on "The Russian Church Community in London" and "Woronzow, Paradise, Father Smirnove, and the Crisis of 1791." The Herberts were the family of the Earl of Pembroke who married Woronzow's daughter. One searches in vain through these memoirs for any indication of Benkendorff's devotion to the Orthodox Church. An account of life on the family estate in Russia mentioned that the summer was divided in two by the feast of Saints Peter and Paul. However, this was not due to the spiritual rhythm of fast and feast, rather the shooting season began after the saints' day. Generally, the few comments about the Church made by Benkendorff's son are more like those of an admiring outsider than a member of the Church.

8. Eugenie Fraser, *The House by Dvina: A Russian Childhood* (London: Mainstream Publishing Co., 1989), 37.

9. Fraser, 44–45.

10. Possibly this is when the iconostasis described in the previous chapter was installed.

11. The Very Reverend Eugene Smirnoff, *A Short Account of the Historical Development and Present Position of Russian Orthodox Missions* (London: Rivingtons, 1903), vii–viii.

12. Smirnoff, ix.

13. Smirnoff, x.

14. Born in Volhynia (western part of Imperial Russia) in 1876, Father Leonid immigrated to America as a missionary and was appointed rector of the seminary in Minneapolis by Bishop Tikhon, the future patriarch and saint. He later received the monastic name of Leonty and was elected metropolitan of the Russian-American Metropolia (1950–1965).

15. The letter is written in Russian. Bishop Raphael studied theology at the Kiev Theological Academy and later taught at the Kazan Theological Academy in Russia.

16. He also published a very interesting article that was the result of his study of the Church Slavonic language and his contacts with Russian believers. He showed that the ecclesiastical language, although superficially very different from modern Russian, is readily understood in the main, even by simple people, because the vocabulary is derived from the same familiar Slavic roots as the ordinary spoken language. (The same cannot always be said for the English language, which in its literary and

ecclesiastical forms uses words derived from Latin roots, which are quite different from the colloquial Anglo-Saxon usages.)

17. In this meeting, they discussed the spiritual situation of the working-class poor in Russia and Britain. Birkbeck was particularly struck by the crowd of hotel staff who mobbed Father John of Kronstadt on both arrival and departure.

18. "This refers to the Contakion of the Departed, 'Give rest, O Christ, to Thy servant with Thy Saints' (*English Hymnal*, No. 744) brought back by Birkbeck from Russia with the Kieff melody, and translated by him. It was first sung in England by command of Queen Victoria at St George's Chapel, Windsor, on the occasion mentioned above." [Footnote in original article in *The Guardian*]

19. This is more commonly rendered in contemporary English use as "God grant you many years."

20. These prisoners would most likely have been subjects of the Austro-Hungarian Empire from the areas now known as Bukovina and Carpatho-Russia.

21. The original text had the word "Galician" ("Galichan") crossed out and replaced with "Ruthenian."

22. An antimension is a covering for the altar table that contains relics.

23. This is the famous Monastery of the Holy Trinity and St Sergius near Moscow.

Chapter 7

1. In *The Brothers Karamazov* (part I, book III, chapter 3), Dostoyevsky's character Dmitry Karamazov makes the statement, "God and the devil are waging war and the battlefield is the heart of man." This has been seen as Dostoyevsky's commentary on individual human behaviour and also on wider social issues including the destabilization of Russian society that was already evident in his lifetime.

2. Of those who joined the French Army, about 4,000 Russian war dead are buried in a cemetery near Rheims.

3. Grace and favour residences are crown property allocated to deserving individuals as a residence. Hampton Court Palace was subdivided into numerous "grace and favour" apartments after it ceased being used as a royal residence in the eighteenth century.

4. Bishop Nicholas of Ochrid was canonized by the Serbian Orthodox Church in 2003 and is now commonly referred to as St Nicholas of Žiča.

5. Some of the territories then referred to as southern Russia are now part of Ukraine.

6. Richard Luckett, *The White Generals* (Taylor & Francis, 1989), 351–353.

7. *Batioushka* means literally "the little father," a term of endearment and respect for a priest.

8. Athelstan Riley was not, in fact, a member of Parliament, but an influential Anglo-Catholic layman who took the interests of the Russian refugees to heart. He was also the biographer of William Birkbeck (see Chapter 6, "Contact with Anglicans").

9. An Established Church is one established by law (i.e., a state church).

10. Share capital is the English equivalent of capital stock in the United States. A company with share capital is one in which the holder of the shares is entitled to a proportion of the company's assets in the event of its winding up. When a company is wound up, it ceases to exist as a legal entity and any assets are distributed to its members in proportion to their share capital.

11. When the Empress Marie was pregnant, she had a vivid dream, or vision, of Blessed Xenia of St Petersburg. As a result, her daughter was named Xenia, with her patron saint being St Xenia the Roman, a monastic saint who had also been the patron saint of the Blessed Xenia.

Chapter 8

1. This amount equals approximately $450 today.

2. For example, at Matins the readings from the Psalter (*kathismata*) and the verses that follow them (*sedalia*) are omitted. "God is Lord" and the troparia are followed immediately by "Praise ye the name of the Lord."

3. Anatoly Vassilisin, who was a member of the London parish until his death in the 1980s, recalled taking part in this service as an altar boy. According to him, it took six and a half hours.

4. See Chapter 7, "The Arrival of Father John Lelioukhin."

5. The Russian Imperial capital St Petersburg was renamed Petrograd in 1914 before being changed to Leningrad by the Soviets in 1924. In 1991, it reverted to its original name of St Petersburg.

6. The Genoa Conference was held in April and May 1922 in an attempt to organize the economic reconstruction of Europe after World War I. This included the controversial issue of trading with the Bolshevik regime in Russia.

7. This may have been Bishop (later Archbishop) Germogen Maximoff, who was living in retirement in the Hopovo convent in Croatia. During World War II he became involved in the formation of an independent Croatian Church. He was shot by the Red Army when it entered Croatia in 1945.

8. It seems likely that Father Vladimir Poliakoff lived in former territory of the Russian Empire that was later annexed by Romania. Because he was not Romanian, either by residence or nationality, the Romanian government would not have wanted him to have the Romanian passport they had issued.

Chapter 9

1. Nashdom Abbey was in Burnham, Buckinghamshire, near Taplow. The house and surrounding formal garden were built between 1905 and 1909 by Sir Edwin Lutyens for Prince Alexis Dolgorouki and his wife. They named it "Nash Dom," which in Russian means "Our House." In 1929 it was purchased by an order of Anglican Benedictine monks, who modified its original name, calling it Nashdom Abbey. The monastery was sold in the 1990s, and was restored and converted into luxury apartments.

2. An *epitemia* is similar to a penance.

3. The official list of parishes and clergy in the Diocese of Western Europe under Archbishop Seraphim in 1929 contains the following entry: "England. London, Chessington and house of Prince V. E. Galitzine—Bishop Nicholas and Priest-monk Vladimir."

4. It seems probable that this was just a down payment, and part of the purchase price was borrowed.

5. Possibly the steep staircases and rooms perched on different levels over the four storeys added to that impression.

Chapter 10

1. Dr Martin Collett, OSB

2. See Chapter 7, "The Evacuation of Southern Russia and the Beginning of the Church Abroad."

3. The Russian couple was Princess Irina Galitzine, the author of this account, and her husband, Prince Nicholas Galitzine.

4. St Sabbas (or Savva) the Sanctified was the founder abbot of a desert monastery in Palestine in the sixth century. He is known as "Sanctified" (*Osviashchenniy*) because he was ordained to the priesthood, which was very rare for monks at that time.

5. A photograph of this icon, held by Bishop Nikodem, appears in Chapter 15, page 450.

Chapter 11

1. Foka Feodorovich Volkovsky was the psalm-reader sent from Russia to serve at the Embassy church in 1897 and remained at that post almost until his death in 1951.

2. The Living Church was the Soviet government's first crude attempt to engineer a Church schism. A highly modernized form of Orthodoxy, which set up a Church organization in opposition to the patriarch, it had virtually no popular support and was soon abandoned by the government, after which the Living Church collapsed.

3. GPU in Russian stands for State Political Directorate. This secret police organization was a predecessor to the more widely known KGB.

4. Metropolitan Sergius (Stragorodsky) was the acting locum tenens of the Patriarchal Throne of the Russian Orthodox Church when, on July 29, 1927, he issued his declaration stating that the Church would be absolutely loyal to the Soviet regime whose interests it shared.

5. "Kulak" refers to relatively prosperous farmers who opposed the Soviets' attempt to forcibly collectivize agriculture during the 1920s.

6. In 1938, £6,000 would have been equivalent to about £255,000 ($400,000) in 2013.

7. Here Father Michael is alluding to the dialectical approach of some philosophers that was adapted and modified by Karl Marx into dialectical materialism. It is interesting that he attempted to draw out the elements of truth that are contained in this teaching—seeking a true "synthesis" rather than simply resorting to outright condemnation.

8. Brawn (*kholodetz*) is a type of meat jelly.

9. At the time of this statement, the youngest daughter of the Ampenoff family was abbess of the convent at Ein Karim near Jerusalem.

10. *Stanitsa* is a Cossack village.

11. Batioushka means literally "the little father," a term of endearment and respect for a priest.

Chapter 12

1. Lienz in Austria was the site of a camp in which the Cossack units were first interred by the British and then forcibly repatriated to the Soviet Union.

2. SMERSH was the umbrella name for three independent counterintelligence agencies in the Red Army.

3. See Chapter 10, "Visit of Archbishop Nestor and Arrival of Father Nicholas Gibbes."

4. The SA was the Sturmabteilung, the original paramilitary wing of the Nazi Party more widely known as the Brownshirts.

5. Metropolitan Evlogy's last years are described by Tatiana Manukhina in an appendix to his memoirs.

6. The fate of people from France who accepted the Soviet invitation to return to Russia is depicted in Régis Warnier's film *East/West* (1999).

7. After serving the interests of Soviet diplomacy for years through prominence in the "peace" movement, Metropolitan Nikolai was deposed by the Moscow Synod in 1959 after protesting the renewed persecutions at that time. He died under mysterious circumstances in 1961.

Chapter 13

1. Before the Revolution, Archbishop Vitaly (Maximenko) had been archimandrite of the Pochaev Lavra and in 1934 he was consecrated bishop for the Russian Church Abroad in North America; not to be confused with Archimandrite (later Bishop) Vitaly Oustinow.

2. He always spelled his surname "Oustinow." This was the same name as the famous film actor and director, Peter Ustinov, who is thought to have been a distant relative.

3. It is not clear when Father Michael was awarded the right to wear a mitre. It may have been during Bishop Nathaniel's visit. Possibly the secretary described him this way specifically to emphasize that he was the senior priest in the parish.

4. During the 1920s an autocephalous Orthodox Church was formed in Poland due to pressure from the Polish government, but virtually all the faithful were Russians living in what had become Polish territory. After communists seized power in Poland, many of these people became "displaced persons"—hence the formation of an exile Polish Orthodox Church, which was known as the "Orthodox Church from Poland."

5. Many of the new immigrants were from Byelorussia, a territory that adjoined Poland, all of which had been under German occupation. The intent was to help them retain a sense of national identity while at the same time preserving the unity of the Church. During the German occupation, a number of bishops were consecrated for the Byelorussian Church, which

had a brief autonomous existence. Many of these bishops found themselves in Germany at the end of the war and joined the Russian Church Abroad. Such, for example, were Archbishops Athanassy of Argentina and Philothei of Germany.

6. Nadine, or Nadezhda, Nicolaevna Legat was the widow of Nicholas Legat, who had a dancing school at 46 Colet Gardens, very close to St Dunstan's Road in London. Nicholas had been ballet master of the Imperial Ballet at the Maryinsky Theatre in St Petersburg. After he died in 1937, his wife Nadine moved to Tunbridge Wells where she continued the work of dance instruction. Both Nicholas and Nadine are buried in Tunbridge Wells Cemetery.

7. Pushkin is considered to be the founder of modern Russian literary language and culture.

8. *Church Life*, the official publication of the Russian Church Abroad, no. 7–8 (1950).

9. He was referring, for example, to Metropolitan Anastassy, who had been a bishop in Russia before the Revolution.

10. Mantle (*milot*)—cf. Elisha receiving Elijah's mantle as a token of taking over his ministry (1 Kgs 19:19).

Chapter 14

1. For more on Archbishop John, see the following sections "Arrival of the Nuns from Palestine" and "Archbishop John (Maximovitch) in England."

2. The reference here is to Archbishop John's time in Shanghai.

3. Archimandrite Nikodem is alluding to the teaching of Metropolitan Anastassy.

4. At the Monastery of St Job of Pochaev, Archimandrite Nikodem also taught the other monks about the Church typicon. He was raised to the rank of Hegumen in 1948.

5. This is in Ozoir-la-Ferrière. See Chapter 7, "Formation of the Parish in London."

6. The parish in Manchester was in the process of acquiring a church house, which was blessed in 1953.

7. In Brazil he received the monastic tonsure with the name Gregory. He later moved to Canada with Bishop Vitaly's brotherhood and subsequently became rector of the church in Edmonton, Alberta.

8. See "Arrival of the Nuns from Palestine" section later in this chapter as well as "Establishment of the Convent of the Annunciation at Willesden" in Chapter 15.

9. See Chapter 7, "The Beginning of Parish Life" and "The Parish and the Church Hierarchy."

10. St Philip's Church was used on alternate weeks by the Russian Church Abroad and the Moscow Patriarchate. Metropolitan Kallistos (Timothy Ware) provided the following clarification as to who was officiating when he made his first visit and later visits: "You say that it is difficult to know whether the service that [you] originally attended at St Philip's Buckingham Palace Road, was celebrated by the Synodal [Russian Church Abroad] or by the Patriarchal jurisdiction. In fact, it was certainly celebrated by the Synodal clergy. There were two priests, with long beards, as well as a deacon. 'I went back the following Saturday, and the service was celebrated by a single priest without a beard': this was Father (later Metropolitan) Antony Bloom. 'Then I returned for a third time on the following Saturday, and the service was celebrated by the two bearded priests with the deacon.' From this it is clear that at the first service the officiating clergy belonged to the Synodal jurisdiction."

11. Mother Maria (Robinson) was later appointed abbess of the convent in Gethsemane and died in 1970.

12. Archimandrite Anthony (Sinkevitch) was later appointed Archbishop of Los Angeles.

13. See Chapter 15, "Establishment of the Convent of the Annunciation in Willesden."

14. In 1994, Archbishop John was glorified as a saint by the Russian Church Abroad at a service held in San Francisco and attended by people from all over the world, many of whom had known him during his lifetime.

15. The Kazan Icon had disappeared from Kazan in Russia just before World War I and was later believed to have been taken to Germany. In the 1950s it became known that the icon was in England, but when enquiries were made by the Russian Church, it appeared that it could not be purchased for less than £25,000. Some questionned its authenticity; working from photographs, some experts said it could be an old and much-revered copy of the original. In any event, the "Black Virgin of Kazan," as it was known in the British press, with its silver and gold cover and surround of semiprecious stones, was an item of great antiquarian value. Besides Archbishop John, other clergy and laypeople travelled to Farley to pray before the icon. Most felt convinced it was the original. It was also taken to the Grand Duchess Xenia in Hampton Court. It has since been returned to Russia.

16. According to the typicon, Matins should be served in the morning before the Divine Liturgy, especially on weekdays when no Vigil is appointed. This can make the morning service extremely long (as, for example, on Mt Athos, where it starts in the small hours of the morning). The Convent of the Annunciation follows the practice of the Russian convents in the Holy Land, where Matins is combined with Vespers on the previous evening. Being a liturgical "purist," Vladyka John did not really approve of this arrangement.

17. This icon of the Mother of God is based on the prophetic vision seen by Moses of the bush that burned but "was not consumed" (Exod 3:2).

18. The first part of Archimandrite Nikodem's address is recounted earlier in the second section of this chapter.

19. In Greek *episcopos*, the same word as "bishop."

20. Dogmatic Hymn, Tone 4.

21. See note 20 for Chapter 13.

22. *Ura*: Hurrah—"exclamation expressing exultation or approbation" (*Oxford Russian-English Dictionary*).

23. See Chapter 12, "Soviet Interference in the Life of Russian Churches Outside Russia," regarding Metropolitan Nikolai.

24. On November 17, 1954, the parish of the Russian Church Abroad established a trust named The Russian Orthodox Church in Exile. Its trustees were Wladimir Kleinmichel, Rufina Ampenoff, Alexei Ananin, Ivan Georgievsky, and Anatole Vassilisin. The trustees of the Patriarchal Parish were Michael Zvegintzov, Alexander Pickersgill, Anna Helena Ertel Garrett, and Laurence Parker Brunt.

25. The books may still be consulted there, although application for a reader's ticket is necessary.

Chapter 15

1. "Postal" fund-raising is the British equivalent of "direct mail."

2. The City of London is the financial district of the capital.

3. See more on Gerald Palmer later in this chapter.

4. Usage of the term *ambó*, or *soleas*, has changed over time and place; in this context, it refers to the raised area in front of the iconostatis and any steps leading up to it.

5. See Chapter 7, "The Revolution and Civil War."

6. Since the church building at Emperor's Gate did not belong to the parish but was held on a lease, this was the lesser rite of blessing of a church building rather than a full consecration. It was a cathedral because the local

bishop (Bishop Nikodem) had his *kathedra* located within that church. *Kathedra* refers to the bishop's seat of authority and is a symbol of his primary responsibility of teaching.

7. See Chapter 10, "Miraculously Renewed Icons of St Savva and St Nicholas."

8. Съборъ, or Sobor, is a Slavonic word that can be translated as "council." It is sometimes used in the sense of a church big enough to hold a council in, which is the meaning intended here. It is interchangeable with cathedral.

9. Under Father Victor, the parish was known as St Andrew's Russian-Serbian Orthodox Church. Father Victor remained there until his death in 1987 and appears to have been well loved by his parishioners.

10. The Troparion of the Kursk icon of the Sign. The full text is "As an invincible rampart and source of miracles, we Thy servants have found Thee, O Mother of God, Most Pure, we put down the assaults of our enemies. Wherefore we pray Thee, grant peace to our fatherland and to our souls great mercy."

11. See Chapter 14, "Archbishop John (Maximovitch) in England."

12. The early ecumenical activities of the Moscow Patriarchate were closely connected with the so-called peace movement, which was an instrument of Soviet foreign policy.

13. The reference is presumably to the war in Vietnam, communist intervention in Africa, and similar activities.

14. As warden of a house for Orthodox boys within a Roman Catholic boarding school run by the monks of the Abbey.

15. The interest of the Russian Church in India was not new, nor was it due entirely to the initiative of Father Lazarus. For example, see Chapter 7, "The Formation of the Parish in London," regarding Father Eugene Smirnoff's encounter with a representative of the ancient Syro-Chaldean (Jacobite) Church who hoped for reunification with Orthodoxy. During the 1930s, Bishop Nathaniel spent time in India as a missionary priest. Father Lazarus had spent time in India and had contact with Russian clergy there before his conversion to Orthodoxy.

16. See the section on Gerald Palmer later in this chapter.

17. A short prayer traditionally sung in Greek in the Russian church, which means approximately "Preserve, O Lord, our Master and Hierarch. Many years to you, Master!"

18. Archbishop Nikon is the author of the biography of Metropolitan Anthony which has been referenced in earlier chapters.

19. Bishop Mikhail Gribanovsky was a highly respected and gifted theologian in the pre-Revolution Church in Russia. Archbishop Nikon

wrote about him in the first volume of his 17-volume biography of Metropolitan Anthony (Khrapovitsky).

20. This would be the Monastery of the Holy Trinity and St Sergius near Moscow. The nearby village was renamed Zagorsk in Soviet times, but its original name of Sergiev Posad was restored in 1991.

21. Metropolitan Anastassy, the primate of the Russian Church Abroad, had been consecrated in 1906 as Bishop of Serpukhov, a vicar of the Moscow diocese and assistant to the Metropolitan of Moscow. He evidently remembered the von Meck family from his time in Moscow.

22. Since the 1960s, this trend has been reversed dramatically.

23. *Writings from the Philokalia on Prayer of the Heart*, trans. E. Kadloubovsky and G. E. H. Palmer (London: Faber & Faber, 1951), 3.

24. Bishop Kallistos (Ware), *The Inner Unity of the Philokalia and Its Influence on East and West* (Athens: Alexander S. Onassis Public Benefit Foundation, 2004). Available at www.myriobiblos.gr/texts/english/wear_innerunity3.html.

25. Leonid Ouspensky and Vladimir Lossky, *The Meaning of Icons*, trans. E. Kadloubovsky and G. E. H. Palmer (Bern: URS Graf Verlag, 1952).

26. Igumen Chariton of Valamo, *The Art of Prayer: An Orthodox Anthology*, trans. E. Kadloubovsky and E. M. Palmer (London: Faber & Faber, 1966).

27. *The Early Fathers from the Philokalia: Together with Some Writings of St. Abba Dorotheus, St. Isaac of Syria and St. Gregory Palamas*, trans. E. Kadloubovsky and G. E. H. Palmer (London: Faber & Faber, 1954), 15.

28. Philip Sherrard (1922–1995) had many talents. He first visited Greece as a soldier in 1946, decided to stay, and married a Greek women. In 1956 he was baptized into the Orthodox Church. He pursued an academic career in both England and Greece, and was well known for his translations of Greek contemporary poetry including works by George Seferis. Like Gerald Palmer, he visited Mt Athos and knew Father Nikon, the hermit of Karoulia. He was buried beside the Orthodox chapel that he built on his property on the Greek island of Evia (Euboeia).

29. Ware, *The Inner Unity of the Philokalia*.

30. Mother Flaviana had painted the Great Feast icons for Emperor's Gate and the icon of All Saints for the Podvoria.

31. In the original: Не говори, что нет спасенья, Что ты в печалях изнемог: Чем ночь темней, тем ярче звезды, Чем глубже скорбь, тем ближе Бог.

32. King Charles I was executed in 1649 just a few yards from where the Cenotaph stands today.

33. A *panagia* is a small icon of the Mother of God worn by Orthodox bishops on a chain. Usually they are round or oval, but Archbishop Nikodem's was an unusual triangular shape.

Chapter 16

1. Derived from the Russian for *self-published*, *samizdat* refers to literature censored by the Communist regime but illicitly published and distributed.

2. In 1987, Bishop Constantine moved first to the Kursk Hermitage in Mahopac, New York, and later to a monastery in Texas, where he died on May 31, 1996.

3. Then still a deacon, Bishop Paul lived briefly in London after World War II; see Chapter 13.

4. As used here, abbot is a translation of *hegumen*, a monastic title ranking below archimandrite. Father Flor was not the abbot in charge of Holy Trinity Monastery.

5. During her imprisonment, the London Cathedral choir and clergy held a moleben on the street in front of the Soviet Embassy to intercede for Irina's safety (see photo page 536).

6. This miraculous icon was treasured in the Russian Church Abroad until 1997, when its owner, Jose Muñoz, was murdered during a visit to Greece. At the same time, the icon was stolen and has disappeared without a trace. Jose Muñoz is buried at Holy Trinity Monastery, Jordanville, New York.

Chapter 17

1. The case involved Count Nikolai Tolstoy's allegations regarding Lord Aldington's responsibility for sending Cossacks and others to their death by forced repatriation to the Soviet Union at the end of World War II. Father Michael had inherited documents from his father, who was a Cossack present at the scene, and so was called to give evidence at the trial. Lord Aldington was awarded substantial damages of £1.5 million, leading the count to declare bankruptcy. Later the European Court of Human Rights ruled that the size of the libel damages amounted to a breach of Count Tolstoy's right to freedom of expression.

2. See Chapter 14, page 419 and the following section "Archbishop John (Maximovitch) in England."

3. Note how many of the experiences of church building mentioned in Father Michael Protopopov's sermon in November 1989 were being repeated here (see first section of this chapter).

4. Among the émigré dissidents who had longed for the overthrow of the Communist regime was the Miller family, mentioned earlier in Chapter 16. They were caught up in these changes when Boris Miller and his son, George, went to Moscow in the early 1990s. George's obituary in *The Guardian* described this part of their story: "Once President Boris Yeltsin broke with communism, George was able to finally step on to Russian soil. By then a member of the executive council of the National Alliance of Russian Solidarists (NTS), he argued for it to join the new government, but his father disagreed, and carried the day by one vote, creating a life-lasting breach. George went to work in the economics ministry, under Anatoly Chubais, the privatization minister. As the reform agenda was discarded, George felt his influence failing. Married with a son and a daughter, he opted for consultancy work, advising western companies on doing business in the new Russia. Back in London, he found a new cause: to support the development of new environmental technologies. . . . But as his health weakened, more ambitious plans were not implemented."

5. The formal name of the ROCOR Commission was Commission of the Russian Orthodox Church Outside Russia on Discussions with the Moscow Patriarchate.

6. See Chapter 12, page 335.

7. Not all of Pavel Lisitsin's philanthropic attempts were as successful. On December 3, 2006, the arts section of the *Daily Telegraph* reported that the British Museum had a large collection of icons that were languishing unseen in a basement. Neil MacGregor, the museum's director, had received a five-page letter from HRH Prince Charles, Prince of Wales, supporting a project suggested by Richard Temple, the founder of the Temple Gallery in Holland Park, for the museum to create a small space—"almost like a chapel of contemplation"—to display this icon collection. Pavel Lisitsin offered to donate the money for such a room. However, MacGregor was not persuaded of the importance of the icons, some of which date from Byzantine times, and turned down the project.

8. Father Avraamy, known as Andrew Neyman before his monastic tonsure, is an English convert to Orthodoxy of Polish origin. He had been a lay member of the parish for many years before joining the monastery of St Job in Munich in the mid-1990s. Later he moved to an Orthodox monastery in Poland. In 2006 he was visiting England for medical treatment and subsequently became an assistant priest at the Greek Orthodox parish in Edinburgh, Scotland.

SOURCES

Chapter 1

The Archives

1. National Archives, Archives of the Russian Orthodox Church in London, RG 8/111, Orthodox Graeco-Russian Church: Memorandum Book, 1721–1870.

The National Archives are located in Kew at Bessant Drive, Richmond, London TW9 4DU; tel. 020 8876 3444; nationalarchives.gov.uk. The RG series of files contains records of the General Register Office. RG 8 contains "Registers of Births, Marriages and Deaths surrendered to the Non Parochial Registers Commission of 1857, and other registers and church records." Within this series are numerous files described as "Archives of the Russian Orthodox Church in London," covering the period from 1713 to 1926.

2. National Archives, RG 8/166, Annual Reports: including Births, Marriages and Deaths etc., 1876–1885.

3. National Archives, RG 8/169, Annual Reports: including Births, Marriages and Deaths etc., 1906–1910.

4. Athelstan Riley, ed., *Birkbeck and the Russian Church* (London: SPCK, 1917), 159.

5. Alexei P. Maltseff (Archpriest), *Pravoslavnye Tserkvi i russkie uchrezhdeniya zagranitsei* [Orthodox churches and Russian establishments abroad] (St Petersburg, Russia, 1906), 202–203.

6. See translation of letters from Metropolitan Arsenius to the Patriarch of Jerusalem in *The Church Quarterly Review*, no. CCXXV, October 1931, 5–14.

7. Steven Runciman, *The Great Church in Captivity: A Study of the Patriarchate of Constantinople from the Eve of the Turkish Conquest to the Greek War of Independence* (Cambridge: Cambridge University Press, 1968), 289–319. See also the same author's essay "The British Non-Jurors and the Russian Church," in *The Ecumenical World of Orthodox Civilization, Russia and*

Orthodoxy, vol. III (The Hague: Walter de Gruyter GmbH & Co., 1974), 155–61. The references in this essay to the unpublished records of the Russian church in London are primarily to the "chronicle" written in the 1920s (National Archives, RG 8/116, compiled by Archpriest John Leliokhine). This chronicle summarizes almost verbatim the information in Maltseff, *Pravoslavnye Tserkvi i russkie uchrezhdeniya zagranitsei*, about Metropolitan Arsenius. However there is no direct reference to the events of 1712–1716 in the original eighteenth-century London documents held in the National Archives files.

Metropolitan Arsenius and the Non-Jurors

1. *The Church Quarterly Review*, no. CCXXV, October 1931, 5–14: letter of February 24, 1728.

2. Runciman, 311–12.

3. *City of London Survey*, Ch. XI, 277–82.

4. Timothy Ware (Metropolitan Kallistos), *The Orthodox Church* (London: Penguin, 1963), 180.

Russian Support for the Church in London

1. M. Constantinides, *The Greek Orthodox Church in London* (Oxford: Oxford University Press, 1933), 11–12.

2. Runciman, 312–16.

3. G. Ivanoff-Trinadtzaty, *L'église russe décapitée* [The beheaded Russian Church], 6–14 and 64–75, in *L'église synodale russe - son évolution et ses relations avec les confessions occidentales à travers les encycliques de 1723 - 1848 - 1895* [The Russian Synodal Church – its evolution and relations with Western confessions shown in the encyclicals of 1823, 1848 and 1895], doctoral thesis for the University of Lyon (France), 1893.

4. Archpriest Eugene Smirnoff, Доклад о состоянии и нуждах церкви Успения Божией Матери, состоящей при Императорском Посольстве в Лондоне [Report on the condition and needs of the Church of the Dormition of the Mother of God attached to the Imperial Embassy in London] (1916) in Eugene Tugarinov, *How Shall We Sing the Lord's Song in a Foreign Land? (*Како воспоем песнь Господю на земли чуждей?*)* (Moscow: Publishing House of St Tikhon's Orthodox University for the Humanities, 2012), 15–16.

Chapter 2

The Graeco-Russian Church at York Buildings

1. Alexei P. Maltseff (Archpriest), *Pravoslavnye Tserkvi i russkie uchrezhdeniya zagranitsei* [Orthodox churches and Russian establishments abroad] (St Petersburg, Russia, 1906), 202–203.

2. National Archives, Archives of the Russian Orthodox Church in London, RG 8/116, Church Chronicle compiled by Archpriest John Lelioukhine, c. 1923, which summarizes earlier material.

3. National Archives, RG 8/111, Orthodox Graeco-Russian Church: Memorandum Book, 1721–1870.

First Russian Clergy: Father Stephen Ivanovsky and the Move to Clifford Street

1. Maltseff, 202–203.

2. National Archives, RG 8/116, Church Chronicle compiled by Archpriest John Lelioukhine, c. 1923.

3. A. A. Sollogub, ed., *Russkaya Pravoslavnaya Tserkov Zagranitsei* [The Russian Orthodox Church abroad] *1918–1968*, vol. 2 (Jerusalem, Russian Ecclesiastical Mission in Jerusalem, 1968), 1045. Article by Archbishop Nikodem Nagaieff (d. 1976) describing the icon painted by Father Stephen Ivanovsky in 1756.

The Ludwell and Paradise Families

1. Gleb Struve, "John Paradise: Friend of Doctor Johnson, American Citizen and Russian 'Agent,' " *The Virginia Magazine of History and Biography*, vol. 57, no. 4 (October 1949), 355–75.

2. Dr. Archibald Bolling Shepperson, *John Paradise and Lucy Ludwell of London and Williamsburg* (Richmond, Va.: Dietz, 1942).

3. Hieromonk Tarasius, *Perelom v Drevnerusskom Bogoslovii* [The turning point in old Russian theology] (Kazan, 1903; reprinted Montreal, 1979), 56–59.

Archpriest Andrew Samborsky

1. Maltseff, 204–206.

2. National Archives, RG 8/116, Church Chronicle compiled by Archpriest John Lelioukhine, c. 1923.

3. A. G. Cross, "Yakov Smirnov: A Russian Priest of Many Parts," *Oxford Slavonic Papers*, New Series 8 (1975): 37–52.

4. Timothy Ware (Metropolitan Kallistos), *The Orthodox Church* (London, 1963), 9.

5. Ada Jane Evelyn (Mrs P. S-M.) Arbuthnot, *Memories of the Arbuthnots of Kinkardineshire and Aberdeenshire* (London, 1920).

6. See "Самборский Андрей Афанасьвич: 1734–1815 [Andrei Afanasievich Samborsky: 1734–1815]," at http://tsarselo.ru/content/0/yenciklopedija-carskogo-sela/istorija-carskogo-sela-v-licah/samborskii-andrei-afanasevich-1734-1815.html.

Chapter 3

A Priest and a Diplomat

1. A. G. Cross, "Yakov Smirnov: A Russian Priest of Many Parts," *Oxford Slavonic Papers*, New Series 8 (1975): 38. Apart from the Embassy church archives, this paper is our principal source of information about Father James Smirnove. Cross has made an extensive study of references to Father Smirnove in contemporary writings.

2. National Archives, Archives of the Russian Orthodox Church in London, RG 8/113, Copy of letter to Count Romanovich Woronsow, Ambassador in London, from Westman, Chief Secretary at the College of Foreign Affairs, stating that annual records of births etc. must be kept by the mission (embassy) priest and sent to the Holy Synod. Note of receipt for this letter dated November 1804.

3. National Archives, RG 8/178 94, Ukases on church and religious matters, 1835–1877.

4. National Archives, RG 8/127, Report of the Church: Births, Marriages and Deaths etc., 1835.

The Russian Church Community in London

1. National Archives, RG 8/173, Documents and correspondence of Jacob Smirnov on church affairs, 1812–1844.

2. National Archives, RG 8/113, Names of children born to Father James Smirnove in London, 1782–1798.

3. National Archives, RG 8/115, Lists of baptisms, marriages, and deaths (with some English translations), including Greeks and other non-Russians, 1807–1846, 8–48.

4. For details of Woronzow's career and views, see Gleb Struve, "John Paradise: Friend of Doctor Johnson, American Citizen and Russian 'Agent,'" *Virginia Magazine of History and Biography*, vol. 57, no. 4 (October 1949), 355–75.

5. M. Constantinides, *The Greek Orthodox Church in London* (Oxford: Oxford University Press, 1933), 17.

The Earl of Guilford: An Extraordinary Convert

Information about Lord North was originally drawn almost entirely from a study by Metropolitan Kallistos (Ware) entitled *The Fifth Earl of Guilford and His Secret Conversion to the Orthodox Church*, kindly made available by Metropolitan Kallistos in manuscript form. Since then, Metropolitan Kallistos's notes were incorporated into Chapter 11 of *Anglicanism and Orthodoxy*

300 years after the 'Greek College' in Oxford, edited by Peter M. Doll (Oxford: Peter Lang, 2006). They have been reproduced here with kind permission of the publisher.

Woronzow, Paradise, Father Smirnove, and the Crisis of 1791

1. Information for this and the following section of this chapter is taken primarily from the articles by A. G. Cross and Gleb Struve previously cited. Both of these articles draw extensively on the Woronzow family archives.

2. Dr. Archibald Bolling Shepperson, *John Paradise and Lucy Ludwell of London and Williamsburg* (Richmond, Va.: Dietz, 1942).

3. Gleb Struve, *Novoe Russkoe Slovo* [New Russian word], New York, August 28, 1949.

The "Priest of Many Parts"

A. G. Cross, "Yakov Smirnov: A Russian Priest of Many Parts," *Oxford Slavonic Papers*, New Series 8 (1975): 37–52.

The New Church at Welbeck Street

1. National Archives, RG 8/175, Correspondence of O Jacob Smirnov regarding the renting of the church and house in Welbeck Street, 1813–1835.

2. National Archives, RG 8/134, Annual Reports: including Births, Marriages and Deaths etc., 1842.

3. National Archives, RG 8/116, Enquiries Register (from 1841) and short Church Chronicle, 1712–1951.

4. Information provided by the City of Westminster Public Library, Marylebone Road, London N.W.1, in a letter dated May 29, 1968, made available to the author by the Rev. S. Newman-Norton (Mar Seraphim).

5. Information provided by the Society of Radiologists, which at one time occupied the building at 32 Welbeck Street.

6. Eugene Smirnoff (Rev.) 1916 report included in Eugene Tugarinov, *How Shall We Sing the Lord's Song in a Foreign Land? (*Како воспоем песнь Господю на земли чуждей?*)* (Moscow: Publishing House of St Tikhon's Orthodox University for the Humanities, 2012), 28–29.

Blindness and Death of Father James Smirnove

1. National Archives, RG 8/131, Annual Reports: including Births, Marriages and Deaths etc., 1839.

2. National Archives, RG 8/115, Death and burial of Archpriest Jacob Smirnov, 1840 16/28, p. 49.

3. Cross, "Yakov Smirnov: A Russian Priest of Many Parts."

Chapter 4

The Priest and People of the Embassy Church

1. N. Talberg, *Istoria Russkoi Tserkvi* [History of the Russian church], (Jordanville, N.Y.: Holy Trinity Monastery, 1959), 735–45.

2. National Archives, Archives of the Russian Orthodox Church in London, RG 8/178, Decrees on church and religious matters, 1835–1877.

3. National Archives, RG 8/115, Lists of baptisms etc. and related information in London, Lisbon etc. Decrees, registers, books etc. received from St Petersburg, 1843–1876, 54–112.

4. National Archives, RG 8/163, Annual Report 1874.

5. National Archives, RG 8/184, Letters to E. I. Popoff, 1854–1869.

6. National Archives, RG 8/111, Orthodox Graeco-Russian Church: Memorandum Book, 1721–1870.

7. National Archives, RG 8/136–155, Annual Reports: Births, Marriages, Deaths, those going to confession and Holy Communion, etc.

8. National Archives, RG 8/186, Letters from Dimitri Tolstoy to E. I. Popov, 1865–1869.

9. National Archives, RG 8/213, Correspondence: E. Smirnov to Russian Embassy, 1877–1921.

10. William Palmer, *Notes of a Visit to the Russian Church in the Years 1840, 1841* (London: n.p. 1882), 551–52.

11. Eleanor A. Towle, *John Mason Neale D.D., a Memoir* (London: n.p. 1906), 175.

12. Harold N. Ingle, *Nesselrode and the Russian Rapprochement with Britain, 1836–1844* (Berkeley, Calif.: n.p. 1976), especially pp. 169–70.

13. Extract from the diary of Dr Robert Lee supplied to the author by the British Institute of Radiology, which formerly occupied 32 Welbeck Street.

14. E. M. Almedigen, *The Romanovs* (London: n.p. 1966), 241.

The Crimean War Prisoners

1. National Archives, RG 8/111, Orthodox Graeco-Russian Church: Memorandum Book, 1721–1870.

2. National Archives, RG 8/180, Russian prisoners of war in England; lists of prisoners of war; correspondence with the church concerning them, 1854–1857.

3. National Archives, RG 8/163, Annual Report, 1874.

4. P. Warner, *The Crimean War: A Reappraisal* (London: n.p. 1972), 196–97.

5. Paul Hayes, *Modern British Foreign Policy: The Nineteenth Century* (London: n.p. 1975), 258, citing Sir Edmund Hornby, expert in Turkish finances.

Rebuilding the Church at Welbeck Street

1. Palmer, 550.

2. National Archives, RG 8/111, Orthodox Graeco-Russian Church: Memorandum Book, 1721–1870, especially pp. 269–75 which comprise Father Popoff's report on the rebuilding work.

3. National Archives, RG 8/189, Letters to E. I. Popov from Empress Maria Aleksandrovna's secretary, 1860–1867.

4. National Archives, RG 8/188, Miscellaneous letters to E. I. Popov, mostly about the new church, 1862–1869.

5. National Archives, RG 8/169, Annual Reports, 1906–1910.

6. National Archives, RG 8/181, Annual Reports: 32 Welbeck Street, details of repairs, etc. prior to commencement of new lease; accounts and correspondence, 1845–1875.

7. "The New Chapel of the Russian Embassy," *Illustrated London News*, April 29, 1865, 392–94.

8. M. Constantinides, *The Greek Orthodox Church in London* (Oxford: n.p. 1933), 19.

Chapter 5

The Anglican Movement Toward Orthodoxy

1. National Archives, Archives of the Russian Orthodox Church in London, RG 8/192, Miscellaneous papers on church matters, including Moscow Metropolitan, 1859–1867.

2. National Archives, RG 8/183, Letters to E. I. Popov from Holy Synod, 1840–1860.

3. National Archives, RG 8/185, Letters to E. I. Popov from A. Tolstoy, 1857–1861.

4. National Archives, RG 8/186, Letters to E. I. Popov from Dimitri Tolstoy, 1865–1869.

5. S. L. Ollard, *A Short History of the Oxford Movement* (London: Mowbray, 1915; reprinted 1963), especially pp. 184–85.

6. William Palmer, *Notes of a Visit to the Russian Church in the Years 1840, 1841* (London: Kegan Paul & Co., 1882), 1–2, 13–14, 387, 551.

7. W. J. Birbeck, ed., *Russia and the English Church* (London: Rivington, Percival & Co., 1895), especially 9, 74–75, 179. Notwithstanding its title, this book in fact comprises the correspondence between Palmer and Khomiakov, together with a few other related materials.

8. Eleanor A. Towle, *John Mason Neale D.D., a Memoir* (London: Longmans, Green & Co., 1906), especially 165–78, 312.

9. A. G. Lough, *The Influence of John Mason Neale* (London: SPCK, 1962), 115–28.

10. *Occasional Paper of the Eastern Church Association*, no. 2, January 1865, cited in *Sobornost,* vol. 9, no. 2 (1987), 23–40.

11. Georges Florovsky, "The Orthodox Churches and the Ecumenical Movement prior to 1910," in Ruth Rouse and Stephen Charles Neill, eds., *A History of the Ecumenical Movement: 1517–1948* (London: SPCK, 1954), 1: 201–205.

12. For additional information about Abbé Guettée, see *La Foi Transmise*, Gascogne, France, no. 26, May 1986.

Stephen Hatherly and the Missionary Plans of Counts Alexander and Dimitry Tolstoy

1. National Archives, Archives of the Russian Orthodox Church in London, RG 8/178 94, Ukases on church and religious matters, 1835–1877.

2. National Archives, RG 8/185, Letters to E. I. Popov from A. Tolstoy, 1857–1861.

3. National Archives, RG 8/148, Annual Reports: including Births, Marriages and Deaths etc., 1856.

4. National Archives, RG 8/192, Miscellaneous papers on church matters, including Moscow Metropolitan, 1859–1867.

5. National Archives, RG 8/189, Letters to E. I. Popov from Empress Maria Aleksandrovna's secretary, 1860–1867.

6. National Archives, RG 8/186, Letters to E. I. Popov from Dimitri Tolstoy, 1865–1869.

7. National Archives, RG 8/188, Letters to E. I. Popov, miscellaneous, mostly about new church, 1862–1869.

8. National Archives, RG 8/228, Correspondence: E. Smirnov to the Economic Council of the Holy Synod, 1890–1913.

9. Stephen Hatherly (Father), "Lecture Delivered in the Greek Syllogos on Wednesday 2nd/14th October, 1874" (London: Saint George Orthodox Information Service, 1974).

10. S. Newman-Norton (Mar Seraphim), "Ex Oriente Lux," *The Glastonbury Bulletin*, October 1978. This study draws heavily on letters written by Dr. J. J. Overbeck to Olga Novikoff, 1867–1904: British Library, Additional MSS 47460–47461.

11. Kallistos (Ware) (Metropolitan), "The Orthodox Church in England," in *A Sign of God—Orthodoxy 1964: A Pan-Orthodox Symposium* (Athens: The Brotherhood of Theologians "Zoe," 1964), 57.

12. E. Cooper, letters to Canon J. A. Douglas, Lambeth Palace Library, J. A. Douglas papers, vol. 4, folios 4–6.

13. Stephen Hatherly (Father), letter published in the *Wolverhampton Chronicle*, October 18, 1871; copy made available to the author by Mar Seraphim Newman-Norton.

Dr Joseph Overbeck and Plans for Western Rite Orthodoxy

1. S. Newman-Norton (Mar Seraphim), "Ex Oriente Lux," *The Glastonbury Bulletin*, nos. 50–56 (July 1978 to February 1980).

2. Simeon S. Bogoslovsky, "Orthodoxy and the Western Rite," *Edinaya Tserkov* [One Church], vol. 6, no. 4 (April 1952), 7.

Death of Father Eugene Popoff: Father Basil Popoff as Rector

1. S. Newman-Norton (Mar Seraphim), "Ex Oriente Lux," *The Glastonbury Bulletin*, no. 55 (October 1979).

2. National Archives Files, RG 8/196, List of communicants, 1866–1867.

3. National Archives, RG 8/166, Annual Reports: including Births, Marriages and Deaths etc., 1876–1885; includes records of service for the priests of the church, 1881–1885.

4. National Archives, RG 8/186, Letters to E. I. Popov from Dimitri Tolstoi, 1865–1869.

5. National Archives, RG 8/163, Annual Reports: including Births, Marriages and Deaths etc., 1874.

6. National Archives, RG 8/178 94, Ukases on church and religious matters, 1835–1877.

7. National Archives, RG 8/169, Annual Reports: including Births, Marriages and Deaths etc., 1906–1910.

8. Ivan N. Ostroumoff, *The History of the Council of Florence* (Boston: Holy Transfiguration Monastery, 1971).

9. S. Weintraub, *Victoria, an Intimate Biography* (New York: Dutton, 1987), 408.

10. Anonymous, "The Russian Church of St Mary Magdalene in Darmstadt" (in Russian), *Vestnik Germanskoi Eparkhii* [Journal of the German Diocese], no. 2 (Munich, 1991), 21–22.

Chapter 6

The Embassy Church and Its People

1. National Archives, Archives of the Russian Orthodox Church in London, RG 8/213, E. Smirnov to Russian Embassy, 1877–1912.

2. National Archives, RG 8/238, Inventory of church articles and vestments contributed in 1879 by Russian Orthodox Church in London to Orthodox Churches in Bulgaria, 1879–1880.

3. National Archives, RG 8/243, Nicholas, Archbishop of Japan to E. Smirnov, 1894–1908.

4. R. Mudie-Smith, ed., *The Religious Life of London* (London, 1904), 97.

5. Count Constantine Benkendorff, *Half a Life* (London, 1955), 149, 208.

6. Prince Mestchersky, Obituary for Father Eugene Smirnoff, *The Christian East* [periodical published by the Anglican and Eastern Churches Association], vol. 4, no. 1, February 1923, 4–5.

7. Alexei P. Maltseff (Archpriest), *Pravoslavnye Tserkvi i russkie uchrezhdeniya zagranitsei* [Orthodox Churches and Russian Establishments Abroad] (St Petersburg, Russia, 1906), 202–209.

8. Eugenie Fraser, *The House by the Dvina: A Russian Childhood* (London, 1984; Corgi edition, 1989), 37, 45. Published by Mainstream. Reprinted by permission of The Random House Group Limited.

Contact with Orthodox in Other Countries and Assistance to Orthodox Missions in the Americas, India, and Spain

1. National Archives, RG 8/169, Annual reports: including births, marriages, deaths, etc., 1906–1910.

2. National Archives, RG 8/213, E. Smirnov to Russian Embassy, 1877–1921.

3. National Archives, RG 8/223, Metropolitan of St Petersburg to E. Smirnov, 1897–1911.

4. National Archives, RG 8/230, Office of the Ober-Procurator of the Holy Synod to E. Smirnov, 1893–1912.

5. National Archives, RG 8/246, E. Smirnov with New York Orthodox Church, 1896.

6. National Archives, RG 8/247, E. Smirnov with Russian Orthodox Theological Seminary, Minneapolis, 1908.

7. National Archives, RG 8/248, E. Smirnov with Nicholas, Syrian Greek Orthodox Church in New York, 1912.

8. National Archives, RG 8/249, E. Smirnov to Russian Orthodox Brotherhood in New York, 1896.

9. Birkbeck Papers, Lambeth Palace Library, Box 5.

10. Eugene Smirnoff (Reverend), *Russian Orthodox Missions—A Short Account of the Historical Development and Present Position of Russian Orthodox Missions* (London, 1903).

11. Eugene Smirnoff (Reverend), trans., *The Offices for the Reception into the Orthodox Eastern Church of Non-Orthodox Christians* (London, 1896).

Contact with Anglicans

1. Athelstan Riley, ed., *Birkbeck and the Russian Church* (London, 1917). This book is a collection of articles written by William Birkbeck and published in a single voume by Riley after Birkbeck's death.

2. *The Christian East*, 1923.

3. Samuel Hoare, *The Fourth Seal* (London, 1930), 15–16.

World War I

1. National Archives, RG 8/213, E. Smirnov to Russian Embassy, 1877–1921.

2. National Archives, RG 8/222, E. Smirnov to Vladimir Metropolitan of St Petersburg, 1913–1916.

3. Birkbeck Papers, Lambeth Palace Library, Box 1.

4. Eugene Smirnoff (Reverend), 1916 report included in Tugarinov, 36–41.

Chapter 7

The Revolution and Civil War

1. From: *The White Generals*, Richard Luckett, Copyright © 1989, Taylor & Francis. Reproduced by permission of Taylor & Francis Books UK.

2. Margarita Kononova, "The Embassy White Guard (1917–1939)," *International Affairs*, vol. 47, no. 6 (Minneapolis–Moscow, 2001), 166–179.

3. C. Nabokoff, *The Ordeal of a Diplomat* (London, 1921).

4. Frances Welch, *The Russian Court at Sea* (London, 2011).

5. Author's interview with Mrs Sophia Goodman, daughter of Count Kleinmichel, 1988, and additional information provided by Mrs Goodman, September 2011.

The Formation of the Parish in London

1. National Archives, Archives of the Russian Orthodox Church in London, RG 8/295, Protocols of the parish councils, 1919–1920. These files, which contain the minutes of the parish council meetings, are also the principal source for the remaining sections of this chapter.

2. National Archives, RG 8/226, Protocols of the parish councils, 1920–1922.

The Beginning of Parish Life

1. Evlogy Georgievsky (Metropolitan), *Put Moyei Zhizni* [My life's path] (Paris: YMCA Press, 1947), 390–391.

2. C. Dobson and J. Miller, *The Day We Almost Bombed Moscow: The Allied War in Russia, 1918–1920* (London, 1986).

3. Richard Luckett, *The White Generals*.

4. N. M. Zernov and M. V. Zernov, eds., *Za Rubezhom* [Chronicle of the Zernov family] (Paris: YMCA Press, 1973), 53. (Recollections of Bishop Nicholas of Ochrid.)

5. Family reminiscences of arrival from Archangel provided by Artemy Ananin.

The Evacuation of Southern Russia and the Beginning of the Church Abroad

1. Luckett, *The White Generals*.

2. Nikon Rklitsky (Archbishop), *Zhizneopisaniye Blazhenneishago Antonia, Mitropolita Kievskago I Galitskago* [Biography of his Beatitude Anthony, Metropolitan of Kiev and Galich], vol. IV, 288–325; vol. V, 5–17, (New York, 1956–1963).

3. Princess Maria Illarionovna, *Put pastirya v nashe vremya* [The path of a pastor in our time]; article about Father Michael Polsky.

4. National Archives, RG 8/293, Miscellaneous documents, 1881–1923.

The Arrival of Father John Lelioukhin

1. Author's interview with Abbess Elisabeth Ampenoff of the Convent of the Annunciation, London, 1988.

2. National Archives, RG 8/172, Records of service of clergymen.

3. National Archives, RG 8/276, Correspondence with the Russian Relief Committee.

4. National Archives, RG 8/299, RG 8/300, Parish register.

5. Georgievsky, *Put Moyei Zhizni*, 380–391.

The Parish and the Church Hierarchy

1. National Archives, RG 8/278, Documents concerning diocesan administration in Western Europe.

2. Rklitsky, *Zhizneopisaniye Blazhenneishago Antonia, Mitropolita Kievskago I Galitskago*, vol. V, 39–42.

St Philip's Church

1. Georgievsky, *Put Moyei Zhizni*, 390.

2. National Archives, RG 8/297, RG 8/298, Account books and miscellaneous documents.

3. Memorandum and articles of incorporation of the London Russian Orthodox Church Community, London, 1921.

Chapter 8

Parish Life, 1923–1925

1. Nikon Rklitsky (Archbishop), *Zhizneopisaniye Blazhenneishago Antonia, Mitropolita Kievskago I Galitskago* [Biography of his Beatitude Anthony, Metropolitan of Kiev and Galich], vol. V (New York, 1956–1963), 211–213.

2. National Archives, Archives of the Russian Orthodox Church in London, RG 8/277, Documents concerning diocesan administration, 1921–1925.

3. National Archives, RG 8/297, Account book and other documents, 1920–1926.

4. National Archives, RG 8/298, Miscellaneous documents, 1920–1927.

5. National Archives, RG 8/172, Records of services of clergymen.

6. V. Timofeyeff (Reverend) and V. Theokritoff (Reverend), *The All-Night Vigil Service of the Russian Orthodox Church* (London: Faith Press, 1924).

7. Vasilii Zakharov, *No Snow on Their Boots: About the First Russian Emigration to Britain* (London: Basileus Press, 2004), especially 159, 162, 240–241.

8. *British Medical Journal*, November 4, 1922, 898.

9. Author's interview with Abbess Elisabeth Ampenoff, 1988.

The 1,600th Anniversary of the Council of Nicaea

1. Rklitsky, *Zhizneopisaniye Blazhenneishago Antonia, Mitropolita Kievskago I Galitskago*, vol. VII, 69–91.

2. Anthony Khrapovitsky (Metropolitan), *Orthodox Life* (1980), no. 4, 34.

A Definitive Statement on Anglican-Orthodox Relations

1. Rklitsky, *Zhizneopisaniye Blazhenneishago Antonia, Mitropolita Kievskago I Galitskago*, vol. VII, 91–95.

Archbishop Seraphim of Finland

1. Evlogy Georgievsky (Metropolitan), *Put Moyei Zhizni* [My life's path] (Paris: YMCA Press, 1947), 426.
2. Rklitsky, *Zhizneopisaniye Blazhenneishago Antonia, Mitropolita Kievskago I Galitskago*, vol. IV, 66–69; vol. VII, 95–96, 199–203, 209–213.
3. Author's interview with Mr Anatoly Vassilisin, 1988.

The Schism in Western Europe

1. Rklitsky, *Zhizneopisaniye Blazhenneishago Antonia, Mitropolita Kievskago I Galitskago*, vol. VII, especially 7; vol. IX, 281–282, footnote.
2. National Archives, RG 8/300, Minutes of parish councils.
3. National Archives, RG 8/293, Miscellaneous documents, 1881–1927.
4. Parish archives from St Philip's Church, 1921–1957.
5. Family reminiscences with Artemy Ananin.

Chapter 9

The Arrival of Archimandrite Nicholas

1. Parish archives from St Philip's Church, 1921–1957.
2. Nikon Rklitsky (Archbishop), *Zhizneopisaniye Blazhenneishago Antonia, Mitropolita Kievskago I Galitskago* [Biography of his Beatitude Anthony, Metropolitan of Kiev and Galich] , vol. V (New York, 1956–1963), 272.

Metropolitan Anthony (Khrapovitsky): Impressions of Abbess Elisabeth

1. Author's interview with Abbess Elisabeth Ampenoff, 1988.

The Consecration of Bishop Nicholas

1. Rklitsky, *Zhizneopisaniye Blazhenneishago Antonia, Mitropolita Kievskago I Galitskago*, vol. V, 273–275.

Parish Life Under the Leadership of Bishop Nicholas

1. Author's interview with Mrs Sophia Goodman, 1988.
2. Author's interview with Abbess Elisabeth Ampenoff, 1988.
3. Author's interview with Mr Anatoly Vassilisin, 1988.

4. Evlogy Georgievsky (Metropolitan), *Put Moyei Zhizni* [My life's path] (Paris: YMCA Press, 1947), 426.

5. Rklitsky, *Zhizneopisaniye Blazhenneishago Antonia, Mitropolita Kievskago I Galitskago*, vol. V, 277–278.

Bishop Nicholas: A Spiritual Portrait

1. Author's interview with Abbess Elisabeth Ampenoff, 1988.

The Death and Testament of Bishop Nicholas

1. Rklitsky, *Zhizneopisaniye Blazhenneishago Antonia, Mitropolita Kievskago I Galitskago*, vol. V, 275.

2. J. A. Douglas (Canon), "Bishop Nicholai. R.I.P.," *The Christian East*, vol. XIII, nos. 3 and 4, (1933), 125.

Chapter 10

A New Rector Comes from France

1. *Tserkovnaya Zhizn* [Church life], official journal of the Russian Church Abroad, 1933, nos. 1 and 6.

2. *Orthodox Life*, no. 4 (Jordanville, N.Y.: Holy Trinity Monastery, 1984).

3. Evlogy Georgievsky (Metropolitan), *Put Moyei Zhizni* [My life's path] (YMCA Press, Paris, 1947), 426, 477.

4. A. A. Sollogub, ed., *Russkaya Pravoslavnaya Tserkov Zagranitsei 1918–1968* [The Russian Orthodox Church Abroad 1918–1968], vol. II, (Jerusalem, 1968), 1098.

5. Nikon Rklitsky (Archbishop), *Zhizneopisaniye Blazhenneishago Antonia, Mitropolita Kievskago I Galitskago* [Biography of his Beatitude Anthony, Metropolitan of Kiev and Galich], vol. VII, (New York, 1956–1963), 230.

6. Recollections of Mr George Orloff in a letter to the author, 1988.

Visits from Archbishop Seraphim of Western Europe

1. *Tserkovnaya Zhizn*, 1935, no. 6.

2. "A 700-year-old Icon brought to London," *The Sphere*, December 18, 1937.

3. *Russki v Anglii* [The Russian in England], October 31, 1937.

4. *Our Lady's Mirror*, Autumn 1937.

5. *The Church Times*, November 26, 1937, 598.

6. *Dereham & Fakenham Times & Journal*, November 27, 1937, 7.

A Closer Acquaintanceship with Father Boris Through His Writings

1. Boris Molchanoff Epokha Apostasii (Archpriest), "The Era of Apostasy," *Tserkovnaya Zhizn*, nos. 5 and 6 (1960); an abridged and updated version of his earlier book, *Taina bezzakonia i Antikhrist* [The mystery of iniquity and the antichrist].

2. Boris Molchanoff Epokha Apostasii, *The Calendar Question*, Montreal, 1982; originally published in Russian as *Understanding Our Orthodox Calendar*.

3. Boris Molchanoff Epokha Apostasii, *Izhe Kheruvimy* [Let us who represent the cherubim], *Vestnik Germanskoi Eparkhii* [Journal of the German Diocese], 1987, no. 4.

Visit of Archbishop Nestor and Arrival of Father Nicholas Gibbes

1. Author's interview with Mrs Sophia Goodman, 1988.

2. J. C. Trewin, *Tutor to the Tsarevich: Compiled from the Papers of Charles Sydney Gibbes* (London: MacMillan,1975), especially 143–145.

3. *Russki v Anglii* [The Russian in England], May 1938.

4. Author's interview with Mrs Antonina Vladimirovna Ananin, 1988.

5. For biographical details of Archbishop Nestor, see www.blackwellreference.com and www.all-creatures.org.

6. *Our Lady's Mirror*, Summer 1938.

7. For more information about the Orthodox presence in Walsingham, see www.Thyateira.org.uk.

Miraculously Renewed Icons of St Savva and St Nicholas

1. *The Old Calendarist*, no. 31 (1973).

2. Irina Galitzine, *Spirit to Survive: The Memoirs of Princess Nicholas Galitzine* (London: Kimber, 1976). Excerpts taken from prepublication manuscript, made available by courtesy of her daughter, Mrs Maria Bond.

Departure of Father Boris Molchanoff

1. Recollections of Mr George Orloff in a letter to the author, 1988.

2. *Orthodox Life*, no. 4 (Jordanville, N.Y.: Holy Trinity Monastery, 1980).

Chapter 11

Recollections of Melvin Mansur

1. Letter dated August 15, 1987, to the author from Mr Melvin Mansur, formerly of London, then of Lexington, Virginia.

Father Michael's Life in Russia

1. Michael Polsky (Archpriest), Положение Церкви в Советской России [The situation of the Church in Soviet Russia] (Jerusalem, 1931). Subsequently reprinted in New York, 1995. Page references are to the 1995 reprint: 7–8, 12–13, 16–17, 17–18, 51.

2. Michael Polsky (Archpriest), О духовном состоянии русского народа под властью большевизма [The spiritual state of the Russian people under Bolshevik rule]. Report to the Second All-Emigration Council of the Russian Orthodox Church Abroad—Belgrade (1938), 3–4, 4–5, 9, 10–11, *passim.*

Father Michael in London

1. Author's interviews with Mrs Sophie Goodman, 1988.
2. Author's interviews with Abbess Elisabeth Ampenoff, 1988.
3. Author's interviews with Mrs Antonina Vladimirovna Ananin, 1988.
4. *Russki v Anglii* [The Russian in England], July 15, 1938, and August 17, 1938.

World War II

1. Anonymous document preserved in parish archives.
2. Author's interview with Mrs Sophia Goodman, 1988.
3. Letter to the author from Mr George Orloff, 1988.

In Memory of Father Michael Polsky

1. Account written for inclusion in this book by Mrs Valentina Bogdan, 1988.

Chapter 12

The Great Betrayal

1. Nikolai Tolstoy, *Victims of Yalta* (London: Hodder & Stoughton, 1977).
2. Nicholas Bethell, *The Last Secret* (London: Deutsch, 1974).

The Fischbek Displaced Persons Camp

1. "Biography of Metropolitan Vitaly," *Orthodox Life*, no. 1–2, 5–6 (1986).

2. L. Tenson, "In Memory of Bishop Nathaniel," originally published in *Vestnik Germanskoi Eparkii* [Journal of the German Diocese], Munich, 1986. English translation in *The Anchor* (Newsletter of the London Russian Orthodox Church), London, June 1986.

3. Paul Pavlov (Archbishop), *Pamyati Druga* [In memory of a friend], *Pravoslavni Vestnik* [Orthodox messenger], Montreal, October 1987.

Soviet Interference in the Life of Russian Churches Outside Russia

1. Timothy Ware (Metropolitan Kallistos), *The Orthodox Church* (Harmondsworth, UK: Penguin Books, 1983), chapter 8.

2. Metropolitan Evlogy Georgievsky, *Put Moyei Zhizni* [My life's path] (Paris: YMCA Press, 1947), 665–672; from the concluding chapter, a description of the last years of the metropolitan's life written by T. Manukhina.

3. Nikon Rklitsky (Archbishop), *Zhizneopisaniye Blazhenneishago Antonia, Mitropolita Kievskago I Galitskago* [Biography of his Beatitude Anthony, Metropolitan of Kiev and Galich] (New York, 1956–1963), 3.

4. N. M. Zernov and M. V. Zernov, eds., *Za Rubezhom* [Chronicle of the Zernov family] (Paris, 1973).

5. Michael Polsky (Archpriest), Положение Церкви в Советской России [The situation of the Church in Soviet Russia] (Jerusalem, 1931). Subsequently reprinted in New York, 1995.

Chapter 13

Departure of Father Michael Polsky

1. Minute book of meetings of the Parish Council of the London Russian Orthodox Church, 1944–1949, held in parish archives.

2. Review written by Metropolitan Vitaly Oustinow, accompanying 1995 reprint of the book, cited at Chapter XI, section 2, item 1.

Pastor of Displaced Persons

1. Mrs Tatiana Danilewicz, "Russians in England," in *Russkoye Voskreseniye* [Russian resurrection], no. 120/121, July (1958). This and the recollections of Mr George Volossevich (from 1988 interview with author) form the basis of this section of the chapter.

2. *Rossianin* (*The Russian*; the name literally means "person from Russia"), London, February 1949, cited in the article "Russians in England" by Mrs Tatiana Danilewicz.

3. Author's interview with Mr George Volossevich, 1988.

4. *Sunday Dispatch*, October 15, 1950.

5. Author's interview with Mrs Sophia Goodman, 1988.

6. Author's interview with Abbess Elisabeth Ampenoff, 1988.

7. *Tserkovnaya Zhizn* [Church life], no. 5–6 (1949); no 3–4 (1959).

8. Paul Pavlov (Archbishop), *Pamyati Druga* [In memory of a friend], *Pravoslavni Vestnik* [Orthodox messenger], Montreal, October 1987.

9. Paul Pavlov, letter to the author, dated August 21, 1987.

10. A. A. Sollogub, ed., *Russkaya Pravoslavnaya Tserkov Zagranitsei 1918–1968* [The Russian Orthodox Church Abroad 1918–1968] (Jerusalem, 1968) 2:1074.

11. Vitaly Oustinow (Metropolitan), *The Liturgical Language of Foreign Converts to Orthodoxy*, report to the Council of Bishops, 1978 (reprinted 1987, Montreal).

12. Galina von Meck, *Farewell to Russia*, unpublished memoirs.

13. Michael Protopopov (Archpriest), *A Russian Presence: A History of the Russian Church in Australia* (Piscataway, N.J.: Gorgias Press, 2006).

Recollections of Paul Uspensky

1. Recollections of Mr Paul Uspensky of Brisbane, Australia, written in Russian in 1987 at the request of Archbishop Paul, as a contribution to the present book.

The *Orthodox Review*

1. *Pravoslavnoye Obozreniye* [Orthodox review], publication of the Russian Orthodox Church in England, 1948–1951.

Visit of Metropolitan Anastassy and the Miraculous Kursk Icon

1. *Tserkovnaya Zhizn* [Church life], no. 7–8 (1950).

Consecration as Bishop and Departure for Brazil

1. Archimandrite Nikodem, report to the London Annual Parish Meeting, 1952.

2. *Tserkovnaya Zhizn* [Church life], August 1951 and September 1951 issues.

Chapter 14

The principal sources of information for this chapter (especially the second, third, and eighth sections) are the reports that Bishop Nikodem prepared and presented each year to the annual general meeting of the parish, which are preserved in the parish archives.

Bishop Nathaniel of Preston and The Hague

1. *Tserkovnaya Zhizn* [Church life], no. 2 and no. 5–6 (1951).

2. *Pravoslavni Vestnik* [Orthodox messenger] (London), no. 1, 1952.

3. *Orthodox Life* (Jordanville, N.Y.), no. 2, 1982.

4. Manuscript found among miscellaneous papers in the church at Emperor's Gate with the notation "Re-typed 15 June 1950. M. Perott."

Archimandrite Nikodem: Life Before Coming to England

1. *Orthodox Christian Witness* (Seattle), January 10/23, 1977.

2. Based on biographical material which originally appeared in *Pokrovski Listok* [Protection newsletter] (Manchester), 1977, a publication of the Parish of the Holy Protection.

3. Manuscript preserved in London parish archives. See also Russian-language websites such as zarubezhje.narod.ru/mp/n_019.htm and beloe.org/t503-topic.

Development of the Parish and Diocese Under Archimandrite Nikodem

1. *Orthodox Christian Witness* (Seattle), January 1977.

2. Author's interview with Abbess Elisabeth Ampenoff, 1988.

3. Recollections written by Tatiana Danilewicz in 1988 for this book.

4. *Bulletin of the Russian Refugees Relief Association in Great Britain* (London), no. 29, 1955.

5. *Pravoslavnaya Rus* [Orthodox Russia] (Jordanville, N.Y.), no. 24, 1976.

Russian London in the 1950s

1. *Bulletin of the Russian Refugees Relief Association in Great Britain* (London), various issues, 1954, 1955, and 1956.

2. T. Matthews, *Russian Wife Goes West* (London, 1955): 199.

3. *Pravoslavnaya Rus* [Orthodox Russia] (Jordanville, N.Y.), no. 24, 1976.

4. Information obtained by Nicolas Mabin during a visit to the offices of the Russian Refugees Aid Society in September 2011.

5. Information about the Russian Refugees Aid Society obtained from www.aim25.ac.uk.

Impressions of a Visit to St Philip's by Timothy Ware

1. Kallistos (Ware), Bishop of Diokleia, "Strange Yet Familiar: My Journey to the Orthodox Church," in his book *The Inner Kingdom* (Crestwood: St Vladimir's Seminary Press, 2000). Reproduced with kind permission of the publisher.

2. Information obtained from rocorstudies.org.

Arrival of the Nuns from Palestine

1. Author's interviews with Abbess Elisabeth Ampenoff, 1988 and 1998.

2. C. J. Birchall (Protodeacon), "Abbess Elisabeth—A Personal Tribute," *Canadian Orthodox Herald* (Montreal, journal of the Canadian Diocese of the Russian Church Abroad), no. 5, May 1999.

3. A. A. Sollogub, ed., *Russkaya Pravoslavnaya Tserkov Zagranitsei* [The Russian Orthodox Church Abroad] *1918–1968*, vol. II (Jerusalem, 1968): 1046–55.

Archbishop John (Maximovitch) in England

1. Savva Saracevic of Edmonton (Bishop), *Blessed John, the Chronicle of the Veneration of Archbishop John Maximovitch* (Platina, Calif.: St Herman of Alaska Brotherhood, 1979): 46 and 372.

2. Tatiana Danilewicz, "Our Mediatrix," *Bulletin of Russian Refugees Relief Association* (London), no. 3, 1956.

3. "La Renaissance Russe" [The Russian Renaissance], *Russkoye Vozrozhdeniye* (Paris), December 1956.

4. Author's interview with Abbess Elisabeth Ampenoff and nuns of the London Convent of the Annunciation, 1988.

5. Constitution of the Sisterhood of St Xenia preserved in parish archives.

Consecration of Archimandrite Nikodem as Bishop of Preston

1. *Tserkovnaya Zhizn* [Church life], no. 9, 1953, and no. 1, 1958.

2. Anonymous manuscript in parish archives (edited); details of publication not known.

3. *Tserkovny Golos* [Voice of the Church] (Geneva), no. 6–7, 1955.

4. *Bulletin of the Russian Refugees Relief Association in Great Britain* (London), no. 42, 1950.

Wanderings in the Wilderness

1. Sollogub, *Russkaya Pravoslavnaya Tserkov Zagranitsei*, 1041.

2. Author's interview with Sophia Goodman, 1988.

3. Account of the Extraordinary General Meeting and correspondence based on *Tserkovny Golos* [Voice of the Church] (Geneva), no. 11, 1956, and a contemporary manuscript account of the meeting written by Tatiana Danilewicz.

4. Letter from Bishop Nikodem to Tatiana Danilewicz dated January 27, 1956.

Chapter 15

The principal sources of information for the first four sections of this chapter are the reports that Bishop Nikodem prepared every year to present to the annual general meeting of the parish, which are preserved in the parish archives.

Opening of the New Church at Emperor's Gate

1. A. A. Sollogub, ed., *Russkaya Pravoslavnaya Tserkov Zagranitsei* [The Russian Orthodox Church Abroad] *1918–1968*, vol. II (Jerusalem, 1968): 1042–46.

2. Account of the consecration written by Antonina Ananin, preserved in the parish archives.

3. Author's interview with Sophia Goodman, June 2010.

Development of Parish Life at Emperor's Gate

1. Ambrose Pogodin (Archimandrite), *St. Mark of Ephesus and the Florentine Union* (Jordanville, N.Y.: Holy Trinity Monastery, 1963).

2. Concerning Father Ambrose's composition of the service to St Augustine, see *St Vladimir's Theological Quarterly*, 52:1 (2008), 122.

3. Ambrose Pogodin (Archimandrite), *Беседы (Омилии) Сватителя Григория Паламы* [Talks (homilies) of Saint Gregory Palamas], translated from Greek into Russian (Montreal, 1963).

4. Information provided by Sophia Goodman, September 2011.

5. Michael Protopopov, *A Russian Presence: A History of the Russian Orthodox Church in Australia* (Piscataway, N.J.: Gorgias Press, 2006).

Establishment of the Convent of the Annunciation in Willesden

Sollogub, *Russkaya Pravoslavnaya Tserkov Zagranitsei,* 1046–65.

Ecumenism and Mission

Orthodox Chronicle (Walsingham, a publication of the Brotherhood of St Seraphim of Sarov), various issues, 1966–1970.

Archbishop Nikon's Visit to England

This entire section is taken from Archbishop Nikon Rklitsky, *Moi Trud v Vinogradnike Khristovom* [My labours in Christ's vineyard], vol. 2 (Jordanville, N.Y.: Holy Trinity Monastery, 1993), 160.

Galina von Meck

1. "Obituary: Galina von Meck," *Times* (London), April 1985.

2. Galina von Meck, *As I Remember Them* (London: Dobson Books, 1973), 60, 78, 124, 215, 319.

3. Galina von Meck, *Farewell to Russia*, unpublished manuscript; extracts quoted with permission of the author's daughter, Anne Courtney.

Gerald Palmer

1. Author's interview with Abbess Elisabeth Ampenoff, 1988.

2. Author's conversations with Gerald Palmer between 1969 and 1975.

3. E. Kadloubovsky and G. E. H. Palmer, trans., *Writings from the Philokalia on Prayer of the Heart* (London, 1951).

4. E. Kadloubovsky and G. E. H. Palmer, trans., *Early Fathers from the Philokalia* (London: Faber & Faber, 1954).

5. G. E .H. Palmer, Philip Sherrard, and Kallistos (Ware), trans., *The Philokalia—The Complete Text,* 4 vols. (London: Faber & Faber, 1979–1995).

6. Philip Sherrard, *Christianity: Lineaments of a Sacred Tradition* (Edinburgh: T & T Clarke, 1998), with foreword by Bishop Kallistos (Ware).

7. Kallistos (Ware) (Bishop), *The Inner Unity of the Philokalia and Its Influence on East and West* (Athens: Alexander S. Onassis Public Benefit Foundation, 2004). Available at www.myriobiblos.gr/texts/english/wear_innerunity1.html.

Father George Cheremetieff as Convent Priest

1. Elisabeth (Abbess), "In Memory of Archpriest George Cheremetieff," *Pravoslavnaya Rus* [Orthodox Russia] (Jordanville, N.Y.), 1971.

2. Author's interview with Abbess Elisabeth Ampenoff, 1988.

3. Recollections written by Tatiana Danilewicz in 1988 for this book.

The Last Years of Archbishop Nikodem

1. *Pokrovski Listok* [Protection newsletter] (Manchester, a publication of the Parish of the Holy Protection), 1977.

2. Antonina Ananin, manuscript account of Archbishop Nikodem's last days.

3. Alexis Pobjoy (Hieromonk), "Obituary of Archbishop Nikodem," *Orthodox Christian Witness* (Seattle), January 23, 1977.

Chapter 16

Archimandrite Alexis as Diocesan Administrator

1. Author's correspondence with Archimandrite Alexis.

2. *Shepherd* (Brookwood, parish newsletter of St Gregory's), various issues, 1980–1982.

3. Author's interview with Mrs Sophia Goodman, 2010.

Bishop Constantine

1. Michael Protopov, *A Russian Presence: A History of the Russian Orthodox Church in Australia* (Piscataway, N.J.: Gorgias Press, 2006), p. 386.

2. *Shepherd* (Brookwood, parish newsletter of St Gregory's), various issues, 1981–1982, 1996.

3. *Orthodox America* (Richfield Springs, N.Y.), no. 141, July 1996.

4. Christopher Wilson, "The Bizarre Tale of King Edward's Bones," *Sunday Express Magazine*, August 24, 1986.

The Russian Dissident Movement

1. Alexander Solzhenitsyn, *The Templeton Prize 1983: Address by Mr. Aleksandr Isayevich Solzhenitsyn* (Grand Cayman, Nassau, Bahamas: Lismore Press, 1983).

2. *Times* (London), May 9, 1983.

3. *Independent* (London), November 26, 2009.

4. *Daily Telegraph* (London), December 3, 2009.

5. *Guardian* (London), February 12, 2010.

Bishop Mark of Berlin, Germany, and Great Britain

1. *Anchor* (London, newsletter of the Cathedral Parish), nos. 2–11, 1986–1988.

2. *Vestnik Germanskoi Eparkhii* [Messenger of the German Diocese] (Munich), various issues, 1986–1988.

3. Biographical material about Bishop Mark taken from the website of the Russian Orthodox Cathedral in Munich: www.sobor.de.

Leaving Emperor's Gate

1. *Anchor* (London, newsletter of the Cathedral Parish), nos. 12–15, 1989.

2. *Evening Standard* (London), May 3, 1989.

3. *Daily Telegraph* (London), February 3, 1990.

Chapter 17

Moving to Harvard Road

1. *Anchor* (London, newsletter of the Cathedral Parish), nos. 14–17, 1989–1990.

2. *Vestnik Germanskoi Eparkhii* [Messenger of the German Diocese] (Munich), various issues, 1991–1995.

3. *Shepherd* (Brookwood, parish newsletter of St Gregory's), various issues, 1995–1996.

4. *Dormition Parish Newsletter* (London), no. 11, March/April 1995.

5. Author's interview with Archbishop Mark, 2010.

6. Author's correspondence with Count Andrei Tolstoy-Miloslavsky, 2010.

Architectural Design and Fund-Raising

1. Author's interview with Mrs Sophia Goodman, June 2010.

2. Author's correspondence with Nicholas Yellachich, 2010.

3. Author's correspondence with Count Andrei Tolstoy-Miloslavsky, 2010.

4. Author's correspondence with Douglas Norwood, 2010.

5. Biographical information about Mikhail Semeonov and Archimandrite Alipy from website: http://culture.pskov.ru/ru/persons.

6. Application from the parish to the Millennium Commission for funding for a Russian Cultural Community Centre and Church, November 1996.

7. Fund-raising appeal from the parish, 1997.

8. Deed dated November 6, 1997, between the Mayor and Burgesses of the London Borough of Hounslow and the Trustees of the Russian Orthodox Church in Exile relating to land at 57 Harvard Road, Chiswick, London Borough of Hounslow.

Building the New Church

1. *Vestnik Germanskoi Eparkhii* [Messenger of the German Diocese] (Munich), various issues, 1998–1999. The accounts of laying the foundation stone, the first Easter service, and raising the cupola are based on articles in nos. 1 and 6, 1998, and nos. 3, 5, and 6, 1999.

2. Author's correspondence with Nicholas Yellachich, 2010.

3. Author's correspondence with Douglas Norwood, 2010.

Convent of the Annunciation: Repose of Abbesses Elisabeth and Seraphima

1. C. J. Birchall (Protodeacon), "Abbess Elisabeth—A Personal Tribute," *Canadian Orthodox Herald* (Montreal, journal of the Canadian Diocese of the Russian Church Abroad), no. 5, May 1999.

2. *Shepherd* (Brookwood, parish newsletter of St Gregory's), March 1999.

3. *Vestnik Germanskoi Eparkhii* [Messenger of the German Diocese] (Munich), various issues, 1999–2000.

4. Author's communication with sisters of the Convent of the Annunciation.

Water Damage and Interior Finishing of the Lower Church

1. Author's correspondence with Nicholas Yellachich, 2010.

2. Author's interview with Archbishop Mark, 2010.

3. Author's telephone interview with Pavel Lisitsin, 2010.

4. Author's correspondence with John Newton & Company Ltd. and materials on its website relating to the remedial work done on the Russian Orthodox Church in Chiswick: www.Newton-membranes.co.uk.

5. Archbishop Mark's invitation to the lesser consecration of the lower church in 2003.

6. *Shepherd* (Brookwood, parish newsletter of St Gregory's), various issues, 2003–2005.

Reconciliation with the Moscow Patriarchate

1. John Maximovitch (Archbishop), *Russkaya Zarubezhnaya Tserkov* [The Russian Church Abroad], 2nd ed. (Montreal: Monastery Press, 1979).

2. *Anchor* (London newsletter of the Cathedral Parish), no. 17, May 1990. This issue contains text of the epistles from the Bishops' Council and Synod.

3. Peter Perekrestov (Archpriest), *"Poslednij arkhierei staroj antonievskoj shkoly* [The last bishop of the old school of Metropolitan Anthony]," in *Russkiy Pastyr* [Russian pastor], San Francisco, 2000, edition 37-.8, 61–98. See pp. 587–588 for description of Archbishop Anthony's last sermon in August 2000.

4. Deeds of the Fourth All-Diaspora Council of the Russian Orthodox Church Abroad (May 7–14, 2006) reported on the official website of the Russian Church Abroad at www.synod.com/synod/eng2006/5endir.html.

5. *Vestnik Germanskoi Eparkhii* [Messenger of the German Diocese] (Munich), various issues, 2002–2007.

Finishing the Upper Church: Installing the New Iconostasis

1. Building appeal fund literature published at the time of the lesser consecration of the lower church in 2003, detailing the work still outstanding.

2. London Russian Orthodox Church Annual Report and Accounts for the years ended 31 December 2004 to 2009, as filed with the Charity Commission. Reports and accounts for the Russian Orthodox Church Abroad (London), registration 234203, can be accessed at www.charity-commission.gov.uk.

3. *Shepherd* (Brookwood, parish newsletter of St Gregory's), various issues, 2006 and 2010.

4. *Daily Telegraph* (London), December 3, 2006.

5. *Vestnik Germanskoi Eparkhii* [Messenger of the German Diocese] (Munich), various issues, 2006–2010. The quotation regarding the change of the church's dedication is taken from p. 596, paragraph 2, issue no. 3, 2008.

6. Annual Report and Accounts of the Russian Refugees Aid Society for 2007 and 2010 as filed with the Charity Commission. Reports and accounts for the Russian Refugees Aid Society, registration 250151, can be accessed at www.charity-commission.gov.uk.

7. Booklet printed by the London parish on the occasion of the blessing of the new iconostasis in 2009.

8. Details of the preparations for the blessing of the iconostasis were taken from the parish website, www.russianchurchlondon.org/En/News, although archive no longer accessible for that date.

Appendix 1

1. National Archives, Archives of the Russian Orthodox Church in London, RG 8/186, Letters to E. I. Popov from Dimitri Tolstoi 1865–1869. Translated by author from original documents in Russian.

ACKNOWLEDGMENTS

I would like to express particular gratitude to the following people for their support and assistance throughout: Archbishop Mark of Berlin, Germany, and Great Britain for his inspiration for this project as well as his continuing encouragement and patience; Nicolas Mabin for his competent and professional help in completing the manuscript; Holy Trinity Publications for agreeing to take on the publishing of this book; and Richard Bowden, the archivist of Howard de Walden Estates Ltd., for arranging for me to visit 32 Welbeck Street where the church of the Imperial Russian Embassy was located for so many years. This is a listed building and so the layout of the rooms is very much as it was in the nineteenth and early twentieth centuries, making it easy to gain an impression of how the building and church would have looked in those days.

In writing this history, I consulted many members of the Russian Orthodox Church Abroad about their recollections of church life in London. In particular, I wish to record my grateful thanks to the following people for providing valuable information for inclusion in this book:

> Archbishop Paul of Sydney and Australia; Archimandrite Alexis (Pobjoy); Abbess Elisabeth Ampenoff and sisters of the Convent of the Annunciation; Count Andrei Tolstoy-Miloslavsky; Mrs Antonina Ananin; Mrs Valentina Bogdan; Mrs Tatiana Danilewicz; Mrs Sophia Goodman; Mr Pavel Lisitsin; Mr Melvin Mansur; Mr Douglas Norwood; Mr George Orloff; Mr Gerald Palmer, Mr Anatoly Vassilisin; Mr George Volossevich; and Mr Nicholas Yellachich.

I also wish to record my gratitude to the following people for providing photographs:

Archbishop Mark of Berlin, Germany, and Great Britain; Archimandrite Alexis (Pobjoy); Deacon Andrew Bond; Mr Antonina Ananin; Mrs Sophia Goodman; Mr George Knupffer; Mr Michael Knupffer; Mr Nicolas Mabin; Mrs Lillia Miller; Mr George Orloff; Miss Elizabeth Palmer; Mr Pavel Shilov; Mr Dmitri Schtipakin; Mr Ioann Suscenko; Mrs Valentina Turner-Udalcova; Mr George Volossevich; and Mr Nicholas Yellachich.

In addition, I also wish to acknowledge the assistance of the following in providing access to valuable source materials:

- Lambeth Palace Library for papers relating to W. J. Birbeck, and the papers of Canon J. A. Douglas
- City of Westminster Public Library for papers relating to Father Stephen Hatherly, made available to the present writer by Mar Seraphim Newman-Norton
- The Institute of Radiology (former occupants of 32 Welbeck Street) for the diary of Doctor Robert Lee
- Mrs Anne Courtnery for the manuscript of the second volume of memoirs of her mother, Galina von Meck, *Farewell to Russia*
- Mrs Lillia Miller, who provided assistance with researching documents in the National Archives
- The Reverend Father Nikolay Savchenko, who provided extensive assistance in accessing and reviewing archival material located at the Russian Orthodox Cathedral in Chiswick

INDEX

Note: Page numbers with *p* indicate photographs. Page numbers with *n* indicate notes.